ROUTLEDGE LIBRARY EDITIONS:
ACCOUNTING

Volume 26

LOCAL AUTHORITY ACCOUNTING METHODS

LOCAL AUTHORITY ACCOUNTING METHODS

Problems and Solutions, 1909-1934

Edited by
HUGH M. COOMBS
AND J.R. EDWARDS

LONDON AND NEW YORK

First published in 1992

This edition first published in 2014
by Routledge
2 Park Square, Milton Park, Abingdon, Oxon, OX14 4RN

and by Routledge
711 Third Avenue, New York, NY 10017

Routledge is an imprint of the Taylor & Francis Group, an informa business

© 1992 Introduction, Hugh M. Coombs and J.R. Edwards

All rights reserved. No part of this book may be reprinted or reproduced or utilised in any form or by any electronic, mechanical, or other means, now known or hereafter invented, including photocopying and recording, or in any information storage or retrieval system, without permission in writing from the publishers.

Trademark notice: Product or corporate names may be trademarks or registered trademarks, and are used only for identification and explanation without intent to infringe.

British Library Cataloguing in Publication Data
A catalogue record for this book is available from the British Library

ISBN: 978-0-415-53081-1 (Set)
eISBN: 978-1-315-88628-2 (Set)
ISBN: 978-0-415-71344-3 (Volume 26)
eISBN: 978-1-315-88327-4 (Volume 26)

Publisher's Note
The publisher has gone to great lengths to ensure the quality of this reprint but points out that some imperfections in the original copies may be apparent.

Disclaimer
The publisher has made every effort to trace copyright holders and would welcome correspondence from those they have been unable to trace.

Local Authority Accounting Methods

Problems and Solutions, 1909-1934

Edited by
Hugh M. Coombs and J.R. Edwards

Garland Publishing, Inc.
New York and London 1992

Introduction copyright © 1992 Hugh M. Coombs and J.R. Edwards

Library of Congress Cataloging-in-Publication Data

(Revised for volume 2)

Local authority accounting methods.
(New works in accounting history)
Includes bibliographical references.
Contents: v. 1. The early debate, 1884–1908—v. 2. Problems and solutions, 1909–1934.
1. Local finance—Great Britain—Accounting—History—19th century. 2. Local finance—Great Britain—Auditing—History—19th century. II. Coombs, Hugh M. (Hugh Malcolm). II. Edwards, J.R.
HJ9779.G7163 1991 657'.835'00941 90–25398
ISBN 0-8153-0685-7 (alk. paper)

All volumes printed on acid-free, 250-year-life paper.
Manufactured in the United States of America.

Design by Marisel Tavarez

CONTENTS

INTRODUCTION

This book may be seen as a companion to Coombs and Edwards, *Local Authority Accounting Methods. The Early Debate, 1884–1908* (1991). The accounting principles and practices in force by the end of the period covered by this book (1934) have survived until the present day, and only recently has their relevance been seriously questioned.

Most of the papers selected for reproduction are concerned principally with the accounting practices of municipal corporations. This approach has been adopted because these corporations—correctly viewed at the time as "vast trading undertakings"—supplied services in the form of gas, water, electricity, and tramways, which meant they were faced with the same pressing problems of profit measurement and asset valuation as their private sector counterparts. The practices developed and discussed in this volume, therefore, enable interesting comparisons to be made with the development of accounting and financial reporting practices of limited companies.

The Sources

This book contains a collection of papers dealing with a range of controversial accounting issues which exercised the minds of local authority officials during the period 1909–1934 and the "solutions" embodied in the Accounts (Boroughs and Metropolitan Boroughs) Regulations 1930. The sources of the material are the printed proceedings of the annual meeting of the public sector professional accounting body—the Institute of Municipal Treasurers and Accountants (IMTA); *The Accountant*; *Knight's Local Government and Magisterial Reports*; and *Local Government Law and Administration in England and Wales.*

It will be noticed that no use has been made of material contained in the public sector journal *Financial Circular* (renamed *Local Government Finance* in 1924), which was heavily utilized for the purpose of the previous volume. The reason is that material contained in *Financial Circular* became of an increasingly routine (short notes, correspondence, brief reports of council/branch meetings, etc.) and legalistic nature, with the more interesting papers published in *The Accountant.* This development may be partly due to the unsuccessful attempt allegedly made by *Financial Circular* to obtain monopoly control of debates surrounding local authority issues and to censor the information it choose to publish, a policy exposed by the leading public sector accountant, George Swainson (1898), which *The Accountant* was naturally happy to make public.

The Discussants

The contributors to the debate were mainly local government officials. The largest number of items reproduced were written by borough treasurers: Allcock (Cardiff), Boucher (Wallasey), Collins (Birmingham), Johnson (East Ham), Larkin (assistant treasurer, Coventry), Murray (ex-treasurer, Glasgow), Patterson (West Ham), A. Wetherall, (Dewsbury) R.A. Wetherall, (Swansea), and Whiteley (Bradford). Two other contributors were borough accountants: Butterworth (Hastings) and McCall (Croydon). Alban was also a local authority accountant (to the Pontypridd and Rhondda joint Water Board), while Andrews was the chief audit clerk at Newport. Two items reproduced were written by town councillors: Nelson, who was chairman of the Gas Finance Committee, Glasgow, and Rodgers, chairman of the Tramways Committee, Newcastle.

The articles were written, in the main, by accountants possessing professional qualifications. Most, naturally, were members of the IMTA, but members of the Society of Incorporated Accountants and Auditors (which merged with the Institute of Chartered Accountants in England and Wales in 1957) also featured strongly: Alban, Collins, Coxall, Henderson, Lamb, Larkin, McCall, A.Wetherall, and Whiteley.[1] Three of the articles included in this volume were written by members of the Institute of Chartered Accountants of Scotland (Kerr, Murray, and Nelson). The single contribution from a member of the ICAEW is the report written by Edward Thomas Pierson, professional auditor of Coventry borough accounts, included as part of item 9.

The contributors to the debate come from a more limited range of backgrounds than was the case for the previous issue, suggesting that local authority accounting had become the domain of specialists employed in that sector of the economy. It is, however, a little curious that more contributions were not forthcoming from chartered accountants working for professional firms in view of their growing involvement in local authority audits.

The Issues

The thirty-one items reproduced cover a wide range of matters. A chronological presentation is employed partly because many of the papers deal with more than one topic, but more importantly because it provides a clearer guide to the development of views on numerous interrelated issues.

The previous volume drew attention to the intense nature of the debates, with colorful and sometimes even insulting language used by the protagonists. Toward the end of the period covered by that volume (1884–1908) one of the participants neatly summed up this attitude using the "story of the two knights who fell to fighting over the question of whether a shield was gold or silver, each of them having seen one side only" (Miller, 1905, p. 15). Throughout the period covered by the present volume (1909–

1934) the debate continued to be vigorous and wide-ranging, but a little less heated than previously, with contributors making a more measured assessment of their opponents' views.

Some of the matters that were of major concern during the period 1884–1908 were far less prominent. The fairly straightforward reason is that these issues had been satisfactorily resolved given the contemporary environment. For this reason nothing is reproduced concerning the local government audit, while the accounting treatment of capital expenditure was also fairly low on the agenda.

The general content of the accounts published by local authorities, in general, and municipal corporations, in particular, is debated in four articles (5, 14, 15, 25), with the following specialist aspects also receiving consideration: the content of the abstract of accounts (20); the need for standardization (26); and an illuminating comparison of the nature and content of municipal accounts with those of limited companies (23). The principles to be followed when preparing borough accounts became the subject of broad statutory regulation in 1930, when the Ministry of Health issued, under the District Auditors Act 1879, the Accounts (Boroughs and Metropolitan Boroughs) Regulations, 1930 (reproduced as item 28). The Order dealt only with borough activities subject to the district audit but, according to a contemporary authority (reproduced as item 29), "the regulations are of great interest and importance, representing as they do, an official pronouncement regarding the application of the principles of accountancy for the transactions of local authorities, and it is probable that many authorities, to whom the regulations do not apply compulsorily, will follow the principles enunciated therein" (MacMillan et al., 1934, p. 27).

A number of issues which received close attention from the literature during the early part of the present century were related to the growth of municipal trading undertakings (water, gas, tramways, and electricity). The pricing of these services was a matter of considerable debate; questions included whether these services should be priced to generate a profit, break-even, or receive a subsidy from the rates. If a profit was to be generated, the question then arose of whether it should be used in the relief of the rates, or to meet future losses, or to finance an expansion of the service. These and related, matters are examined in articles 4, 11, and 12.

The development of trading activities also resulted in growing attention to the need for adequate costing and accounting for their separate activities (Electricity, 17, 24; Tramways, 2, 8, 9, 19), while costing and statistical procedures are considered in a more general context by items 27, 30). The question of whether central establishment charges should be recharged to trading activities, with possible pricing implications, and how central establishment charges should be identified for this purpose also loomed large (7, 22). Where local authorities had decided to supply a particular service, they could either start from scratch or purchase, under statutory authority, an existing company. Some of the important issues in this context are examined in item 13.

Local authorities paid income tax on a range of different types of revenue, and a significant increase in the rate of tax, around the turn of the century, naturally resulted in increased attention being devoted to this topic. It is the subject of two articles (3, 16) and a memorandum produced by the Inland Revenue setting out the official position in 1914 (10). It is also a topic that is touched upon in a number of other articles (e.g., 5). Income tax was of course payable on the profits of trading undertakings, which had implications for policy decisions concerning the price to be charged.

The depreciation question and the related issues of loan periods and the need for a sinking fund receive some attention (1, 18), as do concern with the growing level of municipal debt (6) and the case for the establishment of a consolidated loans fund (21). The book neatly concludes with a broad overview of local authority accounting (31).

Acknowledgments

We are pleased to acknowledge financial support from the Institute of Chartered Accountants of England and Wales, which has helped us to prepare this volume. We are also grateful to the Chartered Institute of Public Finance and Accountancy for permission to reprint articles and extracts from the proceedings of the annual meetings of the IMTA.

NOTE

[1] The IMTA (initially called the Corporate Treasurers' and Accountants' Institute) and the Society were each formed in 1885, and the Society's official history refers to "friendly relations between the two bodies over the course of their concurrent history" (Garrett, 1961, p. 200). It seems that municipal treasurers and municipal accountants qualified, by experience, to become members of the Society at the time of the latter's formation (*ibid.*, p. 5). Later, municipal treasurers who were members of the IMTA were eligible for election as fellows to the Society (*ibid.*, p. 200). Moreover, the Society's charter authorized municipal treasurers, who were also incorporated accountants, to act as principals to local authority employees wishing to take the Society's examinations (*ibid.*, p. 23). The overall result was that a considerable number of the IMTA's members were also incorporated accountants.

References

Coombs, Hugh M., and J.R. Edwards (eds.). *Local Authority Accounting Methods. The Early Debate, 1884–1908.* New York & London: Garland Publishing, 1991.

Garrett, A.A. *The History of the Society of Incorporated Accountants, 1885–1957.* Oxford: University Press, 1961.

MacMillan (Lord) and other lawyers. *Local Government Law and Administration in England and Wales,* Volume I. London: Butterworth, 1934.

Miller, R.F. "Discussion on Municipal Accounts," *Financial Circular,* January 1905: 13–20.

Swainson, G. "The Treasurers' Institute and *The Accountant,*" *The Accountant,* 1898 (1): 204–205.

Glasgow Chartered Accountants Students' Society.

Municipal Finance, with special reference to the Provision and Application of Sinking and Depreciation Funds.

By ALEX. MURRAY, C.A. (*ex-City Treasurer, Glasgow*).

A PAPER read at a meeting of the Society on 9th December 1909, Mr. Alex. Moore, Junr., presiding.

Municipal finance is so wide a subject that it cannot be treated as a whole in the course of a single short paper. It is co-extensive with the sphere of local government, and covers the entire field of municipal administration. No scheme of local improvement can be entered upon without consideration of ways and means, and every minute of a Departmental Committee involves a question of money—of income or expenditure, of borrowing or repaying loans.

The municipality, as a rule, has no capital to start with. All money it requires for capital expenditure must be borrowed. Accordingly every Bill or Provisional Order for sanctioning such expenditure has its financial clauses relating to the borrowing and repayment of the money required, and to rating, or other means of providing for ordinary or revenue expenditure, including interest and Sinking Fund payments.

In this paper we propose to consider only that portion of municipal finance which has to do with the borrowing and repayment of capital. But in discussing this we shall have to take into account the cognate question of the provision of Depreciation Funds, as well as Sinking Funds, out of Revenue.

It is obvious that the first duty of local authorities when proposing to borrow money for capital purposes is to consider in what way the money can be repaid so as to distribute the burden fairly and equitably among those who are to benefit by the expenditure. When a new water supply is to be provided, or a new gas works erected, it is intended to serve future as well as present day needs, and the cost should be apportioned with some attempt at equity as between the present and the future. It should not, on the one hand, press too heavily on present day users or ratepayers, nor, on the other hand, be left to be borne in undue proportion by those of a succeeding generation. It should, as far as possible, be allocated in proportion to the benefit to be derived from it.

It is not always an easy task to determine how this should be done: so many contingencies are involved in the problem that different views prevail as to what is a fair distribution of the burden. The general plan is to fix upon a number of years over which to spread the repayment of the loan. The period will depend upon the view which is taken of the durability and utility of the work on which the money is to be expended. But the problem is by no means a simple one. A building may last for one hundred years, but it does not follow that repayment of the cost should be spread over that period. Long before then the building may cease to be required for the purpose for which it was erected. The structure of a hospital may be quite good fifty years after it has been built, but in less than twenty years it may be condemned by advancing medical science, and a new one has to be provided. A bridge might stand and be perfectly safe for an indefinite period, but by-and-by it has become inadequate for the traffic, and it has to be pulled down and a wider one built; and so on.

In almost every case such contingencies must be kept in view if the distribution of the debt is to be fair and equitable, and local authorities and Parliament must be guided by experience and by common sense in fixing the period within which the debt is to be paid off. A very little consideration will suffice to show that the "life" of the subject is not the only factor to be taken into account. Change of conditions, movements of population, improved methods, new discoveries and inventions rendering appliances, otherwise serviceable, obsolete—all enter into the question, and point to the necessity of providing a good margin. Indeed, there are cases in which the "life" has nothing to do with the repayment of debt. A public park cannot be said to have any limit of "life," but a prudent municipality will wish to have it free of debt within some reasonable time; indeed, Parliament will not sanction a loan on any other condition. And the only question to be considered is what that time should be. There are also cases in which the important question is, not how long the subject will last, but what provision is being made for replacing it. An electric tramway or an electricity supply works is continually wasting in some of its parts, and these must be renewed or replaced from time to time; but, if this is done or provided for, the system may be as good as ever long after the last penny of debt has been paid off. This introduces the subject of Depreciation Funds, which will be noticed later. Meanwhile, let us confine our attention for a little to the single question of repayment of debt.

Having fixed the period within which a loan is to be paid off, the next question is by what method is this to be effected.

There are various methods, all more or less familiar, by which municipal debt may be liquidated. Some of these, though well enough suited to the circumstances of small burghs, would be inconvenient and indeed impracticable in the case of large municipalities. If, for example, a Burgh Treasurer can arrange to borrow £20,000 from one or more lenders, repayable by equal annual instalments, that is quite satisfactory, and nothing more is required, although usually borrowing in that way means paying a higher rate of interest.

But you cannot always find lenders even for small amounts willing to accept repayment of their loans in that way, and when it comes to be a case of hundreds of lenders it is quite out of the question to attempt to do so.

Hence the need for establishing a fund to which a fixed proportion of the loan can be carried yearly or half-yearly, and either applied at once in reduction of debt, or invested at interest until it can be so applied. Such funds are known by different names, as Loans Funds, Redemption Funds, Sinking Funds, &c. In a loose way they are all spoken of as Sinking Funds, and for our purpose it is not necessary to aim at any more exact definition. They are usually of three kinds:—

(1) Equal yearly or half-yearly instalments of principal.

(2) Equal yearly or half-yearly instalments of principal and interest combined—usually called the Annuity System.

(3) Setting aside and accumulating at compound interest a sum sufficient to extinguish the loan in a given number of years. This is the Sinking Fund proper.

Each of these methods has its advantages and disadvantages, and local authorities must choose that which suits them best. One recommendation of the first of these methods is that as the interest charge diminishes year by year, the burden becomes lighter for future ratepayers or users, and is heavier on those who incurred the expenditure; it should therefore act in some degree as a check upon extravagance. On the other hand, in certain cases, where expensive undertakings have to be financed for years before they have become fully productive or advantageous, it would be more equitable to lay the heavier burden on those who are to reap the greater benefit, and so method (2) or (3) may be adopted, although these, and especially (3), have their disadvantages also, which will be noticed hereafter.

Meanwhile, let us consider for a moment how a Sinking Fund operates. In the case of a municipality which borrows for short periods on mortgages or other documents of debt, it may be possible to arrange so that an equal proportion of the loans falls due each year, and in that case there will be little trouble in applying the Sinking Fund. For example, suppose a sum of £100,000 has to be borrowed, repayable in twenty years, the treasurer may arrange his loans so that £5,000 falls due each year. In that case he will pay them off, as they mature, out of Sinking Fund, and no question of accumulation of Sinking Fund arises.

It is otherwise when loans do not mature at dates to suit the Sinking Fund payments. Then an investment must be found for the unapplied balance of the Sinking Fund, otherwise there will be a loss of interest. If this balance is lodged in bank pending the maturity of mortgages it may only earn 1 per cent. interest, while the mortgages are all the while bearing interest at probably 3½ per cent. But a suitable investment is not always available, and that is one of the disadvantages of No. (3) form of Sinking Fund. Take the case of £100,000 loan repayable by setting aside 1 per cent. per annum, and accumulating the amount at 3 per cent. compound interest. This is calculated to extinguish the loan in rather less than forty-seven years. But it is assumed that an investment yielding 3 per cent. is found for every £1,000 every year on the day it is paid into the Sinking Fund, and a very little consideration will suffice to show that in the majority of cases this would be not only difficult, but impossible. And if it were possible it would be exceedingly troublesome and attended with some risk. Suppose Consols were bought at a price to yield 3 per cent., what guarantee is there that at the end of the forty-seven years the whole could be realised without loss? Still there are cases in which that risk must be run.

This form of Sinking Fund becomes still more complicated and difficult in the case of a large municipality like that of Glasgow, where the borrowings amount to several millions, and most of the debt is in the form of stocks, either irredeemable, or redeemable only at the end of periods ranging from twenty-five to forty years. It is unnecessary here to point out the many advantages corporations derive from the issue of stock. It means a wider market, a lower rate of interest, and a great saving of trouble. All the large corporations now borrow by the issue of stock. What usually happens is something like this. Several corporation departments have been spending money on new works, borrowing temporarily, and some are proposing to spend more. A million of money is required, and the market being favourable it is resolved to issue, say, a 3 per cent. stock at par. But the money is required for several departments with different borrowing and rating powers and varying periods of repayment. A separate Sinking Fund is necessary for each department—indeed, for each of its borrowing powers, for the same department may have several different borrowing Acts, and each must be kept strictly within its own limits; but once the stock is issued, every department must either go into the market and buy in stock to absorb the Sinking Fund accumulations, and so raise the price against itself, or find an investment elsewhere. The latter alternative, as we have seen, is attended with much trouble and some risk. The difficulty is, to some extent, met by the creation of a Loans Fund. This introduces a new department which acts as agent or banker for all the spending departments, and stands between them and the creditors. It is constituted under Act of Parliament, with well defined powers and responsibilities, with rating powers greater than those of all the other departments combined, for it can impose a rate known as the "Guarantee Rate," unlimited in amount. It has also a recognised official at its head. In Glasgow this official is known as the City Registrar. The loan or stock in such a case is issued by the corporation acting through the Loans Fund Department. Thereupon the Registrar opens an account with each of the Spending Departments, advances it the money it requires, obtains repayment each half-year of its proportion of interest and Sinking Fund, and sees that it is kept within the limits of its borrowing powers. Thus, inste d of the various departments going into the outside market whenever they require money, and possibly competing with one another, they go to the Loans Department, which has power to borrow not only by means of stock as occasion offers, but also on mortgage, bills, temporary loans, and bank overdrafts. In this way the departmental treasurers are relieved of all anxiety in regard to capital requirements, and are saved much trouble and possibly friction. It should be mentioned, however, that one of the departments of the Glasgow Corporation—the Tramways—is not under the Loans Fund, and is financed separately by the City Chamberlain.

Various attempts have been made to bring the tramways under the Loans Fund, and so have only one borrowing authority for the corporation, but this has always been ɔposed by the railway companies and other large rate-ɩyers, and the desired consolidation has not been effected. he merits of this controversy are interesting, but they do ɔt concern us here.

We have seen that the chief difficulty in the working of a ɩnking Fund is in connection with the investment of the oney, especially when the debt in respect of which Sink-g Fund is payable is in the form of stock, and it may be ɩked how is that difficulty got over by the Loans Fund epartment. In Glasgow this difficulty has not been felt, ecause under its Loans Act of 1883 the corporation has ɔwer to invest its Sinking Fund in statutory securities, and statutory securities" are defined to include its own ecurities. What is done is something like this. The cor-ɔration, in addition to its permanent loans, has always a ɔnsiderable amount of floating debt. When the City egistrar receives Sinking Fund payments from any of the epartments he immediately pays off some of that floating ebt; it may be a temporary loan or a bank overdraft. Next eek, or perhaps next day, a departmental treasurer may equire £50,000 for new capital expenditure, and the City egistrar gives him a cheque for that amount. The Sink-ɩg Fund is thus really used to save new permanent orrowing. It cannot possibly result in a loss either of ɩterest or capital when it is used in that way. On the ɔntrary, the effect almost invariably is a saving of interest.

But while this was the practice, and I suppose also the ɩw, both in Glasgow and Edinburgh, the position until ecently was very different in most of the burghs in Eng-ɩnd. There the corporations were very much hampered in ɩe use of their Sinking Funds. By their local Acts, and ɩe regulations of the Local Government Board, they might ansfer part of a stock, equal to the amount of the Sinking 'und, from an old borrowing power to a new borrowing ower, and then questions arose as to whether the transfer hould be at par or at the market price of the day; or they ɩight use the fund in buying up and cancelling stock, or ɩvest it in statutory securities; but in the one case ɩe stock could not always be got, and in the other there 'as inconvenience and risk of loss. And so some corpo-ɩtions began to ask themselves why they should not be llowed to use their accumulated Sinking Funds in the exer-ise of new borrowing powers. It seemed to them absurd ɔ be compelled to borrow money when they had money of ɩeir own seeking investment. Accordingly, one local uthority after another came to Parliament for powers to se their Sinking Funds for new capital expenditure, and 'arliament had no difficulty in giving the requisite clauses. 'he first to get the clause was the Burgh of St. Helen's, and ɩat was only in 1898. Since then quite a number of other urghs have obtained similar clauses; until now this liberty ɔ use Sinking Funds in the exercise of new borrowing owers may be said to be possessed by all the English munici-palities. It is not to be supposed, however, that the practice is universally approved. On the contrary, at the very time that the English corporations were pressing to obtain the right or privilege so long enjoyed by Glasgow, some very severe strictures of the Glasgow practice were made by some of our own citizens, who now and again criticise the manage-ment of our municipal affairs. On this occasion they challenged the soundness of the finances of the corpora-tion, especially in the matter of its dealings with its Sinking Funds. They alleged that the Sinking Funds existed only on paper, were mere bookkeeping entries, and so on; and in proof of these assertions they pointed to the undeniable fact that the debt of the city, so far from being reduced, was mounting up by leaps and bounds. And when it was explained to them that this was caused by the large amount of new capital expenditure incurred during these years, and that but for the use made of the Sinking Funds the debt would have been greater still, their answer was that the corporation had no right to apply the Sinking Fund moneys towards such expenditure—that it was bad finance, and of doubtful legality—and that the Sinking Funds should have been invested in Consols, or other first-class securities, so as to be available for the redemption of corporation loans when they fell due.

It is interesting to find that no sooner had the English corporations began to follow in the footsteps of Glasgow than a similar outcry arose in England, although this time the objections seem to have originated in the London Stock Exchange, and were put forward professedly in the interest of the stock-holders. It has also to be said that there were in several instances good grounds for the objection, for some of the English corporations, in the prospectuses of their stock issues, had given the public to understand that the Sinking Funds were to be specially invested so as to be available to meet the loan or stock at maturity. And in such a case, whether affecting the value of the security or not, it would have been very like a breach of trust if the Sinking Funds were otherwise disposed of. Anyway, a considerable agitation was got up, and only a little more than a year ago Parliament appointed a Select Committee to inquire into the whole subject. The Committee took evidence, and recently issued its report.

Some of the witnesses who gave evidence before the Select Committee raised many interesting points, which we cannot even glance at in this paper, but we recommend those who would wish to study the question to a careful perusal of the Blue-book. The leading conclusion of the Committee's report, and the one which chiefly concerns us, is as follows:—"The principle of utilising the Sinking "Funds (including Loans Funds and Redemption Funds) "for purposes for which local authorities have borrowing "powers is, if properly safeguarded, financially unobjec-"tionable; and the power of so using these funds is "undoubtedly a great advantage, inasmuch as it affords a "convenient and economical method of exercising new "borrowing powers, without either injuring the credit of "the local authority or prejudicing the rights of the "lender."

One of the objections urged against this method of financing is that it encourages corporations to spend money more freely than they would do if they had to go into the market to borrow for each new expenditure of capital. The answer is that all such expenditure must be within the borrowing powers, and whenever any Sinking Fund moneys are used to save fresh borrowing, the borrowing powers are proportionately reduced. The check upon extravagance, therefore, is operated by the exhaustion of the borrowing powers, and the necessity of going to Parliament from time to time for additional powers. I may add that, in recent years, Parliamentary Committees have been in the habit of scrutinising very carefully every application for new borrowing powers, and, of course, all such applications are advertised and open to the criticism of the ratepayers, of whom, happily, we have a few who always watch what is going on.

Another objection urged against this use of the Sinking Fund moneys is that when a redeemable corporation stock becomes due there will be no provision for meeting it, and the corporation may require to issue a fresh loan or borrow in some other way at a time when money may be dear. There is some force in this objection, as the Corporation of Glasgow found by experience, when, in 1907, it was called upon to redeem its 3½ per cent. stock, amounting to £1,100,000. As a matter of fact, the market was then unfavourable, and the new loan had to be placed at 3½ per cent. interest. A similar difficulty may arise in 1914, when £2,200,000 of 3½ per cent. stock will fall to be redeemed. That undoubtedly is fitted to cause some anxiety, and one can only hope that by 1914 the fates will be propitious. It must not he forgotten, however, that with a Sinking Fund approaching £400,000 per annum, and the prospect of diminished capital expenditure, a large amount of temporary loans and mortgages should be paid off during the next four years, thereby making it easier for the corporation to finance the amount required to meet the maturing stock; and in any case the money can be got at the current rate.

It may be asked, then, What advantage does the lender get from the Sinking Fund, if it is not to be specially invested to meet his loan? The answer is that his security is being improved; the corporation assets in proportion to liabilities are being year by year increased. A lender may not be able to know to what extent this is so—it depends on what proportion of the assets is wasting and what proportion permanent, and also on whether there are adequate Depreciation as well as Sinking Funds. Suppose a million has been borrowed and expended upon various kinds of municipal undertakings—say, parks, streets, tramways, and electricity works—with Sinking Fund periods ranging from twenty to forty years. The lenders have the satisfaction of knowing that at the end of forty years all these assets will be free of debt, and therefore the proportion of the corporation assets to its liabilities will to that extent be better than it is to-day, less what has been lost by waste. And if that waste is being met by adequate Depreciation Funds the financial position of the corporation will have improved, other things being equal, *by a million*.

I see that the Select Committee recommend that in those cases in which a stock is required to be extinguished at a fixed date, any amounts withdrawn from the Sinking Fund should, as a general rule, be replaced at that date, although they recognise that this may operate disadvantageously during the latter part of the life of the stock. There is no doubt that the disadvantage might be considerable, for it would mean that for some years prior to the maturity of the stock the corporation would be unable to use the Sinking Fund moneys for its own capital purposes, and run the risk of loss of principal in any investments it might make of these funds, or submit to a loss of interest if it made no investments. It is therefore a choice of evils, and corporations in the position of having to pay off a stock at a fixed date must consider whether it is safer to run the risk of a loss on their Sinking Fund accumulations or have no fund in hand to meet their obligations when they fall due. The Select Committee seem to incline to the view that the first alternative may in most cases be the safer, and I agree. At the same time it may interest you to know, what I find from a calculation made up by the City Registrar is the case, that if the Corporation of Glasgow had invested its Sinking Funds year by year in Consols for the last twenty years, the loss at present prices would have amounted to *half a million*.

But the proper precaution against being placed at a disadvantage when a stock comes to be redeemed is not the accumulation and investing of the Sinking Funds, but the issue of stocks *redeemable at the option of the corporation*. Most of the stocks issued in recent years are subject to such a condition. The whole of the London County Council's Consolidated 2½ per cent. and 3 per cent. Stocks are redeemable at the Council's option at one year's notice after 1920, and its 3½ per cent. Stock after 1929; but, as a matter of fact, they are not compulsorily redeemable at all. The Glasgow Corporation 2½ per cent. Stocks are redeemable at the option of the corporation—one in 1910 to 1925, the other in 1925 to 1940, *i.e.*, as I take it, they may be redeemed in the earlier year or in any year thereafter, but *must* be redeemed by the last year of the option period. There is a difference of opinion as to the exact meaning of the word "redeemable," some maintaining that it only means that the stock may be redeemed if the issuing authority chooses, others holding that it implies an obligation to redeem on the date specified. The question arose in connection with stocks recently matured, including the Glasgow 1907 Stock, and the opportunity was taken by the Glasgow Corporation of passing a formal resolution to the effect that in the case of its loans "redeemable" means "will be redeemed."

From an accountant's point of view Sinking Funds do not present any great difficulties. The Sinking Fund period is fixed in the Act of Parliament sanctioning the loan, and the auditor's duty is simply to see that the requirements of the Act are complied with. Of course, if the Sinking Fund is cumulative he will see that it is credited with the proper rate of interest; and, if it is invested, he should see that the investments are statutory and the interest regularly received and credited.

It is different, however, in the case of Depreciation Funds. These are not statutory, and it is left very much to the discretion of local authorities what rate of depreciation, if any, is to be allowed. Indeed, as we shall see, great differences of opinion prevail in regard to depreciation. It is all the more necessary, therefore, that auditors should have clear views on the question of principle, so as to be able to advise in what cases depreciation should be allowed; and also, if need be, at what rates, although this is more a matter for experts. A Depreciation Fund, as has been already indicated, is a provision for restoring wasted assets, and is only required where the waste cannot be made good by ordinary repairs. A public park, for instance, does not deteriorate, and a Depreciation Fund is therefore not necessary. The same may be said of a waterworks, provided that the necessary repairs are made year by year. Even in the case of street paving, which is a very wasting kind of asset, if, as is generally the case, it is renewed from time to time at the expense of revenue, no Depreciation Fund is required. And so with various other classes of assets, such as buildings, where, although there may be depreciation going on in the structure, there may be appreciation in the value of the ground; and so on.

In the case of gas works, however, where the plant cannot be permanently maintained by ordinary repairs it is proper to have a Depreciation Fund, as some day the whole plant may have become decayed or obsolete and require to be renewed; and so with electricity works and tramways. And it should be the duty of the auditor to see that year by year an adequate provision is made in the accounts for such contingencies.

A curious point has emerged in the Tramways Department of the Glasgow Corporation, which may as well be considered at this stage. As already mentioned, the tramways are not financed under the Loans Fund, but as part of the Common Good, and on the security of the Common Good Funds. Ever since the undertaking was taken over by the corporation it has been financially successful, and the Committee, before showing any surplus profits, have carried considerable sums year by year from Revenue to the credit of Depreciation Fund and Renewal Fund. These sums were not required to be expended in the immediate future, but were estimated to be necessary, and not more than adequate, to meet repairs and renewals which would be called for in the course of a few years, as parts of the lines and plant came to be worn out. The result was that very large sums had accumulated in the Depreciation and Renewal Funds. The tramways management used these funds for new capital expenditure in extending the system. Although they took fresh borrowing powers from time to time to provide for these extensions, they did not think it necessary to use them so long as they had funds of their own, accumulated from Revenue, which could be so applied. Thus at 31st May 1907, although they had spent about £3,000,000 on the undertaking, they had borrowed only a little over £2,000,000, the difference of nearly a million having been found in the Depreciation and Renewal Funds, accumulated out of Revenue. Of course, they paid Sinking Fund only upon the £2,000,000 actually borrowed from the public.

But about this time the question was raised by some officials of the Scotch Office—"Where have you got the "large sum which you have expended as capital, in "addition to the amount you have actually borrowed, "and why do you not pay Sinking Fund upon it?" They contended that, in using these Renewal and Depreciation Funds to meet capital expenditure, the corporation was really exercising its borrowing powers, and should pay Sinking Fund upon the amount expended just the same as if the money had been actually borrowed. The answer was in effect that Sinking Funds were provided, not in reduction of capital expenditure, but for the purpose of paying off borrowed money, and as this money had not been borrowed a Sinking Fund was not required. Some correspondence followed, and the opinion of the auditors of the Tramways Accounts (Messrs. Kerr, Andersons & Mac' C.A.) was asked upon the point. They reported that they did "not "think that the Sinking Fund should come into operation "as from the date when the capital was expended, but from "the date of borrowing," and they point to the "difficulty "which presented itself of how to charge revenue with a "Sinking Fund on a debt which has no existence." This seems to be common sense, whether it is law or not, and I suppose most of you will agree with the auditors. In the end, however, the Tramways Committee agreed to fall in with the requirements of the Scotch Office, and some curious results followed. In the first place the debt by the Tramways Department to the Common Good, as at 31st May 1908, had to be increased by the sum of £876,708, this being the amount which had been expended for capital purposes out of the Renewal and Depreciation Funds. (Further sums have been since added.) Altogether, by the end of the current financial year, this imaginary debt will amount to over £1,000,000, and on this sum Sinking Fund will be paid, in addition to the statutory Sinking Fund upon the money actually borrowed. The result will be, as Mr. Dalrymple points out, that, assuming the Depreciation and Renewal Funds not to be required during the next ten years, as is possible, all the outstanding loans to the public will have been wiped out, and revenue will be charged annually with Sinking Fund on a debt which does not exist. This is brought about by the circumstances that the Department is now paying Sinking Fund on a sum of over £3,000,000, and applying the whole of the Sinking Fund in paying off a debt which amounts to considerably less than half that sum (actually £1,354,232).

You will have noticed that the discussion turns partly on Sinking Funds and partly on Depreciation Funds, and, that being so, it may be permissible to pursue the subject a little further by way of saying a few words on the subject of Depreciation.

I think the contention of the Scotch Office was based on the very common mistake that a Sinking Fund and a Depreciation Fund are very much the same thing, whereas they are essentially different. A Sinking Fund is for the purpose of paying off debt; a Depreciation Fund is for securing that the subject will be maintained. A Sinking Fund will in due course pay off the debt, but unless you have also a Depreciation Fund, your asset, although free of debt, may be of little value, and you have no funds wherewith to renew or replace it. Hence the need, when you are dealing with a subject which is deteriorating year by year, through tear and wear, for a Depreciation Fund as well as a Sinking Fund.

In the case before us the Scotch Office said in effect:—
"You are using your Depreciation and Renewal Funds for
"purposes for which you have borrowing powers—you are
"in fact exercising your borrowing powers—and, therefore
"you should pay Sinking Fund now. For if you do not, the
"result will be that, instead of paying off the cost of your
"line in the statutory period of 31 years, you may take 40
"years to pay it off. That is to say, by using your own
"funds just now, instead of borrowing, you are post-
"poning the borrowing, and consequently the repayment
"of debt, for perhaps 9 or 10 years, which is unfair to
"the next generation, and contrary to the intention of
"Parliament, which fixed 31 years as the period in which
"the tramways are to be handed over free of debt."

All this sounds very well, but I think there is a fallacy in the argument. It is quite true that Parliament intends that the next generation shall have the tramways free of debt, but Parliament has made no stipulation as to the condition in which the tramways are to be when handed over. In England the tramway owning municipalities act on the supposition that all they require to do is to pay off the debt and leave the next generation to borrow in order to renew the tramways. In some cases what they do is to carry a sum year by year to Depreciation Fund, and out of that to provide their Sinking Fund, whereas in Glasgow, as we have seen, there is provided, not only Sinking Fund, but also year by year a rateable sum deemed ample to maintain and renew the whole system, so that the next generation shall have it as good as new, or funds sufficient to make it so. The English authorities say that Glasgow is doing far too much for posterity—that it is making the present generation pay twice over for its tramways; that no limited companies build up such reserves as the Glasgow Corporation tramways provide; and that in competition with private enterprise the municipalities would be unduly handicapped if they were generally to adopt the Glasgow methods.

This question was discussed at considerable length in the pages of *The Accountant* a few years ago, partly in connection with a correspondence between Mr. Dalrymple and the Borough Treasurer of Bolton, and partly called forth by a paper dealing with this question which I had read before the Glasgow Philosophical Society (Economic Section), and which was noticed in *The Accountant*, I think in 1903. Those who would wish to see what is to be said on both sides may refer to the volumes of that journal for 1903 and 1094.

The bearing of this discussion on the point we have been considering is this. If Glasgow is putting too much of a burden on the present in order to relieve the future, then the action of the Scotch Office is an aggravation of the offence, for it increases the burden. Had Glasgow been like Bolton, it would probably have had no Depreciation or Renewal Fund to use in anticipation of borrowing powers, or if it had any such funds and used them, the attitude of the Scotch Office would then have been justified. They could fairly argue that the tramways at the end of 31 years would be greatly deteriorated, and that it would be unfair to the people of that time to hand them over tramways in that condition, still burdened with debt to the extent of about a third of their cost, and with no adequate provision for their renewal. The logical conclusion would have been "Begin at once and set aside a Renewal Fund," but as I doubt whether it is within the competency of the Scotch Office to insist upon that, I grant that they would be quite justified, as a matter of prudence, in saying "You must begin your payments to Sinking Fund now." That would have been right enough if we had been like Bolton, but as the case stands with Glasgow, it makes no difference whether the tramways when handed over to the next generation, free of debt, are 30, 40, or 50 years old, so long as they are always kept as good as new, or funds are in hand to make them so.

I am sorry to detain you so long on this particular aspect of the question, but I regard it as one in which accountants have a special interest, and auditors of Municipal Accounts some responsibility. Happily, in Glasgow, if there is an error it is on the side of safety; the writing down of Capital Accounts is, if anything, too much rather than too little, and the result of the interference of the Scotch Office is, in my opinion, to make it undoubtedly too much. But in our circumstances the difference is immaterial; it only means so much less of a surplus, or at most a smaller payment to the Common Good. But if we had adopted the English system the difference would have been at once felt by the ratepayers, for, as you probably know, the practice in the English burghs is to apply the surplus in whole or in part in relief of rates.

Now I am not going to discuss whether the policy of applying the profits of municipal trading concerns to the relief of rates is a sound one or not. Much can be said on both sides, and I rather think that even in Glasgow, where hitherto any movement in that direction has been strongly opposed, opinion is coming round to favour it. What I wish to emphasise, however, is this, that if ever that policy is adopted it will be more necessary than ever, especially for auditors, to have clear and definite views in regard to Depreciation Funds. Every accountant knows that until you have provided adequate depreciation you do not show the real profit, and auditors of Corporation Accounts are expected to apply their minds to the question of what is a sufficient provision. Indeed, it is part of their duty to report whether in their opinion the sums written off are adequate.

I do not wish to criticise the accounts of other corporations, but I am safe in saying that in many cases in which sums have been paid over from the "surplus" of trading departments towards the relief of rates, there would have been no surplus had the Glasgow scale of depreciation been applied. It is quite true that in cases such as Bolton a surplus is shown after providing depreciation, but then no Sinking Fund is charged against Revenue (it being paid out of Depreciation Account); while the view I favour is that in Municipal Trading Accounts you ought to provide both Sinking Fund and Depreciation before showing a surplus.

In my former paper, already referred to, I summarised my conclusions on the subject as follows:—

1. All money borrowed for municipal purposes should be paid off within such periods as experience has shown, or, where experience is not available, as prudence suggests, to be fair and equitable as between the present and the future, due regard being had to the character of the undertaking and all the circumstances. In any case, where the subject is of a temporary nature the loan should be paid off within its "life" or period of utility.
2. In undertakings of a permanent character, and especially those in which land is an important factor, the Sinking Fund period should be extended. For a public park 100 years is not too much.
3. In all cases, where practicable, the undertaking should be maintained out of revenue, and where full maintenance is impossible or inexpedient, a Depreciation Fund should be provided to secure reinstatement. If this is done the consideration of the "life" of the subject in relation to the Sinking Fund is eliminated.
4. In estimating depreciation, regard must be had not only to tear and wear, but also, and in a special degree, to the contingency of the work or plant becoming obsolete.
5. In undertakings in which it is necessary to sink capital which will for a time be wholly or partially unproductive, the Sinking Fund may advantageously be postponed or graduated for a period of years.

To this I would now add:—

6. Sinking Funds may, as stated in the recommendation of the Select Committee, be utilised for new capital expenditure with advantage to the local authority and without prejudice to the rights or interests of the creditors, and
7. Depreciation Funds may also be used for new capital expenditure in anticipation of borrowing and without being subject to the payment of Sinking Fund, always provided that the assets on which the money has been expended are fully maintained or provision is made by Depreciation Funds for reinstating them.

I would close these observations with this further quotation from the paper referred to:—

"In laying down these general principles it is assumed (1) that the undertaking is necessary for the well-being of the city, (2) that it is one which the municipality should charge itself with, and (3) that it will be prudently carried out and administered.

"Probably a distinction should be made between remunerative works and those which are a burden on the rates. In a municipal commercial undertaking, by which the public are served as well and as cheaply as they could be by any private company, and especially where they are better and more cheaply served, it is no great hardship if present customers do more than strict theoretical principles might call for, and hand over to their successors an ample margin to provide against unforeseen contingencies. Where, however, it is a case for laying additional burdens on ratepayers it is fair to ask that the allocation of the burdens should be as nearly as may be in proportion to the benefits.

"I need only say further that, in addition to the ordinary contingencies of tear and wear, accident, errors of judgment, and obsolescence, a margin should also be allowed for such risks as a possible decline of population from the decay of trade, the removal of staple industries to other districts, failure of minerals, transfer of shipping to other ports, and other unfavourable changes which may very seriously affect the ability of future ratepayers to bear heavy burdens, and all of which are important elements in determining the proportions in which present day users and ratepayers should share the burden of municipal improvements with those who come after."

Tramways Finances and Policy.

By Councillor JAS. H. RODGERS,
Chairman, Newcastle Corporation Tramways Committee.

A PAPER read at the tenth annual conference of the above Association, held in Glasgow on September 27th, 28th, and 29th 1911.

When the Secretary requested me, some time ago, to read a paper at this important conference on the above subject, I certainly had some hesitation about complying. I felt, in the first place, that after the very excellent paper given last year by our friend Alderman Flint, that to follow this year very much on the same lines would be a mistake; I also felt that I was not capable of dealing with such a large and important question as it ought to be dealt with. However, in a weak moment I was led to give my consent by the advice of several of my personal friends, at least, I thought them such at the time, but since then I have had some doubts about it, or I am sure they never would have advised me to undertake such an arduous task.

Having thus accepted the kind invitation of your Executive to submit to you some of my ideas on Municipal Tramway Finance and Policy, I hope we shall have a real live discussion, and that beneficial results may be the outcome.

During recent years there have been many improvements introduced into municipal life for the benefit of the citizens by municipal corporations, all of which have cost and do cost large sums of money.

We have had established almost in every district throughout the country parks and recreation grounds, art galleries, museums, free libraries, free schools, better lighting and watching, isolation hospitals, better sanitation, and many other equally important and necessary improvements.

The money required for all this generally comes out of the rates, which have, unfortunately, gone up year by year in almost every district throughout the country. It is unnecessary to point out to a conference like this how that continuous increase hampers the proper development of a district. Municipal corporations cannot be blamed if, seeing, as they did, expenditure going upwards in providing those necessary improvements, they turned their attention to see if it were not possible to find some new sources of revenue. This many did, with the result that they secured the monopolies in their respective districts, such as gas, water, electric lighting, and last, but by no means least, the trams. Whether they have generally turned out satisfactory from a money-earning standpoint is very questionable. Personally, I agree with the endeavour, provided always that it is conducted on ordinary business lines.

It is not my intention to review the position of municipalisation generally, but to devote my remarks to the question of municipal tramways.

There are some 88 corporations who at the present time own and work their tramways, whilst there are some 86 others who own them; these are often a short length of line in small urban or rural districts, which are rented or have a working agreement with larger corporations or private companies to work in conjunction with their own lines. My remarks will therefore be confined to the 88 who are at present working their own tramways. I shall endeavour to give a careful survey of their position, and to have a straight talk regarding their policy. If I unfortunately appear somewhat severe in my criticism, I hope those interested will forgive me.

It is right, I think, that the members of this Association, comprising, as it does, Chairmen, Vice-Chairmen, and Members of Tramway Committees, Managers and Officials from the various undertakings, should give some united consideration to this all-important question. We ought not to be satisfied with the knowledge that some 30 of the 88 tramways may be financially sound, whilst the other 58 are either struggling to make ends meet, or are kept going by the assistance of the rates.

I have frequently been amused at these conferences, and elsewhere, by hearing speakers give figures in bulk to prove that the municipal tramways of this country are a financial success, thus:—

Capital Expenditure	£49,568,775
Interest and Dividend	1,163,946
Repayment of Debt and Sinking Fund	1,111,888
Reserve (including Depreciation and Renewal Fund)	761,646
Relief of Rates	346,274
Aid from Rates	64,215

These are the figures published in November last by order of the House of Commons, and are, no doubt, very interesting; but I have seen them quoted to show the success of municipal tramways, and I have seen them given also to prove how rank bad they are. To lump figures together in this way, and use them to prove success or otherwise, is simple folly, *unless* all the municipal tramways were run by a large trust or company, and the successful ones made good the losses of the less fortunate; then, and only then, would such figures be of use in that way.

Seeing then that the tramways in this country are not so federated, but that each must stand or fall by its own earnings (unless assisted out of the rates), the only correct way to my mind is to take separately the financial position of each, and that is what I propose to do.

The first consideration of a Tramways Committee ought to be to make their undertaking financially sound, by the building up of a sufficient Reserve and Renewal Fund.

Their second consideration, to see that the travelling public is supplied with proper accommodation and facilities.

Their third, to see that good conditions of labour are given to all their workers.

And their fourth consideration, to see that when the first three are complied with the ratepayers who backed their bill and over whose streets they run their cars should have some return in the shape of contributions towards the rates.

Do our Committees do this? I am sorry to say many do not; the financial safety seems frequently to be their last consideration, and not the first.

No fewer than 26 of our municipal tramways undertakings are to-day without any Reserve or Renewal Fund at all, whilst many of the others are far from satisfactory in that respect. In coming to this opinion I have not set up a high standard and then judged them by it; I have really taken a very low estimate of what in my opinion the Reserve and Renewal Fund ought to be.

It is somewhat difficult, I admit, to submit figures that will apply alike in every case; districts differ so much in their arrangements, and also in their geographical formation. By some Committees provision is being made in their Reserve Fund for the depreciation of everything—track, car sheds, rolling stock, machinery, and overhead equipment; whilst in others, and I believe this applies to most places, car sheds, rolling stock, machinery, and overhead equipment are kept up out of revenue, and provision is only attempted to be made in their Reserve Fund for track renewals. It is from the latter basis that I propose to judge the financial position of our municipal tramways.

The loans for rolling stock are generally for fifteen years, and I consider that, with care, the life of the cars can easily be extended over that period, and the cost of so doing be a correct charge on revenue. After the 15 years have expired and the original debt is fully discharged, if then new cars are required a loan could be got to replace them.

The same remarks apply to machinery and overhead equipment. The upkeep of these is also in my opinion a proper charge on Revenue Account until the loan period has expired, and then the Committees are free to borrow again if need be.

The track, however, is in a very different position. The money for its formation is borrowed over thirty and sometimes forty years. While the foundation may last that time, I think everyone will admit the rails won't, and will need renewing long before that period is passed. In towns that are hilly, or where a very quick service is given, the wear, I admit, is greater than on the level. This is demonstrated very clearly by the following list, which shows the amount spent on renewals by the places named since their commencement:—

Name	Amount spent	Years opened
Aberdeen	£45,024 ...	12
Bradford	84,397 ...	12
Bolton	53,091 ...	11¾
Birmingham	11,803 ...	4
Burnley	7,770 ...	9
Cardiff	9,255 ...	9
Dundee	8,350 ...	10
Glasgow	238,083 ..	10
Huddersfield	124,615 ...	10
Liverpool	190,321 ...	12½
London County Council ...	45,248 ...	12
Manchester	224,932 ...	9¾
Portsmouth	25,310 ...	9½
Rotherham	9,894 ...	8
Newcastle-upon-Tyne	10,817 ...	9½
Salford	19,051 ...	10
Sheffield	122,529 ...	11½
Sunderland	26,830 ...	10½

Every penny of this money was spent out of their Reserve and Renewal Fund.

How, then, will the following 26 places renew their track when it becomes necessary, seeing they have no Reserve Fund at all?

Barking.	Gloucester.	Oldham.
Bexley.	Handsworth.	Plymouth.
Blackburn.	Haslingden.	Pontypridd.
Bournemouth.	Heywood.	Rochdale.
Colchester.	Ilkeston.	Stalybridge.
Doncaster.	Lincoln.	Wigan.
Dover.	Lowestoft.	Leith.
Erith.	Maidstone.	Perth.
Glamorgan.	Nelson.	

I certainly think they would have been well advised if they had built up their Reserve Funds, even though it had required a rate to do so. It would have divided the cost over some years instead of, perhaps, having to levy a large rate later on, causing the ratepayers of the future to make good this shortage.

I expect it will be suggested by some that when the time does come they can borrow again to relay the track, seeing that a certain amount of the original cost will have been paid off. Well, personally, I deprecate borrowing again whilst the first loan is still unpaid. To do so only means to increase the charges against the undertaking, by adding fresh interest and redemption to your already over burdened systems If you cannot have a satisfactory margin of profit now, how are you going to get it when you increase still further your expenditure on interest and redemption of a new loan? I consider then that at the very least provision ought to be made to defray this cost. It is satisfactory to see that about 67 of the Committees are attempting to do so. Many, I submit, do not place sufficient each year, thus their Reserve and Renewal Funds are far from adequate. It is still very pleasing to know that they accept the principle.

What ought to be the Basis?

We ought, I suggest, to take a life of 15 years for the rails. It may be quite true that on some routes a year or two longer might be possible, but on other routes the rails may have to be relaid two or three times in that period. To take, then, 15 years as the average life I do not consider at all unreasonable.

Many present, I dare say, will have had a similar experience to my own Committee in Newcastle-upon-Tyne, where the rails in some parts of the city are lasting fairly well, whilst others, I am sorry to say, are not. In fact, we are having for the second time to relay some, although we have not yet been running ten years.

What will be the Cost?

It is generally accepted, I believe, that the net cost of relaying will be about £4,000 per single mile of track, but experience shows it is frequently higher. The Inland Revenue Authorities, who are never eager to make allowances, have agreed, I think, to the allowance of £4,400 per single mile of track for this purpose. I have noticed that in several districts where renewals have already taken place the cost is oftener higher than lower. In one town I find, from its published accounts, the cost of relaying a little over six miles was £33,000, which is over £5,000 per mile.

What I suggest, then, is that £200 per mile of single track ought to be set aside each year, and if that amount was invested at 3½ per cent., in fifteen years you would have £3,800 for each mile of track, and thus be able to relay your rails as they were required. I do not think it can be said that I am placing the amount too high; personally, I consider I am keeping the figure very much on the low side.

It must not be overlooked that all the money would not be invested during the fifteen years, some of it would be drawn out long before the time had expired to relay those places that had worn out quicker than the others, thus the interest on such money would not be earned. In that case the money would not represent £3,800 per mile, but something less than that amount.

I consider, then, that it is a low figure, but the reason I am keeping it small is to demonstrate how few of our Municipal Tramways Committees deem it necessary to reserve even this small amount.

In suggesting the placing of £200 per mile of single track per year to Reserve and Renewal Fund, I wish it clearly to be understood I do not suggest that as the maximum but as the extreme minimum.

Many of the Committees, I am sorry to say, appear to think a Reserve and Renewal Fund is quite unnecessary; whilst others seem to think a few thousand pounds is all that is required, and then hand their surplus over to the rates. To give something to the rates no doubt brings them a great deal of *éclat*, but will it be the same when the time comes to relay their rails and they have not the money to do the work? Will they then receive the plaudits and congratulations of the ratepayers, when they have to levy a rate so that the system may be again put into proper working order? I am afraid not. Even if they were only drawing from the rates an equal amount to that which they had given in previous years, the ratepayers would still blame them, and correctly so, for it is not right that the ratepayers of one period should have to pay money to make good that which had been unwisely given to the ratepayers of the past.

There are, I am afraid, several of our Tramway Committees in that position to-day. They have in the past given their profits over to the rates, and now that renewals have to be done their income is not equal to the increased expenditure, with this result—that the present-day ratepayers have to make good the loss.

Last year the following 34 tramways showed a loss on their year's working:—

LIST OF TRAMWAYS COMMITTEES ASSISTED OUT OF RATES, &C.

Name	Amount of Loss	How made Good
	£	
Barking	5,412	Rates
Bexley	933	Do.
Birkenhead	1,115	Do.
Blackburn	181	Do.
Bournemouth	142	Unappropriated Balances
Burton-on-Trent	682	Rates
Colchester	2,170	Do.
Darlington	1,158	Do.
Darwen	390	Do.
Doncaster	135	Do.
Dover	2,622	Do.
Erith	2,878	Do.
Glamorgan	289	Do.
Gloucester	3,179	Do.
Handsworth	1,250	Do.
Haslingden	341	Do
Heywood	675	Do.
Ilkeston	2,471	Do.
Ipswich	2,230	Do.
Lancaster	2,720	Do.
Lincoln	153	Electricity Fund
Lowestoft	2,395	Rates
Maidstone	2,623	Do.
Nelson	784	Do.
Oldham	1,807	Do.
Pontypridd	1,150	Do.
Rawtenstall	296	Do.
Southport..	1,820	Suspense Account
Stalybridge	5,938	Rates
Swindon	2,609	Do.
Wigan	8,670	Do.
Kilmarnock	2,060	Do.
Leith	1,903	Do.
Perth	773	Do.

This is an increase of five over the previous year. I greatly fear that the list will be considerably extended unless some of the Committees alter their present policy of handing over all, or the greater part, of their surplus to the rates, and of granting further concessions to the public and their workmen; the incomes of their systems will not allow them to do so.

I should like now to turn to the separate undertakings, and see how they stand financially. From the information I have had at my disposal, kindly supplied by the various tramway managers, to whom I return my very best thanks, I have endeavoured to class the different undertakings under four heads. I do not suppose I shall give entire satisfaction by doing so, but at any rate we shall be better able to see how each is standing.

In my first list I place thirty tramway undertakings, which I consider are doing well. They are as follows:—

LIST No. 1.

Name	No. of years opened	Miles of Track	Surplus required on basis of £200 per annum per mile of Track	Actual realised surplus	Handed over in relief of Rates	Set aside for Renewals	Total Amount in Reserve and/or Renewal Fund	Total Amount spent out of Reserve and/or Renewals Fund for all purposes
			£	£	£	£	£	£
Birmingham	4	56¼	11,200	65,516	41,103	24,413	126,145	14,880
Bolton	11¼	46	9,200	24,237	8,500	14,990	56,370	96,816
Bradford	12¾	100½	20,000	39,374	20,000	19,374	50,244	84,397
Burnley	9	21	4,200	12,047	4,049	6,466	46,096	7,773
Cardiff	9	31¾	6,360	12,034	nil	12,034	51,014	9,255
Croydon	4¾	17½	3,500	8,459	4,800	3,659	28,347	2,783
Derby	6¾	22	4,400	3,649	nil	3,649	25,630	nil
Huddersfield	10	42	8,400	18,708	6,158	12,250	9,959	124,615
Hull	11¾	29½	5,900	20,000	12,000	8,000	109,000	nil
Leeds	8	108	21,600	87,777	51,888	35,889	4,341	118,270 apart from that spent on track renewals annually
Leicester	7	37	7,400	13,734	nil	13,734	95,426	nil
Liverpool	12½	116	23,200	98,266	32,755	65,511	568,223	190,321
L.C.C.	12	256¾	51,350	192,109	nil	192,109	465,774	45,348
Manchester	9¾	183	36,600	161,250	75,000	86,250	431,182	241,590
Portsmouth	9½	30⅝	6,000	15,656	nil	8,757	75,955	25,310
Preston	6¾	17	3,400	4,370	nil	4,370	25,225	2,378
Rotherham	8	12	2,400	3,646	nil	3,646	16,304	9,894
Sheffield	11½	75½	15,100	39,252	15,476	21,776	77,463	254,409
Walsall	7	19½	3,900	4,772	nil	3,889	27,601	1,912
South Shields	5	10¼	2,050	2,343	nil	1,843	9,470	357
Sunderland	10¾	20	4,000	4,344	2,000	1,941	25,324	26,830
Newcastle	9¾	54	10,800	23,700	nil	23,700	98,557	10,817
West Ham	7	27¾	5,550	8,513	nil	6,923	37,972	3,684 and 1,590 on Top Covers
Wolverhampton	9	21½	4,300	8,266	2,125	6,141	38,455	5,781
Aberdeen	12	27	5,400	11,654	nil	11,654	58,576	45,024
Ayr	9½	5½	1,100	2,191	529	1,962	13,668	nil
Dundee	10¾	28	5,600	7,217	1,000	5,438	50,000	8,350
Glasgow	10	196½	39,300	271,257	68,678	202,579	1,753,747	401,361
Belfast	6	77	15,400	39,147	9,417	29,730	71,436	nil
Nottingham	10	37½	7,500	18,817	15,000	3,817	68,069	4,248

In only three of the above cases will it be seen the Committees placed less than £200 per mile to their Reserve and Renewal Fund.

Sunderland, whilst on the year showing a good surplus, very unwisely, I think, gave £2,000 to the relief of the rates, and only placed £1,941 to their Renewal Fund instead of £4,000.

Nottingham also made a splendid surplus, but I do not consider the Committee was justified in giving £15,000 to the rates and only placing £3,817 to the Renewal Fund; the amount in my opinion ought to have been £7,500 at least.

Derby showed a surplus of £3,649, which was less by £800 than it ought to have been to allow of £200 per mile being set aside for renewals; they, however, placed all their surplus to the fund, which stands at £25,630 in six and three-quarter years.

My second list consists of 14 names of tramways, each showing fairly good results. In my opinion the Committees in charge were not justified in paying the amounts they did towards the rates, taking into full consideration the low state of their Reserve and Renewal Funds. The list is as follows:—

LIST NO. 2.

NAME	No. of years opened	Miles of Track	Surplus required on basis of £200 per annum per mile of Track	Actual realised surplus	Handed over in Relief of Rates	Set aside for Renewals	Total Amount in Reserve and/or Renewal Fund	Total Amount spent out of Reserve and/or Renewals Fund for all purposes
			£	£	£	£	£	£
Blackpool	19	17¼	3,450	8,425	2,425	6,000	5,453	6,105
Bury	6½	20¾	4,150	4,468	1,668	2,800	15,361	nil
Erdington	4	4¼	850	2,473	1,873	600	2,470	nil
Exeter	6	5½	1,100	1,132	nil	1,132	3,832	381
Halifax	12¾	37½	7,500	11,514	4,807	6,707	8,067	8,544
Keighley	6¼	6	1,200	1,205	nil	439	2,644	nil
Northampton	6¾	9	1,800	3,905	1,000	1,200	8,917	nil
Salford	10	38¼	7,650	19,442	18,750	692	46,741	20,051
Southend	9½	7	1,400	4,864	nil	2,000	2,000	1,668
Southampton	11	16	3,200	6,694	2,000	4,694	20,264	nil
Stockport	9½	28	5,600	11,444	7,050	4,012	27,425	4,538
Warrington	9	9⅝	1,925	2,344	2,000	344	9,064	nil
Wallasey	9	12¼	2,450	8,954	6,020	2,000	13,415	1,083 and 15,319 for Cars and Sheds, &c.
York	1	8¾	1,750	1,889	850	1,039	1,978	nil

Blackpool, with only £5,453 in their Reserve Fund, could not afford to give £2,425 to the rates.

Halifax, having made £11,514, ought not to have given £4,807 to the rates whilst having only £8,000 in their Renewal Fund. I certainly expected better things from them after their past experience.

Salford ought to have placed £7,650 at least to their Renewal Fund instead of only £692, and £18,750 to the rates.

Southend, I contend, ought to have built up a Reserve Fund, during the nine and a-half years they have been working, of £13,300, instead of which they have only £2,000, and last year spent £1,668 on track work.

Stockport Renewal Fund is only £27,425, and they have spent £4,538. But in the nine and a-half years they have been running their system it ought to have stood at £53,200, yet they gave £7,050 to the relief of rates.

Wallasey have been running nine years, and in that period ought to have accumulated £22,050, but they only have £13,415 in reserve, and have expended £1,083 on track renewal, and they also gave £6,020 to the relief of rates.

It is a great mistake to risk the financial safety of such splendid undertakings in that way.

My third list contains the names of 16 tramways, all of whom show a surplus on the year's work, but not sufficiently large to allow of the provision of £200 per mile of single track for the Renewal Fund. I therefore contend that, unless that can be done, these tramways are not in a sound financial position. They are as follows:—

LIST NO. 3.

NAME	No. of years opened	Miles of Track	Surplus required on basis of £200 per annum per mile of Track	Actual realised surplus	Handed over in relief of Rates	Set aside for Renewals	Total Amount in Reserve and/or Renewal Fund	Total Amount spent out of Reserve and/or Renewals Fund for all purposes
			£	£	£	£	£	£
Accrington	3¼	10½	2,100	1,754	nil	1,730	6,896	nil
Ashton-under-Lyne	8¾	9	1,800	825	600	200	900	nil
Brighton	9½	17½	3,400	137	nil	137	3,331	Had to draw on fund to make good losses
Burton-on-Trent	7½	9⅞	2,000	318	nil	1,000	7,976	Rate assisted
Chester	8	4¾	950	707	nil	707	1,700	nil
Chesterfield	6¼	5¾	1,150	545	nil	545	4,198	nil
East Ham	9¼	14	2,800	1,167	nil	nil	4,137	£990 of year's profit taken to clear a previous deficit
Great Yarmouth	8¼	14	2,800	1,450	nil	1,250	5,634	nil
Ilford	8	11¼	2,250	679	nil	679	6,919	768
Leyton	4¼	18	3,600	1,317	658	659	1,900	nil
Newport	8	14½	2,900	2,322	nil	2,322	7,685	1,000
Plymouth	11¼	12	2,400	850	850	nil		
Reading	7¼	13½	2,700	2,163	1,500	663	13,631	4,158
Rochdale	9 & 5½	24¾	4,950	1,944	nil	nil	nil	Surplus used in paying over spent capita
Walthamstow	5¾	12½	2,500	1,411	nil	1,411	2,696	nil
Kirkcaldy	8	8½	1,700	512	512	nil	3,139	nil

Ashton-under-Lyne, with only a surplus of £825, paid £600 to the relief of rates, although their Renewal Fund only stands at £900.

Leyton made a surplus of £1,317. They gave £658 to the relief of rates, whilst having only £1,900 in their Renewal Fund after four years working.

Plymouth had a surplus of £850, and gave it all to the relief of rates.

Reading made a surplus of £2,163, but gave £1,500 to the relief of rates, whilst their Renewal Fund was short by £5,000.

Kirkcaldy gave their full surplus of £542 to the relief of rates, the Committee being content with a Renewal Fund of £3,139 for eight and a-half miles of track which has been in use eight years.

It is from the above list, I feel sure, sooner or later, my next will be recruited, unless the Committees responsible alter their present policy and see that their tramways are placed on a good and sound financial basis.

My next and last list consists of 32 tramway undertakings which show no surplus at all; in fact, all but three are a charge upon the rates.

LIST NO. 4.

NAME	Number of years opened	Miles of Track	Surplus	Total amount in Reserve and/or Renewals Fund	Total amount spent out of Reserve and/or Renewals Fund for all purposes	Average number of times population carried per annum
				£	£	
Barking.. ..	7	4½	nil	nil	nil	
Bexley	7½	6½	nil	nil	nil	126
Birkenhead ..	10	24	nil	12,766	4,837	101·55
Blackburn ..	12¾	24¼	nil	nil	8,260	51
Bournemouth ..	8¾	30	nil	nil	2,000 (plus heavy costs of accident, &c.)	139
Colchester ..	6½	8	nil	nil	nil	41·25
Darlington ..	6¾	9	nil	3,816	538	56·23
Darwen.. ..	11	4¼	nil	5,350	5,000	59·5
Doncaster ..	8	10¾	nil	nil	nil	81·23
Dover	13½	7	nil	nil	nil	
Erith	5½	8¼	nil	nil	nil	
Glamorgan ..		¾	nil	nil	nil	
Gloucester ..	7	15	nil	nil	nil	67
Haslingden ..	3	3	nil	nil	nil	
Heywood ..	3	5½				
Ilkeston ..	8	13	nil	nil	nil	58
Ipswich.. ..	7½	14¾	nil	1,402	nil	71·52
Lancaster .	8	4	nil	3,000	nil	32
Lincoln.. ..	5½	3	nil	nil	nil	80 (G.B. Surface Contact)
Lowestoft ..	7¾	5½	nil	nil	350	67·92
Maidstone ..	6¾	7	nil	nil	nil	86
Nelson	8	3¾	nil	nil	nil	44·48
Oldham.. ..	10½	36¾	nil	inl	12,130	102·53
Pontypridd ..	6	8¼	nil	nil	nil	129
Rawstenhall ..	2	11¾	nil	600	nil	
Southport ..	10½	11	nil	417	nil	129·3
Stalybridge ..	7	27¾	nil	nil	nil	104·4
Swindon ..	6½	4½	nil	4,977	nil	
Wigan	10	31	nil	nil	nil	56·5
Kilmarnock .	6½	4¼	nil	1,564	nil	55
Leith	5½	17¾	nil	nil	nil	93·5
Perth	5½	6½	nil	nil	nil	50

Bournemouth was fortunate in having a Reserve Fund, but is now drawing upon it to make good its losses.

Lincoln is fortunate in being able to draw on the profits of the Electricity Department.

Southport is putting its loss to a Suspense Account and living in hopes of one day paying it off out of prospective profits.

I do not really consider it necessary for me to make any comments in submitting the above list; it speaks for itself. I think the Committees would do well to consider their position and see if the losses are not caused by having reduced their fares too low, and by giving other concessions which the moderate amount of traffic they carry does not warrant them in granting. I shall, however, refer to this question later on.

On my fourth list I have placed a column showing the number of times the different places carry their population in the year; it is surprising to find such a small traffic return notwithstanding that many of the places have adopted the halfpenny fare stages, which are *supposed* to increase traffic, if not receipts.

I hope it will not be thought that I am hostile to the municipal trams; I can assure you that I am not; my only desire is to endeavour to obtain a greater interest being taken in the financial position of the several undertakings by the responsible Committees, and to prevent, if possible, the municipal trams becoming a failure and a permanent charge upon the ratepayers; or perhaps handed over to some private company to make a success where municipalisation had failed.

I am a great believer in corporations owning and working their own tramways; but I also believe that when it is done it ought to be done on purely business lines.

Any chairman or manager will tell you that at the present time it is almost impossible to do this. You have members of the Councils voting away the profits to the relief of the rates, irrespective of any future requirements in the way of renewals. This may please their constituents for the time being, and perhaps that is all they really care about; but the time will undoubtedly come when many will have good cause to regret it.

There are others who contend that the ratepayers are not entitled to any financial assistance by contributions towards the rates; that any surplus should be used in giving better and cheaper facilities to the car users, and in granting *extra* good conditions of labour to the employees.

With this policy I also entirely disagree; the ratepayers, I consider, for several reasons have a right to expect a return sooner or later; the streets belong to them, and by placing the tramways in those streets they give them a marketable value.

No corporation possesses the right of disposing, without adequate consideration, of something that belongs to the ratepayers.

Then again the ratepayers backed our bills; without their security we would have been unable to borrow the money for the construction; besides, they are responsible for its repayment. It was the ratepayers who gave us permission to go to Parliament for the powers to establish the tramways; in short they are the owners and we the trustees on their behalf. It is our duty as such to see that the best is made of their estate; to so manage them that they will pay their way, and, when once placed on a sound foundation, any surplus that there is ought to be handed over to the ratepayers as owners.

I believe in giving every facility possible to the public, consistent with the yield of an adequate profit; but I do not see why we should run cars at a loss, or even at a loss of profit, for the sole benefit of the riding public, when frequently one-third or more of those using our cars may be non-residents in our districts.

Why should we run, say, a five-minutes service at a loss, if a ten-minutes service could be run for a profit? Or why should we have halfpenny fares, when it perhaps takes a penny fare to pay the cost? No business company would do it; then, why should the municipal corporations?

The policy of some of our Committees would really make one believe they cannot appreciate the difference between a city like Glasgow, with its population of over a million people, carried over two hundred times every year, and a district with its thirty or forty thousand inhabitants, whose population is only carried by the trams some forty or fifty times in the year. In Glasgow, or two or three other cities with their densely-crowded streets, a halfpenny fare may be both useful and successful; but that, I think, cannot be said of thinly-populated areas.

It is this kind of policy, I feel sure, that is the cause of so many of our tramway undertakings being the financial failures they are.

A very little per care mile run makes a large difference in the profits or losses of a tramway system. Let us take one or two examples: Glasgow runs about 21,000,000 car miles in a year with a traffic return of 10.23 per car mile; if they reduced this return to 9.23 per car mile, by granting concessions to the public, it would only be one penny per car mile less than they at present receive, yet it would represent no less a sum than £87,500 in the year, or more than they at present give to the rates. Then let us take Nelson, a town in Lancashire with a population of 45,000; they run 200,000 car miles in a year, and their traffic return works out at 8.56 per car mile; they run halfpenny fares and made a loss of £784 last year. If they could, by the abolition of the halfpenny fares and by other means, increase their traffic return to 9.56, which is not a large return certainly, being only one penny per car mile more than they receive at present, their traffic revenue would be increased by £833, and their loss would have disappeared. This, I think, proves the importance of being extremely careful in granting innocent-looking concessions.

In no fewer than twelve towns where losses are made each year, the Committees have granted halfpenny fares; whilst in six others, where the profits are not sufficient to make proper provision for track renewals, the Committees have made the same concession.

In only ten places that may be looked upon as financially successful are halfpenny fares allowed; four of these are in Scotland, which, of course, includes Glasgow, and four are in England, viz.: Leeds, Sheffield, London County Council, and West Ham, each serving very large populations: the remaining two are Stockport and Warrington, both of which, I feel sure, would have done better if they had never granted the concession at all.

In the numbers given above, I do not refer to workmen's cars, but only the ordinary daily traffic; nor do I include Manchester, with a circular route with halfpenny sections on the outskirts of the city; or Halifax, Preston, and Perth, with one short route only at that fare.

This goes to prove very clearly, I think, that halfpenny fares ought not to be given, especially by small tramway systems; even the larger ones should be exceedingly careful before granting such facilities.

I shall now refer to what I consider another mistaken policy which some of our Committees have adopted, viz.: the running of cars at cheap fares each morning. I notice in several towns they allow all passengers to travel at half the ordinary fare up to 8 and 9 o'clock in the morning, issuing return tickets at the same rate in many places; that, to my mind, is undoubtedly a great mistake and a decided loss to those undertakings.

We had some time ago a request made by a large and powerful Association in Newcastle to my Committee for this same privilege, and I shall just explain how it would have affected our system had we granted it. I must in the first place explain what we do; but, understand, I do not put it before you as an ideal scheme, although it works fairly well with us.

All cars up to 7 o'clock are workmen's cars, and any person may travel at workmen's rates, the minimum payment on a car being one penny. *Bonâ-fide* workmen may purchase at the Tramway offices twelve tickets for sixpence, which allow him to ride one and three-quarter miles in the morning and evening, or twelve tickets for one shilling, which entitle him to ride three and a-half miles morning and evening.

After 7 o'clock all cars are run ordinary, and each passenger must pay full fare; *bonâ fide* workmen, however, are allowed to travel with their coupons up to 8 a.m.

Between 7 and 9 a.m. we receive in ordinary fares over £90 in cash daily; if we ran those cars at half rates, the same as the places I refer to, we would have to double our number of passengers to receive the same amount of money; to do that, I consider, is absolutely impossible.

The result, we estimated, would work out something like this: the £90 received daily would be reduced to £45 straight away; we might, I say might, for it is very doubtful, have a slight increase in our present numbers, which I estimate might yield, say, £10; thus we would be receiving £55 daily, instead of the £90 as at present, or £35 per day less, which would mean £210 in the week of six days, or £10,920 in the year.

But the request did not stop at that, for it was also suggested that each passenger travelling before 9 o'clock ought to be allowed to take two or four tickets as required, at the same half price, one for morning and evening, and two for dinner time.

If, then, we would sacrifice £10,920 in the year on one service, what was our loss going to be on the four; I put it down at £30,000 at the very least, being several thousands of pounds more than our present surplus; thus a profitable undertaking would have been turned into a losing one.

If that would have been the effect in Newcastle, it must have had a proportionate effect on the finances of those places that have adopted it, and the majority of them cannot afford to do it. It is by this kind of policy, granting concessions in this way, that many of our tramways are in the serious financial state they are to-day.

We all, I believe, excepting six towns, run workmen's cars; I wonder how many make them pay. Very few, I should think, if any.

I do not say we ought not to run workmen's cars, but I do contend that we ought to have a return from these cars, sufficient at least to pay the cost of working them; they ought not to be a charge upon the undertaking.

I am afraid very few can claim that those cars do pay their working expenses; in fact, I have little hesitation in saying that by far the greater number of our tramways are working these cars at a considerable loss.

The loss may not be felt so much by the larger undertakings, but where tramways are established in small, thinly-populated districts, and where revenue is of the greatest importance to them, it then becomes a very serious thing; it is one of the several causes that leaves those undertakings with a debit balance each year.

I fully recognise the difficulty there might be in correcting all this now that the concessions have been granted; but in my opinion it is certainly worth the attempt; especially ought this to be done by those Tramways Committees who are running their service at a loss, and are already a charge upon the rates; the financial stability of their undertaking certainly demands it.

I should now like to turn for a few minutes to another very important question; one that may cause many if not all of the tramway undertakings serious trouble, and great financial loss, unless it is very carefully and firmly handled; I refer to the question of the employees.

We have had recently several strikes, and others threatened, and a general feeling of unrest exhibited by the men.

Personally I think this unrest arises very largely from a misconception on the part of the men; I rather think they have got the idea which is put forward by some members of the Councils and others that they ought to be the first, and last, consideration of the Committees; that the trams are a kind of co-partnership arrangement, they being the only partners, and that any surplus ought to be expended in giving them shorter hours and more money; but should any loss occur, then the ratepayers can make that good.

This, to my mind, is altogether wrong; I believe in dealing with the men fairly and even generously; we ought to give them a somewhat higher wage than that paid in the respective districts to men doing the kind of work from which our employees are generally drawn; we ought to grant them reasonable hours of labour, and these ought to be worked in the least possible compass; we ought to do our very best to ease away any irritation that may from time to time arise. All this ought to be done, with a due consideration as to the proper working of the tramway system.

Thus far, then, should we go, but no further; we have no right, I submit, to raise those men to a position equal with skilled mechanics, who have had several years to serve to learn their trade.

A skilled mechanic has frequently to suffer financial loss from slackness of work, all his holidays, compulsory and otherwise, are deducted from his wages, and he must purchase all his own working apparel, whilst the tramway employee is provided with a full uniform; is allowed holidays each year with full pay; and enjoys regular work, without any lost time, unless it is caused by his own neglect.

If, then, we compare the average income of the two, it will be found that the wages and emoluments of the tram employees, who are generally drawn from unskilled labour, will equal the net income of the skilled artisan; to place him higher still, either by granting more wages or by reducing his hours of labour, would, in my opinion, be not only an injustice to the trained mechanics, but quite unfair to the undertakings we have to manage and direct.

I do not suggest that employees on all tramways are quite free from grievances. That would be almost an impossibility, but I do think that any grievances they may have could easily be put right by a conference between the manager and representatives from Committee and men.

It was most pleasing to see some little time ago that the Committee and employees of the Manchester Tramways agreed to submit to arbitration the men's claims for improved conditions. It was much more satisfactory than if the men had forced a strike, causing loss of money to themselves and loss of revenue to the undertaking, besides causing great inconvenience to the travelling public, such as occurred in Leeds, Glasgow, and Liverpool only recently.

Should it be the misfortune, however, of any tramway to have a strike amongst their employees, I sincerely hope that their Councils will not repeat the action of the Leeds Corporation, and supersede the Tramways Committee by a special Committee to deal with the men, but allow the Tramways Committees and the managers who are responsible for the proper working of the systems to do that. Such action weakens the authority of both the manager and Tramways Committee.

If our Tramways Committees have to deal effectively with the many claims that are constantly being made upon them, by both the employees and the general travelling public, they require, and ought to have, the full confidence and support of the members of our Councils. The working of a tramway undertaking is difficult enough at the best, without making it more so by such action as that of the Leeds Council.

Councils ought not to take fright if their employees cause a dislocation of the regular traffic; it is very inconvenient, I admit; but they ought to have confidence in the Tramways Committees and managers, and feel that they never would have allowed things to go so far as to have a strike of employees, unless they had a good reason for doing so. We can purchase peace at too high a price.

Another drawback Tramways Committee have to contend against is the would-be popular members of the Council or Committee, who are never happy but when advocating further concessions. It is increased wages or shorter hours for the employees, cheap halfpenny fares, or a more frequent service of cars upon some particular route—generally in the locality they sit for—cheaper fares for workmen, free rides for others, and such like demands. Never for a single moment do they consider what the effect of this kind of thing may have on the financial position of the undertaking.

Those members who are really wishful for the success of municipal tramways must stand firm against this kind of cheap popularity; it is certainly not business, nor is it fair to the system or Committee to have to contend against this sort of thing, and be expected to bring out good results at the end of the financial year.

It is certainly not for the benefit of either the employee or the general public to make things so difficult that the tramway undertakings cannot be run financially successful by the corporations. If Committees are driven into excessive expenditure, and their undertakings become a regular charge upon the ratepayers, we can rest assured that in a very little while they will rebel and endeavour to free themselves of the incubus; they will demand that the tramway undertaking shall be handed over to private enterprise to make the best of it, and thus free themselves of the yearly loss.

The position of the corporation would thus be much worse than at the very first, for no company would think of paying the town a rent for the right of running a discredited undertaking, nor would any company, under such circumstances, give the facilities to the public, or the conditions of labour that are now given by the corporations.

Those that are always advocating the concessions I have referred to are not, then, true benefactors to either the public or employees, but rather enemies of both, and certainly no friend of municipalisation; they would do well to read what Mr. Jackson, the Secretary of the Tramway and Vehicle Workers' Union, said the other day at Manchester, regarding those who were endeavouring to persuade the tram employees to strike in that city: "Speeches had been made to induce the tramway men to "come out; the men resented these interferences by out-"siders, and could well manage their own affairs."

Mr. President and gentlemen, I shall now conclude; my only excuse for trespassing so long upon your time is the importance of the subject. I have endeavoured to place clearly before the conference the financial position of each municipal tramway, and I have pointed out what, in my opinion, are some of the mistakes in their policy. I have prepared a schedule of capital expenditure, income, and other items, which I hope will be both interesting and useful.

I hope we may have a good discussion, and that the members will take my criticism in the same spirit that I have offered it, and I can only further hope that it may lead to good results.

SUMMARY OF OFFICIAL RETURNS RELATING TO CAPITAL

	Total Capital Expenditure	Total Income for last year from		Net Surplus Available	Surplus required on the basis of £200 per annum per mile of track	Disposal of Surplus		
		Traffic	Other Sources			Reserve and Renewals	Paid over in Relief of Rates	Paid over for other purposes
	£	£	£	£	£	£	£	£
Accrington	132,822	24,043	467	1,754	2,100	1,730	..	..
Ashton-under-Lyne	107,751	19,779	436	825	1,800	200	600	25 carr for'd
Barking	75,912	3,088	1,541	nil	835	..	..	..
Bexley (1910)	96,984	13,495	1,069	nil	1,300	nil	nil	nil
Birkenhead	366,428	56,717	945	nil	1,800	nil	nil	nil
Birmingham	1,055,540	315,463	3,419	65,516	11,200	24,413	41,103	nil
Blackburn	335,050	54,659	3,707	nil	4,950	nil	nil	nil
Blackpool	283,239	56,651	1,190	8,425	3,450	6,000	2,425	nil
Bolton	538,214	123,602	858	24,237	9,200	14,990	8,500	747 carr. for.
Bournemouth	522,340	89,497	199	nil	6,000	nil	nil	nil
Bradford	944,928	256,063	14,903	39,374	20,100	19,374	20,000	..
Brighton	274,905	49,124	1,623	137	3,400	137	..	..
Burnley	260,470	65,570	247	12,047	4,200	6,466	4,019	..
Burton-on-Trent	106,012	13,990	1,378	318	2,000	1,000 partly ex. rates	..	..
Bury	281,145	60,551	145	4,468	4,150	2,800	1,668	..
Cardiff	780,921	116,806	18,588	12,034	6,360	5,087	..	6,947
Chester (1910)	82,785	12,338	426	707	950	707	..	..
Chesterfield	69,575	11,270	447	545	1,150	545	..	..
Colchester	69,400	9,820	561	..	1,600	..	..	..
Croydon	282,112	85,805	2,356	8,459	3,500	3,659	4,800	..
Darlington	76,269	10,392	517	..	1,800	..	..	..
Darwen	85,735	1,354	242	..	850	..	..	..
Derby	239,301	*43,994	*1,006	3,649	4,400	3,619	..	..
Doncaster	91,395	14,962	341	nil	2,150	nil	..	..
Dover	63,000	11,089	407	..	1,400	..	..	..
East Ham (1910)	186,520	52,502	834	1,167	2,800	..	..	990 to clear prev. deficit 177 carr. for
Erdington	37,490	13,696	..	2,473	850	600	1,873	..
Erith	88,083	11,278	204	..	1,650	..	..	..
Exeter	86,000	16,166	..	1,132	1,100	1,132	..	..
Glamorgan County Council (Swansea)	32,598	396	..	..	150	..	..	..
Gloucester	144,233	14,965	1,002	..	3,000	..	..	..
Great Yarmouth	121,261	23,228	602	1,450	2,800	1,250	..	113 car met'rs 87 carr. for'd
Halifax	400,149	91,526	1,047	11,514	7,500	6,707	1,807	..
Handsworth	126,322	3,122	..	..	..	..	..	..
Haslingden	39,733	6,834	..	..	600	..	..	..
Heywood (with Bury and Rochdale)								
Huddersfield	408,326	92,853	3,332	18,708	8,400	12,250	6,458	..
Hull	488,933	141,988	1,351	20,000	5,900	8,000	12,000	..
Ilford	149,118	28,515	526	679	2,250	679	..	..
Ilkeston	47,578	6,879	158	..	860	..	..	..
Ipswich	114,471	21,157	581	..	2,950	..	..	..
Keighley	46,648	9,407	209	1,205	1,200	439	nil	766 transf'd to Cap.
King's Norton (Birmingham)								
Lancaster	43,330	5,241	136	..	800	..	..	..
Leeds	1,464,902	364,927	5,475	87,777	21,600	35,889 P. Way	51,888	..
Leicester	691,740	122,693	9,705	13,734	7,400	13,734	..	..
Leyton	295,021	56,237	1,267	1,317	3,600	659	658	..
Lincoln (G.B. surface contact)	44,997	6,412	123	nil	600	nil	..	..
Liverpool	1,986,531	582,276	32,538	98,266	23,200	65,511	32,755	..
London County Council	10,709,504	1,969,952	53,052	192,109	51,350	192,109	..	..
Lowestoft	79,235	10,586	310	nil	1,100	nil	..	..
Maidstone	78,748	8,749	651	nil	1,400	nil	..	..
Manchester	1,981,160	799,079	11,015	161,250	36,600	86,250	75,000	..
Newcastle-upon-Tyne	1,184,644	199,947	9,720	23,700	10,800	23,700	..	..
Nelson	36,431	7,576	39	nil	750	nil	nil	..
Newport (Mon.)	189,000	34,092	1,013	2,322	2,900	2,322	..	..

*Electric

Expenditure, Income, &c., to 31st March 1911.

If a Loss on a Year's Working		Paid in Rates		Reserve Fund at present time amounts to	Spent out of Reserve on		
Amount of Loss	Loss made good out of	Last Year	Since Inauguration		Any other Expenditure	Perm. Way Renewals	
£		£	£	£	£	£	
nil	..	406	1,222	6,896	nil	nil	
nil	..	807	6,238	900	nil	nil	
5,442	Out of Rates	..	..	..	..	..	
933	Out of Rates	585	..	nil	nil	nil	
1,115	Out of Rates	1,962	18,507	12,766	nil	4,837	
..	..	13,014	56,500	126,145	3,077	11,803	
181	Previous year's pr'fits	889	10,300	nil	nil	8,260	
nil	..	1,612	..	5,453	4,322	1,783	
..	..	4,435	48,785	56,370	43,725	53,091	
142	Unapprop'd Balance A/c	2,629	19,062	..	£2,000 + of accid	heavy cost ent, &c.	
..	..	12,115	85,217	50,244	..	84,397	
..	..	907	5,591 (Exc. last year)	3,331	3,389 to make good a deficiency	..	
..	..	2,970	17,958	46,096	5,673	2,109	
..	..	494	3,877	7,976	..	..	
..	..	1,573	7,694	15,361	..	..	
..	..	5,288	39,180	51,014	..	9,255	
..	..	333	..	1,700	..	..	
..	..	454	1,859	4,198	..	..	
2,170	Out of Rates	283	1,458	..	..	..	
..	..	2,719	12,630	28,347	..	2,783	
1,158	Out of Rates	92	654	3,816	..	538	
390	Out of Rates	266	2,740	5,350	..	5,000	
..	..	1,211	..	but £25,630 carried for'd	..	..	
135	Out of Rates	..	..	nil	..	..	
2,622	Out of Rates	..	..	..	..	..	
..	..	1,735	7,255	4,137	..	..	
..	..	..	..	2,470	..	..	Working agreement with Birmingham Corporation
2,878	Out of Rates	316	1,684	..	..	..	
..	..	471	3,025	3,832	..	381	
289	Out of Rates	..	..	..	..	..	Working agreement with the Swansea Corporation
3,179	Out of Rates	255	1,715	..	..	..	
..	..	729	4,824	5,634	..	..	
..	..	2,324	29,364	8,067	nil	8,544	
1,250	Out of Rates	..	..	..	..	..	Working agreement with Birmingham Corporation
341	Out of Rates	..	..	..	..	..	Working agreement with Accrington Corporation
							Working agreement with Bury and Rochdale Corporations
..	..	6,458	27,695	9,959	124,615	jointly	
..	..	9,127	69,396	109,000	..	..	
..	..	..	2,500	6,919	..	768	
2,471	Out of Rates	..	..	..	..	..	
2,230	Out of Rates	180	..	1,402	..	..	
..	..	181	1,120	2,644	nil	nil	
							Working agreement with Birmingham Corporation
2,720	Out of Rates	109	1,129	3,000	..	..	
..	..	21,124	139,500	4,341	118,270	..	
..	..	5,029	28,817	95,426	..	..	
..	..	1,358	..	1,900	..	..	
153	Electricity Fund profits	213	1,194	..	..	..	
..	..	..	..	568,223	..	190,321	
..	..	86,896	..	465,774	25,568	19,780	
2,395	Out of Rates	181	1,510	..	..	350	
2,623	Out of Rates	2,484	..	..	..	..	
..	..	41,313	259,097	431,182	19,658	224,932	
..	..	8,612	68,624	98,557	8,697	2,120	
784	Out of Rates	119	..	..	..	..	
..	..	1,165	..	7,685	..	1,000	

and Horse.

SUMMARY OF OFFICIAL RETURNS RELATING TO CAPITAL

	Total Capital Expenditure	Total Income for last year from		Net Surplus Available	Surplus required on the basis of £200 per annum per mile of track	Disposal of Surplus		
		Traffic	Other Sources			Reserve and Renewals	Paid over in Relief of Rates	Paid over for other purposes
		£	£	£	£	£	£	£
npton	133,012	25,199	725	3,905	1,800	1,200	1,000	532 carr. for'd 1,173 Purch'se of Property
ham	631,344	154,920	2,369	18,817	7,500	3,817	15,000	..
ı	427,703	95,975	1,868	nil	7,335	nil	nil	..
th	168,219	34,520	1,716	850	2,400	..	850	..
ridd .. .. (1910)	131,571	21,331	291	nil	1,650	nil	nil	..
outh	696,365	102,930	1,757	15,656	6,000	8,757	..	1,928 Ins'ce Fund
.. ..	187,269	37,491	578	4,370	3,400	1,370	nil	..
stall	170,593	19,566	180	nil	2,350	nil	nil	..
g	227,393	31,373	1,134	2,163	2,700	663	1,500	..
le	350,896	62,046	954	1,944	4,950	nil	nil	1,944 used in paying overspent Cap.
ıam	152,644	33,313	33	3,646	3,400	3,646	nil	..
.. ..	721,338	242,776	5,646	19,442	7,650	692	18,750	..
d .. .. (1910)	1,203,415	296,251	6,585	39,252	15,100	21,776	15,476	2,000 for special purposes
mpton	203,817	55,187	1,362	6,694	3,200	4,694	2,000	..
nd	109,416	28,796	890	4,861	1,400	2,000	nil	1,668 Track improvem'nts
ort	196,179	18,422	nil	nil	2,200	nil	nil	nil
Shields	172,255	29,046	713	2,343	2,050	1,843	nil	500 towards Accident Insurance Fund
idge	279,550	36,479	306	nil	5,450	nil	nil	nil
ort	234,674	55,484	1,158	11,444	5,600	4,012	7,050	382 Accident Insur. Fund
land	299,744	58,889	182	4,344	4,000	1,911	2,000	403
on	44,216	7,374	276	nil	900	nil	nil	nil
ey	176,159	47,033	607	8,954	2,450	2,000	6,020	500 to Insur. Reserve Fund 434 carr. for'd.
ll	179,111	28,265	2,149	1,772	3,900	3,889	nil	883 for new cars & Depôt alterations
amstow	173,000	35,878	686	1,411	2,500	1,411	nil	nil
ngton	102,895	20,367	288	2,344	1,925	314	2,000	nil
Ham	518,039	131,234	1,296	8,513	5,550	6,923	nil	1,590 top covers to cars, &c
.. ..	473,821	62,229	1,250	..	6,200	..	..	..
rhampton (ain system)	255,942	48,909	800	8,266	4,300	6,111	2,125	..
.. ..	112,900	13,138	431	1,889	1,750	1,039	850	..
een	353,078	70,078	1,043	11,654	5,400	11,654	..	..
.. ..	82,789	14,331	675	2,491	1,100	1,962	529	..
e	339,000	61,310	1,018	7,217	5,600	5,438	1,000 common good	779 special
w	3,503,174	946,021	46,911	271,257	39,300	202,579	68,678 common good	..
nock	52,653	7,945	232	..	850	..	..	..
ldy	96,240	14,316	402	542	1,700	..	542	..
.. ..	234,975	30,772	661	..	3,575	..	..	..
.. ..	76,948	8,540	392	..	1,300	..	..	..
t..	1,125,864	213,927	4,374	39,147	15,400	29,730	9,417	..

EXPENDITURE, INCOME, &c., TO 31ST MARCH 1911 (*continued*).

If a Loss on a Year's Working		Paid in Rates		Reserve Fund at present time amounts to	Spent out of Reserve on	
Amount of Loss	Loss made good out of	Last Year	Since Inauguration		Any other Expenditure	Perm. Way Renewals
£		£	£	£	£	£
..	..	1,000	7,200	8,917	..	..
..	..	9,221	68,928	68,069	4,218 Removing centre poles	..
1,307	Out of Rates	2,986	22,228	nil	5,895	6,235
..	..	..	..	..	..	..
1,150	Out of Rates & by a Loan	204	..	..	..	..
..	..	6,211	40,050	75,955	..	25,310
..	..	2,425	nil	25,225	2,378	..
296	Out of Rates	436	780	600	..	..
..	..	1,860	14,075	13,631	1,770	2,388
..	..	1,121	5,740	nil	nil	..
..	..	863	6,056	16,304	nil	9,894
..	..	9,788	63,604	46,744	1,000	19,051
..	..	12,657	96,516	77,463	131,880	122,529
..	..	..	..	20,264	..	..
..	..	363	2,671	2,000	..	1,668
1,820	In suspense	661	4,995	117	..	..
..	..	1,350	4,107	9,470	357	..
5,938	Out of Rates	1,529	9,496	..	..	..
..	..	1,485	10,036	27,425	..	4,538
..	..	3,132	24,853	25,324	..	26,830
2,609 including Depreciation	Out of Rates	254	1,866	4,977	..	..
..	..	978	6,436	13,415	16,402	..
..	..	858	5,908	27,601	1,912 on Cars and Depôt altns.	..
..	..	624	1,440	2,696	nil	..
..	..	676	4,309	9,061	nil	.
nil	..	5,072	15,657	37,972	..	3,681
8,670	Out of Rates	2,609	..	..	..	.
..	..	1,191	8,240	38,455	661	5,120
..	..	276	300	1,978	..	..
..	..	4,195	24,151	58,576	..	15,024
.	..	565	5,070	13,668	..	..
..	..	1,525	13,700	50,000	..	8,350
..	..	61,025	477,350	1,753,747	163,281	238,083
2,060	Out of Rates	147	1,030	1,561	..	..
..	..	306	1,667	3,139	..	..
1,903	Out of Rates	709	2,817	..	..	..
773	Out of Rates	204	1,178	..	..	..
..	..	5,300	..	74,436	..	..

Institute of Municipal Treasurers and Accountants (Incorporated).

South Wales and Monmouthshire Students' Society.

Income Tax as Affecting Local Authorities.

By Mr. F. J. ALBAN, F.S.A.A., A.C.I.S.
(Accountant to the Pontypridd and Rhondda Joint Water Board).

A LECTURE delivered at a meeting of the Society held at Cardiff on 23rd March 1912.

(1) INTRODUCTION—NECESSITY TO UNDERSTAND GENERAL PRINCIPLES.

I must of necessity assume that the student who desires to study the subject of income-tax as it affects local authorities has first of all obtained a fair acquaintance with the broad principles of income-tax as they affect the general public, companies, &c. Taking this essential basis for granted then, I dip into the subject without further explanation.

Legal Authority for Income Tax.—The legal authority for income-tax is the Budget of each year as ultimately enacted and a body of income-tax statutes running from 1842. The statutes are, however, supplemented by a vast quantity of "case law," *i.e.*, Judges' interpretations of the statutes. The essential principle of "case law" is that the decision of a Court is a binding authority for the future in co-ordinate or inferior Courts, and can only be revoked by higher Courts or by statute. Thus, decisions of the House of Lords (as a legal tribunal) are unalterable save by statute. As will be seen, most of the differences between the income-tax assessments of local authorities and those of individuals arise from the authority of "case law."

(2) Why are Local Authorities Assessed to Income Tax?

The outside public are frequently amazed when they realise that local authorities are at all interested in the income-tax, and it does indeed lead to some complication of thought when one considers that the average small ratepayer who is himself exempt from income-tax yet pays tax in his capacity as a ratepayer.

In some respects he is worse off, because the taxpayer in his aggregate corporate capacity is not allowed certain concessions which are invariably given to him in his capacity as an individual.

In some quarters it has been suggested that local authorities should be quite free from income-tax, and should merely hand over to the Inland Revenue authorities any tax received by them in the capacity of collector (*i.e.*, deducted by them from interest, dividends, ground rent, &c.). This would indeed be somewhat on a par with the exemption from local rates which extends to many Government properties in respect of which no contribution or only a contribution based on a reduced valuation (*e.g.*, Post Office property) is made to the local rates.

On the other hand, it might well be argued that such an exemption would give municipal trading undertakings an undue advantage in comparison with their rivals.

The subject leads to many interesting thoughts as to the differences between "taxpayer" and "ratepayer."

We must take things as they stand. Local authorities are assessed, and assessed heavily too—and I pass, therefore, on to a few points relative to such assessments which may profitably receive our consideration.

(3) The Five Schedules.

Income-tax is, for the purpose of convenience in assessment and collection, divided into five schedules; the chief incidents of the respective schedules I have separately tabulated in comparative form, and to this tabulation I venture to refer you.

It is important to note that there are not five separate taxes; it is one tax divided or classified for convenience into five schedules. This fact was brought out in the London County Council case referred to hereafter, and at once gives rise to the broad principle that a person should not be assessed, or at any rate compelled to pay tax, under more than one schedule in respect of the same matter.

(4) Schedule A Allowance for Repairs.

Schedule A calls for some special comment.

As will be seen from the tabulation, it is assessed on the annual value of the ownership of property.

Allowance for Repairs.—Under the general income-tax law the gross annual value of property is subject to a deduction for repairs (including maintenance) as follows:—

House Property 1/6th
Farm Property 1/8th

These deductions are made from the gross assessment and the result is the net assessment—the "net annual value of the property."

By the Finance (1909-10) Act, 1910, relief is extended as follows in the case of:—

(*a*) Land, including farm houses and buildings.

(*b*) Houses the annual value of which does not exceed £8 for income-tax purposes.

Nature and Conditions of Extended Relief.—The taxpayer on proving to the satisfaction of the Inland Revenue authorities that his expenditure in connection with the property, including insurance and maintenance, according to the average of the preceding five years, has exceeded the one-sixth or one-eighth can make a claim for the return of tax in respect of the property up to a maximum of

House Property—an additional one-twelfth of the gross annual value,

Farm Property—an additional one-eighth of the gross annual value,

making in each case a maximum allowance for repairs and maintenance of 25 per cent.

This additional relief takes the form of a definite claim for repayment of tax. Each case is considered on its merits, and it does not necessarily follow that the taxpayer will be entitled to the maximum allowances.

Local authorities may, like other taxpayers, take advantage of this additional allowance.

(5) The Rules into which Schedule A is Divided.

Schedule A is assessed under a number of rules.

Rule No. 1 is applicable to all lands, tenements, hereditaments, or heritages capable of actual occupation, of whatever nature, and for whatever purpose occupied, and of whatever value, except the properties included in rules Nos. 2 and 3.

In practice all lands, &c. (note that the term "land" includes all below the surface, *e.g.*, mines, mains, &c., and all above, *e.g.*, buildings, &c.), which are rateable for purposes of local rates are construed as being within this rule. Thus—

(*a*) Hereditaments in respect of which no question of profit arises, *e.g.*, sewers, are assumed to have an annual value, the underlying idea being that all land, &c., has an inherent value quite apart from the question of profits.

(*b*) Land (including the buildings connected therewith) held for the purpose of trading concerns, other than those specified in Rules 2 and 3, is assessable under this rule, although the concerns are also assessable in respect of profits under Schedule D, as explained later.

(*c*) All houses, &c., are assessable under the rule.

Annual value for the purpose of this rule is the rack ent at which the property is worth to be let by the year, and theoretically is identical with the value for local ating purposes.

This "annual value" is regarded as equivalent to ncome and is taxed accordingly. Thus a person who wns and occupies his own house is regarded as having in income equivalent to the annual value of the property and he is assessed thereon.

Any annual charges on the property, *e.g.*, mortgage nterest, ground rent, &c., are (in the case of individuals) leducted from the annual value for the purpose of arriving at the "income" from the property, it being ightly considered that the beneficial interest in the proerty to the extent of the mortgage interest or ground ent is vested in the mortgagee or ground landlord.

The case is fairly simple as applied to houses and lands, but when applied to sewers, &c., many difficulties arise, n fixing upon the "annual value."

Rule No. 2 relates to tithes, &c., and directions are given as to how the "annual value" thereof is to be calculated.

Rule No. 3 relates to quarries, mines, railways, gasvorks, waterworks, and other concerns arising out of ands.

Concerns included in this rule are to be assessed under he rules applicable to Schedule D, and for all practical purposes may be regarded as Schedule D assessments. The annual value is in these cases based on the "profits," generally those of the preceding year.

6) THE SCHEDULE A ASSESSMENTS ON LOCAL AUTHORITIES.

The Schedule A assessments on local authorities may be divided into five classes—

(1) *On lands, buildings, &c., occupied by the local authority, but not owned by them, e.g.*, property rented for offices.

In this case the occupier in the first instance pays the ax (for exceptions see tabulation), and then deducts tax rom the next payment of rent.

The occupier paying tax under this section is merely a ollector for the Inland Revenue, and the power which he possesses to recoup the tax paid from the landlord leaves him in the position of having personally borne no tax.

There are exceptions in the case of property let at a ent which does not represent the full annual value. The occupier can only deduct tax on the amount of rent paid, and where a fair rent is not paid the balance of tax falls on the occupier.

(2) *On lands, buildings, &c., owned by the local authority, but not occupied by them, e.g.*, Houses for working classes, slaughter-houses, gymnasia, estates, &c.

In this case the occupier pays tax, and then deducts tax from the rent paid to the local authority; or the local authority, as landlord, pay tax direct. (See tabulation.)

Tax is thus borne by the local authority, but if the rent is used to pay interest it may be set off against the tax deducted from such interest. (London County Council, first case, paragraph 12; Customs and Inland Revenue Act, 1888, Section 24.)

(3) *On lands, buildings, &c., owned and occupied by the local authority, e.g.*, public offices (in respect of which no assessments under Schedule D have been made)—

In this case the local authority pay tax direct; this tax may not be set off against interest paid. (London County Council, second case.)

(4) *On lands, buildings, &c., owned and occupied by the local authority for the purpose of municipal trading concerns.*

This section may be roughly subdivided into two main classes, *e.g.* :—

(*a*) Those which are wholly assessable to Schedule A (under Rule 3) although profit-making concerns, *e.g.*, gasworks, waterworks, iron works, &c. These are assessable under Schedule A because they are "concerns arising out of land"; they are, however, assessable on profits according to the rules of Schedule D, and for all practical purposes may be regarded as Schedule D assessments.

(*b*) Those which are also assessable under Schedule D on profits, *e.g.*, tramways, electric lighting concerns, and businesses generally.

In this case there may be Schedule A assessments (Rule No. 1) on the property in addition to the Schedule D assessments on the profits; the practice is not uniform, for although theoretically *all* lands, &c., should be assessed to Schedule A (Rule No. 1) it is often not the practice to so assess land held by trading concerns, these being only assessed under Schedule D.

Any such Schedule A assessments may be deducted from the Schedule D assessments on profits, and thus are in effect merged therein and double assessment is prevented; put simply, the total assessment is merely a matter of apportionment between Schedules A and D. (See Par. 7.)

Many students are greatly puzzled at this apparent duplication of assessments.

(5) *On properties owned and occupied by the local authority for the purpose of carrying on special statutory duties, e.g.*, sewers. (Rule No. 1.)

In the case of a statutory body owning an undertaking not carried on with a view of profit, and not in fact producing any profit, the hereditaments must be valued at the rent a hypothetical tenant would be expected to give if called upon to perform the statutory duties which the body has to perform. (See Par. 8.)

(7) The Deduction of Schedule A Assessments from Schedule D Assessments in Trading Concerns.

Where properties are occupied for trading purposes the assessment on which tax is actually paid under Schedule A (*i.e.*, the net assessment) may be deducted as rent from the balance of profits for assessment under Schedule D.

It was formerly the practice to ascertain the average profits under Schedule D, and then deduct from such average when ascertained the actual Schedule A assessment for the year of assessment.

This produced inequalities where the Schedule A assessments varied from year to year.

The practice is now to charge against each year's profits comprised in the average the actual Schedule A assessment on which tax has been paid in each of these years, thus arriving at the net average for Schedule D.

It should, however, be noted that while Schedule A is taken *before* arriving at the average, the allowance for wear and tear (see Paragraph 16) is deducted *after* the average is struck.

(8) Schedule A—The Assessment of Sewers.

That the sewers of a local authority should be assessable to income-tax seems somewhat anomalous.

As far back as 1901 it was decided in *Ystradyfodwg and Pontypridd Main Sewerage Board v. Newport Union* that sewers which were partly above ground were assessable for purposes of local rates.

Based on this rule, an assessment was also made for income-tax purposes, which ultimately became the subject of a House of Lords decision in 1907 in the case of *Ystradyfodwg and Pontypridd Main Sewerage Board v. Benstead (Surveyor of Taxes)*.

The facts in this case were as follows:—

A sewer was vested in and under the control of a sewerage board for a united drainage district as the local sanitary authority for the purposes of such sewer. The sewer, which was about seventeen and a quarter miles in length, was constructed partly underground, partly on the surface, and partly in an artificial embankment; and no change was made by reason of its construction in the assessment under Schedule A of the Income Tax Act, 1842, of the owners or occupiers of the lands over, through, or under which the sewer was constructed. The sewerage board derived no profit from the sewer.

It was held that the sewer was a hereditament capable of actual occupation, of which the sewerage board were in occupation, and that the board were assessable to income-tax under the Income Tax Act, 1842, Section 60, Schedule A, No. 1, upon the annual value of the sewer.

Schedule A, No. 3, applies to the properties therein specified when such properties are used as trading concerns for the purpose of earning profits, and a sewer vested in a public authority and out of which no profit can be made as assessable under No. 1 and not under No. 3.

It was the contention of the sewerage board that if they were assessed at all they should be assessed under No. 3 (on profits—which were *nil*) and not on No. 1 (annual value).

It was felt that the decision in the foregoing case very largely extended the liability of ratepayers to income-tax, and a question on this point was addressed to the Government in the House of Commons. The reply of the Chancellor of the Exchequer was as follows:—

> "There is no reason to apprehend that the decision referred to will seriously affect the liability of sewers to assessment to income-tax. The sewer in question was not wholly an underground sewer. It was in part carried above ground, or along specially constructed embankments, and it had attached to it certain appurtenances in the shape of an outfall, with sluices and other apparatus. It had been held by a judgment of the Court of Appeal to be assessable to rates, and thereupon the Inland Revenue claimed that it was assessable also to income-tax on the principle that whatever is a proper subject of rates is also a proper subject of taxes. So far as sewers are concerned, the Board of Inland Revenue will be satisfied to treat the judgment of the House of Lords as no more than an affirmation of that principle, and will not regard it as requiring them to depart from existing practice under which sewage works, pumping stations, and so on are assessed both to rates and to income-tax, but purely underground sewers to neither."

How far this dictum will stand is not clear. It will be within the memory of the members that as recently as March 21 1911 the House of Lords decided, in the case *West Kent Sewerage Board v. Dartmouth Union Assessment Committee and Others*, that all sewers whether over or under ground are rateable whenever the occupation of them is valuable within the meaning of the authorities dealing with rating.

In reviewing the case, an eminent legal authority says that it involves a complete change of rating practice, inasmuch as the decision applies to all sewers, whether payment is or is not made in respect of them, and that it would therefore seem to be the duty of Assessment Committees to see that they are rated. He suggests that the annual value of occupation should be based on a percentage of the cost of constructing the sewer.

Having regard to the view which the Crown has ıvariably taken, that what is liable to rates is also assess- ›le to income-tax, one wonders will the Income Tax ıthorities follow this ruling in the case now quoted ıd further complicate the relations between imperial and cal exchequers by assessing the poor ratepayers in :spect of the presumed annual value of their sewers?

(9) SCHEDULE D.—THE AVERAGE SYSTEM.

Profits under Schedule D (including those assessed ıder Schedule A, but according to the rules of Schedule as before referred to) are assessed on "statutory" or ısumed figures. The profit or income for the year of ıssessment is deemed to be either :—

(*a*) the average profits of the three preceding years (or shorter period if the undertaking has been first estab- shed since that time), *e.g.*,

Schedule D. Profits in respect of trades, manufactures, professions, employments and vocations, *e.g.*, tramways, electric lighting, &c.

Schedule D. Profits on foreign possessions.

Schedule A. Tithes in kind.

Schedule E. Income of subordinate officials (by practice, not by law).

(*b*) the profit for the preceding year, *e.g.*, cemeteries, ıs and water undertakings, bridges, ferries, canals, ›cks, fishings, rights of market and fairs, &c.

The effect of the Finance Act, 1907, on Corporation ıcome Tax so far as it relates to the former right of :payment on profits afterwards proved to be over-assessed ı average, is as follows :—

Formerly, under Section 133 (1842 Act) and Section 6 853 Act), when it was discovered that the profits were ss than the assessment a new average could be taken, :cluding the first year of the old average and bringing to account the profit or loss for the year of assessment.

A return of tax could then be claimed between the old ıd the new average.

Legally, when the profits for the year of assessment ıceeded the new average, no allowance could be obtained, ıt

In practice the Inland Revenue allowed a return of tax ı the difference between the actual profits and the old ᵥerage.

The general effect of the sections was that the taxpayer ›uld claim adjustment where his profits were lower than ıe assessment, but the income-tax authorities had no ›rresponding right where the profits were higher.

Now, these sections are repealed, but adjustments are :rmitted in the first three years and the last three years a business, so that, in effect, the taxpayer pays in the ›ng run (though not in each individual year) under the ᵥerage system on the exact amount of profits he earns.

(10) EXEMPTIONS FROM INCOME TAX.

Amongst the properties which are specifically exempted from payment of income-tax may be mentioned :—

(*a*) Colleges and halls in universities (Schedule A).

(*b*) Hospitals (Schedule A). Hospitals are not the less exempt because fees are taken from patients, but they are not exempt if wholly self-supporting; the apartments and buildings of a County Lunatic Asylum occupied by salaried officials having an income of more than £150 a year are not exempt.

(*c*) Public schools (Schedule A), including schools maintained partly by charitable endowments and partly by fees charged for instruction.

(*d*) Almshouses (Schedule A).

(*e*) Rents of land or interest applied to charitable purposes (all schedules); in *Rex v. Special Commissioners; ex parte University College of North Wales*, 1909, the "advancement of education" was held to be included in this clause.

(*f*) All places of worship (except as to interest or ground rent paid).

(*g*) Literary and scientific institutions, comprising any building the property of any literary or scientific institution used solely for the purposes of such institution, and in which no payment is made for instruction by lectures or otherwise, provided that the same be not occupied by any officer thereof, or by any person paying rent for the same. (Schedule A.)

The above has been held to include free public libraries (buildings used solely for the purpose). (*Mayor of Manchester v. McAdam*, House of Lords, 31st August 1896.)

(*h*) Crown Property.—To obtain exemption buildings must be used solely for Crown purposes; thus police stations, assize courts, and burgh court buildings are exempt.

Only the parts used exclusively for the service of the Crown are exempt.

Municipal buildings, so far as they are used for civic purposes, are liable for taxation in the ordinary way, but those parts used for Crown purposes (*e.g.*, police courts) are exempt.

(*i*) Interest on Police Pension Fund investments.

This exemption appears to be a concession. It is not extended to other thrift funds (see par. 35).

(11) EXEMPTIONS AND ABATEMENTS FOR LOCAL AUTHORITIES.

The question has been raised on a number of occasions, "Are not many of the smaller local authorities (including "overseers) exempt from taxation (particularly as regards "Schedule A), on the ground that their total income from "all sources does not exceed £160?"

Section 8 of the Finance Act, 1898, in laying down the existing scale of abatements for income-tax (beginning at

£160 from £400 income) expressly uses the word "individual," and not "person." Corporations as "persons" seem therefore to be certainly excluded from the benefit of this section.

It is therefore suggested that local authorities are governed by the 1894 Act (which related to "persons" which includes corporations). By the latter Act total exemption is granted in respect of incomes of less than £150 a year, and abatements in respect of incomes under £500.

Surveyors have contested this view, and cases which have come before local Commissioners have been decided in the Crown's favour (see Paragraph 24 as to overseers); on the other hand, the Inland Revenue Board wrote a letter to the clerk of a rural sanitary authority, dated November 13th 1891, in regard to waterworks constructed to serve a number of townships in the union, where the Surveyor insisted that the authority was assessable on the full profits derived from each, without any abatement whatever. The Board said that they were advised in the circumstances that the rural sanitary authority could not properly be regarded as assessable to income-tax in respect of the aggregate profits of the waterworks for the general townships so as to deprive any township of the right to exemption or abatement.

In *Curtis v. Old Monkland Conservative Association* (House of Lords, December 1905) a claim for exemption on the point under consideration was made, but the claim was disallowed.

This, however, was an unincorporated association, and in a case, *Market Harborough Advertiser Company v. Mylam* (King's Bench Division, January 1905), the question whether such a company was a "person" within the section was expressly left undecided.

Section 19 (8) of the Finance Act, 1907, is now no doubt intended to meet the point in question. It reads:—"Section 34 of the Finance Act, 1894, shall cease to have "effect so far as it gives relief or abatement to persons "who are entitled to relief under Section 8 of the Finance "Act, 1898."

It is probably intended by this enactment that *claims* to exemption or abatement of *individuals* alone should be recognised, but, if so, it is not clear that effect is really given to this intention.

(12) London County Council Cases—The First Case.

A knowledge of the decisions in the London County Council cases is nowadays regarded as the A B C of the student studying municipal income-tax; some of the principles fought for seem so equitable that it is difficult to realise how keen was the fight to establish these principles.

In tracing briefly the various principles which these cases have established, it is necessary to consider particularly Section 102 of the Income Tax Act, 1842, and Section 24 of the Customs and Inland Revenue Act, 1888.

Section 102 of the 1842 Act, after providing that tax on annuities, yearly interest, &c., should be assessed on the payer, and that the payer might recoup himself by himself deducting tax on paying the payee, enacts:—

> "Where any creditor on any rates or assessments not chargeable by this Act as profits shall be entitled to such interest, it shall be lawful to charge the proper officer having the management of the accounts with the duty payable on such interest, and every such officer shall be answerable for doing all acts, matters, and things necessary to a due assessment of the said duties, and payment thereof, as if such rates or assessments were profits chargeable under this Act, and such officer shall be in like manner indemnified for all such acts, as if the said rates and assessments were chargeable."

By the Customs and Inland Revenue Act, 1888, Section 24, Subsection (3), it is provided that—

> "Upon payment of any interest of money or annuities charged with income-tax under Schedule D, and not payable or not wholly payable, out of profits or gains brought into charge to such tax, the person by or through whom such interest or annuities shall be paid shall deduct thereout the rate of income-tax in force at the time of such payment, and shall forthwith render an account to the Commissioners of Inland Revenue of the amount so deducted, or of the amount deducted out of so much of the interest or annuities as is not paid out of profits or gains brought into charge, as the case may be; and such amount shall be a debt from such person to (His) Majesty and recoverable as such accordingly."

The facts in what is known as the "first London County Council case" (finally decided by the House of Lords in 1900) were as follows:—

The County Council paid out of their Loans Fund on stock (approx.)		£1,140,000
The funds for payment of these dividends were obtained from		
(1) Interest received on loans advanced to other local authorities out of the Loans Fund. This is already taxed under Schedule D, because the borrowers deduct income-tax when they pay their interest to the Council	500,000	
(2) Rents received. These are already taxed under Schedule A, because either the Council's tenants deduct the "property tax" on paying their rents to the Council, or as regards weekly property the Council pays property tax direct to the Crown	100,000	
		600,000
and the balance ...		£540,000

was provided from the rates.

The stock and the dividends thereon were by various Acts made a charge upon the land rents and property belonging to the Council, and on the rates to be levied by the Council.

The dividends were paid out of a Loans Fund, the accounts of which were kept separate as required by Treasury regulations as regards capital and revenue.

On paying the dividends the Council deducted tax, and the question at issue was as to how much of such tax they were entitled to retain under Section 24 of the Customs and Inland Revenue Act, 1888, and how much they should hand over to the Crown.

The Council contended that to the extent of £600,000 the interest had been "paid out of profits or gains brought into charge," and they were therefore entitled to retain a corresponding amount of tax, and only to account to the Crown in respect of £540,000.

The Crown contended first of all that they were entitled to the whole of the tax deducted from the £1,140,000.

Later they agreed that some proportion of the interest (previously taxed under Schedule D) could be set off, but they were not prepared to allow a set-off in respect of *rents* (which had been taxed under Schedule A).

Observe that the Inland Revenue authorities contended in effect that Schedules A and D related to two separate taxes—that tax paid under Schedule A could not be set off against tax payable under Schedule D.

They read the words of Section 24, "such tax" as meaning "income-tax under Schedule D" and "brought into charge" as "brought into charge under Schedule D."

They were only prepared moreover to allow a proportion of the *interest* on the ground that such interest being payable indifferently out of—

(*a*) Interest received; and

(*b*) The remainder of the Consolidated Loans Fund (both capital and income) only a proportionate part was payable out of profits charged.

The Queen's Bench Division thought Schedules A and D were distinct, and gave judgment for the Crown, holding that the suggested allocation of interest was the correct method; also that Schedule A and Schedule D were distinct, and that Section 24 of the Act of 1888 had no reference at all to Schedule A.

The Court of Appeal was unanimously of the same opinion as the lower Court as to Schedule A and Schedule D being distinct. Collins, L.J., thought that the London County Council might have appropriated, and would have been justified in so appropriating their funds as to put themselves in a position to prove that they had actually applied certain specific sums of the Consolidated Loans Fund in a particular manner, and thus entitled them to retain tax on certain portions of the dividends paid, but they had not done so. Vaughan Williams, L.J., was of the same opinion; he, however, held that in applying the third alternative (above) regard was not to be had to any part of the fund which was capital, but only to such part as was income.

The County Council appealed to the House of Lords, which unanimously allowed the appeal, and reversed the decision of the lower Courts.

Lord Macnaghten dismissed the idea of having regard to both the capital and income of the Loans Fund as "an ingenious but not very businesslike suggestion" and "not open to argument." He called attention to the fact that in Section 24 of the Act of 1888 the word "payable" was first used, and later the word "paid," and drew the conclusion that so far as interest was in fact paid out of profit (whether in law payable thereout or not) the person paying might deduct and retain the tax. He then proceeded:—

> "Income-tax, if I may be pardoned for saying so, is a tax on income. It is one tax, not a collection of taxes essentially different. There is no difference in kind between the duties of income-tax assessed under Schedule D and those assessed under Schedule A or any of the other schedules of charge."

Again,

> "But to read the enactment (the Act of 1888) as imposing a double duty would be contrary to the whole scope of income-tax legislation, and whimsical in the highest degree, when you consider that the double burden would necessarily fall upon the fundholder, in whose case the collection of duty is certain, while a person chargeable under Schedule D would be expressly exempted from double duty."

Lord Davey, in the course of a like judgment, alluded to the view of Collins, L.J., that the London County Council might have made some appropriation of their funds; he (Lord Davey) thought it difficult to see how any account-keeping by the debtor could alter the rights of the Crown.

The case may be said to have established the following principles:—

(1) That the income-tax, although assessed and collected under five schedules, is one tax.

This practice has invariably been observed in ordinary cases. In the case of the mortgagor of property income-tax paid under Schedule A on the annual value of the mortgaged property is set-off against income-tax under Schedule D on the yearly interest of the borrowed money, and the mortgagor deducts and retains the latter by reason of his having paid the former. In assessments on the profits of trading undertakings, also, the value of property on which tax is paid under Schedule A is allowed by the Revenue authorities as a deduction from the profits to be assessed under Schedule D.

(2) The right to "deduct and retain" tax from the interest or other annual payment holds good, even if the profits or gains out of which it is payable are not exclusively charged therewith.

(3) The "Birmingham compromise," which was extensively followed prior to the London County Council case, disappeared. It may be of interest to explain that the compromise rested upon the principle that, because the interest on corporation loans was partly charged on the rates and partly on the security of property and profits, the corporation might retain a certain proportion only of the tax deducted by them from interest on loans.

So far the decisions were very satisfactory to local authorities, but they left untouched the important question of the right to set-off tax paid on premises owned and occupied by the local authority against tax deducted from interest payable. This point gave rise to

(13) THE SECOND LONDON COUNTY COUNCIL CASE, which was determined by the House of Lords in 1907. These were the facts:—

The Council paid interest on stock (which was charged indifferently on the whole of the land rents and property and on the rates) to the amount of	£1,371,000
This was paid out of rents, &c. (already taxed and the right to set off which was settled in the previous case) to the extent of	838,000
Leaving payable out of rates	£533,000
The Council were assessed to Schedule A in respect of premises occupied and owned by them on	£118,000

The question at issue was whether the County Council were entitled to retain tax on £118,000, and only to pay to the Crown tax in respect of the balance, viz., £415,000 (£533,000—£118,000).

The Council relied on the right which a mortgagor in the occupation of property mortgaged has to retain tax deducted from the interest payable to his mortgagee, because he has already paid tax on the annual value of the property.

The Crown relied on the words "paid" in Section 24 of the Act of 1888. The King's Bench Division held that the substance of the matter should be looked at; that the Council in effect raised £118,000 out of rates to pay for their occupation of the land, &c., in question; that the land had no real value to them, being charged to its full value, and tax paid on it under Schedule A; that if they had to hand over tax on the whole £533,000 the Crown would be getting tax twice on £118,000.

They, therefore, held that the Council were entitled to the relief claimed. This was confirmed by the Court of Appeal, but the House of Lords decided to the contrary.

Loreburn, L.C., said that the only question was as to £118,000.

> "This," he continued, "is not paid out of profits and gains brought into charge. It is paid out of rates; and on the rates which the Council pays over to its creditors it is bound by the proviso at the end of Section 102 of the Act of 1842 to deduct the tax and pay it over to the Crown. It is said that the effect of this conclusion will be to tax the same income twice over. I cannot see this. The County Council pays tax on £118,000, the annual value of their own land, which they occupy. The holders of consolidated stock pay tax on £118,000, the annual interest of the debt due to them from the County Council. It seems to me that the two incomes are different, and the persons who receive and enjoy them are different, and the persons who pay income-tax on these two incomes respectively are also different."

Lord Macnaghten said the stock and dividends were charged "indifferently" on the whole of the lands, rents, and property, and on the rates.

> "I cannot understand," he said, "what the property in the occupation of the Council has to do with the matter. It stands apart. It is quite true that this property is charged in favour of the holders of metropolitan stock, but the charge is not, and never can be, operative. It is superseded by the charge on the rates and vanishes altogether. The 'profits and gains' derived from the property in the occupation of the Council are charged at their source in the hands of the Council under Schedule A. The stream flows no further. The Council are secure in the full and beneficial enjoyment of the property which they occupy. What possible claim can there be to relief or indemnity as regards income-tax in respect of this property?"

He thought Channell, J., had misapprehended Lord Davey's observations as to the income of incumbered property being the income, less interest, on the incumbrance. That proceeded on the assumption of the interest being a real burden. If such interest was discharged by a person other than the owner the burden was nominal. In the present case the property never contributed, and was worth as much as if it was not charged. Collins, M.R., he said, had likewise accepted those remarks of Lord Davey. He himself agreed that the Crown could not ask for the tax twice, but here it only received it once. By the contention of the Council there might be taxable income and the Crown might still receive no tax on it. For example, suppose the dividend on stock was £100,000; if there was no property in their occupation, and the dividend was raised entirely by rates, the Crown would receive tax on the whole, but if they acquired and occupied property, the amount would gradually diminish, and when the annual value reached £100,000 would vanish altogether. The property itself pays tax under Schedule A, whoever may be the owner and occupier, but they would lose tax on the dividends, if, when collected, it went to recoup the Council for tax under Schedule A.

The result of this case is therefore that corporations have to pay on the "annual value" of properties which they own and occupy, although the property may be of no annual value to them.

An obvious injustice is thus created.

On behalf of the Crown it is contended that there is no absolute analogy between the case of an ordinary owner-occupier who has a mortgage on his premises and who is allowed to deduct and retain tax on his interest, and thus recoup himself for the Schedule A tax paid, and of a local authority.

In the former case the interest must be paid out of taxed income (except to the small extent, comparatively, to which exemption or abatements are allowed), but corporations have in the rates a source of untaxed income; therefore an indefinite application of the principle contended for by the County Council would cause the tax receivable by the Crown in respect of dividends paid to gradually vanish as the County Council acquired more property.

For example (taking small figures for simplicity's sake),

A local authority's total annual interest on rate fund is £20,000.

They own no property and we will assume they have no trading undertakings.

The local authority deduct tax on the £20,000, and pursuant to Section 24 of the Customs and Inland Revenue Act, 1888, hand the same over to the Crown.

After a while the local authority proceed to acquire offices of their own. We will assume the offices cost £10,000 and the annual value is £400.

The local authority borrow £10,000 at 4 per cent., the annual interest being therefore £400.

It is obvious that in this case there is no annual value in the buildings vested in the local authority. The annual value of the property is £400, and the local authority pay interest in respect of the property to the extent of £400. The tax should rest on the real recipient of the annual value, *i.e.*, the mortgagee.

Under the ruling in the London County Council case, the local authority is assessed on tax deducted from interest (including interest on the loan borrowed for the offices) . . . . £20,400, and also on the annual value of the offices £400, and the ratepayers have to find tax on £400 in respect of an annual value from which they really receive no benefit. Under like circumstances an ordinary owner-occupier would be allowed to retain the tax on the interest on the loans borrowed for the offices.

It seems evident to this point that the local authority have an equitable claim to be allowed the set off.

What real reason, then, actuates the Crown in its apparently unjust demand?

It will be observed that in his judgment Lord Macnaghten says—

> "He himself agreed that the Crown could not ask for tax twice, but here it only received it once. By the contention of the Council there might be taxable income and the Crown might still receive no tax on it. For example, suppose the dividend on stock was £100,000, if there was no property in their occupation, and the dividend was raised entirely from rates, the Crown would receive tax on the whole, but if they acquired and occupied property the amount would gradually diminish, and when the annual value reached £100,000 would vanish altogether. The property itself pays tax under Schedule A, whoever may be the owner and occupier, but they would lose tax on the dividends if when collected it went to recoup the Council for the tax under Schedule A."

Lord Macnaghten appears to ignore the fact that if the local authority acquired property they would ordinarily need to borrow for the purpose, and thus the Crown would receive in tax on interest an equivalent amount to the tax in respect of the Schedule A assessment.

But suppose the property was purchased directly out of rates, I think it clear that the position indicated by Lord Macnaghten would then apply.

For instance, if the local authority under the circumstances given were assessed in respect of interest at...	£20,000
The local authority acquire property of the annual value of £400 out of the rates, *i.e.*, without borrowing, and demand to set-off the same against an equivalent amount of interest.	
Prior to the acquisition of the property the *Crown* would receive tax on interest (from the local authority)	20,000
Annual value of property (from the owner of the property)	400
	20,400
but if the local authority were allowed the set-off claimed, the Crown would only receive :	
Tax on interest less set-off of £400	19,600
Annual value of property	400
Total	£20,000

The local authority would have deducted from interest tax on £20,000, and thus tax on £400 would go into the local authority's pocket, because in this case the local authority do derive benefit from the property—the annual value is really vested in them.

The same principle is *gradually* applied as the local authority *repay* their debt.

It seems clear, therefore, that to obtain an amendment of the law as now declared by the highest tribunal, viz., the House of Lords, corporations must confine their claim to set-off Schedule A tax on property in their occupation and ownership against assessments on interest paid, to the interest on the outstanding loans borrowed for constructing or acquiring the particular building, &c., taxed under Schedule A, otherwise the corporation would make a profit on the tax deducted and retained from interest which, it must be remembered, they simply collect on behalf of the Crown.

Of course, this argument is directed purely and simply to the particular point under consideration and ignores the "one entity" business.

After all, we must remember that the income tax is necessarily not run on scientific lines.

Extreme amalgamation and extreme division both operate to reduce the aggregate yield to the Crown of the income-tax. For instance, if a man having an annual income of £1,000, leaves the same to two sons who each receive £500, the Crown loses tax because of the abatement which is allowed to each of the sons by reason of their respective incomes being below the £700 limit. Again, if two businesses are amalgamated, one of which makes a loss and the other a profit, the Crown loses, because now the whole concern pays only on the net profit after deducting losses, while formerly the Crown received tax on the whole profit of the one concern, but did not make any contribution towards the loss of the other.

It should be observed that where trading departments pay a proportion of the rent of central offices, &c., owned and occupied by the local authority, such rent may be charged as a trading expense before arriving at profits for income-tax purposes.

It should be clearly understood, too, that the injustice of the London County Council's second case applies to property owned and occupied on *rate* funds. All Schedule A assessments in the case of trading departments may be set-off against the Schedule D assessment on profits.

(14) The Transfer of Taxed Profits to Rate Funds.

Arising out of the first London County Council case, the Inland Revenue Commissioners issued an instruction to their Surveyors to the following effect :—

> "From the principle laid down it follows, on the one hand, that interest which is in fact paid out of profits or gains assessed under any schedule of the Income Tax Act should be excluded from the further assessment on interest paid, whether the profits or gains so applied in paying the interest are pledged to secure the payment or not. Where interest is in fact paid out of a mixed fund consisting partly of assessed profits and partly of unassessed rates, the Board are willing that, for the purpose of income-tax assessment, the interest should be regarded as being paid in the first instance out of the assessed profits. Thus, if taxed rents, or surplus gas or water profits which have been charged with income-tax are carried into a borough fund, or into a district fund out of which interest is paid, you may regard the interest paid out of the fund into which the profits have been carried as having been in fact paid out of the taxed profits, either wholly, if the amount of the taxed profits is not less than the amount of the interest or to the full amount of the taxed profits in cases where the amount of the interest paid exceeds such taxed profits.
>
> "On the other hand, it follows, from the principle laid down, that the whole of the interest paid otherwise than out of taxed profits is chargeable, and that no set-off or deduction can be allowed, because the authority liable to the payment of the interest has been charged, and has paid income-tax in respect of property or profits which have not, in fact, been applied in payment of interest."

Having regard to the varying interpretations placed on this circular by different Surveyors the Board in April 1903 pointed out—

> that in some cases adjustments had been made by Surveyors on the basis that the whole of the taxed income of a corporation should be set off against the total amount of interest paid, without regard to the question of separate funds, but that this principle was, in the opinion of the Board, an erroneous one, and was not intended to be deductible from their prior circular of August 1901. They further stated that in their opinion no set-off or deduction could be allowed in respect of profits which had not in fact been applied in the payment of the interest in question, and that the surplus taxed income remaining to any particular fund, such as the general district fund after payment of the interest chargeable to that fund, could not be allowed as a set-off against the interest charged upon and paid out of any other fund.

It will thus be observed that the Board were of opinion that complete pooling of the funds of a local authority was not permissible. With this question I deal later.

But they agreed that if taxed profits were applied in relief of a rate fund, the interest paid out of that fund might be regarded as paid out of such taxed profits to a corresponding extent, and the local authority could accordingly retain the tax deducted from such interest.

Arising out of this latter aspect an interesting question was put by Mr. Roger N. Carter, F.C.A., in a lecture delivered in 1909, viz. :—

A municipal gas undertaking is assessed for 1909-10 on the basis of 1908 at £20,000
It makes, and carries to the rates, a profit of... £50,000
Is interest on the non-productive fund paid out of taxed profits to the extent of £20,000 or £50,000?

(15) THE POOLING BASIS.

As intimated in the preceding paragraph the pooling uestion is another matter concerning municipal income-ax assessments which has been the subject of controversy or many years.

Briefly, the proposition is that a municipal corporation hould be treated as one entity and assessed as such, and ıot as a number of separate entities having separate funds r undertakings, *e.g.*, that a corporation which possesses Borough Fund and a General District Fund, and also arious trading undertakings, should be treated for ncome-tax purposes as a whole and not as a separate ody in respect of its Borough Fund, and another separate ody in respect of its General District Fund, and again separate body in respect of each of its separate trading ndertakings.

In support of this contention it is pointed out that—

(*a*) There should be similarity of treatment between ndividuals and local authorities; under Section 101 of he Act of 1842 and by the Customs and Inland Revenue ct, 1890, a "person carrying on two or more distinct trades, chargeable under Schedule D, is allowed to set-off the loss of one department against a profit in another, or against other income." He can pool his rofits and losses, and pays only on the net profit.

Again, by Section 192 of the Act of 1842, it is understood hat a person shall include "bodies corporate."

(*b*) A corporation should be regarded as one entity, not s a number of separate corporate bodies (*i.e.*, one for ublic health purposes, another for borough fund purposes, another for gas purposes, and so on). The general ody of ratepayers is the same in each case, although the ıcidence of rating may be unequal.

(*c*) The debt of local authorities is in most cases harged indifferently on all their funds and revenues, *e.g.*, Stock Regulations, 1891, Articles 4 (1) and (2).

But apart from these general statutes the particular ocal authorities which have contested this pooling question have contended that in their particular case their ınds were one entity, because of the provisions contained ı local Acts charging interest on indebtedness indifferently on all funds, revenues, and profits of the corporation. The division of the accounts into funds is to a great tent for administrative convenience only.

Where a local authority, under the principle of each ınd being assessed separately, pays on profits in some epartments, whilst there are losses exceeding those profits in others, many ratepayers, as such, are called upon to pay in full income-tax in regard to which, as individuals, they are (by reason of the smallness of their income), either entitled to total exemption or partial abatement.

Against the "pooling basis" it may be urged :—

(*a*) That for some purposes, *e.g.*, rating, &c., the different funds are legally regarded as separate entities.

(*b*) The amalgamation of numerous concerns under one body and the consequent pooling of profits and losses necessarily tends to a reduction of the yield from taxation.

(*c*) That corporations, by their own actions, *e.g.*, estimates, rates, loans, and statutory procedure generally, distinctly act as separately constituted authorities, in regard particularly to Borough Fund and District Fund.

Several cases have been fought on this point, and in some instances the decisions of Local Commissioners have been in favour of the local authority (*e.g.*, Blackpool). But of late years interest has chiefly been concentrated on the *Leeds* case, which is generally regarded as a test case on the question.

This case has now been fought as far as the Court of Appeal.

The facts are shortly as follows :—

Leeds Corporation v. Sugden.

The Corporation were assessed to Schedule A in respect of their waterworks, gasworks, tramways, markets, electric lighting undertaking, and annual value, in the sum of £270,036. By their Act of 1901, loans originally raised on various securities were charged indifferently on all the undertakings, and on the rates; there was also to be established a Dividends Fund, out of which interest was to be paid. The total interest was £285,446, thus showing £15,410 in excess of tax-paid income.

The position was as follows :—

	Taxed Income.	Dividends Fund.	Difference.	
	£	£	£	£
Waterworks ...	88,498	64,236	24,262	
Gasworks	48,345	43,702	4,643	
Tramways	25,320	19,092	6,228	
Electricity	8,748	19,258		10,510
City Fund and Rate	63,105	19,719	43,386	
Consolidated Rate Fund	36,020	119,439		83,419
	£270,036	285,446	78,519	93,929

The Crown sought to tax the sum of £93,929 on the ground that to that extent the interest was not paid out of taxed profit. The Corporation tendered tax on the £15,410, contending that, except as to this sum, the interest was paid out of profits taxed.

The King's Bench Division (14th February 1911) decided in favour of the Crown. Hamilton, J., said that it had been contended that the Corporation must resort to its income before resorting to rates, and that in contemplation of law that must be deemed to have been done which ought to have been done. He did not understand that to be contested, if it could be shown that on the provisions of all the Leeds Acts it could be established that the Corporation could lawfully apply all and any of its incomings to the discharge of all and any parts of the interest upon the whole unified loans. But he did not think that was so. It was manifest that, if so, interest payable out of the consolidated rate (where there was differentiation) might have been applied out of the Borough Fund (where there was no differentiation). Lord Davey's expression (London County Council case) that it was enough "if the interest is charged upon, or payable, out of the taxable income" might seem to support the argument for the Corporation, as it was (in certain remote contingencies) so charged, but this must be read in connection with the exposition of Lord Macnaghten in the subsequent case: "It is quite true that this property is "charged in favour of the holders of the Metropolitan "Stock, but the charge is not and never can be operative."

In the Court of Appeal, however, this judgment was reversed (29th July 1911), Kennedy, L.J., dissenting.

The Master of the Rolls said that in the Leeds Act of 1901 some of the sections were inconsistent, and as to one section he had been unable to understand it at all. He had, however, come to the conclusion that the interest on the loans was no longer payable out of the net receipts of each separate undertaking.

Farwell, L.J., said the contention of the Crown amounted to a claim for the payment of tax twice over.

So far, then, the law as declared by the Court of Appeal is in favour of pooling.

But it will be observed that the decision is largely based on the provisions of the local Act of Leeds, and the fact that not only future indebtedness, but also past indebtedness, was made a common charge upon all funds and revenues was strongly pressed as an argument in the Corporation's favour.

The judgment of the Master of the Rolls (reported in the *Financial Circular* of September 1911) almost wholly rests on the provisions of the Leeds Act of 1901.

Can the decision, then, be treated as of general application? I presume that but few authorities have provisions in local Acts exactly identical with those of Leeds. Still it is valuable to have a verdict that in certain circumstances the whole of the funds of the local authority may be pooled.

It is of interest to note that the London County Council have recently been allowed to set-off a loss on steamboats against profits on tramways on the ground that both concerns (1) were "trades," &c., and (2) were chargeable under Schedule D.

(To be continued.)

Institute of Municipal Treasurers and Accountants (Incorporated).

South Wales and Monmouthshire Students Society.

Income Tax as Affecting Local Authorities.

By Mr. F. J. ALBAN, F.S.A.A., A.C.I.S.
(Accountant to the Pontypridd and Rhondda Joint Water Board.)

(*Continued from page* 30.)

(16) DEPRECIATION ALLOWANCES FOR INCOME-TAX PURPOSES.

To a body of accountants it is unnecessary to elaborate the point that depreciation is a necessary trading expense, and as such should be charged in the Profit and Loss Account before any figure of profit is arrived at.

It is only in comparatively recent years, however, that the Inland Revenue authorities have recognised the principle that proper allowances should be made for depreciation in framing income-tax assessments.

The Customs and Inland Revenue Act, 1878, reads :—"The Commissioners shall, in assessing the profits or "gains of any trade . . . chargeable under Schedule "D, or the profits of any concern chargeable by reference "to the rules of that schedule, allow such deduction as "they may think just and reasonable as representing the "diminished value by reason of wear and tear during the "year of any machinery or plant used for the purposes "of the concern."

In applying this section many difficulties were experienced, *e.g.* :—

(1) The allowance was left to the discretion of the local Commissioners, and thus lack of uniformity in making allowances became a pronounced cause of complaint.

(2) Difficulties arose in deciding what the term "machinery and plant" covered.

Largely at the instance of the Institute of Municipal Treasurers and Accountants (Incorporated), the Inland Revenue authorities framed in 1907 a scheme for determining the allowances to be granted for wear and tear in respect of tramways, light railways, and gas, water, and electricity concerns.

The following is a brief summary of the scheme :—

(A) *Tramways Undertakings.*

Permanent Way.

(1) Life of permanent way.

If 50,000 car miles per annum to be considered				16 years.
75,000	,,	,,	,,	14 years.
125,000	,,	,,	,,	12 years.

over 125,000 given special consideration.

Special circumstances (exceptional gradients, wood sets, c.) to be given special consideration.

(2) The cost of renewals, including sets or other paving, but excluding concrete foundations, to be taken at £4,400 per mile of single track (until general renewal of track takes place).

(3) No allowance to be made for expenditure on repairs or maintenance of permanent way, but an amount to be allowed based as follows :—

Renewal	£4,400
Estimated cost of repairs £100 per annum (life say 16 years)	1,600
	£6,000

Amount to be allowed per annum in lieu of depreciation 1/16th)—£375.

(4) Repairs to be arrived at on average of the last three years (or less, if the trams not running three years).

Repairs for foregoing purpose include renewals at unctions, &c., which occur at frequent intervals.

Repairs allowance to be reviewed every five years and any necessary adjustment made.

(5) An account to be kept, and in ten or fifteen years or on general renewal the allowance to be reconsidered, but no re-opening of past allowances is to take place.

(6) Extensions and improvements to be excluded from working expenses for income-tax purposes.

(7) These regulations apply to overhead trolley systems. Other systems to be specially considered.

(8) *Cables.*—Repairs and also 3 per cent. (diminished value) depreciation to be allowed.

(9) *Overhead Equipment.*—No depreciation allowed. All expenditure on maintenance and renewals to be charged as and when incurred.

(10) *Cars.*—Usually all expenditure on maintenance and renewals to be treated as working expenses, and charged against revenue as and when incurred.

But depreciation to be allowed if circumstances justify it on the basis of 7 per cent. (diminished value).

(11) Repairs to be allowed as a deduction in computing assessable profits.

General Plant.—

(12) Repairs and also 5 per cent. depreciation (diminished value) to be allowed for all other plant and machinery, including standards, brackets, and workshop tools, but excluding loose implements, office furniture, and small articles, which require frequent renewal.

(B) *Electric Light Undertakings.*

(1) *Cables.*—Repairs and 3 per cent. (diminished value) depreciation to be allowed.

(2) *Plant.*—Repairs and 5 per cent. depreciation (diminished value) to be allowed.

(3) *Conduits.*—No depreciation allowed, but all maintenance expenses to be charged as and when incurred.

(4) *Meters, Loose Tools, and Office Furniture.*—As number 3.

(C) *Gas and Water Undertakings.*

(1) No depreciation to be allowed under any circumstances in respect of any portion of these undertakings.

(2) All expenditure on repairs and renewals (but excluding extensions and improvements to be charged as working expenses as and when incurred).

(3) Exceptional expenditure on *bonâ fide* renewals to which full effect cannot be given in any particular year owing to profits being insufficient to be carried forward to following years, like unallowed depreciation under Section 26, Finance Act, 1907.

The foregoing scheme has been generally considered to be favourable to tramways and electric lighting concerns, but considerable exception has been taken in the case of gas concerns (chiefly by companies) to the total elimination of percentage allowances for depreciation. Of course, the scheme is not binding on the Local Commissioners, who have to determine what allowances shall be made, and in several cases gas companies have been successful in obtaining percentage allowances, despite the opposition of the Revenue.

Having regard to the saving clause as to carrying forward exceptional expenditure (see item No. 3 under Gas and Water Undertakings) the only advantage of a percentage allowance appears to be that the money representing the allowance is in the hands of the undertaking for some little time longer than would otherwise be the case (*i.e.*, before the actual renewals for which the allowance is made take place), and thus some gain in bank interest might be effected.

(17) Carrying Forward Unallowed Depreciation.

Reference has been made in the foregoing scheme (see Gas and Water, No. 3) to the fact that unallowed renewals may be carried forward to succeeding years, if necessary, like unallowed depreciation under Section 26 (3) of the Finance Act, 1907. The concession thus given is a most valuable one, and removes many grievances previously experienced.

The section is to the following effect :—

"Where as respects any trade, manufacture, adventure, or concern, full effect cannot be given to the deduction for wear and tear in any year owing to there being no profits or gains chargeable with income-tax in that year, or owing to the profits or gains so chargeable being less than the deduction, the deduction or part of the deduction to which effect has not been given, as the case may be, shall, for the purpose of making the assessment for the following year, be added to the amount of the deduction for wear and tear for that year, and deemed to be part of that deduction, or if there is no such deduction for that year be deemed to be the deduction for that year, and so on for succeeding years."

(18) INCOME TAX SCALE OF DEPRECIATION FOLLOWED FOR RATING PURPOSES.

It is interesting to note that the foregoing scale of depreciation allowances is now being followed in some assessments of the various undertakings for local rating purposes.

(19) ALLOWANCES FOR DEPRECIATION OF BUILDINGS, &c.

It will have been observed that the foregoing allowances apply only to machinery and plant.

It is often asked, "Should not some allowance also be made in respect of the depreciation of buildings?"

This matter received the consideration of the Departmental Committee on Income Tax, 1905, whose report, as follows, is self explanatory.

[The additional allowances made by the Finance (1909-1910) Act, 1910 (paragraph 4) should also be noted.]

(74) "A further legislative step in the direction of making allowance for depreciation was taken in 1894, when, by the Finance Act of that year, a deduction of one-sixth from the rack-rent value of buildings was authorised as an allowance to cover maintenance and repairs. Although nothing was specifically said on the point, it may be inferred that the allowance was intended to cover also eventual replacement of buildings. For Sir W. Harcourt stated in the House of Commons that the rate of allowance was taken at one-sixth pursuant to Mr. Hubbard's recommendation of 1861, and a reference to Mr. Hubbard's arguments shows that he adopted the figure of one-sixth of gross value as calculated to cover 'the ultimate renewal of the fabric when decayed by age as well as current repairs.'"

(75) "We find, however, that in the case of owner-occupiers of trade premises, Section 9 of the Finance Act of 1898 directed that, in estimating the amount of profits for Schedule D assessment purposes, only the net amount assessed under Schedule A should be allowed as a deduction instead of the full annual value, thereby limiting the allowance for wear and tear of buildings to any actual expenditure for repairs charged in the Trading Accounts. Having regard to the fact that, as a rule, the amount of wear and tear of mills, factories, and similar premises greatly exceeds that of residential and other buildings, we are of opinion that the full annual value of premises so occupied should be allowed as a set-off in computing the liability under Schedule D, instead of such allowance being restricted to five-sixths only of the full annual value assessed under Schedule A."

(20) INTERDEPARTMENTAL TRANSACTIONS.

In the assessments of municipal trading undertakings some considerable attention has to be given to what are known as "interdepartmental transactions" with the view of eliminating from the income-tax assessment any profits which may be made by one department out of another.

For instance, if the municipal gas undertaking supplies the public lighting of the town at a price which gives to the gas department a profit, it is in the circumstances unfair that the gas department should pay income-tax on this profit, for the profit is really a transfer from one pocket to another pocket of the same person.

Similar instances occur in connection with water undertakings, electric light undertakings (supply of public lighting to the local authority, and also supply of current to the municipal tramways department, if any), &c.

It seems to me also that the same point is involved where a joint Board—say a Gas Board or a Water Board —is appointed by two or more authorities, and provides the public services for those local authorities, but I do not know of any cases in which under such circumstances the profits on supplies to the constituent authorities have been allowed to be eliminated.

In order to eliminate the element of profit the cost of the commodity must be arrived at; this must necessarily be a matter of estimate, but it is surprising how assessments can be cut down by making an intelligent endeavour to arrive at the actual cost.

The following is a form of gas assessment (given by the late Mr. Swainson of Bolton in a paper by him some years ago) :—

Income-tax Assessment, 1890-1.

Receipts	£126,740
Expenditure	77,689
Net income	49,051
Less profit on gas supplied to street lamps and other committees of the corporation ... ... (A)	1,998
Net assessment for gas profits	£47,053

(A) arrived at as follows:—

As 126,740 (receipts) is to 77,689 (expenditure) so is 5,161 (the receipts from gas supplied to corporate departments) to X (the cost of producing the gas supplied to corporate departments).

X equals 3,163.

The profit is therefore 1,998, which is eliminated from the assessment as shown above.

The objection to this method is that it assumes that the cost of the commodity supplied to the corporate departments is in exactly the same ratio as the cost to the outside public, whereas it is apparent that certain expenses (*e.g.*, cost of collections, bad debts, &c.) are entirely absent with regard to the interdepartmental supplies.

I now append an assessment, approved by a surveyor of taxes, showing how departmental profits on public lighting were arrived at in connection with a gas department.

Manufacture cost (less railway wagons hire purchase disallowed)	£10,668
Distribution cost	876
Management cost, less cost of collection and bad debts	1,094
Rates, &c. (less income-tax)	1,038
Stable Account	40
	13,716
Less Residuals	3,202
Net Cost	£10,514

Total Consumption ... ... 93,889,000 c.f.
Public Lighting Consumption ... 10,654,000 c.f.
10,654/93,889 of £10,514 ... = £1,193
(Cost of public lighting).

With regard to electric lighting assessments it is important to remember that in many cases the public lighting mains are distinct from the ordinary mains, and the expenses in connection with the former are directly charged to Public Lighting Account. I append an example of a calculation of profits on public lighting which has been accepted in the case of an electric lighting department.

Expenditure	£4,998		
Total Units *made* (ignoring losses in transmission)	1,308,510		
Average Cost per unit *made* (excluding cost of public lighting)	0.916d.		
Units *used* for Public Lighting	101,252		
Cost of Public Lighting—			
101,252 units at 0.916d.	£386	0	0
Attending and repairs (allocated separately, public lighting mains being distinct from other mains)	189	0	0
	575	0	0
Received in respect of Public Lighting	827	0	0
Profit	£252	0	0

I do not for a moment suggest that these examples are by any means perfect; numerous points can be raised, for instance, I understand that some surveyors have claimed that in arriving at the cost ot (say) public lighting, a proportion of the allowance in respect of wear and tear should be added. This seems reasonable.

With regard to interdepartmental charges as between tramways and electric lighting concerns it is important to notice that the exact cost of the current as supplied by the one department to the other is not in some cases comparable with the cost of current supplied to other consumers, inasmuch as the tramways department possesses separate cables, &c., and, apart from the upkeep of these, necessarily bears its own losses on transmission.

I have often seen it suggested that, while interdepartmental profits may thus be eliminated in regard to supplies to Rate Funds, the same rule should not be applied to transactions between trading undertakings, *e.g.*, tramways and electric light. In practice I have not found this objection to be raised, and I do not see, in equity, that it should be.

(21) INCOME-TAX ON INTEREST FROM SINKING FUND INVESTMENTS.

Some years ago a few cases came to my knowledge where the Inland Revenue authorities allowed income-tax in respect of Sinking Fund investments to be set off against the tax deducted from interest, dividends, &c., paid in respect of a debt, so that in effect the Sinking Fund investments produced their income gross.

Of late years, however, this practice has been stopped, and I understand that the Board of Inland Revenue maintain that interest on accumulating Sinking Funds cannot be set off in this way, the reason being, I presume, that the interest on the Sinking Funds is statutorily applicable for purposes of the Sinking Funds, and cannot, in fact, be used to pay the interest on debt.

The matter is of some importance to local authorities because the present high rate of tax materially reduces the yield of investments.

Arising out of this matter it is of interest to note the varying treatment which is accorded to interest received from Sinking Fund investments. In many cases the Sinking Fund yields interest in excess of the rate on which the Sinking Fund was originally calculated. The interest is treated in one of two ways:—

(*a*) Some corporations carry to each Sinking Fund the exact amount yielded by the interest, and thus the amount in the fund is in excess of the amount actually required.

(*b*) Others carry the whole of the interest to a Suspense Account, and carry therefrom to each Sinking Fund the exact amount of interest required, leaving the surplus of interest as "interest in excess of requirements and unappropriated."

If the balance is applied directly or indirectly in relief of rates or Revenue Account (*e.g.*, applied in reduction of annual contributions to Sinking Fund) cannot such balance be set off against a corresponding amount of the tax which the corporation deduct from the interest paid?

I have not entered into the question of the legality of the procedure above quoted. I believe that under the Stock Regulations issued pursuant to the Public Health Acts (Amendment) Act, 1890, one must (theoretically at any rate) earmark against each Sinking Fund the specific Sinking Fund investments by which it is represented, and it is, therefore, feasible that each particular Sinking Fund is legally entitled to the *exact* yield of its investment, although such yield may be in excess of requirements.

(22) Deduction of Tax on other Interest Received.

Dealing with the question of deducting tax on interest, the case of *Poole Corporation v. Bournemouth Corporation* (Chancery Division, 1910) is of interest.

> "A local authority purchased a tramway undertaking and raised the whole of the purchase price by a loan repayable in the usual way by half-yearly instalments of principal and interest extending over thirty years, and, on completion of the purchase, let the undertaking to another local authority under an agreement which provided that the rent should be such a sum as should enable the lessor authority to repay the principal and interest of the loan and certain costs by half-yearly instalments within the period of thirty years. Under this agreement the lessee corporation claimed that they were entitled to deduct income-tax from the whole amount of the half-yearly rent paid by them, while the lessor corporation contended that the rent should be such a sum as would be sufficient, after deducting income-tax, to pay the actual interest and instalment of capital of the loan.
>
> "It was held, that upon the true construction of the agreement, and having regard to Section 40 of the Income Tax Act, 1853, the lessee corporation were entitled to deduct income-tax as claimed by them."

If such interest is carried to a Rate Fund, it seems that the local authority might properly claim to set-off the same against the tax deducted from interest on debt paid out of the fund, but where, as I apprehend would generally be the case in arrangements of the kind in question, the interest is statutorily required to be carried to an accumulating Sinking Fund, no such set-off appears to be practicable.

(23) Bank Interest Received—Generally.

It is the well-known custom of banks not to deduct tax when charging or crediting interest. Hence, as regards interest received by a corporation, an assessment is made on the corporation in respect thereof. The assessment is made by virtue of the third case in the rules relating to Schedule D (Section 100, Income Tax Act, 1842), the third item of which includes "Interest on money not being annual interest." As a rule this does not really matter, because the bank interest received, so taxed, may be set off against—

(*a*) Interest paid to mortgagees, &c. (if the bank interest is used to pay such interest); or

(*b*) The Schedule D assessment on profits.

But in some cases such a "set-off" is not possible.

In the case of *Glamorgan Quarter Sessions v. Wilson (Surveyor of Taxes)* (King's Bench Division, March 2, 3, 8, 1910)—

> The Quarter Sessions of a county had deposited with a bank sums raised by them as a Compensation Fund under the Licensing Act, 1904. The bank interest on such deposit was paid by the bank without deduction of income-tax.

On behalf of Quarter Sessions it was contended—

(*a*) The Quarter Sessions was a judicial body, and could not be assessed.

(*b*) That they had no beneficial interest in the Compensation Fund, but had only the power of distributing it between the persons to whom it belonged, and that the distribution was made by the Court's judicial decision under power given them by the Licensing Act, 1904.

The Surveyor maintained that—

(*a*) There was no statutory exemption in favour of Quarter Sessions; and

(*b*) It was immaterial for what purpose the interest was intended.

It was held that Quarter Sessions were properly assessed to income-tax.

(24) Bank Interest Received by Overseers.

Overseers have of late years been frequently assessed on the bank interest received by them (under the 3rd rule, Schedule D, before referred to).

Against such assessments it has been contended:—

(i) That the overseers should be treated as a "person" and consequently if their total income is less than £160 or £150 per annum should be totally exempt.

(ii) That as the interest arises from receipts in respect of rates and is applied in relief of rates it should, like rates, be exempt.

(iii) That banker's interest on poor rate is exempt by Section 86 of the Poor Law Act, 4 & 5 William IV, Chap. 76, which exempts poor law mortgages, instruments, contracts, agreements, &c., from "Stamp Duty."

Contention (i) is dealt with in paragraph 11. With regard to (ii) and (iii), which have been overruled in cases contested before local Commissioners, it appears to have been the practice of the Inland Revenue Department in years back to exempt this interest from assessment; in 1906 the City Accountant of Dublin was granted exemption from tax on interest received on Poor Rate Account, but he himself says, "So far as I can judge the exemption is a concession."

(25) BANK INTEREST PAID.

With regard to bank interest paid (without deduction of tax, as is the general custom) an injustice may arise in the case of an assessment on profits if the profit exceeds the total interest, including bank interest. In this case the assessment is on the profits and the party assessed is presumed to recoup himself as far as possible by deducting tax from the interest paid. The tax is deducted as a matter of course from the interest paid to mortgagees and stockholders, but as regards bank interest no such deduction is made, and accordingly an amount of tax equivalent to the bank interest should, in equity, be either—

(*a*) refunded to the corporation by the Inland Revenue (the Inland Revenue will receive tax on the item in the bank's profits); or

(*b*) allowed as a deduction from the Schedule D assessment.

(See paragraph 26 as to the treatment of Public Works Loans Commissioners' interest.)

But in making an application of this kind I received the following communication from the Commissioners:—

Cardiff, August 9th 1911

"Dear Sir,—

Bank Interest Claim.

I am directed by the Board of Inland Revenue to acquaint you that your claim on behalf of the Pontypridd and Rhondda Joint Water Board may be preferred when the loan has been in existence for at least twelve consecutive months.

It is not the practice to admit claims in respect of loans which have been in existence for any shorter period.

Yours faithfully, H. EDWARDS.

"F. J. Alban, Esq."

Ordinarily speaking, of course, bank interest paid without deduction of tax should be allowed as a debit to Profit and Loss Account for income-tax purposes, but this is of little avail where the profits are assessed on the average of the previous three years, or on the basis of the previous years' profits, as is the case in the instance I have cited.

The law on the subject appears to be as follows:—

In *Goslings and Sharpe v. Blake* (Court of Appeal, 24th and 25th June 1889) it was decided that the provision for deduction of tax contained in Section 40 of the Act of 1853 only applied to annual interest, and that in case of loans for short periods the tax must not be deducted by the borrower, but the interest must be returned for assessment by the lender. This case was before the Act of 1888 (see paragraph 12). But in the case of *The Lord Advocate v. Lord Provost, &c., of the City of Edinburgh* (Court of Session, Scotland, 3rd March and 15th October 1903, and 6th July 1905), it was held that the Act of 1888, Section 24, applies to any interest of money, whether yearly interest or not, which is not payable or not wholly payable out of profits or gains brought into charge, and that the corporation was bound to retain and render an account of the income-tax on the interest on the temporary loans, so far as the interest is not paid out of profits already charged with tax.

It seems clear, therefore, that tax may be deducted on payment of bank interest, although I suggest that a custom has been established, in which the Inland Revenue authorities have acquiesced, that, as a matter of convenience, tax shall not be deducted, but shall be accounted for in the bank's profits.

I submit this view with a certain amount of doubt, as the Inland Revenue Department on the 1st February 1907 wrote the following letter in the case of *De Peyer v. The King* (Court of Appeal, February 1909):—

"In the case of interest on a fixed sum advanced for a period of a year or more at a fluctuating rate, it is doubtful whether the interest is 'annual,' so as to entitle the borrower to deduct tax on payment to the bank (Section 40), and in view of this doubt, if the interest has been paid out of taxed sources and has been taken into account in computing the bank's liability to assessment, the Board, as a concession, admit a claim from the borrower, if supported by an adequate certificate from the bank. They have extended this concession to cases where interest is paid in full at varying rates on fluctuating advances or overdrafts on current account, although in such cases the interest is clearly not annual. And, strictly speaking, the borrower has no title either to deduct tax on payment, or to claim repayment from this department, on the ground that such deduction has been refused by the bankers, but this extension is subject to the proviso that the interest has been paid over one or more years, so as, in fact, to constitute an annual charge on the taxed income of the borrower. It is under this concession that your claims have been admitted for 1906 and past years, but in no case can the Board extend the concession to a case where the advance or overdraft bearing interest has not continued for one year at least."

(26) PUBLIC WORKS LOANS COMMISSIONERS' INTEREST.

Those members who have to pay Public Works Loans Commissioners' interest (which is paid in full without deduction of tax) will know that the interest so paid is as a rule excluded from the assessment on interest, or deducted from the Schedule D assessment, or allowed in some other way.

I understand that on one occasion a borough treasurer, apprehending some difficulty in this respect, deducted tax on making a payment of Public Works Loans Commissioners' interest; ultimately, however, the Board of Inland Revenue gave the following undertaking:—

"The corporation will not by paying the Public Works Loans Commissioners' interest in full be placed in a worse position than they would be if they were to deduct the tax from such interest."

(27) THE SUCCESSION RULE.

Where there is a change in the proprietors of a business, although the nature of the business remains the same, the succession rule applies, *i.e.*, the assessment is made on the basis of bringing the past profits into average notwithstanding the change in *personnel* of proprietors. The Inland Revenue authorities look at the *business* rather than the *proprietors* for the time being.

The succession rule does not apply if the profit "has fallen short from some specific cause" since the change took place, or by reason of it; in this case the business is to be assessed as a new one on the actual profit made.

The succession rule affects local authorities who purchase from companies undertakings, such as tramways, waterworks, &c., and in this connection the case of *Stockham v. Wallasey Urban District Council* (King's Bench Division, December 1906) is of interest.

The facts are complicated, but the following brief statement is substantially correct:—

"A local company had bought both a tramway undertaking and an omnibus undertaking. Wallasey Council eventually bought the tramways part of the company (under statutory powers). It was a four-mile horse tramway with nine cars. The Council made ten miles, and ran twenty electric cars, and consequently the profits of the Council greatly exceeded the profits of the old company. The Council, however, succeeded in the view that they should be assessed on past results as a succession. Bray, J., agreed that a person could not succeed to part of an undertaking, but here he thought there were two undertakings, and the Council have succeeded to one of them."

(28) ASSESSMENTS OF MUNICIPAL WATER UNDERTAKINGS.

With regard to the assessment of water undertakings, it seems clear from the decisions in *Glasgow Corporation Water Commissioners v. Inland Revenue* (Court of Session, 1875), and *Glasgow Corporation Water Commissioners v. Miller* (Court of Session, 1886), and other relevant cases, that the following rules may be laid down:—

(*a*) Where a municipal corporation possesses waterworks for a supply of water within its boundaries, and is empowered to levy a "compulsory rate" on all dwelling-houses within its boundaries, income-tax is not payable on the rates so raised.

(*b*) So far as the corporation sells water to manufacturers and others for purposes not included in the "compulsory rate," and so far also as it supplies water outside the limits of its district, it is a trader, and becomes liable to income-tax on the surplus profits from such transactions.

(*c*) A "compulsory rate" is one which the ratepayers have to pay (1) whether they are willing to pay it or not, and (2) whether they take water or not.

A non-compulsory rate is one paid only by those who pay it as a *quid pro quo* for water they are supplied with: it is not properly a rate at all, and such a rate is not exempt from income-tax.

The following very recent case is interesting:—

In the King's Bench Division (February 1912) Mr. Justice Hamilton considered the appeal of the Wakefield Rural District Council against the income-tax assessment as to alleged profits on the Council's water undertaking. The appellants have a large number of parishes in their area, and they supply water to nine parishes, the water being bought from the Wakefield Corporation.

There was a profit in respect to four parishes, receipts balanced with expenditure as to two parishes after allowances for establishment charges, and in the remaining parishes there was shown a loss, the consumers only paying a water rate.

The point in question was whether the net profit on the whole undertaking was chargeable, or whether, as was argued by the Inland Revenue Commissioners, the profits in the four parishes were chargeable without regard for the loss that was sustained respecting the other parishes.

His Lordship, in delivering judgment, remarked that the Commissioners had found that the water undertakings respecting the several parishes were separate concerns, but his view was that the whole constituted one concern, and might be regarded as analogous to mines and ironworks, docks, and so forth.

The supply was a joint one, but the impulse by which the water was circulated was a common impulse, and he could not accept the view of the Solicitor-General that the tax should be allocated between the parishes that showed a profit.

The appeal was allowed.

(29) THE PREPARATION OF ACCOUNTS FOR INCOME TAX PURPOSES.

In preparing the accounts of a trading department for income tax purposes one of two methods may be employed:—

(1) To take the net profits as shown by the complete Profit and Loss Accounts, add back the various items charged in the Profit and Loss Account which are disallowed for income-tax purposes, and deduct those items of income upon which tax has already been paid by way of deduction, or which are assessed to taxation under any other schedule.

(2) To take the gross profits as shown by the Profit and Loss Accounts; charge against the same only those items which are allowed as proper expenses incurred in carrying on the undertaking; and credit only those items of income which have not already been subjected to taxation or which are not taxable under any other schedule.

The first method is to be commended, as it clearly shows what items have been deducted or included. Of course, municipalities invariably adopt this method, as their accounts are freely published; but private firms and companies cannot as a rule, having regard to trade competition, &c., afford to disclose much detail.

(30) Deductions Allowed and not Allowed in Computing Profits for Income Tax Purposes.

A statement is appended of the items which are allowed and not allowed for income-tax purposes; some of the items, of course, refer to individuals rather than local authorities.

(A) *Deductions allowed.—*

(1) Repairs of premises occupied for the purpose of the trade, &c., and for the supply or repair of implements, utensils, or articles employed, not exceeding the sum usually expended for such purposes according to the average of the three years preceding.

(2) Debts proved to be bad, also doubtful debts according to their estimated value.

(3) The rent of premises used solely for purposes of business and not as a place of residence.

(If the local authority pays the Schedule A tax of property which it holds as tenant, such tax should be deducted from the landlord in making the next payment of rent; thus the local authority acts merely as the collector for the Crown.)

(4) A proportion not exceeding two-thirds of the rent of any dwelling-house, partly used for the purposes of business.

(5) The annual value of any premises occupied by the owner solely for the purposes of business, and not as a place of residence, according to the amount on which duty has been paid under Schedule A. (This clearly shows that the Schedule A assessment on a trading concern is ultimately merged in the Schedule D assessment on profits. (See Par. 7).)

(6) A proportion not exceeding two-thirds of the annual value (according to the amount on which duty has been paid under Schedule A) of any dwelling-house occupied by the owner, and partly used for the purposes of trade. One-third of all gas, electricity, rates, water, and other like charges, is usually also disallowed.

(7) Any other disbursements or expenses wholly and exclusively laid out for the purpose of the trade, &c.

The following deductions may also be claimed:—

(8) Revenue expenses, although not included in the accounts of undertakings, such as:—

(*a*) A proper proportion of salaries of borough officials.

(*b*) A proper proportion of town hall expenses.

(*c*) A proper proportion of rent of municipal offices.

(*d*) Actual renewals (subject to scheme before mentioned), whether paid direct from revenue or from any Suspense or Reserve Account.

(9) The profit on interdepartmental supplies. (See Paragraph 20.)

(10) Bank interest paid in full without deduction of tax. (See Paragraph 25.)

(11) Public Works Loans Commissioners' interest paid in full without deduction of tax. (See Paragraph 26.)

(12) There may also be set off in Rate Fund Accounts against the tax deducted from interest paid any taxed profits transferred by trading departments which are used to pay such interest.

(B) *Deductions not allowed.*

(1) Interest on capital, any annual interest annuity, or any other annual payment payable out of the profits or gains, or for any royalty, or other sum paid in respect of the user of a patent. (The duty on such interest, patent, royalty, or other annual payment should be deducted from the person to whom the payment is made). Bank interest and public works loan board's interest, paid in full without deduction of tax, are usually allowed.

(2) Sums paid as salaries to partners, or for drawings by partners.

(3) Sums invested or employed as capital in the trade or business, or on account of capital withdrawn therefrom. (Thus capital expenditure must be eliminated from the Profit and Loss Account for income-tax purposes.)

(4) Sums expended in improvements of premises or written off for depreciation of land, buildings, or leases.

(5) Loss not connected with or arising out of the trade, &c.

(6) Expenses of maintenance of the persons assessable, their families, or private establishments.

(7) Income-tax on profits or gains, or on the annual value of the trade premises. (This is an appropriation of profits, not a charge against profits.)

(8) Premiums for life insurance, or wear and tear of machinery and plant, but allowances may be claimed in respect of these items. (In the case of municipal trading undertakings, certain renewals may be charged as expenses in arriving at profits. (See Paragraph 16).)

(9) Loss recoverable under an insurance or contract of indemnity.

In considering the deductions allowed, it is instructive to note the case of *Dillon (Surveyor of Taxes) v. The Corporation of Haverfordwest* (Queen's Bench Division, 5th February 1891). The Corporation, by a private Act of Parliament, were empowered to sell gas, provided they first lighted the public streets; they claimed to deduct the cost of such lighting from their profits. It was held that no such deduction could be made, as the public lighting was not an expense necessarily incurred in *carrying on* their trade, but was only an expense necessary to enable them to *enter on* that trade.

(31) Assessment of Burial Boards—Profit Assessable Irrespective of its Application.

In *Paddington Burial Board v. Commissioners of Inland Revenue* (Queen's Bench Division, 13th and 14th March 1884) the Burial Board claimed that they were not liable to be assessed to income-tax on their gains, on the ground that such gains could not be "profits" because they were applied in aid of the poor rate. The Court held that the Board clearly made a profit, and the destination of it was immaterial, and therefore gave judgment for the Crown.

(32) Assessment of Cemeteries.

It was held in *Edinburgh Southern Cemetery Company v. Kinmont* (1889) that, when a cemetery company under its contract of co-partnery had power to sell and dispose to any person of the use of a piece of ground in the cemetery for burial purposes in perpetuity, that the proceeds of such sales of the right of sepulture during the year were assessable for income-tax without deduction of any part thereof in respect of its being a realisation or conversion of capital, and that being income derived from a trade carried on by the use of the land they fell to be assessed under Schedule A, No. 3, Rule 3, of the Income Tax Act, 1842.

(33) Contributions under National Insurance Act, 1911.

It is understood that contributions under the National Insurance Act, 1911, paid by employers in respect of persons employed by them, will be allowable as a business expense in estimating the assessable profits under Schedule D.

(34) "Adding Back" Income Tax.

Whichever method be adopted in "adding back" (see Paragraph 29), it is important to only add back the expenditure which is actually included in the Profit and Loss Account; this may seem self-evident, but the item "Income-tax" is subject to great misconception in this respect.

For instance, if a trading department is assessed to income-tax at, say, £1,000, it is quite easy to add back the whole £1,000, forgetting that perhaps £800 was recouped by deductions from interest on debt, ground rent, &c., leaving only the £200 as the net debit to Profit and Loss Account; this latter amount, £200 only, should be added back to the profit and loss balance. The Surveyor usually inquires, "What amount is charged in the account for income-tax?" and it is particularly easy to fall into the error of giving in answer the gross amount. This mistake has come under my notice in a number of cases.

The same point applies as regards Schedule A tax, where ground or lease rent is payable. The amount to be added back is the Schedule A tax as reduced by the amount deducted from the ground rent, &c.

In a test case set by our Institute in 1906 (Final Examination)—the example being the assessment of a corporation's electricity undertaking—the income includes "gross" rents of property, whilst the expenditure includes "income-tax on profits."

In such circumstances, as the rent is credited in gross, the property tax (paid by the owner either direct or by deduction by tenants) must have been included somewhere in the expenditure, and as the only item of income-tax referred to in the question is the "tax based on profits" the "property" tax (or Schedule A) must be specially written back and the assessment increased accordingly.

(35) Deductions from Salaries under Superannuation and Thrift Acts.

From the municipal officer's personal point of view it is interesting to note that in *Beaumont v. Bowers* (Queen's Bench Division, May 1900) it was held that compulsory deductions from an officer's salary under the Poor Law Officers' Superannuation Act, 1896, could be treated as a "deduction" for the purpose of estimating the liability of the recipient of the salary to income-tax.

This decision was overruled in *Bell v. Gribble (Surveyor of Taxes)* and *Hudson v. Gribble* (Court of Appeal, February 1903)—cases arising on a thrift fund established under the Manchester Corporation Act, 1891.

TABLE OF THE VARIOUS SCHEDULES

Sch.	Levied in respect of	Paid by
A (Property or Landlord) Tax.	The Annual Value of the property (ownership) in all lands, tenements, hereditaments, &c., in *United Kingdom*. "Annual value" is regarded for income-tax purposes as equivalent to "*Annual Income*." Annual value exists, although no profit can be made, so long as the occupation is "valuable." (Thus in the case of a Statutory Body owning an undertaking not carried on with a view to profit and not, in fact, producing any profit, the hereditaments must be valued at the rent which the hypothetical tenant would be expected to give if called upon to perform the statutory duties which the particular body has to perform. (*Ystradyfodwg and Pontypridd Main Sewerage Board v. Benstead*).	*Landlord*, Assessment is made on Landlord in cases of (*a*) dwelling-houses annual value of which is under £10; (*b*) lands (including buildings) let for under one year; (*c*) in other cases where landlord so requests in writing before 31*st July*. In other cases assessment is made on occupier, who, however, may deduct tax paid by him from next payment of rent; or in some cases (Section 10, Act 1898) any subsequent payment of rent.
B (Farmer's Tax).	The Annual Value of the Occupation in all lands and houses used for agricultural purposes.	Occupier. (This tax is analogous to that under Sch. D., and is in respect of the Occupier's estimated profits from his farming business.)
C	Annual amount of all profits arising from interest, &c., payable out of public revenue.	Receiver (generally by way of deduction from income).
D	(*a*) The Annual Profits or gains arising or accruing to any person residing in the United Kingdom. (1) From any kind of property whatever, whether situate in the United Kingdom or elsewhere. (2) From any Profession, Trade, Employment, or Vocation, whether the same is carried on in the United Kingdom or elsewhere. (*b*) The Annual Profits or Gains accruing to any person whatever, whether a subject of His Majesty or not, although not resident within the United Kingdom, from any property whatever in the United Kingdom, or any trade, &c., exercised within the United Kingdom. (*c*) All interest of Money, Annuities, and other Annual Profits, and gains not charged by virtue of any of the other Schedules.	Recipient.
E	Annual amount of income arising from every public office or employment, or profit and annuities, &c., payable out of public revenues, except annuities charged under Sch. C.	Receiver.

UNDER WHICH INCOME-TAX IS LEVIED.

Basis of Charge and Incidence of Assessment.	Exemptions, Allowances, &c.	Remarks.
Lands and dwelling-houses—Annual Rental (less repairs), determined as follows :— (*a*) In London—Gross Value as fixed by Assessment Committee. (*b*) In Scotland—Assessment for Rating Purposes is conclusive evidence of Annual Value if made by Surveyor of Taxes. (*c*) In England, provinces—As determined by District Commissioners—need not necessarily be identical with Gross Poor Rate Value. *Tithes (in kind)*—Average profits of three preceding years. *Do. (compounded for)*—Average profits of preceding year. *Profits of Manors*—Average receipts of seven preceding years. *Lease renewal fines*—Receipts of preceding year. **Stone, Slate, Limestone, and Chalk Quarries*—Profits of preceding year. **Coal and other Mines*—Average profits of five preceding years: General Commissioners have option to assess on profits of preceding year. **Iron, Gas and Water Works, Docks, Ferries, Bridges, &c.*—Profits of preceding year. **Railways*—Assessed by Special Commissioners on profits of preceding year. NOTE.—If business commenced within periods named, then from time of commencement. **Assessed according to the rules of Schedule D.*	*Repairs* (deducted from Gross Assessment)—1/8th for lands (including farmhouses and buildings, 1/6th for houses and buildings (excluding farm houses); under Finance (1909-10) Act, 1910, the above allowances are extended in the case of (*a*) lands, including farm houses and buildings, and (*b*) houses the annual value of which does not exceed £8 for income-tax purposes; to a maximum of 25% in each case on proof of corresponding expenditure. Claim for repayment must be made. *Land tax, drainage rate, losses by flood, tempest, &c.* (if owner abates portion of rent). *Voids* *Usual exemptions and abatements* (where total income under £700, for life insurance, children, &c.) *The net assessment under Sch. A.* is deductible from profit in lieu of rent where Trader owns business premises. In this case the Sch. A Assessment may be regarded as merged in the Sch. D. Assessment. *Exempt*—Almshouses; Hospitals; Free Libraries; Public Schools; Buildings belonging to, and used solely for the purpose of Literary or Scientific Institutions.	Assessment made every five years cannot be increased save for structural improvements, but may be reduced because of deterioration of property.
1/3rd of gross annual value for Sch. A. (with option of assessment under Sch. D if tenant gives notice to Surveyor within two months after commencement of year of assessment). If profits or gains fall short of the amount, *actual* amount of profits or gains.	Losses by flood or tempest (if owner abates portion of rent). Voids. Usual exemptions and abatements.	Assessment made once every five years. If rent remitted assessment may be reduced. Profits of nurseries and market gardens estimated according to Sch. D—but charged under Sch. B.
Actual Income.	Usual exemptions and abatements.	Where Interest does not amount to £2/10/0 in half-year, no deduction is made, but interest is included in Sch. D. Except on coupons issued by the National Debt Commissioners from which the tax is to be deducted, although they do not amount to £2/10/0.
In respect of trade, manufacture, professions, &c.—Average profits for three years preceding year of assessment; or proportionate average where set up during period. Profits of uncertain annual value not otherwise assessed.—Profits of preceding year. Profits of Foreign Securities.—According to full amount received or to be received in United Kingdom in current year without any deduction Profits of Foreign Possessions.—According to average amount received in United Kingdom during three preceding years. Other Annual Profits or Gains.—Average or otherwise, as equitable.	Usual exemptions and abatements. See detailed list of deductions allowed, and not allowed, in computing profits. Note deduction of net Sch. A Assessment where trader owns business premises.	
Actual income for the year current. Additional or supplemental assessment may be made for additional income. The three years' average system is allowed by practice of Inland Revenue officials (*i.e.*, not by law) in the case of subordinate officials.	Usual exemptions and abatements.	Includes salaries of Government Officials, Directors, Managers, &c., of Public Companies, &c.

The Limitation and Application of Profits from Municipal Undertakings.

By Bailie WALTER NELSON, C.A., J.P.
(Chairman of Gas Finance Committee, Glasgow.)

A PAPER read at the annual meeting of the Institute of Municipal Treasurers and Accountants (Incorporated) held at Cardiff on the 4th and 5th July 1912.

At this season of the year the attention of a reader of one or other of the journals dealing with municipal enterprise is arrested by such head-lines as these:—

A Record Year at X.

A Profitable Year at Y.

Relief of Z's Rates.

A perusal of the articles under these head-lines leaves one in doubt as to whether the ratepayers of the cities thus brought into prominence are to be envied, or the users of the commodities yielding the profits commiserated.

The policy and action of municipal authorities has in recent times been sharply criticised, not only by local ratepayers, but by the trading community, and has led to inquiry by Parliament itself.

There would appear to be good ground for comment when we consider the magnitude of municipal indebtedness,

which in 1883-1884 amounted to	£193,000,000
and in 1903-1904 was	£469,000,000
an increase, in twenty years, of	£276,000,000

The increase is in large measure attributable to local authorities having become traders in many departments of commerce, including Waterworks, Gasworks, Electrical Works, Tramways, Steamboats Harbours, Markets, Fire Insurance, Telephones, Industrial Dwellings, Milk Supply, Entertainment Purveyors, and it may almost be said Bankers, as some authorities are prepared to receive deposits at short notice and low rates of interest.

Municipal activity is said to be directed towards works which are productive and non-productive. The classification is perhaps scarcely accurate, as several so-called "non-productive" departments, such as Health Administration, Parks, Baths, Street Improvements, and others, clearly contribute—in a sense akin to the supplies of such commodities as Water and Lighting, or of the service of Tramways—to the comfort, or convenience for traffic and trade, of the citizens.

For general purposes the non-productive works may be differentiated from the productive, as being that class whose cost is represented by a tax on the whole community instead of by a tax or rate on the individuals using them. In common parlance, the productive works are those which fall within the category of "profit earning" departments, and form the class which comes under the term "Municipal Trading."

It is no part of this paper to enter into the merits or demerits of municipal trading. Most of those present will be acquainted with the Report of the Joint Select Committee on Municipal Trading, the Report on the Repayment of Loans by Local Authorities, and the Report of the Departmental Committee on the Accounts of Local Authorities.

I desire simply to recall the views of the London Chamber of Commerce as expressed by Mr. Sydney Morse in his evidence before the first-named Committee (Answers 832 and 833):—

"We desire to put this principle forward, as the principle to be adopted, that the action of municipalities in trading should be restricted to matters undertaken in the public interest and without a view to profit; in fact, if I may put it in another way, to matters in respect of which it is reasonable that a rate should be made." . . . "We say that, as a principle, municipal trading should be restricted to those matters which are undertaken in the public interest and without a view to profit."

And in juxtaposition I give the views of Mr. Bernard Shaw, as stated in his book entitled "The Common Sense of Municipal Trading," Chapter I:—

"As far as their legal powers have gone, municipalities have always traded, and will always trade, to the utmost of the business capacity and public spirit of their members." . . . "It is waste of time to force an open door, and in all public services in which the determining factor is practically unlimited command of cheap capital combined with indifference to dividend, the door is more than wide open: it has been carried clean off its hinges by the victorious rush of municipal socialism under the reassuring name of Progressivism."

One matter of importance has undoubtedly been elicited from the Parliamentary inquiries to which I have referred, and that is an expression of doubt as to whether the Trading Accounts of local authorities have been properly framed so as to show clearly the net results of the trading.

Several prominent public men, who are by no means adverse to modern municipal government and enterprise, have stated candidly that examination of the accounts of many municipal trading works by competent accountants would disclose losses instead of profits.

It is a truism of commerce, under present day conditions, that the difference between earning profits and making losses depends on unremitting attention to details, on prudent selection of the staff, and particularly of the captains of industry, on close devotion of the workers, and on careful periodical examination of the accounts.

Most of the leading municipalities in the United Kingdom, and many of the smaller boroughs, endeavour to keep and present the accounts of their Trading Departments so as to show the true results of their trading.

I take it that we are all in agreement on these points, viz.:—

(1) That separate accounts of all trading undertakings should be kept.

(2) That the yearly accounts when brought to a balance should present a true and correct view of the whole transactions and the results of trading during the year.

(3) That every receipt properly applicable to the year should be brought into the accounts and that every charge which the undertaking ought to bear is duly debited.

(4) That sums written off as irrecoverable, and abatements or modifications made from standard prices or rates—particularly where such abatements are granted to other departments of the municipality—are so dealt with only by the express authority of the Council or the responsible Committee.

(5) That the Capital Account should set forth clearly the capital expenditure for the year and the source from which that expenditure has been met.

(6) That the Balance Sheet should exhibit a complete statement of the whole assets and liabilities of the undertaking and disclose specifically the amount set aside or applied by the Council in reduction of debt through the medium of sinking fund or otherwise.

It would appear that the practice followed in the treatment of certain charges, which are legitimate expenses of working, varies; and there is also variation in the method of dealing with certain classes of receipts.

For example, in the matter of expenditure, an item commonly omitted from the Revenue Account is a share of the general staff expense of the local authority. Clearly, whether the Trading Department has a separate establishment of its own or not, the general staff expenses (Town Clerk's office) City Treasurer's office, and other main establishment outgoings, should be fairly allocated as between the Rating Departments and the Trading Departments.

The same remark applies to the expenditure in the maintenance of the Town Hall or Council Chambers, which may be looked upon as of the nature of a rental to be allocated in just proportion to each of the Municipal Departments. Then, in some instances, the assessments to rates of the properties of municipal undertakings are modified where the assessment authorities are the owners of the undertakings.

Again, a common bone of contention between the Department charged with the Supervision and Maintenance of Streets, and a Tramway Department, is the question of payment for street improvements or street widenings.

These widenings may be:—

(1) Those undertaken solely for the benefit of the Tramways, in which case the whole cost should be borne by the Tramway Department.

(2) Those undertaken to cope with existing road traffic concurrently with Tramway construction, in which case the Street Improvement Department would appear to be liable for the whole cost.

(3) Those undertaken in anticipation of an increasing road traffic, and to permit of the more efficient working of the Tramways, in which case the cost may be apportioned as between the two departments, either in equal shares or in such shares as may be agreed on as fair in the circumstances by the City and Tramway Engineers jointly.

Then, in the matter of revenue, it is too commonly the practice to depart from standard prices in dealing with other departments of the municipality.

In some cases these other departments are supplied free of charge, or there are undercharges, or, again, there are overcharges. In all three cases the proper term for such a policy is "malpractice."

I think the view of all sagacious Councillors, and certainly of the members of an Institute like ours, will be that a full and fair accounting should always be made as between departments for services rendered or products sold.

Granting that there may sometimes be difficulty in fixing a reasonable price, owing to the large consumption of the product by the Corporation, as compared with other customers, all that should be conceded, if there is to be a true accounting, is "*the most favoured nation terms.*"

These can easily be calculated where there is a standard sliding scale in, say, the cases of gas, electricity, and water; but if there be no such scale, then the actual cost of production of the commodity may fairly be taken.

Assuming that the Revenue Account of the undertaking presents no difficulty in respect of the matters above mentioned, and that all ordinary expenditure has been paid or provided for, the balance is usually carried to a net Revenue or Profit and Loss Account.

Against this balance are charged the rentals of leased property (if any), interest on loans, and provision for depreciation.

Thereafter the surplus on the Profit and Loss Account is carried to an Appropriation Account, which is debited with Sinking Fund instalments, and, if there be a surplus or deficit, such surplus or deficit is carried off to Rate Account or otherwise disposed of by the municipality in accordance with the powers given it by statute.

I am aware that difference of opinion exists as to the legality and propriety of debiting revenue with depreciation where a statutory Sinking Fund is in force.

The subject has been fully discussed at previous meetings of this Institute; the views of the public have been expressed from time to time in the Press; and wordy war rages on the problem on the occasion of the presentation of the annual accounts of trading departments in many Town Councils.

The Departmental Committee on the Accounts of Local Authorities was evidently reluctant to give a lead on the question, and contented itself with stating that "the "repayment of debt, so far as it goes, may properly be "regarded as provision for depreciation; but it is possible "that the period allowed for repayment may be excessive, "and therefore in some cases further provision for "depreciation may be necessary."

The weight of professional expert opinion is in favour of a provision for depreciation.

The wear and tear of fixed assets is essentially an element in the cost of the year's trading; and provision for this depreciation, including possible obsolescence, should not be determined or affected by the result of the trading. It should form a charge on the Revenue Account of each year before the balance of net profit is struck, and should not be treated as an appropriation of any balance of net profit available.

It appears to me that a fair rule on this thorny question is: —

> In all cases, where practicable, the undertaking ought to be maintained from year to year in complete and efficient working order out of revenue. Where it is impracticable to secure full maintenance out of the year's trading, a Depreciation Fund should be provided to secure reinstatement. If this course be followed, consideration of the "life" of the subject in relation to the Sinking Fund becomes eliminated.

There are, of course, undertakings which do not call for depreciation. As an example, we have waterworks where the upkeep charges —apart from the replacement of sections of mains—vary little from year to year. Moreover, the "life" of these mains may usually be taken as of equal duration with the period allowed for the repayment of the capital borrowed.

The case is different with Gas Works, Electrical Works, and Tramways. Here the "life" of much of the working plant, and in some instances of the buildings falls far short of the periods given by Parliament wherein to pay off the Capital debt. Moreover, the probability of obsolescence, in the case of many of the assets of such undertakings, must not be lost sight of.

While admitting that the circumstances of each understanding must be fairly considered, and that it would be unreasonable to lay down a general standard or scale of depreciation, I may say that the city of which I am a representative has put into practice, after full inquiry, scales which it may be worth giving here.

It may be added that the question of depreciation was fully discussed before the Committees of both Houses of Parliament when Glasgow was promoting a Consolidation of its Gas Acts in the Session of 1910, and that the scale for the gasworks buildings and plant, hereinafter mentioned, has obtained the express imprimatur of Parliament.

The Consolidation Act was not an unopposed measure, and it is significant that Parliament took occasion to review the powers of utilising profits from their gas undertaking then held by Glasgow. Under its main Gas Act of 1869, Glasgow had power to carry any balance of profits to the credit of the Corporation for their general purposes—in other words, might apply these profits in aid of rates, if so minded. By the Act of 1910, that power was taken away, and the Corporation expressly directed to apply profits to the reduction of the gas charges throughout the limits of supply.

Scale of depreciation in force in Glasgow gas undertaking:—

On gasworks	$1\frac{1}{2}$	per cent.	per annum.
On chemical works ...	3	,,	,,
On pipes	2	,,	,,
On meters	6	,,	,,
On stoves	10	,,	,,

Scale of depreciation in force in Glasgow electricity undertaking:—

On land and buildings ...	1 per cent.	per annum.	
On machinery and plant, electrical instruments, transformers in consumers' premises, &c.	3½	,,	,,
On accumulators ...	5	,,	,,
On mains and cables ...	2½	,,	,,
On meters	4	,,	,,

Scale of depreciation in force in Glasgow tramways undertaking:—

On permanent way ...	£440 per mile of single track		per annum.
On electrical equipment of line	4.3	per cent.	,,
On buildings and fixtures ...	2½	,,	,,
On power station and sub-stations' plant	7.4	,,	,,
On workshop tools and sundry plant	7½	,,	,,
On cars	7½	,,	,,
On electrical equipment of cars	8.79	,,	,,
On other rolling stock ...	10.15	,,	,,
On miscellaneous equipment	7½	,,	,,
On office furniture	7½	,,	,,

A net surplus from trading is sometimes realised in connection with municipal undertakings other than water, gas, electricity, and tramways, but, in the absence of complete official information as to the accounts of these "minor" undertakings, I have thought it well to confine my remarks to the four main enterprises above mentioned.

Two factors influence the "profits" or net surpluses from trading—assuming the balance on the Trading Account has not been inflated by reason of inadequate provision having been made for depreciation, or from want of attention to those items of charge or under-charge to which I have referred in an earlier part of this paper.

These factors are (1) the interest on the money borrowed on behalf of the undertaking, and (2) the sums which require to be set aside for repayment of debt.

With regard to interest, municipalities have been able to borrow at considerably keener rates than ordinary commercial companies. The rates, in recent times, have ranged from 3 per cent. to 3½ per cent.—most of the larger municipalities have borrowed, on the average, at or slightly under 3¼ per cent.

The outlook for the future is not so bright, and unless existing municipal enterprises are well and economically managed, and their plant kept up to a high state of efficiency, the public may not respond so readily as they have done in the past. When new loans fall to be marketed, the effect of any distrust on the part of the public will be reflected by a demand for higher rates of interest.

With regard to Sinking Fund instalments towards repayment of debt, local authorities have usually a choice of one of three methods, viz.:—

(1) Equal yearly (or half-yearly) instalments of principal, generally known as the instalment system.

(2) Equal yearly (or half-yearly) instalments of principal and interest combined, *i.e.*, a terminable annuity—the annuity system.

(3) The setting aside and accumulating at compound interest a sum sufficient to extinguish the debt within the allotted number of years. This is the Sinking Fund proper.

Where the second or third method of debt repayment is adopted the combined items of loan interest and Sinking Fund charge will remain constant until the end of the repayment period, when both will disappear, and then the "profits" will suddenly be greatly increased.

Where the instalment system is adopted the Sinking Fund charge will remain constant until the end of the period, but the loan interest item will diminish steadily, and the "profits" tend to increase by degrees.

Each method has its advantages and disadvantages, and local authorities will choose the one which is likely to suit best the circumstances and finances of their undertakings. The instalment system has in recent years been frequently adopted, particularly by those municipalities which have been authorised to institute a Loans Fund.

With regard to the period for repayment, this is usually supposed to be calculated according to the estimated "life" of the undertaking, or at a little less than that "life," in order to provide for a margin of safety.

In fixing the period for repayment, Parliament usually endeavours to strike a happy medium whereby the interests of the present ratepayers or users (who naturally desire that the repayment should be as long as possible), and the interests of future ratepayers and users (which demand that the burden of an expensive loan shall be removed as early as possible) are harmonised.

Sixty years is about the maximum period allowed for the repayment of local loans, whatever the estimated "life" of the undertaking may be.

This period appears a short one in the case, say, of waterworks, especially where the water is conveyed for a great distance from the city or area served by the undertaking. Moreover, in the case of nearly every expensive undertaking of this character, provision has to be made considerably in excess of present needs, and these works do not usually become fully productive for a considerable number of years after construction.

It would appear more equitable in the case of waterworks for Parliament either to postpone the operation of the Sinking Fund for a period of from five to ten years after date of completion of the whole works, or alternatively to extend the period for repayment to, say, eighty years.

On the other hand, the periods allowed in the case of gas works, electrical works, and tramways are, in the main, liberal.

It is admittedly difficult, if not indeed impossible, to generalise regarding the policy which should be followed by municipalities in making contributions to the rates out of the net surpluses of their trading departments.

The circumstances of the locality in which the operations are being carried on, the fact of there being competitive industries in the district served by the undertaking, the extent to which the undertaking is supplying districts beyond the city proper, the risks attending the carrying on of the enterprise, are all factors which have to be taken into account.

While the policy followed in Scotland has mainly been towards appropriating surpluses in reduction of the price of the commodities or services, in England it is openly claimed that municipal undertakings have, in the main, been entered upon by the municipalities with the view to the application of the profits in aid of rates.

There is no doubt that, at the inception of municipal trading, it was held out by the local authorities when promoting bills for the different classes of commercial or quasi-commercial undertakings, that the commodities or services would be capable of being supplied to users at cheaper quotations than were obtainable from existing trading concerns in private hands, and that a considerable margin would be available thereafter for the benefit of the ratepayers. There is diversity of opinion as to whether the promise first named has been made good. Generally speaking, the quotations of local authorities for their commodities show substantial reductions on former time prices, and closely approximate, and in some instances are under the prices quoted by up-to-date competitive public companies.

Having agreed, however, to the general experience of the past twenty years, and to the tendency nowadays towards increasingly large, and sometimes arbitrary, transfers to Rate Accounts, it is claimed that some limit should be put upon the allocation of "profits" towards rates.

This claim, to my mind, is well founded, but it is by no means easy to indicate what the limit should be, and Parliament would appear to be too busily occupied with questions of Imperial finance to take up seriously the defining of a limit such as is desiderated.

From a careful examination of the accounts of trading departments of the principal municipalities in the Kingdom some helpful information is obtainable; and the suggestions which, as a result of that examination, I throw out for the consideration of the Institute are these:

(1) That having in view the interests both of users and ratepayers, a limitation on the sums which a municipality is entitled to treat as profits from its trading departments is desirable.

(2) That the fairest basis is to allow a definite percentage on the actual capital sums expended on the undertaking, which percentage should be chargeable (primo) with the annual amount of interest due and paid in respect of the debt of the undertaking (secundo) with the annual amount of Sinking Fund instalment due and paid or set aside in respect of the undertaking (tertio), any surplus, after defraying the charges first and second named to be treated as surplus profit available as the municipality may deem best, either in aid of rates, or as a Reserve Fund, or for reduction of the price of the commodity or service, or in the reduction of debt.

(3) That, having regard to the character of the undertakings after-named, and to the periods allowed them respectively wherein to pay off their debts, the percentage should not exceed the sums hereinafter stated, viz.:—

In the case of	Water Works	... 5	per cent.
,,	Gas Works	... 7	,,
,,	Electrical Works	... 7	,,
,,	Tramways	... 7	,,

(4) That if the Revenue Account of the undertaking should show a surplus at credit after provision is made for the percentages last stated, such surplus should be applied towards depreciation, if depreciation has not been already charged to the year's trading; and if any sum thereafter remain over, such sum should be carried forward to the Trading Account of the succeeding year.

Bradford Chartered Accountants Students' Society.

Some Features of Local Authorities' Finance.

By F. Ogden Whiteley, A.S.A.A.
City Treasurer of Bradford.

A lecture delivered to members of the above Society on 5th February 1913.

Synopsis.

Constitution of Local Authorities.
Character of Expenditure:—
Capital.
Revenue.
Sources of Income:—
Borrowings.
Imperial Subventions.
Miscellaneous.
Rates.
Internal Audit.
Methods of Accounting.
Balance Sheets.
Trading Undertakings.
Professional Audit.
Government Returns.
Banking Arrangements.
Income-Tax.

Mr. Chairman and Gentlemen,—I thank you for the invitation extended to me to address you this evening, and, although the various phases of Municipal Accountancy and Finance have been lectured upon until they are almost threadbare, I hope some profit may accrue from a general survey of municipal matters in their financial aspect.

I propose, therefore, to address you discursively, rather than to give you a lecture in set form, and to ask you to take with me a short survey of some of the outstanding features of the financial operations of a local authority—and more particularly of a municipal corporation—with which some, if not all, of you will doubtless, during your professional career, have to deal, either as the officer responsible for the accounts, or in the professional audit of them, and that audit (to be efficient) must necessarily go far beyond the mere examination of the Account Books.

The financial operations of a community are regulated by legislation contained, on the one hand, in general statutes applicable alike to all authorities of similar constitution; and, on the other hand, in local Acts of Parliament promoted by the corporation, or other governing body of the locality concerned; and it will, I think, be well to give some consideration, in the first place, to the history of municipal development and legislation.

The history of Egypt and Assyria gives us no account of strivings, between one school of thought and another, as to the relation between "depreciation and sinking fund," or the more intricate questions as to income-tax; and even the municipal affairs of Greece and Rome (empires which have had so much influence upon the development of western civilisation) are shrouded in almost as deep a gloom, and we are led to seek such assistance as will shed a glimmer of light upon the evolution of English local government finance in the conditions existing prior to the epoch-marking Municipal Corporations Act of 1835, and to trace the development from that great landmark being placed upon the Statute Book to the present time.

The early awakening ideas of communal life found their expression in communities of "tons," who governed themselves with somewhat primitive ideas of democracy. They appear to have had their periodical assemblage, to settle their local grievances and make regulations for their conduct, and presided over (as the equivalent to our mayor to-day) by a "town reeve," thus laying the foundation of the modern town council.

The next step appears to have been the constitution of a *district* local government, known as the "hundred moot," presided over by the shire-reeve, which designation has since been abbreviated to the term "sheriff." The hundred-moot found its ultimate development in our present county council and assizes, and when we bear in mind that only so recently as 1835 did our present popularly-elected borough councils, with their aldermen and mayors, come into existence, and the old court-leet, with the borough-reeve at its head, and with its constables and jury, lose its sway as the local representative of the law, order, and administration, we must appreciate the enormous strides which have brought us, in a matter of seventy-five years, to the measure of public ownership and control, not only of civic and public health administration, but of gigantic trading undertakings, which are vested in and exercised by our city council to-day as the local governing authority. The court-leet appointed from amongst the citizens, officers (who generally held the office in an honorary capacity) to attend to the necessities of the community in various directions, but their functions appear to have been largely supervisory of the obligations imposed upon the citizens themselves in the maintenance of roads adjacent to their property, and other duties. There were, however, certain matters of expense for the community to meet, and "myslayers" were appointed to assess, levy, and collect the moneys required from the citizens, of which an account was required to be kept and produced in the court-leet for the audit of all whom it might concern. Thus, at any rate early in the sixteenth century, we find the existence of an officer corresponding to your city treasurer and accountant of to-day, though with functions and responsibilities of apparently much less diversity and onerousness.

Side by side with the Municipal Corporations Act of 1835 should be placed the Public Health Act of 1848, which constituted local boards of health responsible for the sanitary and public health administration of their districts, and which duties, in the larger areas governed by municipal corporations, were placed upon the corporations. These Acts, however, soon became ineffective to meet the strong tide of evolution, and were replaced, respectively, by the Municipal Corporations Act of 1882 and the Public Health Act of 1875, which—with a number of subsequent subsidiary and amending Acts, which have since been produced with rapid succession—form the broad basis of our civil and public health administration of to-day.

Broadly speaking, the Municipal Corporations Acts include :—

- Administration of justices in local courts, sessions, and assizes.
- Expenses of police, including prosecutions, maintenance and transport or punishment of offenders.
- Municipal elections, and preparation of ward rolls.
- Provision and maintenance of town hall, city court, and other public properties.
- Coroner's inquests.
- Remuneration of recorder, stipendiary magistrate, town clerk, treasurer, clerk of the peace, clerk of the justices, &c.

The Acts provide that, for each borough, the treasurer shall keep a borough fund, into which shall be paid rents of municipal properties and other moneys receivable under the Act, and upon which shall be charged the expenditure under the foregoing headings, *and all other expenses of carrying into effect the Municipal Corporations Acts, and all expenses charged upon the Borough Fund by any Act of Parliament, or otherwise by law.*

The expenses of the council in promoting local Acts are chargeable upon the borough fund and borough rate, and the following general statutes provide that the costs of carrying them into effect shall also be charged upon such fund and rate :—

Inebriates Act, 1888.
Baths and Washhouses Acts.
Education Acts.
Libraries Acts.
Unemployed Workmen Act, 1905.
Children Act, 1908.
Costs in Criminal Cases Act, 1908.
Rivers Conservancy Acts.
&c.

The Public Health Acts make provision for such purposes as hospitals, public health inspection, cleansing, sewerage and sewage disposal, and the improvement and maintenance of highways, the costs of which are, subject to certain exemptions, to be charged upon and paid out of the district fund, any deficiency of such fund being met from the proceeds of a general district rate.

The costs of giving effect to the following Acts, amongst others, are also chargeable upon the district fund :—

Housing of Working Classes Acts.
Museums and Gymnasiums Act, 1891.
Contagious Diseases (Animals) Acts.
Housing, Town Planning, &c., Act, 1909.
Electric Lighting Acts.
&c.

In practice, however, the general principle of charging upon the borough rate the costs of civil government, and upon the general district rate matters of public health, is not strictly applied.

Parliamentary Committees have, from time to time, approved, in local Acts of various corporations, the raising of moneys for certain public health purposes upon the *borough rate,* and for administrative purposes upon the *general district rate*, and the purposes chargeable upon the respective funds in different towns are almost as variable as the number of municipalities. For example, it is provided in the Bradford local Acts from 1871 onwards, that the expenses of *sewage treatment* shall be charged upon the *borough rate,* whilst the cost of the sewers *to convey the effluent* to the disposal works is charged upon the *general district* rate.

The cost of Bradford street improvements authorised between 1873 and 1897 is charged upon the borough rate, whilst previous and subsequent expenditure for the same purpose is made chargeable upon the general district rate, so that the cost of street improvements appears in the detailed purposes of both rates. Similarly, hospitals and parks (though really public health purposes) are charged upon the borough rate. Whatever substantial justification there may have originally been for requiring municipal corporations to make two separate rates to meet different portions of their expenditure does not now exist, and the Royal Commission on Local Taxation, which reported in 1899, recommended that *one consolidated rate for all purposes (including also poor law purposes) should be made by each corporation*; whilst in the same year the London Government Act, 1899, provided that in all London boroughs there should be *one general rate for all purposes levied by the corporation*, the guardians and other spending authorities precepting the corporation for the amounts of their requirements. In this matter (amongst many others) we are awaiting a long-promised Parliamentary measure of local taxation reform.

Over and above the civil and public health administration, regulated by general statutes I have referred to, we should consider some of the functions exercised by local authorities under their local Acts and certain general "enabling" Acts and Provisional Orders issued thereunder, the bulk of which have come into existence, or made their influence felt, within the generation immediately past. Of these the principal are the Waterworks Clauses Acts, 1847 and 1863; the Gasworks Clauses Acts, 1847 and 1871; the Tramways Act, 1870; the Electric Lighting Act, 1882; and the Light Railways Act, 1896; and although the rights of providing services made available under these Acts have in some cases been granted to companies or independent commissions, it is so generally recognised to-day that the provisions of these services is inseparable from the best interests of the community, that the towns in which they are not owned and controlled by the municipality are in an exceedingly small minority. The powers to establish and maintain other services—such as public milk supply, promenades, gardens, conditioning houses, &c.—have been obtained under local and general Acts, whilst under the Education Acts of 1902, and subsequently, the entire system of public education (including the medical examination of children) has been vested in the local governing council.

The magnitude of the operations of local authorities throughout the country may be gauged from the fact that their revenue income for the year ended 31st March 1910 amounted to no less than 127 million pounds, of which 63 millions were raised by rates, 21 millions by Imperial grants, and 33 millions from trading undertakings, this income representing substantially, of course, the expenditure in the carrying on of the various undertakings, and the civil and public health administration of the country. The outstanding debt of local authorities (including the amount raised for acquisition and development of trading undertakings) amounted in 1910 to no less than 536 million pounds, as compared with 137 millions thirty years ago, an increase of 400 million pounds, or 290 per cent. The National Debt in 1910 was 762 millions, as compared with the local authorities' total debt of 536 millions. It should, however, be borne in mind that the municipal debt has been entirely incurred for constructional purposes, and valuable assets exist side by side therewith; the major portion is represented by trading undertakings which would (if the opportunity were given) be bought up with avidity by companies at prices much in excess of the gradually reducing debt. The National Debt, on the contrary, has been largely contracted in the prosecution of devastating wars, the money having been blown away into "eternal nothingness."

In considering the comparative desirability of corporation securities it is a fictitious basis to have regard to the "debt per head," without, at the same time, ascertaining for what purpose that debt has been created. Bradford's "debt per head" is £28, but £18 of that is represented by trading undertakings, which last year produced a net surplus of £93,000 after paying interest on borrowed money, setting aside £118,000 for reduction of debt, and supplying efficient services at much lower prices than private companies. The debt upon these undertakings amounts to five million pounds, no less than two millions having been provided from revenue in reduction of debt in accordance with the terms under which the borrowings were authorised, and £140,000 set aside to Reserve and Renewal Accounts. If the undertakings had been in the hands of companies, instead of the corporation, the total cost of the undertakings (£7,000,000) would probably still have been outstanding, but would have been veiled under the more palatable term of "capital."

The Local Government Act of 1888, which constituted county councils in their present form, relieved Courts of Quarter Sessions of their administrative functions, the county council exercising administrative control over and within the districts of various classes of minor authorities within its area, such control lessening in each upward grade of local status. Certain large cities and boroughs, however, having a population of over 50,000, were by that Act constituted separate counties in themselves, and denominated county boroughs, and these are independent of any control by the County Council of the geographical county in which they are situate. The Local Government Board were, by the Act, empowered to also confer county borough status upon any borough subsequently reaching the population limit referred to. County boroughs, however, when formed as such, do not reach a complete state of autonomy in local affairs, a considerable measure of control being exercised by various Government Departments—such as the Local Government Board, the Board of Trade, the Home Office, and the Treasury—and the tendency appears to be in the direction of a tightening rather than relaxation of such control.

Under the Local Government Act of 1894, the scheme of county government was developed by the abolition, as such, of local boards of health, and the constitution of certain new classes of local authorities, viz.:—parish meetings, parish councils, and urban district councils, each exercising—within its own area—a measure of public health and other administration and control, but all subordinate, in a greater or less degree, to the county council.

Having regard to the wide field of operation of the major authorities, which I have briefly outlined, I propose to consider the financial operations incident thereto under certain broad divisions, giving separate consideration to certain features of the trading undertakings which are not common to the accounts of the purely administrative concerns.

Character of Expenditure.

The Acts of Parliament to which I have referred prescribe that, to the extent of the inability of the two general funds, in any year, to meet the amounts payable thereout, the citizens shall be called upon to provide the money in the shape of rates. For the construction, however, of substantial works, which are not only costly in their character, but the benefit and value of which will extend over a considerable period of years, it would obviously be inequitable to ask the ratepayers of one year to bear the entire cost, and provision is accordingly made that a local authority may—with the approval of Parliament under local Act, or with the sanction of the appropriate Government Department—borrow the sum necessary, and charge to the ratepayers the annual interest thereon, together with such instalments of principal as may be necessary to discharge the loan within a period specified in the sanction to borrow—such period being fixed with due regard to the probable "life" or duration of the asset to be acquired, but in no case greater than sixty years, with the one exception of housing schemes, for which sanction may be afforded to spread the cost over a period of eighty years.

The expenditure of a local authority, in its non-trading aspect, may, therefore, be classed generally under the headings of "Capital" and "Revenue." Bearing always in mind, however, that for no subject or asset is it intended that there shall remain a permanent capital charge or debt, capital expenditure becomes nothing more than *deferred revenue* expenditure.

All expenditure incurred by a local authority must be for a purpose permissible by law; must generally be authorised by the council of the authority; must be charged to the proper fund and appropriate account, and (except the expenditure be covered by a specific authorisation to borrow) must be met during the year in which it is incurred, or included in the next succeeding rate. In this aspect it will be seen, therefore, that the expenditure of a local authority differs entirely from that of a trading undertaking, and may better be compared to the domestic arrangements of an individual in using his income in the best possible manner for the comfort and convenience of himself and his family. He would not borrow money and contract a mortgage upon any of his domestic equipment which he could reasonably pay for out of his income, but if he sought to expend (say) £1,000 upon the acquisition of his house, he might find it convenient to borrow the money, and spread the repayment over a number of years, rather than cripple the current resources requisite for the comfort of himself and his home.

Income.

The sources of income of a local authority may be divided under four headings :—

Borrowings.
Imperial Subventions.
Miscellaneous.
Rates.

Having determined to carry out works which are (to use the definition of the Public Health Act) of a *permanent* character, it is essential either to obtain power to borrow by local Act, or—as is the usual practice—to apply to the Local Government Board under the provisions of the Public Health Act, or other Act governing the purpose of the expenditure, for sanction to borrow; the application being accompanied by a detailed estimate of the cost, plans and specifications, and a copy of the resolution of the council authorising it. If the application be made under the Public Health Acts, the Board will usually send one of its inspectors to hold a public inquiry in the locality, and to hear evidence in support, or opposition, tendered on behalf of the council, or by, or on behalf of, any ratepayer or ratepayers within the authority's area. The inspector's duty, after hearing the evidence and making such inquiries as he may deem necessary, is to report to the Board whether he considers it advisable, in the interests of the community, that the application be granted. The Board very properly declines to give sanction to borrow for the replacement of an asset previously acquired out of loan, *to the extent that any part of the original loan remains outstanding*, and they decline to sanction loans—even if for a legitimate purpose—to the extent that the work has been, or will be, performed by permanent employees of the council. An application for sanction to borrow under the Education Acts must first be submitted to, and approved by, the Board of Education, and the Local Government Board usually accepts the Education Department's recommendation without holding a local inquiry. After consideration of the report of their inspector, or of the Board of Education, the Local Government Board decides whether or not the local authority shall be empowered to borrow money. If the Board declines, and the expenditure is for a proper statutory purpose, the local authority may, if they choose, carry out the work, *but must pay the cost out of current revenue.*

Assuming, however, as is usually the case, that the Board issued its formal sanction, such sanction is always coupled with a restriction as to the period within which the money shall be repaid, and such repayment may be effected either—

(1) By equal annual instalments of the principal sum, with interest upon the remaining balance; or
(2) By such equal annual sum as will within the prescribed period pay off the principal money, with interest at the agreed rate; or
(3) By means of a sinking fund which, accumulated at compound interest, will provide the amount borrowed at the expiration of the loan period, interest upon the loan being meantime paid annually upon the full amount of the loan.

Much discussion has taken place on different occasions as to the financial advantages of the respective methods, it being contended by some that the first-named is, in the aggregate, cheaper than the second and third. The example which I have put into your hands, however, will show at once that this is not the case; actuarially all three methods are, and must be, equal at any given rate of interest upon the principal and accumulations, and the choice by the local authority of the method to be employed is a matter rather of policy.

In the "Instalment" method the charges are proportionately greater in the earlier years than in the other methods, as I have shown upon the diagram, but they are proportionately less in the latter period of the loan, and prudence would usually direct, therefore, that the Instalment method should be adopted in the case of an undertaking where the income or benefit is likely to decrease as time goes on, and/or where the cost of repairs and maintenance is likely to be an increasing quantity. In the case, however, of an undertaking where the income or benefit is likely to increase to a greater extent than the cost of maintenance, the Annuity or Sinking Fund method (under both of which the annual charges are uniform throughout the period of the loan) should, in justice to the ratepayer of the present day, be applied. A good instance of the former class of undertaking would be a refuse destructor, and a waterworks might be taken as typical of the latter, as, with the exception of the pipes, depreciation does not materially arise, whilst the earning capacity is usually an increasing quantity.

The local authority would similarly be advised in its choice of the available methods of borrowing by the conditions of the money market prevailing at the time; thus, if money were cheap and the market favourable, an issue of stock for a long term would usually be a wise policy, whilst with *dear* money, and stringent conditions, it would be advisable to take loans only on short terms of, say, three or five years.

The borrowing of money for a local authority by the issue of six months' or twelve months' bills is occasionally of service, but not generally advisable. This power, if possessed by an authority, may be of service in raising moneys required pending an issue of stock, or the borrowing by short term . ans. Any moneys borrowed for capital expenditure, but remaining unexpended when the work is completed, must be repaid to the lenders or carried to the sinking fund for ultimate liquidation of the debt. This will usually have the effect of proportionately shortening the period of revenue contributions, but if such balance should represent any material proportion of the original sum borrowed, or if any substantial sum be realised from the sale of lands acquired but not required (as occasionally arises in the case of street improvements), the Local Government Board will consider a proposal for a proportionate reduction in the annual contributions, so that the total sum necessary shall be standing in the sinking fund at the expiration of the period originally authorised.

Imperial Subventions.

Prior to the passing of the Local Government Act of 1888 the Imperial Government made certain grants to local authorities in aid of expenditure borne by them in respect of services which were wholly or mainly *national* in character. Under the Act of 1888 these grants were withdrawn, and certain licence duties (including liquor, game, dogs, guns, carriages, &c.), together with a proportion of the probate duties (now estate duties) were paid over to the local authorities in substitution therefor.

The income fı .he licence duties, &c., is applied mainly to the relief of the following services :—

Police.—One-half cost of pay and clothing.

Pauper Lunatics.—Payment to Guardians of 4s. per week each in respect of pauper lunatics, where the net cost to the Guardians is equal to or exceeds that amount.

Cost of Union Offices.—Payment annually to the Board of Guardians of a sum equal to the cost of the union offices during the year ended 31st March 1889, as certified by the Local Government Board.

Cost of Criminal Prosecutions.

Cost of Revising Barrister.

By the Customs and Inland Revenue Act of 1890, additional duties, known as the Local Taxation (Customs and Excise) Duties, of 6d. per gallon on spirits and 3d. per barrel on beer, were imposed, and the proceeds divided between the local authorities of England, Scotland, and Ireland. Out of the English share (80 per cent.), £300,000 is allocated to police superannuation, and the residue applied to purposes of higher education.

Under the Finance and Revenue Acts of 1907 to 1911, the sums payable to the councils in respect of liquor licences, Customs and Excise duties, and certain other licences were, in consequence of increased duties imposed for the benefit of the Imperial Exchequer, stereotyped at the amounts paid to the councils in the year ended 31st March 1909. The sum receivable by Bradford amounts to £45,000 per annum.

In addition to the proceeds of the above licences, &c., local authorities receive grants, subject to efficient service, in aid of education, which, apart from certain grants for special subjects, are as follows :—

Annual Grant.—Being 21s. 4d. per unit of average attendance of children over five years of age, and 13s. 4d. for children under five years of age.

Fee Grant.—10s. per unit of average attendance.

Aid Grant.—4s. per unit of average attendance, plus three-fourths of the difference between the produce of a rate of 1d. in the £ and 10s. per child in average attendance.

Special Grant.—To local education authorities whose rate for elementary education exceeds 1s. 6d. in the £, a grant representing approximately three-fourths of such excess, the total sum available, however, being limited to £350,000 per annum.

Various returns have been prepared showing that the amounts of the grants from the Government, and the proceeds of the assigned revenues, do not now bear the same relative proportion to the amount of expenditure upon the services aided.

The Municipal Corporations Association prepared such a return in 1910, which showed—for fifty-two of the principal towns of the country—that in the year ended March 1908 the cost of the services in respect of which grants were made prior to the passing of the Local Government Act of 1888 (other than education) had increased, as compared with the year ended March 1892, by no less than 74.5 per cent., while the Exchequer grants had increased by 18.7 per cent. only.

The total cost of education in England and Wales during the year ended 31st March 1906 was £20,956,166, of which 47 per cent. was raised from local rates and 53 per cent. from Government grants. The total cost during the year ended 31st March 1910 was £23,080,779, of which the amount borne by the rates represented 51 per cent. and from Government grants 49 per cent.

Whilst the major portion of the expenditure of a local authority is of a local nature, other portions are directly national in their character, whilst others, again, may be regarded as partly *national* and partly *local.* The relation between the Imperial and local authorities, in bearing the cost of the second and third of these classes of service, has been the subject of serious consideration for many years.

In 1897 a Royal Commission was appointed to inquire into the present system under which taxation is raised for local purposes, and the Commission sat almost continuously for four years, and issued several valuable reports, besides many volumes of evidence. Both the Majority [illegible] Minority Reports of the Commission agreed in their main recommendation, namely, that substantial additions should be made to the sums allocated from Imperial revenues in aid of local expenditure. They expressed the opinion that, in regard to what they called "preponderatingly national" or "onerous" services (poor law, education, police, main roads, and others), generally speaking one-half of the expenditure should be met from Imperial sources. No action has, however, been taken upon the weighty and valuable conclusions of the Commission in this connection, except the appointment, early in 1911, of a Departmental Committee "to inquire "into the changes which have taken place in the relations "between Imperial and local taxation since the report of "the Royal Commission, and to make recommendations "on the subject for the consideration of His Majesty's "Government with a view to the introduction of legisla-"tion at an early date." That Departmental Committee is still sitting, and although it has issued one large volume of evidence, recent inquiries in Parliament have been unable to elicit from the Chancellor of the Exchequer any assurance of the issue of a report, and consequent legislation, in the immediate future.

Local authorities are possessing themselves in as much patience as possible, with the hope that legislation—adju[illegible] upon a more equitable basis the financial relations between the Imperial and local authorities—may not be far distant. The Chancellor of the Exchequer, in submitting his Budget of 1910, referred to this question, and said :—"Whoever stands in this box next year will "have to deal with this problem, and deal with it "thoroughly," and—although the Government has its quiver pretty full—as much pressure as possible is being brought to bear to secure the promised reform.

Miscellaneous Income.

The miscellaneous income of a corporation includes rents of properties, fees for various registrations and licences, cemetery dues, bathing charges, slaughter-house tolls, library fees and penalties, certain fines and fees imposed by the Court of summary jurisdiction, and sundry other items accruing to various departments for work done and services rendered.

As before mentioned, any deficiency of the borough fund and district fund (other than moneys properly chargeable to Capital Account), after receipt of subventions and miscellaneous income, must be met from rates.

Rates.

Prior to making a rate the local authority is required to cause an estimate to be prepared of their expenses for the ensuing year, or half-year, together with any expenses incurred within six months prior to the making of the rate and not otherwise provided for, and such estimate must be duly approved by the council. As it is not competent to legally include in a rate any sums paid more than six months prior to the making of the rate, it will be at once seen that a rate must be made upon the basis of the estimated *receipts and payments,* in order that at the end of the year there may be no substantial overdraft on Revenue Account. In one town within my knowledge the estimates were, for many years, made upon the basis of *income and expenditure,* and a surplus was always shown at the end; but whilst such surplus was theoretically correct, there was an accumulated bank overdraft on Revenue Account which represented 1s. in the £ on the rates, and it was necessary to increase the rates 2d. and 3d. in the £ for several years in succession to clear the bank. Not only had the accountant taken credit for all stocks and stores purchased for usage, but not actually used, but when the council—without borrowing powers—purchased a fire engine, having an estimated life of ten years, he charged to the first year's rates one-tenth only of the cost as *expenditure,* leaving the other nine-tenths to increase the bank overdraft; and similarly in various other directions.

After approval of the estimates the council may proceed to make their rate at such an amount in the £, upon the value of the property assessable thereto, as will, in their opinion, produce the amount estimated to be required. For the purposes of the borough fund, the council must charge upon the overseers of the respective parishes within the city, or borough, such proportions of the whole sum as the assessable values of the respective parishes bear to the whole, and the amount of the borough rate requirements is thereupon to be raised by the overseers as part of the poor rate. For the purpose of assessing the contributions upon the several parishes the corporation are to be guided by the valuation lists in force, made under the Union Assessment Committee Act of 1862, or, if they think that valuation is not a fair criterion, they may cause an independent valuation to be made. Upon the receipt of the corporation's precept, and similar precepts issued by the poor law guardians—or frequently in anticipation of them—the overseers proceed to make a poor rate at such a poundage as may be necessary to meet the total of such precepts, together with their own expenses.

A general district rate is made, levied, and collected *by the corporation* from the occupiers of all kinds of property assessable to any rate for the relief of the poor, but subject to partial exemptions to the occupiers of land, lines of railways, canals, land covered with water, &c., which are assessable only upon one-fourth part of such value.

The needless cost and annoyance to the ratepayers of a dual collection, and the existence of boards of overseers as separate and independent authorities, have been obviated in a large number of towns, as at Bradford, by securing power of appointment of overseers and of assistant overseers by the corporation, and requiring the overseers to collect the general district rate together with, and substantially as part of, the poor rate. It is thus rendered possible for the overseers to be practically a committee of the council and to collect on one demand note all the rates payable in the township by the same staff as collect the water, gas, electricity, and other charges due to the corporation.

Internal Audit.

The Municipal Corporations Act requires that all payments to, and out of, the borough fund shall be made to and by the treasurer; and similarly, in regard to all the revenues of the corporation, moneys received and receivable are so received and receivable *on behalf of the treasurer*, and for his satisfaction. And in order that he may present his accounts promptly and clearly to the professional auditors from time to time, it is necessary for the treasurer to have a departmental audit staff, whose duties shall be to conduct a continuous audit of the revenues of the corporation, ascertaining that in every department the debits created are in strict accord with the scales of charges approved by the respective committees from time to time, and applicable thereto; that such amounts are duly accounted for by the issue, when paid, of progressively numbered counterfoil forms of receipt, provided from the treasurer's department; that all moneys represented by the counterfoils of such receipts are punctually paid to the proper account at the bank, and are debited to the proper Cash Books; and that all arrears are rigorously followed up with the narrowest practical margin of time. The audit includes the record of all tickets, or other forms having a cash exchange value, from their issue by the printer to ultimate disposal, or destruction (if unused). This internal audit not only keeps daily pace with financial transactions—which, in Bradford, represent an income of over two millions per annum—but renders the duties of the professional auditor easier and less irksome. The professional auditor is, of course, at all times entitled to test the work of the internal audit staff, as and where he may choose.

Methods of Accounting.

Principles of accounting do not vary, but the way in which those principles are most effectively applied is dependent to a large extent upon the character of the business or undertaking, and the purposes for which that undertaking exists. The purposes of accountancy are not limited to ascertainment of " profit and loss," but are to afford to the person, or the corporation, whose accounts are concerned, such information as to the financial operations as may enable him or them to most efficiently carry on the concerns, or to secure economy with efficiency in the discharge of public or private functions and obligations.

I need not discuss the relative merits of the systems of " receipts and payments " and " income and expenditure " respectively, as I am a strong adherent to the latter, except to say that, in connection with rate-aided funds, it is necessary, besides a record of income and expenditure, to provide a record of receipts and payments for comparison by the various committees, with details of the estimated receipts and payments upon which the rates are based, in order to show where excesses have arisen, or savings have been effected. In the accounts of these funds, also, the term " expenditure " bears in certain respects a meaning modified somewhat from its proper acceptance in connection with a trading undertaking. Whilst I bring into account all moneys receivable and payable—whether actually received and paid, or not—and the value of all saleable commodities (*e.g.*, grease and manure produced at the sewage works), and charge in the accounts only such consumable stores as have been actually used during the period of account, I do not carry forward the residual value of what I may call " domestic equipment," such as garden seats in various parks, tools, implements, &c., but include such charges as *expenditure.*

Except in cases of specific contracts entered into by the council, no goods are permitted to be ordered, or work to be done, without proper approval by the committee, and authentication by the chairman in a Requisition Book, in which the head of the department has to set out the dates and particulars of supplies. When the invoices therefor have been examined, certified, and passed forward to the finance department, the Requisition Book is also submitted, so that the entries may be compared with the accounts and the items marked off and initialled by the treasurer's clerk. The Requisition Book then shows, at any time, and particularly at the end of the year or half-year, what work has been performed and goods supplied, *but not invoiced,* with the approximate value thereof. The invoices, after examination with the Requisition Book and contracts (if any) are checked as to their arithmetical accuracy, and submitted, with a schedule, to the committee concerned for approval, each account being initialled by the chairman and the schedule signed by him. The accounts are subsequently presented to the Finance Committee for approval, and the schedule containing the list of accounts authorised to be paid by the treasurer is signed by three members of the council and forwarded by the town clerk to the bank as their authority for payment of cheques drawn by the treasurer in discharge of the accounts. Salary and wages sheets are prepared in the various departments, and forwarded to the finance department for examination as to rates of pay and arithmetical accuracy. They are then handed to a clerk responsible for summarising and drawing cheques therefor, such summaries being examined with the pay sheets *by the audit staff* and initialled. Payment of wages is made by clerks quite independent of those who prepare and check the wage sheets and summaries, or draw the cheques. The invoices and wages sheets are then forwarded to the accounting section for journalising, and posting into the Ledgers, which are arranged in columnar form. The Cash Books are independently made up from the schedules of accounts prepared for the committees, and are proved with the Ledger balancings.

Income.

The income is carried into Cash Books and Ledgers from departmental returns of amounts earned and cash received; these returns are prepared weekly and certified by the audit staff.

The foregoing methods are varied, in regard to the accounts of trading undertakings, by the direct introduction of all earnings from the Day Books and rentals into the respective Journals and Ledgers; all amounts earned, but not subsequently collected, being written off, for appropriate reasons, after submission to and approval by the Finance Committee. The principal Stocks and Stores Accounts are kept in the treasurer's department, and physical tests of various sections of each are made monthly at the respective stores, an explanation being called for in respect of any appreciable deficiency or surplus revealed thereby.

Balance Sheets.

Upon the assets side of a municipal Balance Sheet the heading usually found will be "Property, Assets, and Outlay." Inasmuch as it would obviously be impracticable to make a revaluation, year by year, of such subjects as sewers and street improvements, the actual expenditure is maintained, on the one hand, so long as the subject remains of service and value; whilst on the liabilities side is retained the amount of outstanding loans and the total of the amount provided through the Sinking Fund Account and utilised (or available for utilisation) in repayment of debt. This latter sum represents, of course, a surplus, to the extent that the value of the undertakings exceeds the debt outstanding. In the case of a trading undertaking, any amount which it is considered necessary to provide for depreciation in supplementation of the sinking fund contribution, is set aside as a separate Reserve and Renewals Account, instead of being written off the amount of the assets. In this connection I may briefly refer to the contention which has been urged from time to time as to the necessity for a full provision for depreciation *over and above* the contributions to sinking fund. That position is an untenable one, for whilst one freely admits that a sinking fund *is not* a depreciation fund, it in a large measure performs the same function. The loan period is ostensiby fixed according to the estimated life of the various parts of the undertaking, and if, and when, any portion requires replacement, there is neither legal nor politic objection to borrowing again the cost of reconstruction *to the extent that the outstanding debt upon the original plant has been discharged.* If the operation of the sinking fund is as swift as the depreciation of the asset, no further provision is necessary, except to meet abnormal repairs and maintenance, with a prudent provision for contingencies. If, on the other hand, the asset is wasting away more quickly than the operation of the sinking fund, a supplementation should be made, so that, when the time for reinstatement arrives, additional provision shall have been made equivalent to the shortage of the sinking fund to meet the cost of reinstatement. To provide an ample sinking fund, and an ample depreciation fund in addition, as has been strongly argued in certain directions, is to impose upon the users of the commodity—or the ratepayers—of one generation, not only the cost of producing those commodities, but also the money necessary to buy a new concern when the present one is worn out, and to make a present of it, free of all encumbrance, to the next generation.

All other items in the Balance Sheet follow substantially the lines of every standard Balance Sheet, except that in many cases additional detail is provided, so that "He who runs may read."

The balance of assets upon Revenue Account will, in a non-trading fund, include the value of the plant acquired from time to time out of the rates, together with the current surplus (if any) shown in the body of the Revenue Account.

Government Returns.

Somewhat elaborate returns to the various Government Offices are provided for in general and local Acts, in order that the central supervisory departments may be satisfied that the financial transactions of the undertakings are kept substantially within the four corners of the law. Upon an application being made for borrowing powers under the Public Health Acts, the Local Government Board requires to be satisfied, not only that the limit of debt under that Act to the amount of two years' assessable value of the district is not exceeded, but also that due provision is being made for repayment of existing loans in accordance with sanctions previously granted. Similarly, in respect of all moneys borrowed under local Acts, a return is required to be made annually, and verified by statutory declaration, of the amounts set aside to the sinking funds, and their application. The Local Government Board are also to be furnished with what are known as the Local Taxation Returns, containing a comprehensive and detailed record of the whole of the financial transactions of the corporation. Annual financial returns are to be made to the Board of Trade in respect of tramways, light railways, gas and electricity undertakings, whilst returns of police expenditure, and of the police superannuation fund, are to be made to the Secretary of State for the Home Department. The Board of Education require to be furnished with various returns upon which the different grants are based. Each of these departments is also furnished with a copy of the Treasurer's Abstract of Accounts, and you may take it from me the various returns are subjected to the closest scrutiny and comparison with the abstract.

Banking Arrangements.

Not the least important feature in connection with this subject is that of banking arrangements. When it is remembered that a corporation of reasonably large dimensions will have a banking turnover—taking debits and credits together—of perhaps five millions a year, it is necessary that the arrangements with the bank should be most carefully considered, and that in any comparison of quotations submitted by different bankers the probable aggregate effect should, so far as is possible, be reduced to a parity, having regard to the character of the turnover and the duration and volume of aggregate debits and credits during the whole year. The various Acts authorising the establishment of trading and other undertakings require that separate accounts shall be kept in regard thereto, and in the keeping and balancing of such separate accounts it is a material advantage to have a separate fund at the bank. This should not, however, have any bearing upon the banker's allowances and charges, inasmuch as the arrangements with the bankers should be to treat the daily balances of the corporation's accounts *in the aggregate*, and if the commission charged upon payment of cheques be by way of a percentage the amount of all transfers between one account and another should be excluded. A bank may stipulate fixed interest rates of charge upon aggregate overdrafts, and allowances upon aggregate credits respectively, or it may offer (within certain minimum and maximum limits) rates bearing a definite relation to, and varying with, the Bank of England rate of discount for the time being. The effect of aggregation, although in the interest of the corporation as a whole, will be that the funds which are practically always overdrawn, such as those of gas and electricity, will, during the period the accounts as a whole are in credit, be subjected to only a small rate of interest upon their overdrafts, whilst the accounts which have regular credit balances suffer proportionately, and it is necessary, in order that each account may, as far as possible, receive the benefit of the pooling, to make an equitable adjustment at the end of the quarter or half-year between the respective funds of the benefit and advantage accruing to the corporation by the aggregation.

The charges upon cheques cashed by the bank may be either by way of a percentage upon the amount, or by an agreed annual sum in lieu of percentage, and if the latter can be fixed at a sufficiently reasonable figure there are many advantages in its acceptance. It is also desirable to make the best possible terms with the bank as to charges upon cheques and bills forming part of the moneys paid to the corporation's credit.

In order to check the bank, a daily record must be kept of the character of the credits as between cash, local, country, Scotch, and Irish cheques, and bills maturing at the expiration of given periods, and also to keep a daily summary of the whole of the accounts, in order to see whether the aggregate represents a credit or debit balance.

For the purpose of checking the interest charges I adopt a decimal Pass Book, containing debtor and creditor columns, followed by columns showing the balance and the number of days for which such balance has remained undisturbed; and again the product of the two, so that the running total of the products represents the aggregate amount of credit or debit balance for one day. A further column is provided which shows the product of the amount of cheques upon which interest is chargeable by the number of days to be charged. For example, a credit of £2,952 may include country cheques of £750, upon which two days may be charged for collection, and a Scotch cheque of £100, upon which four days may be charged for collection; the product against the credit would, therefore, be £1,900, and a deduction of the total of the *charges products* from the total *interest products*, if the account is in credit, or an addition if the account is in debit, will give a total product which, if multiplied by double the rate of interest and divided by 73,000, reveals the interest allowable or chargeable. With this method, however, you are all doubtless familiar.

Trading Undertakings.

The principle of municipal ownership of trading undertakings is that of the provision by the people for themselves of services essential to the life, health, and prosperity of the community, rather than—as in the case of a private company—the provision of the same services for the purpose of making a dividend. Moreover the highways which provide the means of communication of those services throughout the city, either upon lines or through pipes, are already the property of the community. It is, therefore, theoretically sound to supply the services at "cost price," *i.e.*, such prices as will meet the cost of production and distribution, together with interest upon the debt and the necessary provision for repayment thereof, leaving a reasonable margin to meet contingencies. There is, however, some weight in the argument adduced in favour of a moderate contribution to relief of rates, by reason of the fact that in the borrowing of moneys for municipal trading undertakings there is given to the lender, as security for his money, not only the undertaking itself, but also the entire rateable value of the city. Whilst, in consequence of that collateral security, it is possible to borrow moneys for such undertakings at rates varying from 3 per cent. to 3½ per cent, it is probable that at least ½ per cent. more would have to be paid in the absence of such added security. The ratepayer *quâ ratepayer*, however, carries an obligation for the debt, and in the event of failure of the revenues derived from the trading departments to meet the charges incident thereto the ratepayer would have to make up the difference. Because he holds the dog the profits are greater, and he thinks, therefore, that he is entitled to some share of the profits. He must not, however, lose sight of the fact that of every sovereign of profit made by the ratepayers, *out of themselves*, the Inland Revenue Department comes down and carries away fourteen pence to swell the Imperial resources.

In order to afford a proper basis of comparative costs and results of the different classes of municipal trading in various towns, the Municipal Treasurers' Institute—in conference with the respective Associations of Engineers and Managers—have agreed, for each of such undertakings, a standard form of setting and classification of accounts. As the various items in the Revenue Account are calculated to the standard unit of comparison in each case, the engineer is now able, with facility, to see whether his costs of working are high or low in comparison with other towns, and to act accordingly.

In my own printed accounts I have also published—after the Balance Sheet of each trading fund—statistical information covering the respective periods the undertakings have been operated by the Corporation, or for twenty years in those cases where the undertakings have been established much longer than that period.

Professional Audit.

As you are doubtless aware, the audit of municipal accounts (over and above the internal audit to which I have referred) is of three kinds:—

1. That of the District Auditor of the Local Government Board.
2. Of Elective Auditors.
3. Of Professional Auditors.

The accounts of the minor authorities, and of county councils, are subject to the Local Government Board audit, as are also the accounts of all education authorities, and of overseers in respect of rate collection. I cannot, perhaps, more explicitly deal with this question than by quoting from the report of the Select Committee of both Houses of Parliament, which considered the matter in 1903. In their report the Committee state:—

> "A uniform system of audit should be applied to all the larger local authorities."
>
> So far as the elective audit is concerned, "The evidence shows that no effective system of audit is thus supplied. The auditors are poorly paid or unpaid altogether; little interest is taken in their election; and, although in some cases they are able to lay a finger on a particular irregularity, it is not clear that they could not make the same discovery in the capacity of active ratepayers. No complete or continuous audit is ever attempted by them."

Dealing with the Local Government Board audit, the Committee say:—

> "This audit is carried out by District Auditors, who, as a rule, are not accountants, and are not, in the opinion of the Committee, properly qualified to discharge the duties which should devolve upon them. The duties of the auditors seem to be practically confined to certification of figures, and to the noting of illegal items of expenditure. To apply this system of audit to municipal corporations would arouse strenuous opposition from them, and the course may be considered impracticable; but, in addition to this, the fact that District Auditors are not accountants seems to unfit them, as a class, for the continuous and complicated task of auditing the accounts of what are really great commercial businesses."

The Committee recommend, *inter alia*, that:—

> "The existing systems of audit applicable to corporations, county councils, and urban district councils in England and Wales be abolished, and that auditors, being members of the Institute of Chartered Accountants or of the Incorporated Society of Accountants and Auditors, should be appointed."
>
> "The auditor should have the right of access to all such papers, books, accounts, vouchers, sanctions for loans, and so forth, as are necessary for his examination and certificate."
>
> "He should be entitled to require from officers of the authority such information and explanation as may be necessary for the performance of his duties."

"He should certify :—

(i) That he has found the accounts in order, or otherwise, as the case may be;

(ii) That separate accounts of all trading undertakings have been kept, and that every charge which each ought to bear has been duly debited;

(iii) That, in his opinion, the accounts issued present a true and correct view of the transactions and results of trading (if any) for the period under investigation;

(iv) That due provision has been made out of revenue, for the repayment of loans; that all items of receipts and expenditure and all known liabilities have been brought into account; and that the value of all assets has in all cases been fairly stated."

"Auditors should be required to express their opinion upon the necessity of reserve funds, of the amounts set aside to meet depreciation in addition to the statutory sinking funds, and of the adequacy of such amounts.

"After careful consideration, the Committee are of the opinion that, in view of the thoroughness of the above audit, powers of surcharge and disallowance could be altogether dispensed with in the case of the major local authorities. These powers could not, it is believed, be applied to municipal corporations, in view of the strong objection expressed by them; and it is doubted whether their retention in the case of other authorities would compensate for the loss of uniformity which would result. The power of disallowance, applying as it does only to illegal expenditure, and not to unwise undertakings and enterprise, does not afford any real safeguard to the ratepayers whose interests are affected."

Income Tax.

Section 40 of the Income Tax Act of 1842 provides that "All bodies corporate . . . shall be chargeable with "such and the like duties as any person will, under and "by virtue of this Act, be chargeable with," and proceeds to make the treasurer of the corporation answerable for doing such things as may be necessary precedent to assessment, and for paying the tax as and when due.

Returns for assessments have, therefore, to be made to the Surveyor of Taxes annually in respect of the various trading undertakings, and of any moneys paid, from which tax has been deducted. The returns for the trading undertakings follow the accepted lines, with which you are familiar, except that a deduction is allowed for the proportion of any profits which may have been made upon the sale of commodities or residuals to other (non-trading) departments of the corporation, on the ground that a person cannot make a profit out of himself.

Prior to 1909 each corporation made, through its financial officer, the best terms possible with the Surveyor of Taxes, as to allowances to be made for depreciation of plant. In that year, however, overtures were made by the Municipal Treasurers' Institute to the Board of Inland Revenue, through its Superintending Inspector, with the result that a scheme of depreciation allowance, applicable to the undertakings of all corporations (but capable of certain elasticity to meet local requirements), was agreed upon, and this has been found to be very satisfactory in practice.

Notwithstanding the provisions of Section 40, to which I have referred, corporations have had, and are still having, to wrest from the Board of Inland Revenue a recognition of their right to be treated, in all cases, as a *person* would be treated. Section 101 of the same Act provides that persons carrying on two concerns may set the losses sustained in one against the profits acquired in the other concern; and Section 102, in dealing with the deduction of tax from interest and other annual payments, states that in every case where a sum shall be payable out of profits or gains brought into charge by virtue of the Act, no assessment is to be made upon the person entitled to such interest, but the whole of such profits or gains shall be charged with duty upon the person liable to such annual payment, and the person so liable to make such annual payment, whether out of profits or gains charged with duty, or out of any annual payment liable to deduction, or from which a deduction has been made, shall be authorised to deduct tax at the current rate in force, *and, having paid upon the profits or gains, shall be acquitted of any further payment.*

Corporations contend, therefore, that the Inland Revenue authorities are wrong in their present practice of assessing each undertaking separately, and of allowing a corporation to retain only such of the tax deducted by them from interest on loans raised for the purposes of each undertaking as is paid out of the profits of that undertaking, but that, speaking generally, a corporation should be regarded as one entity, although carrying on several businesses, and, therefore, entitled to retain, from the amount deducted from interest, a sum equal to the whole of the income-tax paid by the corporation in respect of the whole of their properties and undertakings. In other words, *a corporation should be regarded as one entity*, and be called upon only to pay tax either upon its total profits and property, or upon its total interest, whichever is greater; and that any charge beyond this is a double assessment.

This question is now before the Courts upon an appeal taken by the Association of Municipal Corporations, at the joint expense of all the large corporations, and the case of Leeds has been chosen as a test case. In the High Court the decision of the Judges was in favour of the Crown, but the case was taken to the Court of Appeal, where the judgment of the Divisional Court was reversed, and a decision given in favour of the Corporation. The Crown have given notice of appeal to the House of Lords, and we are awaiting the decision of the highest tribunal upon this important question.

Conclusion.

I am afraid I have wearied you with my remarks upon a subject which, though part of my daily life, is probably not of such general interest, but I thank you for the courtesy and sympathy with which you have listened to me.

LOAN OF £1,000, REPAYABLE WITHIN 5 YEARS, WITH INTEREST AT 3 PER CENT.

DIAGRAM showing comparative cost each year, of repayment by "Annuity" and "Equal Instalment" methods.

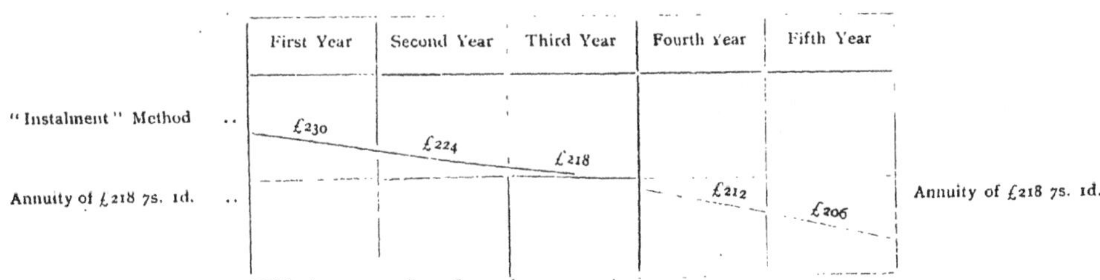

REPAYMENT OF A LOAN OF £1,000 within 5 years—with interest at 3% per annum.

Year	Sinking Fund or "Annuity" method.	"Instalment" method (*i.e.*, equal annual instalment of principal with interest on remaining debt).			"Annuity" Method.		Comparative amount on hand at end of each year by adopting "Annuity" method.	Interest earned thereby.
	Annual Payment.	Principal.	Interest.	Total.	Less.	More.		
	£	£	£	£	£	£	£	£
1	218,355	200	30	230	11,645	—	11,645	—
2	218,355	200	24	224	5,645	—	17,640	350
3	218,355	200	18	218	—	355	17,814	529
4	218,355	200	12	212	—	6,355	11,994	535
5	218,355	200	6	206	—	12,355	—	361
	1,091,775	1,000	90	1,090	17,290	19,065		
						17,290		
						1,775		1,775

The Association of Midland Local Authorities.

Municipal Debt.

By ARTHUR COLLINS, A.S.A.A., Deputy Treasurer of the City of Birmingham.

AN ADDRESS to the members of the above Association at their meeting in Wednesbury on the 23rd May 1913.

This subject is perpetually coming forward for consideration; although theoretically local authorities are not permitted to have irredeemable debt, yet as fast as one loan is redeemed another is incurred, and therefore few, if any, Councils have no debt—the majority always will have debt to provide for.

Let us face the debt now outstanding against local authorities. It amounts to about 540 millions sterling. (The National Debt is about 700 millions.)

What conclusions can be drawn from this fact, and what considerations should prevail to guide local administrators in this matter of loan indebtedness in the future? These are the questions which this short paper will raise, in non-technical terms. I scarcely need to add that my views are quite personal and have no official significance.

The debt of local authorities is represented by the following items:—

TOTAL LOANS OUTSTANDING AT THE END OF THE YEAR 1909-10 IN ENGLAND AND WALES.

Purposes.	*Amounts.*
Baths, Cemeteries, Harbours, Docks, Piers, Canals and Quays (other than the undertakings of the Port of London Authority), Markets	£63,000,000
Undertakings of the Port of London Authority (Docks, Quays, &c.)	23,000,000
Elementary Education (including Industrial Schools)	41,000,000
Highways, Bridges and Ferries, and Sewerage and Sewerage Disposal Works...	101,000,000
Other Purposes	92,000,000
Total non-trading Debt... ...	320,000,000
Gas Works, Waterworks, Tramways, Light Railways and Electric Light Undertakings	216,000,000
Grand total of Local Debt (in 1909-10)	£536,000,000
In 1912-13, say	£540,000,000

Dealing first with debt on trading undertakings, totalling 216 millions. Have we got value remaining for this? Exclude purely local considerations, and judge the matter broadly. It is not enough to reply that even this position (of having such a large debt) is better than having limited companies in possession, for that is not altogether a financial consideration; it is rather one of sentiment, even though it may involve better public services, greater facilities for the public, and perhaps cheaper rates. That reply also excludes two or three factors which will come more and more into prominence during the next ten years, namely : (*a*) excessive capitalisation for goodwill or premiums on compulsory purchases; (*b*) capital outlay now become obsolete; and (*c*) capitalisation of sundry expenses which a prudent private trader would write off out of profits at once.

If the tests suggested by these groups of cases be applied to the several classes of trading undertakings, it will probably be found that water and gas undertakings are not over-capitalised. They have, generally, been owned by the local authorities many years, have substantially reduced their debt by sinking funds, and the capitalisation did not suffer in the old days quite so severely from having to be compulsorily acquired from a company in possession. Gas undertakings, however, will, it is feared, have a fairly rough time during the next ten years in having to discard the old carbonisation processes which are quickly becoming obsolete, and this tendency requires special consideration.

It is by this time common knowledge that electric plant does not survive the periods of the earlier loans granted for these purposes, and one's general experience suggests that quite 50 per cent. of the electric plant laid down within the last ten years is obsolete, and to a large extent scrapped, although twenty-five years may be the equated loan period granted, and still running. Tramways rolling stock and equipment is fast evolving into new types, which will hasten the present trend towards obsolescence, and both electric and tramways undertakings being more recent acquisitions of local authorities, are in many towns burdened with a heavy price paid for purchase which can only be called goodwill, or watered capital, under certain conditions to be mentioned.

However, the capital has been raised, and must be redeemed. Is the provision for redemption sufficient? Will the past policy of capitalisation serve for the future?

So far as municipal trading undertakings are concerned, there has been too great a tendency to rely wholly on the sinking fund, and otherwise leave the debt to take care of itself. There is need for a longer view, to augment the sinking fund by reserve funds, safeguarding against that remarkable gain of invention upon expectation, by which a scheme or process thought to be good for ten years is now out of date in six or eight years.

There are clear and unmistakable signs that this need for speeding up the reduction of outstanding capital is being recognised by local authorities, but many are delaying, and paying undue regard to cheap prices of supplies or profits to rates. They are, it is feared, mortgaging the potential income or funds of the future for the benefit of the present.

It is not necessary to reopen the old question asking whether sinking fund is the same as depreciation. It is by this time well understood that in principle the two can never be the same, although it may sometimes happen accidentally that the period granted for the loan, which determines the sinking fund, is exactly equal to the life of the assets.

Whilst this may be true of a loan for a specific purpose, such as a tramcar, it would not hold good with many classes of assets, including land, a tramshed and tramcars, all turned into one loan for twenty-five or thirty years. It is clear that the tramcars will be obsolete before that loan is paid off, and to buy new cars in the absence of some reserve fund new capital will have to be raised, and so the interminable borrowing goes on.

In fairness to the officers of local authorities, it may be said to be the general opinion amongst them that they would prefer to maintain fair prices and an adequate reserve fund with or without contributions to rates, instead of cutting things so fine for the benefit of the present customers that they have no stand-by in the form of reserve fund available to meet new developments without increasing their capital. The necessity for constant reborrowing or new capitalisation does, in fact, hinder the officers of a trading department in introducing improved methods and systems in their works. With a reserve fund available they have greater freedom in introducing new inventions.

The first point, then, which this paper would endeavour respectfully to impress upon a body of gentlemen whose votes determine these matters, is that the present time is notably one for extreme caution in disposing of surplus profits of municipal trading undertakings. Whilst one is a firm believer in the right of the ratepayer to have a reasonable return from the consumer upon the outlay which the ratepayer has at risk in the trading undertaking, prices should be so fixed as not only to give the ratepayer this return, in the form of reasonable contributions in relief of rates, but also to make full and sufficient reserves for the purposes previously mentioned. No municipal trading undertaking is, in one's opinion, justified in charging such prices as to result in a loss.

A great deal may, of course, be said in favour of including goodwill as an asset to the trading undertaking to set against the outstanding debt. Where the goodwill arises because a local authority has had to buy out a company at a price which exceeded the value of its solid assets, the goodwill really represents the purchase-price of the future dividends which the company might have earned had the local authority not bought it out. This is a fair argument so long as the local authority continues to make out of the trading undertaking a surplus which otherwise the old company would have had for distribution amongst its shareholders, but we in the public service know how very often a company's profits cannot be maintained under corporation management, for reasons quite apart from the difference between a corporation committee and a board of directors. Prices are at once expected to go down. That is often done without full consideration. The corporation cannot pay those workmen in the new department the rate of wages which was ruled by the dividend of the company. The public is not content with a service which runs no risks of loss in any branch, and one not prepared to take a bad class of trade for the benefit of the town, even though it reduces the profits of the good class of trade. These and other important features of corporation management do not assist a local authority in maintaining a financial return from the purchased undertaking justifying the price paid. On these grounds, therefore, it behoves a local authority to be conservative in fixing its prices and regulating its expenditure, more particularly its capital expenditure, so as not to make the productive value of the concern so small that the goodwill becomes in every respect a fictitious asset, so far as the ratepayer who has found the capital is concerned.

Turning now from municipal trading undertakings to the other services which local authorities provide, such as Baths, Parks, Municipal Buildings, Sewers, Streets, Roads, &c., it is found that the loan indebtedness thereon exceeds £320,000,000 sterling. There is one feature of this capitalisation which has already been referred to briefly, but not explained under the heading of trading undertakings in preceding paragraphs. That is the tendency to capitalise small schemes of incidental expenditure in the acquisition or development of a municipal undertaking of any kind, which any private trader would at once pay out of revenue. There is that small class of capital outlay which requires a few hundred pounds only (or even less), strictly of a capital nature, if the term be pressed, and which, consequently, owing to the rigidity of our line of demarcation between capital and revenue, innumerable authorities defray by loan instead of out of current funds. The objection urged against the non-capitalisation of this outlay is that it is a way of increasing the rates which everybody wants to reduce, and also that as the future ratepayer will benefit by it so ought he to pay his share of it.

The influence which such arguments have on the mind of a local administrator must always depend, of course, on his individual point of view. The official mind, however, sees that these little schemes and improvements average themselves, taking many years together, and cost, by capitalisation, practically double the prime cost. Had the schemes been taken in fair order, and paid for a few at a time out of revenue year by year, the good results would still have been achieved. The fixing of a limited figure below which expenditure of that kind is not to be capitalised, has a steadying effect upon the quality or merit of the schemes of small outlay proposed to be incurred, and the municipal officer, therefore, is often impelled to regret that this tendency to excessive capitalisation was not corrected by reasonable legislation, or departmental order, or Council resolution, many years ago.

Again, how many members of local councils have observed that everything which can be connected with a capital expenditure scheme, however remotely sometimes, is in many towns capitalised. For instance, many committees permit incidental expenses of an officer or a member of the council who happens to have made a journey having a close or distant connection with a new loan to be charged to that loan. We ratepayers of to-day are thus diligently paying into sinking funds our quota in repayment of the cost of solid or liquid refreshment enjoyed by our municipal representatives on deputations ten or twenty years ago. The life of the asset for which the loan was sanctioned is, may be, sixty years, and so these travelling expenses, a small printing bill, a few books, an advertising charge, a petty cash disbursement, all figure in the capital outlay, and must stand to-day for very considerable sums in the loan indebtedness of 500 odd millions, upon which these discursory remarks have dwelt.

It is with some diffidence that one ventures in an assembly of this kind to remark that this is one of the incidents of municipal management where the Local Government Board auditor would undoubtedly insist not necessarily upon surcharging (for that process in items of this nature is undignified, unnecessary, and offensive), but he would insist on charges of this kind being defrayed out of revenue and not out of capital. Personally, one is of opinion that the time is not far distant when the Local Government Board will require an account from local authorities of the money they have spent in future against every loan sanctioned by the Board. It will be remembered that at present the Local Government Board only make inquiries of this kind when the amount of the loan sanctioned has been exceeded, so that one part of a scheme in a loan not fully spent may be omitted or modified, and expenditure of another kind, including these incidentals, in perfect good faith, may have been subsituted. From the financial point of view, however, it is a short-sighted policy to resort to capitalisation in these petty cases, and one which results only in building up for the future a burden of debt posterity will find to be burdensome.

From these remarks it will have been gathered that the second point which one has ventured to urge for the favourable consideration of this meeting is to endeavour to correct any tendency which a local authority may have towards adopting a loose (which means a less prudent) distinction between charging to posterity and charging to ourselves, and the impression one would leave upon your minds is that there is too widespread an idea that we are doing a great deal for posterity. That was all right so long as we seemed to be reaching the point of maximum development in communal undertakings, but we are at the commencement of a new era of municipal development which is tending more and more towards a wider system of provision for indivduals by the community, and one has a shrewd suspicion that in forty or fifty years' time posterity will be busily engaged in revising past notions of what communal management and institutional treatment involved, wishing heartily that the loans outstanding on such matters as old-fashioned street construction, sewage treatment, housing and town planning, poor law institutions, massive infectious diseases hospitals, and the like, had been provided for by the generations which incurred them.

As a practical step towards improved methods of control which a town council may exercise on its capital outlay, the general instructions issued to committees may be reviewed, and brought up to date by regulations dealing with the following matters:—

(1) To prevent the expenditure of money on Capital Account until the town council and Local Government Board have sanctioned a loan.

(2) To fix a limit on small sums which should not be charged to capital.

In this direction, it has been found, in many towns, most useful to call upon the Finance Committee to review all proposals involving new capital outlay, and report on the financial aspects to the town council.

In any case, one's object is attained if these very casual observations should lead any of the Midland local authorities to useful conclusions in deciding to strengthen their procedure for keeping a firm hand upon the reins which regulate the rate of increase in their municipal debt.

Institute of Municipal Treasurers and Accountants (Incorporated).

The Apportionment of the Central Establishment Expenses of Local Authorities.

By C. H. PATTERSON
(Borough Treasurer of West Ham).

A PAPER read before the members of the above Association at the twenty-eighth annual general meeting, held at Tunbridge Wells, 3rd and 4th July 1913.

Having been invited to present a paper on establishment charges, I have prepared a few notes to place before the Institute in the hope of doing something to promote a common understanding as to what these charges properly are and how they should be distributed. Most of those who have any acquaintance with this matter must hope that authorities may come more into line with each other with regard to it, and that, by the adoption as far as possible of uniform methods, comparison between the financial returns of different local bodies may be facilitated. At least, I may succeed in provoking a useful discussion.

I have felt some diffidence in accepting the invitation to write on this subject, for whilst all financial officers are familiar with the principle of allocation itself, there is much diversity of procedure in the allocation of establishment expenses, and it arises in part from differences of local circumstances which are of such a character as almost to prohibit the laying down of general rules.

Authorities and their departments differ in size and constitution, and the expenses of differently constructed departments are incommensurable. The mere disparity of size involves often a radical difference in constitution. Official titles nominally the same imply a different grouping of duties in different places, and it is not always easy to distribute the cost of services. It would be interesting to have a complete or even a representative return of what is done by way of apportionment throughout the country. Such information as has been obtained shows that "many "authorities seem to have attempted no apportionment "between the different departments, and in others there "is reason to suppose that the allocation may have "tended to favour one fund at the expense of another." (Report of the Departmental Committee on the Accounts of Local Authorities, 1907.)

Whilst it must be admitted that complete uniformity is an unattainable ideal, it seems to me evident that there are certain valid principles, and that these principles need to be more widely recognised and should be more generally followed.

Let us first define our terms.

The expression "central establishment expenses of a local authority" may with advantage be employed to designate the working expenses (official, clerical, accommodation, and other) of the main and central departments (as the town clerk's office, borough treasurer's office, borough engineer's office), the departments which not only carry out the general municipal business, but also discharge certain functions that directly assist the various revenue-earning undertakings, special services or subsidiary departments of the authority, and are necessary to their proper working. These *expenses* as far as they are allocated (charged) may be called *charges*.

Central establishment expenses usually include the following items, viz. :—

Salaries of chief officials and staffs.

Accommodation Expenses of town hall or municipal offices (viz., rent, rates, taxes, insurance, loan-charges, repairs, furnishing, attendance, cleaning, lighting, heating, &c.).

Printing and Stationery (relating both to council and to committee purposes).

Audit, costs of, both general and internal.

Law and Parliamentary Expenses.

It should be noted that I am not dealing in this paper with the establishment expenses of revenue-earning undertakings or other non-central departments themselves. Such departments or undertakings often have their own establishments, the expenses of which are allocated to the several headings of expenditure in their Revenue and Trading Accounts, or partly distributed in the cost of works rechargeable. In this paper I am dealing only with the expenses of the central department, of which department I have given a definition in a previous paragraph.

Now, it will be found that the central expenses here enumerated are incurred for two groups of objects, more or less defined and separable, viz. : (1) The general work of the authority ; (2) the work done on behalf of the various sectional departments.

Whatever principle of allocation is adopted, the central expenses can never be wholly distributed amongst the various surrounding departments, revenue-earning undertakings, &c., which are assisted. There is always left a residuum. This residuum, in proportion as our allocation has approached accuracy and completeness, may be assumed to represent the expenses incurred in performing those duties which belong to the primary business of the corporation itself. Thus, the whole of the central department may be considered itself to be of service, consisting of certain primary and certain secondary functions, the expenses of the latter only being allocatable over the surrounding departments.

Looked at in one way, indeed, the central department does not generically differ from the surrounding departments, for the provinces of these also sometimes overlap, and apportionments occasionally have to be made between them. But, of course, it is as part of its normal function, and not merely occasionally, that the central establishment overlaps the others. It is a service to serve the others. It regularly assists them, does accountancy, legal, and engineering work for them, and in theory, at all events, they are co-ordinated under it.

You sometimes hear it said, "But why apportion at all? If no trading departments existed the central department would still exist. All expenses come out of one pocket," &c. The answer to this is that there is a need for apportionment, a need which always existed, and which has become imperative and obvious as a consequence of the modern development of municipalities. Legislation of recent years has tended to abolish *ad hoc* bodies, as notably in the case of education, whilst at the same time new public services, including revenue-producing undertakings, have been continually added to the work of local bodies. As soon as revenue-producing undertakings were added, it became plain that true statements of profit and loss could not be made unless each undertaking were charged with its own apportionment of central expenses. Without allocation the sectional profit and loss statement is illusory. When education was added, which had already been separately administered, the allocation of central expenses in continuation of separate treatment was only natural, but it was also seen to be indispensable to a true knowledge of the cost of education. In paragraph 69 of the Report of the Departmental Committee on Accounts, we read :—

> "In regard to all undertakings for which a clear and true statement of profit and loss is required, it is obviously essential that each should bear its proper charges and should not be allowed to profit at the expense of other services, funds, or accounts. The expenses of a central establishment, too, should clearly be divided in fair proportions among the various departments, in accordance, so far as possible, with the benefit which they have derived from it ; and in our opinion both the Capital Accounts and the Revenue Accounts should bear their proper proportion of these charges."

It has, in fact, been generally conceded that, although there is no legal compulsion to apply apportionment, there is nevertheless a business necessity to apply it, in a number of clear cases. A department taking out costs of works done by direct labour always adds a percentage for central establishment charges, and similarly I think it may be laid down as one of the principles for a universal basis which we are trying to establish, that a proportion of central expenses should always be charged on all trading undertakings, and also on education, which is so clearly a distinct service.

It is especially desirable that a trading undertaking should be above reproach in these matters, and should be able honestly to justify its existence by a genuine statement of profit and loss. The dangerous critics are those who have facts on their side. If a trading department really is "supported by the rates," though only to the extent of its fraction of central establishment charges, hostile critics have an opening which enables them to attack the whole principle of municipal enterprise. It is not worth while to give them this advantage.

The public services of a municipal body, however, form a series or gradation, at one end of which are trading undertakings, and at the other end services like roads or drainage, which are common necessities, and involve no considerations of profit-earning. Education, for obvious reasons peculiarly attaching to it, stands apart, and suggests no doubt; and trading concerns, as I have said, ought also unquestionably to be charged. But in our series there are intermediate services, such as housing and water supply, which are not always expected to yield a profit. And in regard to these, and even sometimes in regard to trading services properly so-called, two objections are raised when it is proposed to charge them with a proportion of central expenses. It is said, first, that a certain department may be run not primarily, or not at all, for profit, but for the public good, and therefore that it has a right to derive free benefit from the services of the central department. The statement that a certain department is run for the public good seems to imply that there are certain other departments which are run for the public detriment. All departments, including the central department, are run for the public good, and none of them has a right on that ground to claim that it may cast part of its burden on any of the others. Nor should a department escape from complete accountancy merely on the ground that it is not run for profit. If at any time it should receive help from a collateral service it would have to account for it, and it ought also to account for help received from the central service.

It is next said, sometimes, that no proportion of the salaries of the chief officials of the central department should be apportioned over the surrounding departments, because it is part of their general duty to aid the work of these departments. Now, it is quite true that it is part of their general duty, and even that, so far as I am aware, the salaries of chief central officials do not at present automatically increase with the addition of each new trading or other service to the work of a corporation. Nevertheless, extra work is done, assistance is rendered, central staffs, requiring organisation and supervision, usually have to be increased; and the simple fact is that, whether or not as part of their general duty, and whether or not extra remuneration is given, the chief officers do render services which the other departments, were they independent, would have to provide on their own account; and therefore there should be apportionment.

Having thus disposed of these general objections, let us next endeavour actually to determine, as far as we can, what other services besides education and trading should bear their proportion of the central expenses, and how much farther we should proceed with our apportionment.

As to this part of the subject I think it is generally agreed the apportionment should certainly be made as between the accounts of separate funds, as, district rate fund and borough rate fund, or similar funds in counties or urban district councils.

We then come to the sub-accounts included within these generic funds. Should the sub-accounts be separately charged, or which of them should be charged? To give a complete and satisfactory general answer to this question is most difficult, because of the diversity in form of published accounts, and the differences of local circumstances. Any movement towards uniformity in the matter of establishment charges would be assisted if local authorities were generally to adopt the recommendation of the Departmental Committee on Accounts as to the keeping of separate accounts. In paragraph 66 of this report the following remarks occur :—

> "The line of demarcation between Trading Accounts and other accounts is not always very distinct, and there may be some difficulty in determining the extent to which separate accounts should be kept in regard to certain services which are carried on by local authorities under their general statutory powers, and which, though not expected to be profitable, might be expected to support themselves independently of the rates. To this class belong, for example, housing schemes and water supplies carried on under the general law; and again, all such works as are re-chargeable, partly or entirely, to other authorities or to private persons, as in the case of private street works and improvements.
>
> "Such undertakings as these should be dealt with in separate Revenue Accounts, bringing out the surplus or deficiency in each case. This system, as a general rule, should apply also to public libraries, baths and washhouses, parks and recreation grounds, burial grounds, and other such services, which, though in different degrees productive of revenue, are regarded normally as a direct charge upon the rates."

The proposal which I would make as to the sub-accounts is that all those sub-accounts should be charged that have a separate Revenue Account. I would make the possession of a Revenue Account the test. It will be remembered that in the form of accounts adopted by the Institute provision is made for separate Revenue Accounts for public libraries, and for baths and washhouses, and it would be necessary to apportion the establishment expenses under these two heads. It will also be noticed that the Departmental Committee go further, and include parks, recreation grounds, cemeteries, and other such services, as requiring separate Revenue Accounts. Stables and farm accounts, workshop accounts, and accounts similar to these, also obviously need to be charged with central expenses, for although they are merely nominal accounts exhausted by a charge upon the other heads of service, and do not appear under such headings in the account, yet buying and selling take place, and dealings with stock and commodities, and there is need of a profit and loss statement. It is necessary in these accounts to ascertain the full expense of the work done and the supplies given in order that the proper cost thereof may be charged.

Wherever there is a separate Revenue Account or a separate result is required to be shown, it would appear to be necessary to that extent to include separate establishment expenses and to apportion central expenses, although, of course, the question may still be asked, Which are the accounts for which a separate result should be shown? And to this question, for reasons already stated, there can hardly be at present a satisfactory general answer.

In considering how far allocation is to be carried, we arrive at certain obvious limits. There is a line beyond which we cannot go, and there is a line beyond which it would not be worth while to go. There are many small services, as to which it would be a waste of time to make separate allocations. But what is a small service in one municipality may be a large one in another. Such considerations as these make standardisation difficult. All that can be said generally is that allocation should not be pushed to extremes, because in the extremes it is less valuable both in itself and for purposes of comparison. Neither should it be neglected, as it often is, for this also destroys the basis of comparison. It is to be hoped that allocation may be extended over the main services everywhere to a reasonable extent and with more consistency than obtains at present, so that as far as possible the accounts of local authorities may be brought more into line, in order that useful comparisons may be made. In determining whether to allocate in any given case, the purpose to be served should be considered, and how far it is really necessary to define the costs of the service. It may be that this utility will indicate the general utility, and that what is best to be done with reference to a particular case will be found to be best as regards the general purposes of comparison.

It is important that all expenses of the central establishment should be *somewhere* shown, as a total or in summary, and should then be distributed, as far as is required, by entries *per contra*. In the Institute's standard forms of accounts provision is made to show separately in the borough fund, and in the district fund, the establishment expenses relating to each, but it would be much more satisfactory if these expenses were all grouped as a total in the accounts of one fund and allocated thence, so that a complete summary of all expenses might be visible at a glance, together with the allocation of the same.

Then there is the question whether or to what extent the Capital Accounts should bear a proportion of central establishment expenses. By a recommendation of the Departmental Committee it is suggested that capital should be charged in these matters as well as revenue. It would, however, be difficult for any local authority to arrange for this to be done, in view of the recent practice of the Local Government Board, who, when sanctioning loans for expenses of a capital nature, exclude from their sanctions any charge for the services of permanent officers or workmen, and would presumably exclude also their requirements and the costs of their accommodation in connection with the works. In view of this attitude of the Local Government Board it would appear that the only course left open to local authorities is to charge the Revenue Accounts of the particular services for expenses of this nature incurred in connection with capital outlay. The trading undertaking or other department which has services rendered to it by the central establishment in connection with its capital works should certainly be charged for those services somehow, and if the Local Government Board refuse to permit the charge to be made in the Loan (Capital) Account, it must be made in the Revenue Account. To charge these expenses vaguely to the corporation would be to allow them to escape from the particular departmental accounts in which alone they have special relevance, and thus to deprive those accounts of value and meaning.

As regards the authority for making the apportionment, there being no statutory compulsion to distribute these expenses, I think it desirable that the Finance Committee should be authorised by the council to make an equitable apportionment by arrangement with each committee concerned, subject to the arbitrament of the council.

As to any universal basis of apportionment, I have already pointed out that, by reason of the diversity both in local circumstances and in systems of accounts, there is difficulty in framing regulations capable of general application.

Establishment expenses are of a varied nature, and by no means all capable of clear calculated apportionment. As far as apportionment can be calculated with precision or within the limits of reasonable approximation it is well to calculate it. Otherwise resort must be had to conjectural estimates or agreed figures. It is by the latter method that *salaries of chief officials* must be dealt with, as they can hardly be apportioned by time.

With respect to *staffs*, the salaries of those members of the central staff who are exclusively engaged on work relating to some non-central department should, of course, be wholly allocated to the department for which they are working, so long as they are thus exclusively engaged. With regard to the others, an apportionment on time should be made, and to this end an office diary might be kept where there is continual variation in the duties of individual members of the staff.

As to *accommodation expenses* (rent, rates, repairs, and general cost of premises and their upkeep), in this case it may happen in many places that a preliminary apportionment is necessary, as a number of different departments, some of them non-central, may be housed under one roof. First of all, therefore, eliminate the accommodation expenses of the non-central offices and departments, showing likewise the separate cost for each department in the central establishment. This may be done proportionately on the space occupied, having regard also to the location of the rooms or offices. The further apportionment with reference to staff units will then present but little difficulty, and its mode will best be suggested in each case by local circumstances. Calculation might be facilitated by assigning to each member of the staff a figure representing accommodation cost, arrived at by dividing the total cost by the number of staff, and making, if necessary, exception for any individual member specially accommodated.

Printing and stationery can to a great extent be allocated initially instead of subsequently, if the order or the invoice be marked with the name of the service, so as to indicate as far as possible the purpose for which the goods are required. To the expenditure thus earmarked must be added in the Allocation Account an approximate sum for the general expenses of the department under this heading.

The apportionment of *expenses of committees* will have already been exhausted under the three previous headings.

Audit.—Internal audit could be dealt with under staff. External audit includes auditors' fees or stamp duty, plus accommodation expenses, if any, and could be apportioned in the former case on time occupied, and in the latter case by a proportionate division of the total amount of the stamp duty.

Law expenses, if they are not Parliamentary, will be to a great extent definable from the bill of costs, but Parliamentary expenses are sometimes incurred collectively, whether in reference to the promotion of one Bill for a number of different municipal objects, or in reference to the opposition to a Bill from several municipal points of view. The proper distribution of the expenses of promotion is usually, and rightly, provided for by a clause in the Bill itself. The expenses of opposition, however, which, by analogy, should also be apportioned, are usually charged against the municipality as a whole. This practice is undoubtedly in many cases wrong. Those departments which are interested in the opposition, and on whose account it was undertaken, ought as a general rule to be charged with their respective proportions of the costs of it. This rule should apply without exception to revenue-earning undertakings, whenever it is clear that if they were not attached to the municipality, but were acting independently, they would themselves of their own initiative incur the expenditure in Parliamentary opposition as a matter of commercial policy.

In conclusion, perhaps, I may hope that I have at least called attention to the difficulties of the subject and opened the way to discussion. It is recorded (I am well aware) that a certain pilot said that he knew all the rocks on the coast, and then, when the ship struck, remarked that that was one of them. But, unlike him, perhaps, I may claim that my few remarks are not so belated as to be entirely useless.

The end towards which our efforts should be directed is to secure a uniform basis of apportionment. Of the obstacles in the way of this I am, as I said before, not ignorant. These cannot be removed until they are generally known, and my object has been to contribute, in however small a degree, to such a mutual interchange of information and of opinion as may ultimately lead to a proper settlement of the question.

VOL. XLIX.—NEW SERIES.—NO. 2019.] SATURDAY, AUGUST 16, 1913. [PRICE 6d.

Leading Article.

Tramway Finances.

IN another column of the present issue we reproduce the reports recently made to the Tramways Committee of the Coventry Corporation by the General Manager, Mr. T. R. WHITEHEAD, and the professional auditor, Mr. E. T. PIERSON, F.C.A., as to making provision in the accounts for renewals, and on other questions of financial policy. These reports would have proved interesting reading at any time; but they are especially important now, as having a distinct bearing on a point raised in the recent Telephone Award; and, further, because the unfortunate results achieved by municipal tramway undertakings in many cases where they enter into active competition with motor omnibuses, have emphasised the importance of sound finance, even in the case of undertakings municipally owned.

In the reports before us, it is pointed out that the tramway undertaking was acquired by the Corporation at a price arrived at by arbitration, having regard to the fact that the plant then stood in various stages of expired life. Had a Loan been authorised at the time which would have provided not merely for the payment of the arbitration price, but also for the setting aside of a Sinking Fund equal to the deteriorated state of the plant acquired, the position of affairs would have been very much more straightforward than that which now obtains. But, as matters were arranged when the tramway undertaking was acquired, there can be little doubt that the majority of those concerned, and also those ratepayers who thought anything about the matter, were under the impression that the Loan then authorised represented the total capital commitment of the Corporation in connection with the tramway scheme. The Corporation is now naturally finding itself face to face with the difficulty that, whatever may be the average life of a tramway plant, stated in general terms, the average life of the plant which was in point of fact acquired, was less than the normal average life by the amount of the working life that had already expired. Accordingly, rates of depreciation which would have been quite adequate in the case of a new undertaking are inadequate in its particular case. Doubtless, also, the Corporation has been suffering from the old practice of the Local Government Board in granting Loans for equated periods to cover a miscellaneous equipment, each part of which has a different term of working life; and the further fact that leave to borrow for renewals is only granted to an amount equal to the extent to which provision has been made for the repayment of the Loan out of which the superseded plant was constructed. But its chief difficulty was, no doubt, the difficulty experienced by all purchasers of a second-hand plant; that, if they pay a fair price for such plant as it stands, the outlay then incurred is not the sum-total of the capital outlay they will have to make, but merely a first instalment of such capital outlay.

Another point arising under these circumstances is the question as to how far it is possible to obtain a proper allowance for wear and tear in respect of income-tax assessments. Normally, such an allowance, even if made upon quite generous lines, will be based upon the average working life of the equipment of a description similar to that employed in the case under review; but it is unlikely in the extreme that credit has been given for the fact that what is material to such an issue is not the average working life of such equipment in general, but the estimated unexpired life of the actual equipment then in existence. This point is not directly raised in the reports before us, but it would be sure to be of interest to our readers, if any reliable information were forthcoming as to how the deductions allowed for wear and tear in connection with income-tax assessments have been arrived at in the case of the Coventry tramways since the Corporation took them over.

On the question of municipal tramways generally, it may be remembered that, when we were discussing in these columns some years since the importance of due provision for depreciation, if suitable efficient tramway services were to be maintained, some of the advocates of municipal trading at all costs expressed in these columns the view that there was no real need to provide for more than the barest maintenance, in that when a local authority took over a tramway system it thereby secured an effective monopoly of tramway conveyance, and accordingly need not fear competition thereafter, even if its particular system of traction should become obsolete. At the time this extraordinary view was expressed, we protested against it, as being fundamentally unsound, and as representing an unprincipled view of the responsibility which a local authority acquiring a monopoly of any description acquired along with the attendant privileges; but, of course, we were no more able than those who thought differently from us to forecast what the future might have in store, in the way of new modes of mechanical transport. Then discussion seemed to centre round the relative advantages of different methods of organising tramway systems, and in particular on the respective advantages of the overhead system, the culvert system, and the stud system; but the advent of the motor omnibus has entirely altered the condition of affairs by rendering a tramway undertaking—no matter what system of traction it may adopt—liable to competition within its own area. Thus, in the year 1911-12 the Barking District Council lost £5,000 on its tramways, in the year 1912-13 this loss was increased to £7,200, and there can be little doubt that in each successive year the loss will get bigger. Whether or not these figures are arrived at after what we should regard as due provision for depreciation, we do not know; but in any event they are sufficiently unsatisfactory. Nor are such losses in connection with municipal tramways confined to Barking. Ilford is certainly no better off; and, as of course everybody knows, the London County Council's tramway system is barely able to make both ends meet, without making any provision whatever for future renewals. Last year the tramway systems of Gloucester, Colchester, Lancaster, Oldham, Wigan, and Swindon, to mention no others, all showed balances on the wrong side; and there can, we think, be little question that a similar fate will sooner or later overtake every tramway system which is subject to the competition of the motor omnibus, unless some new invention of first-class importance again turns the balance in their favour.

How different the position would have been in all these cases had provision been made at the time the tramways were first taken over for the building up of a proper reserve for future renewals! In many instances, no doubt, the cost of such a Reserve might have been recognised from the first as being prohibitive; in which event it is only fair to suppose that the tramways would not have been taken over at all. But had proper Reserves for renewals been set aside from the first, the local authorities that now find themselves hopelessly crippled by the competition of motor omnibuses would each have been possessed of a very considerable fund, which they might (had they thought fit) have employed in themselves providing a local omnibus system, which would in all probability have very effectively discouraged outside companies from venturing in. Further, had not these various local authorities been over-occupied with mutual jealousies, they might have co-operated, and established through systems of tramways and omnibuses on sound business lines, which (if properly managed) would have enabled them to preserve, in fact, the monopoly which they never had except upon paper. Matters have, however, now gone too far for retreat to be possible. Rate-payers must reconcile themselves to the fact that—whether with or without their consent, and whether with or without a full disclosure of the facts beforehand—they stand committed to an expensive system of tramways which, under modern conditions, can only be run with the help of grants in aid from the rates. It is a question, which sooner or later will have to be considered very seriously, whether in some cases it would not be cheaper for the ratepayers to let their tramway systems for what they would fetch; and thus, at least, put a limit on the loss that will hereafter fall upon the public funds.

City of Coventry Tramways Department.

REPORT OF GENERAL MANAGER AND PROFESSIONAL AUDITOR AS TO MAKING PROVISION IN THE ACCOUNTS FOR RENEWALS, AND OTHER QUESTIONS OF FINANCIAL POLICY.

(*a*) Report of General Manager as to life of plant and associated considerations.
(*b*) Report of Professional Auditor as to financial policy.

(*a*) GENERAL MANAGER'S REPORT.

To the Chairman and Members of the Tramways Committee of the Coventry Corporation.

Gentlemen,

I beg to report that I have conferred with the professional auditor upon the subject of the resolution dated the 12th November 1912 in reference to making provision in the accounts for renewals and other questions of financial policy, and it has seemed convenient that I should report as to the life of the plant and associated considerations, and that the auditor should deal with the questions of financial policy.

To arrive at a basis for considering the subject I have deemed it necessary to go into considerable detail in preparing calculations relating to the life of the various parts of the plant. These calculations I have summarised in as concise a form as possible, and to the tabulations have added particulars relating to the Sinking Fund for Renewals, which theoretically should have been established at the commencement of the life of the various parts of the plant referred to, and the total which would have been accumulated at 31st December 1911 when the Corporation took over the undertaking.

I have also ascertained the annual charge which would be requisite now to provide a Sinking Fund for Renewals, owing to no provision having been made in the past. These particulars are contained in Schedule No. 1 attached hereto.*

Schedule No. 2 sets forth the amount of expenditure which has to be incurred upon renewals in various years.

Schedule No. 3 gives an analysis of the capital expenditure, showing the amount of such expenditure, also that portion thereof which will need to be renewed, and the remaining portion, which consists of non-recurring expenditure, together with a statement of the Sinking Fund apportioned under the respective heads.

Having regard to the policy of the Committee respecting the future provision of power, I have included nothing in the renewable expenditure in respect of buildings and power station plant.

* See page 218.

The estimated cost of renewing the plant is based purely upon actual renewals, and nothing is added for any improvements which may be ultimately decided upon, such as heavier rails, larger cars, and the like. With regard to the track, it has been assumed that the existing concrete foundation will not require renewal, and allowance has only been made for removing and replacing such portions as may be disturbed in removing the steel sleepers and for fixing the anchor chairs, &c., and it has also been assumed that 75 per cent. of the old sets will be used again in the reconstruction.

It is a matter of some difficulty to estin[illegible] the actual economical life of tramway track and cars, as the service and speed of cars, the amount and type of vehicular traffic, and the degree of maintenance exercised all have a direct effect on the life to be obtained. The figures given represent the life which, in my opinion, should be fully obtained with the conditions existing in Coventry.

The total annual charge, as shown in Schedule No. 1 (Col. 6) is £3,233. The estimated life of the assets to which this annual charge relates varies between 16 and 30 years, with an average life of 20 years. If a charge distributed evenly over a period of 20 years is substituted for the varying periods in the schedule it would show the following results:—

Period of Sinking Fund for Renewals, 20 years.
Period expired at 31st December 1911, nine years.
Period unexpired at 31st December 1911, 11 years.
Annual charge (at 3½ per cent.) on £87,375—£3,252.
Total Sinking Fund which would have been accumulated at 31st December 1911, about £33,000.

Theoretically the cost of the undertaking to the Corporation is less by this last-named sum (representing the estimated expired portion of life at date of purchase) than it would otherwise have been, and on this account it might be considered that the interest on the sum of £33,000, upon the above basis, shoul[illegible] [illegible] a charge for the next eleven years on the revenue of the undertaking, and if this were done there would be an annual charge of £4,242, as follows:—

Annual Sinking Fund Contribution for 11 years, from 31st December 1911	£3,252
Interest on £33,000, at 3 per cent., per annum	990
	£4,242

Upon the Sinking Fund basis there are other alternative methods for providing for renewals which could be set out. However, the professional auditor, in his report, deals fully with the question, and I concur with his remarks upon the subject. This report and attached schedules are intended to indicate the basis for consideration of the actual financial policy to be adopted.

It will be noted that the Sinking Fund established for the repayment of the loan for the purchase of the undertaking will not be completed until August 1942, but long before that time it will be necessary, as shown in the schedules, to replace the bulk of the plant, and therefore it seems essential that a separate provision should be made for such renewals.

I am,

Your obedient Servant,

T. R. WHITEHEAD,

General Manager.

Priestley's Bridge, Coventry,

May 30th 1913.

(*b*) PROFESSIONAL AUDITOR'S REPORT.

To the Chairman and Members of the Tramways Committee of the Coventry Corporation.

Mr. Chairman and Gentlemen,

1. I beg to report that I have conferred with the general manager upon the subject of the Committee's resolution of the 12th November last, and approved of the course he proposed to adopt in ascertaining particulars as to the life of the varied assets belonging to the Tramways Department, and I have examined the detailed calculations, which have necessarily been involved. The same appear to have been well considered, and represent probably as sound a basis for the consideration of the subject as it is possible to secure.

2. It appears that the Committee have to consider and decide upon two important points of policy, viz.:—

(*a*) The funds which have to be provided for the purpose of renewals.

(*b*) The method of treatment in the accounts of such provision.

3. By the general manager's report it will be seen that in order for the Corporation to be possessed of the undertaking with adequate provision in hand to cover proportion of "life" expired, there should have been in a Sinking Fund at 31st December 1911 an accumulation of £34,923, or, upon an equated basis, the sum of £33,000.

4. It also appears that before the Sinking Fund already established has run its course, which will be in 1942, outlay to the extent of £87,375 will be necessary in order to maintain the undertaking upon its present basis, without making any allowance for improvements. It appears essential, therefore, that provision must be made by way of additional loan, or out of revenue, or partly by both, for this sum.

5. Seeing that the arbitration price is fixed upon the basis of the undertaking being in a certain condition when taken over, viz., with the plant in various stages of expired life, it is reasonable to assume that the Corporation should be in a position to borrow and add to Capital Account, as and when required, a sum equivalent to the amount which theoretically should have been in the Sinking Fund at 31st December 1911, viz., £33,000, thus leaving a balance of outlay to be found over a period of years amounting to £52,452.

6. Schedule No. 2 of the general manager's report shows the years in which renewals are likely to fall due, and I have made calculations for the purpose of finding the regular annual amount, which will, with interest, be required to provide the necessary funds, as and when required, in accordance with such schedule.

7. I do not consider that an ordinary equated Sinking Fund will serve the purpose of providing the sums which will be necessary from time to time to meet the outlay specified in the last-named schedule of the general manager's report. The money should be accumulated so as to be immediately available as required. I have therefore assumed the funds to be set aside will be left on deposit at the bank, and carry compound interest at 3 per cent.

8. Assuming funds set aside to be earning interest in accordance with the preceding paragraph at the rate of 3 per cent. per annum, I find that in the period from 1912 to 1917 a sum of £5,092 per annum will provide for the requisite expenditure up to that date, and also a proportionate share of the expenditure to be incurred after such date.

9. From the year 1918 onwards to 1926 the annual instalment required would be reduced to £2,432, after which a sum of £70 per annum would suffice.

10. This calculation is based upon a new loan being raised in 1917 for £8,442, being a proportionate part of the £33,000 referred to in Paragraph 3, a further sum of £23,278 being raised in 1924, and £1,280 in 1929. It does not take into account the comparatively small sum of £2,027, shown by Schedule 2 to be required in 1934.

11. On the other hand, other sums will have to be provided in the subsequent years in respect of Sinking Fund upon the further moneys borrowed, and also further provision for depreciation, because as soon as a unit of plant has been brought into use, from that moment provision requires to be made for such depreciation.

12. So far I have dealt with the first point under consideration, viz., the particulars of the funds which have to be provided for the purpose of renewals. There

SCHEDULE No. I.

Description 1	Estimated net cost of Renewal. 2	Total estimated life 3	Life expired at 31st Dec. 1911. 4	Life remaining at 31st Dec. 1911 5	Annual Sinking Fund Charge invested at 3% 6	Total Accumulated Sinking Fund to 31st Dec. 1911 7	Annual Charge from Dec. 31, 1911 to accumulate full cost of renewal at date of renewal 8
PERMANENT WAY.	£	Years	Years	Years	£	£	£
1899 Track:—							
Burges to Ford Street	1,042	16	12	4	52	738	249
Ford Street to Bell Green	9,361	18	12	6	400	5,677	1,447
Ford Street to Gosford Green (Via Payne's Lane .. Ford Street to Stoke (Via Far Gosford Street.. ..	9,470	18	12	6	404	5,734	1,464
1905 Track:—							
Coventry Station to Bedworth .. .. Broadgate to Allesley Road..	25 492	20	7	13	945	7,239	1,626
Spon End to Earlsdon	10,032	20	7	13	373	2,857	642
	£55,307				£2,174	£22,245	£5,428
Cars:—	£				£	£	£
4 Tram Cars	1,960	18	16	2	84	1,687	966
5 " "	2,450	20	9	11	91	924	191
8 " "	4,320	20	12	8	161	2,285	485
2 " "	1,080	20	10	10	40	461	94
7 " "	3,780	20	11	9	141	1,805	372
3 " "	1,620	20	10	10	60	692	141
6 " "	3,240	20	5	15	121	641	174
5 " "	2,975	20	5	15	111	590	160
40	£21,425				£809	£9,085	£2,584
OVERHEAD EQUIPMENT.	£				£	£	£
Poles.							
1895 Construction	3,403	30	16	14	72	1,451	119
1899 "	2,703	30	12	18	57	809	116
1905 "	1,331	30	7	23	28	214	41
	£7,437				£157	£2,474	£363
Cables.	£				£	£	£
1895 Construction	350	30	16	14	7	141	10
1899 "	897	20	12	8	33	468	101
1905 "	486	20	7	13	18	138	31
	£1,733				£58	£747	£152
Test Tables, Conduits and Feeder Pillars.	£				£	£	£
1899 Construction	608	30	12	18	[illegible]	184	26
	73	20	12	8		43	8
1905 "	696	30	7	23	15	115	21
	96	20	7	13	4	30	6
	£1,473				£23	£372	£61
Summary.	£				£	£	£
Permanent Way	55,307				2,174	22,245	5,428
Cars	21,425				809	9,085	2,584
Overhead Equipment	7,437				157	2,474	356
Cables	1,733				58	747	152
Test Cables, Conduits and Pillars	1,473				35	372	61
Total ..	£87,375				£3,233	£34,923	£8,581

SCHEDULE No. II.

Year ended 31st December	Amount of Renewals falling due at end of each year	Year ended 31st December	Amount of Renewals falling due at end of each year
	£		£
1912	—	1924	36,016
1913	1,960	1925	3,753
1914	—	1926	6,215
1915	1,042	1927	—
1916	—	1928	—
1917	18,831	1929	3,311
1918	—	1930	—
1919	5,290	1931	—
1920	3,780	1932	—
1921	2,700	1933	—
1922	2,450	1934	2,027
1923	—		Total £87,375

SCHEDULE No. III.

CAPITAL EXPENDITURE.

Items	Amount Expended	Amount Renewable	Amount no Renewable
	£	£	£
Amount of Award	202,132	87,375	114,757
Stores	2,714	—	2,714
Cost of Arbitration	6,820	—	6,820
Stamp Duty on Purchase ..	2,021	—	2,021
	£213,687	£87,375	£126,312
Sinking Fund for 30 years invested at 2½% (2·2777 per £100)	£4,867	£1,990	£2.877

remains to be treated the second point, viz., the method of treatment in the accounts of such provision.

13. I consider that a proper amount should be charged in the accounts for depreciation, and in considering the amount to be so charged it is only fair and reasonable to reckon the Sinking Fund instalments as part of the provision for depreciation. The difference between the total depreciation provision required and the amount thereof appropriated to the ordinary Sinking Fund represents a sum which can be set aside towards the provision of the renewals now under consideration. Should the sum so set aside be insufficient to meet the cost of such renewals, any deficiency in the provision should be taken out of the ultimate net profits of the undertaking.

14. The amount to be set aside in any undertaking to provide for depreciation is one upon which there are frequently differences of opinion amongst experts, but it will perhaps be a safe method to adopt, as the amount to be set aside, the sum which would be allowed as a deduction for the purpose of income-tax. The exact sum so to be allowed necessarily varies from year to year, but the allowances my firm have secured in connection with the undertaking during the past three years have averaged £9,289 per annum. As I understand, it is not likely the power station plant will be renewed, the depreciation in respect thereof (£720) could well be excluded, leaving the sum of £8,569, which, I suggest, is a sum which could fairly be taken as chargeable against revenue for depreciation for present purposes.

15. Of this amount there has already been appropriated £4,929 by way of annual charges in respect of the existing Sinking Fund, leaving a further £3,640 to be set on one side towards creating the proposed fund for provision of renewals. This is less by £1,452 than the amount required for the first six years, as specified in Paragraph 8 (viz., £5,092 and this deficiency therefore represents the burden of renewals to be borne out of surplus profits (if any), or to be otherwise provided for.

16. For convenience I summarise the figures thus:—

Present annual charge in Revenue Account for Sinking Fund		£4,929
Further charge now proposed		3,640
Total chargeable in Revenue Account in respect of depreciation		8,569
Further annual amount required to complete necessary provision		1,452
Total annual requirement for each of the first six years		£10,021
Sinking Fund	£4,929	
Additional requirements	5,092	
	£10,021	

17. The profits available for the first six years, judging by the accounts to 31st March last, however, are not likely to be sufficient to meet the above sum. It therefore appears that to charge depreciation as herein specified would result in an annual deficit, to be made good out of the rates or carried forward until such time as the profits were adequate to make good the same.

18. There is no statutory requirement to compel the Committee to provide for depreciation other than by way of the Sinking Fund, although the course above set forth is the proper one from a sound financial point of view. As an alternative it is possible to adopt the course of not making what I might term a "scientific charge" for depreciation, but to set aside the whole of any surplus profits to reserve, towards meeting the required sums, unless and until, in course of time, the profits are more than sufficient to make good the inadequate provision of earlier years.

19. Another course is to fix upon some modified figure for the first few years, in the hope that increasing profits will permit of any deficiency of provision to be made good later on.

20. For example, it might be argued that, seeing the undertaking has so recently come into the hands of the Corporation, and important matters of policy relating to extensions, &c., remain to be dealt with, the Committee would be wise to defer dealing with a complete scheme such as above indicated, and at present to limit themselves to the consideration of the course to be adopted up to the year 1917, when a substantial outlay will be necessary according to the manager's calculations.

21. To provide for such outlay, viz., £18,831, the proportion which could be raised by way of loan, as indicated in Clause 5, would be £8,442, leaving £10,389 to be provided. This would involve an annual charge upon the department of £2,581, allowing for interest upon such amount set aside at the rate of 3 per cent. per annum.

22. I think it desirable to add that, since the preparation of the above report, the Town Clerk informs me that in reply to an inquiry addressed by him to the Board of Trade, the latter have stated they would not in ordinary circumstances be prepared to sanction any loans for the purposes indicated. This reply seems to render it incumbent upon the Committee to adopt all reasonable precautions for the provision of adequate funds to provide for renewals.

23. I strongly deprecate the debit of sums for capital outlay to the Revenue Account. Any such course seems to me to be irregular. In my opinion the charges against revenue should only be such as are proper charges for the year. Any capital outlay for which it is not intended to obtain a loan should be provided out of the proposed Reserve (for Renewals) Fund. Undoubtedly the right course is to charge a regular sum in the accounts, as herein recommended, and utilise the funds so set aside for the purpose of renewals, leaving all other sums (for extensions and the like) to be provided by way of new loans.

I am,

Mr. Chairman and Gentlemen,

Your obedient Servant,

EDW. THOS. PEIRSON, F.C.A.

Professional Auditor to the Corporation.

Coventry,

30th May 1913.

Income Tax.

Official Allowances in respect of Depreciation of Machinery and Plant.

(To the Editor of The Accountant.)

SIR,—I have laid before the Board of Inland Revenue your letter of the 9th ult., on the subject of allowances for income-tax purposes in respect of depreciation of machinery and plant in the case of certain industries, and in reply I am directed to inform you that such allowances fall to be made by the General Commissioners of Taxes or by the Special Commissioners of Income Tax, as the case may require. The Board, however, have always endeavoured, wherever practicable, to secure a measure of uniformity in the treatment of claims to these allowances, and the following represents the usual practice in regard to various industries, including those to which you specifically refer :—

I.—*Shipping Industry.*

(*a*) The normal rates of allowance for depreciation are as follows :—

On Steamers 4% } On the original cost price of the vessel
On Sailing Vessels 3% } *plus* subsequent capital expenditure.

Exceptional cases are dealt with specially by the Commissioners concerned.

(*b*) Allowances are made year by year until the total cost of the vessel, less the breaking up value (taken at the rate of 4 per cent. in the case of steamers and 3 per cent. in the case of sailing vessels) has been allowed.

(*c*) The net expenditure on the renewal of engines and boilers and the net cost of any structural improvements such as the lengthening or strengthening of a ship, is not allowed as a deduction for income-tax purposes, but is added to the prime cost of the ship and depreciation allowed on the total amount.

(*d*) Where a vessel changes hands, allowances for wear and tear are granted to the new owner not exceeding the actual cost to him of the vessel (less breaking up value).

II.—*Paper Mills.*

No objection is raised on behalf of this Department where the Commissioners grant an allowance not exceeding 7½ per cent. in respect of machinery in mills which run by day and night, or an allowance not exceeding 5 per cent. in mills working by day only, provided that all additions to, and renewals and replacements of machinery and plant, are charged to capital.

III.—*Printing Works.*

No objection is raised where the Commissioners grant allowances not exceeding 5 per cent. in respect of engines, boilers, and shafting, and 7½ per cent. in respect of printing and binding machines. Type is, as a general rule, dealt with by way of an allowance for actual cost of renewal, but if depreciation is insisted on, no objection is made to an allowance not exceeding 10 per cent. Special and delicate machinery is dealt with by the Commissioners according to the facts of each case.

IV.—*Flour Mills.*

No objection is raised where the Commissioners grant an allowance not exceeding 5 per cent. on the engines, boilers, and main shafting, or an allowance not exceeding 7½ per cent. on the other more perishable machinery.

The above allowances in the cases of Paper Mills, Printing Works, and Flour Mills, are calculated on the written-down value, *i.e.* on the balance of value left at the end of the year preceding the year of assessment, after deducting from the prime cost the sums allowed for depreciation, and adding the net sums spent on additions and renewals.

In all cases where an allowance is made for depreciation, the cost of renewals and replacements, less any allowance made for obsolescence, is necessarily treated as capital expenditure.

V.—*Railway Wagons.*

I enclose for your information a copy of a scheme, dealing with the determination of the allowances to be granted for income-tax purposes in respect of payments made in acquiring wagons under hire-purchase agreements. It should be noted that the scheme does not remove the matter from the jurisdiction of the Commissioners.

VI.—*Tramways and Light Railways, Gas, Water and Electricity Undertakings worked by Municipal Corporations and Companies.*

I enclose leaflets giving particulars of schemes under which the allowances for income-tax purposes in respect of the depreciation of those undertakings may be dealt with, when the Commissioners offer no objection. It should be observed that in each case, the scheme must be adopted, if at all, in its entirety, and that the corporations and companies concerned will not be entitled to allowances in respect of " permanent way " or any other special subject while rejecting the remainder of the scheme.

I also enclose a copy of a scheme for determining the income-tax allowances to be granted for wear and tear and maintenance of gas undertakings other than those owned by municipal or other public authorities.

I am, Sir, your obedient servant,

J. S. CHAPMAN,
Secretary.

Inland Revenue,
Somerset House, London, W.C.
6th May 1914.

RAILWAY WAGONS.

HIRE-PURCHASE.

Scheme for determining the Income Tax allowances to be granted in respect of payments made in acquiring wagons under hire-purchase agreements.

1. The lessee of wagons under a hire-purchase agreement shall furnish to the Surveyor of Taxes a copy of the agreement together with a certificate from the wagon builder, or other satisfactory evidence as to the price at which the wagons would have been sold for cash at the date of the agreement, hereinafter referred to as the initial value.

2. The difference between the initial value and the aggregate amount payable under the agreement shall be treated as " hire " and allowed in equal annual amounts spread over the term of the agreement.

3. Depreciation shall also be allowed on the initial value from the beginning of the agreement in accordance with the provisions of the Income Tax Acts at a rate to be settled by agreement between the lessee and the Crown or by appeal to the Income Tax Commissioners.

4. In the event of any wagons under a hire-purchase agreement being purchased outright before the termination of the agreement or being returned to the lessor, the allowance for hire shall cease from the date of such purchase or return, and if returned the allowance for depreciation shall thenceforth cease.

5. If any such wagons shall be " refinanced " the allowance for hire under the agreement thus terminated shall cease and a fresh allowance shall be made for the period of the new agreement to be determined by taking the difference between the amount at which such wagons are refinanced at the date of the new agreement and the aggregate amount payable under the new agreement, and spreading the said difference evenly over the term thereof. The allowance for depreciation to be continued without reference to the new agreement.

6. Where any wagons are the subject of hire-purchase agreements current at the date of this scheme or during any of the preceding years upon the average profits of which any income-tax assessments are computed, and no allowances for hire have been made in respect of the payments under such agreements, the amount which would have been allowable annually for hire had this agreement been in force at the date of the hire-purchase agreement shall be ascertained and the appropriate amount shall be allowed annually for the remainder of the term of the hire-purchase agreement. Provided that, where the depreciation allowance in respect of such

wagons has been calculated on the aggregate amount payable under the agreement, the total of the amounts allowable as hire under this clause shall be deducted from the said aggregate amount in computing future allowances for depreciation.

Should satisfactory evidence of the initial value of the wagons at the date of the agreement not be available, such value may be computed from the aggregate amount payable under the agreement on the basis of a five per cent. interest table.

7. Where any wagons are the subject of hire-purchase agreements current at the date of this agreement, and allowances have been made in any previous year in respect of the payments under such agreements otherwise than in the form of depreciation, the aggregate amount of such allowances shall be deducted from the aggregate amount allowable under this scheme as "hire" in respect of such agreement, and the balance only shall be allowed in equal annual amounts spread over the remainder of the term of the agreement. Provided that, any adjustment of the capital value on which depreciation is allowable rendered necessary by the operation of this clause, shall be made as provided in Clause 6.

GENERAL.

8. The cost of reconstruction and all renewals of parts shall be allowed as repairs, except so far as they constitute an extension, enlargement, or other similar improvement of value.

9. Where such reconstruction and renewals are allowable under this scheme they shall be allowed notwithstanding that the cost thereof may not have been debited in the company's accounts against revenue.

10. Where "dead-ends" are converted into "spring-buffers" the total cost of such conversion shall be allowed less £5 per wagon, which latter sum shall be treated as the capital value of the improvement, such sum to be added to the value of the wagons for the purpose of computing the annual allowance for depreciation.

11. This scheme shall take effect for 1913-14 and for years preceding where appeals are now awaiting settlement, and in calculating the assessable liability shall be applied to each of the five years or other period on the average of which the said liability falls to be computed.

12. The rate of depreciation when agreed upon shall apply to all wagons whether the subject of hire-purchase agreements or not.

(WE) desire to adopt the above arrangements and hereby undertake to fulfil the conditions thereof.

Dated ....

Extracts from a Circular of the Board of Inland Revenue to Surveyors of Taxes as to Allowance of Income Tax in respect of Depreciation of certain Undertakings.

TRAMWAYS.

PERMANENT WAY.—ALLOWANCE FOR MAINTENANCE TO COVER DEPRECIATION.

Life.

1. The life of the permanent way is to be taken as 12, 14 or 16 years, according to the traffic thereon. The classification is to be based on the average car mileage per mile of track per annum of the financial year preceding the year of assessment, viz. :—

(1) Not exceeding 50,000 car miles per mile of track—16 years.

(2) Over 50,000 and not exceeding 75,000 car miles per mile of track—14 years.

(3) Over 75,000 and not exceeding 125,000 car miles per mile of track—12 years.

(4) Over 125,000 car miles per mile of track—special consideration.

2. Where there are special circumstances, such as exceptional gradients, and the compulsory use of wood-paving, &c., tending to show that the car mileage does not fairly represent the wear and tear of the track, each such case is entitled to special consideration.

Cost of Renewals.

3. The cost of renewals, including setts or other paving, but excluding concrete foundations, should be taken at £4,400 per mile of single track until the general renewal of the track takes place.

Basis of Computation of Depreciation Allowance.

4. No allowance should be made in computing the assessable profits in respect of any expenditure on repairs or maintenance of the permanent way, but the allowance for depreciation should be computed at such a sum per annum as will in the aggregate over the determined life of the permanent way be equal to the cost of renewal as above fixed plus the estimated repairs for that period :—

Cost of renewal per mile (as above) ..	£4,400
Add for example :—	
Estimated cost of repairs at £100 per mile per annum, for an undertaking with a life of 16 years	£1,600
	£6,000
Amount to be allowed per annum in lieu of depreciation 1-16th	£375

5. The amount to be added in respect of ordinary repairs should be determined by taking the actual average expenditure as shown in the accounts of the undertaking for the last three years, *i.e.* the three years preceding the initiation of the scheme, or such period less than three years as the undertaking has been in existence. If at the beginning of any year of assessment for which the allowance is being computed the mileage of the track differs from the average mileage during the three years above mentioned, the allowance under this head should be increased or diminished proportionately.

6. Repairs under this head should be understood to include renewals of special track work at junctions and cross-overs, which occur at frequent intervals.

Periodical adjustment.

7. Inasmuch as the expenditure on repairs is expected to increase as the track begins to wear, in which case the figure to be adopted under this head, which is to be based on past experience, will be unsatisfactory, the amount of such estimate should come up for revision at the end of every five years, and an adjustment should be made by increasing or diminishing the allowance as the circumstances require, having regard to the basis of calculation

outlined above. The whole amount to be allowed for repairs in each year of the quinquennium can be varied only with variations in the mileage of the track, *i.e.* the amount to be allowed *per mile of track* is a constant quantity.

8. A strict account should be kept by the Corporation and the Surveyor of the annual allowances, and of the actual expenditure on repairs and renewals; and at the end of ten or fifteen years (*i.e.* the second or third revision) or at such time as the general renewal of the track shall have taken place, the amount to be annually allowed should be re-considered and increased or diminished for succeeding years as the ascertained facts shall show to be necessary, provided that under no circumstances shall the allowances for previous years be re-opened.

9. All expenditure on extensions and improvements should be excluded from the working expenses for income-tax purposes; and the necessary additional allowance for depreciation on the lines suggested above (*i.e.* mileage) should be at once allowed on such expenditure, and added to the sum already allowable.

10. The allowance of £4,400 for renewal of permanent way mentioned above is intended to apply to overhead trolley system. Special arrangements should be made, on the lines of the foregoing, in the case of the conduit, surface contact, or other system. The number of such cases is very small. As the circumstances vary very considerably in each case, the amount to be allowed for renewals should in the first instance be arrived at by arrangement with the Chief Inspector of Taxes.

Cables.

11. In addition to repairs, depreciation should be allowed at the rate of 3 per cent. per annum on the written down value.

Overhead Equipment, i.e. Trolley Wires and Connections.

12. No depreciation should be allowed; all expenditure on maintenance and renewals should be charged as working expenses, as and when incurred.

Cars and other Rolling Stock.

13. Subject to the ensuing clause, expenditure on maintenance and renewals should be treated as working expenses and allowed in lieu of depreciation.

14. Depreciation, however, should be allowed in lieu of renewals where the circumstances justify such an allowance, provided that a strict account is kept of all renewals, and that if such renewals are charged to Revenue Account they shall be shown separately in such account and added back in computing the assessable profits.

15. The allowance in such case should be 7 per cent. per annum on the written down value.

16. In any case the annual expenditure on repairs is to be allowed as a deduction in computing the assessable profits.

General Plant and Machinery.

17. All other plant and machinery, including standards, brackets, and workshop tools, but excluding loose implements, office furniture, and small articles which require frequent renewal, should be bulked together and depreciation allowed thereon at the rate of 5 per cent. per annum on the written down value, in addition to the cost of repairs.

. . . .

25. In all cases where depreciation allowances are granted, a strict account should be kept of the annual expenditure on renewals (and repairs in the case of tramway tracks), including replacements due to obsolescence, and of the amounts allowed for depreciation and obsolescence, whether under this arrangement, or under any arrangement made prior hereto, and a readjustment should be made for the future, if necessary, at the end of every five years, as detailed under Tramways (Permanent Way), subject, however, to the special provisions applicable to Tramways (Permanent Way).

26. Where depreciation allowances other than those for the permanent way of tramways are granted, renewals should be carefully distinguished, and, if charged against revenue, they should be notified to the Surveyor, in order that they may be added back in arriving at the income-tax liability.

27. "Written down value" means original prime cost, plus subsequent additions, less all allowances actually granted by the Revenue in respect of wear and tear.

28. These proposals are to take effect for the year 1908-9, and for years preceding in cases where claims of depreciation are at the present time awaiting settlement.

29. The computations necessary for any future adjustment should be duly made, agreed and recorded each year, whether the accounts for the particular year under review show any assessable income-tax liability or not.

30. Where, in any cases, allowances for depreciation have been made which are now to be discontinued, and they have not been exhausted by renewals already effected, the amount of such unexhausted allowances should be determined by agreement between the Surveyor and the Corporation or Company, and deducted from the expenditure on future renewals as and when they are effected.

31. All cases of dispute should be referred to the Board through the Chief Inspector of Taxes.

GAS AND WATER UNDERTAKINGS.

18. No depreciation should be allowed in any circumstances in respect of any portion of these undertakings.

19. All expenditure on repairs and renewals, but excluding extensions and improvements, is to be charged and allowed as working expenses, as and when incurred.

20. Provided that whenever any exceptional expenditure on *bonâ fide* renewals is incurred, and full effect cannot be given to its deduction in that year owing to the profits or gains chargeable with income-tax in that year being less than the amount so expended, the balance of the said expenditure which has not been allowed may be carried forward and allowed in the following year or years, as is provided in the case of unallowed wear and tear by Section 26 (3) of the Finance Act, 1907.

. . . .

28. These proposals are to take effect for the year 1908-9, and for years preceding in cases where claims of depreciation are at the present time awaiting settlement.

29. The computations necessary for any future adjustment should be duly made, agreed, and recorded each year, whether the accounts for the particular year under review show any assessable income-tax liability or not.

30. Where, in any cases, allowances for depreciation have been made which are now to be discontinued, and they have not been exhausted by renewals already effected, the amount of such unexhausted allowances should be determined by agreement between the Surveyor and the Corporation or Company, and deducted from the expenditure on future renewals as and when they are effected.

31. All cases of dispute should be referred to the Board through the Chief Inspector of Taxes.

ELECTRIC LIGHTING UNDERTAKINGS.

Cables.

21. In addition to repairs, allowance for depreciation may be granted at the rate of 3 per cent. per annum on the written down value.

Plant and Machinery.

22. On all other plant, exclusive of loose tools, meters, and office furniture, depreciation may be allowed at the rate of 5 per cent. per annum on the written down value, in addition to the cost of repairs.

Conduits.

23. No allowance should be made for depreciation; but annual expenditure on repairs and renewals may be allowed as working expenses, as and when incurred.

Meters, Loose Tools, and Office Furniture.

24. No allowance should be made for depreciation; but annual expenditure on repairs and renewals may be allowed as working expenses, as and when incurred.

. . . .

25. In all cases where depreciation allowances are granted, a strict account should be kept of the annual expenditure on renewals, including replacements due to obsolescence, and of the amounts allowed for depreciation and obsolescence, whether under this arrangement, or under any arrangement made prior hereto, and a readjustment should be made for the future, if necessary, at the end of every five years, by increasing or diminishing the allowance, as the circumstances require.

26. Where depreciation allowances are granted, renewals should be carefully distinguished, and, if charged against revenue, they should be notified to the Surveyor, in order that they may be added back in arriving at the income-tax liability.

27. "Written down value" means original prime cost, plus subsequent additions, less all allowances actually granted by the Revenue in respect of wear and tear.

28. These proposals are to take effect for the year 1908-9, and for years preceding in cases where claims of depreciation are at the present time awaiting settlement.

29. The computations necessary for any future adjustment should be duly made, agreed and recorded each year, whether the accounts for the particular year under review show any assessable income-tax liability or not.

30. Where, in any cases, allowances for depreciation have been made which are now to be discontinued, and they have not been exhausted by renewals already effected, the amount of such unexhausted allowances should be determined by agreement between the Surveyor and the Corporation or Company, and deducted from the expenditure on future renewals, as and when they are effected.

31. All cases of dispute should be referred to the Board through the Chief Inspector of Taxes.

GAS UNDERTAKINGS OTHER THAN THOSE OWNED BY MUNICIPAL OR OTHER PUBLIC AUTHORITIES.

SCHEME FOR DETERMINING THE INCOME TAX ALLOWANCES TO BE GRANTED FOR WEAR AND TEAR AND MAINTENANCE.

Plant, Machinery, and Mains.

1. No depreciation shall be allowed in respect of the Plant, Machinery, and Mains, other than as specified hereinafter, but in lieu thereof all expenditure on repairs and renewals is to be charged in the company's accounts for income-tax purposes and allowed as working expenses, as and when incurred. All expenditure on extensions and improvements, where debited against revenue, to be distinguished and excluded from the said allowances.

2. Provided that whenever any expenditure on such renewals is incurred, and full effect cannot be given to its deduction in the year when incurred, owing to the profits or gains chargeable with income-tax in such year being less than the amount so expended, the balance of the said expenditure, which has not been allowed, may be carried forward and allowed in the following year or years, as is provided in the case of unallowed wear and tear by Section 26 (3) of the Finance Act, 1907.

Gasholders.

3. In addition to repairs, depreciation shall be allowed at the rate of 3 per cent. per annum on the written down value. Such value not to include tanks, except where constructed of steel or iron, and in no case is the cost of excavation to be included in the value upon which the depreciation allowance is computed.

Meters (Ordinary and Prepayment), Cookers and Gas Fires.

4. In addition to repairs, allowance for depreciation shall be granted at the rate of 10 per cent. per annum on the written down value.

Services and Fittings.

5. No depreciation shall be allowed in respect of services and fittings, but in lieu thereof all expenditure shall be allowed as a trading expense as and when incurred.

"Services" are to be understood as representing the pipes which connect the street mains with the properties served.

"Fittings" are the pipes, pendants, and brackets within such properties, supplied by and at the cost of the company.

Where Fittings so supplied are removed by the company at any time they shall be brought back into stock, if of any value, and re-issued without any charge against revenue except for the cost of repairs necessary to enable them to be re-issued. In the event of their not being re-issued, revenue shall be credited with the scrap value.

General.

6. In all cases where depreciation allowances are granted, renewals, if charged against revenue, shall be carefully distinguished and notified to the Surveyor in order that they may be added back to profits for the purpose of arriving at the income-tax liability.

7. If new works are erected, wholly or partially, on a new site, in place of old works abandoned or demolished, a reasonable allowance shall be granted for renewals in respect of the displaced plant, so far as it is actually renewed, such allowance to have regard to the original cost of the displaced plant, less any depreciation that may have been granted, but such allowance shall not include the cost of preparing the new site or erecting foundations for the new plant.

8. All renewals of parts which do not destroy the identity of the original article shall be allowed as repairs, except so far as they constitute an extension, enlargement, or other similar improvement in value.

9. Where renewals are allowable under this scheme in lieu of depreciation, they shall be allowed notwithstanding that the cost thereof may not have been debited in the company's accounts against revenue.

10. " Written down value " means original prime cost, plus subsequent additions (including renewals which have not been allowed for income-tax purposes), less all allowances actually granted for income-tax purposes in past years in respect of depreciation.

11. " Expenditure " includes the sum expended on materials, labour, and incidentals.

12. This scheme shall take effect for the year 1912-13, and future years, and for years preceding where claims of depreciation are now awaiting settlement.

13. Where, in any case, allowances for depreciation have been made which are now to be discontinued, and they have not been exhausted by renewals already effected, the amount of such unexhausted allowances shall be deducted from the expenditure on future renewals as and when they are effected.

We desire to adopt the above arrangement and hereby undertake to fulfil the conditions thereof.

On behalf of

Dated the day of 191

Chairman.

Secretary.

APPENDIX.

Application of Electricity Revenue.

The terms of reference were :—

To consider the application of electricty revenue and submit a memorandum upon the subject with special reference to :—

1. The appropriation of revenue moneys for expenditure of a capital nature.
2. The provision of a " working balance."
3. The desirability of securing wider powers for the disposal of profits.

The Council beg to report that :—

1. The general law upon the subject is contained in Section 7 (1) of the Electric Lighting (Clauses) Act, 1899, which provides that :—

Where a local authority are the undertakers the following provisions shall have effect :—

(1) All moneys received by the undertakers in respect of the undertaking, except (*a*) borrowed money, (*b*) money arising from the disposal of lands acquired for the purposes of the special order, and (*c*) other capital money received by them in respect of the undertaking, shall be applied by them as follows:—

(*a*) In payment of the working and establishment expenses and cost of maintenance of the undertaking, including all costs, expenses, penalties and damages incurred or payable by the undertakers consequent upon any proceedings by or against the undertakers, their officers or servants, in relation to the undertaking.

(*b*) In payment of the interest or dividend on any mortgages, stock, or other securities granted and issued by the undertakers in respect of money borrowed for electricity purposes.

(*c*) In providing any instalments or sinking fund required to be provided in respect of moneys borrowed for electricity purposes.

(*d*) In payment of all other their expenses of executing the special order not being expenses properly chargeable to capital.

(*e*) In providing a reserve fund, *if they think fit*, by setting aside such money as they think reasonable, and investing the money and the resulting income thereof in Government securities, or in any other securities in which trustees are by law for the time being authorised to invest other than stock or securities of the undertakers, and accumulating it at compound interest until the fund so formed amounts to one-tenth of the aggregate capital expenditure on the undertaking.

The reserve fund shall be applicable to answer any deficiency at any time happening in the income of the undertakers from the undertaking, or to meet any extraordinary claim or demand at any time arising against the undertakers in respect of the undertaking, and so that if that fund is at any time reduced it may thereafter be again restored to the prescribed limit, and so on as often as the reduction happens.

The undertakers *shall* carry the net surplus remaining in any year, and the annual proceeds of the reserve fund when amounting to the prescribed limit, to the credit of the local rate as defined by the principal Act, or at their option shall apply that surplus, or any part thereof, to the improvement of the district for which they are the local authority, or in reduction of the capital moneys borrowed for electricity purposes.

Provided always that if the surplus in any year exceed five pounds per centum per annum upon the aggregate capital expenditure on the undertaking, the undertakers shall make such a rateable reduction in the charge for the supply of energy as in their judgment will reduce the surplus to that maximum rate of profit.

Any deficiency of income in any year when not answered out of the reserve fund shall be charged upon and payable out of the local rate.

This section is usually incorporated in Local Provisional Orders, but is not applicable to the county of London.

The Act extends to Scotland and Ireland.

2. It will be seen that the appropriation clauses are mandatory except as to the reserve fund, with the result that every local authority is more or less in difficulty as regards the provision of a working balance, also it will be observed that whilst the undertakers are given the option of applying, if they see fit, surplus profits to the improvement of the district for which they are the local authority, they are not allowed, as is commonly the case in connection with gas and water undertakings, the option of applying such profits in extending and improving the undertaking.

3. With the object of ascertaining the practice adopted by authorities owning electricity works inquiries have been addressed to the financial officers of 162 authorities, and replies received from 146.

4. From the information obtained it appears that :—

(*a*) With very few exceptions the local Provisional Orders are substantially identical with those of Section 7 (1) of the Electric Lighting (Clauses) Act, 1899, quoted above.

The variations are as follows :—

In three instances powers have been obtained to expend surplus profits upon extensions and improvements of the undertaking. (Leeds, St. Marylebone, and West Bromwich.)

In two instances powers have been obtained to form a Renewals or Depreciation Fund. (St. Marylebone and West Bromwich.)

In one instance power has been obtained to provide a "working balance" out of surplus profits. (Stoke-on-Trent.)

In four instances powers have been obtained to increase the reserve fund to one-fifth of the aggregate capital expenditure of the undertaking. (Burnley, Devonport Leeds, and Norwich.)

(*b*) In five instances objection has been taken to the expenditure out of revenue for works of a capital nature.

(*c*) In no case have legal proceedings been taken against any authority.

(*d*) The method of appropriating surplus profits in aid of rates varies in practice, but the greater number adopt the principle of allocating the profits in the year following that in which such profits arise.

5. The Council takes the view that an amendment of the law is desirable, and consider that local authorities should have the power :—

(*a*) To apply surplus profits (within the limits of the proviso) in enlarging, extending, or improving the undertaking.

(*b*) To raise capital for providing a "working balance," or, alternatively, to reserve money for that purpose out of the surplus profits of the undertaking.

6. The Council understands that the Incorporated Municipal Electrical Association are promoting an Electricity Bill (otherwise known as the "Wiring and Fitting" Bill) in this session of Parliament to provide, *inter alia* :—

(*a*) *Application of Revenue.*

To apply the whole or any portion of the net surplus to any of the purposes of the undertaking, including the formation of a fund for working capital, provided that the fund so formed is not to exceed a sum equivalent to one-half of the gross annual revenue—Clause 7.

(*b*) *Working Capital.*

The power to borrow for working capital repayable within ten years with suspension of sinking fund for two years—Clause 8.

7. The Council are, however, of opinion that the Institute should express their approval of the above proposals as contained in the Bill, and, if considered desirable, address a representation upon the subject to the Board of Trade.

8. The Council takes the view, in the event of the present Bill not being proceeded with, that members of the Institute would be well advised to seek the necessary powers themselves when next promoting a Bill in Parliament, making use of the above-mentioned instances as precedents.

The Council have embodied the substance of the information received from the various authorities in paragraph 4 of this report, and do not consider it to be necessary to add a long appendix with the details of each case.

The President read an address, and papers were read by Mr. H. E. Haward (Comptroller London County Council) and Mr. F. Ogden Whiteley (City Treasurer of Bradford) which will be reproduced in these columns in due course.

The following officers for the ensuing year were elected : Mr. E. A. Coombs, Kensington ; Vice-President, Mr. J. W. Forster, Tunbridge Wells ; Secretary (re-elected), Mr. H. J. Hoare, Devonport ; Treasurer, Mr. H. M. Stevens, Brighton ; Hon. Editor of "Financial Circular," Mr. Whiteley, Bradford.

VOL. LI.—NEW SERIES.—No. 2069.] SATURDAY, AUGUST 1, 1914. [PRICE 6d.

LEADING ARTICLES

The Profits of Municipal Trading Departments.

AS we stated in an article which appeared in these columns last week, during the past year the Sub-Committee of the Council of the Institute of Municipal Treasurers and Accountants has been considering the question of the application of credit Revenue balances in the case of electricity departments of Local Authorities, and its report upon the subject was given in full in our issue of the 11th ult.

The terms of reference to the Sub-Committee were that it should consider the application of electricity revenue, and submit a memorandum upon the subject with special reference to (*a*) the appropriation of revenue moneys for expenditure of a capital nature; (*b*) the provision of a working balance; (*c*) the desirability of securing wider powers for the disposal of profits.

The report before us points out that the general law upon the subject is contained in Section 7 (1) of The Electric Lighting Clauses Act, 1899, which states clearly how the moneys received by the undertaking on Revenue Account are to be dealt with in all cases where the general Act applies, and is not superseded by some special Act governing the particular undertaking in question. Under this section such moneys are applicable in the first instance towards the payment of the working and establishment expenses of the undertaking, including the cost of maintenance ; then to the payment of interest on borrowed moneys; then towards providing the statutory sinking funds; then in payment of all other expenses of executing the special Order, not being expenses properly chargeable to capital. Further (if they think fit) those responsible for the undertaking may set aside a reserve fund to be invested in Government securities, to accumulate at compound interest until such time as the fund so formed amounts to one-tenth the aggregate capital expenditure of the undertaking. This reserve fund may be employed to make up any deficiency occurring in the income of the undertaking from time to time, or to meet any extraordinary claim or demand; and, having been depleted in any such way, it may thereafter be reinforced until such time as it again amounts to the aforesaid maximum of 10 per cent. The section then goes on to say that any net surplus remaining after providing for the aforesaid items (including the income derived from the investments of any reserve fund amounting to the maximum of 10 per cent.) shall be applied to the credit of the local rate, as defined by the principal Act, save in so far as it may be employed in " the " improvement of the district governed by " the Local Authority," or in reduction of the capital moneys borrowed for electricity purposes ; but if the surplus in any year (meaning, presumably, the net surplus) exceeds 5 per cent. on the aggregate capital expenditure of the undertaking, it is provided that the undertakers must make such a rateable reduction in the charge for the supply of energy as will in their judgment reduce the surplus to the maximum rate provided, *i.e.* 5 per cent. Any deficiency of income in any one year, not answered out of the reserve fund, is to be charged upon and payable out of the local rates.

The statutory provisions which we have thus summarised above are set out in full in the report of the Sub-Committee, and were reproduced in our columns in full on page 63 of our issue of the 11th ult. As the Sub-Committee very properly points out, they differ from the customary provisions in the case of gas and water undertakings, in that they do not give a Local Authority the option of applying any portion of its profits in extending or improving the undertaking ; but it is, we think, quite arguable, on the principle that the greater includes the less, that power to use surplus profits in the improvement of the district for which they are the Local Authority includes *inter alia* the power to use surplus profits for the improvement of anything in that district, including the electricity undertaking itself. It is doubtless unsatisfactory that so important a matter should be dealt with in such vague terms; but we cannot help thinking that most kinds of capital expenditure directly connected with an electricity undertaking might be regarded just as much as an improvement of the district as might be (say) the widening of a street, or the laying down of a tramway. However that may be, any doubts that may be felt upon this point could, we think, usually be got over in practice quite easily by applying the surplus profits of one trading department towards meeting capital expenditure in another trading department, of a description that could fairly come within the heading of " improvements." Thus each department might in turn apply its profits towards the improvement of something connected with some other trading department, in such a way that the expenditure could fairly be claimed as an improvement of the "district."

What, however, the report before us very properly points out cannot be done in the existing state of the law is to apply surplus profits of an electricity undertaking towards the provision of a working balance, or balance of working capital. It is an absurd oversight on the part of the law that municipal trading undertakings are apparently expected to be able to carry on their operations without working capital, and, further, without borrowing for the purpose of providing such a working capital. Indeed, bank overdrafts for this purpose have been decided to be illegal borrowings! In practice the difficulty can usually be dodged by refraining from exercising up to the hilt the right obtained to incur capital expenditure, while yet exercising the right obtained to exercise borrowing powers. That is to say, by exercising borrowing powers slightly ahead of the incurring of the capital expenditure in respect of which these borrowing powers were authorised the trading departments of a Local Authority can in practice usually contrive to squeeze out a working balance sufficient to carry it along; but this clearly is at best a subterfuge, and, as the Sub-Committee points out, the difficulty should be met by statutory powers being granted to a Local Authority to borrow for working capital purposes on reasonable terms. A suggested loan term of ten years, with a sinking fund suspended for two years, seems to us by no means unreasonable, in view of all the circumstances. Another way for obtaining a working balance indirectly is to apply for borrowing powers to meet the cost of renewals to the fullest possible extent, while yet taking a somewhat generous interpretation of the meaning of "maintenance." It is clear that, under the heading of Maintenance, the trading department of a Local Authority could, if it were so minded, charge against revenue the full cost of all renewals that involved no actual extension of the original undertaking. At the same time, it is often practicable to reborrow for renewal purposes, at all events up to a point.

Upon the whole, it seems to us that the statutory provision most in need of amendment to enable the practical requirements of the normal situation most readily to be met is some relaxation of the provision that the reserve funds accumulated out of profits must be invested in Government securities. If it were not compulsory that the reserve fund should so be invested, it would become an exceedingly simple matter for a Local Authority speedily to build up a working balance out of reserved profits, while there can be little question that in the long run it is desirable that the working balance should consist of reserved profits, rather than that it should consist of borrowed capital.

On the question of the desirability of wider powers being granted to electricity departments as to the disposal of profits, some limitation ought to be placed upon the exercise of such powers in the interests of consumers of electricity. While some Local Authorities run their trading departments exclusively in the interests of their consumers, others—and among them many of the largest—seem to regard them primarily as a means of raising money independently of the ratepayers. While we take the view that, if ratepayers are responsible for deficiencies, and have to guarantee interest on capital —and the repayment of capital, should the trading profits prove inadequate to provide for both—they are entitled at least to something by way of compensation for the financial risks they undertake, we certainly think that the only really strong argument in favour of permitting municipal trading at all is the argument that the customer (or consumer) is entitled to be considered, and not merely regarded as someone out of whom trading profits can be extracted. In the case of electricity undertakings (and for that matter gas and water undertakings) owned by capitalist companies, the consumer is very effectively protected against excessive charges. We think it only right that he should have at least equal protection in the case of public-service undertakings that are municipally owned; but, as regards that portion of surplus profits which (under any circumstances) is judged to belong to the undertakers themselves, rather than to the consumers, we see no particular reason why those responsible for the management of the undertaking should not be given a fairly free hand as to the disposal or application of these surplus profits. The fact that even under the existing law they may apply them, or any part thereof, to the improvement of the district for which they are the Local Authority seems to suggest that this has been conceded by the Legislature as a question of principle. We are inclined, however, to agree with the Sub-Committee whose report is now before us, that the application of the principle might, with advantage, be made more clear. Probably it will be some while before Parliament finds time to pass a general Act dealing with the question. In the meantime, we think that individual Local Authorities would be well advised to endeavour to secure a reasonable and businesslike treatment of the position in any special Act that they may have occasion to promote.

Observations on the Transfer of Undertakings to Public Authorities.

By R. Kerr, C.A.

A paper read at a meeting of the London Chartered Accountant Students Society, held at the Institute of Chartered Accountants, on 11th March 1915, Mr. A. E. Cutforth, A.C.A., in the chair.

In choosing the subject of to-night's paper I was actuated partly by the reason that the subject is one which must be of some interest to each of us, whether or not we propose to make accountancy our profession. When we leave the City at night we become private citizens, and most of us as such have an interest in the undertakings which many of our local authorities control for the supply of our water, our gas or electricity, or the means of conveyance to our homes by tramway. We may sometimes speculate how, and in what manner, the undertakings were acquired by the local authorities concerned, and I will endeavour to-night to outline briefly—from the point of view of an accountant—the principles usually applied in assessing the consideration payable for undertakings supplying a service of public utility.

Before passing to a consideration of the principles which govern the assessment of price it would be well to explain that when it is proposed to form a public authority or board to acquire an existing business, it is necessary to seek powers from Parliament in order to carry out the objects desired. It will not be necessary nor profitable to attempt to particularise the various legal formalities which precede the passing of a Bill under the provisions of which a local or public authority will enter into possession of the undertakings proposed to be transferred.

The purchase price will either be named in the Act or be left to be agreed between parties or to be assessed by a Court of Arbitration.

My observations will be directed to three distinctive methods of determining the purchase price, viz. :—

1. By agreement;
2. By arbitration under the Lands Clauses Acts; and
3. By arbitration under the Tramways Acts.

Of the three methods mentioned, purchase by agreement is without doubt the most economical, inasmuch as the heavy expenses incidental to arbitration need not be incurred; that this is a material consideration is well illustrated by the Metropolitan Water Board arbitration, which cost upwards of a quarter of a million sterling. There is also this advantage, that if agreement be arrived at between parties it must be assumed that each is satisfied as to the fairness of the price agreed upon, whereas this can seldom be said to result when the price is determined by arbitration. In cases of mutual agreement, there are, of course, no rigid rules which can be laid down as to the method which should be employed in assessing a purchase price, but I think we may assume that such price is almost invariably based upon the revenue-earning capacity of the business in question, and in this way is similar in principle to the usual practice in arbitration under the Lands Clauses Acts. The services of accountants are almost invariably requisitioned to assist on the one side in the preparation of the claim for compensation, &c., and on the other side in the investigation of the accounts and criticism of the claim. I think, in the latter case, we must regard the duties of the accountants engaged as the more onerous, inasmuch as they must approach their task without the active co-operation and goodwill of those conversant with the details of the business, which would not unnaturally be placed at the disposal of the accountants who might be acting for the other side. As a convenient way of considering this matter, let us put ourselves in the place of accountants acting on behalf of a hypothetical purchasing body. Our instructions would probably be very general and might embrace an inquiry into and report on the accounts, history, and prospects of the undertaking in question, and comments on the claim, if any, advanced by or on behalf of the proprietors. Our attention would, I think, be primarily directed to the question of ascertaining the maintainable income, because, in the absence of any special reasons to the contrary, *earning* capacity must largely be the measure of value to be applied to assets of a revenue-producing character.

The term "maintainable income" is one which occurs frequently in these cases, and I want you to consider its meaning. It is not every concern that has a maintainable income. The term, I think, can be applied only to undertakings which supply a service of public utility. It would not apply to the income of an ordinary commercial company, because the security of such income is frequently open to vicissitudes in public tastes and other risks; but an undertaking which supplies for profit any service of public utility, such as a water company, an electricity company, a dock company, &c., may be said to have a maintainable income, because such income is not dependable to any large extent on variations in public taste. A water company has, other things being equal, the most stable of all incomes, as, in spite of the progress of modern invention, no universal substitute for water has been or is ever likely to be discovered. The maintainable income, as I understand it, of a concern of this nature, is the income which under normal circumstances it will be able to earn in perpetuity, or for its lifetime, with the *resources* it has at its command at the date of the inquiry, due regard being had to statutory obligations.

If we can ascertain the probable maintainable income we shall be able, by capitalising such income, and allowing for any exceptional factors, to arrive at a figure which might be advanced as a basis upon which to negotiate a purchase price.

What would be the ordinary process we would employ to arrive at a figure of maintainable income? We should have to analyse carefully the composition of the Revenue Accounts for a consecutive period of years to the date of the last available accounts, and the maintainable income would be based on the average of such experience over a selected period after making such adjustments to the accounts as we considered necessary or desirable in order to show the true position. Our adjustments might take the form of allocating expenses to the year's results which ought properly to bear the expense, and similarly with income. We might find as a result of our inquiries that amounts had been charged to capital which were properly chargeable against revenue; and, *vice versâ*, it might be our duty to relieve the Revenue Account of expenditure which was properly attributable to capital. Exceptional items in the accounts can best be discovered by preparing analytical tables for a series of years and inquiring into variations which become visible on a comparison between one year and another, but, of course, a close examination of the books is also necessary. It will probably be found that the most difficult question we have to deal with on Revenue Account is to determine a fair charge against profits in respect of maintenance, renewals, and depreciation. An accountant is not expected to deal authoritatively with questions of maintenance and depreciation, and he would be well advised to consult an engineer with a view to assessing the charge which should be made against profits. The engineer would have to decide from figures and statistics supplied by the accountant and from his own personal experience and inspection what sum should be spent annually on the undertaking so as to enable it to earn year after year the same income as it had done in the past. The accountant would then substitute the figure so obtained for the annual expenditures on maintenance and provision for depreciation which had been charged in the books, and, subject to the verification and adjustment of other items of income and expenditure, he would be in a position to arrive at an average income, based on past results, which might be regarded as the maintainable income.

The choice of a period upon which to base an average is one which requires careful consideration, and the accountant, whilst indicating his preference, would be well advised to illustrate the variation which would result from lengthening or shortening the period of average selected. The usual period taken is either five or seven years, but the period of average must largely be governed by the circumstances affecting each individual case. In order to obtain a capital value for the maintainable income, it is customary to apply thereto a multiplier which will vary somewhat according to the nature of the business and the degree of security it offers. For instance, the multiplier in the case of a water company would probably be higher than in the case (say) of an electricity company, because, for reasons already indicated, the income of a water company, in the absence of special circumstances, offers the maximum security obtainable in a commercial business.

Again, as the purchase consideration has to be translated into terms of money, financial considerations enter into a determination of the number of years' purchase. For instance, the market price of Consols to-day, taken at (say) 75, gives thirty years' purchase of its income; whereas, taken at the market prices current fifteen years ago, the number of years' purchase was more than thirty-six, although the security is much the same to-day as it was then. Reference must accordingly be made for this purpose to the current market prices of securities of a similar class and stability, and it would be well to work out the results on several alternative bases. Having arrived by this means at a capitalised value of the maintainable income, we should have to review the position and see whether the procedure we have followed and the results attained have given due consideration for all the assets we propose to purchase.

It is possible that an undertaking may possess assets of value which do not contribute to the general or maintainable income, and a consideration for purchase should not be suggested without allowing for the value thereof. As an instance of the nature of such assets, the concern may be possessed of undeveloped land which, whilst being held in anticipation of future extensions, may not for the moment be revenue producing. A purchase, therefore, based entirely on income would not give due consideration for unproductive assets which might eventually prove to be valuable. If it be demonstrated that value does attach to unproductive assets, an adjustment could be made either by adding a lump sum to the capitalised value of income, or by adding to the maintainable income the estimated *annual* present value of such assets. I do not propose to carry you beyond this point except to remark that the accountant must be prepared to draw up a clear and full report on the results of his whole investigation, in which he would set out all material factors bearing on the matters referred to him. I need scarcely emphasise the importance of presenting a report which can be substantiated as to facts and in which the manner of dealing with such facts is logically explained. A report which is confused and ill-arranged is often regarded as valueless, no matter how sound the opinions expressed therein may be.

Before leaving this section of my paper, I may say that, although purchase by agreement is perhaps not of so frequent occurrence, where the interests concerned are large, as purchase by arbitration, we have a comparatively recent instance in the amalgamation of the London dock undertakings under the Port of London Authority. The purchase price for the undertakings of the dock companies was fixed by agreement between the Board of Trade and the companies; and, I believe, the President of the Board of Trade, when explaining how the purchase price was arrived at, stated in Parliament that, on account of the uncertainty and expense attendant on public arbitration proceedings, the Government was not prepared to proceed with the scheme unless the principle of purchase by agreement was accepted by Parliament.

I will now pass to purchase by arbitration under the Lands Clauses Acts.

Many of the remarks I have already made will apply equally to this section of my paper, and I propose further to illustrate their application by a brief reference to the case of the Metropolitan water companies, which were acquired by the Water Board by arbitration under the Lands Clauses Acts. I have ventured to introduce this case as I think it will be more convenient to follow the principles which govern a concrete example rather than to deal with generalities only. For similar reasons, when I come to deal with arbitration under the Tramways Acts, I will refer to the recent case of the acquisition by the Post Office of the National Telephone Company's undertaking. Both cases are well known to the public, and the extracts I will quote are taken from the printed proceedings of the public inquiries. I propose to deal rather more fully with the Telephone case, as in the latter a reasoned judgment was delivered by the Court of Arbitration, which was not the case with the Water Board.

The Metropolitan Water Board was constituted under the Metropolis Water Act, 1902, and Section (2) of the Act provides that :—

> "The Water Board shall pay to each company as compensation for the transfer of their undertaking such sum as may be agreed on between the Board and the company, or, in default of agreement, as may be determined by arbitration under this Act."

Section 23 nominated Sir Edward Fry, Sir Hugh Owen, and Sir John Wolfe Barry to form the Court of Arbitration constituted under the Act, and Subsection 8 provided that :—

> "The Court of Arbitration shall determine the value of the undertaking of each Metropolitan Water Company as if, with the necessary modifications, the law of compensation for the purposes of the Lands Clauses Acts were applicable to the case."

As you will have observed, the Act made provision for the settlement of terms by agreement between the Board and the companies in the matter of purchase price, but advantage does not appear to have been taken of this method, and the Court was finally called upon to assess the price to be paid to each of the companies.

Under the provisions of the Act, the Arbitration Court had to determine the amount of compensation payable to each company for the transfer of its undertaking, but inasmuch as a company can only exist through its shareholders, the task which the Court had to accomplish was in effect to assess the compensation payable to shareholders. I make that distinction, because several of the Metropolitan water companies were restricted by statute from distributing in dividend amongst their shareholders more than a fixed rate on the subscribed capital, although, in certain cases, the maintainable income was considerably in excess thereof. Where such in fact was the case compensation would be limited to the capitalised value of the maximum statutory dividends, and not the capitalised value of the maintainable income. The dividend or income-earning capacity of the undertakings was the test of their value.

It is impossible to say what was the exact method adopted by the Court in attributing the values stated in the awards, as a reasoned judgment does not appear to have been given, but a broad indication may be gathered from the course of discussion before the Court and from the method in which the claims and counterclaims were drawn up. It would seem that the general course of procedure was to endeavour to establish the amount in each case of the maintainable income and subject to the question of surplus or undeveloped assets, liabilities as to future capital expenditure, restrictions as to dividends, &c., to apply a number of years' purchase to such maintainable income commensurate with its security.

The maintainable income of undertakings like water companies, with obligations for the supply of water to an ever-increasing community, is not an easy thing to determine, with fairness alike to the buyer and seller. Many considerations have to be taken into account, such as, on the one side, the imminence and probable productivity of additional capital expenditure to meet the requirements of the service, and, on the other, the prospect of enhanced profits owing to the progressive character of the business.

To illustrate the wide divergence of view which had to be adjusted by the Arbitration Court, I quote the following figures, taken from the proceedings in connection with one of the water companies. The company in question claimed as compensation a total of, approximately, £4,300,000 The Water Board, on the other hand, offered a sum of £1,500,000, or a difference of £2,800,000.

I observe from the printed proceedings in this case that the company's claim was prepared in the following manner :—

After giving a condensed account of the history and capital of the company, the statement of claim sets out the profits, as published, for the last financial year, and, in adjustment, adds thereto :—

(1) An allowance for unproductive capital expenditure; and

(2) Sundry adjustments.

Deductions were made for debenture interest, &c., and the balance representing the net income was compared with and showed a considerable excess over the maximum statutory dividend which the company was entitled to distribute. Then comes the statement of claim, as follows :—

(1) The maximum statutory dividend capitalised on the basis of an equivalent investment. (The rate taken by the company was 2¾ per cent., which is equivalent to 36.36 years' purchase.)

(2) An allowance for recoupment of loss of interest pending re-investment at 1 per cent. on the amount claimed, as compensation for loss of dividends.

(3) An allowance for cost of re-investment to cover brokerage and stamp duties, taken at 1 per cent. on the same figure.

(4) An allowance to cover costs, charges, and expenses incurred and to be incurred in consequence of the passing of the Act up to and including the dissolution of the company—taken at ½ per cent. on the above figure.

That completes the claim, and the important item in it is, of course, the amount claimed as compensation for loss of dividends. The company's contention, in effect, was that the maximum statutory dividend has been earned and distributed for the past twenty years, and further, that the net income, taken on the basis of the last year's results, showed a material excess over the amount required to pay the maximum dividend, and that therefore such dividend might be regarded as being well secured. The company asked for the income to be capitalised on the basis of an equivalent investment, and it will be found that the rate applied in the claim, namely, 2¾ per cent., or 36.36 years' purchase, represented approximately the average yield of trustee securities immediately before the outbreak of the Boer War in 1899. At the time of the arbitration markets had not had time to recover from the effects of the war. The other items in the claim call for no special comment beyond the remark that it is the usual practice to claim for an allowance under these heads, and consideration was presumably given to the claims in the final award.

Let us now turn to the answer of the Water Board to the claim of the company, as the two, read together, give a fair presentment of the divergence in view which usually exists between parties in cases of this nature.

The answer of the Water Board embraced objections under twenty-four heads, which may be summarised, broadly, as follows :—

(1) That the income as shown by the company's accounts, and also the maximum dividend, could not be maintained, because of :—

(*a*) Inadequacy in the sources of supply of water.

(*b*) Inadequacy in the charge for maintenance.

(*c*) Liability to competition.

(2) That effect should be given to the Sterilisation and Sinking Fund Clauses, inserted in recent Acts.

I should, perhaps, explain that a sterilisation clause is sometimes inserted by Parliament in Bills promoted by private undertakings, and, its effect is to withhold from the proprietors of such undertaking in the event of a purchase by a public authority, any gain or advantage which may subsequently accrue from the works or powers to be authorised by the Bill.

(3) The number of years' purchase, viz. : 36.36 years was excessive.

(4) The sums claimed as allowances for recoupment of loss of interest and costs of re-investment were excessive.

The summary I have given indicates the extent of cleavage between parties which had to be bridged by the Court of Arbitration. Evidence was led on each side from eminent members of our profession, and elaborate tables relating to the accounts, water consumption, &c. &c., were put in. The result of the arbitration in this case was that the Court awarded the company an amount which represented a reduction of approximately 20 per cent. on the company's claim, but no explanation was given in the award as to the reasons which influenced the Court in reducing the amount claimed by the company nor the directions in which the claim was affected.

If one might hazard a guess it is probable that the Court took the view that the maximum statutory dividend was not so well assured for the future as to justify the application of a rate of interest so low as that afforded by trustee securities such as Government and corporation stocks, railway debentures, &c.

I think that considerable weight was placed by the Court on the fact that, although the company was able to point to a prolonged period of prosperity there were indications that the demand for water in the district, owing to the continued growth of population, was likely shortly to overtax the existing sources of supply. The company's works, in themselves efficient and well maintained, were ill adapted for the purposes of extensions which, it was foreseen, would have to be made in order to meet the company's statutory obligations. These factors, although indefinite in character, would, if their probability became established, have a considerable effect on the minds of the arbitrators, and it is not unlikely that, in place of the $2\frac{3}{4}$ per cent. or 36.36 years' purchase, claimed by the company, a lower capitalisation, such as (say) $3\frac{1}{4}$ per cent. or about 31 years' purchase, was substituted.

Before leaving the subject of the Water Board arbitration cases, I wish to emphasise the nature of the consideration paid for the transferred undertakings. It was in effect compensation to the shareholders of the individual companies for loss of future income, due regard being had (1) to the stability and source of such income, and (2) to the liabilities for the maintenance of a public service attaching to companies of this nature. The consideration was not based upon the amount or then value of capital expenditure, except in so far as the assets represented by such expenditure were still undeveloped or partially developed.

Let us now turn to the last main section which I want you to consider, and that is, purchase by arbitration under the Tramways Acts, with special reference to the case of the National Telephones. Under this method, in contradistinction to the one we have just been considering, the question of income need not be considered, as the purchase consideration was based upon what is known as the "then value" of the assets transferable. The value of the telephone undertaking was assessed under the terms of a purchase clause, almost similar in wording to Section 43 of the Tramways Act of 1870, incorporated in the purchase agreement between the company and the Postmaster-General. Section 43 of the Tramways Act states, *inter alia* :—

> "Where the promoters of a tramway in any district are not the local authority . . . the local authority . . . may within six months after the expiration of a period of 21 years from the time when such promoters were empowered to construct . . . by notice in writing require such promoters to sell their undertaking . . . upon terms of paying the then value of the property and plant (exclusive of any allowance for past or future profits, &c., . . ."

The main terms of this clause were, with slight modification, incorporated in the telephone purchase agreement already referred to, and an almost similar clause appears in the Electric Lighting Act of 1888. The telephone arbitration will therefore have an important and far-reaching effect on the electricity supply companies serving the Metropolitan area, whose properties will probably be subject to an almost similar valuation on the expiry of their tenure in 1931, and it is possible that some of us here to-night may be intimately connected with the arbitration proceedings which are likely to take place about that date.

It would at first sight seem a hardship that a remunerative business worked up by the energy and foresight of a company should receive no consideration beyond the bare value of tangible assets, when it falls to be transferred to a public authority. As a matter of fact, however, these companies, under the operation of purchase clauses, have a fixed tenure of life which, in the eye of the law, is sufficiently prolonged to enable shareholders to reap adequate benefit from their enterprise in the shape of dividends during the period of tenure. At the end of the period of tenure a company would, under the provisions of the Tramways Act, get the then value of the assets, but no consideration for goodwill.

It has long been an accepted maxim in cases of this nature that the then value of property, plant, &c., *in situ*, adapted to the requirements of the business, shall be arrived at by ascertaining a figure of replacement cost and by deducting therefrom depreciation calculated according to the life and age of the respective parts. The principle is clear and simple, but, as you can well imagine, questions of a complex character arise in practice not only where the undertaking transferable is a large one, but also with smaller concerns. Consider the difficulties underlying the ascertainment of the replacement cost of the National Telephone Company's undertaking, a vast organisation covering, metaphorically, the whole of the United Kingdom. The method which the Telephone Company adopted in preparing its claim was to rely on its own experience of cost, for the reason that the greater part of the undertaking had been constructed by the company itself, and it was argued that the best evidence of the replacement cost was the actual cost. The Post Office, on the other hand, relied largely on evidence of well-known contractors, and also on its own experience as regards telephone construction. Shortly after the opening of proceedings both parties fell into line in agreeing that the arbitrators had to decide three main issues :—

(1) What should be fixed as the "plant cost," *i.e.* price of all materials, including cost of transport to the various sites throughout the country, and the cost of the labour in placing them in position.

(2) What should be added to the "plant cost" in respect of expenses of supervision, engineering, ordering and storing, cost of raising capital, interest during construction, obtaining wayleaves, &c., obtaining subscribers' agreements, &c.

(3) Having arrived at (1) and (2), the hypothetical replacement cost, what should be deducted in respect of depreciation in view of the fact that none of the plant that was being taken over was actually new.

The question of plant cost, as will be readily understood, introduced into the case an overwhelming mass of figures submitted by the company through its officials, as representing its actual experience, but fortunately during the Long Vacation, which intervened whilst the case was being heard, the parties were able to come to an agreement under this head.

As regards the second and main division into which the case fell, viz., the additions which should be made to "plant cost" in order to arrive at total cost, I propose to comment briefly on one or two of the items which may be of interest to you professionally and which from the reports of the case appear to have been the subject of considerable discussion. Let me, however, first deal with an interesting point which arose in connection with the method adopted by the company in preparing its claim.

The items of expense for which allowance was claimed were twelve in number, and in the statement of claim submitted by the Telephone Company additions were made in respect of these items to the agreed plant cost by means of successive percentage additions. The percentage addition for each successive item was taken not on the agreed plant cost figure, but on plant cost plus the percentages added for each of the preceding items on the list. Let me illustrate my meaning : for instance, head office administration came sixth upon the list, and the addition made in respect of that item was calculated on plant cost plus the sums already added for items 1, 2, 3, 4, and 5. This method, which has been termed the snowball fallacy, is open to the grave objection that, if any percentage addition be faulty, the error becomes magnified by each subsequent addition superimposed thereon. It will be appreciated that the allowance which should be made in respect of each head of expense could in any event be assessed approximately only, and that every endeavour should in consequence have been made to limit and confine as far as practicable the effects of possible errors. A sounder method would have been to base each percentage addition on an agreed figure.

As regards the items of expense added to plant cost in order to arrive at total cost, I propose to discuss two only, viz., cost of obtaining subscribers' agreements and cost of obtaining capital, inasmuch as the principle of their inclusion in the cost of plant was not accepted by the Court without considerable discussion.

Those who have had the good fortune to be subscribers to the National Telephone Company will probably recollect entering into an agreement with the company as to conditions of service, &c. I am afraid I am not aware of the steps which used to lead up to the signing of these agreements, but apparently they gave rise to considerable expense, which had to be paid by the Telephone Company, and in their statement of claim the company included, as part of the cost of plant, the costs of obtaining agreements with current subscribers. The Postmaster-General objected on the grounds that the cost of obtaining agreements could have no relation whatever to the value of plant and equipment. With the latter view the Court disagreed, for the reason that, unless permission were duly obtained from subscribers, the instruments and connections could not legally be placed in position without constituting a trespass. It was held, therefore, that it was a necessary step in the construction of plant to obtain these agreements, and that the cost of obtaining them was an element in the cost of plant. I must say I find it difficult to appreciate to the full the arguments in favour of including this item as part of the construction cost of plant. It might well be regarded as being somewhat akin to the cost of advertising which a commercial company might incur in establishing or extending the sale of its manufactures. The benefits which flow from successful advertising are directly reflected in increased revenue earnings, and the same may be said of every new telephone agreement obtained. If the cost of obtaining such agreements is to be considered as a capital charge it might, in my opinion, not unfairly be regarded as forming part of the goodwill of the business which in transfers of this nature is expressly excepted from the consideration payable.

The other question to which I would refer is whether the cost of obtaining capital is an element in the cost of plant. On this question the Court was divided, and I think I can best indicate the view of the majority by quoting an extract from the award.

> "The method described by the House of Lords for ascertaining value is to consider what it would cost to construct the plant. It has been said that the cost of obtaining capital cannot be an element added to the value of the plant. The thing transferred here is the plant *in situ*, and the cost of construction, less depreciation, is the method by which the value has to be ascertained. It follows that every expense which is necessary in order to construct is an element to be considered, and it has to be considered because it is necessary in the process of construction."

The majority therefore held that the cost of raising capital was an element in the cost of plant.

As representing the opposite view, the following is an extract from the judgment of one of the arbitrators, who differed from his colleagues as to the propriety of including this item as part of the cost of plant :—

> "To find out what it would cost to construct is one of the steps to ascertain the value of the plant. It seems necessarily to follow that only those expenses which bear on the value of the thing constructed can be properly so taken into account. These expenses, forming the actual cost of construction, having been

> ascertained, represent the value. That value has then to be expressed and paid in the current coin of the realm. How or where that current coin is obtained, or what is paid for obtaining it, has nothing in the world to do with the value of the thing which is the subject-matter of the payment."

These are the opinions of eminent men directly differing on a question of principle as to what may or may not be included as part of the cost of plant. If I may venture to express an opinion, I agree with the view that the cost of raising capital is an element in such cost. The argument for the other view assumes, first of all, the construction of the plant, and secondly the payment for it. But, as we all know, the expenditure on the construction of a large piece or pieces of plant is incurred from day to day, and the money has to be found *during* construction, otherwise the plant would never be completed. It appears to me one of the *vital* factors in construction that capital in the shape of current coin is ready and available from time to time as required to pay for obligations incurred, and without such capital the plant could not be constructed. Therefore, to my mind, the reasonable cost of obtaining the requisite capital must be regarded as forming part of the cost of plant.

There is now left to consider only the last and final main division into which this interesting case was divided, viz.:—

> What should be deducted from the hypothetical replacement cost in respect of depreciation, in view of the fact that none of the plant that was being taken over was actually new?

I need not enlarge here on the facts which have to be determined before depreciation can be calculated, viz., the cost, life, and age of plant. As regards the life, it was argued in this case, on one side, that the physical life was the proper one to adopt, and, by the other side, that the effective life was the correct one to take. The physical life of plant is the period during which it would, if properly maintained, continue to perform the services required of it. The effective life is a shorter one, which introduces the question of probable or possible obsolescence. On this question the Court was unanimous, and it decided that the physical life was the proper one to take for the purpose of calculating depreciation in cases of this nature. It was pointed out that consideration could only be given to obsolescence where in fact it had been proved to exist, otherwise questions would be introduced which could not be supported by any evidence other than hope or expectation.

The cost and life of the plant having been determined, and its age proved by evidence, all the factors material to a calculation of depreciation were available. There had then only to be determined the principle upon which depreciation should be taken. Two methods were advanced for the consideration of the Court. The first method, the one adopted by the company, sought to measure depreciation on the principle that, if a sinking fund were created and invested at compound interest, at any period during the life of such plant the amount of the accumulated sinking fund would represent the measure of depreciation. This method may be illustrated by a curve, the slope of which is slight during the early period of the life of the plant, but whose gradient becomes progressively more steep as the life advances. Accountants are familiar with the method as applied to the depreciation of leasehold properties, and also in the amortisation of mortgage debentures of public companies. It is not used, I believe, by public companies for the depreciation of plant in their books, but I understand that engineers frequently apply the principle when asked to advise whether it would be more economical to replace existing plant with a more modern and up-to-date article. It was urged against this method that a sinking fund, dependent upon compound interest, would not represent the actual depreciated value of the plant until the last penny of compound interest is earned, viz., at the very end of the period of life, and that any curtailment in the operation of the compound interest period would prevent the accumulated fund being a measure of depreciation at that date. The other method, the one advanced by the Post Office, may be termed the straight-line method, which is perfectly familiar to us in commercial practice. By it the plant is considered to depreciate equally from day to day and year to year throughout the period of its life. This was the method finally accepted and applied by the Arbitration Court, and I think it will be agreed that in comparison with the other there are fewer objections to be urged against its adoption. It is impossible for anyone to assess in figures the exact measure of depreciation at a given moment; all methods must to a certain extent be approximate, and the straight-line method is not immune from criticism, but it is a common-sense way of dealing with the problem, and it does not open up such a wide field for the possibility of error as the sinking fund method. Those who are familiar with the operation of sinking funds well know how heavy is the accumulation of the fund in the later years, and were plant to be depreciated on that principle any mistake in estimating the life of the plant—and such are bound to occur in practice—would have more far-reaching effects than if the straight-line method were employed.

That, gentlemen, brings us to the end of our consideration of the Telephone case, which I trust I have not dealt with in too great detail.

We have discussed to-night the course of procedure usually adopted when the purchase price of an undertaking is fixed by agreement; we have seen that where arbitration is resorted to under the Lands Clauses Acts the fundamental basis of the purchase price is the revenue-earning capacity of the undertaking to be transferred; and, finally, we find that the purchase price of an undertaking transferable under Clause 43 of the Tramways Act of 1870, or under similar provisions, is what is known as the "then value" of the assets, which, according to established practice, has to be assessed by ascertaining the replacement cost and making a suitable deduction therefrom in respect of depreciation.

The Progress of Ideas in Municipal Accountancy.

By J. H. McCall, F.S.A.A.
(Borough Accountant, Croydon)

A paper read at the annual meeting of the Institute of Municipal Treasurers and Accountants (Incorporated), held at Folkestone, on 30th June and 1st and 2nd July.

My friend and predecessor, Mr. Gunner, has urged me on several occasions, in view of my exceptional experience as he was pleased to call it, to prepare a paper on the progress of ideas in municipal accountancy. In the meantime, Mr. Carson Roberts has published his book on the Accounts of Local Authorities, which happily provides me with a text for a paper on the subject. Before introducing this subject, it is perhaps necessary for me to strike a personal note in order to elucidate the opinions which I may express.

The Influences at Work in Commercial Accountancy.

Twelve years ago I left the municipal service, and if I can correctly recall my impressions of that day, I think I may claim to have been moulded to the municipal type. I had passed such examinations as were usual. I was very much impressed with the dignity of the Institute, and most important of all, I was firmly convinced that the municipal accountant, by his professional training and experience, was sufficiently equipped to compete with the commercial accountant in his own domain. It was with these feelings that I started to work for one of the largest firms of Chartered Accountants in the City of London. My eight years' experience with that firm was sufficient to correct false impressions of the past, and what is more important than even that, it gave me the opportunity of seeing the activities of accountancy applied to commercial concerns. I hope my remarks will not be thought derogatory to great cities like Liverpool, Manchester, and Birmingham when I say that the City of London is the real home of accountancy. The reason for this is that it is the home or headquarters of every conceivable kind of business, national and international. Many of the great industrial concerns of this nation have their head offices in London. There are the great financial houses which cluster round the Money Market; there are the great financing companies with their tentacles in every other country in the world. In addition to these great English limited companies, there are the great United Kingdom branches of foreign houses, and last but not least, the companies and agencies in which the United States element is predominant. In the midst of all these financial, commercial, and international agencies of work, the accountant takes a very important part. In fact, the practising accountant in the City of London must be prepared to deal with every conceivable class of accounts. Much could be said about the romance of business, and perhaps some day a man, with the necessary imagination and talent, will write the romance of accountancy. It is our part, however, to observe the forces at work which have raised accountancy from its obscure origin and placed it in the front rank of the commercial professions, which play so very important a part in the business of the Empire.

First of all, I think the commercial accountant owes a great deal of his success to the atmosphere which is already created for him in the great business world. He comes into close touch with the great captains of industry; with daring financiers and keen adventurers; with an unlimited variety of businesses, all operating for the main object—money making. In this world the race is to the swift and the battle to the strong. The highest price is paid for brains and ideas. In addition to these factors the ever-changing circumstances of business, with its rapid development and its frequent variations, demand from the accountant methods that must be flexible, elastic and adaptable. He must not go to the market with old-fashioned ideas and cut-and-dried methods unless he desires to be relegated to the side-streets with other pieces of antique. There is, further, a considerable formative influence in the profession by reason of the accountants themselves being brought into close touch with one another. This influence is more potent than lectures or other means of disseminating ideas, for it may be justly claimed that the greatest accountants in the City of London are just those men who have no time for academic discussions. The commercial student of accountancy is thrice blessed if it is his lot to be cast so favourably in the City of London. He lives in the right atmosphere of progress; he receives the influence of great men; and he is particularly favoured with the very fine literature of his profession.

I think I may say without fear of contradiction that the brain output of any society is the measure of its strength and efficiency. In any association of men whose interests are peculiar and similar the result has always been, in civilised countries, literature on the subject. We can say without hesitation that the literature of the commercial accountant has always been sufficient for present-day purposes. With the proper atmosphere, with the influence of great examples, and the benefit of an excellent library, it cannot be wondered that accountancy as a profession has developed so favourably in the commercial world.

These, gentlemen, are the impressions made upon my mind during my eight years' experience in the City of London. By the curious element of chance, I returned to municipal service two years ago. My early impressions of the municipal service had almost been effaced from my memory, and I came back to it strongly imbued with commercial ideas, so I think it will be of interest to you if I relate how I regard municipal accountancy from this new standpoint.

Adverse Conditions in Municipal Accountancy.

In the first place, I can see that the conditions under which the profession of municipal accountancy is developing are very different from those conditions which obtain in the commercial world. No one can say that the operations of the municipality, even if the trading undertakings are included, are conducted with the business view of making money. The personalities who are most active in its sphere take no personal risks and have no capital involved. The ratepayer is a very different kind of being to a shareholder; consequently administration has become not a means to an end, but the end itself. I am glad to think, however, that the profession is well represented in its leaders, and in this respect may compare very favourably with the commercial branch of the profession. Our geographical position presents a difficulty which it is difficult to overcome. It is not possible for that daily contact and association of ideas which has proved so great an element in the success of commercial accountancy. I have been particularly interested in gathering up the literature of the past ten years, and am astonished at the miscellaneous output which loses a great deal of its value because it remains miscellaneous. My impression is that very much more could be done and should be done in the future in the direction of official publications. If individuals are too busy, or if they are not sufficiently inclined to produce publications at their own personal risk, then I think something might be done in producing official publications on every branch of the municipal accountant's work through the medium of the Institute. I venture to suggest that if that had been done in the past we should not have been in the present unpleasant position of not being in possession of a municipal library of accountancy which does justice to the intelligence possessed by the members of the profession. I have met here with a great difficulty with regard to my position. When I was appointed I was told by the Finance Committee that they had chosen a man with business experience with the object of putting "some ginger" into a large department. I am not sure that I really appreciate what is meant by putting "some ginger" into a department, but I think I understand that one of the right and proper things to do is to encourage one's staff to educate and qualify themselves in their work. In this matter of education I was very disappointed to realise what a small library we have dealing with the various aspects of municipal accountancy. However much financial officers have been losers in this matter, there is not the slightest doubt that the auditors of Corporations, whether professional, or auditors of the Ministry of Health, have suffered from the same cause It is not to be wondered at, then, that after many years of waiting, a district auditor should have ventured on the production of a book which professes to deal with the accounts of local authorities. Personally, I think Mr. Carson Roberts is to be congratulated upon his effort to supply a need—that is, some volume which can be placed in the hands of every audit clerk on the staff of the Ministry of Health.

I think it will be recognised that clearly there is need for some reform in the matter of account-keeping of local authorities. One only has to consider the appalling number of rules and regulations issued from Government Departments, with their limitations and restrictions, which, were they made to applv to commercial affairs, would be sufficient to strangle any business. It is curious to see how little the representatives of the ratepayers are trusted to use their common sense in the spending of their own money. The ratepayers, one would think, have an inherent right to spend their own money according to the wishes of the majority; but the Government says that they may subscribe to a joint fund, and then may only spend it in a certain way subject to innumerable regulations. No commercial concern is treated in this manner. Take, for instance, the question of borrowing money. The Government says the local authority may borrow money for certain purposes, and at the same time places innumerable difficulties in the way of borrowing that money. A banking concern may borrow an unlimited amount of money on merely receiving it over the counter, and, in many cases, not even giving a formal receipt or acknowledgment. A local authority must for every amount that it borrows from individuals execute a mortgage deed and pay stamp duty. This may serve as a very good illustration of the monstrous method of conducting business with the aid of a plentiful supply of red-tape. We have received just recently the financial regulations setting forth the rules for the keeping of the accounts of an Assisted Housing Scheme. There is not only the separation of accounts demanded in consideration of the Ministry of Health audit, but a schoolboy's catalogue of particular accounts which must be kept; all this emanating from the department of the Government which apparently is regardless of any economy in the spending of tax-payers' money. In my opinion, the axe should be laid at the root of the tree—we need more simplification and less Government control in the affairs of local government; and it has been suggested that, if the huge staff that is employed on this unnecessary legal control could be turned on to the departments who are responsible for the national waste, their time would not be wastefully employed. I think it is well to bear this in mind before considering what Mr. Roberts has to tell us in the matter of municipal accountancy.

The Scope of Carson Roberts "Accounts of Local Authorities."

His book covers a wide field, taking in its stride the principles of bookkeeping, organisation of accounts, financial matters, and auditing. It is difficult sometimes to separate the matters falling under these respective headings, and it must be admitted that the whole question of accountancy is viewed from the somewhat restricted standpoint of an auditor. The publishers tell us that the book has been prepared primarily for use by district auditors, and those qualifying for appointments as district auditors, and although the book is published with the concurrence of the Local Government Board, it must not be assumed that the opinions and suggestions which it contains have necessarily received official approval. The author in his preface states that his object is "to get at the "problems and difficulties which abound in the accounts "of larger authorities, to discuss options and important "openings for variations of practice, and to deal with "the questions of principle of a financial as well as of an "accounting order." He states that these problems have as yet received little or no attention in the books dealing with accounts, and with this statement I am in full agreement. He recognises that he is dealing to a large extent with debatable matters, and that he feels "it "would be absurd to expect the suggestions offered or the "solutions put forward to appeal to every reader, even "when supported by argument." There seems to be a touch of sarcasm here, for he goes on to say that, in dealing with some questions he "has not hesitated to depart "from the beaten tracks, or even to question official pre-"cept or regulation." It may be in this case he is thinking, not of municipal accountants, but of district auditors and other officials of the Ministry of Health. We will now specifically examine what Mr. Roberts has to say with regard to bookkeeping.

Questionable Bookkeeping Points in the "Recognised System."

His first chapter deals with what he calls the general outline and structure of the "Recognised System." It comes somewhat as a shock to read that there is a recognised system at all, and one is quite curious to learn to what extent this system has received recognition. He states in the second chapter that the system, that is, the recognised system, is, "in so far as "its components have been developed, in complete accord "with the regulations issued by the Local Government "Board wherever the method of bookkeeping has been "developed in Accounts Orders—for instance, in relation "to Income Accounts and Poor Relief Expenditure "Accounts." It is also "recommended for general "adoption in the ordinary Rate Fund Accounts by the "Committee appointed in 1906 to report thereon." Up to this point, at any rate, the system may be described as the recognised system. We therefore find that what is called the recognised system is one which has parts in accord with regulations, and parts recommended by a Committee so far back as 1906.

An examination of the system itself will show how far it has been recognised by the great corporations. For instance, in his classification of books and documents, the primary books of account include *Debtors' Accounts* and *Creditors' Accounts*, and by this Mr. Roberts means not some summary of debtors and creditors prepared for the purpose of completing the accounts at the end of the year, but personal accounts which are operated upon right through the year, as "it is from the personal "accounts and from them alone that the actual liability "and asset balances are carried to any Balance Sheet." Now I venture to suggest that if this is part of the official recognised system, it has not been adopted in most of the large corporations which are not subject to the district audit. On the question of *separate banking accounts*, I am very pleased to see that we have no talk of advantages and disadvantages, but a distinct opinion "that separate "banking accounts are never advantageous, leading as "they do to unnecessary confusion and elaboration." Mr. Roberts would have one Cash Account for loan money, and the details of expenditure of course set out in the detailed Ledger Accounts. "Separate banking accounts for loan money" he tells us, "may safely be described as a misguided effort whenever they occur."

Loan and Capital Accounts. In dealing with capital expenditure we may safely say that Mr. Roberts is fairly astride his particular hobbyhorse. No method of stating capital expenditure seems satisfactory to him; even the commercial system is unappropriate, assuming, as he does, that the capital assets in the Balance Sheet are shown at what is supposed to be their current value—that is, at their original cost less the estimated depreciation. The secret of the author's standpoint is to be found in the word he uses to describe capital expenditure, that is, "deferred" expenditure. It would be well for us to examine closely what is intended in this particular phrase.

Capital Expenditure in the commercial sense means the expenditure necessary to place a company or firm in a position to earn revenue. In the case of a company this expenditure includes not only money provided by shareholders, but raised by mortgages, debentures, or other forms of loans, sometimes referred to as Loan Capital. The term "capital expenditure" as applied to Municipal Authorities has its root idea in the economic and commercial theories, but is necessarily restricted by legislation. For practical purposes it may be taken to mean all expenditure for which a sanction to borrow the necessary money may be obtained. Where money has actually been borrowed it is described in the Government forms as "expenditure out of loans." As the principles which have governed the decisions of the Government to sanction the borrowing of money are not inconsistent with commercial ideas, it seems to me somewhat futile to describe any of the expenditure out of such loans as deferred expenditure. So long as we understand capital expenditure in this sense and record it as such in our books, there does not appear to me to be any cause for alarm; but the author seems to think that a Balance Sheet should be a statement of liabilities and assets, the assets being split up into two categories—the first relating to what he calls abiding or realising assets, which may be stated on the Balance Sheet at their original cost, and a second class of assets generally relating to the Rating Fund, which he ungrammatically calls deferred expenditure. These should be placed on the Balance Sheet at the original cost less the amount of loan repaid at that date. No other method will suit Mr. Roberts; even the commercial Balance Sheet is full of faults in his opinion. We may well ask what it is that produces this particular dogma. It seems to me that Mr. Roberts thinks erroneously that a Balance Sheet is a statement of liabilities and assets. In his exemplification of a Balance Sheet arrangement he draws the line at what he calls "Total Liabilities" and "Total Assets," and places under the line Fund Balances, Surpluses, Deficiencies, Reserve Funds, &c., and he says "There can be no doubt that balances "of all kinds would be rendered far more intelligible "and useful, especially if fund balances in hand, such as "Reserves for Contingencies, Redemption, Renewal, or "Depreciation Funds were not mixed up with the liabilities, and if the deficiencies were not classed as assets; "much the best plan is to show them for what they are, "as the balancing items of the Balance Sheet, and this is "done most clearly by adding surpluses below 'Total "'Liabilities' and deficiencies below 'Total Assets,' "just as the balances of the ordinary personal accounts "and fund accounts are shown."

To build on a fundamental fallacy like that is asking for criticism. In the commercial world a Balance Sheet is taken to be a classified summary of the debit and credit balances in a set of books. The great aim in setting out the Balance Sheet is to so describe each set of balances that there is no misunderstanding on the part of anyone who reads such Balance Sheet. This seems to be a much better way than the adoption of a cast-iron classification which is open to all sorts of objections.

There are many other instances which illustrate the statement I made previously, that, however much the system described is recognised elsewhere, from the point of view of being put into practical operation by the great Local Authorities it cannot be said to have received such recognition.

The Organisation of Accounts—Questionable Points.

When we turn to the questions of the organisation of accounts, we find a very wide divergence of opinion. Mr. Roberts throughout his book strongly insists upon the keeping of *personal accounts*. I may say incidentally that I am in agreement with him in this respect, although I do not attach the same importance to it. He would have all tradesmen's invoices filed away alphabetically so that they may be easily checked over with the credit entries in the Tradesmen's Ledger. He would go a step farther and cut out of the system any *expenditure Analysis Books*, and have in their place analysis columns in the personal accounts, the totals of such analysis columns being posted periodically to the expenditure accounts in the Ledger. Now this method, I think, so far as I have been able to gather, is an unknown one in the commercial world. I believe there are one or two Metropolitan Boroughs which have adopted it, and from what I can hear, it works very well. But what is at the bottom of the idea? Simply this. Arrangements to make the work of auditing the accounts easy. The whole question of organisation is looked at from the standpoint of an auditor who has had no practical experience in the keeping of accounts. Every auditor knows in his own heart that fifty per cent of the work performed by his staff is "swank." Much of it could be cut out, but whether it is desirable to cut out any of it is quite another matter. It is plain on the face of it that if you cut out your expenditure analysis books and confine the audit operation to an examination of the personal accounts from a legal standpoint, it would be very satisfactory to a district auditor. Another matter which is emphasised by Mr. Roberts is the importance of having *one cash account* for practically all purposes. "Attempts to maintain cash separation," he says, "upon which the less "efficient accounting systems of the past largely "depended almost invariably lead to confusion. "Attempts to use Cash Accounts as guides invariably "lead to delay in the completion of those Ledger Accounts "which can alone act as true guides to the financial "position of any fund. This serious defect always "results from any useless duplication in account keeping. "The above remarks apply to columnar separation as "well as to the plan of keeping several Cash Accounts." When he comes to the splitting up of the cash for the Balance Sheet purposes, he says, "All that it is necessary to do is to list on the last page of the Cash Book "the several items which are separately shown upon the "Balance Sheet, and agree their total with the general "cash balance." In his opinion "the idea that each "Cash Account separation aids Ledger balancing by providing opportunities for sectional treatment is quite "unfounded. The fact is, it makes balancing more diffi-

"cult." Here again, the point of view is that of the auditor. In my own experience, an audit clerk considers an undue number of pass-books attaching to any system of commercial accounts as a great nuisance—and perhaps he is right. But, after all, systems of accounts are not modelled with the view of making the work of an auditor easy, and this principle is recognised in commercial circles. There are differences of opinion as to the advisability or otherwise of keeping separate accounts at the bank, and it seems to me that the auditor who dogmatises on this subject, and who is without knowledge of what is involved in keeping and balancing the manifold accounts of a great corporation, loses very much in his general argument. I think the few matters enumerated will be sufficient to show that there will be considerable difficulties to overcome before the system laid down by the author can be recognised—if ever it can be—by the large Local Authorities.

The Theory of Double Entry Restated.

Now let us turn to the point of view of the author with regard to the theory and practice of accounting in its application to the accounts of Local Authorities. The author thinks that insufficient attention has been given to the theory and principles of double entry. He says that "The theory should not be neglected, for it is only "those who have fully grasped the theory and princi- "ples of this system as well as its purposes and results "who are able to state what new accounts should be "opened in the Ledger to deal with each new set of "transactions or facts which come to be recorded; to "decide what is the correct debit and what the correct "credit for each item, including extraordinary as well "as the ordinary; to clear up the confusion into which "any set of Ledger Accounts has been brought; and to "explain why corrections are necessary. These are the "powers which the district auditor must possess in order "to be fully equipped for his work." He tells us that the double-entry system was designed in the 15th century or even earlier; he might have added that the knowledge of it has taken half a millennium to reach the Ministry of Health. He says, "The clear expositions of "these principles do not abound in works on account "keeping." So far as I have been able to gather from my own reading, very clear expositions have been given of the principles of double entry which have been available to the student of accountancy for many years past. He is correct, however, when he thinks that in the great majority of cases the system is learnt from Ledgers kept by others. "Thus practice or custom comes to be "regarded as law by the student; but knowledge of prac- "tice or custom is of little help when new facts outside "the ordinary scope present themselves, and the confused "and meaningless entries which are so often met with "in Ledger Accounts are very often attributable to this "defective training." He would supply this supposed deficiency by stating in his own peculiar way the theory underlying bookkeeping by double entry. Following on his outline of the principles of double entry, he sets out in detail the principles which should govern the keeping of Ledger Accounts. It is rather curious that when he criticises the method of recording entries through the journal, instead of relying upon his exposition of the theory, he says, "Journals of this nature "have no place in the system with which we are con- "cerned, and the results just described are a clear "contravention of the requirements of the Local Govern- "ment Board." I think, perhaps, it would have been better if he had not mentioned the requirements of the Local Government Board in an attempted scientific explanation of the principles of double entry.

"Make-shift Methods" of Accounting Officers Criticised.

The author makes a vigorous attack upon the makeshift methods of accounting officers. He points out two defects which he considers the most dangerous, and at the same time the most prevalent in the accounts of Local Authorities, which are to be found on the income side. They are (1) Failure to keep the primary records which are necessary for securing a complete account of income and (2) Failure to keep clear and proper accounts with the debtors, and to present a continuous record of outstanding claims. He points out that the practice of keeping Cash Ledgers supported by Income Account Books is the reason for this failure. "The Ledger system," he says, "limited to cash transactions, could "in theory be accompanied by a full set of Income "Account Books and primary records, but in practice "one omission almost invariably leads to another, and "makes it a very difficult matter to prevail upon the "accounting officers to require the authorities to keep "the necessary accounts and records." In dealing with Expenditure Accounts he is even more emphatic in his protest against the prevailing practice, that is, of posting from Cash Accounts and adding on liabilities at the close of the financial period. "It is clear this cannot "rank as an adequate system because it does not keep a "record of accounts with tradesmen; moreover, there is an "indefensible duplication of charge which has to be "compensated by a set of entries to which no proper "meaning can be attributed." He would have separate accounts with tradesmen which could be directly referenced from the Trade Ledger to the expenditure accounts running throughout the year, claiming that it is of "value to accounting officers in so far as it gives a "better opportunity for detecting double charge, "deviation from agreed scale of charge, arithmetical "errors in extension, and omission of trade discounts and "allowances for returned empties or of other credit items."

Rate Collection Recommendations.

By far the most important portion of the book is devoted to an examination of the present systems of Rate Accounts. Here Mr. Roberts is at his best, and although much of what he says with regard to waste duplication applies to rural parishes and other small authorities, he does not hesitate to condemn in the main the whole system at present obtaining in the matter of rate collection. This criticism is, of course, not directed against accounting officers, but against the complicated rules and regulations of Accounts' Orders which have emanated from time to time from the Local Government Board. Mr. Roberts looks forward to the time when separate rating bodies will cease to be appointed for rural parishes, when the district will be the only rating unit throughout the country. This change will probably be accompanied by a unification of the rating authorities and of the rates themselves in the urban areas such as that which took effect in the London boroughs at the beginning of this century. These changes would result in reducing the rating authorities from a little under sixteen thousand to under two thousand, and make a much greater reduction in the number of rates levied. He anticipates another change which is highly probable, and that is "the "giving effect to special reliefs granted to railways, "&c., in the valuation instead of in the collection column "of the rate books. At present these reliefs involve the "making of separate accounts of different patterns of a "considerably complicated design—sometimes three rates "in one parish." But without waiting for these important and necessary changes, many things can be done, in his opinion, by means of certain modifications and alterations in the present systems. He strongly advocates "that wherever two authorities are collecting "rates in one area, wherever different collectors make "demands upon the same ratepayers, and wherever "different rates are separately levied or dealt with in "separate sets of account books, though by the same "officers, there is room for a great improvement of system. "The existing separations involve considerable duplica- "tion of work, and multiplication of demands, which is "more objectionable from the ratepayer's point of view "by reason of the much greater risk of error, leakage or "loss." He would set up a revenue office distinct from the collecting staff and directly supervised by the chief accountant of the authority or by the chief revenue officer. This officer and his staff should have no part in the handling of the cash, but the work should be such as to establish the correctness and promptitude of all accounts kept by collecting officers, including the cashiers of the central office. He sets out in detail what he considers to be the duties of collectors and the duties of the rating office. All this, of course, is pure theory, but the most important part of his book is the suggested change from the form of the rate book itself. He would split it up into two or three books, taking the small rate book, with which is combined the valuation list, the irrecoverable rates book, and the recoverable rates book. I think a great and useful work will be attained by Mr. Roberts if, in drawing attention to this very important section of account keeping of Local Authorities, he uses influences with the powers that be to initiate reforms of the system itself, and to allow more freedom in the matter of the bookkeeping.

Financial Problems Discussed.

Mr. Roberts in his chapter on financial problems makes reference to one or two points of interest. "The main objects," he says, "of all legislation connected with the regulation of local finance have been :—

(1) To prevent any postponement of charge or of payment whereby a part of the burden proper to a financial period is cast upon the ratepayers of a later period.

(2) To secure an equitable distribution of cost in all cases where the benefit of expenditure extends over a considerable number of years.

(3) To limit the rate of expenditure by a particular authority or upon a particular object, or

(4) To secure proper distribution of charge as between different funds or different groups of ratepayers.

Most of the statutory provisions and decisions thereon are directed to protect future ratepayers from being charged with debt incurred before their time, but there are a few which protect present ratepayers from being overburdened; it is always the cash and not the revenue position which the law has brought under review in this connection. It is no longer date of payment which governs the incidence of charge in the accounts of the more important local authorities; it is the revenue position which is dealt with in the accounts." "With these divergent principles in operation, it is not surprising," he says, "to find that the safeguards have ceased to be appropriate." He sees some difficulty in relation to bank over-drafts, and suggests that "provision for a working "balance is clearly the first purpose to which the pro- "fits of any trading undertaking should be applied; and "it may be right to assume that this is implied on a "reasonable interpretation of the statutory clauses relat- "ing to the disposal of such profits." "The power to "include in rating estimates sufficient reserve to cover "contingencies also appears to be desirable." Mr. Roberts also deals with loans and sinking funds, and strongly advocates the application of sinking fund accumulations to new capital purposes. His notes on income-tax add nothing new to the stock of common knowledge on that subject. I do not think Mr. Roberts himself would claim originality for many of the ideas incorporated in his work, and I venture to suggest he has largely drawn upon all the available literature of the last twenty years. As the object of this paper has been generally to trace the progress of ideas in municipal accountancy, it may now be asked how far this book has gained a place in the development of such ideas. The processes in the evolution of an idea are fairly simple. In the first place it must be born in the mind of some individual. Its struggle for existence depends upon the mental ability of that individual to express the idea intelligently. The growth of the idea depends upon its ability to stand the test of criticism; and also depends upon its self-evident usefulness. Writers of books need not necessarily be persons with original ideas, but they serve a very useful purpose if they make a collection set out in some scientific arrangement. Mr. Roberts has, if I may say so, gathered his ideas, some of which are excellent. If I might say a word of criticism as to the arrangement of the book, it does not rank high in the literature of accountancy for two reasons. First, the language of the book is not the language of accountants; he uses phrases in relation to accounts that are unheard of in the world of accountancy; many of his paragraphs are too heavy and involved in their structure to be of much use to the student. In the second place, the arrangement of the book, in my opinion, is not scientific. The principles of bookkeeping, financial problems, the organisation of accounts and audit matters are mixed up together from beginning to end.

Conclusions Drawn from the Points Discussed.

This leaves us, gentlemen, very much where we were at the commencement. There is not the slightest doubt that there is an abundance of ideas which have been expressed and discussed from time to time, but, if I may say so, the real principles of pure accountancy have been buried beneath the litter of extraneous subjects. I venture to think that the legal aspect of things in the future will be relegated to its proper place, and that for the dogma of standardisation and uniformity there will be substituted the primary principles which underlie all systems of accounting. In conclusion, on behalf of the students of this Institute in whom I take the keenest interest, I should like to say one or two things about the examinations. The "final" covers three days of six hours each. On looking at the last examination papers I find that six hours are applied to questions on bookkeeping and accounts, three hours to local authority finance—if it can be called finance—three hours to auditing, and no less than six hours to law. In my opinion too much time is devoted to this so-called law section. The enormous amount of study necessary for this section seems to be out of all proportion to is usefulness, and most of the time expended might be much more usefully devoted to the study of the principles of bookkeeping and accountancy on a broader basis.

It is without doubt very necessary for the student to possess a knowledge of those branches governing his acts as an officer in the Finance Department of a Local Authority. I quote from the syllabus, but how many officers in the finance department are really concerned with matters requiring a knowledge of the law of realty, the study of which might very well occupy the labours of a year.

I would also suggest the cutting out of the law of property so that the "Honours" subjects might be compulsory and not supplemental.

I take this opportunity, gentlemen, of thanking you for the opportunity of ventilating what are my private opinions, and to say for the information of a larger audience that my views regarding the book of Mr. Roberts are not to be taken as having received the official approval of the Institute.

The Published Accounts of a Municipality.

By SYDNEY LARKIN, Esq., A.S.A.A.
Assistant City Treasurer, Coventry.

A lecture delivered to the members of the Midland Students' Society of the Institute of Municipal Treasurers and Accountants (Incorporated), at the Council House, Coventry, on Saturday, 24th April 1920, Mr. Harry Lord, City Treasurer, Coventry, in the chair.

1. *Introductory.*

This subject is approached from two points of view (which, although in practice separate, are fundamentally the same), viz. that of the student preparing for examinations and that of the financial officer whose duty it is to construct the accounts of a municipality for publication.

It is essential that a candidate sitting for an examination in accountancy should have very clear and distinct ideas as to the principles on which accounts are drawn up, and should be able to apply those principles without hesitation to the various questions with which he may be faced in the examination room.

As regards the financial officer, he, too, should naturally be guided by the same idea of what he is undertaking, but he should also be actuated by the constant desire to follow his accepted principles more closely, and, if it is apparent that the principles formerly followed are wrong, to change them. By these means alone can published accounts be brought to the highest level of conciseness and usefulness. They will also automatically tend more and more to uniformity.

An essential preliminary to carrying out the line of action here indicated is the critical study of the accounts of one's own and other boroughs with a view to adopting the best methods of expressing the result of the operations which the financial officer is daily recording.

2. *Purpose of Published Accounts.*

In addition to carrying out the requirements of the Municipal Corporations Act, the published accounts serve two purposes. Primarily, they inform the public as to the financial position of the borough, and, secondly, they afford to the official a useful and ready means of reference for various particulars wanted from day to day.

The form in which the accounts are published should, therefore, in view of the first-named purpose, be one of the greatest possible simplicity, and, in view of the second purpose, should nevertheless contain all essential information in its most convenient form.

3. *General Arrangement.*

Although a municipal corporation is one body, and for that reason the accounts should be drawn up with such a degree of uniformity as will enable its financial position as a whole to be seen, yet its activities are so varied that it is both necessary and convenient to show the accounts of each separate section as complete in itself. It is desirable, therefore, that the various sections should be arranged in some logical sequence in the volume containing the published accounts.

The following arrangement is based on that idea :—

1. Preface or introduction.
2. General summary of Income and Expenditure on Rate Accounts.
3. Borough Fund Account.
4. Accounts subsidiary to the Borough Fund.
   Free Libraries Account.
   Education Committee Account.
   Police and Police Pension Fund Accounts.
   Exchequer Contribution Account.
   Accounts of Trading undertakings connected by law with the Borough Fund.
5. District Fund Account.
6. Accounts subsidiary to the District Fund, e.g. those of Trading Departments connected by law with the District Fund.
7. Loan Accounts, common to both funds.
8. Aggregate Balance Sheet.
9. Statements of Loans, &c.
10. Index to Contents.

It will be found that items peculiar to different localities can generally be fitted into the above arrangement.

The accounts of the Education Committee, although recording part of the expenditure out of the borough rate, are so evidently distinct that it is not thought that there will be much difference of opinion on the question of their separation from those relating to the Borough Fund. The total amount paid out of the proceeds of the borough rate for the purpose of education would, of course, be included in the Borough Fund Account. The same remarks apply to the Police Accounts, which, at present, are required to be restricted to cash receipts and payments.

The above outline shows the general arrangement of the accounts. It is necessary next to consider the most reasonable method of setting out the different parts of which each of the above sets of accounts is built up. The order adopted is largely arbitrary, but the following appears to be justified on chronological basis :—

1. Loan Account.
2. Capital Expenditure Account.
3. Revenue, Net Revenue and Appropriation Accounts.
4. Reserve Fund Account and any other subsidiary or suspense accounts required by local circumstances.
5. Balance Sheet.

Both the general arrangement and the detailed arrangement are points of comparatively minor importance. They are, however, matters which are worthy of consideration, and the value of an abstract of accounts may be somewhat impaired by the lack of principle in building up the volume. In any case, whatever detailed arrangement is decided upon should be applied strictly to each set of accounts.

In this survey of the subject, the items mentioned will be considered in the order suggested.

4. *Preface to Abstract of Accounts.*

It is a fairly general practice for the detailed statement of accounts to be prefaced by a report or general statemetn by the treasurer. This, in many instances, is in stereotyped form year by year with the necessary alteration substituting the new figures for the old. It frequently gives, in such cases, the expenditure and income of the various committees of the Council with the loans outstanding, perhaps comparing the results with those of the previous year. The outstanding feature of this type of report is its dulness. The persons who are really interested in this sort of thing will extract the information and make the comparisons for themselves ; those who are not interested will probably fail to have their interest aroused by the style of document one has in mind. A preface is, in any case, only read by a few, but it may be presumed that those few are worth providing for. It is therefore suggested that an effort should be made to put, each year, some distinctive note into this part of the abstract. It is an opportunity that should be taken to call attention to (*a*) any improvement in the form or arrangement of the accounts, as compared with previous publications ; (*b*) any outstanding financial feature of the year, e.g. the effect of some particular legislation either local or general, or of some particular event or change of policy ; (*c*) in the absence of anything that would come under (*a*) or (*b*), or in addition to them, an analysis of the cost of a special branch of the municipality's activities. The aim should be to make the preface " live," the success or otherwise of the effort depending, of course, to some extent on the author's personality.

This part of the abstract is also a convenient place in which to introduce certain statistical information. It is desirable that the statistics should not be lengthy, but should be confined to items which are almost certain to be required by the various officials and others in the course of their duties. The following might well be included :—

1. Area of the borough.
2. The population at the last three census dates and the present estimated population.
3. Total rates in the £ levied in the borough during the last ten years, distinguishing the separate rates, and showing any differential rates.
4. Rateable value and produce of a penny rate during the same period.

Voluminous statistics should be avoided in the same way as voluminous accounts. They defeat their own objects. Similarly, the preface or introduction should be concise.

5. *General Summary of Income and Expenditure on Rate Accounts.*

There are two types of individual who study abstracts of accounts, viz. those who are interested in details and take no notice of the broad features of the accounts, and those who take a more intelligent view of the financial affairs and wish to have before them the whole position at a glance.

The point in connection with local authority finance most frequently lost sight of is that the local bodies are spending bodies first of all, and that only part of the money spent is raised by local rates or local services.

The form of summary statement here submitted is designed to show the total expenditure—whether out of rates or out of imperial subsidies. It also shows exactly how the money provided by the rate has been utilised.

A similar statement would be drawn up for the District Fund Revenue Account.

BOROUGH OF BLANKTOWN.

General Summary of the Borough Fund Revenue Account for the year ended 31st March 1920.

Committee	Income other than rates and Government Grants	Expenditure	Net Income		Net Expenditure			
					Out of Local Rates		Out of Imperial Taxes	
			Amount	Rate in £	Amount	Rate in £	Amount	Rate in £
	£	£	£	Pence	£	Pence	£	Pence
Baths	4,146	6,146	—	—	2,000	1.00	—	—
Education	6,972	120,978	—	—	58,000	29.00	56,006	28.00
Estates	3,042	2 103	1,839	.92	—	—	—	—
Finance..	1,207	14,992	—	—	11,854	5.93	1,931	.97
Markets	4,255	2,863	1,392	.70	—	—	—	—
Watch	2,858	27,421	—	—	14,345	7.17	10,218	5.11
Water	4,000	—	4,000	2.00	—	—	—	—
	27,380	174,503	7,231	3.62	86,199	43.10	68,155	34.08
	Deduct—Net Income..				7,231	3.62		
					78,968	39.48		
	Income in excess of Expenditure for the year				1,032	.52		
	Amount raised by Rate				80,000	40.00		

6. *The Double Account System.*

Before proceeding to discuss the first section in the detailed accounts which, in the suggested arrangement before mentioned, is called the "Loan Account," it may be remarked that that account is placed first because, at the first inception of an undertaking, it is usual to borrow the money necessary to acquire it. This does not apply to the rate funds, but, inasmuch as uniformity of arrangement is a convenience, the same principle is advocated.

The term "Loan Account" may not be a familiar one. The usual account including the record of loans is one called the "Capital Account," and is used in the method of presentation of accounts known as the double account system. By the irony of fate, possibly because the word "double" is used in each, this system has achieved a reputation for orthodoxy as solid as that of double entry. The system is based on the separation of capital and revenue items and depends for its existence on various statutory and other prescribed forms of accounts incidental to public undertakings. The idea underlying the separate statement of the Capital Account (in the form so familiar to all) was that it might be clearly shown that the money raised for the purpose of acquiring capital assets had been so utilised, and that the balance only, which was brought into the General Balance Sheet, was used as "working" capital.

Having regard to the fact that the loans raised by a municipal corporation are for specific purposes, it would appear that the inventors of the double account system had hit upon a method of presentation of accounts most suitable to such a case, and a great majority of accountants have adopted that view. The fact is, however, that the form of the double account system, as originally devised, is not at all suitable to the accounts of a local authority, and the attempts on the part of financial officers to adapt it are highly ingenious.

The special points arising in connection with the Capital Accounts of a local authority are :—

1. The loans are raised for specific purposes, and there is no balance for working capital. Any loan raised for that purpose would be treated quite differently in the accounts.
2. The loans are gradually paid off.
3. The expenditure out of loans is of varying character and in some cases is of such a nature that its retention in the Balance Sheet is purely temporary.
4. Capital assets are acquired by other means than by expenditure out of loans.

These points, in the main, were not apparently in the minds of the original framers of this system. One of the reasons for not adopting the double account system for ordinary commercial Balance Sheets is that no provision is made for depreciating the assets. *Per contra*, it might be said that it is equally unsuitable for municipal accounts on account of the difficulty of showing the gradual liquidation of debt.

To illustrate the unsuitability of the form of the double account system, the following example of a "Capital" Account has been extracted from an abstract of accounts :—

CAPITAL ACCOUNT.

Dr. For the year ended 31st March 1919. *Cr.*

	Expenditure to 31st March 1918 Expended during year	Expended during the year	Total to 31st March 1919		Receipts to 31st March 1918	*Additions or §Reduction during year	Total to 31st March 1919
	£	£	£		£	£	£
To expenditure to 31st March 1918	692,235	—	692,235	By Loans	556,155	* 5,000 § 3,450	557,705
" Extensions	—	5,675	5,675	" Loans repaid	151,179	* 3,450	154,629
			697,910				
Less—Plant abandoned			3,484				
" Total expenditure..			694,426				
" Balance of Capital Account			17,908				
			£712,334				£712,334

In order to indicate the various methods of dealing with this form of account and the serious endeavour made by accountants to cope with the difficulties involved, it is worth mentioning that, in this instance, the amounts carried to the Balance Sheet were £694,426 (total capital expenditure) and £712,334 (total loans raised). In the same volume from which the above form was taken there were other Balance Sheets giving figures corresponding to £694,426 (total capital expenditure) and £557,705 (loans outstanding) in one case, and £17,908 (balance of Capital Account) in another.

The above example is rendered comparatively simple by the exclusion of all details, but it is still not easily understood by the average lay student of accounts, nor does it (except in the case where the balance of the Capital Account is transferred) have any proper connection with the Balance Sheet. In the other two cases the "account" so-called is merely a statistical statement explaining two items in the Balance Sheet.

7. *Loan Account.*

There are two reasons for departing from the ordinary practice of mixing up capital expenditure with loans received in published accounts. One is that the relationship between the two gets smaller as time goes on. As is pointed out later, all expenditure of a municipal corporation is, strictly speaking, expenditure out of revenue. It may be thought desirable to spread the cost of any particular item over a period of years, and the most convenient method of doing this is to raise a loan for the purpose. The loan having been repaid, however, the expenditure in question is simply expenditure defrayed out of revenue and bears no relationship to the loans of the corporation, i.e. the existing loans. This would lead one to inquire at what stage the framers of the example of a "Capital Account," as shown above, would cease to accumulate the total of loans received as shown on the right-hand side of the account. There is one point in the specimen account given which is worth preserving, viz. the Loan Account (for such it is) is given without recourse to the ordinary debit and credit arrangement, the words "additions" and "reductions" being used instead. In the specimen Loan Account given below, which would, of course, be taken from the Ledger, a similar nomenclature and arrangement is adopted.

LOAN ACCOUNT.

For the year ended 31st March 1919.

	Balance at 1st April 1918	Transactions during year		Balance at 31st March 1919
		Increase	Decrease	
	£	£	£	£
Redeemable Stock	140,000	—	—	140,000
Annuities (Capitalised) ..	10,000	—	—	10,000
Short Term Mortgages ..	230,000	5,000	1,000	234,000
Instalment Loans	156,155	—	2,000	154,155
Capital Money Appropriated	20,000	—	450	19,550
Totals	£556,155	£5,000	£3,450	£557,705

The balance at 31st March 1919 would be carried to the Balance Sheet and the whole account is comparatively simple. That is the second reason for departing from the usual form of account.

8. *Capital Expenditure Account.*

The debit side of the old "Capital" Account is treated in a similar manner. The following example will give the information required. As has been pointed out, capital expenditure is not necessarily paid for out of loans, and the two matters should not be confused.

CAPITAL EXPENDITURE ACCOUNT.

Dr. For the year ended 31st March 1919. *Cr.*

	Expenditure to 31st March 1918	Expenditure during the year	Total to 31st March 1919		
	£	£	£		£
To Expenditure	692,235	—	692,235	By Plant abandoned (during year)	3,484
" Extensions	—	5,675	5,675	" Balance carried forward	694,426
	£692,235	£5,675	£697,910		£697,910

The balance carried to the Balance Sheet is £694,426 and is also carried forward to next year's account. It is, in addition, made quite plain that the plant abandoned was an item of that particular year.

The points in this account are (1) that all capital expenditure, whether out of loan or out of revenue, is debited to it; and (2) that it shows all reductions in the total expenditure whether by sale, by being scrapped, or by any other means.

9. *Revenue Accounts of Rate Funds.*

The great variety of items comprising the rate funds affords corresponding scope to the skill of an accountant in drawing up the Revenue Accounts so as to show in the clearest manner the cost of, or income accruing from the various services. Generally speaking, the interest of the public lies in the detailed items of the Rate Accounts rather than in the results thereby differing from the interest shown in the accounts of the trading undertakings, where the results are all-important and the details ignored. The reason for this is, of course, that the Rate Accounts are made up of a great number of small sub-accounts, each of which may be regarded as complete in itself.

It therefore becomes apparent that, in drawing up the Rate Fund Revenue Accounts, care should be exercised that the classification and analysis adopted is such as to afford all information that could reasonably be looked for in the most concise form.

The transactions attributable to the funds are, in the first instance, related to various committees of the Council, and the income and expenditure of each committee should be so arranged as to lead up to a separate total. The order in which the different committees are placed is often fixed arbitrarily, but there is no reason why a regular arrangement should not be adopted, and an alphabetical arrangement would appear to be almost the only one for which any advantage can be claimed. This is particularly so where all committees are on one fund.

Then, again, a committee may control various departments or its financial transactions are naturally grouped under separate main heads of account denoting particular services rendered. Each of these departments or services should give its separate total, so that its financial result is clearly shown.

The classification and analysis to which income and expenditure are subject will bear some relationship to the annual local taxation return and to the various returns made to Government Departments in respect of claims for grants. It is desirable that the published accounts should show all the information necessary for the local taxation return and, although the detailed returns for grants will be made up from the books of the corporation, their heads of account will be, in many instances, too minute for the published accounts. In such cases the general headings only would be published.

In order to bring the accounts into line with the local taxation return it is suggested that the income from investments of sinking funds (and any other extraneous item paid into the sinking fund in the course of the year) should be shown on both the income and the expenditure side of the published account. This will enable a figure to be shown for each department representing the whole of the provisions for repayment of debt during the year and not merely the amount provided out of revenue.

In framing Revenue Accounts an attempt should be made to standardise the heads of account, not only as to their nomenclature but also as to the order in which they run. This may appear to be a matter of small moment, but it facilitates reference, and it is of a great convenience in the actual work of bookkeeping. From the point of view of " elegance," also, some congruity should be preserved in the arrangement of heads of account.

The columnar form for Revenue Accounts will be found suitable in all cases where there are several similar branches of the same department or committee. It is recommended not only on account of its general conciseness, but also to enable the comparative results of the branches to be clearly shown. The columnar form of Revenue Account is applicable to—

Housing schemes.
Libraries.
Bathing establishments.
Hospitals.
Cemeteries.

Some abstracts of accounts are amplified by the inclusion of the results of the previous year, or, in some cases, the estimates of the current or succeeding year. These additions of the accounts are of doubtful value and tend rather to confuse the lay mind.

10. *The Balance of a Revenue Account.*

An annual Revenue Account, in its clearest form, shows the result for the year and the surplus or deficiency is carried to the Balance Sheet, where its net effect can be seen. If the practice is adopted of bringing forward to the Revenue Account the balance of the previous year, the actual result of the year is obscured. This applies more particularly to a Rate Fund Account. In the case of a trading undertaking the more strictly correct method may be followed of carrying the balance of the net Revenue Account to an Appropriation Account, which will show in what manner the surplus is disposed of or the deficiency made good as the case may be. If a balance remains on this account it may be carried forward to the next year's Appropriation Account.

11. " *Profit and Loss.*"

Attention may be drawn to the use of the above terms in municipal accounts. Owing to the peculiar nature of these accounts as regards questions of reserves for depreciation and similar matters and the effect of sinking fund provision on the finances of an undertaking, it is perhaps not fitting that words of such exact meaning in the popular mind as " profit " and " loss " should be used to express the amount by which the recorded income for the year exceeds or falls short of the recorded expenditure. " Surplus " and " deficiency " are in more general use and are more elastic in their interpretation.

The " Profit and Loss Account " of the commercial world is, by almost common consent, the " Net Revenue Account " in municipal affairs.

12. *Revenue Accounts of Trading Undertakings.*

It is hardly possible to deal adequately with this branch of the subject. Standard forms have been suggested and are generally adopted either wholly or in a modified form. It is well to add that there should be a clear distinction in the system of bookkeeping between income and expenditure, and the published accounts should show the gross figure in all cases except those in which refunds or other similar items are clearly more properly treated as deductions from income or expenditure. As an example, reference may be made to the income from gas residuals, where, as is well known specific expenditure is incurred to produce the income. The method sometimes adopted of debiting, in the books, this expenditure to the Trading Account of the particular residual in respect of which it was incurred and carrying to the Revenue Account only the " profit " shown on that account, is not only productive of illusory figures but it also rather spoils the effect of the whole account. This is only by way of illustration. The same principle is sometimes adopted in regard to other items, such as works executed for customers.

A supplementary item, often inserted in the accounts of trading undertakings, is the " per unit " figure for each item of income and expenditure. Good as may be the intention of the accountants who adopt this feature, the method will be regarded by students of costs as altogether too crude to be valuable.

13. *Income and Expenditure and Receipts and Payments.*

The general rule for municipal accounts is that they should be kept on a system of income and expenditure and their publication would follow the same basis. Income and expenditure should, however, not be followed too closely. In some accounts receipts and payments are much more convenient, e.g. Exchequer Contribution, Police and Police Pension Fund, Reserve, &c., Funds, and Trust Funds.

There are, too, many other items encountered in different places in the accounts which are more usefully confined to actual receipts and payments, or to a modified form of income and expenditure. The great point to be kept in mind when dealing with municipal accounts is that there is no question of profits involved, in the sense in which profits are regarded in an ordinary dividend earning concern.

Dividends and interest on investments are an example of income which is conveniently confined to receipts. The only exception to be recommended is where a dividend is due within the financial year but for some reason does not arrive. Credit would naturally be taken for the amount due. Another example was found during the recent war, where certain sums were claimed from the Government in respect of occupations of premises and other things. In the majority of instances the actual sums received were the nearest approach to income that could be arrived at. Government grants, too, are much more usefully treated on a cash basis.

The subject of this paragraph may possibly be thought to be outside the scope of the matter under consideration, and to relate more to accounting than to publication, but it is desirable that some discussion should ensue as to what meaning should be attached to the words income and expenditure. To adopt a strict interpretation is not only a difficult matter, but it would seem also either to detract from the utility of the information given or to be a perfectly futile procedure. The question of rents receivable will serve as an example. Let it be assumed that the following rents are due on the dates named :—

		Amount due.
Jan. 1	Half-yearly rents	£100
Feb. 2	Annual rents	100
	Half-yearly rents	300
June 24	Annual rents	100
July 1	Half-yearly rents	100
Aug. 2	Do.	300
		£1,000

It is submitted that for the purposes of the accounts of a corporation it is sufficient that income of £1,000 is brought into account for the year, the various items being credited as and when due. But to treat the matter as one of " income " in its strictest form it is also necessary to bring into account, at the 31st March, roughly,

9 months of annual rents due 24th June ;
3 months of rents due 1st Jan. ;
and 2 months of rents due 2nd Feb.

If no change has taken place during the year, the same amount is involved at the beginning as at the end of the year, leaving the income at £1,000. That means extra work with no result. If, on the other hand, an additional annual tenancy is created on the 1st January, for example, there would be three months' rent accrued due on the 31st March, which might be regarded as income. Seeing, however that nothing is due or receivable from the tenant in the financial year closing, what advantage can be claimed by bringing in the quarter's income and introducing a fictitious debtor, who, so far as one can see, owes nothing ?

14. *Income Tax.*

From the point of view of income-tax, the published accounts are, of course, of great importance, inasmuch as they serve as the basis on which assessments are made. It is, therefore, desirable that the accounts should be, so far as possible, in suitable classification to enable the income-tax authorities to make their computations without the necessity of asking for long lists of particulars and other matters explanatory of the items printed in the accounts.

It is, however, in the actual statement in the accounts of the amounts paid by way of income-tax that there appears to be scope for improvement, or, in any case, some consideration.

In the first place, it is perhaps well to remember that income-tax is a tax on income and, therefore, an appropriation of part of the income (either real or imaginary) of the corporation. It is, in the second place, to be noted that there is only one income-tax and only one corporation, although the corporation may have to submit to two or more separate assessments, depending on the number of " funds " which, by law, it possesses.

In some specimen forms of published accounts issued by the Institute of Municipal Treasurers and Accountants a few years ago, items of expenditure occurred in the various Revenue Accounts called "rates and taxes." This expression is often met with in abstracts of accounts. Sometimes it is enlarged into " Rents, Rates, Taxes, and Insurance." It will, probably, not be seriously contended that income-tax is of the same nature as rates, from whatever point of view it is regarded. It is clear that income-tax cannot be called a working expense (as expenditure on local rates undoubtedly is), and that since it is a tax on profits it should appear separately or in the Net Revenue Account along with other items which are similarly charges on the gross profits of an undertaking. If, as often happens in the case of small trading undertakings in particular, there is no charge on the concern for income-tax, none would appear in the accounts. In these cases, of course, the assessed profits are less than the interest, and one is led to consider whether it is not more correct to treat the income-tax of any one fund as a whole. This is, no doubt, a question of bookkeeping rather than one of the presentation of accounts, but the two matters are not unconnected. The suggestion that, after all, it *is* one corporation we are dealing with, and one income-tax, is rather repugnant to some persons, who are always terrified lest some advantage might accrue to one department at the expense of another. This attitude was exemplified some years ago by the arguments that raged over the question as to whether stock should be transferred at par value or at issue price, when redemption funds are utilised in lieu of borrowing. The principle suggested here is that if, for example, there is no net charge for income-tax on the District Fund Accounts of the corporation, no charge for income-tax should appear in, say, the accounts of the gas undertaking, which forms part of the district fund. If, on the other hand, a net charge exists, the various departments liable should be arrived at by the process of elimination of those which (on their own basis) are not liable. The actual charge should be apportioned among the departments in proportion to the liabilities respectively shown when treated individually. The amounts of tax payable in respect of " non-trading " properties in the corporation's own occupation would appear to be proper items to be deducted and separately stated before the apportionment is made, these payments being more in the nature of an imposition than a tax on income.

15. *Subsidiary Accounts.*

Theoretically, every Balance Sheet (by means of its accompanying accounts) should show continuity with the one preceding it. To attain that end it would be necessary to publish separate accounts for each item in the Balance Sheet, treating them in exactly the same way as is customary in the matter of the Loan, Capital Expenditure, and Revenue Accounts. Such a procedure would, however, so burden the accounts with unnecessary detail that it is not one likely to be followed, although some published accounts (chiefly relating to gas undertakings) treat sundry debtors as a separate account, and occasionally detailed Stores Accounts are shown. Nevertheless, such accounts as Investments, Cash, Stores, Debtors, and Creditors are generally not shown in detail, inasmuch as they are only component parts of the Capital, Revenue, Sinking Fund, Reserve Fund, and other Accounts, all of which would be separately published, showing the connection between one year and another and between themselves.

16. *Sinking Fund, &c., Accounts.*

Sinking Funds and Redemption Funds are generally part of a common fund in respect of the whole of the mortgages or stock of the corporation. Where there are Sinking Fund moneys in hand, it is considered necessary to show separately the portions of the Sinking Fund relative to particular departments or funds.

BOROUGH FUND SINKING FUND ACCOUNT.

Dr. For the Year ended 31st March 1920. *Cr.*

	£			£
To Loans repaid during the year	8,000	By Balance brought forward..		5,200
" Balance carried forward	1,700	" Contributions during the year:—		
		Town Hall ..	£500	
		Asylum	1,000	
		Police Station ..	3,000	
				4,500
	£9,700			£9,700

It is not desirable to complicate an account of this nature with details of cash in hand, &c. These particulars appear in the Balance Sheet.

If the Sinking Fund is formed in connection with loans raised by means of short term mortgages, it is probable that the whole of the fund in hand will be utilised each year in the redemption of debt, and in that case, of course, a separate Sinking Fund for each set of accounts is redundant. The amount appearing in the Loan Account as a reduction in the amount of loans outstanding would agree with the amount stated in the Revenue Account or Net Revenue Account, as the case may be, as provision for repayment of debt.

The correct statement of the Loan Account and Sinking Fund Account, together with the corresponding entries in the Revenue Account and Balance Sheet, is intimately connected with the detailed loan statement usually inserted at the end of the published accounts and will be again referred to.

17. *Reserve Fund Account.*

Here, again, a plain statement of the balances at the beginning and end of the year, together with the transactions during the year, is all that is necessary.

RESERVE FUND ACCOUNT.

Dr. For the Year ended 31st March 1920. *Cr.*

	£		£
To Renewal of Works ..	25,000	By Balance brought forward	23,000
" Loss on realisation of investments	100	" Contribution from Revenue	10,000
" Balance carried forward	9,000	" Dividend on 5 per cent. War Stock	500
		" Dividend on Corporation Stock	500
		" Bank Interest	100
	£34,100		£34,100

The chief reason for stating the interest accruing to the fund in detail is to show at a glance what is taxed and what is untaxed.

18. *The Balance Sheet.*

The Balance Sheet is the point where the results of all the various transactions are brought together and their general effect on the finances of the fund or undertaking is shown. In the construction of a Balance Sheet there is a great diversity of practice both as to principles and as to form, and the usefulness of the document is thereby largely affected.

A Balance Sheet, in the commercial world, is generally recognised as a more or less tentative statement drawn up at a certain point in the history of an undertaking, and often does not represent the facts of the case or even anything approaching them. In an ordinary non-municipal undertaking there is always the question of the disposable value of the business, either as a going concern or in liquidation, and Balance Sheets appear to hover between the two extremes, which are, of course, always possibilities.

The properties* of a municipality, however, are not of the same nature, and the question of disposable value does not enter into the minds of the persons responsible for the accounts. It will be apparent, therefore, that the Balance Sheet of a municipality can approximate the truth to a greater extent than can that of an ordinary concern, and at the same time retain its usefulness.

19. *Basis of Valuation of Capital Expenditure.*

The Departmental Committee appointed in 1906 to inquire into the accounts of local authorities were "strongly of opinion that original cost, when known, "is the only satisfactory basis for the statement of the "values of assets on the Balance Sheets; and this view "is acted upon by almost all local authorities." The Committee, however, suggested that the distinction between capital expenditure on assets which have "an abiding or realisable value" and capital expenditure on works, "the permanent retention of which on the Balance Sheet would be undesirable," should be duly noted on the face of the accounts, and further suggested that the latter class of capital expenditure should be written down each year by the amount of repayment of the corresponding loan.

This course does not appear to add to the simplicity of the accounts from the point of view of the public nor to add to their clearness from any other point of view. So long as the capital expenditure is shown in sufficient detail, indicating fully the items on which the expenditure has been incurred, any attempt to explain to the public that "Erection of Hospital, £10,000," represents an asset of abiding value, while "Widening High Street, £10,000," is of another class of expenditure, is obviously superfluous. When it is also remembered that the original cost of widening High Street was £20,000, the statement becomes useless.

The recommendation of the committee to divide the capital expenditure into two classes was no doubt due to the confusion of thought caused by the insistent impression that a corporation is always likely to be absorbed or wound up with certain financial results to the shareholders.

It is not likely that anyone would be deceived by the nclusion of all capital expenditure at cost. The fallacy of the committee's recommendation lies in the words "permanent retention on the Balance Sheet." It would not be suggested that either the hospital or the widening of High Street should figure "permanently" on the Balance Sheet. A destructive fire would be an effective cause of the removal of the hospital therefrom, and the total repayment of the loan would operate in the case of the street widening. The recommendation that the expenditure on street widening should be written down by the amount of loan repaid, besides causing a useless value to be assigned to the expenditure year by year, would act in diverse ways, depending on the terms of the loan raised for the purpose. An equal instalment loan, an annuity loan, and a fixed term loan would all give different results, and while in the case of the first two the accounts would show the amount yet requiring to be provided out of revenue, the third case certainly would not.

It may, therefore, be laid down that all capital expenditure should be included in the accounts at cost price and, in the case of expenditure which is represented by works of a non-realisable nature (a description which is sufficiently accurate to convey a fairly exact idea of the class of expenditure referred to), should be continued at that figure until the whole of the loan has been repaid. When the redemption is complete the expenditure should be

*It will be understood that this statement does not refer to such asset as are usually disposed of by a local authority.

written out, together with the corresponding amount of debt redeemed.

Where, however, the expenditure is represented by a real asset (such as land, buildings, machinery, &c.),the cost price should only be retained so long as the asset continues to "live." If at any time it, or any portion thereof, is sold, destroyed, scrapped, or otherwise brought to the end of its existence, a corresponding adjustment should be made in the Assets Account. No alteration should be made in the records relating to the respective loan and its repayment until the repayment of the loan has been fully provided for. The clearness of the accounts would be seriously impaired by an attempt to adjust the Loan Account to the reduced value of the asset. In the circumstances mentioned it would, of course, be proper to make any provision that might be necessary to clear the loan off by means of a transfer from other funds, such as Reserve or Revenue, and, no doubt, that course would be pursued in practice.

In most cases the asset will be maintained during the whole of the period of the loan and will, therefore, remain in the Balance Sheet at its original figure. When the appropriate loan is wholly repaid the asset will have been provided out of revenue and should be described as such, the amount of debt redeemed in respect thereof being transferred to the account generally known as Capital Expenditure defrayed out of Revenue.

In this connection it may be remarked that the account "Capital Expenditure defrayed out of Revenue," is strictly limited to expenditure on a fixed and definite asset. Revenue expenditure on a strip of land thrown into the street (for which it is decided not to borrow) would not be credited to that account.

20. *Valuation of Investments.*

The valuation of investments of municipalities is a matter to which attention has been given on many occasions during recent years, but it does not appear that anything has been accomplished, generally speaking, beyond calling attention, by means of foot-notes, to the fact that the market value of the securities mentioned in the Balance Sheet is considerably lower than that actually assigned to them in the accounts. That course of action, sufficient though it may be from the auditors' point of view, does not affect the situation, since it leaves things exactly as they were before. If the Balance Sheet states that the Reserve Fund of a certain undertaking amounts to £100,000, wholly invested, and a foot-note to the Balance Sheet intimates that the market value of the investments allocated to the Reserve Fund is £66,000 it means that the Balance Sheet is incorrect and that the Reserve Fund is actually £34,000 less than it is stated to be. It is difficult to justify the retention of the investments at their original figure in such a case, particularly as the adjustment necessary to exhibit the true position involves no more than a book entry reducing the sum standing to the credit of the Reserve Fund by the amount of depreciation that has taken place.

The matter has, however, a more serious aspect when it is regarded from the point of view of a Sinking Fund. Where the Balance Sheet states that the amount of Sinking Fund available is £100,000 (wholly invested, as before) and the foot-note calls attention to the "estimated market value," a state of affairs is indicated which demands a remedy. If the justification of retaining the valuation at £100,000 is difficult in the case of the Reserve Fund, it is surely impossible in the case of a Sinking Fund. It is, in fact of the highest importance that deficiencies in the market value of investments of this nature should be written off out of revenue year by year. It may be contended that the market value will perhaps recover before the realisation of the investments is necessary. In that event, the corporation will certainly not be in any embarrassing position by reason of the low book value of these assets.

The distinctive feature of these investments is that they are held, primarily, for the purpose of conserving certain principal moneys and not for producing income. Where, therefore, it is essential that the value of the principal should remain intact it may be taken as a rule that any depreciation should be made good.

There is, on the other hand, a different class of investment which is, as a matter of fact, made for the purpose of producing income and which is only on rare occasions liable to be sold in the market, and there is no advantage obtained in adopting any other than the cost price for Balance Sheet purposes. The commonest examples of this class occur in bequest funds and in the Police Pension Fund. Another example occurs in the investments

BALANCE SHEET NO. 1.

Liabilities.	£	*Assets.*	£
Capital—		Capital—	
Loans outstanding	144,000	Capital Expenditure	200,000
Sundry Creditors	1,000	Cash in hand	5,000
Loans Repaid	50,000		
Expenditure defrayed out of Revenue	10,000		
	205,000		205,000
Sinking Fund—		Sinking Fund—	
Amount available	11,000	4 per cent. Victory Bonds	10,000
		Cash in hand	1,000
	11,000		11,000
Reserve Fund—		Reserve Fund—	
Balance of Fund	12,000	4 per cent. Funding Stock	10,000
		Cash in hand	2,000
	12,000		12,000
Revenue—		Revenue—	
Sundry Creditors	2,000	Sundry Debtors	2,000
Bank Overdraft	6,000	Stock of Materials	8,000
Surplus	2,000		
	10,000		10,000
	£238,000		£238,000

BALANCE SHEET No. 2.

Liabilities.			£	*Assets.*		£
Loans outstanding			144,000	Capital Expenditure		200,000
Sundry Creditors—		£		Sundry Debtors		2,000
On Revenue Account..		2,000		Stock of Materials		8,000
On Capital Account		1,000		Investments—	£	
			3,000	4 per cent. Victory Bonds (Sinking Fund)	10,000	
Surplus—				4 per cent. Funding Stock (Reserve Fund).. ..	10,000	
On Revenue Account..		2,000				20,000
Capital outlay defrayed out of Revenue..		10,000		Treasurer—		
Provision for Repayment of Debt—	£			In hand on Capital Account	5,000	
Loans Repaid	50,000			Do. Sinking Fund Account	1,000	
Sinking Fund available	11,000			Do. Reserve Fund Account	2,000	
		61,000			8,000	
Reserve Fund		12,000		Overdrawn on Revenue Account	6,000	
			85,000			2,000
			£232,000			£232,000

belonging to the Borough Fund which have been acquired out of the proceeds of the sale of corporate estate and from other sources. In this instance, investments are sometimes realised and, when that is done, the actual excess, if any, of the book value over the amount of cash realised should be charged against the current year's revenue.

21. *The Form of the Balance Sheet.*

There are many forms in which a Balance Sheet may be constructed, two of which may be noted here as being typical. One is that in which the various "sections" of the Balance Sheet are treated distinctly and separately balanced, and the other is that in which the assets and liabilities are classified according to their character, irrespective of whether they may be earmarked to any particular "section." The usual "sections" are Capital, Sinking Fund, Reserve Fund, and Revenue.

Each type has its adherents, but it is rarely that the first-mentioned is carried out in its entirety, the division being usually confined to Capital and Revenue.

Examples of the two forms are appended.

There is not much doubt that the second form has something to recommend it from the point of view of simplicity, and, although the first example is elaborate in its explanation of its analytical correctness, it is not the prime function of published accounts to teach people how to dissect a Municipal Balance Sheet. It should, of course, yield to such dissection, and the second example does this. There are two further points in favour of the simpler form, viz.: (1) It conforms more to commercial usage—an aspect which may appeal to some people—and (2) the number of main headings is reduced to a minimum, thereby greatly facilitating the preparation of an Aggregate Balance Sheet in an intelligible form.

It is important that, whatever form is decided upon, strict uniformity should exist in all the Balance Sheets in any one volume of accounts, with a view, of course, to their ultimate collation in the statistical table known as the Aggregate Balance Sheet.

22. *The Aggregate Balance Sheet.*

This is simply a summary of the various Balance Sheets, and, in itself, bears no relationship to the accounts. It cannot be said to be of any particular value even for the purpose of forming an opinion of the general financial position of the corporation, in spite of the fact that it is generally for some such purpose that the Aggregate Balance Sheet is drawn up. The totals, however, form an imposing array, and, so long as individual Balance Sheets are constructed in a sufficiently concise form, there is no difficulty in its preparation. It should naturally be in columnar form (a form which gives it whatever value it may claim) and so occupies a single opening in the volume of accounts.

23. *Loan Statements.*

The detailed statement of loans should be made to fit in with and amplify the particulars as to the provision for repayment of debt given in the accounts. No undue economy should be exercised in allocating space to this important section of the published accounts. Although not actually part of the accounts, as such, the loan statements are of the highest importance, and any annual abstract not including such statements loses much of its value. It is essential, however, that the statistics should be so arranged as to be intelligible and easily referred to, and, to carry this out, it is well studiously to avoid anything in the nature of a large folding sheet which often so largely figures in this part of an abstract. The particulars may be repeated, if necessary, in various forms, under different groupings, so as to give at a glance whatever information is likely to be required.

The first grouping would show the detailed loans, &c., relevant to each separately published section of the accounts and would give information on these lines:

Columns—

1. Sanction—
   (*a*) Purpose.
   (*b*) Date.
   (*c*) Amount.
2. Loans, &c., raised—
   (*a*) Date.
   (*b*) Amount.
   (*c*) Term.
   (*d*) Source of borrowing, &c.
3. Amount provided for Repayment—
   (*a*) To beginning of year.
   (*b*) During year.
   (*c*) To end of year.
4. Amount remaining to be provided for.

In the case of a trading undertaking, a single plain statement is sufficient and would lead up to totals corresponding with figures in the main body of the accounts. In the case of a rate fund, it is convenient to insert subtotals for each department or undertaking comprised in the fund.

The column headed "Source of Borrowing, &c.," is intended to differentiate between Stock, Short Term Mortgages, and Instalment Loans (particularly loans from the Public Works Loan Commissioners). Capital moneys utilised in lieu of borrowing are conveniently classed with the loans, and, also, land appropriated for other purposes; these sources would be, therefore, indicated under this heading.

Some exception might be taken to including the capital money and land appropriated (particularly the latter) among borrowings. It must be repeated, however, that all expenditure of a corporation is revenue expenditure, some being provided for out of current income and the other being deferred to the future. In this connection the position of a loan and of land appropriated for a capital purpose (irrespective of the fact that they are both the subject of a Government sanction) is precisely similar, and they are, therefore, classed together.

Every loan sanctioned and intended to be borrowed or already borrowed and to any extent outstanding should appear in this statement.

The totals lend themselves to further classification in a new statement which would specify the several Acts of Parliament authorising the borrowings. These particulars are wanted at local inquiries and at other times when dealing with Government departments.

The columns suggested are:—

(1) Act under which sanctioned, and purpose.

(2) Total amount sanctioned for each purpose.

(3) Total amount borrowed for each purpose.

- (a) Debt.
- (b) Capital moneys appropriated.
- (c) Land appropriated.

(4) Total amount outstanding for each purpose.

- (a) Debt.
- (b) Capital moneys appropriated.
- (c) Land appropriated.

(5) Sinking and Redemption Funds in hand.

The totals only of each purpose under each separate Act would be given on a line. For instance, under the Public Health Act, street improvements would appear. Under the Bigtown Corporation Act, 1890, street improvements carried out under that Act would be inserted, and soon. The totals of all the street improvements picked out from the various General and Local Acts would agree with the totals under street improvements in the first mentioned statement.

A third suggested statement is framed to supplement the Aggregate Balance Sheet and gives in convenient form an analysis of the outstanding debt of the corporation. The columns would be headed:—

1. Account.
2. Total Debt.
3. Redeemable Stock.
   - (a) 2½ per cent.
   - (b) 3 per cent.
4. Short Term Mortgages.
5. Instalment Loans.
   - (a) P.W.L.C.
   - (b) Others.
6. Capital Moneys Appropriated.
7. Land Appropriated.

24. *Standardisation of Published Accounts.*

It is often suggested and, indeed, advocated, that a universal standard form of accounts for municipalities should be adopted, mainly on account of the advantage which would accrue to those who have occasion to compare the abstracts of various towns. Superficially, it would appear that there is a good deal to be said in favour of this. It is, however, clear that the only satisfactory standard form would be the perfect form, and none would be so rash as to agree that that happy stage in the art of presenting accounts has been reached or ever will be reached. There is no objection to be taken to the issue by some authority—either a Government department or an organisation of accountants—of a "suggested" standard form, leaving it optional to the municipality, to adopt it wholly or in part, but what it is feared is in the minds of those who are most enthusiastically in favour of the standard form is that it should be compulsory. The obvious reason for opposing anything of that nature is that the standard form would be the end of all things in the matter of published accounts—that while the municipal financial officer might continue, for the time being, to exercise his brains in the internal organisation of the departments under his control, in improving his system of bookkeeping, and in advising his corporation in general financial matters, he must cease to use any intelligence in the work of presenting his accounts to the public.

Income Tax in relation to the Accounts of Local Authorities.

By G. R. Butterworth, F.S.A.A., F.I.M.T.A.
(Borough Accountant, Hastings.)

A lecture delivered before the London Students' Society of the Institute of Municipal Treasurers and Accountants, on 10th December 1920.

Mr. Chairman and Gentlemen,

My subject to-night is "Income-tax in Relation to Local Authorities' Accounts." As this subject was suggested to me as being one upon which the London Students' Society would like to have some information, I felt it to be my duty to respond to your Secretary's wishes.

Many years ago, as a student, I suggested to the Council of the Institute that a useful paper might be given by a member of the Institute on the subject of the "Duties of the Chief Financial Officer of a Local Authority."

If I remember rightly, I was told that the subject had already been dealt with, and that the duties were well known. I was not satisfied at the time, and I venture to think that it would still be useful to students if they could be told exactly what those duties should comprise. I mention this because I think that it is right that students should wish to know something of basic principles.

I realise that a great deal has been written on the subject before us, and that most useful books have been published which give all the essential details for students, notably the joint work by our Ex-President, Mr. Whitley, and Mr. Wm. Whittingham.

My task is difficult, because of the necessity for concentration. However, I will endeavour to treat the subject as simply as possible, and try and remember that I am addressing students, some of whom may not, as yet, have had the opportunity of giving the matter much study.

Local authorities are affected by all the schedules under which income-tax is payable.

Schedule A deals with the ownership of land and property.
Schedule B with the occupation of land and buildings connected therewith.
Schedule C with the income derived by way of interest, dividends, &c.
Schedule D with income not covered by other schedules.
Schedule E with the assessment of salaries, &c.

It should be borne in mind that there is only one tax, the various schedules merely afford a convenient classification for the purposes of assessment and collection.

The complication that arises in the assessing of a local authority to income-tax is due to the fact that the authority is not treated as one corporate body or entity, but as a number of bodies depending upon the number of its separate Rating Funds.

This is a matter of supreme importance to local authorities, as will be seen later. In the meantime, by way of illustration, it may be pointed out that whilst a firm like Harrods, Ltd., are entitled to set off the loss of one department against the profit on another, a local authority has not that privilege, unless the undertakings are connected with the same Rating Fund.

A few years prior to the war several important test cases were taken to the House of Lords, which, for the time being, have settled the main principles of assessment, viz. the two cases taken by the London County Council, and what is known as the Leeds Test Case.

The first County Council case settled the right to set off Schedule A assessments in respect of property owned but not occupied by the Council, against the tax deducted from the dividends on Metropolitan Stock.

In the second case, it was decided that no set off could be allowed in respect of property owned and occupied by the Council.

The Leeds Test Case was fought on the question as to whether the whole of the accounts of a Corporation could be pooled for income-tax purposes. The House of Lords decided that the separate rating funds of each local authority should be regarded as separate entities.

Although the second County Council case and the Leeds Test Case did not end as we could have wished, we owe a deep debt of gratitude to the Executive of our Institute for all that was done in connection with those cases, and for the evidence submitted by the Institute to the Royal Commission on Income-Tax last year.

It is obvious that I could not, within the confines of this paper, deal with all the points that arise in settling the liability of a local authority to income-tax.

I therefore propose to indicate briefly the method of procedure, and to refer to the principal rules which now govern settlements.

Schedule A Assessments.

During the course of a financial year the first matters to be dealt with are the Schedule A assessments.

In the metropolis the gross annual value, according to the valuation list in force for Poor Rate purposes, is taken as the gross value for income-tax purposes, and in the provinces the rack rent or gross estimated rental, according to the Poor Rate valuation.

To cover the cost of maintenance and repairs, these gross values are reduced by one-eighth in the case of lands, including farm-houses and farm-buildings, and by not more than one-sixth in respect of houses and buildings.

It is important to see that the properties are not over-assessed, and that payment is not made for void periods. It should also be noted that public parks, public schools, Police Courts, and Police Stations, are exempt.

We will now divide the Schedule A assessments into groups:—

(*a*) Property owned and occupied in respect of non-trading undertakings.
(*b*) Property owned and occupied in respect of trading undertakings.
(*c*) Property occupied, but not owned.
(*d*) Property owned, but not occupied.

Under (*a*) fall such properties as town halls, fire stations, depots, stables, &c. These assessments are not as a general rule available as "set off" against the Interest on Rating Funds. There are partial exceptions in the case of public baths, town halls, and properties let subject to a rental to other departments.

Under (*b*) the buildings connected with gas works, waterworks, and markets, are not always assessed under Schedule A, but in the case of tramways, electricity undertakings, &c., the buildings are now assessable. In cases where Schedule A assessments exist, they may be deducted in arriving at the Schedule D assessment.

Under (*c*) the tax is paid by the authority, and recovered by deducting the amount so paid from the rent.

Under (*d*) the occupier or the authority may be assessed. In either case the amount is allowed as a "set off" against interest.

In connection with the question of "set off," there is an important exception in the case of assessments of property acquired under part 1 of the Housing of the Working Classes Act, 1890.

Schedule B Assessments.

The next class of assessments to be considered are those under Schedule B. This tax falls upon the tenant. Schedule A is charged upon the ownership, and Schedule B on occupation.

Assessments are based on the annual value of agricultural land and the buildings connected therewith. Corporations are affected in respect of land acquired for sewage works, &c.

Tax assessed under this schedule is allowable as " set off " against the interest on loans.

Schedule C.

Local authorities are assessed under this schedule in respect of the interest received on investments. Tax is deducted at source, and only the net interest is received. Charitable institutions being exempted from assessment the tax deducted should be recovered. This applies to Police Pension Funds, Scholarship Funds, &c.

Schedule E.

Returns have to be compiled, and are forwarded to the Surveyor of Taxes quarterly, showing the amounts actually paid to workmen who are in receipt of a wage at the rate of £150 per annum. Returns have also to be made annually of the amounts payable to the official and clerical staff, including school teachers. In the latter case the returns are based on the estimated payments, the actual figures being given after the close of the financial year.

Assessments under Schedule D.

Assessments under Schedule D remain to be dealt with. They include the following:—

(*a*) Gasworks,
Waterworks.
Cemeteries.
Markets.
Slaughter Houses.
Interest from which tax has not been deducted at source.
Bank interest.
Income not included under other schedules.

(*b*) Tramways.
Electricity undertakings.

Properties included in Group (*a*) are assessed on the figures for the previous year. Group (*b*) on an average of the three preceding years.

We have now to take each of the Trading Accounts separately, and ascertain the assessment under Schedule D. The principles to be followed are as follows:—

Start off with the *Gross Profit* as shown by the accounts. I assume that the correct proportion of general establishment charges has been charged to the Revenue Account. The additions to the Gross Profit include:—

(*a*) Income-tax.
(*b*) Rents from which income-tax has been deducted before payment.
(*c*) Insurance premiums paid to authority's own Insurance Fund.
(*d*) Interest allowed by bank (less commission charges).
(*e*) Expenditure of a capital nature charged to Revenue.

The items to be deducted from the Gross Profit include:—

(*f*) Bank interest.
(*g*) Obsolescence.
(*h*) Interest on loans from the Public Works Loan Commissioners.
(*i*) Profit derived from supplies to non-trading departments.

Some explanation is necessary as to the procedure to be followed in arriving at the Schedule D assessments.

In the first place it is necessary to start off with the *Gross Profit* as shown by the accounts, because the Net Revenue Account includes Loan Charges and other items which do not enter into the calculation in arriving at the *profit for income-tax purposes.*

Additions to Gross Profit.

(*a*) *Income-tax* is added because the amount is included in the Revenue Account, and is not allowable as a working expense.

(*c*) *Insurance Premiums paid to Corporation's own Fund* are not allowed as expenses. In lieu thereof, the actual disbursements out of the Insurance Fund in respect of each undertaking are allowable.

Insurance premiums paid to companies are allowed as working expenses.

(*d*) *Interest allowed by Bank.*—This income is liable to assessment, and, as it appears in the *net Revenue Account*, must be added to the Gross Profit.

(*e*) *Expenditure of a Capital Nature Charged to Revenue Account.*—This is not allowable as a working expense, but depreciation on the amount so expended is usually obtained in due course.

Deductions from Gross Profit.

(*f*) *Bank Interest Paid.*—This expense, being included in the net revenue, should be deducted from the Gross Profit.

(*g*) *Obsolescence.*—Obsolescence may be claimed in addition to depreciation as and when it occurs. For the benefit of junior students, I may say that obsolescence is the going out of use of plant and machinery before the full amount of depreciation has been allowed. (I deal with depreciation at a later stage.) The method to be adopted in arriving at the amount is as follows:—

		£
Cost of Machine		1,000
Less Amount allowed by way of depreciation	£600	
Amount realised by sale ..	200	
		800
		£200

The amount to be deducted from the Gross Profit for the year is £200. Where the whole of the machinery is merged for the purpose of calculating depreciation, the £200 allowed as " obsolescence " must be taken out of the aggregate written down value, otherwise there would be a double allowance.

(*h*) *Interest on Loans obtained from the Public Works Loan Commissioners.*—This interest is paid gross, i.e. without deduction of tax. If this item were not allowed, a double assessment would arise.

The following examples illustrate this point.

No. 1.

	£
Profit, Schedule D	50,000
Gross Interest on ordinary loans from which Tax has been deducted and retained by the Authority	40,000
Amount on which Tax is actually paid by the Authority	£10,000

No. 2.

	£
Profit, Schedule D	50,000
Gross Interest paid to the Public Works Loan Commissioners	40,000

In this case, the authority would be called upon to pay tax on £50,000, unless they claimed a " set off " in respect of the interest paid *gross.*

(*i*) *Profits on Supplies to Non-Trading Undertakings*—This allowance is claimed on the ground that no person can make a profit out of himself, therefore an authority selling, say, electricity to the Waterworks Department (both undertakings being chargeable to the District Fund), is not assessable in respect of such profit.

Particular attention should be directed by the student to the methods to be adopted in calculating the amount of profit on these supplies.

Three methods are permissible:—

(1) Cost of supply to non-trading departments as compared with total cost.

(2) Calculating profits on the basis of units or quantity supplied to non-trading undertakings, as compared with total supply.

(3) By allocating the total costs between fixed expenses and variable expenses, the cost as regards variable expenses to be on the basis of units supplied, and the fixed expenses on the basis of kilo watt capacity.

I must refer you to the rules governing these methods of calculation, the working out of which is a very involved and lengthy process.

It is important to note that the sale of commodities by an undertaking chargeable to one fund cannot be allowed in respect of sales to an undertaking chargeable to another fund.

For instance, if the Water Undertaking is chargeable to the District Fund, the profit on water supplied to properties attaching to the Borough Fund cannot be allowed.

Depreciation and Renewals.

So far, we have not dealt with Depreciation or Renewals. In the case of tramways and electricity undertakings, depreciation is allowed on agreed bases, but in the case of Waterworks and Gas Works the actual cost of renewals is allowed as and when incurred.

The Depreciation bases are as under:—

Tramways.

Permanent Way	An allowance based on the average car mileage per mile of track.
Cables	3% on written down value.
Plant and Machinery ..	5% on written down value.
Trolley Wires and Connections	Actual cost of maintenance and renewals as and when such expenses occur.

Electricity Undertakings.

Cables	3% on written down value.
Plant and Machinery ..	5% on written down value.
Meters and Office Furniture	Actual cost of maintenance.

Gas Works and Waterworks.

It should be noted that where the actual cost of repairs and renewals in any one year is greater than the profit, the excess is to be carried forward to succeeding years until the full allowance has been absorbed.

It will now be convenient to give figures showing how the Schedule D assessment is arrived at, and for that purpose I have selected one undertaking of each class.

WATERWORKS.

Assessment, year ended 5th April 1920.

		£	£
Gross Profit, year ended 31st March 1919			50,000
Add Income Tax		1,500	
Rents paid from which Tax has been deducted		400	
Fire Insurance Premiums paid to Corporation's own Fund		300	
Interest allowed by Bank		1,500	
			3,700
			53 700
Deduct Rents received, less Tax		300	
Income derived from supply of Water to Non-Trading Departments, less cost of water sold		1,000	
			1,300
	(a)		52,400
Deduct Cost of Renewals applicable to general supply			3,200
			49,200
Deduct Schedule A Assessments			2,000
Net amount on which Tax is payable under Schedule D			£47,200

ELECTRICITY UNDERTAKING.

Year ended the 5th April 1920.

Gross Profit, year ended 31st March 1919		75,000
Add Income Tax	2,500	
Rents paid (net)	200	
Fire Insurance Premiums (own fund)	400	
		3,100
		78,100
Deduct Profit on Electricity supplied to Non-Trading Undertakings	3,500	
Interest on Deposits	50	
Bank Interest and Commission	350	
		3,900
Profit for the year		£74,200

Profit, year ended 31st March 1920	74,200
" " " " 1919	60,000
" " " " 1918	50,000
	3)184,200
Average for three years	61,400
Deduct allowance for depreciation.. ..	20,000
Net amount on which Tax is payable under Schedule D	£41,400

It must not be assumed in the two examples of Schedule D assessments given that I have exhausted the items to be added back or deducted. I have merely endeavoured to give a general idea. The exact figures will depend upon the method of keeping the accounts and the particular items of Income and Expenditure applicable to such accounts.

For instance, if the General Administration Charges have not been apportioned to the various departments, the proper proportion of those expenses should be deducted from the gross profit. The cost of management and Registration of Stock should also be charged against the gross profit.

It is now necessary to carry the Schedule D assessments on trading undertakings a stage further to arrive at the amount of profit legally available as a "set off" against the rate fund interest to which the undertaking is chargeable. I therefore give the following examples, using as a basis the figures given in the preceding examples of the assessments to Schedule D.

WATERWORKS.

		£	£	£
Total Profit, item (a) in preceding statement				52,400
Add	(a) Rents received (gross)			429
				52,829
Deduct	(b) Interest on Loans from which Tax has been deducted by the Authority..		25,000	
	(c) Sinking Fund—Contributions ..	10,000		
Less	(d) Net Income on supplies to non-trading departments	1,000		
			9,000	
	(e) Rents paid (gross)		571	
				34,571
Amount available as "Set-off" against Rating Fund Interest				£18,258

ELECTRICITY WORKS.

		£	£	£
Profit for the year (not the three years' average)				74,200
Deduct	(f) Interest on Loans from which Tax has been deducted by the Authority..		30,000	
	(g) Sinking Fund—Contributions ..	27,000		
Less	(h) Profit on supplies to non-trading departments	3,500		
			23,500	
	(i) Rents paid (gross)		285	
				53,785
Amount available as "Set-off" against Rating Fund Interest				£20,415

The "set off" against Rating Fund Interest is that portion of the profit on an undertaking which is available in payment of the interest on the Rating Fund. It is not necessary that there should be an actual transfer of the profit to the Rate Account.

Taking the figures relating to the waterworks, the item marked

(*a*) *Rents received,* is added back because tax has already been borne by the undertaking.

(*b*) *Interest on Loans.* This amount is deducted because the authority has the tax in hand.

(*c*) *Sinking Fund Contributions.*—This must be deducted because it is assumed that it is a charge against the profits of the undertaking. If there is no legal liability to charge the undertaking with these contributions the amount should not be deducted.

(*d*) *Profit on Supplies to Non-Trading Departments.*—This amount is deducted from the Sinking Fund contributions because, although the profit is not assessable to income-tax, it is regarded as being applicable to the payment of the Sinking Fund.

(*e*) *Rents Paid.*—This item is deducted because tax has been retained by the authority.

A further important point is that if the amount of the Sinking Fund contributions, less the profit on supplies to non-trading departments, is less than the wear of the year, the latter figure must be substituted in compiling the profits available for "set off."

"Set Off" Against the Interest on Rating Funds.

I will assume that the whole of the Schedule D assessments have been compiled, and that the available "set off" against the Rating Funds has been ascertained. It now remains to prepare a final statement, bringing into account the interest on the Rating Funds. Here again I shall not attempt to exhaust the items which may affect the compilation of such a statement.

BOROUGH FUND.

	£	£
Interest		10,000
"Set off" in respect of Trading Undertakings—		
Tramways	10,000	
Cemeteries	1,500	
Gasworks	2,000	
"Set off" on Fund Account—		
Schedule A assessments	1,000	
" B "	100	
Bank Interest	500	
		15,100
Amount by which Interest liability is exceeded by "Set off"		£5,100

DISTRICT FUND.

	£	£
Interest		75,000
"Set off" in respect of Trading Undertakings—		
Water	18,258	
Electricity Works	20,425	
Markets	1,500	
"Set off" in respect of Fund Account—		
Schedule A assessments	9,000	
" B "	800	
		49,983
Net amount on which Tax is payable		25,017

It will be observed that by the division into funds the surplus of £5,100 on the Borough Fund Account is not deductible from the surplus of £25,017 on the District Fund Account.

Anomalies and Reform.

I have given you a general idea of the principles and methods of assessment.

I now propose to deal with some of the anomalies which exist, and indicate methods of reform. In doing so I shall refer to some points not previously dealt with.

Schedule A.

I have told you that certain properties, such as schools and police stations, are not assessable.

It is difficult to understand why schools should be exempt whilst the buildings in which the Education Committee's administrative staff are housed are chargeable.

The Union Office of the Poor Law Guardians is not assessable, but the Town Hall is.

The present exemptions are made on buildings occupied in connection with services which are semi-national in character.

It would appear that the principle ought to be extended to other buildings which are so used.

As the result of a case taken to the House of Lords in 1911, sewers are now assessable under Schedule A. It is contended that they should not be assessable, inasmuch as they are not rent-producing, nor is there any valuable occupation; in this respect they are in the same position as public parks, which are not assessable.

Schedule B.

It is contended that lands from which no income is derived, and which have no connection with farming, horticulture, and afforestation, should be exempt from taxation under this schedule.

Schedule D.

One Corporate Body.

It is claimed that a local authority should be treated as one corporate body and entity, and not as a number of bodies depending upon the number of its separate Rating Funds.

The partial effect of the division is shown in the illustration previously given, where tax on the Borough Fund assessment of £5,100 would have been saved but for this arbitrary division. Moreover, the position is aggravated by the lack of uniformity. In some boroughs the water undertaking is connected with the Borough Rate, whilst in others it is chargeable to the District Fund, and this applies equally to other trading undertakings.

Bank Interest.

Another effect of this division into funds is that the assessments for bank interest are made separately for each fund, consequently, where interest is received on one fund and paid on another, an assessment is made on the amount received, and no set off allowed in respect of the interest paid. It is claimed that the whole of the bank interest should be pooled in arriving at the assessment.

Sinking Fund Contributions.

In regard to the deduction of the Sinking Fund contributions, in arriving at the set off against Rating Fund interest, it is contended that local authorities are placed at a disadvantage as compared with the private taxpayer.

Local authorities should not be placed in any worse position because they are legally liable to make provision for the liquidation of debt.

Interest on Statutory Accumulating Sinking Funds and Reserve Fund.

The interest is deducted at source, consequently the local authorities pay the tax, but they are not allowed to treat this interest as a "set off" against Rating Fund interest.

The Inland Revenue Department contend that the interest earned must be accumulated, and is, therefore, not actually available for payment of Rating Fund interest. This also applies to Statutory Reserve Funds.

It is contended that the interest earned on these funds should be available as a "set off" against any other liability which the authority may have for income-tax.

Where the interest earned is in excess of the requirements of a Sinking Fund, and such interest is transferred in aid of rate, an allowance should be claimed in respect of such interest.

Property Owned and Occupied by a Municipality.

I have previously stated that the Schedule A assessments on properties owned and occupied by a municipality are not as a rule allowed as a " set off " against Rating Fund interest, the contention of the Board of Inland Revenue being that there is no *actual income* from these properties out of which interest could be paid.

It is claimed that a municipality should have the ordinary right possessed by the owner-occupier.

If a man buys a house, and borrows money to pay for it, he is entitled to retain the tax deducted from the interest paid, because he is not, to the extent of the interest paid, the beneficial owner of the property. The fact that he occupies the house makes no difference to his claim.

The following rule governs the exceptions under this head :—

No "set off" is in law due in respect of the net Schedule " A " assessment on such property as a town hall. As a concession, however, if such properties produce incidental income from casual lettings, a proportion of the net Schedule "A" assessment is to be admitted as a " set off," such proportion to be approximately the same as that borne by the total lettings to the sum of the net Schedule " A " assessment, plus the running expenses (including repairs and general establishment charges) of the premises, e.g. :

	£
Schedule "A" net	400
Total expenses	800
	£1,200

Lettings, £300. Allowance, £100.

Sale of Grave Spaces.

The amount received for the sale of grave spaces is included as income in arriving at the Schedule D assessments on cemeteries.

It is contended that this income should not be taxable.

Three Years' Average.

As previously stated, the assessments on certain undertakings are based on an average of three years' profits, in other cases on the profits for the year.

There is no apparent reason for this anomaly, and it is contended that uniformity of practice should obtain, and that the three years' average principle should be applied to all trading undertakings.

Depreciation and Renewals.

Here again we have two principles at work, viz. (*a*) depreciation calculated on a fixed percentage on written down value, and (*b*) repairs and renewals as and when incurred.

The disadvantage of the latter principle is that fluctuations in the amount allowed occur from year to year, according to the amount spent on renewals, and the undertaking will also be affected, adversely or otherwise, by any variation in the rate of tax.

Profits on Non-Trading Supplies.

In calculating the assessment of a trading undertaking, only profits arising from the sale of commodities to non-productive departments of the same fund can be allowed, supplies to another fund being treated as if they were made to another person.

It is contended that this is against the general principle laid down that " a corporate body shall be regarded as a person."

Finance Act, 1918, Section 24 (4).

Attention is directed to the above Act which, in effect, allows for depreciation on buildings connected with electricity and tramway undertakings.

The section is important, because in many cases no assessment had been previously made under Schedule A in respect of the lands and buildings attached to these undertakings.

General.

With income-tax at 6s. in the £, it behoves local authorities to see that they are not contributing more than their fair share to the National Exchequer.

Under present conditions income derived by means of a compulsory Water Rate is not assessable, whereas income derived from a Water Charge is. Therefore, where a deficiency arises in connection with a water undertaking and that deficiency is thrown upon the Rate Fund, there is no liability to taxation in respect of the amount raised by means of the District Rate.

Now, as nearly all ratepayers are water consumers, and both rate and charge are payable on the basis of rateable value, it is obviously bad finance to make a profit out of the water supply involving a heavy payment of income-tax.

I know that in the illustration I have given showing the " set off " against the District Fund the " set off " from the water undertaking is required, but circumstances might have been otherwise.

The question of profit-making in relation to payment of income-tax should also be borne in mind in connection with other trading undertakings. It is also important to note the effect, from the income-tax point of view, of the policy of utilising Sinking Fund accumulations for new capital purposes; the saving in some boroughs must be very great.

Care must also be exercised to take advantage of the provisions of any local Act, which may make all the difference to the amount to be allowed as a " set off " against the Rating Fund. For instance, in the case of a trading undertaking, where there is a distinct provision that the Sinking Fund shall be defrayed out of Borough Fund or District Fund.

In the matter of income-tax in relation to Municipal Accounts we are governed by law rather than by common sense. We must, therefore, take advantage of the law where it is on our side.

Conclusion.

It may be, and has been urged, that authorities should only be assessed in respect of the interest on loans, and that they should be allowed as a " set off " Schedule A assessments in respect of properties owned but not occupied by them.

Had this been the law, this paper would have been unnecessary, and you might now have been listening to a more able writer on some other topic of greater interest.

My object has been to arouse interest in the subject, and to induce you to look into the matters I have touched upon.

The best plan is to read up the subject and work out examples from actual figures. In that way you will get the principles firmly fixed in your mind, and be prepared for that time when the duty may devolve upon you of settling the liability to income-tax of a municipal authority.

Electricity Accounts of Local Authorities and Costs in connection with the same.

By W. A. Henderson, A.S.A.A.

A lecture delivered before the London Students' Society of the Institute of Municipal Treasurers and Accountants, on 9th December 1921.

In accordance with the request of your Executive Committee, I am proposing to give you some information which I trust will be of use to you in connection with the above.

It is not my intention to go into many of the legal aspects which financial officers encounter in connection with the accounts which have to be prepared for an electric lighting undertaking. Neither do I propose to outline the bookkeeping work which follows the usual methods common to the recording of transactions in a trading concern. I shall, however, if you desire, be pleased to give you my opinions on the matter in the discussion which I trust will follow the reading of my paper.

The public general legislation relating to the supply of electricity in the United Kingdom is comprised in the Electric Lighting Acts, 1882-1909, and which have now been added to by the Electric Supply Act, 1919. This last Act of Parliament has been enacted for promoting, regulating, and supervising the supply of electricity. Powers are given to Commissioners who act under the general direction of the Board of Trade.

The principal Act dealing with the accounts of an electricity undertaking is the Electric Lighting (Clauses) Act of 1899. Therein is contained the general rules which have to appear in any Provisional Order or License which is obtained either by a municipal undertaking, a commercial undertaking, or other persons desiring to give a supply of current. These directions are, however, often slightly varied by Provisional Orders, where the applicant can make a good case and not bring such diversion into conflict with the general Statutes. Where such deviations cannot be obtained at the time of applying for the Order or License, they are often obtained by private Acts.

The Board of Trade require annual financial statements of electricity undertakers, and a prescribed form has been prepared which appears in many respects to be now very much out of date. You will no doubt be acquainted with this form and, therefore, I do not propose to go through the items *seriatim*, but only to deal with some of the difficulties which beset a financial officer when setting out his books of account in order to supply the information required each year.

It is probably not necessary for me to mention that the books should be so devised as to enable all information to be arrived at to :—

(1) Compare estimates with actual cost,

(2) Comply with the electrical engineer's requirements to promote economical working,

(3) Supply the required information for financial statement, and

(4) Enable a comparison with a commercial undertaking.

Capital Account.—For two distinct purposes it is necessary to know what is the aggregate capital expenditure on the undertaking, and these are :—

(1) To be certain that the reserve fund does not exceed one-tenth of that amount.

(2) To ascertain when the surplus available to be carried to the credit of the local rate in any year exceeds 5 per cent., so as to be in a position to advise the responsible authority that such excess must be used for the reduction of the price of the supply of energy.

As far as I have been able to ascertain, the Electric Lighting Acts give no definition of capital expenditure or aggregate capital expenditure, and it would appear that such items are covered by capital assets and outlay, and when such capital moneys have been spent, it continues to remain in the Capital Account even if any particular assets may become obsolete, sold, or destroyed. You will appreciate that this has an important bearing on the calculation of the reserve fund. In some Provisional Orders an amendment of the clause dealing with sums available for the relief of rates is made, the percentage being only to "apply to so much of the undertaking "as shall for the time being remain in the hands of the "undertakers." It appears to me that this is a correct method of dealing with this, as when a reserve fund is based upon a percentage, it should be on the capital assets in use and not the capital outlay, which may include costs of assets which have entirely disappeared.

The prescribed form of accounts does not provide for the reduction of assets, and so, in order to be in a position to give effect to the proviso, if necessary, further accounts have to be kept than in the ordinary case where the percentage is based upon capital assets and outlay.

It is therefore very necessary to keep detailed costs of all capital works, and that these costs should be reduced to jobs, as it would be impossible to comply with the Government requests when sanction for loan capital is applied for without doing so.

These details, however, have all to be so arranged that they can be brought into the Capital Account in the prescribed form, which has to be kept upon the double account system.

The question often arises as to whether a particular item should or should not be included in the Capital Account, and this may be either governed by the particular item concerned or a ruling by the Government Department. As an example, the Ministry of Health have always held, and the Electricity Commissioners now follow the rule, that they will not sanction money for the purposes of expenditure incurred where the same is executed by permanent employees of the Council. Of course, if an item is a capital item, there can be no doubt that the correct cost must be all the costs incurred, and in such cases the total value should be taken to the Capital Account, and for any sum which will not be allowed by a Government Department as a charge against the loan sanction a contribution should be made for capital purposes from Revenue Account.

There is also another item which occurs to me as being difficult to understand. It is the item "Value of surplus land sold." It is obvious that the value of the land may be one item, whereas the sale price may be quite different. As the accountant is compelled to only show the sum which has passed through the accounts as the result of the transaction, it is not clear why the word "Value" is inserted. Where such transactions take place it will be seen that in the Capital Account the value of the land sold has to be transferred to a sinking fund or to the account for the reduction of borrowed money, so that although the capital assets have been reduced in value, they still are taken into the total expenditure of capital assets right through the history of the undertaking.

A further item of expenditure shown in the Capital Account which occurs to me to be quite wrong is the item "General Stores (cable, mains, lamps, &c.)." I am of opinion that stores as such cannot form a portion of the Capital Account until they are actually earning revenue. Whilst it may be suggested that in cases where machinery is purchased, and spare parts are provided in the contract for purchase, such spare parts are part of the capital cost, my opinion is that such stores, until they are actually being used for production, are properly included in a Stores Account and are in the nature of a Suspense Account.

Revenue Account—Expenditure.—Turning now to the Revenue Account. The headings taken on the expenditure side generally set out the most useful heads of expenditure, but I have often thought it is very unfortunate that the divisions between the Trading Account and the Net Revenue Account have not been differently grouped. For instance, in the Trading Account it occurs to me that instalments of money repaid should be equal to the depreciation of the undertaking during the year before arriving at the gross profit. If the actual sum paid to lenders or contributed to the Sinking Fund Account is not sufficient, then an additional sum should be provided, charged to the Trading Account, and carried to reserve, so that if the life of the asset has expired before the expiration of the loan period, sufficient reserve will be established to enable the outstanding balance of loan to be repaid. Again I think the item representing payments to the Inland Revenue, in respect of tax due to the Crown, should be taken out of the Trading Account and brought into the Net Revenue Account.

It is also very necessary to always remember that for income-tax purposes items of renewals, as distinct from items of repairs, should be kept separate, and although I do not propose to here deal with income-tax questions, unless this further dissection of the Revenue Account is recorded, considerable trouble will be incurred when the annual return is made.

Bulk Supplies.—In the early future it is anticipated, if super-stations come into force, "generation expenditure" will be practically eliminated and substituted by the item of "purchase of electricity in bulk." As to how a basis of charge will be ascertained it is not easy at the present time to forecast, but it may not be out of place at this juncture to give a little information, as undoubtedly the financial officer will be required to give an opinion on any contract containing financial clauses which is proposed to be entered into for the supply of energy in bulk. From my experience the most satisfactory method is to arrange for a supply to be at a fixed rate of charge, measured by the usual mechanical arrangements as to quantity and other technical requirements.

The usual method of registering bulk supply where it is taken direct from a generating station is to meter the current when entering the consumer's terminals. In view of the fact that electrical meters are not the most accurate recorders, it is usual to have three meters to record the current passing and average the records taken. In such cases it is usual for one meter to be the property of the supplying body, the second to be the property of the consuming body, and the third being joint property. It will also be necessary to have demand indicators fixed to register the amount of current passing over at any one time. It is a matter for negotiation as to when the meter reading and the demand indicator registrations should be recorded.

The readings for any considerable supply are usually recorded in kilo volt amperes corrected to kilowatts by the reading of the power factor indicator. I do not think, however, it is necessary to go into any explanation of the technical terms, as both are the registration of quantities.

The form of charge then is usually arrived at by:—

(a) A fixed charge per kilowatt or per kilo volt ampere of the maximum supply demanded in the period fixed for these two to be taken.

(*b*) A price per unit, subject to a fixed or average price for coal, with a calorific value of twelve thousand British thermal units per pound. When the coal price varies consequential alterations occur in the standard price. The price fixed for the units consumed may be either for the whole of the units consumed or on a sliding scale decreasing with quantities used.

In these abnormal times, however, with continuous alterations in cost of labour and material, it is usual for the supplying body, after fixing the normal terms of the contract, to insert clauses safeguarding them against increases, and *per contra* for the bulk consumer to require entries in the deed to cover him should decreases occur. Generally, these items are limited to a cost of coal and the labour connected with delivering it at the generating station. Now anyone who has had any experience in checking coal accounts delivered in large quantities knows the difficulties connected with this examination. It is therefore suggested that there should be provided, in the agreement for the supply, a method of charge whereby the trucks of coal or the barge loads of coal are measured on delivery. The coal supplier may have an arranged rate for weights taken at the colliery, but these weights may become very different ones, especially with the conveyance of small coal, by the time that they are delivered into the bunkers for consumption at the station. The cost of the wages and the increases attendant thereon chargeable to the coal account will easily be possible of check as they occur. Where the contract provides that a general increase or decrease of wages is to affect the cost of bulk supply apart from coal, a further clause is necessary so as to definitely set out which men would be considered as allocable to general cost, so that such increases or decreases of wages can be easily attached to the particular men engaged. These few points are worth closely considering as they often form an important part of the calculation to arrive at increases or decreases to be charged to the person purchasing bulk supply. I would also advise that provision should always be contained in the contract to enable an entire audit to be available where necessary, if the supplying authority desire to obtain an increase or the purchasing authority have grounds to believe they are entitled to a decrease in the charges made.

I have obtained a copy of the evidence in an arbitration case between a Council and a tramway company as to the price to be charged, and although, of course, there was no agreement as to price, yet the parties seemed to be quite in agreement as to the formula.

It was in the following form :—

From the annual loan charges ... ... — — —
Deduct the proportion in respect of mains, house services, and meters ... ... — — —

— — —

Analyse the revenue charges and apportion them as between standing charges and running expenses—Add to the figure already obtained the standing charges... — — —

— — —

The figure thus obtained is divided by the number of kilowatts forming maximum demand and multiplied either (*a*) according to the Council's contention—by the maximum demand of the tram company, or (*b*) according to the tram company's contention, by their demand when the maximum demand on the plant was reached.

The next step is to find the loan charges on mains, &c., for the exclusive use of the company and add them to the figure already obtained.

The total up to this point we will call "D." Then divide the running expenses by the number of units sold and we get a figure which we will call "E."

Now, it is plain that the company must pay "E" for each unit taken, plus "D" for their whole supply (for the year), while their demand remained practically stationary, plus a profit.

So far as the actual payment is concerned, "D" may be paid as a whole or divided by a number considerably less than the annual requirements in units.

Thus if the user consumed 400,000 units, the first 250,000 of them might be charged at $\frac{1}{250000}$ "D" more than the others.

You will naturally ask how the revenue charges are to be apportioned between standing charges and running expenses, but as I find that the engineers were far from able to agree on that point, I am not going to attempt to lay down any rule. Doubtless you are thinking this is a very complicated matter, but more complications follow. The next complication is with regard to coal and the price per unit may rise and fall according to the price per ton of coal. Yes, say the engineers, but what is a ton of coal? Eventually they may agree that a ton of coal is the quantity of material which will produce, say, 12,000 British thermal units, so that you may find you have a rather intricate calculation to make in order to find the price of a "ton of coal," particularly in cases where you have, say, a coal strike on and the Council generating electricity has been compelled to use a variety of combustible material of various heat values and costing various prices.

Revenue Accounts—Income.—I propose generally dealing with costs and the necessary statistics under a separate heading, so that I will now deal with one of the items on the income side of the Revenue Account which is of paramount importance. I refer to the revenue from current supplied to the consumers. Numbers of methods are in vogue for recording transactions, the more important of which are :—

(1) By personal accounts on card index ;
(2) By columnal accounts in bound Ledgers.

In the second case many authorities have a combined Ledger showing the units and charges horizontally across the book, with columns for cash posting and the other necessary columns opposite. This makes a very unwieldy book, and from experience I can state it is not as easily worked as by dividing the information as between sheets so far as the dissected charges and costs are concerned, and only bringing into the Personal Ledger the consumers in alphabetical street order, with columns for the name and address, cash columns for arrears brought forward, the quarterly charge, total charges receivable, on the debit side, with the cash received, bad debts, &c., and arrears on the credit side. It is then possible to repeat the last five columns three times and so obtain the whole of the accounts for a year on one page of the Ledger. Personally I do arrange for the dissected quarterly charges to be made up on loose sheets, which facilitates balancing, easily localises errors and enables the castings and summaries to be carried out much more expeditiously than if they are entered up in the Ledger as a whole. I would also suggest to you that when you are dealing with the keeping of the Consumers' Ledger, you should collect all the Council's own properties together under one heading. This is very useful for income-tax purposes, preparation of local taxation returns and preparation of the financial statement. I would advise you to adopt a similar principle with regard to other charges against local authorities where they are required. On the local taxation return this is not specially provided for, but the omission seems to be overlooked because Note 3 on the face of the Return states "Amounts received from other "local authorities . . . are to be shown as separate "items of receipt."

Net Revenue Account.—On the Net Revenue Account I am not able to follow what was in the person's mind who drafted the *pro forma* accounts when he inserted the following items in the way he did :—

(1) Interest on mortgage debt accrued due to date.

(2) Instalment of principal of money borrowed.

If it is necessary to calculate the interest up to the date of the closing of the accounts it occurs to me equally necessary to charge up the instalments of principal to the same date. It may interest you to know that in order to prevent any difficulties, not only so far as the Electricity Accounts of my authority are concerned, but with all loan accounts, I arrange for my loans to fall due for interest and repayment of principal on the 30th September and 31st March in each year, so that my figures do not conflict with the return and yet give the true revenue charge for the year. You will also see that this arrangement is of considerable advantage to me in connection with cash balances, and, if I can possibly avoid it, I shall not alter unless compelled to do so in the future by lenders.

Sinking Funds and Reserve Funds.—In the statutory form this is a very mixed account, and whilst one can fill in the figures required by the Board of Trade, neither of them are records such as most accountants would keep. It is hardly worth criticising as I propose to suggest quite a different form.

Alternative Form of Statutory Accounts.—Generally speaking the forms of accounts attached to the Report of the Departmental Committee on the Accounts of Local Authorities meet many of my objections to the present statutory forms, and I should welcome their substitution as a step forward in the right direction. They, however, are still not comparable with a private undertaking, and when all electricity undertakers have to publish their accounts in one way it is certain many of the criticisms lodged against municipal undertakings will be swept away. It should be possible to analyse all accounts where a monoply supply is given, such as electricity, and this is not, as far as I know, available to the ordinary person. Uniformity would meet the case.

Accounts not usually set out in Provisional Orders.—There are now just two or three special items which I will refer to which may be of interest and enable a discussion to arise. The first is the question of a Working Capital Account. As far as I have been able to gather, there is no authority in any of the Acts to enable an undertaking to retain a working balance, and the terms of the model order either dispose of surplus from year to year, or direct that a contribution shall be made from the Rate Fund, upon which the undertaking relies for making good deficits. This is undoubtedly a weakness which should be remedied, and in any provisional order which is to be obtained it is trusted that every opportunity will be taken to have a clause inserted to enable this to be done.

The second point is the provision of reserves to equalise expenditures which have to be incurred from time to time, but which actually accrue from year to year. For example, pointing and repairs to the brickwork of a building. In my opinion there should be set aside, each year, a sum to meet the cost when such works are required, and thus equalise the charge over several years' working.

The next is the question of providing capital assets with revenue moneys. My opinion is that these items should not be charged up in any portion of the Revenue Accounts in any particular year, but should be taken to a Suspense Account and charged up to the Revenue Account over a period of years. In my own authority, when this was done to some considerable extent some while back, the Government auditor objected to the course and drew attention to the fact that one of the terms of the Provisional Order for dealing with moneys paid by the undertaking stated that money so paid could only be charged in respect of payment of "all "other their expenses of meeting the Order not being "expenses properly chargeable to capital."

In view of these terms it was impossible to argue the matter, and as no sanction had been obtained prior to the works being carried out, it was necessary to charge the whole of these capital works into one year's Revenue Account, thus precluding comparison of workings from year to year.

Stores Accounts.—Reverting to my criticism of the present Statutory Form, there is no valid reason for ever charging up the purchase of stores to Capital Account or Revenue Account. Stores are as liquid as cash and should always be a suspense item. It is salutary, inasmuch as the likelihood of items being attached to capital is precluded.

Works Chargeable.—Such items as these should always appear under a separate heading. There is no cause to attach either items of income or expenditure to any nominal head. It should be plain on the face of the account what has been expended and what is recoverable, and the dangers attached to any other method are too apparent to elaborate upon them.

Disposition of Surplus.—This controversial subject has been the cause of many a heated discussion. The provisional orders as a rule are quite definite, that after meeting revenue charges and providing a Reserve Fund up to a fixed amount, the balance is to go to the relief of the rate upon which the account would be chargeable if a loss was incurred. Some have argued that all the ratepayers, being the persons who risked loss in trading, should have the benefit of a surplus. Others, that the consumers who contribute the electricity revenue should have their charges abated, so that after making all provision that a careful person would make, any surplus available should abate the charges. A third idea is that the second of the above should occur until the price charged is a reasonably low figure and then the balance carried to the relief of rates.

Estimates of Income and Expenditure.—Compilation of estimates for the year's working and for new extensions, and the comparison of such with actual costs and revenue derived, are not kept by all undertakers. One knows that a trading undertaking is not similar to a Rate Fund and that increased business may or may not incur additional costs, but it is advanced that where actual result cannot be known until after the accounts are balanced, the responsible officer is in an unfortunate position unless, from period to period, he is advised how he is progressing as compared with his considered estimate. I shall deal with this matter on costs, but in my opinion there is no question that such estimates should be prepared and periodical comparisons made.

Depreciation.—Depreciation of assets is a subject to which sufficient consideration has not been given. Theoretically, the period of the loan sanction is the life in the undertaking of most assets, although not so far as land and buildings are concerned. Actually, this is not so, and therefore the scientific way of dealing with the item is to value the assets at each balancing period. Then compare the figure provided or redeemed to date for loans raised with the reduced value of the assets, and, on the result, make adjusting entries either to decrease or increase the Surplus Assets Account. If this system was permitted I should advocate a separate account being kept of this adjustment. Unless this is done, if a municipal concern is compared with a commercial one and the figure of redemption of debt in the former, which may be equivalent to 5 per cent. of the capital, compared with depreciation in the latter, which may be only 2 per cent. of the capital, the reason for the above opinion is obvious. In some municipal undertakings where an equated period has been taken for the loans advanced, it is certain that it would be extremely difficult to ascertain, if a financial inquiry was held when a loan was required to replace an asset purchased, what was the actual outstanding balance of loan on that particular asset.

Cost Accounting.—Costs of an electricity undertaking, in my opinion, form one of the most important parts of the financial officer's duty. Such costs, however, must be so compiled as not only to show the financial aspect, but also to enable the electrical engineer or manager to gauge how he is proceeding and whether he is obtaining the greatest amount of efficiency from his fuel and plant. I speak with a good deal of knowledge on this point, as some years ago in conjunction with an electric engineer, by adopting an efficient method of costs, an undertaking which was running at a loss was converted into a profit making business with greater efficiency all round.

The essentials of a costing system are similar in an electricity undertaking to any other, and briefly they are:—

(1) That an efficient stores system is in vogue.
(2) That labour costs are promptly analysed.
(3) That direct charges are promptly ascertained.
(4) That they are not made so unwieldy that they lose their usefulness.
(5) That they are an integral portion of the accounting system.

The subject of costing is one large enough for a paper on its own account, but there are one or two things peculiar to electricity undertakings which deserve attention.

First the Coal Account, which is such a vital item in the costs. It is desirable, in my opinion, to enter this account up in detail for the kind of coal, weight, cost per ton, and value. Probably various kinds will be bought, and this will be useful to compare prices and obtain average costs. Each week, or at least each month, the stock in hand should be ascertained by measurement, and the value of the consumption ascertained by adding together the stock at the commencement to the payments and outstandings, and deducting the outstandings at the commencement plus stock on hand at the end of the period, the cost of the last to be based on the average, unless a closer figure is ascertainable. Now the records of the generating station cannot give one the sales of units owing to losses in distribution. This last figure is, however, able to be closely estimated, and what may be termed an estimated actual sold units can be known in the periods to be reviewed. From this data the cost per unit in pounds weight of coal and cash can be calculated. If distribution losses are too variable, the usual method adopted is to base cost on actual generated units as well as estimated sold units. It gives the authority the following information:—

(1) Whether the coal is satisfactory;
(2) If the stoking is being done properly and if the mixing of coal, where performed, is advantageous.

Both these factors are most important, and I have known savings effected upon unsatisfactory returns being made during a year's working, whereby the man and machine handling were localised to quantities used, which completely changed the aspect of the consumption in a month.

Now as regards other revenue costs. In any system which is instituted it is necessary to be careful, whilst obtaining essentials, not to overweight them with numerous job numbers. Special costs are undoubtedly necessary and savings can be made from prompt returns. A system with which I have had close experience provided for the main headings of the Board of Trade return with a very few additional items as the costing headings. Where any particular cost was required a sub-number was given at the start of the job and a column provided in the Cost Book and so earmarked in the revenue cost which it ordinarily fell under. At the end of any particular job the detailed cost was then ascertainable, and could be easily scrutinised without unnecessary labour to collate the items of revenue cost whilst not disturbing the main heading. Sub-costs are very useful in some works such as boiler scaling, engine overhauls, or repairs to mains where cable is used. I am aware accountants do not all agree with the method outlined, but my own experience has shown me that it is labour saving without losing effectiveness. When every working day revenue job has to have a distinct number, the work becomes cumbersome and does not reflect credit on the management.

When capital costs are considered here it is essential to keep jobs separately, but the general system outlined above can be followed with advantage. It is, however, desirable to sub-divide such items as boilers and machinery, mains and electrical equipment. In the case of mains, I would advise a division as between high tension, low tension, and service mains, the last being divided as between individual services. It is apparent that, in the case of service mains, to record the whole of the expenditure of such in one section enables a ready comparison to be made with the amount sanctioned and yet have the cost of each service.

The only other question, I think, in connection with costing is the question of "on cost," and I do not think any useful purpose could be served in dealing with these items through the cost accounts except by way of memoranda. These expenditures have to be brought to the various heads of account in the statutory form, but of course this does not preclude the comparison of the costs, either in revenue or capital, being compared with what a person outside the undertaking would charge to carry out works. The "on cost" can be readily obtained from the allocation of the establishment and other charges by a fixed percentage based on experience.

I would advise the record kept of all expenditure and income being reduced at the end of each year to cost per pence of units sold, and that these should be tabulated from year to year. In this connection, tables prepared by the London County Council and also the *Electrical Times*, the former so far as London and the Home Counties are concerned, and the latter for all undertakings of the Kingdom, provide very useful headings to select a table applicable to an undertaking. If these are kept from year to year they are of great benefit to those concerned in the trading results.

Attached is a statement found to be very useful for comparison purposes and also a sample Cost Sheet prepared monthly for an electrical engineer's guidance.

In conclusion it is desirable to remember that costs and statistics prepared therefrom should be limited to those which serve a really useful purpose, and the preparation of elaborate returns, whilst not only costly, are often so cumbersome that they become misleading and useless. Undoubtedly, it may be advanced that in an electricity concern careful watching is more important than with the manufacture of goods, as a storage for practical purposes is regarded to-day as impossible. But in an electricity concern the current sold is similar to the sale of other goods, and the use of statistics is to watch the cost of production against sales. All municipal accountancy should, of course, be moulded with this view in end, no matter whether for a trading undertaking or for a Rate Fund. Regard must always be given to the fact that unless the costing and the accountancy serve a useful purpose during the financial year and at its end, the labour expended is entirely wasted.

Comparative Annual Statistics of Electricity Undertaking.

	1917-18	1918-19	1919-20	1920-21
	£	£	£	£
Capital Expenditure				
Trading Account—Income ..				
Do. Expenditure ..				
Gross Profit				
Percentage of Expenditure to Income				
Do. Gross Profit to Capital Expenditure ..				
Loans—Interest				
Do. Repayment				
Profit before deducting Repayment of Loans				
Net Profit for Year				
Total Units generated or purchased in bulk				
Total Units lost in distribution ..				
Units consumed on Works ..				
Units sold—				
Public				
Private—Night Lighting ..				
Do. Day Lighting and Power Supply ..				
Total ..				
Average price obtained for Current:				
Private (all services)				
Public Street Lighting ..				
Public and Private				
Private—Night Supply ..				
Do. Day & Motor Supply				
Cost per Unit Sold :—				
Generation :				
Coal				
Oil				
Waste, Water, and Engine Room Stores				
Wages				
Repairs and Maintenance ..				
Distribution :				
Wages				
Repairs, Mains, Meters, &c. ..				
Works Costs—				
Rents, Rates, and Taxes ..				
Establishment Charges and Management				
Total Running Costs—				
Interests and Repayment of Loans				
Irrecoverables, &c.				
Total Cost per Unit Sold— ..				
Coal consumed				
Average price per ton of Coal consumed				
Lbs. weight of Coal consumed per unit sold..				
Water used from Mains ..				
Water used from Artesian Well (estimated)				
Number of Street Lamps in Lighting at 31st March ..				
Number of Units consumed per Lamp (average)				
Revenue derived per Lamp (average) for Current ..				
Average cost per Lamp for Carbons, Maintenance, and Repairs				
Total average cost per Lamp ..				
Number of Consumers				
Average number of Units sold per Consumer				
Total connection of Units sold per Consumer				
Total connections, 8 c.p. equivalent (30 watts)				
Length of Frontage along which Mains are laid				
Load Factor				
Maximum Load				
Capacity of Plant				
Average Loan Indebtedness ..				
Instalment of Loans Assets purchased with Revenue Moneys				
Percentage of Loan Indebtedness (representing Provision for Depreciation)				

	1917-18	1918-19	1919-20	1920-21
	£	£	£	£
Interest on Loans, plus amount of Net Surplus for period or minus Net Deficiency ..				
Percentage of Loan Indebtedness (representing amount available for Dividend) ..				
Amount available for Dividend if the undertaking were a Company, the repayment of Loans being regarded as Depreciation				

Weekly Statement of Progress.

Works Cost Sheet.

Week ended

GENERATION.

Job No.		By Contract	Stock	Wages	Direct Charges	Total
		£ s d	£ s d	£ s d	£ s d	£ s d
1	Unloading Coal ..					
2	Removing Ashes ..					
3	Well Pump ..					
4	Boilers					
5	Engines					
6	Condensing Plant ..					
7	Dynamos					
8	Rectifiers					
9	Accumulators ..					
10	Switch Gear ..					
11	Cleaning Flues ..					
12	Cleaning Station ..					
13	Cleaning Plant ..					
14	Station Lighting ..					
15	Holiday Pay ..					
16	Sick Pay					
17	Station Motors . ..					

Works Cost Sheet.

Week ended

REPAIRS AND MAINTENANCE.

Job No.		By Contract	Stock	Wages	Direct Charges	Total
		£ s d	£ s d	£ s d	£ s d	£ s d
24	Holiday Pay ..					
25	Sick Pay					
26	Foundations ..					
27	Buildings					
28	Flues and Shafts ..					
29	Well Pump ..					
30	Water Pipes ..					
31	Feed Pumps ..					
32	Heaters					
33	Boilers					
34	Steam Pipes ..					
35	Engines					
36	Exhaust Pipes ..					
37	Condensing Plant ..					
38	Engine and Boiler Drains					
39	Dynamos					
40	Rectifiers					
41	Station Cables ..					
42	Switches and Switch Gear					
43	Instruments ..					
44	Accumulators ..					
45	Tools					
46	Travellers & Cranes					
47	Coal Conveyor ..					
48	Bunkers					
49	Station Motors ..					
50	Steam Valves ..					
51	Turbo Alternator ..					
52	Stokers					
53	Boiler Furnaces ..					
54	Cooling Towers ..					
	Carried forward ..					

DISTRIBUTION COST SHEET.

Week ended

Job No.		By Contract	Stock	Wages	Direct Charges	TOTAL
		£ s d	£ s d	£ s d	£ s d	£ s d
160	Returned empty Cement Sacks ..					
181	Wages Distribution					
182	Repairs H.T. Mains and Conduits ..					
183	Repairs, Arc Mains					
184	Inspecting Gas Road Covers and Ventilators					
185	Repairs L.T. Mains and Boxes ..					
186	Disconnecting and Reconnecting ..					
187	Repairs, Transformers					
188	Repairs, Services ..					
189	Repairs, and Refusing Consumers' Premises					
191	Repairs to Tools ..					
192	Reading Meters ..					
193	Meter Changing, &c.					
194	Re-testing and Repairs					
196	Sick Pay					
197	Holiday Pay ..					
200	Establishment—Stores					
201	Stocktaking ..					
202	Office and Management					
203	Publicity, &c. ..					
	Carried forward ..					

PUBLIC LAMPS COST SHEET.

Week ended

REVENUE.

Job No.		By Contract	Stock	Wages	Direct Charges	TOTAL
		£ s d	£ s d	£ s d	£ s d	£ s d
64	Incandescent Street Lighting					
65	Maintenance, Arc Lamps					
66	Trimming Arc Lamps					
67	Repairs, Mechanism					
68	Repairs, Globes ..					
69	Switch Wiring in Arc Lamp Posts ..					
70	Holiday Pay ..					
71	Sick Pay					

CAPITAL COSTS. ....(Head of Expenditure). For Week ended........................

Job Number	101 Material	101 Wages	111 Material	111 Wages	121 Material	121 Wages	131 Material	131 Wages	141 Material	141 Wages	151 Material	151 Wages	Total Material	Total Wages	Relay	Direct Charges	Total
	£ s d	£ s d	£ s d	£ s d	£ s d	£ s d	£ s d	£ s d	£ s d	£ s d	£ s d	£ s d	£ s d	£ s d	£ s d	£ s d	£ s d

The Redemption of Loans (including its relation to Depreciation Fund).

BY ARTHUR COLLINS, F.S.A.A., F.I.M.T.A.

Consulting City Treasurer, Birmingham; Financial Adviser to Local Authorities.

(1) Your excellent scheme for joint printing of lectures and its programme of classified subjects, covering almost the whole range of the Institute's syllabus for the examinations, is specially designed to provide students all over the kingdom with printed material for the purpose of their studies and examinations. One has therefore to see to it that this lecture covers many elementary points which in an extempore address would no doubt be "taken as read." At the same time, let me confess that one of the advantages of being always a student is this—that the elementary bases must never be forgotten or overlooked. Text book study is never stale.

(2) The first phase of this address, i.e. the redemption of loans, is fully reviewed in a Government publication entitled "The Report of the Select Committee on the Repayment of Loans by Local Authorities." This report, issued in 1902 (Cd. No. 239), contains everything of importance relating to the subject up to that time—and as this is mostly true of other similar Government reports, one may perhaps be pardoned for advising (in parenthesis) the student members of our Institute to take advantage of any Government publication of this kind, on our own subjects, as the foundation of their studies in that particular field.

(3) Another Government publication, to which reference must be made, is "The Report of the Select Committee on the application of Sinking Funds in Exercise of Borrowing Powers"—issued in 1909 (Cd. No. 193).

(4) A third Government publication which everyone might advantageously consult is the white paper on "Local Authorities (Borrowing Powers)" issued in 1914 (Cd. No. 179). This return shows:—

(*a*) The *limitations* placed by various Acts of Parliament upon the borrowing powers of each class of *local authority* in the *United Kingdom*, specifying each local authority separately, and

(*b*) the cases in which by subsequent *public Acts of Parliament* provision has been made whereby money for various purposes is to be excluded from being reckoned as part of the *debt* of a *local authority* for the purposes of the limitation on borrowing previously imposed by *parliament*.

(5) Every student preparing for the examinations of our Institute will be familiar with the text-book, "Biddell's Loans of Local Authorities," issued in 1904. It is a matter for regret that this book has not been brought up to date, but the fine publication of my former deputy and the now acting treasurer of the city of Birmingham (Mr. Johnson) entitled "The Finance and Law Relating to Local Authorities Loans and Borrowing Powers," issued at the end of last year, may be said to bring the subject substantially up to date. The Scottish practice is also excellently codified in the publication of my old students, Messrs. Alban and Lamb, and comparative study of the methods of our canny brethren cannot fail to broaden one's views.

A lecture delivered before the London Students' Society of the Institute of Municipal Treasurers.

(6) The temporary provisions of the Local Authorities (Financial Provisions) Act 1921, as far as they affect the debt and loans of local authorities, should also be consulted.

(7) Proceeding then on the assumption that the student has been, is, or may become broadly familiar with the technical and detailed information to be found in these publications, one may make a reference to the main features of the subject, and then endeavour to show how the stress of war conditions has necessitated certain departures from the methods formerly obtaining.

(8) The subject of this address starts at the point of "redemption" and there is therefore no need to traverse the proceedings in obtaining a loan sanction from the Ministry of Health, including :—

(*a*) Preparation of plans, reports, and detailed estimates for approval of the local authority, and their formal resolution that powers be sought to borrow.

(*b*) The dispatch to the Government Departments concerned of the copies of the resolutions, plans, estimates and other information required by them, including return as to local debt and proof of the issue of statutory notices (e.g. to land owners) in certain cases.

(*c*) The holding of an inquiry locally by a Government inspector, in certain instances subject to the relaxation now permitted by Section 6 of the Local Authorities (Financial Provisions) Act 1921.

(*d*) The report of the inspector holding the inquiry and the subsequent decision of the department stating, if favourable, the amount of the loan they sanction and the period during which the loan is to be redeemed.

(9) There is, however, this peculiar feature common to Municipal Finance as opposed to the financing of industrial concerns (excluding, of course, redeemable debenture issues) that the question of repayment is an essential element in the negotiations leading up to the raising of the loans. A great proportion of Government and industrial capital involves no undertaking to repay the capital invested. A waterworks or gas company, for example, is under no obligation, under the general law, to provide for the redemption of its capital, but a municipality undertaking the same services must make that provision for all its debt.

(10) This feature is emphasised in paragraph 2 of the 1902 report :—

> " It has been the policy of Parliament for many years to require that local loans should be repaid within a limited number of years, and to prevent the establishment by any local authority of a permanent debt.
>
> " To secure this object each general statute which confers borrowing powers upon local authorities specifies a maximum period for the repayment of loans raised under such powers. Within the limits thus established a discretion is, in English and Irish Acts, as a rule left to the Government department specially concerned with the matter for which the loan is required, to decide the exact term of the redemption of each particular loan. In the case, however, of most of the loans raised by metropolitan boroughs this discretion is, in the first instance, exercised by the London County Council.
>
> " In Scotch law a different principle prevails."

Periods for Repayment.

(11) Regarding the periods for prescribed repayment of loans, the following selected extracts of the 1902 report speak for themselves, special attention being paid to paragraph 6 :—

> *Par* 4. . . . . . it is obvious that the discretion left to the Government Departments which fix the actual period for the repayment of each loan is a very wide one. Although some other departments have duties in respect of certain loans, by far the greater part of the work of controlling the borrowings of local authorities falls, in England and Wales, upon the Local Government Board.†
>
> The board has a staff of engineering and medical inspectors amongst whose duties is that of holding local inquiries, when directed to do so, into the circumstances under which it is sought to spread the expense of any work over a number of years by raising a loan for such work. Such an inquiry is in most cases obligatory under statute, if the new loan required will cause the indebtedness of the district to exceed one year's assessable value. At these inquiries the question of the probable durability and continuing utility of the work is gone into by the inspector, and it is his duty and that of the chief engineering inspector to advise the board as to the period for which the loan should be sanctioned.
>
> *Par.* 5.—The Local Government Board and the Board of Trade hold that the maximum periods mentioned in general Acts refer to the most durable items of the work for which borrowing powers are sought. It is therefore their practice to examine each item of the estimates for such work, and to assign to each group of items an appropriate term for the repayment of the loan required for it. In order to avoid a multiplication of separate loans, the course usually adopted is to grant an equated period for the whole loan, which is arrived at by considering the sums required fo- each group of items, and the term assigned to that group. The result of this severance and equation is to reduce the periods allowed below the maximum periods mentioned in the Acts, but equation is not practised where the sums included in each group are large, and the local authority express a preference for separate loans.
>
> *Par.* 6.—The Local Government Board, being charged with the general supervision of local finance, takes into its consideration in fixing the period for redemption not only the probable useful life of each part of an undertaking for which a loan is desired, but also the probable future condition of localities with regard to debt, in order that the ratepayers of the future may not be unduly burdened, and so rendered less able to discharge efficiently the duties that are likely to come upon them.
>
> *Par.* 7.—In addition to their borrowing powers under genera statutes, most of the more important municipal authorities have acquired the right to borrow for various purposes under local Acts, and have so borrowed large sums to be repaid within periods fixed by or under those Acts. The committee have been unable to discover any general principles by which the periods allowed by local Acts are fixed.
>
> *Par.* 11.—Standing Order 172 of the House of Commons provides that "in the case of all Bills whereby any municipal corporation, district council, joint board or joint committee, or other local authority, in England or Wales, are authorised to borrow money for any matter within the jurisdiction of the Board of Trade or the Local Government Board, estimates showing the proposed application of the money for permanent works shall (except so far as the exercise of the borrowing power is made subject to the sanction of the respective boards) be recited in the Bill as introduced into Parliament, and proved before the Select Committee to which the Bill is referred."
>
> There is no doubt that one of the objects of this Standing Order is to provide the committee dealing with a Bill with materials upon which to found a judgment upon the question of the appropriate period to allow for the loans sought by the Bill. The committee are of opinion that this Standing Order is not satisfactorily complied with in many cases. The estimates as set out in many Bills are too general, and the proof of them is usually merely formal.
>
> If a Bill is unopposed the preamble is taken as proved, and as the estimates and other particulars are recited in the preamble, no further compliance with the Standing Order is called for.
>
> *Par.* 12.—In addition to the statutory limitations upon the periods for repayment already mentioned, there is a further provision, acting as a check in the case of some loans, to which the committee desire to call attention.
>
> If the borrowing authority obtains the loan from the Public Works Loan Board, the period for repayment is determined by the Commissioners who are empowered by Statute to make regulations governing all the conditions of these loans.
>
> Section 11 of the Public Works Loans Act, 1875, directs the Commissioners in making such regulations to have regard to the durability of the work and to the expediency of the cost being paid by the generation of persons who will immediately benefit.
>
> The general policy of the Commissioners is "to hold out inducements to accept short periods for repayment instead of throwing as much of the burden as possible upon posterity." One of these inducements is the acceptance of a lower rate of interest for a short term than for a longer one.

† References to the Local Government Board now apply to the Ministry of Health.

(12) A practical point arises just now in drafting bills for borrowings under Local Acts, as referred to in paragraphs 7 and 11 of these quotations; it is advisable to suggest to the local authority for consideration the inclusion in the clause of the draft bill in the column specifying the amount of borrowing powers of only the first instalments of the borrowings that are deemed to be immediately necessary, leaving subsequent borrowings to be a matter for the sanction of the Ministry of Health or other appropriate department. The ordinary course, i.e. to include authority for all borrowings that can be foreseen over a very considerable period, or for the complete cost of a lengthy job to be carried out by instalments is a very convenient one, but it has the great disadvantage of including in the bill a large sum of money which under present conditions is apt to frighten both the local ratepayers (at a town's meeting) and the legislators. Of course the local council should always be advised of the potential total cost of any scheme. The course now suggested, therefore, has two material advantages :—

(*a*) it helps to remove misapprehensions at the town's meetings as to extensive new powers of spending.

(*b*) it helps to get the bill through committee and Parliament, in these present abnormal times, by reducing the positive commitments in the bill and leaves discretionary power in the State Departments.

(13) This course is not convenient if a longer period of repayment is desired than the Ministry or other Department of State can grant under the general law; it may also prove to be possible to obtain Parliamentary sanction to such longer *periods* in the Local Act, where exceptional circumstances justify the proposal, leaving the Ministry to approve of such sums, with this war period attached, as experience may prove to be necessary and desirable.

Methods of Repayment of Debt by Local Authorities.

(14) The methods actually adopted by local authorities for the repayment of debt are as follows :—

(1) The instalment of principal system, under which an equal yearly or half-yearly instalment of principal is repaid to the lender throughout the prescribed period for the loan, together with the interest on the amount of the loan outstanding from time to time.
(2) The annuity system, under which an equal yearly or half-yearly sum to cover both principal and interest is paid to the lender throughout the prescribed period for the loan.
(3) The sinking fund system, under which such a sum is set aside to a fund each year as will be sufficient to repay the loan within the prescribed period for the loan.

(15) For the sake of completeness it may be added that the Sinking Fund system may again be sub-divided into two parts :—

(*a*) The accumulative Sinking Fund, broadly equivalent in effect to the annuity system.

(*b*) The non-accumulative Sinking Fund broadly equivalent in effect to the instalment system.

(16) The advantages and disadvantages of the respective methods are fully tabulated on pages 74–75 of the text book referred to in paragraph 55, but I shall in a later paragraph ask you to consider these methods in their relation to the question of depreciation. (*See* paragraph 53.)

(17) The 1902 report gives instructive examples showing the relative cost to the ratepayers of the several methods, both for specific years, and for the whole period of the loan.

(18) The instalment method, while throwing heavier burdens on the earlier years, is in the *aggregate* cheaper than the annuity and sinking fund methods, as of course the earlier the repayment of principal the less the interest payable.

(19) It may be suggested that this saving, looked at from the ratepayers' point of view, is more apparent than real, because it is said that the extra money extracted from the ratepayers by the instalment method during the earlier years of the loan would have earned more interest to the ratepayer if left with him than is saved to the Local Authority as representing the ratepayers in aggregate. This thesis would involve an analysis of the use to which the many different classes of ratepayers would put their money, thus left with them, and interesting though the task of exploration would be, it might still only leave one with an opinion and not with proof. For example, what conclusion would one reach in the case of the man who would have put his share of the saving on a horse ?

Loans Funds, Redemption Funds, and Sinking Funds.

(20) The terms " Loans Funds," " Redemption Funds " and " Sinking Funds " are apt to provoke some confusion in the mind of the young student, and for his information the following definitions and explanations are furnished from the 1909 report :—

(*a*) " Loans Fund " is the title given by numerous Local Acts (passed in 1880 and subsequent years, and containing what are usually known as the Model Stock Clauses or similar provisions) to the fund to be established for the redemption of the stock issued by Municipal Corporations under the authority of those local Acts, and for the payment of dividends on the stock. It is, therefore, not solely a Sinking Fund for the discharge of capital. Accounts are kept as part of the Loans Fund Account, showing separately the amounts set aside for redemption of stock and for payment of dividends.

(*b*) " Redemption Fund " is the title given by the Stock Regulations of the Local Government Board, issued under the Public Health Acts Amendment Act, 1890, to the fund to be established for the redemption of stock issued by a local authority under those regulations. The same title is given by the Stock Regulations of the Board, issued under the Local Government Act, 1888, and the Metropolis Water Act, 1902, to the accounts to which are carried the moneys required to provide for the redemption of stock issued under and subject to those regulations by County Councils and the Metropolitan Water Board. Thus, generally speaking, a " Redemption Fund " is a sinking fund applicable to the redemption of stock under the Board's Stock Regulations. The same title is given, however, to the fund established for redemption of stock under the Liverpool Corporation Loans Act, 1891, and to the fund established under the Leeds Corporation (General Powers) Act, 1901, for the redemption not only of stock but also of other classes of corporation debt.

(*c*) " Sinking Fund " (the term used in the Local Taxation Returns) is the term generally applicable to the fund set aside for the repayment of debt; but when used in contradistinction to " Loans Fund " or " Redemption Fund " it would generally apply to a fund set aside for the repayment of ordinary mortgage or debenture debt under Local or General Acts, although it would also apply to a fund set aside for redemption of debenture stock under the Local Loans Act, 1875, or a few special stocks under local Acts.

(21) Local Acts provide many variations in detail of these terms, including various " Consolidated Loans' Funds." No doubt many of you have paid more than passing interest to clause 36 of the Swansea Act of 1921, as set out in the Institute's *Financial Circular*, particularly in view of the observations of our friend, the City Chamberlain of Edinburgh, Mr. Robert Paton. There is an example of the advance which Scotland has made in the consolidation of its loans funds. In England, we do not advance money for working capital from the loans fund.

(22) It cannot too often be made clear by those who direct the studies of juniors in our service that the repayment of a loan does not necessarily mean redemption.

Repayment depends on the terms arranged with the lender. A loan from him may run for three years only, say, and repayment to 10 different lenders for three years each might take place, either by lump sums out of new borrowings, or partly out of Sinking Funds, or partly by instalments of principal, and yet redemption would not be effected till the 30th year. Funds for redemption proceed on the basis of the sanctioned period and not on the terms which happen to be made with any lender.

(23) Whatever may have been the pre-war views of local Government officers as to the caution exercised by Parliament and Government Departments in limiting periods for repayment, it happens to have proved to be fortunate in the light of post-war conditions and problems, that the authorities were guided, not merely by the anticipated life of the works and assets in respect of which loans were sanctioned, but also by considerations of future financial burdens. The responsibilities falling so heavily upon local councils in connection with unemployment, the higher cost of labour and materials, and all other post-war circumstances, would leave local authorities in a position even more difficult than the present, had not a considerable portion of loan debt already been paid off in those pre-war days, which in this respect were truly "the good old days."

(24) When special reasons have been adduced to satisfy Parliament that exceptional provisions for the redemption of debt should be granted the relief has taken the form of :

(*a*) granting longer periods in approved cases.
(*b*) suspension of Sinking Funds, and
(*c*) capitalisation of interest in the case of works, e.g. waterworks, requiring a long period to construct, and/or built for the needs of many years ahead.

(25) The last two factors will be dealt with later, but on the point we are now discussing, namely the period sanctioned for the loan, the periods of redemption (*a*) set out in the appendix to the 1902 report, may usefully be compared with (*b*) the periods which have been granted during the last few sessions of Parliament. For one's own professional use in Parliamentary work, my staff keep up for me a table of such periods for reference and the circumstances of each case arising in Parliamentary committee for years past; by way of illustration, the following instances of periods granted, after due consideration of all the facts, by Parliamentary Committees during the 1921 session are taken from this list :—

Taf Fechan Water Supply Board.	For purchase of loan and construction of works.	70 years.
Do.	For payment of interest during construction	60 years.
Manchester Corporation.	For construction of Waterworks	80 years.
Do.	For payment of interest on capital during construct'n	80 years.
Halifax Corporation.	For the purchase of loans and construction of works	70 years.

(26) Applications for abnormal periods of redemption should of course be made with great caution, and the mere fact that the annual burden is thereby made lighter and longer does not of itself justify the representation to the Parliamentary Committee. In all the above cases, good reasons, apart from the one just mentioned, were given and the need proved.

SUSPENSION OF SINKING FUND AND CAPITALISATION OF INTEREST DURING THE CONSTRUCTION OF WORKS.

(27) The battle, in municipal finance, between "present" and "future," as exemplified by the present heavily-burdened ratepayer on the one hand, and posterity on the other, reaches its climax when we discuss this branch of subject. It is of course an important matter of public policy. Parliament has a most careful regard for the ratepayer of the future, and naturally so, for he is entitled to be protected against a legacy of debt incurred by his predecessors, except on clear proof that it is fully justified.

(28) The 1902 report deals with the subject as follows : *Par. 24.*

"The committee have considered the question of the proper date for the payment of the first instalment of the sinking fund.

"As a general rule such instalment should be paid within a year of the borrowing. The committee, however, think that that requirement need not be insisted upon in the case of a loan for new works from which a cash return may be reasonably expected when they are completed ; and that in that case the payment of the first instalment may be properly deferred during some portion of the time allowed for the construction of the works. Such works, even if the return from them is not sufficient to make them profitable in the ordinary sense of the word, will be at any rate a lighter burden on the rates when completed that the instalments of repayment cause them to be during construction. Future ratepayers will have whatever return there may be from the work to assist them in the payment of instalments."

(29) Fortified by this expression of opinion, it became the practice of Parliament, in approved cases, to concede a strictly limited permission to suspend sinking funds during the construction of works.

(30) The capitalisation of interest during construction has to be viewed from different standpoints, and concessions in this regard were and are most jealously guarded and only granted in isolated cases by Parliament.

Par. 25 of the 1902 report said :—

"Some local authorities desire in the case of reproductive works not only to defer the payment of the first instalment in respect of capital, but also to pay interest during construction out of the money borrowed. This would relieve those whose representatives decide to borrow for such works from immediate liability to contribute anything in respect of the borrowing and should not in the opinion of the committee be ever permitted.

"During the construction of works the district has in many cases the advantage of the expenditure within it of much of the money raised by the loan, and this may fairly be taken into consideration as some compensation for the fact that nothing is being earned by the works in the interval."

(31) Many students will at once recall the power conferred on limited companies by the Companies Act, 1907, and now codified in the Companies (Consolidation) Act, 1908, Section 91, reading as follows :—

"Where any shares of a company are issued for the purpose of raising money to defray the expenses of the construction of any works or buildings or the provision of any plant which cannot be made profitable for a lengthened period, the company may pay interest on so much of that share capital as is for the time being paid up for the period and subject to the conditions and restrictions in this section mentioned, and may charge the same to capital as part of the cost of construction of the work or building, or the provision of plant:

Provided that—

(1) No such payment shall be made unless the same is authorised by the articles or by special resolution;

(2) No such payment, whether authorised by the articles or by special resolution, shall be made without the previous sanction of the Board of Trade;

(3) Before sanctioning any such payment the Board of Trade may, at the expense of the company, appoint a person to inquire and report to them as to the circumstances of the case, and may, before making the appointment, require the company to give security for the payment of the costs of the inquiry;

(4) The payment shall be made only for such period as may be determined by the Board of Trade; and such period shall in no case extend beyond the close of the half-year next after the half-year during which the works or buildings have been actually completed or the plant provided;

(5) The rate of interest shall in no case exceed four per cent. per annum or such lower rate as may for the time being be prescribed by Order in Council;

(6) The payment of the interest shall not operate as a reduction of the amount paid up on the shares in respect of which it is paid.

(7) The accounts of the company shall show the share capital on which, and the rate at which, interest has been paid out of capital during the period to which the accounts relate."

(32) Post-war conditions—in relation both to construction costs and rates of interest—have made it almost impracticable to complete certain existing schemes, or the inauguration of new schemes of any magnitude, without a revision of pre-war restrictions on the capitalisation of interest and/or the suspension of sinking funds.

(33) The problem is now not confined to two factors, i.e.

(*a*) suspension of sinking fund, during construction.

(*b*) capitalisation of interest, during construction.

Regard must be also had to:

(*c*) abnormal cost of construction, and

(*d*) the abnormal rates of interest that have had, during the latter part of the war, and since, to be paid for the capital moneys required.

(34) Assume for example—as has happened within my experience—that a local authority has to pay 7½ per cent. interest on money to enable urgently essential public works to be completed. For these works a loan period of 60 years is granted. The authority may have prepared parliamentary estimates before the war, on a 3½ per cent. basis, and even in 1918 might perhaps reasonably assume that over the whole term the *average* rate of interest it will need to pay will not exceed 5 per cent. The 7½ per cent. loans are repayable within say 10 years and may then be renewed perhaps at 4½ per cent. It has been suggested that the difference between the estimated future normal rate for the particular local authority concerned (say 5 per cent.), and the abnormal rate (7½ per cent.) paid during the 10 years, should not fall upon those 10 years exclusively, but should be spread over the whole period. The point is, of course, partly met by the capitalisation of interest during construction, but if we assume the construction period to be 4 years, it can be seen how strong the claim is that the case is not fully met.

(35) The difference between the original and the revised estimates of loan charges is much greater than would at first sight appear. The result may conceivably work out as follows (and the example, although happily on the extreme side, is one which came within my personal experience):—

Pre-War Figures			Post-War Figures		
Construction Cost (Estimated) ..		£400,000	Now Estimated at ..		£1,000,000
Annual Loan Charges (during first 10 years, after which interest rates were subject to revision)—					
	%	Total		% (on pre-war) Estd. Cost	Total
	£ s d	£		£ s d	£
Interest (4%) ..	4 0 0	16,000	(7½%) ..	18 15 0	75,000
Sinking Fund (say) ..	0 12 0	2,400		1 10 0	6,000
	£4 12 0	18,400		£20 5 0	81,000

Increased Loan charges per annum £62,600

Do. per £100 pre-war estimated construction cost .. .. £15 13s. (%)

(36) The suspension of sinking funds and the capitalisation of interest as well as relief in respect of temporary abnormal interest rates, during construction of works, thus become problems formidable even to a large local authority with great financial and rating resources. The cases are more numerous than one would think, a considerable number being in my hands at the present time. Many large constructional works of local authorities were overtaken by the war, and there are several ways of relieving the financial situation which time prevents one from reviewing in an address of this nature.

Application of Sinking Funds to New Capital Purposes.

(37) The application of sinking funds to new capital purposes is a subject upon which one could dilate at considerable length, but the 1909 report, referred to in paragraph 3, exhaustively reviews the whole subject as it stood at that time. The conclusions of that committee were as follows:—

"The conclusions to which your committee have come may be summarised as follows:—

(1) The principle of utilising sinking funds (including loans funds and redemption funds) for purposes for which local authorities have borrowing powers is, if properly safeguarded, financially unobjectionable; and the power of so using these funds is undoubtedly a great advantage, inasmuch as it affords a convenient and economical method of exercising new borrowing powers.

(2) In those cases in which the stock is required to be extinguished at a fixed date, your committee are of opinion that any amounts withdrawn from the fund should as a general rule be replaced by that date, and that any departure from this principle should require the previous consent of the Local Government Board.

(3) While satisfied that the ordinary method, prescribed in Local Acts and by the Stock Regulations of the Local Government Board, of utilising loans funds and redemption funds, set aside for the repayment or redemption of loans raised by the issue of stock, is theoretically free from objection, your committee feel a preference for the system prescribed by the London County Council (Money) Acts, in so far as that system involves the approval of a Government Department as a necessary precedent to the exercise of the power, and requires that all moneys used from the funds must be replaced before the expiration of the life of the stock. At the same time we recognise that this last condition may operate disadvantageously during the latter part of the life of the stock.

(4) With regard to the operation of the system prescribed by the Local Acts and Stock Regulations, your committee are of opinion that, while in the majority of cases there may be no real objection to the transfer of stock at par value, nevertheless there should be some limitation to prevent the transaction working unfairly as between different accounts; and we suggest that with this object the Local Government Board should take such administrative action as we have previously indicated.

(5) Your committee consider that a loans fund set aside in respect of loans raised by irredeemable stock may, subject to proper restrictions and conditions, be utilised for borrowing powers.

(6) With regard to sinking funds set aside in respect of loans raised on mortgage, the funds should not be used for borrowing powers where the mortgage earmarks the borrowing power under which the loan is raised; and where a loan is by the mortgage charged on specified rates or revenues, the sinking fund should not be used for any borrowing power under which the loan is required to be charged on different rates or revenues.

(7) Sinking funds set aside in respect of loans raised under and subject to the provisions of the Local Loans Act, 1875, should not be used in the exercise of borrowing powers.

(8) Returns should in every case be made to the Local Government Board clearly showing—

(i) The amount of the sinking funds, loans funds, or redemption funds invested, and the securities in which investments have been made;

(ii) The amount of stock or debt cancelled; and

(iii) The amount applied in the exercise of borrowing powers.

Moreover, the accounts should be audited by an independent auditor, who should make a special report in every case in which he is of opinion that there has been any irregularity in the transactions of the local authority in regard to the use of the sinking funds or to the provision made for the repayment or extinction of debt.

(9) The terms of prospectuses should be strictly adhered to, and reasonable information as to the contributions to and management of the sinking funds should be placed at the disposal of the ratepayers of the locality; and, where stock has been or is proposed to be issued, of the Stock Exchange."

(38) It is my experience, however, that in practice the Stock Exchange attach considerable importance to redemption funds being used for the redemption of stock. It may only be a sentimental point, and it may on the other hand be a justifiable expectation, especially where it promotes business and keeps the stock at a good price, this being in many instances regarded as advantageous to the status of the local authority and worth something on future issues of their securities. Some stocks (i.e. particularly those of smaller authorities) would rarely "move," but for the application of the corporation's own sinking funds.

(39) It will be within your knowledge, too, that a number of corporations have in prospectuses of stock issues in recent years definitely undertaken to apply their redemption fund to the purchase and extinction of stock when purchasable in the open market at, or under, Par.

(40) In connection with Government finance, students will no doubt be aware of the undertaking given by the Government in connection with the issue of 5 per cent. War Loan Stock (1929-1947) to the following effect:—

> For the purpose of providing against depreciation in the market price of the loans the Treasury undertake to set aside monthly a sum equal to one-eighth of 1 per cent. of the amount of each loan to form a fund to be used for purchasing stock or bonds of either loan for cancellation whenever the market price falls below the issue price. Whenever the unexpended balance of such funds reaches £10,000,000 the monthly payments will for the time being be suspended, but they will be resumed as soon as the unexpended balance falls below £10,000,000.

It should be observed that this provision is not necessarily a charge against the Government's "Revenue Account" or "Annual Budget."

(41) The utilisation of sinking funds is of itself worthy of a separate lecture. In estimating the relative advantages of the several courses available, i.e.

(*a*) to purchase the authority's own stock in the open market for redemption.

(*b*) to apply to new borrowing powers.

(*c*) to invest the sinking fund with other local authorities, regard must be paid to a variety of local and general circumstances obtaining at the time, and the assessment of the value of these elements is a fine art.

(42) The method of investing sinking funds—or any capital moneys not immediately required—with other local authorities (or in other securities) is a proposal calling for the closest investigation by the financial officer. The credit of a big town's credit is usually several points higher than that of a small town, and, taking legitimate advantage of this circumstance, the financial officer may find it possible to make loans from his sinking funds on terms mutually advantageous to all parties concerned, securing to his authority for 10, 15 or 20 years at the present good rate of interest, leaving a gain of a fraction of £1 per cent. or more by raising new capital for the purposes of his own local authority at a lower rate than that received on the sinking fund invested. A large and financially sound municipality may thus use its important asset, viz. "credit," to the definite advantage of its ratepayers. Of course this can only be regarded as a general proposition, subject always to the local circumstances in each case, but it is within one's knowledge that transactions of this kind of late have been effected with substantial annual gain.

Relation of Loan Redemption to the Depreciation Fund.

(43) This is a thorny side of our subject. In "Municipal Finance for Students"—a book written more years ago than one now cares to contemplate—the elementary phases of this subject were reviewed, and for the information of students, old and young, one may add that the essence of one's conclusions substantially still seems to me to be justified by further experience.

(44) We can probably assume with safety that the periods prescribed in the case of local authorities for the redemption of loan debt do not exceed the estimated lives of the subjects of the loan. The provision in that event statutorily required to be made by a local authority for the redemption of loan debt is now almost universally regarded as equivalent in effect to the writing down of such assets year by year, according to the lives of the assets, which are the subject of the debt.

(45) In pre-war days some critics of municipal finance, especially of trading departments, contended that local authorities ought to provide not only for redemption of loan debt but also for depreciation as an additional and inevitable working expense. They suggested that the redemption of loan debt was not relevant to the question of depreciation, as such redemption was a statutory requirement peculiar to local authorities. This is not now so seriously argued in any responsible quarter, and it seems to be more generally agreed that, on the strict condition that the loan period does not exceed the life of the asset, a double charge—depreciation and loan repayment—is not necessary.

(46) Difficulties arose because of the practice (now discontinued, speaking generally) of equating periods for the redemption of loans for divers objects—short-lived and long-lived assets being merged in one equation. The method of "equating" is well known to those present, and the net effect was that certain short-lived assets needed renewal before the equivalent sinking fund had been completely created.

(47) Although in theory the sinking fund should be deemed to accumulate on the same actuarial basis as the original equation, i.e. for the short-lived assets first, the Government Departments, in allowing the local authority

to borrow for the renewal of an exhausted asset before the expiration of the equated period, restricted the loan to the amount actually provided in the sinking fund. The current Revenue Account had thus to be drawn upon for the renewal of the short-lived assets; this could not be regarded as a satisfactory financial policy.

(48) It may also be the case that obsolescence in some cases may march in advance of the provision for repayment of debt.

(49) That renewals or depreciation funds should be created to meet the contingencies mentioned in the foregoing paragraphs is a fundamental element of sound finance, and this view is taken in the recommendations contained in the 1902 report:

"That the sanctioning authority should be empowered to fix the method of repayment in all cases and to provide for the establishment of a Repairs Fund where necessary."

(50) It may be permissible to remark that, engaged as one has been on many occasions in parliamentary proceedings or arbitrations connected with the purchase by local authorities of public utility undertakings owned by companies, e.g. tramways, electric lighting, gas and water undertakings, one generally finds that only nominal provision, if any, has been made by companies in respect of depreciation. In many cases it would appear that the local authorities have repaid the company not only the whole of their capital but a substantial additional amount for goodwill. Everything depends on the terms of purchase which determine the basis of the purchase price, e.g. on the net maintainable revenue, which may have no relation to the capital expended.

(51) Practical experience shows that the compulsory redemption of debt (i.e. capital) by local authorities is a salutary and effectual method of providing for depreciation.

(52) Departing for a moment from the "loan repayment *versus* depreciation" aspect which is peculiar to local authorities, let us consider what is the proper basis for charges to revenue in respect of the depreciation of industrial plant.

(53) Broadly speaking, the bases generally regarded as available for adoption for the annual charge against Revenue Account are:—

(1) On fixed original cost or "straight line" provision —equivalent to the "instalment" method of repaying debt.
(2) On the reducing balance of cost.
(3) On the annuity or sinking fund.
(4) Charging renewals to Revenue Account as they arise.
(5) Annual re-valuation, the depreciation thus ascertained being charged to Revenue Account

(54) Of these, (4) is (subject to minor exceptions) not financially sound, and (5) may be ideal but is generally impracticable. (2) may produce inadequate provision unless a very high percentage is used for the commencing basis, in which event the charges in the early years are all the higher.

(55) We are therefore left with (1) and (3), the latter being virtually the method most generally followed by local authorities. While there is plenty of technical literature upon this controversy, let me recommend to those present who have not already studied them Mr. P. D. Leake's valuable research works on the subject, although we may not necessarily accept all his views.

(56) It is instructive to consider the judgment delivered in 1913 in the case of the *National Telephone Co. v. H.M. Postmaster-General.* The Court had to determine the "then value" of plant, &c., on the basis of a clause in an agreement which substantially followed Section 43 of the Tramways Act, 1870. The question of the method of calculating depreciation, assuming life and age to be agreed, gave rise to great divergencies of view between the parties. The Postmaster-General contended that the depreciation was properly measured by the ratio which the expired life bore to the whole life of the plant; or, in other words, that the value on the "appointed day," viz. 31st December 1911, was represented by the proportion which the life still anticipated bore to the whole life. This method of calculating depreciation has been called the "*straight line method.*"

(57) The company urged that, when the life of a class of plant was, as far as possible, ascertained, a sinking fund should be formed by the investment every six months of an amount which, accumulating at compound interest, would produce at the end of the estimated life an aggregate sum equal to the original value of the plant when new. At any point in the life (they contended) the difference between the original value and the amount which at that point had been accumulated in the sinking fund was the value which should be paid by a purchaser. The company's witnesses were, however, compelled to admit that they had never known the method adopted as between a vendor and a purchaser of plant. The Court rejected the sinking fund method and adopted the straight line method.

(58) So far as industrial plant is concerned, the sinking fund method, generally adopted by local authorities, is not in accord with this recorded case; if a local authority sells a trading undertaking by arbitration to a company, the straight line method of depreciation might be regarded by the tribunal as settled by this precedent. This, however, is only a suggestion of an interesting analogy on which one could not express a general opinion. A useful discussion, however, might range round this question, should the instalment method be adopted in connection with provision for redemption of debt raised for provision of plant?

(59) In view of the schemes, e.g. joint electricity, &c., now being framed, the whole question is worthy of careful consideration, to ensure that the burden of depreciation, including obsolescence (so far as these factors not covered by provision for repayment of debt), is adequately provided for, and equitably distributed in point of time and from year to year between the parties benefiting by the use of the plant.

(60) No one is more fully cognisant than the writer that this paper should be supplemented by further lectures on several of the principal sections before it could be regarded as completely covering the subject. Our Joint Students Society Committee is, however, a live body, and one has only to dare to mention subjects for future lectures to be challenged at once for additional contributions—that is if the hardy adventurer who makes the suggestion is given even so much as an option in lieu of the fine of another address. Let me therefore say that my opinion, expressed above, is entirely without prejudice. If prizes were given for spilling ink on lectures to students I know of one deserving but indigent lecturer who might hope thereby to secure that provision for old age which he lost by relinquishing a municipal post with a superannuation scheme.

Tramways Accounts and Costs.

By E. J. Johnson, O.B.E., F.I.M.T.A.,
Borough Treasurer, East Ham.

(1) Legislation Governing Tramways.

The principal Acts governing the power of Promoters to purchase, construct, or lease tramways, are the Tramways Act, 1870, and the Light Railway Acts, 1896-1912, and, under the former, applications for Provisional Orders are made to the Board of Trade, who may settle and prepare an order, which has to be confirmed by Parliament before it becomes operative, but under the latter Acts, if application for an order is confirmed by the Board of Trade, no Confirming Act is required.

It has not been considered necessary to delve very deeply into the general legislation for the purpose of this lecture, inasmuch as this aspect has been dealt with exhaustively in previous lectures, but the following material points might be mentioned :—

Powers to Construct, Place or Run upon Tramway.

The earlier portion of the Tramways Act, 1870 (Part 1), with the Board of Trade rules made thereunder, governs applications for Provisional Orders authorising tramways. This procedure was first introduced by this Act in substitution for the necessity of promoting Bills. Parts 2 and 3 of the Acts contain general provisions for the construction and working of tramways and applies to all tramways whether authorised by Provisional Order or by Special Act, and under Section 64 the Board of Trade have power from time to time to make rules to be laid before Parliament for carrying the Act into effect.

There is no provision authorising a local authority to place or run carriages upon a tramway, or to demand or take tolls and charges in respect of the use of such carriages, but this provision is usually obtained by Provisional Order or Special Act.

Leasing of Tramways.

Where a local authority has so contracted or acquired a tramway, it may, with the consent of the Board of Trade, subject to the provisions of the Act, by lease, to be approved by the Board, grant to any corporation or company the right of user of the tramway. The lease must be made for a term, not exceeding 21 years, but may be renewed with the consent of the Board for a similar term.

How Expenses are to be Defrayed.

(*a*) Where the local authority in any district are the promoters of any tramway, they shall pay all expenses incurred by them in applying for and obtaining a Provisional Order, and carrying into effect the purposes of such Provisional Order out of the local rates, and any such expenses shall be deemed to be purposes for which such local rate may be made, and to which the same may be applied.

(*b*) Where the local rate is limited by law to a certain amount, and is by reason of such limitation insufficient for the payment of such expenses, the Board of Trade may, by the Provisional Order, extend the limit of such local rate to such amount as they shall think fit, and prescribe for the payment of such expenses.

(*c*) Such local authority may, for the purpose of such Provisional Order, borrow and take up at interest, on the credit of such local rate, any sums of money necessary for defraying any such expenses, and for the purpose of securing the repayment of any sums so borrowed, together with such interest as aforesaid, such local authority may mortgage to the persons by or on behalf of whom such sums are advanced, such local rate ; but the exercise of the above-mentioned power shall be subject to the following regulations :—

1. The money so borrowed shall not exceed such sum as may be sanctioned by the Board of Trade.

2. The money may be borrowed for such time, not exceeding thirty years, as such local authority with the sanction of the Board of Trade, shall determine ; and subject as aforesaid to the repayment within thirty years, such local authority may either pay off the moneys so borrowed by equal annual instalments, or they may in every year set apart as a sinking fund, and accumulate in the way of compound interest by investing the same in the purchase of exchequer bills or other Government securities, such sums as will be sufficient to pay off the moneys so borrowed, or a part thereof, at such time as the local authority may determine.

Separate Accounts Necessary.

Local authorities shall keep separate accounts of all moneys paid by them in applying for, obtaining and carrying into effect any such Provisional Order, and in the repayment of moneys borrowed, and of all moneys received by them by way of rent or tolls in respect of the tramway authorised thereby.

Appropriation of Surplus.

When, after payment of all charges incurred under the authority of this Act, and necessary for giving effect to such Provisional Order, there shall be remaining in the hands of such local authority any of the moneys received by them by way of rent or tolls in respect of the tramway authorised by such Provisional Order, such moneys will be applied by them to the purposes for which the local rate may be by them applied.

Local Authorities and Local Rates Affected.

In England and Wales under Schedule "A," Part I of the Tramways 1870 Act, it provides

A lecture delivered before the London Students' Society of the Institute of Municipal Treasurers and Accountants.

amongst other matters that the local authorities and local rates affected are as follows :—

(*a*) In Municipal Boroughs.	The Borough Fund or other property applicable to the purpose of the Borough Rate or the Borough Rate.
(*b*) In Urban Districts.	The General District Rate.

Consequently any surplus or deficit may be transferred to the Rate Fund concerned.

(2) Standard Form of Accounts.

In July 1907 the Departmental Committee on the Accounts of Local Authorities, before whom representatives of the Institute of Municipal Treasurers and Accountants gave evidence, issued their report which embraced a standard form of Abstract of Tramway Accounts for publication by local authorities. Doubtless, this form of accounts is well-known to all the members of this Society, therefore I will not recapitulate in detail the actual form of accounts to be kept but refer to the services to be incorporated therein ; it is advantageous for comparative purposes to show in a separate column the average expenses and revenue per day against the respective services, together with figures relating to the previous year printed in italic type.

Revenue Accounts Expenditure.

Traffic Expenses.

(1) Superintendence.—Salary of traffic superintendent and assistants.

(2) Wages of Motormen and Conductors.

(3) Wages of other traffic employees.—Depot clerks, traffic regulators, pointsboys, &c.

(4) Cleaning and Oiling Cars.—Should include wages of car cleaners and the cost of all cleaning materials and utensils.

(5) Cleaning, Salting and Sanding Track.—Should include wages of men employed in this work, together with the cost of tools and materials.

(6) Fuel, light and water for depots.

(7) Ticket Checks.—Should include wages of inspectors, clerks in punch and ticket office, cost of tickets and conductors' punches.

(8) Uniforms and Badges.

(9) Miscellaneous.—Should include amongst other items the cost of Inland Revenue and police licences for cars.

(10) Salaries of General Officers and Staff.—Should include salaries of general manager, and all officers and clerks not engaged exclusively in other sections, together with a proportion of the salaries of the borough treasurer and any of his staff engaged on the service.

(11) Proportion of through-running expenses for services linked with other authorities' systems. (A special paragraph showing the principal bases for agreements between various authorities who have inter-running facilities is set forth separately, together with two complete claims showing the adjustment between certain authorities under two different methods.)

(12) Store Expenses.—Salaries of stores and time-keepers, and expenses in connection with the stores.

(13) Rents.—Rentals of offices, shelters and wayleaves.

(14) Rates and Taxes.—Should include all local rates and taxes.

(15) Printing, Stationery and Advertising.

(16) Fuel, Light, &c., for Offices.

(17) Other establishment charges.

(18) Law Charges.—Should include all legal expenses, except those referred to in No. 19, together with a proportion of the salaries of the town clerk and any of his staff engaged on the service.

(19) Accident Insurances and Compensations.—Annual premiums of cash in transit, third party, workmen's compensation and employers' liabilities policies. Or, if the Corporation accept the risk direct, the amount of claims, legal and general expenses paid in connection therewith should be herein included,

(20) Fire and other Insurances.

(21) Miscellaneous.

(22) National Health and Unemployment Insurance.—Corporation's contributions in those cases where the gross amount of wages is not charged to the respective accounts may, with advantage, be included as a separate item under this heading.

General Repairs and Maintenance.

(23) Permanent Way.—All expenditure in connection with repairs and maintenance of track, also wages, materials, &c.

(24) Electrical Equipment of Line.—Cost of repairs to overhead or surface contact lines, also wages, materials, &c., and repairs to rail bonding, cable section boxes, &c.

(25) Buildings and Fixtures.—Cost of repairs to buildings and fixtures, such as workshops, offices, shelters, car sheds, gas and water pipes and other fittings.

(26) Workshop Tools and Sundry Plant.—Expenditure for repair of workshop tools, machinery and appliances. (Ordinary craftsmen's tools should be charged direct to the account upon which they are used.)

(27) Cars.—Should include all expenditure for repairs to cars, fittings and electrical equipment, also wages, tools, &c.

(28) Other Rolling Stock.—All expenditure for repairs to sundry vehicles, such as water cars, snow ploughs, lorries, &c., also wages and materials, but no vehicle used exclusively in respect of the before mentioned accounts should be charged direct to this account.

(29) Miscellaneous equipment.

Superannuation.

(30) Corporation's contribution to the Superannuation Fund.

(31) Allowance to officers and servants.

Power Expenses.

(32) Cost of Current.—

In a large number of towns the current for tramways is supplied through the Corporation's electricity undertaking at a price agreed, but in those cases where the tramway authority provide their own power, it is usual to set forth in the accounts an abstract showing the expenditure under various headings such as :—Salaries and wages, fuel, water, repairs of electrical plant, buildings, &c., together with the average cost per unit and per car mile.

REVENUE ACCOUNT—INCOME.

(1) *Traffic Revenue.*

This should include gross income for the year as per detailed summary of traffic receipts. (A special paragraph has been devoted to a system in operation showing how these figures are arrived at.)

(2) *Sundry Revenue.*

Advertisements on cars, tickets, &c. It is usual for the Corporation to appoint advertising contractors to obtain advertisements, and the Corporation to allow them a certain percentage of the gross receipts therefor as commission.

The balance of the Revenue Account is transferred to the Net Revenue Account.

NET REVENUE ACCOUNT.

Set forth below are the principal items which should be included :—

Expenditure.	*Income*
1. Deficiency brought forward—previous year (if any).	1. Revenue Account—balance transferred therefrom.
2. Interest on loans (including income-tax).	2. Transfer from Borough or District Fund in aid of deficiency (if any).
3. Interest on over-draft from bankers (if any).	3. Bank Interest (if any).
4. Contributions to Sinking Fund.	4. Rent of leased lines.
5. Instalments of loans.	
6. Rent of leased lines.	
7. *Renewals Fund.* A separate paragraph upon this subject is set forth elsewhere.	
8. *Reserve Fund.* A separate paragraph upon this subject is set forth elsewhere.	
9. Borough (or District) Fund Amount transferred in aid of rates (if any).	

The balance (if any) of this account should be carried to the Reserve or Renewals Account, though, where circumstances warrant it, some portion is taken to the relief of local rates.

APPROPRIATION ACCOUNT.

It is often found in practice that the repayment of mortgage loans, contributions to Sinking Funds, and Reserve or Renewals Fund, is included in an "Appropriation Account" in lieu of the net Revenue Account, and gives a clearer idea as to the comparison between the accounts of a municipality and a company—it being considered to some extent that interest as a charge against net Revenue Account would be comparable with the amount available for payment of dividends of a company, though care must be used if the same is quoted, having regard to the different bases of payments of interest.

SINKING FUND ACCOUNT.

Expenditure.	*Income.*
Redemption of Loans.	Dividends from investments.
	Net Revenue Accounts—Amount transferred therefrom in respect of contributions during the year.

The balance of this account is taken to the Balance Sheet.

RESERVE AND RENEWALS ACCOUNT.

Expenditure.	*Income.*
1. Cost of laying new feeder cables.	Dividends from investments (if any).
2. Reconstruction of cars.	Net Revenue Account—amount transferred therefrom.
3. Provision of new equipments for cars.	

NOTE.—In general practice the Renewals and Reserve Accounts are merged, though, according to the standard form, it is provided that they should be kept distinct.

Should there be a deficiency the same should be carried forward with a view to the amount required being met out of the rate affected, and in the event of there being a balance the same should be carried forward and of course shown in the Balance Sheet, though, as stated previously, according to the policy of the Corporation is more often appropriated in aid of rates.

CAPITAL ACCOUNT.

The principal heads of services incorporated in the Capital Account—it is advisable to have the separate assets valued where a portion of the undertaking has been acquired from a company and shown distinct from the expenditure for construction by the local authority—are as follows :—

Expenditure.	To 31st March 19..	From 1st April 19.. to 31 March 19..	Total	*Income.*	To 31st March 19..	From 1st April 19.. to 31 March 19..	Total
To Acquisition of undertaking where acquired from Compy.				By loans raised viz. :			
Land				Stock			
Buildings & fixtures				Mortgages ..			
Permanent Way ..				Revenue contributions to capital :—			
Electrical equipment of line ..				1.—Excess expenditure above amount of sanctions which it has not been considered sufficiently important to obtain a further sanction			
*Power station and Sub-stations plant				2.—Expenditure of a capital nature, e.g. slight extension of car sheds and improvements of electrical equipment &c.			
Workshop Tools and sundry plant ..							
Cars (including electrical equipment of cars) ..							
Other rolling stock				Other Items :—			
Miscellaneous equipment							
Offices & depots ..							
Office furniture ..							
Parliamentary expenses ..							
Preliminary expenses							
Balance unexpended at 31st March 19 .							

Note.—The proceeds of realisations or sales of property should be shown as deductions from the specific items on the other side of the account, where statutory provisions do not prescribe a different treatment.

* This item applies only to systems having a separate tramway power station.

Alternative form of Capital Account.

The form of this account, whilst being the recognised standard, is not generally adopted by municipalities, and from the perusal of various Abstracts of Accounts, it appears to be the practice to include in the Capital Account the actual cash position of the respective sanctions, delineating, on the expenditure side, deficiency at the close of the previous year, and the expenditure during the year; and on the contra side, the balance available at the close of the previous year and the income during the year.

The material difference between the two forms, it will be observed, is that with the former the balance on the debit side of the account will show the total capital expenditure which is carried to the Balance Sheet in one amount; whereas, under the latter system, the detailed capital outlay under the various services is shown in the Balance Sheet.

BALANCE SHEET at close of Financial Year.

Liabilities.	£ s d	£ s d	*Property Assets and Outlay.*	£ s d	£ s d
Loans :—			Capital outlay as per Capital Account :—		
Stock (at par value)			Acquisition of undertaking where acquired from company		
Mortgages			Land		
			Building and fixtures		
Sundry Creditors :—			Permanent Way		
			Electrical equipment of line		
			*Power station and sub-stations plant ..		
			Workshop tools and sundry plant ..		
			Cars (including electrical equipment of cars)		
			Other rolling stock		
			Miscellaneous equipment		
			Offices and depots		
			Office furniture		
Total Liabilities.			Parliamentary expenses		
Renewals Fund :—			Preliminary expenses		
(balance at credit thereof)			Works in progress		
Reserve Fund :—			Stores on hand		
(Balance at credit thereof)			Investments (at cost)		
Net Revenue Account			Sundry debtors		
(balance at credit thereof)			Unexpired licences		
Revenue contributions to capital.. ..			Cash		
Redemption of Debt :—					
Debt extinguished					
Sinking Fund available					
			*This item applies only to systems having a separate tramway power station.		

(3) Principal Books of Account.

The chief books of account which it will be found necessary to keep in order that the details for the before-mentioned accounts may be readily ascertained, commencing with the books of first entry are :—

(1) Works Costing Accounts.

(*a*) Maintenance Works Ledger with analysis columns.

(*b*) Works Ledger, for Works Accounts which do not require analysing.

These accounts are built up principally from :—

1. Wages Journal prepared from time books and/or time sheets filled in by the men or by the time keeper, and extended and agreed with the wages sheets by the office staff.

2. Haulage Journal, compiled from the returns of the foremen and time keepers.

3. Material Journals for materials issued out or returned to stock and purchased direct from tradesmen.

summarised either monthly, quarterly, half-yearly, or yearly, as found most convenient, and transferred to the various accounts in the Analysis or Impersonal Ledger.

The subsidiary forms and books required in connection with Cost Accounts I have not thought it necessary to give in consequence of the explicit and able manner this question was dealt with recently in the lecture on "Cost Accounts" to this Society by Mr. C. A. J. Hunter, Senior Assistant Accountant, Borough Treasurer's Department, West Ham, but nevertheless have set forth in the Appendix extracts of a few of the most important.

It is most essential that the foreman should have a Works Order which will bear a distinctive number issued to him in respect of each of the works, and he in turn inform his gangers thereof, so that such reference number is inserted on all requisitions, good received, &c., notes and time record sheets.

Furthermore, in respect of Maintenance Accounts an "Allocation Sheet" giving series letters and numbers applicable to various services as set forth in the Appendix should be issued to *all those* concerned with the same object in view.

(2) Expenditure Analysis Book. I will not dwell upon that very contentious matter as to the indispensability of detailed Creditors Accounts although my own opinion is, after many years' experience of both methods, that the result does not warrant the labour entailed, upon the assumption that detailed personal accounts are not kept, this book would be posted direct from the accounts passed for payment, and if the ledgers are kept, as they should be, on the self-balancing principle, agreed monthly with the order on the borough treasurer.

The monthly totals, when agreed, would then be posted to the various accounts in the Impersonal Ledger.

(3) Income Analysis Book.

If a similar system prevails as in the case of creditors and no detailed debtors accounts are kept, the books will be posted direct from the Cash Book, and the monthly totals, when agreed, posted to the Impersonal Ledger in the same manner as expenditure. It should be here noted that the main item of income, traffic receipts, is not posted in this ledger, but to a deposit account in the names of the outdoor cashiers in the General Ledger, who are debited with the amount collected from the conductors and credited with their payments either direct to the bank or the chief cashier. The contra entry to the debit entry, viz. the amount collected from the conductors, is credited to a special Personal Account for conductors raised in the General Ledger.

(4) Salaries Journal.

(5) Mortgage Ledger.

(6) Sinking Fund Ledger.

(7) Investment Ledger.

(8) Main Cash Book, to be compiled from the

(*a*) Cash Receipts Analysis Book.

(*b*) Cash Payments Analysis Book.

The subsidiary Cash Book, duly analysed to enable sectional balancing, to be summarised either weekly or monthly as deemed to be most convenient; and the periodical totals posted to the Main Cash Book.

(9) Analysis or Impersonal Ledger.

Contains the impersonal or working accounts necessary to be opened in order to supply the requisite detail for the publication of the Abstract of Accounts and the various statistical returns.

(10) General Ledger.

The accounts which would be found in this Ledger include :—

(*a*) *Deposit Accounts* of officers' responsible for the receipt of cash.

(*b*) *Special Personal Accounts.* Such as Conductors' Accounts, previously referred to, Income Tax Commissioners, Contractors' Deposits.

(*c*) *Interest on and Repayment of Loans Accounts*

(*d*) *Sinking Fund Accounts* for contributions and interest

(*e*) *Adjustment and Suspense Accounts.*

(*f*) *Ledger Accounts,* i.e. totals or bulk accounts, under which class would be found, if the self-balancing system is in operation, a bulk account for each of creditors, debtors, Sinking Funds, investments, mortgages &c., supplying the necessary balances for the Balance Sheet without recourse to the subsidiary ledgers.

(*g*) *Reserve and Depreciation Accounts.*

and finally the REVENUE ACCOUNTS and BALANCE SHEET.

(4) Income Tax.

Tramways undertakings are assessed for income-tax purposes under Schedule D. The assessment is calculated upon the average profits of the three preceding years.

The following scheme for determining allowances to be granted for wear and tear, which came into operation in 1908-1909, brought about a uniform method of arriving at such allowances. Prior to this time the allowances were left to the discretion of local Commissioners, the results of which proved unsatisfactory.

Permanent Way. Allowance for Maintenance to Cover Depreciation.

(*a*) *Life of Permanent Way.*

The life of the permanent way is to be taken as 12, 14 or 16 years, according to the traffic thereon.

The classification is to be based on the average car mileage per mile of track per annum of the financial year preceding the year of assessment, viz. :—

Average Car Miles per mile of Track. Over	Average Car Miles per mile of Track. but not exceeding	Estimated life of Track.
1	50,000	16 years
50,000	75,000	14 ,,
75,000	125,000	12 ,,
125,000		Special consideration.

Where there are special circumstances, i.e. exceptional gradients, compulsory use of Wood Paving, &c., tending to show that the car mileage does not fairly represent the wear and tear of the track, each such case is entitled to special consideration.

(b) *Cost of Renewals.*

The cost of renewals, including setts or other paving but excluding concrete foundations, should be taken at £4,400 per mile of single track, until the general renewal of the track takes place.

This allowance is intended to apply to the overhead trolley system. Special arrangements should be made in the case of the conduit, surface contact or other systems. A strict account should be kept of the annual allowance and of the actual expenditure on *repairs and renewals*, the allowances being open to revision at the end of 10 or 15 years or when the general renewal of the track takes place, but allowances in respect of previous years shall *not* be reopened.

(c) *Repairs.*

The amount to be added in respect of ordinary repairs should be determined by taking the actual average expenditure as shown in the accounts of the undertaking for the last three years, and the repairs should include renewals of special track work at junctions and cross-overs.

Inasmuch as the expenditure on repairs is expected to increase as the track begins to wear, the amount allowed in respect of repairs is subject to revision at the end of every five years. Should the life of the track and track mileage not have been altered during the five years, the allowance will remain fixed for that period.

No allowance should be made in computing the assessable profits in respect of any expenditure on repairs or maintenance of the permanent way, but the allowance for depreciation should be computed at such a sum per annum as will, in the aggregate over the determined life of the permanent way, be equal to the cost of renewal plus the estimated repairs for that period.

(d) *Extensions and Improvements.*

Expenditure on extensions and improvements should be excluded from the working expenses for income-tax purposes. The necessary additional allowance for depreciation on the lines suggested above (i.e. mileage) should be allowed on such expenditure, and added to the sum already allowable.

(e) *Revised Scheme of Annual Allowances for the Wear and Tear of the Permanent Way.*

The revised scheme of annual allowances in respect of the wear and tear of the Permanent Way came into operation 1st April 1920.

The cost of the Permanent Way laid prior to 1908 is to continue to be taken at £4,400 per mile of single track until the *renewal* of any portion of the track takes place.

From the date of the renewal of the track or any portion thereof, such renewal shall be regarded as a new track and annual allowances in respect thereof shall be granted on the basis of the sum *actually expended* and of the agreed life.

The cost of constructing new track since 1908 or of renewing any track should exclude expenditure on concrete foundations, but the cost of renewing the concrete foundations is allowed as a trading expense unless they are an improvement on the old foundations.

The cost of repairs is allowed as an expense based upon the *actual amount expended* on repairs in each of the three preceding years.

Cables.

Depreciation at the rate of 3 per cent. per annum is allowed on the *written down value* in addition to repairs.

" Written down value " means the original prime cost, plus subsequent additions, less all allowances actually granted in respect of wear and tear.

Overhead Equipment.

Overhead equipment, i.e. trolley wires and connections, no depreciation allowed. Expenditure on maintenance and renewals should be charged as working expenses as and when incurred.

Cars and Other Rolling Stock.

Expenditure on maintenance and renewals should be treated as working expenses, but depreciation at 7 per cent. per annum on the " written down value " is allowed in lieu of renewals where circumstances justify such an allowance in addition to the annual expenditure on repairs.

General Plant and Machinery.

Depreciation at the rate of 5 per cent. per annum is allowed on the " written down value " of plant and machinery, including standards brackets and workshop tools, but excluding loose implements, office furniture and small articles which require frequent renewals in addition to the cost of repairs.

Wear and Tear Allowances—Machinery and Plant.

Where full effect cannot be given to the wear and tear allowance in respect of machinery and plant owing to the insufficiency of profits during the year, the difference may be carried forward to the succeeding year.

Depreciation on Buildings.

Provision is made for the depreciation of buildings by Section 24 (4) of the Finance Act, 1918, the full annual value of the buildings being allowed as a deduction in lieu of the net annual value.

CORPORATION'S CLAIM SHOWING A LIABILITY TO PAY UPON AN ASSESSMENT OF £6,321.

The following is a detailed statement showing the compilation of a Corporation's claim in respect of income-tax, the result of which shows a liability to pay upon an assessment of £6,321.

	£	£	£
Gross profits, as per Abstract of Accounts	15,410	15,705	10,879
Items Added Back.			
Repairs and maintenance of Permanent Way ..	2,898	1,730	2,367
(Other items if any)	—	...	—
	18,308	17,435	13,246
			17,435
			18,308
			3)48,989
Assessable profits on basis of three years' average			16,330

Allowance for Depreciation and Renewals.

Permanent Way.

Under paragraph 1 of the circular issued by the Board of Inland Revenue, the life of the permanent way is to be taken to be 12, 14 or 16 years, according to the traffic thereon, the basis of classification being a sliding scale calculated on the average car mileage per mile of single track during the financial year preceding the year of assessment.

The actual number of car miles run during the year ending 31st March was 1,201,970, while the length in miles of single track was 14.25 miles, the average car miles run per mile of single track being, therefore, 84,348.

The case accordingly falls within Class 3 of the Board's scale (i.e. over 75,000 and not exceeding 125,000 car miles per mile of track) and the life must be calculated at 12 years.

For the purpose of calculating the allowance for depreciation the cost of renewing the track, including setts or other paving, but excluding concrete foundations, is to be taken at £4,400 per mile of single track, £4,400 by 14.25 62,700

To this is to be added the estimated cost of repairs during the whole life of the asset (12 years) calculated on the basis of the average expenditure on repairs during the 3 years preceding the adoption of the scheme, as follows :—

	£
Expenditure during year (1)	2,124
,, ,, ,, (2)	2,010
,, ,, ,, (3)	3,150
	3)7,284

Amount forward 16,330

	£	£	£
Brought forward ..			16,330
Average for 3 years for 14.25 miles of single track ..	2,428		
Estimated cost of repairs during life of track, £2,428 by 12		29,136	
		91,836	
Amount to be allowed per annum in lieu of depreciation (1-12th of £91,836)		7,653	
Cables.			
Depreciation to be allowed on the basis of 3 per cent. on the " written down " value.			
" Written down " value at 31st March	1,932		
Less depreciation allowed	58		
	1,874		
Add expenditure during the year	—		
" Written down " value at 31st March	1,874		
3 per cent. on £1,874 ..		56	
Overhead Equipment (i.e. trolley wires and connections)			
No depreciation to be allowed, all expenditure on maintenance and renewals to be charged as working expenses as and when incurred.			
Cars and Other Rolling Stock.			
Depreciation claimed on the basis of 7 per cent. on the " Written down " value.			
" Written down " value at 31st March	24,708		
Less depreciation allowed..	1,729		
	22,979		
Add expenditure during year	990		
" Written down " value at 31st March	23,969		
7 per cent. on £23,969 ..		1,678	
General Plant and Machinery. (Including standards, brackets and workshop tools, but excluding loose implements, office furniture and small articles which require frequent renewal)			
Depreciation to be allowed at 5 per cent. on the " Written down " value.			
" Written down " value at 31st March	12,632		
Less depreciation allowed..	632		
	12,000		
Add expenditure during year	573		
	12,573		
Amount forward			16,330

	£	£	£
Brought forward ..			16,330
Deduct overhead trolley wire and double suspensions	133		
" Written down " value at 31st March	12,440		
5 per cent. on £12,440 ..		622	
			10,009
NET ASSESSMENT for the Year			£6,321

SET-OFF OF PROFITS AGAINST RATING FUND INTEREST.

It is important to note that where the profits exceed the amount of contributions to sinking funds (including repayment of loans) *or* the wear and tear allowance, whichever is the greater, together with the interest paid in respect of loans,. the balance is available as a set-off against the appropriate Rating Fund interest.

CORPORATION'S DETAILED CLAIM SHOWING DEPRECIATION ALLOWANCE OF £1,914 IN EXCESS OF PROFITS.

	£	£	£
Gross profits, as per Abstract of Accounts	4,493	3,661	—
Items Added Back.			
Repairs and maintenance of permanent way	6,423	6,218	11,012
Bankers' interest	340	287	25
(Other items if any)	—	—	—
	11,256	10,166	11,037
			10,166
			11,256
			3)32,459

Assessable profits on basis of three years' average 10,819

Allowance for Depreciation and Renewals.

Permanent Way.

Under paragraph 1 of the circular issued by the Board of Inland Revenue, the life of the permanent way is to be taken to be 12, 14 or 16 years, according to the traffic thereon, the basis of classification being a sliding scale calculated on the average car mileage per mile of single track during the financial year preceding the year of assessment

The actual number of car miles run during the year ending 31st March was 1,379,511, while the length in miles of single track was 14.25 miles, the average car miles run per mile of single track being, therefore, 97,148.

Amount forward .. 10,819

	£	£	£
Brought forward ..			10,819
The case accordingly falls within Class 3 of the Board's scale (i.e. over 75,000 and not exceeding 125,000 car miles per mile of track) and the life must be calculated at 12 years.			
For the purpose of calculating the allowance for depreciation the cost of renewing the track, including setts or other paving, but excluding concrete foundations, is to be taken at £4,400 per mile of single track, £4,400 by 14.25 .. .		62,480	
To this is to be added the estimated cost of repairs during the whole life of the asset (12 years) calculated on the basis of the average expenditure on repairs during the 3 years preceding the adoption of the scheme, as follows:—			
Expenditure during year (1)	6,044		
" " " (2)	5,810		
" " " (3)	6,423		
	3)18,277		
Average for 3 years for 14.25 miles of single track ..	6,092		
Estimated cost of repairs during life of track, £6,092 by 12		73,104	
		135,584	
Amount to be allowed in lieu of depreciation (1-12th of £135,584)		11,298	
Cables.			
Depreciation to be allowed on the basis of 3 per cent. on the " written down " value.			
" Written down " value at 31st March	1,425		
Less depreciation allowed..	43		
	1,382		
Add expenditure during the year	—		
" Written down " value at 31st March	1,382		
3 per cent. on £1,382 ..		41	
Overhead Equipment (i.e. trolley wires and connections)			
No depreciation to be allowed.			
All expenditure on maintenance and renewals to be charged as working expenses as and when incurred.			
Cars and Other Rolling Stock.			
Depreciation claimed on the basis of 7 per cent. on the " Written down " value			
Amounts forward		11,339	10,819

	£	£	£
Brought forward ..		11,339	10,819
" Written down " value at 31st March	15,531		
Less depreciation allowed..	1,087		
	14,444		
Add expenditure during year	3		
	14,447		
7 per cent. on £14,447 ..		1,011	
General Plant and Machinery. (Including standards, brackets and workshop tools, but excluding loose implements, office furniture and small articles which require frequent renewal)			
Depreciation to be allowed at 5 per cent. on the " Written down " value.			
" Written down " value at 31st March	8,070		
Less depreciation allowed..	403		
	7,667		
Add expenditure during year	—		
" Written down " value at 31st March	7,667		
7 per cent. on £7,667 ..		383	
			12,733
Deficit—Depreciation allowance in excess of profits ..			1,914

(5) Depreciation and Renewals Funds.

The necessity of making provision for depreciation and renewals *depends largely* on the period allowed for the repayment of the loans borrowed to meet the expenditure on the particular assets, together with the policy adopted by the undertakers for meeting the expenditure on renewals.

The ascertained sum required annually to meet the depreciation should be charged to Revenue Account. If the loan period corresponds with the life of the asset the depreciation *may* be covered by the contribution to the sinking fund in respect of the loan, but if not, further provision should be made to meet the necessary depreciation.

By way of illustration let me refer to the permanent way of a tramways undertaking which generally involves a large expenditure. Loans have been granted in the past for a period of thirty years, but the life of which (excluding the concrete foundations) is approximately twelve to fifteen years. It will therefore be seen that to be financially sound some further provision must be made in addition to sinking fund.

The *actual* life of the asset and the corresponding loan period are the material factors.

It is absolutely essential that at the end of the life of an asset sufficient moneys must have been accumulated to execute the renewals or repay the outstanding debt.

Although the amount contributed to the sinking fund be equal to the amount required for depreciation, it should be borne in mind that the renewal of worn-out parts and probably other contingencies must be charged to Revenue or a still further provision made annually to meet such expenses as and when incurred.

Arguments have been put forward that local authorities should provide for depreciation in addition to the repayment of the debt within the life of the asset, but it should be borne in mind that this would cause a double burden, and may impose a charge on present-day ratepayers for the purpose of accumulating a legacy for the next generation. It is, however, advisable that the finances be so arranged to provide over a very long period an undertaking free of debt without the necessity to reborrow when renewals take place.

Extract from Report of Departmental Committee.

This matter has been considered by the Departmental Committee on local authorities accounts and their report reads as follows :—

The question how far the repayment of debt may be regarded as covering provision for depreciation is one which has given rise to serious differences of opinion in many quarters. The distinguishing feature of the capital out of which the assets of a local authority are acquired is its temporary character. The capital is required to be repaid within a period which is supposed to be not greater than the life of the asset, the calculation of the period including a certain allowance for obsolescence and reasonable contingencies. When the asset is exhausted further borrowing for its renewal is allowed, according to the practice of the Local Government Board, to the extent of the provision which has then been made for the repayment of the capital.. The general object of provision for depreciation is to ensure that an asset which ceases to be of value will, at the time of its exhaustion, cease to be represented by a charge upon the revenue ; and the question how far this purpose is met by sinking funds and redemption funds depends mainly on the correspondence of the life of the asset with the period allowed for the repayment of the capital debt. It cannot be maintained that in any given case this correspondence will be precisely accurate. Such assets as land or buildings may be entirely freed from debt at a period when their value is by no means exhausted, and may even have increased, while on the other hand it is possible, or may even be probable, that as regards a new kind of undertaking, the period allowed for repayment of debt might have been too long. Although in general the loan repayment may provide sufficiently for depreciation, it may, in some cases, be a matter of prudence to make further provision to a limited extent to meet unforeseen expenditure or to equalise the cost of repairs falling on a series of years, or again to provide for renewals in cases where subsequent experience has proved that too long a period was in fact granted originally for the repayment of the debt. The repayment of debt, as far as it goes, may properly be regarded as provision for depreciation; but it is possible that the period allowed for repayment may be excessive and, therefore, in some cases, further provision for depreciation may be necessary.

Period of Sanction reduced for Re-construction where period of Original Sanction not expired.

It is possible under exceptional circumstances where it is necessary to reconstruct the track and the original sanction has not expired, with the view of obviating the charge upon Revenue Account in respect of the amount of loan debt outstanding, to obtain sanction for the reconstruction for a shorter period of years. The immediate financial advantage of this is considerable, and no doubt is conceded, having regard to the unfortunate financial position of tramway funds generally as well as the fact that the effect of the heavy general traffic on the routes was unforeseen when the track was laid down, otherwise a period of 30 years would not have been allowed.

(6) WORKING CAPITAL.

(*a*) *Authority to obtain Short Term Sanctions Authorising Loans.*

The question of borrowing for the provision of working capital for tramway undertakings, of recent years, owing to the abnormal deficits of many undertakings, is one no doubt which has caused many financial officers to have serious thoughts as to the advisability of borrowing on short term loans for the provision of working capital, and it is obvious that Parliament realised the position, consequently provision was made in the Local Authorities (Financial Provisions) Act, 1921, authorising local authorities to borrow for the purpose of providing temporarily for any current expenses that may be incurred in the execution or performance of any of their powers and duties. Such borrowing may require the consent of the Ministry and, of course, is limited to the aggregate amount authorised by their sanction.

(*b*) *In certain cases period of Loan may be extended to Ten Years.*

The amount borrowed shall be charged on the funds, rates and revenues of the local authority *pari passu* with all other mortgages and other securities affecting the same. All sums borrowed, together with the interest thereon, shall be repaid out of Revenue of the local authority received in respect of the financial year in which the expenses are incurred, and in cases where any money borrowed before the 1st April 1923 the Minister may, if satisfied that the particular circumstances of the case justify such a course, extend the term within which such repayment is to be made—for a period not exceeding 10 years from the date on which the money is borrowed.

The power under this Act is in addition to, and not in derogation of, any other powers of borrowing exercisable by the authority.

(*c*) *Necessity to Borrow obviated by Quarterly Payments of Deficiency raised by Rate.*

I believe in some towns the necessity for borrowing for working balance is, to a large extent, obviated by the payment quarterly of any amounts agreed to be raised by rate to meet deficiencies in lieu of waiting until the close of the year.

(*d*) *Advantage of General Pass Book with Analytical Columns.*

In the case of one authority, even though the deficiency on the Tramways Fund is somewhat considerable, advantage is not taken of the provisions of the beforementioned Act, inasmuch by the whole of the Corporation's cash passing through one Pass Book with analytical columns for various funds, a daily balance of the respective funds is extracted and a transfer made at the close of the year in respect of interest due to the general fund, particularly at the present time, with the bank rate and correspondingly the banking terms being at a low rate, it obviously would not be advantageous to borrow for a given period.

I realise that this method is not carrying out the law, and that it is open to objection by the auditors, but the financial advantage to the Corporation is considerable, and providing the general balance in the Pass Book is in the Corporation's favour, no question can arise with the bankers upon that delicate question of payment in respect of interest on overdraft.

Furthermore, in those cases where tramways and electric light undertakings are run jointly, it frequently happens that the electricity undertakings in the original instance bears the expenditure for a considerable amount of the store's materials used in connection with tramways' maintenance, and unless this aspect of the position is looked into it might be possible, in the event of the provisions of this Act being utilised, for obtaining a working balance for the Electricity Fund, that the latter may bear an undue proportion.

(7) COMPILATION OF TRAFFIC RECEIPTS AND TICKET STOCK ACCOUNT.

As the chief source of income is from traffic receipts an efficient system of check is necessary. That this is well met by the punch and ticket system is shown by it being universally adopted.

The tickets are lettered with a series letter and numbered up to 10,000 in a series for each class of ticket. Those required for immediate use are kept in lockers; each locker containing a series letter of all valued tickets to be issued to conductors. The number on the locker to correspond with the number on the ticket box containing the tickets to be issued to conductors.

Tickets not required in the lockers for immediate use form the reserve stock from which the lockers are replenished.

When the tickets are issued in the box to the conductors, for which they have to sign, a summary way-bill is enclosed giving for each class of ticket a series letter, quantity, and first and last numbers. Against these are columns required to be filled in by the conductors upon the conclusion of his shift, namely, the first number returned in the box and the number sold, together with the amount thereof extended. The cash handed to the outdoor cashier is also signed for on this way-bill.

Ticket Stock Books are kept showing the stock of tickets on hand, in reserve, lockers (including boxes) separately in order that the stock may be more easily verified by the internal audit section. The Reserve Stock Book is debited with the tickets purchased and credited with the tickets transferred to lockers. The Locker Stock Book is debited with the tickets transferred from reserve stock and credited with sales as shown by the summary of way-bills, either daily, weekly, or monthly, as found convenient, referred to later.

In order that a complete check may be put upon the stock a daily ticket sheet, treating with tickets only, is kept in the office for each box issued, which has to be completed upon the return of the box to the office.

The headings of the form are as follows :—

1. Section.
2. Box number.
3. Tickets issued.
4. Total tickets as per way-bills and date.
   (*a*) Emergency tickets issued.
   (*b*) Tickets sold.
   (*c*) Thick and lost tickets.
   (*d*) Tickets returned in boxes.
5. Total tickets and date.
   (*a*) Tickets issued from lockers.
   (*b*) Tickets in boxes.

This form not only checks the tickets stocked but does in fact lock up the whole of the daily summaries of way-bills, the total of the tickets-sold column must agree with the tickets issued as shown on the way-bill summary.

When the total way-bills returned by the conductors have been checked as to tickets returned, cash extensions, and with the Outdoor Cashier's Cash Book, &c., they are summarised under routes on to a daily total sheet, the daily summaries are again summarised into monthly totals.

These monthly totals which form the basis for the ledger entries are under the following principal headings.

(*a*) Passengers.

(*b*) Value of tickets issued for cash or vouchers, &c.

(*c*) Cash vouchers, &c., paid in by conductors.

(*d*) " Overs."

(*e*) " Shorts."

The first item (*a*), Passengers, is purely statistical. So far as the other items are concerned, I think it would be clearer if the entries necessitated by the other items were journalised as follows :—

Conductors' Account.
  Dr. to Traffic Receipts.
 For value of tickets sold.

Cashiers Account.
  Dr. to Conductors' Account.
 For cash vouchers, &c., paid in by conductors.

Conductors' Account.
  Dr. to Traffic Receipts.
 For "Overs" paid in by conductors.

A separate book is kept of conductors' deficits or shorts, a notification of each is sent to the conductors for special collection, and the entry for the cash collected will be exactly the same as the cash vouchers, &c., collected in the first instance. Any short once incurred which is subsequently remitted would, of course, have to be debited to Traffic Receipts Account and credited to Conductors' Account.

The other item calling for special comment would be " vouchers." When the vouchers are sold, which should be through the office only, the sale is recorded in the Voucher Sales Book and the cash received is credited to a Voucher Account in the General Ledger. The vouchers handed in by the conductors to the cashier, who in turn delivers them to the office, resulting in the entry Crediting Cashier's Account and Debiting Voucher's Account.

In some authorities the conductor is handed an envelope in which he puts his vouchers, &c., seals and returns it in his box to be dealt with by the office, and not paid into the outdoor cashier. This method avoids duplicate handling of vouchers and consequent queries, as these vouchers are easily lost by a gust of wind blowing them about, or mislaid. In this case the Journal entry would be in lieu of crediting the Cashier's Account, Conductor's Account would be credited.

The balance of vouchers should always be a liability representing the value of vouchers sold, not yet presented.

The balance of Traffic Receipts Account, is, of course, transferred to Revenue Account, and the balances of Conductors' Account and Cashiers' Account are taken to the Balance Sheet.

Ticket Staff and Cashiers—Members of Treasurer's Staff.

The above system of dealing with Traffic Revenue is based upon the assumption that the ticket staff and cashiers are members of the Treasurer's Department, but in cases where the staff are members of the Tramway Manager's Department, the same system should be in operation with the difference that the whole of the section way-bills traffic receipt analysis, Ticket Stock Books, and actual stock of tickets would be subject to periodical audit by the internal audit section of the Treasurer's Department.

All bank " paying in " books would be issued from the latter department, and the cashiers pay into the Corporation's banking account daily, the tramway manager or cashier not being authorised to withdraw any money from the bank. Each cashier would have receipt and deposit books for alternate shifts to be sent with a carbon copy of the bank paying in slip to Treasurer Department daily for audit purposes.

(8) TRAFFIC RECORDS.

If the ticket staff and cashiers are members of the Treasurer's Department, returns should be sent to the tramway's manager showing :—

Daily Returns.

(*a*) The number of passengers on the various routes and the traffic receipts thereof together with the total passengers and traffic receipts on all routes combined.

(*b*) Report any question with reference to conductors which it is necessary for action to be taken by Inspectors, &c.

Weekly Returns.

Statement showing total number of passengers, differentiating those who tendered tokens, and the various fares obtained on each route, together with total traffic receipts thereot.

Mileage Records.

The compilation of mileage records is a matter for the tramway's manager and is based upon the daily or shift reports of the motormen, compared with the traffic regulator's reports and checked with the traffic superintendent's records.

(9) BASIS AND ADJUSTMENT OF THROUGH-RUNNING ACCOUNTS WITH OTHER AUTHORITIES.

Frequently authority is obtained either by special Act or Provisional Order, authorising running powers over other authorities' lines, and inasmuch as there is a tendency for local authorities to unite in this direction, I thought it might be advantageous to some if I set forth details of two different schemes showing the principal clauses in the agreements and the financial result thereof to the various authorities concerned.

SCHEME NO. I.

Service of Cars.

The service of cars to be provided by each authority in proportion to length of route, viz. :—

(*a*) 47.659% of total
(*b*) 26.186% ,,
(*c*) 26.155% ,,

subject to periodical adjustments of mileage owing to it being practically an impossibility to arrive at the exact percentages in the framing of the time tables or in actual operation, provision being made should any authority be unable to provide the proper proportion of cars allocated, and an opportunity given for the same to be made up, or failing that, the other authorities are allowed to claim from the defaulting authority their full working costs for all excess mileage run in their stead.

Appropriation of Fares Collected.

The fares collected are retained by each authority pending periodical adjustment which usually takes place quarterly : a statement of the receipts to be furnished to each weekly.

At specified times what is known as a " Special check " is taken for a week over the whole of the route to ascertain the value of each authority's area, and it might be mentioned that there are special Journey Way-Bills issued to each conductor with specific instructions to insert the fares received at the end of the respective stages.

The Journey Way-Bills are summarised in most minute form, and upon the result of this " Special Check " the receipts are divided, consequently any balances due to or from an authority are dealt with.

Maintenance of Track and Cars in Working Order, &c.

Each authority is responsible for the keeping of its own cars and track in working order.

Accidents.

Each authority is responsible for accidents in whatever area they are running at the time.

Compilation of Account under the above method for one quarter.

Authority.	Time-table miles in each area.	Actual miles run by each Authority.	Actual miles in ratio of time-table Miles.	Difference.	
				To be run.	Run in excess.
A	394,928	399,207	391,544	—	7,663
B	213,501	219,485	211,671	—	7,814
C	209,276	192,006	207,483	15,477	—
	817,705	810,698	810,698	16,477	15,477

Authority.	Amount due to each authority at p.c.m. earned during special check week.	Actual Receipts.	Proportionate amount due to each authority.	Difference. Amount due to c.d.
	£ s. d.	£ s. d.	£ s. d.	£ s. d.
A	391,544 at 20.630=33,656 9 5	31,332 11 6	32,782 9 11	1,449 18 5
B	211,671 at 20.543=18,118 3 1	17,549 17 1½	17,647 13 5	97 16 3½
C	207,483 at 13.062=11,292 5 3	12,546 15 4	10,999 0 7½	—
	810,698 63,066 17 9	61,429 3 11½	61,429 3 11½	1,547 14 8½

	Difference. Amount due from
A	—
B	—
C	£1,547 14 8½

From the above mileage account it will be observed " C " authority is still to run 15,477 miles and pay £1,547 14s. 8½d. received in excess.

Scheme 2.

Service of Cars, Maintenance of Track, and Accidents.

The service of cars is provided by each authority in proportion to the length of route in each area, viz. :—

(*a*) 40.015% of total
(*b*) 34.913% „
(*c*) 25.072% „

The same provisions apply to adjustment of mileage maintenance of track and accidents as in Scheme 1.

Pooling of Fares Collected.

The fares collected are retained by each authority. The total receipts on the whole route are " pooled," but in the case in question the earning value of each authority's area is considered to be equal and the pool is shared out quarterly according to the car mileage due to each authority.

Compilation of Account under above method for one quarter.

Authority.	Time-table miles in each area.	Actual miles run by each Authority.	Actual miles in ratio of time-tables Miles.	Difference.	
				to be run.	run in excess.
A	145,178	31,866	144,600	112,734	—
B	127,709	235,208	127,201	—	108,007
C	92,001	96,362	91,635	—	4,727
	364,888	363,436	363,436	112,734	112,734

Authority.		Amount due to each authority at flat rate.	Actual Receipts.	Difference:	
				Amount due to.	Amount due from.
		£ s. d.	£ s. d.	£ s. d.	£ s. d.
A	144,600	11,867 8 0	2,923 18 10½	8,943 9 1½	—
B	127,201	10,439 9 1½	19,635 14 5	—	9,195 5 3½
C	91,635	520 10 8	7,268 14 6	251 16 2	—
363,436 at 19.697d. =		£29,827 7 9½	29,827 7 9½	9,195 5 3½	9,195 5 3½

From the above it will be observed that although " A " is to receive £8,943 9s. 1½d. from " B " they still have 112,734 miles to run and "C" is to receive £251 16s. 2d. from " B," in addition to having run 4,727 miles in excess.

(10) Joint Undertakings for Tramways and Electricity Supply.

There are one or two towns where the tramways and electricity undertaking, so far as their administration is concerned, is still under one manager, whose appointment is " Tramways Manager and Electrical Engineer," and the undertakings are combined, but even though the accounts of both undertakings are kept separate, providing that a good system of allocation is in operation, particularly where a number of officials and workmen, and administration services are chargeable upon a basis according to " User " to each undertaking, there should be little or no difficulty in arriving at the correct debits and credits applicable to the respective undertakings.

(11) Statement as to Borrowing Powers, &c.

Incorporated with the account should be a statement as to borrowing powers under the following headings :—

Borrowing Powers Authorised.			Borrowing Powers Exercised.	Borrowing Powers remaining to be exercised.
Act. Order of or Sanction.	Period of Loan.	Amount		
		£	£	£

N.B.—This might with advantage be enlarged to embrace sufficient data to show the net debt outstanding.

(12) Statistical Information.

It is customary to incorporate with the Abstract of Accounts statistical information as follows :—

Date of commencement of undertaking.
Population.
Miles of track in operation (showing single and double track separately).
Capital expenditure at end of year.
Amount of debt redeemed.
Percentage of debt to capital outlay.
Net debt at close of year.
Total amount applied in aid of rates.
Total amount received from rates.
Traffic Revenue.
Revenue from other sources.
Other receipts.
Total Revenue.
Working expenses.
Surplus.
Interest on loans.
Contributions to Sinking Fund and loan instalments.
Net surplus or deficit.
Number of units of electric current used.
Number of car miles run.
Number of passengers carried.
Number of passengers carried per car mile.
Traffic receipts per car mile.
Total cost per car mile.
Revenue per passenger.
Total cost per passenger.
Average number of cars in use per day.
Average Traffic Revenue per car run per day.
Average Traffic Revenue per car mile.
Average Traffic Revenue per car run for the year.
Average Traffic Revenue per day.
Average Traffic Revenue per week.
Average Traffic Revenue per mile of route.
Average total Revenue per car mile.
Average total Revenue per head of population.
Total number of passengers carried (showing dissection between various routes).
Average number of passengers carried per car mile.
Average number of passengers per day.

Average fare per passenger paid to Traffic Revenue.
Average working cost per passenger.
Average gross expenditure per passenger.
Average surplus per passenger.
Scale of fares.
Cost per mile for current.
Percentage of total expenses to Total Revenue:—
Working expenses.
Interest on capital.
Sinking Fund contributions.
Instalment of loans.
Surplus.
Number of cars in stock.

(13) ASSESSMENT OF UNDERTAKINGS TO LOCAL RATES.

Assessment of Undertaking to Local Rates.

The method of arriving at the gross and rateable values of a tramway undertaking is somewhat complicated, but it is not my intention to weary you with any details, as no doubt you are familiar with the same, and probablythe subject will be dealt with in the lecture which I understand is to be given you in the very near future.

In passing I think mention should be made of the fact that throughout the Country, excluding London, the National Union of Assessment Committees and the various railway companies have agreed to a reduction of between 21 per cent. to 31 per cent. from the rateable values of railways, taking effect for a short period of years from the 1st April 1922, and it may be advantageous to municipalities if the assessments of their trading undertakings were looked into, particularly as in the majority of towns considerable losses have taken place in recent years.

Allowance of 75 per cent. under Public Health Act, 1875, is not applicable.

No portion of the rates on tramway undertakings constructed under the Tramways Act, 1870, is assessed to the general district rate at *one-fourth* as in the case of tracks constructed under the Light Railway Acts: the reason for this is not fully understood, and appears to me to be an anomaly which is somewhat unfair and inequitable.

All railway tracks are eligible for such an allowance.

(14) UNFAIR BURDEN UPON UNDERTAKING OF ENTIRE COST OF CONSTRUCTION AND MAINTENANCE OF TRACK.

Construction and Maintenance of Whole Width of Track should not be borne by the Undertaking.

It is generally known that the tramway authority is responsible for the whole cost of laying foundations and surfacing of roads as well as the entire maintenance thereof including 18 inches either side of the outer rails which, in many instances, constitutes over 50 per cent. of the roadway. I venture to suggest that the time has arrived when this very serious burden should again be pressed before Parliament by municipalities, with a view to being relieved of such burden. It is obvious that since the enactment was passed the nature and volume of traffic has been practically revolutionised by the introduction of heavy mechanically propelled vehicles which was not foreseen.

The merits or demerits of the case for submission is primarily one for engineers to deal with, but the financial burden to-day for the reconstruction and maintenance of tram tracks to withstand the effect of the present day traffic is causing many authorities to talk of "Scrapping the Trams," though, having regard to the large number of passengers they can convey, as compared with other forms of passenger vehicles, it would entail a serious inconvenience to the public if this were carried out. Local authorities would not object to pay increased fees for Revenue licences somewhat in proportion to that paid by owners of other passenger vehicles who are free to use the same track and possibly cause the necessity for repairs equally as much as other mechanically propelled vehicles.

APPENDICES.

(1)

STORES REQUISITION. No.....

To the storekeeper,

Please Supply for { Works Order No.....
Maintenance Service No.....

Material.		Purpose required and Description of Work.
Quantity.	Description.	

Signature............... Date...........

(2)

TRANSFER NOTE (Distinctive colour paper).

To the Storekeeper.

The undermentioned material has been transferred from works at................

Works Order No.....

Maintenance Service No.....

To Works at Works Order No.....
Maintenance
Service No.....

Quantity.	Description.	Quantity.	Description.

Sent by........................ Date.............
Received by..................... Date.............

(3)

MATERIALS AND STORES RECEIVED THIS DAY.

To the Storekeeper. Date......

Quantity.	Descripion.	Received from.	Where used.	Works Order No......... Maintenance Service No. E.......

Signature.....................

Note.—A delivery note must vouch each consignment of goods and accompany this return.

(4)

RECEIPT DELIVERY NOTE.

To...........

.Please receive the undermentioned materials per............

Quantity.	Description.	Description of Work and Works Order No. Maintenance Service E. No.....	Cart No. and Contractor.	Remarks.

Signature of Storekeeper............Received by..

Date................ Date..........

N.B.—This Note to be returned immediately to Storekeeper's Office.

ALLOCATION SHEET.

E *Traffic Expenses.*

1 Salaries
Wages—
2 Motor Inspectors
3 Shed Foreman and Traffic Regulator
4 Inspectors
5 Motormen
6 Conductors
7 Car Washers
8 Greasers
9 Track Cleaners
10 Pointsmen
11 Miscellaneous (small and sundry)
12 Fuel
13 Light
14 Water
15 Uniforms, Waterproof Clothing, &c.
16 General Stores and Cleaning Materials
17 Electrical Engineer's Disbursements (proportion)
18 Licenses—Police and Inland Revenue
19 Tickets and stationery
20 Punches

K *Management.*

1 Salaries
2 General Establishment Charges

F *Car Shed.*

1 Lighting
2 Cleaning
3 Repairs

G *Maintenance and Renewals.*

1 Permanent Way
2 Electrical Equipment—Overhead Lines
3 ,, ,, Feeders
4 Car Equipment
5 Car Repairs (General)
6 Tools and Implements
7 Oil and other Lubricant

H *Capital.*

1 Permanent Way
2 Electrical Equipment—Overhead Lines
3 ,, ,, Feeders
4 Car Equipment
5 Cars
6 Car Shed
7 Tools
8 Furniture
9 Uniforms, &c.
10 Fixtures and Fittings

The various service headings and numbers can be increased to suit requirements.

Week ending............................ TIME BOOK.

Workmen		Occupation.	Employment.		Chargeable to.	Friday	Saturday	Sunday	Monday	Tuesday	Wednesday	Thursday	Time total.	Rate of Wages.	Amount	Totals.
No.	Name.		How.	Where.									hrs. dys.	hr. dy.	£ s d	£ s d

INVENTORY...................... 19.... Sheet No.......

....

Name of Yard or Foreman, and Number of Rough Inventory Sheet.	Stores Ledger Folios.	Material.	Quantity.	Value as per Inventory		Depreciation during year		Present Value.		
				at	Amount	at per cent.	Amount	at	Plant	Material
			T. c. qr. lb No.		£ s d		£ s d		£ s d	£ s d

Abstracts of Accounts.

By A. Wetherall, F.I.M.T.A., F.S.A.A.
Borough Treasurer, Dewsbury.

Introduction.

The preparation and publication of the Annual Abstract of Accounts is *the* job more than any other which is associated directly and personally with the office of Chief Financial Officer. This attitude of mind is particularly true of the average municipal finance student. If he permits himself to indulge in day-dreams of the future when his ambition shall have been achieved, the Abstract of Accounts will loom large in the picture. It is regarded by him with much the same feelings of veneration and pride as, we can believe, the poet regards the privately-published book of his verse. Later on, I believe, it assumes its proper proportion as part of the work of the office. But the " Abstract " is not published solely for the edification of the Chief Financial Officer; it is published in pursuance of a statutory duty. It is open to the inspection of any ratepayer who may if he choose acquire a copy at a reasonable cost. Yet the " Abstract " has not become a " best seller," and the ratepayer who may be jealous of his right of inspection is certainly not " thronged " when he chooses to exercise it.

Members of the Council are usually given a copy " free of charge," and as there is no condition attached to the gift that it shall be studied, it is usually accepted. That it is not considered vital to their needs is shown by the fact that more than one economy Committee has suggested that the expense of the " Abstract of Accounts " might be saved.

Quite apart from the statutory duty imposed on the Treasurer an " Abstract of Accounts " is becoming increasingly necessary by reason of its great convenience.

Where copies of the accounts are required, as, for example, for the purpose of assessing the liability of the Corporation to income-tax, the " Abstract of Accounts " affords a convenient basis.

It is also a very convenient form in which to compare the expenditure of the Corporation with previous years. It contains under one cover, in handy form, the accounts contained in numerous and bulky ledgers. It is also a convenient statistical record for use in the Finance Departments of other Municipalities.

What is an Abstract of Accounts ?

The expression " Abstract of Accounts " is very often restricted in its meaning to the annual volume issued by the municipality or larger district council—in fact, in my introductory references, it is this kind of " Abstract " I have had in mind—but the expression has a much wider significance than this. It

A lecture delivered before the Yorkshire Students' Society of the Institute of Municipal Treasurers and Accountants.

would, perhaps therefore, be desirable to consider exactly what an " Abstract of Accounts " of a local authority is, and what are the statutory requirements relating thereto.

The dictionary definition of " Abstract " is " summary " ; " abridgment " ; " essence." The " Abstract of Accounts " of a local authority is, therefore, a summary of the accounts of that authority, and this summary should be the *essence* of the accounts themselves. That word " essence " gives us the aim. Picture to yourselves, in imagination, the accounts of the authority as contained in the various ledgers, placed in a retort, heated by the flame of enthusiasm, and the torch of accountancy qualification, and the " Abstract " being distilled off.

It will be seen that an " Abstract of Accounts " is not necessarily required to be printed or published.

STATUTORY REQUIREMENTS AS TO " ABSTRACT OF ACCOUNTS " OF LOCAL AUTHORITIES.

The statutory requirements as to the " Abstract of Accounts " are as follow :—

Boroughs. (*a*) Municipal Corporations Act, Section 27 (2). " After the audit of the accounts for the second half of each financial year, the Treasurer shall print a full Abstract of his accounts for that year."

(*b*) Public Health Act, 1875, Section 246. " The accounts of the receipts and expenditure of the Borough Council, acting as an Urban Authority under the Public Health Acts . . . are to be published in like manner, and at the same time as the municipal accounts."

County Councils. The Local Government Act, 1888, Section 71 (2). " The provisions of the Municipal Corporations Act, 1882, with respect to . . . . the accounts of the Treasurer of the Borough and to the inspection and abstract thereof shall apply to the accounts of a County Council . . . "

Urban District Councils. Public Health Act, 1875, Section 247 (10). Provides that " after receipt of the Auditor's Report on the Accounts the Local Authority . . . shall publish an ' Abstract ' of such accounts in some one or more of the local newspapers circulated in the district."

Rural District Councils, are similarly required by the Local Government Act, 1894, Section 58 (2) to publish an " abstract " of their accounts in one or more of the local newspapers circulated in the district.

Parish Councils. Parish Councils have been relieved of the necessity of publishing an "Abstract of Accounts," but they are required to lay before the parish meeting, held next after the completion of the audit, a copy of the financial statement as certified by the District Auditor.

With regard to the " Abstracts " required by statute to be published in local newspapers, it will be obvious that it is not conveniently possible to publish an " abstract " of the whole of the accounts of the larger urban district councils, and these authorities, generally speaking, publish their abstracts in book form in the same manner as the Town Councils.

It will have been noticed that in the case of parish councils, publication consists of laying before the next parish meeting the financial statement signed by the Auditors. This financial statement is an " Abstract of Accounts," and it will therefore be desirable to consider what statutory obligations there may be upon local authorities to prepare " Abstracts of Account " apart from the duty of publication.

Local Taxation Returns. Extensive powers have been given to the Ministry of Health by the Local Taxation Returns Acts, 1860 and 1877, and by Section 25 of the Municipal Corporations Act, 1882, to require Annual Returns to be made to them of any receipts or expenditure of the local authority. Forms are provided for the purpose of these Returns, and these, when completed, are, of course, " Abstracts of Account." In the case of some authorities, i.e. where the form of accounts is prescribed by the Ministry of Health, the financial statement submitted to the Auditor in the form prescribed is accepted in place of the Return.

Electric Lighting. A form of " Abstract " has in this case been prescribed by the Board of Trade.

Gas Works. The Annual Return to the Board of Trade is required under the Gas Regulation Act, 1920 The Return provided in this case is not a full " Abstract of the Accounts." The statutory forms prescribed for Gas Companies are generally followed by local authorities in their published accounts, and these follow ordinary commercial practice.

Tramways. Separate accounts are required to be kept by Section 20 of the Tramways Act, and Annual Returns are required.

Forms of Claims in Respect of Grant-aided Services. In the more recently-established grant-aided services the basis of the claim for grant is an " Abstract of Accounts " duly certified by the Auditors.

LIMITATIONS OF THE STATUTORY ABSTRACT.

The statutory provisions relating to " Abstracts of Account " and their publication, refer to accounts of " receipts and expenditure " except under Section 58 of the Local Government Act, 1894, where the words " receipts and payments " are used. The terms " receipts and expenditure " are not co-relative, but the Local Government Board when appealed to with regard to the Accounts of County Councils, explained that the accounts should be kept on cash lines. That, of course, was prior to the Report of the Departmental Committee on the Accounts of Local Authorities. The Committee decided that accounts on full income and expenditure lines were the only adequate accounts in the case of the larger local authorities, although they recognise "that it is not practicable at present to apply the complete system of income and expenditure to the fund accounts, which deal mainly or entirely with rates." This puts the onus on the local authorities, but the Returns required by the Ministry of Health and other Government Departments are now accepted, if prepared on lines of "income and expenditure," and, indeed, if the accounts of the authority are prepared on "income and expenditure lines," the Returns should be similarly prepared.

WHAT THE ABSTRACT SHOULD CONTAIN.

Having regard to the limitations of the statutory Abstract of Accounts," and also to the convenience and usefulness which we have seen are to be obtained from the "Abstract of Accounts," what should the "Abstract" contain?

The Departmental Committee, previously referred to, have expressed their opinion as follows :—

"The essential elements of a proper Abstract must comprise sufficiently detailed income and expenditure accounts for each separate fund (including the revenue and net revenue accounts of each trading undertaking, the capital and loan expenditure accounts, and accounts of the sinking funds and reserve funds); a short summary of all the income and expenditure; the separate and aggregate Balance Sheets; and a tabular statement in regard to the authorised loans and the provisions made for their repayment."

"The Regulations should not preclude any reasonable sub-division of the entries, provided the standard arrangement be preserved, nor the addition of statements giving information upon any special matters which local circumstances may render desirable (paragraph 127)."

Also (paragraph 78), "We are . . . strongly of opinion that in any abstract of the accounts a great mass of detail is much to be deprecated. It renders the accounts confusing and unintelligible to the ordinary ratepayer; while those more skilled in matters of account should be enabled to ascertain any particulars they may require, without undue difficulty, by inspection of the accounts themselves."

I do not think anyone will quarrel with the items recommended by the Committee for inclusion. The list is not intended to be exhaustive. With these recommendations as a starting point, the following is suggested as an outline of the items which should comprise the "Abstract of Accounts." Subject to anything I may have to say later on the question of arrangement, I have placed the items in what I conceive to be the logical order. :—

No. 1. Contents.

No. 2. Treasurers' and Auditors' Reports.

I am not satisfied that a report by the Treasurer is necessary, or that it is really desirable. It seems to be a reflection on the Abstract if explanation is necessary, and there is a very great danger that the report, by becoming a mere mass of figures, may be less illuminating than the accounts themselves. There is a tendency nowadays to provide a preface to the "Abstract" and for this there is, perhaps, more to be said. In it new features of the accounts can be pointed out, and new tendencies indicated.

No. 3. Summarised Revenue Accounts.

These are a concession to the man-in-the-street, who is not likely to proceed further than the earlier pages of the book. The new form of local taxation return, known as the epitome of accounts, is frequently published ***in extenso***, and although there is no objection to this, it does seem that the necessity for this tabloid abstract applies more particularly to the rate funds.

No. 4 Abstract Proper.

The accounts under this heading will include

(*a*) Rating fund or funds, revenue account, capital account, sinking fund and balance sheet.

(*b*) Accounts in association with one or other of the rating funds (particularly those under the adoptive Acts). With regard to these accounts, the Departmental Committee reported :—

"This system (i.e. separate revenue accounts, bringing out the surplus or deficiency in each case) as a general rule should apply also to public libraries, baths and wash-houses, parks and recreation grounds, burial grounds, and other such services, which, though in different degrees productive of revenue, are regarded normally as a direct charge upon the rates. In these cases it does not seem to the Committee to be necessary to prepare separate net revenue accounts and balance sheets in addition to the separate revenue accounts of income and expenditure." (Paragraph 66.)

(*c*) Trading undertakings. Revenue account and net revenue account, capital account, sinking fund and balance sheet, with accounts of statutory reserve and renewal funds in addition.

(*d*) Accounts which are required either by statute or by reason of their nature to be kept separate from the rating funds.

No. 1. Exchequer Contribution.

This applies only to County Boroughs and County Councils. Owing to the nature of the transactions recorded, it is regarded as sufficient to show the account in cash form. This account is part of the Borough Fund.

No. 2. Education Accounts.

These are required to be kept separate by the provisions of the Education Act, 1902. In Boroughs, these accounts are associated with the Borough Fund but the Audit provisions are different! The accounts will be sub-divided into elementary and higher education respectively, showing for each a revenue account, capital account, sinking fund, and balance sheet.

No. 3. Housing Accounts (a) Assisted Scheme.
(b) Dwelling-house Improvement Fund.

These accounts are associated with the District Fund. In addition to the usual revenue account, capital account, sinking fund and balance sheet, the will usually be a Repairs Fund, which should be shown.

No. 4. Private Street Works Accounts, Stable Accounts, Plant Accounts, and similar Special Accounts involving Apportionment of Charges.

In most of these cases, a separate revenue account will be sufficient.

(c) Accounts which are not associated with any one fund and which must be kept separate by reason of statutory provision or on account of their special nature.

No. 1. Consolidated Loans Fund.

No. 2. Mortgage Sinking Fund (this applies particularly in the case of authorities having power to issue a common form of mortgage).

No. 3. Insurance Funds and other similar funds established by special statutory provision.

With regard to the arrangement of this part of the Abstract, it is submitted that where there is more than one rating fund the Borough Fund should logically come first. The accounts under (b) should immediately follow the revenue account of the Rate Fund with which they are associated, and the accounts under (c) and (d) should also be identified with the particular funds with which they are associated.

No. 5. Aggregate Balance Sheet.

The value of a statement in this form was appreciated by the Departmental Committee, but they have given no indication as to the form they would suggest. The columnar form is, perhaps, preferable, and the distinction between capital and revenue should be observed as in the separate Balance Sheets of the services.

No. 6. Loan Statement to show Loans sanctioned, Loans raised, Provision for Redemption of Debt, Sinking Funds invested, and Loans outstanding.

No. 7. Statistical Records.

There is great diversity of practice as to the statistics shown. It is thought that the following should be given :—

(a) General statistics, e.g. Area, Population, Rateable and Assessable Values, Net Loan Debt, Rates in the £, Rate Collection Statistics.

(b) Statistics *re* Trading Undertakings.

(c) Statistics *re* Rate Fund Services. To some extent this is supplied in No. 3, where the Epitome is published. It should, however, be possible to extend this very considerably, and also to secure some uniformity when the Institute has completed its labours with regard to the compilation of these records.

No. 8. Estimates for Rates.

It is very convenient to have these bound up in the " Abstracts of Accounts." Where the Estimates are prepared before the actual close of the year's accounts, it is also convenient to have " the estimated actual " expenditure and income corrected to the figures as subsequently ascertained.

No. 9. (a) Accounts of Charities administered by the Corporation.

(b) Accounts of Overseers of the Poor of the Parishes comprised in the Borough.

(c) Accounts of Joint Boards and Committees of which the Authority is a constituent part.

No. 10. Index.

A full and complete Index is very necessary. It is convenient to show this in columnar form giving a reference to the revenue account, capital account, balance sheet, estimates, and special accounts, &c., in respect of each service.

Special Features of the Final Accounts of Local Authorities.

I cannot regard my task as complete without taking one of those excursions into municipal accountancy which I have said is the peculiar liability of those who treat of " Abstracts of Account." I do not propose to go very far, but in view of the fact that so much of the Abstract consists of revenue accounts, capital accounts, and balance sheets, it seems to me that something must be said of the special features of these accounts and statements when applied to the transactions of a local authority.

Revenue Accounts.

The revenue accounts should follow commercial lines; that is to say, they should be summaries of the nominal accounts of the fund or undertaking concerned. Nominal accounts, you will remember, tecord transactions relating to income and expendirure. In the case of the trading undertakings, the revenue account shows the result of the employment of capital; and may be correctly described as a " profit and loss account," although I admit that

that expression is ambiguous even when applied to ordinary commercial accounts.

With regard to rate fund services and other non-trading undertakings, the correct designation is, revenue account.

The question arises as to the extent to which it is necessary to give detail. From the point of view of what I have called the "Statutory Abstract," the summarised revenue account included under Part 3 is sufficient, but a too brief summary tends to destroy the value of the Abstract for some of those extra statutory purposes to which it is applied. Generally speaking, I think too much detail is shown. It is not necessary, for instance, in my opinion, to give every nominal account which is shown in the ledger. One of the authors I have mentioned earlier gives two instances of excessive detail which I will also include as horrible examples. They are "milk for cats" (this under the heading of police expenditure) and "rug for Borough Accountant's Department." What is more important to my mind than the question of detail is that there should be a logical classification of the expenditure and income. In many instances the items appear to have been put together quite promiscuously, as if a spare column in the ledger amongst the rates, taxes, insurance, and similar establishment expenses had been utilised for, say, printing and stationery, and the order of the ledger had been slavishly followed in the Abstract. Another point is that items are frequently shown as income which should strictly be deducted from the expenditure. Items like "salary overdrawn," or "stamps supplied to Overseers," should not be shown as income.

Frequent changes in the classification of expenditure and variations in the extent to which detail is shown may render comparison difficult, and thus diminish the usefulness of the Abstract. Great care should always be exercised in making any changes in the form of the Abstract generally.

The special features of the revenue accounts are :—

(1) Rates income. This income is not the result of the employment of capital, but the result of a statutory levy. This is merely a difference of nature, and does not involve any special treatment. In the case of the rate funds it will be about the largest item of revenue.

(2) Government Grants. The present system of Government Grants does permit of the amount due in respect of a particular service being ascertained at the close of the year. Formerly, at least in some cases, it was not possible to ascertain this, and the difficulty thus occasioned was perhaps the biggest obstacle to the adoption of proper revenue accounts.

(3) It is very convenient to arrange the revenue accounts in departments or services according to the different Committees of the Council which administer them. In some cases this is carried too far, as, for instance, where the ordinary costs of a service is shown under one Committee and the loan charges in respect of that service shown in another portion of the "Abstract" under the Finance Committee. It is desirable that the whole cost of a service should be capable of being ascertained on one inspection.

In at least one case within my knowledge, it is the practice to carry the amount of the estimated rate aid required for a particular service to the credit of that service in the revenue account, thus showing a separate surplus or deficiency in respect of each service. This does not seem to serve any useful purpose, and, moreover, it is technically incorrect. There is, perhaps, something to be said for the practice so far as the Committee estimates are concerned.

Capital Accounts.

The capital account of a Municipality should be shown on the double-account system. If this is carried out strictly, the capital expenditure is shown in detail in each year's published accounts, with columns for (1) expenditure up to the commencement of the financial year; (2) expenditure during the year, and (3) total. This involves a lot of detail, which is avoided in some cases by carrying forward a balance from the preceding Abstract. It is, however, very convenient for reference, to have the capital accounts shown in this form. It is not, perhaps, necessary to show the loans in similar detail; loans in respect of a particular service being shown in one sum, except in the case of loans raised during the financial year, which should be identified with a particular sanction.

The special features of the capital account are :—

(1) The item of debt redeemed. The statutory requirement to redeem the loan debt by annual contributions from revenue does not apply to those companies who publish their accounts on the double-account system. In the case of local authorities it is consequently necessary to show on the credit side of the capital account, not the loans *raised* in respect of a particular service, but the loans *outstanding*, and to show, in addition, the amount of debt redeemed in respect of that service.

(2) Extinction of Assets. In certain cases, expenditure out of loan in respect of, e.g. costs of Act, is sometimes extinguished out of the surplus represented by debt redeemed in respect of that particular expenditure. As I have shown elsewhere, the retention of such expenditure as an asset can be justified, but there is something to be said for the extinction in certain cases, as for example, e.g. where an Act has been repealed by a later one. Expenditure on street improvements, particularly reconstruction of road surface, is

also frequently extinguished when the loan debt is repaid. Some authors get over the difficulty by attempting to distinguish between "assets" and "deferred expenditure," but it seems to me that such a distinction cannot logically be maintained.

(3) Gifts. In many towns, valuable public properties have been acquired by gift from public spirited individuals, and in some Abstracts of Account assets of this kind are not included. In my view they should be shown in the Balance Sheet at the actual value, if known, or at an estimated value if more accurate information cannot be obtained. It is rather a delicate matter, perhaps, to put an estimated value upon a gift, but at least a note may be made on the Balance Sheet of the existence of the asset.

(4) Expenditure out of Revenue. Many authorities provide expenditure, which is, undoubtedly, of a capital nature, out of current rate, and where this is done the expenditure should be shown in the capital account, otherwise the existence of a valuable asset will not be disclosed on the Balance Sheet. I have known cases where income has been shown in the revenue account as being derived from certain property which did not appear either in the capital account or the Balance Sheet of the authority.

Balance Sheets.

Where the double-account system is in operation, the capital account and Balance Sheet are connected by the inclusion in the latter of the balance on the capital account. In municipal accounts, it is customary to show the assets and capital outlay; the loans out of which they have been acquired, and the amount of debt redeemed or other surplus representing gifts, &c., on their respective sides, instead of showing the balance of the capital account. There is, of course, no violation of principle in this. In any event, it is desirable that the capital portion of the Balance Sheet should be kept separate from the revenue portion.

The Balance Sheet is a statement of assets and liabilities. It is not an account, and, therefore, no question of form arises so long as the assets and liabilities are clearly distinguished. Generally speaking, the form adopted is that which shows the liabilities on the left-hand side and the assets on the right-hand side. I do not accept the view expressed by a former Municpal Accountant (Mr. J. C. Howarth, "Municipal Balance Sheets"), who stated that the "prevailing practice in England in commercial concerns is to place assets on the right-hand side and the liabilities on the left, while municipalities, as a general rule, adopted the contrary practice, i.e. with the assets shown on the left-hand and the liabilities, per contra," nor do I accept the further view expressed by him, "that the latter method of treatment is the best." The best method, other things being equal, is obviously the arrangement which is in common use.

Having regard to the fact that some of the capital expenditure of the Corporation is not represented by tangible assets, as that term is generally understood, it is advisable to describe the items on the left-hand side as "assets and capital outlay"; the liabilities side should be headed "liabilities and credits," following ordinary commercial practice.

Second Day—Thursday, 21st June, 1923.

AFTERNOON SESSION.

The PRESIDENT: Gentlemen, I will call on Mr. Wetherall, the Borough Treasurer of Swansea, to read his paper.

Mr. R. A. WETHERALL (Borough Treasurer, Swansea), then read the following paper on :—

A "REAL" CONSOLIDATED LOANS FUND.

1. One of the chief functions of the Chief Financial Officer is the administration of the debt services of the Local Authority he serves. It is the discharge of this particular function more perhaps than any other, with the possible exception of rating, which makes the Chief Financial Officer a specialist.

2. The Institute has already interested itself in the question of the consolidation of rating funds and the levy of one local rate for all local purposes with the result that the power to effect this is now being given to authorities who care to apply for it.

Possibly in the near future the benefits to be derived from the consolidation of rates, of which presumably Parliament has been amply satisfied in individual cases, will be made generally available by the operation of a general Act.

3. It is the object of this paper to examine the possibilities of a similar process of consolidation applied to the loan debt of a Municipality in order to secure similar benefits in the administration of the debt service.

The analogy with rating must not be pressed so far as to convey the impression that this paper is intended to compare in any way with the very exhaustive Memorandum on Consolidated Rating issued by the Institute—my object will be achieved if discussion of the question is stimulated.

A "Real" Consolidated Loans Fund (*continued*).

4. Apart from the similarity of the general nature of the two problems the circumstances which give rise to the problem of the administration of debt services are the same as those which called for the introduction of a consolidated rate. Thus we have :—

(i.) The provisions of the general law with regard to borrowing and debt redemption which are applicable to all local authorities.

These are more or less out of date and certainly not adapted to present conditions when borrowing by a local authority is no longer an infrequent and isolated experience but a daily necessity.

(ii.) The provisions secured by private legislation by progressive Municipalities modifying the general law to meet present day needs and pointing to the need for

(iii.) the "something more" which is suggested by the expression "real" Consolidated Loans Fund.

5. The progress of ideas with regard to Local Authorities' debt redemption outlined in the preceding paragraph would seem to be as follows :—

(i.) The Public General Acts which provide for the exercise of borrowing powers by a local authority appear to regard each act of borrowing as a separate and isolated occurrence.

With a view to securing proper control over a power which might otherwise be abused, a separate application has to be made in respect of each borrowing power; separate sanctions are issued and different securities are given in respect of different classes of loans.

Moreover although the language of the Acts is none too clear in this respect there are indications of an intention that a separate provision should be made for the repayment of *each loan* and that the amounts so provided should be rigidly applied to the repayment of the particular *loan* in respect of which it was provided.

A "REAL" CONSOLIDATED LOANS FUND (*continued*).

(ii.) The later provisions mark the period covered by the authority given to local authorities to issue Stock and the development of borrowing by short term mortgage. In each case we have a common security with a single redemption fund which is available for new capital purposes but the new security must be identified with the old.

Moreover the Interest Funds and the Redemption Funds for Stock and Mortgages respectively are required to be kept separate and distinct.

(iii.) The present suggested solution of the problem envisages borrowing by a local authority as a more or less continuous process—a necessary incident of municipal activity.

If a local authority borrows money on twenty different sanctions in a year it exercises not twenty different rights but the same right twenty different times.

In the same way a loan raised two years ago for the purpose of providing a public park is directly connected with a loan proposed to be raised to-day for a public baths or public elementary school.

6. It will be necessary to consider each of these phases in greater detail and as a first step it is proposed to deal with those Public General Acts which authorise a Municipality to borrow and the conditions under which the power to borrow is given.

There are three principal Acts to which attention must be given and in each instance the power conferred authorises borrowing by *mortgage* of the rates.

7. COMMISSIONERS CLAUSES ACT, 1847.

The provisions of this Act were incorporated in private Acts obtained by bodies of local Commissioners who administered certain local government services either alongside of the Municipality or in districts which had not obtained a Charter of Incorporation. The provisions were also incorporated in certain general Acts and particularly in the Burial Acts and the Tramways Act of 1870. The functions of these Commissioners have in most cases been absorbed by the Municipality but the provisions may still apply to loans borrowed under sanctions which are not yet fully redeemed.

The Act provides for :—

(a) Form of mortgage.
(b) Transfer and form thereof.
(c) Registration of mortgages and transfers.
(d) Appointment of Receiver.

but the sections which really concern the subject under consideration are Secs. 80, 84 and 85. (See Appendix A).

8. Public Health Act, 1875.

A large proportion of the borrowing by Municipalities is made under the provisions of this Act.

The Act provides :—

(a) Form of mortgage.
(b) Transfer and form thereof.
(c) Registration of mortgages and transfers.
(d) Appointment of Receiver.

Section 233—Borrowing Powers and Section 234—Regulations as to Exercise of Borrowing Powers (See Appendix B).

9. Municipal Corporations Act, 1882.

The power to borrow under this Act is restricted to the amounts necessary for the purchase of land or for the building of any buildings which the Council are by that Act authorised to build.

There is no limitation of the amount of loans which may be sanctioned under the Act.

The maximum period allowed for redemption is 30 years.

Sections 112 and 113 provide with regard to the redemption of the debt (See Appendix C).

A "REAL" CONSOLIDATED LOANS FUND (*continued*).

There is no provision as in the Public Health Act, 1875, that the Sinking Fund may be applied from time to time in paying off the debt as occasion arises.

Neither is there any provision for the repayment to mortgagees within the period authorised for the loan.

10. LIMITATIONS AND RESTRICTIONS IN THE METHOD OF BORROWING BY LOCAL AUTHORITIES UNDER THESE ACTS.

The three Acts quoted all provide for the borrowing to be exercised by mortgage of the rates and appear to contemplate that the borrowing shall be for the whole period of the loan.

The latter difficulty arises from a confusion in the language of the Acts between the obligations of the local authority to its ratepayers and its obligations to the mortgagees.

Both the Act of 1847 and the Act of 1875 provide for re-borrowing for the purpose of discharging loans raised under the respective Acts but there is no corresponding provision in the 1882 Act and there would seem to be no doubt in this latter case that the borrowing must be for the whole period of the loan.

The sole object of the borrowing powers conferred is to enable the authority to spread the cost of land and buildings and other permanent works over a term of years which is determined by the estimated life of the asset which has to be acquired.

As a means of securing that the cost of this expenditure should be equitably distributed over such period certain methods of repayment are prescribed.

The mortgagee however is in no way restricted in his security to the amounts provided annually out of the rates and it would be more correct to speak of methods of redemption (of the expenditure which has been met out of the loan) than of methods of repayment of loans.

The form of mortgage is virtually the same in each case although the security is different in that it provides for the charge to be upon a particular rate fund.

A "REAL" CONSOLIDATED LOANS FUND (*continued*).

An authority exercising its powers under these Acts will have some of its mortgages secured on the borough fund and borough rate, and others on the district fund and district rate.

All mortgages secured on the same rate fund rank *pari passu*.

11. PERIOD OF LOAN.

The Acts prescribe in each case a maximum period within which the loan is to be repaid.

Section 80 of the Commissioners Clauses Act provides for reborrowing when such borrowing can be effected at a lower rate of interest for purposes of paying off any loans then being in force.

The Public Health Act, Section 233, also authorises reborrowing but the sanction of the Ministry of Health must be obtained in the same way as is required for the original loan. Such sanction must apparently be obtained before the loans, for the discharge of which it is proposed to reborrow, are actually repaid.

I cannot admit the doubt which has been expressed in some quarters as to the necessity for such sanction, but I can readily agree that the requirement is ignored in practice and that if it were to be enforced the advantage of borrowing by short term mortgage would largely disappear.

As previously mentioned the Municipal Corporations Act, 1882, contains no provision as to reborrowing. The method of repayment to be prescribed by the sanctioning Authority is either by instalment or sinking fund or both. As will be seen later the sinking fund cannot be applied without the approval of the sanctioning Authority and this confirms the view already expressed that the borrowing under this Act must be for the whole period of the loan.

12. METHOD OF REPAYMENT.

The Commissioners Clauses Act prescribes a sinking fund as a means of repayment but it is a sinking fund quite different from that which is ordinarily understood by the term.

A "Real" Consolidated Loans Fund (*continued*).

A prescribed part of the loan has to be set apart each year and accumulated by compound interest *or otherwise* until the amount is sufficient to discharge the principal monies.

There is, however, no provision for paying into the sinking fund interest on such part of the sinking fund loans as have been applied in repayment of loans so that the date by which the sinking fund would mature is obviously dependent upon whether or no it is so applied.

The Public Health Act, 1875, prescribes the following alternative methods :—

(1) By instalments, (2) by annuity, (3) accumulating sinking fund.

The Act also authorises the application of the sinking fund in or towards the discharge of the loans for the repayment of which the fund has been established.

The Municipal Corporations Act, 1882, as already mentioned provides that the method of repayment shall be prescribed by the sanctioning Authority and may be by :—

(1) Instalment, (2) Sinking Fund, or (3) by both.

The sinking fund contributions are required to be invested and the consent of the sanctioning authority is required to the transfer of such securities.

Another important question which arises in the exercise of these borrowing powers by mortgage is as to whether the Acts require that the loans raised shall be identified with a particular sanction to borrow thus involving a separate sinking fund for each loan.

13. Short Term Mortgages.

There is no necessary relation between the period for which a loan is sanctioned and the term within which the mortgage is to be repaid and, as between borrower and lender, this latter may be regulated by the terms of the mortgage.

It is a common practice to borrow money on mortgage for short terms which may (subject to the restrictions imposed by the

A "Real" Consolidated Loans Fund (*continued*).

Acts) be redeemed from time to time out of sinking fund or replaced by new borrowings.

The method is decidedly advantageous to the borrowing authority especially on a falling market and has proved very popular with investors.

It does, however, involve the problem of reborrowing and renewal of loans to meet amounts falling due for repayment within the period of the sanction as well as the actual provision for the redemption of the loan by sinking fund at the end of the sanctioned period.

14. Borrowing by Stock Issue.

The second phase of the development of local authorities' borrowing is marked by the Local Government Act, 1888, which authorises a County Council to exercise its borrowing powers under the Act by means of an Issue of Stock.

This Act also authorises borrowing by way of mortgage (including the power to reborrow) but from our present point of view it is the power to issue Stock which is its chief characteristic.

This Act was followed in 1890 by the Public Health Act Amendment Act which extended the power to issue Stock to Urban Authorities who undertook the formality of adopting part five of the Act.

Prior to 1890 this power had been obtained by many Authorities under local Acts which incorporated model stock clauses. These are, however, very similar to the stock regulations, 1891 to 1921, which govern the issue of Stock under the Public General Act.

The following are the points connected with Stock Issue which are particularly relevant to our subject.

(1) The period for which the Stock is issued is fixed by the Consent Order and may not exceed 60 years.

(2) This period is irrespective of the period fixed by the various sanctions to loan which may be included in a Stock Issue.

A "Real" Consolidated Loans Fund (*continued*).

(3) Stock and interest thereon is charged indifferently on all revenues of the Authority.

(4) The Stock Regulations since 1901 have authorised the utilization of redemption fund for new capital purposes.

15. Common Form of Mortgage.

The principal features of Stock Issues, viz. :—the common security; common redemption fund; and the power to apply sinking funds to new capital purposes, have since been extended to borrowing by mortgage but the powers are not generally available. Many Authorities are empowered by local Act in the exercise of any statutory borrowing powers to issue a common form of mortgage charged indifferently on the funds and revenues of the Corporation. This permits a complete consolidation of the mortgage loans of the Corporation, but until existing mortgages charged on separate rate funds are cleared these must continue side by side with the new consolidated mortgages.

In practice where this power has been obtained the distinction between the two classes is often ignored and the whole of the mortgages regarded as consolidated.

The powers obtained under this head usually include also the power to reborrow and the power to renew loans by endorsement on the mortgage deed, also the power to apply sinking funds to new capital purposes.

16. A Local Authority possessing the powers I have indicated will thus be enabled to exercise its borrowing powers either by Stock Issue or Mortgages with a separate sinking fund and redemption fund for each and with power to apply such funds to new capital purposes.

Having regard to the fact that such Authorities will for some years to come have also mortgages outstanding on the Borough Fund and District Fund respectively it will be seen that there must be at least four distinct funds for debt redemption and for interest.

A "REAL" CONSOLIDATED LOANS FUND (*continued*).

17. In these circumstances the application of sinking funds to new capital purposes results in numerous sub-divisions of the original borrowing which may become inconvenient, and in any event there is not complete consolidation so long as the various redemption funds have to be kept separate.

18. In the same way there will be four separate pooled funds for the payment of the interest on loans and dividends on Stock:—The Borough Fund pool in respect of mortgages issued on the security of Borough Fund and Borough Rate; District Fund in respect of mortgage loans secured on the District Fund; Consolidated Mortgage Interest Fund for interest on mortgage loans issued in common form and charged indifferently on all the funds and revenues of the Authority; and a Dividends Fund for the payment of dividends on the Stock Issues.

19. It will I think be agreed that the modern development of borrowing by short-term mortgages renders it necessary that the distinction between Borough Fund and District Fund for purposes of interest on loans and debt redemption should not be maintained—the consolidation of the Rating Funds where the power has been obtained will automatically effect its abolition, but there will be a difference of opinion to the desirability of abolishing for purposes of debt service the distinction between mortgages and stock.

20. The third stage will, however, only be reached when we have a real consolidation of the whole of the debt services of a Local Authority, and in order to achieve this the process of borrowing must be regarded as one and indivisible whether exercised by issue of mortgages or stock.

Such a consolidation requires that all capital monies however raised should form a pooled fund, and that all monies provided for the redemption of debt should be paid in to the same pool and become available for new capital purposes.

Out of this pooled fund the repayment of loans (as distinct from redemption of loans) is to be financed; redemption of loans and stock to be effected; capital expenditure met and any surplus funds invested.

A "REAL" CONSOLIDATED LOANS FUND (*continued*).

21. It would appear that such a consolidation has already been achieved by the Edinburgh Corporation, but it is well known that Scottish Local Authorities have many legislative advantages over the English, and the powers conferred in that instance go very much further than the outline I have just suggested. In order that the issue may not be confused I have chosen an English precedent, or at least what is hoped may become a precedent.

Clauses 145 and 146 of the Torquay Corporation Bill in the present Session of Parliament furnish a convenient text. (See Appendix D).

22. Such a clause will enable the Authority to form a complete pool of capital monies (including the amounts contributed for debt redemption) out of which any statutory borrowing power may be exercised; loans redeemed; loans repaid to be reborrowed; and any surplus funds may be invested.

It also necessarily involves a pooled interest fund which will result in an average charge for interest in respect of all borrowings. Moreover, by enabling the existing unapplied redemption funds to be carried into the loans fund and so available for the redemption of all Stock or other securities issued by the Corporation applies immediately the same principle to all existing loans.

There is thus secured complete consolidation of the debt service of the Local Authority.

23. Two questions immediately suggest themselves :—

(1) Is the principle sound? and

(2) Does the consolidation secure simplicity with efficiency?

24. There can, I think, be no question but that the principle of consolidation of debt is a sound one. It is perhaps necessary that the central authority should exercise a control over the powers given to Local Authorities to borrow money by requiring a separate application for each borrowing, but the application is merely a separate incident in a process which must be regarded as permanent and more or less continuous.

A "Real" Consolidated Loans Fund (*continued*).

The Authority borrowing money whether it does so as a Municipality, as an Urban Authority, or as a Burial Board, is still a Local Authority exercising one of its functions for the benefit of the inhabitants at large, and although it is necessary in view of the separate incidence of the rating to preserve an equal charge in respect of its different loans there is no reason at all why the mortgagees or other lenders should be restricted in their security to a particular fund or rate.

25. Pooling of Debt Service — Interest and Dividends.

If the view suggested in the preceding paragraph is the correct one there should be no difficulty about the principle of pooling all interest charges. The only question involved is one of accounting.

If a Local Authority 25 years ago raised a loan of £20,000 for the erection of a Town Hall, by means of an issue of 3% Stock, and is now compelled to pay 6% for a similar sum raised on mortgage for the erection of an Elementary School, is it correct from the accounting standpoint to say that the administrative service should be charged with interest at the rate of 3% per annum, and the Education Service with interest at the rate of 6% per annum. (In this case the dice is loaded against the Chief Financial Officer, who suggests to his Authority that the interest charge should be averaged because of the fact that some proportion of the cost of the Education service is met by Government Grant. The difficulty of accepting an average figure may be even greater if say a 6% Stock has been issued particularly for housing purposes and the average rate paid in respect of other borrowed money is lower).

It is submitted that the question of whether or no there is a Government Grant in respect of a particular service should not enter into the question although it is recognised that the Government has set local authorities a very bad example in this respect in their attempted restriction of the full effects of consolidation of rating funds in regard to income tax liability.

A "Real" Consolidated Loans Fund (*continued*).

It is quite true in the case I have mentioned by way of illustration that the local authority has on two separate occasions borrowed money for two separate and distinct purposes, but in doing so it has exercised one statutory right (that of borrowing for permanent works) and in each case it has done so in discharge of one of its functions as a Municipality.

I submit, therefore, that the correct view to take is that it has borrowed £40,000 at an average rate of 4½ per cent. and the different services should be charged accordingly.

26. This view has already been accepted, in effect, by the powers conceded under the Stock Regulations to apply redemption funds to new capital purposes.

Under these regulations it is competent of the local authority to apply the redemption fund provided in respect of the Town Hall borrowing to the new capital purpose of an Elementary School and by way of effecting this to treat as redeemed at par so much of the Town Hall debt and a similar amount of Stock as transferred for the purpose of the new expenditure on a school.

It must however be borne in mind as an indication of the attitude likely to be taken up by the Ministry of Health on this clause that the Stock regulations have been amended since 1921 as regards the transfer of Stock in the exercise of new borrowing powers so as to provide that such stock shall be transferred at a price to be fixed by the Minister of Health.

It would seem also that the same view is accepted in the practice which exists of arranging mutual loans although I admit that in that case it is induced by quite other motives.

In that case the local authority having £20,000 to invest in respect of its Redemption Fund looks round for another authority to which it is prepared, in consideration of an equivalent loan, to lend the amount at the lowest possible rate of interest which, after tax deduction, will give a net rate equal to that on which the Redemption Fund is based.

A "Real" Consolidated Loans Fund (*continued*).

27. Pooling of Debt Service—Sinking and Redemption Funds.

I do not know whether the view is anywhere held in these days that a separate Sinking Fund has to be established for each separate loan raised by a local authority and that the amount to the credit of such Sinking Fund can only be applied to the redemption of the loans in respect of which it was established.

It is, I believe, generally accepted that under the general law only one Sinking Fund is required in respect of loans raised on each separate rate fund.

It is understood that there must be sub-divisions of that Sinking Fund for accounting purposes because of the varying periods for which loans may be granted.

Where a common form of mortgage is used only one Sinking Fund is required.

A separate Redemption Fund has always been maintained in the case of stock issues.

28. Where, however, the power to utilize Sinking Funds for new capital purposes is combined with power to issue a common form of mortgage it has been suggested that the authority has power in effect to pool its Sinking Funds and Redemption Funds at least in certain circumstances.

29. Consider the case of an authority with a stock issue which has transferred stock in the execution of new borrowing powers extending beyond the period of stock redemption. At the date of redemption the sum of say £50,000 has to be borrowed to meet this transferred stock remaining unredeemed.

The Sinking Fund in respect of consolidated mortgages could be applied to such purpose.

30. The Torquay proposal is much more clear and much more direct but it is none the worse for that.

The principle involved is that of the utilization of Sinking Fund for new capital purposes. This has been declared by the

Joint Select Committee appointed to report on the subject to be financially unobjectionable.

The principle has been conceded by the Stock Regulations and by Local Act in the case of Redemption Funds and by Local Acts so far as Mortgage Sinking Funds are concerned.

The proposal to pool both Sinking Funds and Redemption Funds and to use the pooled Fund for new capital purposes is merely an extension of the principle and given a common security with an assurance of the necessary safeguards which will presumably be introduced in the scheme which is to be submitted to the Ministry of Health, there does not seem to be anything very revolutionary in the suggestion.

31. An important feature of the proposal is that the Sinking Fund or Redemption Fund as an intermediary between the contributions from the Revenue Accounts and the actual redemption of loan is abolished.

The contributions are carried to the Consolidated Loans Fund direct and the debt is to be considered as having been redeemed to an equivalent extent. There will consequently be no necessity to identify a new borrowing power with the various securities which may have been allocated in the exercise of the old borrowing power whose redemption moneys it is now proposed to apply to the new capital purpose.

32. It also seems to follow that the charge to revenue in each year will be for an amount equivalent to the Sinking Fund instalment with interest on accumulations; that any interest on investments of the Consolidated Loans Fund will not be required to be carried to the Sinking Fund and that consequently such income will be available so far as tax liability is concerned for the payment of interest on loans.

33. I do not know how far it may be necessary to modify this view of the powers sought by the scheme which is required to be approved by the Ministry of Health before the Consolidated Loans Fund can be put into operation but it is clear that no considerable advance will have been made upon existing powers unless it is accepted in full.

A "REAL" CONSOLIDATED LOANS FUND (*continued*).

34. Although recent precedents in the general direction of consolidation of debt have applied exclusively to mortgages it is interesting to note that the City of Leeds General Powers Act, 1901, secured the principle of a consolidated debt, with a Consolidated Redemption Fund which might be used in the exercise of new borrowing powers, but that Act contained a general code of provisions with regard to the raising, repayment, and redemption of loans by the Corporation which make it necessary to show as part of the Redemption Fund all the separate sub-divisions of that Fund and to identify the amounts applied to new capital purposes with the particular sub-divisions of that fund and to indicate the nature of the securities which had been transferred.

35. This restricted view of the limits within which the consolidation of the debt should be permitted gives no advantage over the powers possessed by the local authority having power to issue a common form of mortgage in conjunction with its powers under the Stock Regulations and would lead to much complication in the Sinking Fund accounts. In fact I find that a recognition of these difficulties, as far back as 1910, induced our friend Mr. Mitchell, then Assistant City Treasurer of Leeds, in the course of an address to the Lancashire and Yorkshire Students' Societies to suggest in anticipation the solution which is now being sought by the Torquay Corporation. (I may add that since I made this discovery I have been of the opinion that the invitation to introduce this subject at the Annual Meeting of the Institute was sent to me in error).

36. If the scheme is approved in full it will, without doubt, secure the utmost simplicity in the administration of the loan debt and its service, and that without any loss of efficiency.

37. There are, however, special difficulties with regard to its operation and particularly on the inception of the scheme.

There is, for instance, some doubt having regard to the special conditions applying as between borrower and lender, as to whether loans advanced by the Public Works Loan Board in-

A "Real" Consolidated Loans Fund (*continued*).

cluding the half proceeds of Savings Certificates, could be brought into the scheme. The deprivation which this involves however cannot be regarded as a serious obstacle to the scheme.

A similar doubt is suggested with regard to the inclusion of Housing Bonds in a scheme of this kind,

(i) Because their availability is restricted to Housing purposes, whereas the Consolidated Loans fund is a mixed fund.

So far as this objection is concerned it should however be possible to devise a formula which would permit of their being included in the scheme.

(ii) Because the security given to the holders includes the Government subsidy in respect of Housing and this is not available as part of the ordinary security given by the Corporation Loans.

(iii) Because of the fact that the rate of interest in respect of the issue of Housing Bonds is fixed by the Ministry of Health.

The advantage in this respect of consolidation would be with the Ministry of Health, but there are special reasons why the Assisted Scheme accounts should not be given the benefit of an average rate of interest so far as the Bonds are concerned, which do not apply for example to the case of 6% Housing Stock.

Briefly these are (1) the borrowing is of the nature of a joint borrowing with the Government and Municipality on terms which are determined by the Government. (2) The security given is, as has just been shewn, an extended one; (3) Special privileges are given to holders which do not apply to other Corporation loans, e.g., interest paid in full without deduction of tax in certain cases and the right to tender bonds in purchase of houses under the Corporation or any other assisted Housing Schemes.

38. The existing loans and stock of the Corporation also give rise to some difficulty.

A " REAL " CONSOLIDATED LOANS FUND (*continued*).

The clause provides that the amounts unapplied at March 31st, 1924, of any sums provided for redemption of debt shall be carried to the Consolidated Loans Fund where it becomes available for any of the purposes of the Fund, and, not merely available but indistinguishable from other monies in the Fund.

It will, therefore, be necessary for the old debt to be dealt with on exactly the same lines as the future advances out of the Consolidated Loans Fund, i.e., the actual liability of the Corporation to the Stockholder or Mortgagee will be shewn in the Balance Sheet of the Consolidated Loans Fund and the liability of the various services in respect of the net debt outstanding will be shewn in the respective Balance Sheets as an amount due to Consolidated Loans Fund.

39. This does not settle the further question of priorities which is a legal one. The question will arise where there are loans outstanding with different securities. Mortgage loans, secured on either Borough or District Fund, issued prior to a Stock issue or to mortgages in common form would have a priority over the loans secured on a common security so far as the particular funds on which they are respectively secured are concerned.

40 Another question which arises is as to the treatment of discount or premium (including discount or premium on redemption) and other costs of issue.

Under existing conditions any premium on issue of Stock is, or may be, applied to the costs of issue and a discount on redemption is similarily available either for the reduction of the amount of discount on original issue or of the costs of such issue.

The discount and other expenses of issue are apportioned over the various services covered by the borrowing powers exercised by the stock issue and are redeemed over the period of the stock issue or, as is now provided by the stock regulations, over the period at the expiration of which the Authority has the option to redeem the stock.

It is clearly anomalous that the discount and expenses of issue should be in this way charged on the services whose borrowing powers were exercised by the original issue for the longer or shorter periods mentioned when as a matter of practice some portion of the stock may have been transferred to other services.

It seems, therefore, to be necessary under the suggested scheme that the discount on stock issue and the costs of such issue, as reduced by premiums on issue or discount on redemption, should be regarded as a purpose for which a borrowing power has been exercised in respect of the Consolidated Loans Fund and that the debt service in respect of this borrowing power should be charged to management expenses and apportioned with other such expenses of the Loans Fund, over all the different services according to the net debt outstanding.

41. Another important question is as to the Investment of Consolidated Loans fund monies.

The fund must provide not merely for the redemption of the debt but also for the repayment of Mortgages, Bills and other securities which may have to be met during the currency of the loans in the exercise of which they have been issued. Prudence therefore suggests that some portion of the fund should be kept available in some form of investment.

How should the income derived from such investments be applied?

It would seem that the amount of the Consolidated Loans Fund which is invested at any particular time must represent amounts credited to the fund for redemption of debt and not so applied, and that from the point of view of the various services it will represent in a technical sense an overborrowing.

In these circumstances it would appear that the proper course would be to credit the income to the Consolidated Interest fund in reduction of the amount paid for Interest and Dividends.

42. The point it has been endeavoured to establish so far is that the setting up of a "real" Consolidated Loans Fund involves no new principle. The principle of a common security, and that of the application of sinking funds to new capital purposes in lieu of borrowing are both generally accepted.

A "REAL" CONSOLIDATED LOANS FUND (*continued*).

The feature of the proposal that is new is that for purposes of accounting, securities issued by the Corporation in respect of borrowing powers exercised—whether short dated or long dated securities—should not be identified with a particular service, but should be regarded as representing a duly authorised borrowing power conferred upon the Corporation as a local authority.

It is remarkable that the objections which may be urged against the scheme should apply particularly to long dated securities.

It is however the merest accident that at a moment favourable to a stock issue certain particular borrowing powers are available. Is it not moreover a matter of common practice that a stock issue is made the opportunity for funding debt which already exists in an unfunded state. Many a service now enjoying the advantage of a three per cent. stock must have had the same borrowing powers originally represented by short dated securities.

In fact the whole practice of borrowing by a local authority is inconsistent with the view that the advantage or disadvantage of a particular issue should attach to a particular service or services.

43. There may be some hesitancy about imposing this view of borrowing by a local authority upon services in respect of past issues of stock which were made on the basis of an entirely opposite view even though that view may now be accepted as a wrong one.

It is however submitted that even this, what may be called, vested interest should not survive the period covered by the option of the authority to redeem the Stock.

44. It is hoped that there is nothing in the views here expressed which may be regarded as involving a suggestion that obligations to existing stock and bond holders should not be faithfully carried out.

I do not think that a Local Authority would be permitted by any scheme of this kind to avoid its contractual obligations; I am quite sure that this Institute would not countenance such a suggestion even in order to secure the benefits of a *real* Consolidated Loans Fund.

A " REAL " CONSOLIDATED LOANS FUND (*continued*).

APPENDIX " A."

COMMISSIONERS CLAUSES ACT, 1847.

Sec. 80. If the Commissioners can at any time borrow or take up any sum of money at a lower rate of interest than any securities given by them and then being in force shall bear, they may borrow such sum at such lower rate as aforesaid, in order to pay off and discharge the securities bearing such higher rate of interest, and may charge the rates and other property which they may be authorised to mortgage or assign in security under this or the special Act, or any part thereof, with payment of such sum and such lower rate of interest, in such manner and subject to such regulations as are herein contained with respect to other moneys borrowed on mortgage or assignation in security.

* * * *

Sec. 84. In order to discharge the principal money borrowed as aforesaid on security of any of the rates the Commissioners shall every year appropriate and set apart out of such rates respectively a sum equal to the prescribed part, and if no part be prescribed one twentieth part of the sum so borrowed respectively, as a sinking fund to be applied in paying off the respective principal monies so borrowed, and shall from time to time cause such sinking fund to be invested in the purchase of exchequer bills or other Government securities, or in Scotland deposited in one of the banks there incorporated by Act of Parliament or Royal Charter, and to be increased by accumulation in the way of compound interest or otherwise, until the same respectively shall be of sufficient amount to pay off the principal debts respectively to which such sinking fund shall be applicable, or some part thereof which the Commissioners shall think ought then to be paid off, at which time the same shall be so applied in paying off the same in manner hereinafter mentioned.

* * * *

Sec. 85. Whenever the Commissioners shall be enabled to pay off one or more of the mortgages or assignations in security which shall be then payable, and shall not be able to pay off the whole of the same class, they shall decide the order in which they shall be paid off by lot among the class to which such one or more of the mortgages or assignations in security belong, and shall cause a notice, signed by their clerk, to be given to the persons entitled to the money to be paid off, pursuant to such lot, and such notice shall express the principal sum proposed to be paid off, and that the same will be paid, together with the interest due thereon, at a place to be specified, at the expiration of six months from the date of giving such notice.

APPENDIX "B".

PUBLIC HEALTH ACT, 1875.

Sec. 233. Any Local Authority may, with the sanction of the Local Government Board, for the purpose of defraying any costs, charges and expenses incurred or to be incurred by them in the execution of the Sanitary Acts, or of this Act, or for the purpose of discharging any loans contracted under the Sanitary Acts, or this Act, borrow or re-borrow, and take up at interest, any sums of money necessary for defraying any such costs, charges and expenses, or for discharging any such loans as aforesaid.

An Urban Authority may borrow or re-borrow any such sums on the credit of any fund or all or any rates or rate out of which they are authorised to defray expenses incurred by them in the execution of this Act, and for the purpose of securing the repayment of any sums so borrowed, with interest thereon, they may mortgage to the persons by or on behalf of whom such sums are advanced any such fund or rates or rate.

Section 234 provides :—

Regulations as to Exercise of Borrowing Powers.

The exercise of the powers of borrowing conferred by this Act shall be subject to the following regulations, namely :—

(1) Money shall not be borrowed except for permanent works (including under this expression any works of which the cost ought in the opinion of the Local Government Board to be spread over a term of years).

(2) The sum borrowed shall not at any time exceed, with the balances of all the outstanding loans contracted by the local authority under the Sanitary Acts and this Act, in the whole the assessable value for two years of the premises assessable within the district in respect of which such money may be borrowed.

(3) Where the sum proposed to be borrowed with such balances (if any) would exceed the assessable value for one year of such premises, the Local Government Board shall not give their sanction to such loan until one of their Inspectors has held a Local Inquiry and reported to the said Board.

(4) The money may be borrowed for such time, not exceeding sixty years, as the Local Authority, with the sanction of the Local Government Board, determine in each case; and, subject as aforesaid, the Local Authority shall either pay off the moneys so borrowed by equal annual instalments of principal or of principal and interest, or they shall in every year set apart as

a sinking fund and accumulate in the way of compound interest by investing the same in the purchase of Exchequer bills or other Government securities, such sum as will with accumulations in the way of compound interest be sufficient, after payment of all expenses to pay off the moneys so borrowed within the period sanctioned.

(5) A Local Authority may at any time apply the whole or any part of a sinking fund set apart under this Act in or towards the discharge of the moneys for the repayment of which the fund has been established. Provided that they pay into the fund in each year and accumulate until the whole of the moneys borrowed are discharged, a sum equivalent to the interest which would have been produced by the sinking fund or the part of the sinking fund so applied.

(6) Where money is borrowed for the purpose of discharging a previous loan, the time for repayment of the money so borrowed shall not extend beyond the unexpired portion of the period for which the original loan was sanctioned, unless with the sanction of the Local Government Board; and shall in no case be extended beyond the period of sixty years from the date of the original loan.

APPENDIX "C".

MUNICIPAL CORPORATIONS ACT, 1882.

112. (1) Where the Treasury approves a mortgage or charge under this Part they may, as a condition of their approval, require that the money borrowed on the security of the mortgage or charge be repaid, with all interest thereon, in thirty years, or any less period, and either by instalments or by means of a sinking fund or both.

(2) In that case the sums required for providing for the repayment of the principal and interest of the money borrowed shall be by virtue of this Act a charge on all or any of the following securities, namely, the land comprised in the mortgage (without prejudice to the security thereby created), or any other corporate land, or the borough fund, or the borough or other rates legally applicable to payment of the money borrowed, or of the expenses which the money is borrowed to defray, as the Treasury direct.

113. (1) Where money borrowed under this Part is directed to be repaid by means of a sinking fund, the Council, shall, out of the rents and profits of the land on which, or out of the borough fund or rates, on which, the sums required for the sinking fund are charged

A "REAL" CONSOLIDATED LOANS FUND (*continued*).

under this Act, invest such sums, at such times, and in such Government annuities, as the Treasury direct, and shall also from time to time invest in like manner all dividends of those annuities.

(2) The annuities shall, in the books of the Bank of England, be placed to the account of the Corporation, and in the matter of this Act or of any previous Act under which the investment is made.

(3) The dividends of the annuities shall be received and invested by such persons as the Council by power of attorney under the Corporate seal from time to time appoint.

(4) No transfer shall be made of the annuities, or of any part thereof, without the consent in writing of the Treasury, addressed to the Chief Accountant of the Bank of England.

(5) The direction in writing of the Council by power of attorney under the Corporate seal, with the consent in writing of the Treasury shall be sufficient authority to the Bank for permitting any such transfer.

APPENDIX "D".

TORQUAY CORPORATION BILL — SESSION 1923.

CONSOLIDATED LOANS FUND.

145. (1) Notwithstanding anything contained in the Public Health Acts (Amendment) Act, 1890, or in any other Act or Order on or after the thirty-first day of March, one thousand nine hundred and twenty-four the Corporation may if they think fit establish a fund to be called the Consolidated Loans Fund to which shall be paid as and when they are received :—

(a) All moneys borrowed by the Corporation whether by issue of stock or other security together with any moneys temporarily borrowed without security in connection with the exercise of duly authorised borrowing powers;

(b) All moneys of a capital nature received by the Corporation whether from the sale of capital assets or otherwise except such as are applied by the Corporation with due authority to another capital purpose; and

(c) The appropriate sums provided in each year out of other funds of the Corporation to comply with the terms and conditions as to repayment attaching to their several borrowing powers :

And there shall also be carried to the credit of the consolidated loans fund the unapplied balances of all moneys borrowed or received and of all sums provided by the Corporation as aforesaid before the thirty-first day of March one thousand nine hundred and twenty-four.

A "Real" Consolidated Loans Fund (*continued*).

(2) The moneys of the consolidated loans fund shall be used or applied by the Corporation :—

(a) In the exercise of any duly authorised borrowing power by transfer of the required amount to the appropriate fund and account of the Corporation; or

(b) In the redemption of stock or any other securities issued by the Corporation the purchase of stock for extinction or the repayment of any moneys borrowed by the Corporation;

And any moneys of the consolidated loans fund not used or applied in these ways may be invested in any Government or other securities in which trustees are by law for the time being authorised to invest and the sums realised by the sale of such securities shall be repaid on receipt to the consolidated loans fund and the moneys of the consolidated loans fund shall not be used or applied otherwise than as provided in this sub-section.

(3) Subject to any priority existing at the passing of this Act all stock of and loans to the Corporation and the dividends and interest thereon shall be charged indifferently on all the revenues of the Corporation and shall rank equally one with the other without any priority whatsoever.

(4) Save as in this section expressly provided all the obligations of the Corporation to the holders of stock or other securities of the Corporation shall continue in force.

(5) The powers conferred by this section shall not be put into operation by the Corporation except in accordance with a scheme to be approved by the Minister of Health and such scheme may make provision for any matters incidental to the establishment and administration of the consolidated loans fund.

Security for Principal Moneys.

146. (1) All principal moneys shall be and the same are by virtue of this Act charged indifferently upon all the revenues of the Corporation.

(2) The interest from time to time payable on any such principal moneys shall rank equally with the interest or dividends on all other securities of the Corporation created or granted in pursuance of any statutory borrowing power and all such interest and dividends shall be the first charge on all the revenues aforesaid.

The President: Gentlemen, the paper is now open for discussion. Time, however, is very short this afternoon and we have here in our midst a representative of the Ministry of Health.

In your name I welcome him here this afternoon as the first representative of that Ministry ever to attend a Conference of this Institute. To my mind it is a new era of the interest the Ministry takes in the affairs of the Conference and I am now going to ask Mr. Carson Roberts, as one particularly interested in this subject, to open the debate.

Mr. A. CARSON ROBERTS (Ministry of Health) : Mr. President, firstly, let me thank you and your Executive Committee for the honour you have done me and the privilege you have given me to-day. I have heard it suggested that anyone from my Department venturing to come among the financial officers of the chief local authorities in their collected strength would be a Daniel entering the lions' den. I cannot say that being here helps me in the least to appreciate what the feelings of that gentleman may have been on that memorable occasion. I do not know any body of men with whom I can be more thoroughly at home, with whom I have more opinions in common, or to whom I can speak my mind more freely. But, in order that I may speak it quite freely I beg you to note that I come here to express my own views and not as one charged to convey any official rulings or messages.

If a visitor may have that privilege, I should like to compliment Mr. Wetherall on the really excellent paper he has just read. His conception of an Ideal Loan Fund, is also my conception. In regard to the constructive part of what he has said I agree not only with the outline but also with the detail. If, in what I have to say, I go rather further than he has gone, and, if I take hold of the subject in perhaps a rather bolder way, he will clearly see that there is nothing which is even indirect criticism, it is only supplementary.

I am going to disarm criticism connected with existing Acts and Regulations by adopting the convenient assumption that we have a clean slate on which to construct our ideal. After that, we can consider how it can be attained with the law as it stands, what alterations are wanted, if any, and finally, by what means we can graft the new system on to an old system which has the complications of the past, the obligations of the past and the vested interests of the past to deal with. I would submit that

A " REAL " CONSOLIDATED LOANS FUND.—DISCUSSION (*continued*).

that is the best way of discussing the subject: we must paint the ideal first and then talk about how to attain it.

I.—THE IDEAL LOAN FUND.

As regards this ideal, in the first place I would like to draw on my clean slate Mr. Paton's chart, nothing more lucid have I ever seen. Incidentally I would include loans from the other funds such as the Pensions funds and the Insurance funds and so on—this, I believe, he intends though his chart doesn't shew it. Then I would touch on the accounting side to make the picture clearer. This is a wonderfully simple thing to deal with, to my mind—indeed, The Consolidated Loan Fund is beautifully simple in all respects, if one gets hold of its conception properly.

EFFECT ON ACCOUNTS.

The Ideal Loan Fund which I would depict would form a separate section of the accounts, producing a separate Loan Fund Balance Sheet. So far as the other Accounts and Balance Sheets of the Authority are concerned the Loan Fund can be treated as the only lender. All the entries appearing in the other accounts will thus follow the beautifully simple lines which are available when all the loans have been obtained for the full periods of the borrowing powers with an arranged system of repayments, and it will be possible without any extra trouble to base the discharge of the capital outlays upon either the instalment or the annuity system as the Authority may elect.

It is therefore, only necessary to consider the Loan Fund Ledger itself. Its Balance Sheet should take the following simple form :—

Outstanding Loan Balances	Outstanding Advances to
Stockholders A Stock ...	Trading Undertakings ...
B Stock ...	Services ....
Annuity Holders	Other Authorities ....
Mortgagees	Deferred Financing Charges
Loans from Funds of the	(Discounts and Expenses
Authority	of Issue)
Bank Overdraft	Sinking Fund Investments..

A " REAL " CONSOLIDATED LOANS FUND.—DISCUSSION (*continued*).

The Accounts of the Loan Fund ledger should also contain an Interest Account and a Financing Costs Account, the net results of which will require annual (or half-yearly) apportionment to the other accounts as described later.

I submit that with this short statement and Mr. Paton's diagram we have a full and a clear picture of a Loan Fund and its working. The conception includes, as will be seen, a separate financing agency, which, of course, will be the Finance Committee guided by one of you. This Central Control will make all the contracts with lenders and handle all transactions with them. It will also make all the necessary advances to borrowing accounts out of its general pool, which will be the Loan Fund. It will meet all charges for interest and expenses as they fall due, and apportion them between the borrowing accounts on some equitable system.

The conception also includes a complete absence of any ear-marking of loans to borrowing powers. This pooling of loan money is in fact the key to the whole position.

THE ADVANTAGES OF POOLING LOANS.

1. The greatest advantage of the Loan Fund system is that it frees your financing from all its present trammels. Thus financing costs are reduced in several ways :—

(a) A loan pool can be fed in the best market at all times, and experience has proved that the average rate of interest thus paid is materially lower than that which has to be paid when ear-marked loans are arranged.

It enables the Authority to suit its borrowings to the convenience of the lenders as regards amounts, periods and repayments, and this in itself means lower interest. The Authority can keep an open door to receive loans whenever lenders come to offer them. If they flow in too freely, it is only necessary to reduce the tap rate of interest. It should never be necessary to turn a lender away, provided he is satisfied with the interest offered.

A " Real " Consolidated Loans Fund.—Discussion (*continued*).

Specific loans fitted to the requirements of the borrowing powers can only be obtained in a narrow market. The ordinary lender does not like to take his loan back bit by bit, and lenders will seldom advance money for the full period of the loan sanction at the same rate as they will lend with the privilege of recall on six months' notice.

(b) The loan pool also throws open large possibilities in the way of loan conversion when interest rates are low. It places the Authority in a position to issue long period Stock when money is cheap, and thus to fund its short term debt. It should never be necessary to take on high rates of interest for long periods.

(c) With a well managed pool, it is possible to do more than fund existing debt when interest rates are low; it is possible to provide in advance the estimated requirements of several future years. Even Stock issues need no longer be limited to existing borrowing powers. This may appear to be an over bold development of the scheme. But I am ready to shew that within reasonable limits it is a perfectly sound and proper part of the plan.

2. It provides the Authority with the best and most convenient way of employing not only its sinking funds but also its various other capital funds—Pension funds, Insurance funds, Reserve funds, and special Capital Receipts which call for investment.

In some of these cases it enables the Fund in question to earn gross interest when it would otherwise only be able to earn taxed interest.

3. It can, as Mr. Paton has pointed out, also provide the best means of employing surplus revenue funds. If each main cash account transfers to the pool any balance on hand in excess of its requirements, considerably more than bank interest may be earned on these balances.

4. It provides the Authority's own ratepayers with a safer and cheaper means of investing their savings than they would

otherwise have at hand. And a scheme which is convenient and useful to the lender is always advantageous to the borrower. This is at the root of the success of the mortgage pools of the North. It tends to advance the best corporate spirit and gives to the inhabitants an added interest in the well-being of their town.

5. The establishment of the principle that loans are not earmarked removes all need for any statutory powers to transfer sinking funds to new capital purposes. This power flows automatically from the pooling of loans. There must be no misconception : *loan pooling in itself frees the sinking funds.*

6. All need for any rule as to the valuation of transferred stock is also removed. Each borrowing account is charged with the exact amount of the advance it receives : it has no concern with the source of the money. Discounts, premiums, and variations in market values are matters which only concern the Loan Fund and therefore they cause no complication.

7. Another series of advantages arise on the side of simplification. I say without hesitation that with a properly managed loan pool the accounting work can be brought to the ultimate maximum of clearness and simplicity.

(a) Each borrowing account obtains the full advantages of a series of loans covering the exact periods of its borrowing powers and repaid either on the simple instalment or the annuity system as may be decided by the Authority.

These repayments (to the pool) are governed by schedules exactly similar to those included in the mortgage deeds of the P.W.L.C., only that the interest column is omitted.

You are therefore freed from all that horrible complication which in the past has attended the compilation of accumulating sinking funds—that mass of " barbed wire and fishhooks," as Mr. Paton described it most aptly and delightfully in a letter I received not long ago.

(b) Each borrowing account is also enabled to obtain its loans just as and when it needs them. This can be carried to any degree of accuracy in fitting the advances to the demands of the loan expenditures. Interest of course must run from the dates of the advances.

(c) There is very great simplification in the calculation of income-tax set-off, and the disability attaching to the income of accumulating sinking funds is removed.

The last named are in themselves no mean advantages.

II.—ATTAINING THE IDEAL—THE SNAGS AND THE BOGIES.

1. The greatest snag has been the earmarking of loans to Borrowing Powers.

Gentlemen, in my opinion useless and unnecessary earmarking is one of the greatest sources of trouble in your field of work.

Why have we inherited all this complication of separate rates for special purposes? Why, because Parliament earmarked one rate to one group of services and another to another group calling them Lighting Rates, Highway Rates, Library Rates, Sewer Rates, General District Rates, Special Expenses Rates and so forth.

We know now that this was unnecessary, and that the reliefs which the different groups of ratepayers enjoy can be given equally well and without any of the trouble in one General Rate, and we are now laboriously engaged upon equating these reliefs piecemeal, town by town.

The earmarking of cash is another folly. I have known many authorities, whose ledgers include all the separate fund and service accounts that are useful or desirable, insisting upon the keeping of a score or several score of separate banking accounts—another interesting relic of the darker ages, and one which, as you and I know, can cause infinite trouble.

The earmarking of loans is in fact a greater folly. It is it, and it alone, which has prevented the proper development of the

Loan Fund system. What it is worth while to talk about is, how to get rid of it, not who is to blame for it. But I really can't refrain from pointing out that you or your predecessors must take a proper share of this blame. It is the Local Acts and the Stock Regulations which now stand in the way of complete pooling. The Stock Regulations allow complete pooling inside each class of Stock but they bar pooling of Stock of different classes or of Stock with other loans. Can you claim that you have ever moved for the pooling of Stock with other loans, even in connection with Local Bills? Twenty years ago, would your predecessors have given us the stuff which Mr. Wetherall has given us to-day or which Mr. Paton gave us last November or which Mr. Collins has embodied in the Torquay Clause?

It is now 29 years since I began advocating the principle I am talking of to-day, and I belong to the crew of the Department which you would make the scapegoat for the delay. But 29 years ago I was busily engaged in preaching the advantages of loan pools to the financial officers in a County which is fond of claiming that it leads the way. My efforts resulted in the formation of many mortgage pools and in the freeing of much sinking fund money, and this luckily occurred at a time when Consols stood at 100-114. The Local Government Board of that day had full knowledge of this and raised no objection.

Truth to tell, the movement is still in its infancy, and there is much need for clearer conception of its attributes on both sides.

I am well aware of all the good pioneering work which has been done—in one direction by the London County Council which has developed on the side of combined borrowing on wider security, and on the other by the towns of the North and elsewhere, with their mortgage pools, in some of which the ideal principles are well developed. But is it not right that you should pioneer, and that general legislation should follow and benefit by the experience of local legislation?

We mustn't let the Dominions get ahead of us in this matter. A few years ago I was consulted about local legislation in Canada whereby several Municipalities were combining to establish one loan pool with a Joint Control Board and united security—the scheme is now at work. I mention this particularly because it helps the mind a good deal in grasping the conceptions which are at the root of Loan Consolidation. There they have a Finance Control which acts for a number of Authorities, and the distinctions upon which Loan Consolidation is founded stand out more clearly. The division between loans and borrowing powers is made wider, and the idea of earmarking the one to the other more impossible.

Someday we may see this scheme in operation in England—London has already its advantage on the point of combined security. The large Boroughs will no doubt continue to handle their own finance, but we may have Finance Controls acting (say) for Administrative Counties, and surely it is absurd to complicate this development by earmarkings.

2. The delay in this development has been attributed to confusion of thought in connection with raising and repayment of loans, on the one hand, and spreading of capital charges by the help of borrowing powers on the other.

This distinction between the obligations to the mortgagees and the obligations to the ratepayers is, as Mr. Wetherall has pointed out, of primary importance for the proper conception of a Loan Fund. Unfortunately the expressions which our language provides—" loans," " borrowings "—apply equally to both, and that is why the statutory provisions are ambiguous, even when it is clear that the distinction was present in the minds of those who framed them.

But believe me the greatest confusion of thought is that which sets up unnecessary earmarkings of loans to capital purposes.

3. Power to invest Reserve Funds, Pension Funds, and other Capital Funds in loans to the Authority itself is necessary to the complete development of the Ideal Loan Fund, but much can be done without that power. This power is, however, now being granted in local legislation, and this indicates that there is no real objection to its extension on more general lines.

A " Real " Consolidated Loans Fund.—Discussion (*continued*).

4. There is one other Snag or Bogie.

I allude to a fear that the Money Market will not regard Loan Consolidation with favour, and that it may make it more difficult for Local Authorities to raise loans on advantageous terms.

In so far as this fear is based upon the effect which would be produced by dissipating the fallacy that a sinking fund is provided for each loan (whereas, as we know, these funds are related to the sanctioned spreadings of expenditure and not to the loans), the sooner the myth is dispelled the better.

I assert without hesitation that never in the case of any Local Authority has there been such a thing as a Stock Redemption Fund in the sense which the money market attaches to the expression. If the Stock Regulations are calculated to create the impression that any such fund is provided, the sooner they are revised the better. If any prospectus has held this out as an attraction, it is a deceptive and incorrect prospectus, and the Authority must get out of its trouble as best it can. The recent issues of 20 year Stocks have served to explode any fallacy which may have existed in this regard.

The so-called Stock Redemption Fund is, as we know, an aggregation of the sinking fund provisions in respect of the borrowing powers to which the Stock is for the time being attached. These sinking fund provisions in connection with Housing expenditure will only provide 12½ per cent. of the Stock total at the end of 20 years. Moreover, where long term Stocks are concerned, the whole or any part of these sinking fund provisions may be in use for other capital purposes when the Stock redemption date arrives, or, to state the matter more correctly, the Stock is liable in law to be detached from the purposes in respect of which the sinking funds have been compiled, and thereupon the sinking funds cease to have any connection with the Stock redemption.

But even when this fallacy has been disposed of, I know that it is still important to take this snag or bogie into serious every year in such form as the Secretary for Scotland shall prescribe. The Act authorises the Secretary for Scotland to prescribe the form of abstract of accounts and in pursuance of this power such a form has duly been prescribed.

(2) The accounts of Burghs in Scotland are regulated by the *Town Councils (Scotland) Act*, 1900, which laid down in some degree of detail the accounts to be kept and required that such accounts should exhibit a complete state of affairs. The Secretary for Scotland in 1902 prescribed a model form for Burgh accounts in accordance with the powers given to him in that behalf, but this has been revoked in favour of a new model form, incorporating the changes necessitated by the Local Government (Scotland) Act, 1929, and published in November, 1930.

(3) The Third Schedule to the *Local Government (Scotland), Act*, 1929, provides that an Abstract of the Accounts of every County Council and Town Council shall be made up, balanced and signed in such manner as the Secretary of State may prescribe.

16. The foregoing statutory provisions have been amplified and/or modified by a series of Statutory Rules and Orders which prescribe in some measure of detail the forms of accounts to which they relate. In a number of cases the prescribed form has become the basis for the publication of those accounts in the Abstract (*e.g.*, Housing (Assisted Scheme) Accounts) and to that extent has been the means of achieving a high degree of uniformity. Scotland appears to be in advance of England as model forms and abstracts have been prescribed by the Central Departments.

17. The following is a list of the Statutory Rules and Orders in force in England and Wales which I believe is comprehensive :—

Local Government Board.—General Order—Accounts (Urban District Councils, etc.), 22nd March, 1880.

Local Government Board.—General Order—Accounts (Urban District Councils, etc.), 8th March, 1881.

It is that of how a Loan Consolidation Scheme can best be grafted on to the things that are in the many cases where financing transactions have already reached a complicated stage. How are the vested interests of the past to be dealt with?

This subject has two sides : firstly there are the vested interests of lenders; and secondly there are the vested interests of the several undertakings and services.

In regard to the first there is little to be said. If you have entered into special contracts with any lenders you cannot vary the position without their consent. The contractual obligations concerned will relate either to priorities, to securities, or to application to special purposes.

It is only the last which can bar the inclusion of the loan in a consolidation scheme, and earmarking to purpose is not necessarily involved when different security or prior lien is given. A lender may have a limited security or a priority of claim, but what is there in this to bar pooling his loan with other loans in regard to the purpose to which it is devoted?

Again, variations in security which do involve earmarking can often be abolished easily enough by consent. Any lender is ready enough to allow his security to be extended to embrace all the revenues of the authority, as a general mortgage does.

When we turn to the vested interests of the undertakings and services a number of special questions arise, we are in fact brought face to face with all the apportionment problems.

I admire the broad-minded way in which Mr. Wetherall has dealt with this part of the subject. But I anticipate that he will be criticised by some of his colleagues for some of his suggestions.

Let us go straight to the real root of the trouble. If we had been discussing this question prior to the Housing Schemes of 1919, I believe there would have been a more or less general acceptance of Mr. Wetherall's solutions. Prior to 1919 there was no reason to suppose that his equitable scheme would not work fairly as between the several accounts. But we cannot be blind to the fact that Local Authorities have recently been urged, pressed or even forced into borrowing large sums for the purposes of Housing when loans were abnormally costly.

Let me point out, however, that there is a perfectly simple way of respecting these or any other vested interests or disinterests now or hereafter attaching to particular funds or accounts without in the least upsetting the scheme of consolidation.

The interest charges on the loans now earmarked to any purpose can be dealt with specifically so long as these loans remain undischarged. The necessary adjustments in the interest apportionment calculations would not be difficult, and they would seldom extend over many years, the remainder of five in the case of certain bonds—the remainder of 20 in the case of certain Stocks.

Of course it would be absolutely purposeless and quite inadvisable to bring into any Consolidation Scheme those instalment or annuity loans covering the whole period of the borrowing powers which are at present earmarked to the particular services upon which they have been expended. In the future all borrowing powers can be exercised on these simple lines in so far as the borrowing account is concerned, but in most cases it will be between the pool and the borrowing account that this will be arranged and there will be no need to impose upon the lender any conditions in regard to taking his loan back bit by bit.

Subject to these two qualifications it appears to me to be a simple matter encugh to graft a Loan Fund system upon any set of loan accounts.

The Principles of Apportionment.

It is necessary that the principles, on which interest and other expenses should be apportioned and in which profit and loss items should be treated, should be defined. The Torquay Clause puts it up to the Local Authority to suggest, and to the Minister to approve, these principles. I take it no one will demur to that.

But the Torquay Council would no doubt welcome any guidance this Institute has to offer on the Scheme it is to propound.

Mr. Wetherall has covered most of this ground. His rules, as I understand him, are the three following :—

1. All Interest inwards and outwards to be dealt with together, and the net amount to be apportioned annually in proportion to the extent of the loan fund employed for the purposes of each account during the year. (Mr. Lambert has given a useful discussion of the actual procedure for putting this rule into application.)

2. Expenses of running the Finance, including annual contributions for the discharge of Discounts and Stock Expenses —to be dealt with on the same lines.

3. The profits on buying in Stock below par to be applied in discharging the discount liabilities still standing on the books (purchases above par—presumably the converse).

This covers all the ground with the exception of the profits and losses on sinking fund investments. What of them? I don't propose to offer any suggestion, but should be very glad to hear what the Institute consider to be the right principle. Are these profits or losses to be the affair of the year in which they are realised or is there to be some system of periodic revaluation of the investments in order to avoid the risk of heavy disturbance in the incidence of annual loan service charges?

It is about the first of Mr. Wetherall's rules that there will be controversy between the advocates of (i) the average or pro ratâ system and (ii) the specific or earmarked system. I should like to make quite clear the suggestions which I am now submitting for removing this difficulty, and, therefore, I venture to recapitulate. I suggest :—

1. That the loans covering the whole periods of particular borrowing powers and repayable on an agreed instalment or annuity system should never be brought into the pool—no useful purpose would be served by bringing them in.

2. That the consolidation scheme should in each case specify the existing loans in respect of which the interest charges are to be earmarked to particular accounts.

By virtue of these arrangements it becomes possible for each Authority to maintain, to any extent that is desired, the existing connection between loans and borrowing purposes, in so far as interest charges are concerned. Naturally the schemes propounded would have to deal even-handedly with the several classes of borrowing accounts, but it would be for the Authority, in each case, to decide to what extent the vested interests of the past are to be taken into account. There will be cases in which the facts are such that there is no call to make any adjustments in the interest aportionments, and in these cases the schemes may provide for pro ratâ charge forthwith.

3. The right of each trading account or other separate service to exercise a borrowing power by a specific whole period mortgage should, I think, be maintained for all time.

This would remove the objection, which some feel, to binding (say) a Water Undertaking to accept the average interest rates of the pool, when at the time when its borrowing powers are exercised the advantage of a whole period loan at low interest is attainable.

I see no objection to according this privilege and to keeping the loans so raised outside the scheme of consolidation. I am convinced that it is a privilege which would soon fall into disuse and be forgotten. I say this because I feel sure that the loan pools will be managed in such manner as to take full advantage of the possibilities of funding short-term debt whenever low interest rates are available. In fact, the only effect of including this provision would be that of protecting borrowing accounts from mismanagement of their finance by the Central Control. If the pool is well managed, no borrowing account could ever obtain any advantage from taking up a specific loan in place of borrowing from the pool. The average interest rate on the consolidated debt will sometimes be raised above the level at which loans could have been effected when certain borrowing powers were exercised; but, if the funding powers are applied when it is expedient to use them, both to the existing debt and to some extent with regard to prospective needs, this average rate will always compare favourably with the rate at which a loan for the whole loan period was obtainable.

THE BORROWING LIMITS OF A LOAN FUND.

As already suggested the Loan Fund can borrow without continuous reference to the extent of the authorised borrowing powers. Provided the cash balance is kept within the limits of the sinking fund contributions of the year, the borrowing powers will not have been exceeded when the account closes. Moreover, the power to borrow for the purpose of discharging loans as they mature can be used to any extent that is reasonable and proper in view of approaching redemption dates.

As temporary bank accommodation is one of the ways in which borrowing powers can be exercised, the Loan Fund can, without difficulty, be so managed that it carries no balance pro or con at any time. In general, and subject to the questions of policy referred to below, this is the simplest and best line to adopt in managing a Loan Fund.

It is also true that investment of money is no necessary part of the Loan Fund system. This system in fact enables the Authority to avoid any form of investment and the expense connected therewith, and *to keep its outstanding loan debt at the lowest possible level* at all times.

On the other hand the system does not in any way reduce the power of the Authority to invest Sinking Funds, Pension Funds, Reserve Funds or any other funds eligible for investment. Indeed, if no limit be imposed, it would give to Local Authorities a power to hold investments against loans to an extent far in excess of that which any Council could desire. It is clear that any Authority could bring its list of sinking fund investments alone up to about half its loan debt; and, when we consider what Pension Funds (where they exist) will amount to in 30 or 40 years, it will be seen that many Councils at that time could have investment lists far in excess of their total loan debt. They could thus become large lending corporations while still retaining power to be large borrowers.

The Loan Fund system is in no wise involved in the large questions of policy which here arise. These questions can be dealt with entirely apart from it. All that it does is to simplify the position ; it has no other bearing whatsoever on these questions.

To my mind the only advantage, which a Local Authority can derive from refraining to discharge loan debt to the full extent that the Loan Fund permits, comes when the money market offers long term loans at low interest. The power to take up such loans (e.g. by Stock issue) is otherwise limited to the unexercised borrowing powers plus the existing loan debt which is eligible for redemption at short notice. To such extent as the Authority holds Loan Fund (i.e. Sinking Fund) unapplied this power is extended. Thus it may be possible to provide loans of low interest to cover capital requirements which are in sight, though borrowing powers have not actually been acquired.

To what extend this new power, which the Loan Fund system brings, should be given to Local Authorities is a question which must present itself when Consolidated Loan Fund Regulations come to be framed. There can be no difficulty in so framing these Regulations as to provide any safeguard which Parliament or the Government Department concerned may think necessary.

It hardly appears to be necessary to refer to the need for paying regard to the dates when important loan or stock redemptions mature. To what extent it is of advantage to hold invested as well as uninvested balances with a view to redemption or new capital requirements is a matter of opinion upon which sound advice is desirable in connection with each case. We must not forget, however, that, at the time when new loans involve high interest, the realisation of investments will usually involve loss, and that the losses which can occur in this way are often matters of much more serious consequence than the payment of high interest on loans of short duration, such as money bills and bank overdrafts.

Sinking Fund Investments.

It is important to note that power to invest sinking funds in the Authority's own securities is no part of the Loan Fund system here described. Not only is it unnecessary to the scheme; it would, indeed, be a source of much useless trouble and complication.

That it is entirely unnecessary, when the loans cease to be earmarked, will be seen on consideration of the design of the system. The total debt is distributed to the borrowing accounts and the repayment contributions provided by each account reduce pro tanto the amount allocated to that account. Thus the sinking fund contributions (if not invested) are forthwith applied to the purpose for which they were provided, and Loan Fund money is thereby set free to equal amount.

That it is a useless complication can best be appreciated by considering its effect upon debt returns (or loan statements) and upon balance sheets. Without it, there are no sinking fund entries to make (except when some of the money is invested outside). With it, we may have to set out an unexhausted sinking fund balance in connection with each borrowing power, and to shew a large number of sinking fund items on the balance sheets with per contra entries of the Authority debtor to itself.

The proper development of the Loan Fund system does not call for this power, but it does call for power to invest other Capital Funds in the Authority's own securities.

The Local Authorities Concerned.

The advantages of the Pooling System are by no means confined to those Authorities which have established a practice of raising short term mortgages from local investors or to those which issue Stock. There is no Borrowing Authority which cannot obtain material advantage from an adoption of the plan.

It may safely be stated that it is capable of effecting an important reduction in the interest burden in every case, by reason of the wider market which it throws open and the greater attractions which it offers to investors. This is particularly true in those cases where all the borrowings have hitherto been from the P.W.L.C., the Ecclesiastical Commissioners, the Insurance Companies or other lending Corporations which have been willing to take their loans back by instalments spread over the sanctioned periods.

The PRESIDENT: Gentlemen, on my left we have a very eminent Past President of this Institute and I am going to ask Sir Harry Haward to address a few words to us upon this very important subject, for I believe there is no one in the Institute more able than he to express a competent opinion.

Sir HARRY HAWARD: At this late hour of the Conference I do not propose to trouble you with many remarks on this important matter on which we have had such an interesting and clear paper and such a masterly address from my friend Mr. Carson Roberts. The matter is one of great complexity supposing that the principle be admitted, and really the most practical way of handling it, I suggest, would be to ask the Council to take it into consideration and draw up a report or scheme for dealing with it. It seems to me quite impossible in a meeting like this to discuss the ramifications and details of this most complicated question. I am not particularly competent to deal with it for this reason, that fortunately in the case of the London County Council we have had, ever since I was connected with the Council, a Consolidated Loans Fund and we have not experienced the difficulties which face so many of you gentlemen here in your financial transactions. We have had this Consolidated Loans Fund, but rather unfortunately, I think, some ten or fifteen years ago, as the result of the Report of the Committee on Local Authorities' Accounts, we decided to appropriate the nominal amount of consolidated stock, not to the different services for which the stock had been raised, but at any rate to the different main funds for which the stock had been raised, for example the General County Rate Fund, the Special County

Rate Fund, the Tramways, the Housing, and so on. Thus of course we have become involved in the difficulties relating to discounts and premiums and losses or gains on the realisation of the investments and so on, all of which we used to avoid by treating the Consolidated Loans Fund as the financing fund. That is a small matter compared with the difficulties with which you are faced in earmarking all monies raised to these different borrowing powers in the way that has been described. But there is one point on which I do not at present quite see eye to eye with the author of the paper or with Mr. Carson Roberts. I suppose it is because I am rather old-fashioned or at any rate I have lived so long under one system that I find it difficult to reconcile myself to this novel idea of an average rate of interest to be varied every year; and the particular paragraph in Mr. Wetherall's paper, to which I take exception—there are other minor paragraphs—I fasten upon this because among other reasons time is limited—is at the end of paragraph 25, where Mr. Wetherall says this : " I submit, therefore that the correct view to take is that it has borrowed £40,000 at an average rate of 4½ per cent. and the different services should be charged accordingly." You will recollect that he has referred to a loan of £20,000 raised 25 years ago for the erection of a Town Hall by means of the issue of three per cent Stock and a loan of similar amount raised quite recently at six per cent. He says the proper way to regard that, is that forty thousand pounds has been raised at an average rate of 4½ per cent. Now that I cannot swallow, and whether it is due to the fact that nearly all our obligations are long term obligations or not I cannot say, because for the most part the London County Council adopted the view that it was best to create your asset when you incurred your liability. If you had a permanent work to construct, it was better to arrange the finances for the whole sanctioned term of borrowing. I admit in a period such as we have been passing through of high rates of interest this sound maxim may need some qualifications. But if I take the cost of money which was raised twenty or thirty years ago at three per cent. and raised for the purpose of building working class dwellings, well, the Local Authority proceeded on the basis of fixing the rent to meet its outgoings and those outgoings depend on the rate of interest which was fixed at three per cent. for the whole period of the loan. Would it be fair, would you expect the Housing Committee to agree that the rate of interest of three per cent. on which the rents have been fixed, should be turned at the present time into a rate of 4½ per cent. because money that was being raised to put up an Elementary or Secondary School now was costing six per cent.? That I think is a matter that will have to be considered, and I am not quite sure that Mr. Carson Roberts thought interest should be averaged in such a case. I think he said that long term borrowings should be eliminated from this average rate of interest. If so, I have not so much to say against the proposal because it seems to me not of so much importance that you are averaging the rate of interest in the case of these short term borrowings. The other point relates to the question of Stock which you are bound to redeem at a fixed date, I take it that that would come within the description of direct contractual obligations which must be respected and in regard to such Stock it would be right that the sinking fund should be intact at the date when you are required to pay off the Stock-holders. That was a distinct reservation made by the Committee who reported on the use of Sinking funds for capital purposes. I think I am right that they made a reservation on that point. They thought it only right and proper that the Sinking fund belonging to Stock which you were obliged to redeem on a certain date should not be used for purposes which would carry you beyond that date. That I think is a matter which wants careful examination, and it is one of the "snags" you may meet in considering the effect of such a proposal as this on the money market. Those are the only points I have to raise but I would suggest very respectfully to the Institute that if this matter is to be profitably pursued it should be taken up by a small Committee of the Council and thoroughly thrashed out.

The PRESIDENT : Gentlemen, if it would meet with your wishes, shall we adjourn this discussion until ten o'clock to-morrow morning for half an hour? It is a most important matter and we should not like to dismiss it.

Mr. ALLCOCK (City Treasurer and Controller, Cardiff) : I sincerely hope you will not postpone the discussion. The first paper I read to this Institute was treated in the same way and I think we should go on for another half hour and conclude the subject. It is not fair to Mr. Wetherall that while we have these facts in our minds we should defer the discussion until to-morrow morning.

The President : I am in the hands of the meeting entirely, and I must say I do not wish to burk discussion. It is in view of the other engagements some have, even at this table here, that this should be publicly discussed in the morning, when we shall be free.

Mr. Allcock (City Treasurer and Controller, Cardiff) : I move that the discussion continues now.

Mr. R. Geoffrey Johnson (City Treasurer, Sheffield) : I will second that.

The President : I will put the resolution to the meeting " that we proceed with the discussion."

The resolution was put to the meeting and lost, only 33 voting for it, and the proceedings were adjourned until 10-0 a.m. the following day.

COSTING AND ALLOCATION OF CENTRAL ESTABLISHMENT CHARGES

By WM. C. COXALL, F.S.A.A., F.I.M.T.A.

The standardisation of the treatment of central establishment charges presents a most difficult problem. In this paper the past and present practice is described, and then the author goes on to make some suggestions for the future. He believes that the solution is to be found in the application of proper costing methods.

WHEN your Secretary invited me to write this paper I think he must have felt very much like King Pharaoh, of whom it is recorded in sacred writings, his task-masters did say, "Thus saith Pharaoh, I will not give ye straw. Go ye, get your straw where ye can find it, yet not ought of your work shall be diminished."

Few subjects are more difficult of scientific treatment or ultimate solution on a uniform or standardised basis, but we ought, none the less, to strive to reduce the perplexities to the utmost minimum.

Comparatively speaking, little has been written upon the subject; the only previous papers one has been able to discover are those written by—

(*a*) the late Mr. C. H. Patterson, of West Ham, and read at the annual meeting of the Institute in 1913.

(*b*) Mr. A. H. Dunn, of Newport, and read to the South Wales Students' Society on the 18th October 1919.

A Retrospect.

The Executive Council of the Institute, ever in the vanguard, in March 1903 passed the following resolution :—

> "That in the interests of sound finance and accuracy of account keeping, it is desirable that all trading and other undertakings of a corporation should bear their proper share of Establishment Charges, i.e. not only those charges which relate to the undertaking proper, but also those of the Central Departments, where such Departments render the undertaking any service whatever."

In the year 1903 a Joint Select Committee was appointed to investigate the subject of "Municipal Trading," and whilst scarcely a reference to this subject was made in the evidence submitted, or in the subsequent report of the Committee, there is an important appendix given on page 233 *et seq.* of the report, setting out an abstract of the accounts of every Municipal Trading Undertaking then in existence.

In the last column of this appendix is given :—

> *Column* 21.—"Average annual amount (if any) of General Legal and Establishment Charges of the Corporation, charged to the undertaking."

This column gives a very comprehensive indication of the practice then in force—twenty-two years ago.

It is impossible to set out in a concise way the information there given, but the following facts have been aggregated therefrom :—

Undertaking	Total No. of Undertakings	No. of Undertakings charged with an amount for Central Establishment charges in Col. 21	No. of Undertakings not so charged
Water	193	113	80
Gas	97	66	31
Electricity	102	51	51
Tramways	45	19	26
Markets	228	47	181
Baths	138	17	121
Cemeteries	143	45	98
Miscellaneous, e.g. Housing, Ferries, Docks, &c. ..	43	20	23
Total	989	378	611

These undertakings were owned by 298 Local Authorities, of which 136 did not charge any amount to any of their trading concerns.

The amounts transferred vary in ratio tremendously, some being as low as ½ per cent., others as high as 5 per cent. on income or working expenses.

The overall average was 9 per cent. on income and 1.4 per cent. on working expenses.

From the 13th March to the 31st July 1906 the Departmental Committee appointed to inquire into the accounts of Local Authorities sat to examine expert evidence, and in 1907 issued their report.

Many of the eminent men who appeared as witnesses were closely examined upon this question, and the following is a short epitome of the opinions expressed by them :—

(*a*) Proportions should be charged to all trading undertakings, but a scientific basis of apportionment unattainable.

(*b*) Method of apportionment should be on the basis of "services rendered."

A lecture delivered before the North-Eastern Students' Society of the Institute of Municipal Treasurers and Accountants.

(c) General Rules should not be laid down by the auditors, but by the Finance Committee, or apportionments, when made, should be approved by that Committee.

(d) The auditors should have the right to report as to the equity of such apportionments.

(e) Divergence of opinion, as to whether the apportionment should apply to Capital Accounts.

In answer to the following written inquiry by the Departmental Committee :—

"Are proportionate amounts of the central establishment, debited to the different funds or undertakings, and if so, how are the proportions arrived at ?"

the following replies were received :—

Boroughs.—"The answer is generally in the affirmative. The amount charged is based either on a fixed proportion or (more usually) on an estimate of the services rendered ; this estimate is approved by the Finance Committee.

"In about ten of the boroughs, no proportions are charged to the different funds ; but in three of these cases, each Department has its separate staff and is substantially independent of the central establishment.

"In only one of the six metropolitan boroughs is a complete apportionment of the establishment expenses made ; in others the apportionment is practically limited to the important trading undertakings."

Counties.—"An apportionment of the central establishment expenses is made, though sometimes only partially, in almost every county, the amounts being usually arrived at by computation of the services rendered. In the case of the London County Council, the whole question of the allocation of establishment expenses is under the consideration of the Finance Committee. Proportionate amounts of the central establishment expenses are charged in the case of certain accounts. With regard to the education, works, tramway, steamboat, and working class dwellings services the administrative work is mainly carried out in separate establishments, apart from the central offices, and the whole cost of these separate establishments is charged direct to the respective undertakings.

"As regards trading undertakings, a proportionate part of the central office expenses is charged, based as far as possible on actual cost of the services rendered. As regards other services of which a separate account is kept, the principle which has generally guided the Council is to charge the *extra* cost to which the Council has been put by the new service. A rough apportionment is made of establishment expenses between general county account (the account charged with expenditure to which the whole area of the administrative county is assessed), and special county account (the expenditure under which the City of London is exempt)."

Urban Districts.—"Proportionate amounts are almost always charged where the Authority carry on waterworks or other trading undertakings. The charges are generally settled by the Council annually on the basis of the estimated value of the services rendered."

Rural Districts.—"The reply is generally in the negative, though where there are waterworks that account is, on the whole, usually charged for the services it receives."

The ultimate report of the Departmental Committee on this matter was as follows :—

"In regard to all undertakings for which a clear and true statement of profit and loss is required, it is obviously essential that each should bear its proper charges and should not be allowed to profit at the expense of other services, funds, or accounts. Among the many difficult questions involved in this requirement, reference may be made to the allocation of expenditure for which more than one Department are jointly responsible, as in the case of a street improvement which is partly necessitated by tramways, or the allocation of capital expenditure incurred in pursuance of housing schemes ; the settlement of an equitable basis for amounts chargeable to a department in respect of services or commodities received from another department ; the rental of property belonging to the Authority, and (in London, where the borough councils are in most cases the assessment authorities) the assessment to the rate of the property of the various undertakings. The expenses of a central establishment, too, should clearly be divided in fair proportions among the various departments in accordance, as far as possible, with the benefit which they have derived from it ; and in our opinion both the capital accounts and the revenue accounts should bear their proper proportion of these charges."

"The information we have received appears to show that *sufficient attention has not been paid to questions of this kind by Local Authorities.* As regards establishment charges, for example, many Authorities seem to have attempted no apportionment between the different departments, *and in others there is reason to suppose that the allocation may have tended to favour one fund at the expense of another.*

"It is plain that all these questions (and there are many others of a similar character) have an important bearing on the accuracy of the statement of profit and loss. It is equally plain that they are questions which cannot be dealt with adequately by general regulations ; *each case must be treated separately on its own merits and in accordance with the particular circumstances.*"

Finance Committees

"The settlement of such questions as these, which cannot be left satisfactorily to the executive committees who are naturally interested in showing economical results in the departments for which they are responsible, is one of the most important functions of a Finance Committee.

"In our opinion, it should be compulsory for every Authority of sufficient size (as is now the case with County Councils under Section 80 of the Local Government Act, 1888) to appoint a Finance Committee with general powers of control and supervision over all matters of finance."

In chronological order, we now come to the paper of the late esteemed Borough Treasurer of West

HAM in 1913 from which are selected the following more important items.

1. It would be interesting to have a complete return of what is done by way of apportionment throughout the country.

2. Central expenses are incurred for two groups :—

(a) The general work of the Authority—Primary function.

(b) Work done for various sectional departments —Secondary function.

3. There is always left a residuum, which in so far as allocation has approached accuracy, may be said to represent expenses incurred in performing the *primary* duties of the corporation.

4. Dealing with the usual form of objection to apportionments, he said :—

Objection 1.—All expenses come out of one pocket. Why apportion at all ?

(a) If there is no legal compulsion to apply apportionments, it is nevertheless a business necessity, e.g. works done by direct labour for comparison with contract work.

(b) Dangerous critics are those who have facts on their side.

It is not worth while to give them this advantage.

Objection 2.—Certain departments are run for the public good and have therefore a right to free benefit of central services.

(a) This contention implies that some departments are run to the public detriment. All departments are run for the public good.

(b) No department should escape from complete accountancy methods.

Objection 3.—Chief Officials' Salaries should not be apportioned over surrounding departments because it is part of their duty to aid these departments.

(a) Extra work is involved, increased staffs are necessary, and were the departments independent, they would have to provide additional expert assistance.

5. He recommended the possession of a separate Revenue Account for the test as to the necessity of apportionment and especially stressed the example of Education Accounts.

In determining whether to allocate in any given case, the purpose to be served should be considered.

6. All central expenses should be shown in summary in one account or fund, and then distributed.

7. Capital Works Accounts should bear their fair share even if not permitted by Government sanction, and be afterwards provided as a Revenue Contribution to capital.

8. (a) Apportionment should be calculated with precision and close approximation.

(b) Salaries of chief officials can only be dealt with by approximation.

(c) Staff salaries should be based on time apportionment and *diaries should be kept for this purpose*.

(d) Rent, Rates, Repairs and general cost of premises should be apportioned on "space" basis.

Space might be apportioned to each staff member by dividing the total cost by the number of staff.

(e) Printing and stationery should be charged direct as far as possible and the remainder apportioned approximately.

(f) Expenses of committees to follow previous headings.

(g) *Audit*.—Internal audit dealt with under staff. External audit on time basis or proportion of Stamp Duty.

(h) *Law expenses*—

Parliamentary will be definable by the Bill of Costs.

Expenses of opposition.—The usual practice to charge to the municipality as a whole is wrong; they should be charged to the departments concerned.

Mr. DUNN's paper in 1919 included, *inter alia*, the following points :—

(1) *General principles*.

(a) That the separate Rate Fund Accounts are charged with all proper expenses so as to give full effect to the principle of differential rating where such is provided for by the statute.

(b) That the accounts of the various trading undertakings and special services are made as complete as possible.

(c) That, in order to facilitate comparisons as between town and town, standardisation of details should be aimed at.

(d) That apportionments are not carried to extremes.

(e) That the larger trading undertakings—for example, Electricity Works, Water Works, Gas Works, and Tramways—should be fully charged no one will deny. All other sub-accounts should be charged that have a separate Revenue Account.

(2) *Method of Allocation*.—Charge direct as far as possible. Bring all other items into a total or summary in one fund and therefrom distribute them.

(3) *Methods in applying above principles*.

(a) To estimate the values of services rendered and/or expense incurred on behalf of the particular departments and services, and to charge such amounts to the accounts concerned. The estimate may take the form of a fixed sum of money or a fixed percentage of the total.

(b) To apportion the charges on the basis of revenue expenditure.

(c) To apportion the costs of rate and similar collections over the accounts concerned on the basis of the total amount collected.

(d) To apportion rent, or its equivalent, on the basis of floor space occupied by the several departments.

Attention is also drawn to the methods suggested in Whiteley and Whittingham's "Income Tax in relation to Local Authorities," pages 66-72, for securing due allowance for central charges, where no transfers have been made in the actual books of account.

To complete this portion of my paper, it is essential to mention the Exchequer Grants Audit Committee presided over by Lord Meston.

In the annual report of the Institute, 1921, page 49 *et seq.*, is given a résumé of evidence given on behalf of the Institute by the then president, vice-president, and Mr. J. Gronow, and paragraphs 13 and 14 deal with the recommendations made respecting allocation of central charges to grant-aided services.

Paragraph 13 *reads* :—

"That as the apportionment of administrative expenses between the various grant-aided funds presents great difficulties which have for some time past been under consideration by the Ministry of Health in conference with an Advisory Committee representing, *inter alia*, the Institute, under these circumstances the witnesses suggest that tentatively there should be an extension of the principle now applicable to grants-in-aid of housing by the application of a percentage upon the amount of the grant-in-aid (as determined by expenditure qualifying for grant) in respect of administrative expenses."

Paragraph 14 *reads* :—

"That for the purpose of such tentative allowance, 5 per cent. upon the amount of all grants be added to the said grants as representing, approximately, the equivalent of the present corresponding grant for general administration expenses on housing, other than expenses specifically allotted thereto.

This Committee has not yet reported, and it would perhaps be unwise, therefore, to enter into any detailed analysis of the effect of these suggestions upon the National and Local Budgets.

Present Day Practice.

Research and exhaustive inquiry has failed to discover any Government return which would give me similar useful information of the practice in vogue to-day comparable with the statement given in the "Municipal Trading" Report of 1903 already referred to, and much as I dislike throwing additional burdens upon my colleagues, I felt compelled to seek assistance by way of *questionnaire*.

The following inquiries were therefore addressed to eighteen County Boroughs, five non-county Boroughs, two Metropolitan Boroughs, two Urban District Councils, and two Scottish Burghs—Total, twenty-nine, and replies were received from twenty-three of them.

Having regard to the expense, it is not considered worth while to print an epitome of the replies as an appendix to this lecture, instead, the position indicated is shortly stated below.

Q. (1) Assuming the undermentioned to be a definition of complete centralisation—

"Executive Departments issue orders, prepare Stores Warrants, Wages Books, and all other primary records, and receive minor cash sales, but all further financial transactions, both on income and expenditure, are carried out by the Finance Department."

please state upon what particular points your system departs from the above.

R. The majority of replies indicate that centralisation as indicated is in operation.

Q. (2) Do you act for all departments in :—

(*a*) Income Tax matters.
(*b*) Loan and stock management.

R. It is gratifying to know that every reply is in the affirmative.

Q. (3) What is the scheme or method of allocation of central charges, e.g. :—

(1) Rent.
(2) Rates.
(3) Heating and Lighting.
(4) Cleaning.
(5) Loan Charges on Central Buildings.
(6) Other expenses.

R. It is impossible to set out concisely the replies, as nearly every Authority's practice differs, probably on account of varying circumstances as to building accommodation, &c.

Percentage and lump sum methods are used.

Heating, Lighting, and Cleaning is frequently based on building space occupied.

"According to services rendered" is a recurring phrase.

Q. (4) Does such scheme apply to :—

(*a*) Trading Undertakings.
(*b*) Rate Funds.
(*c*) Other accounts (if any).

R. The replies are in the affirmative in most cases.

One reply indicates that all such expenses are charged to Trading Undertakings and none to Rate Funds!

Q. (5) Is such allocation further sub-divided in the Rate Funds under service headings ?

R. There are eight negative and five affirmative replies.

Q. (6) (1) Is the same basis used for :—

(*a*) Income Tax settlements.
(*b*) Government Grant claims.

(2) If not, please indicate variation of method or system for purposes under (6) (1).

R. There are three negative and eleven affirmative replies, and one is negative as to Income Tax but affirmative as to Government Grants.

Q. (7) Does the scheme vary in treatment as to the—

Town Clerk's Department.
Borough Treasurer's Department.
Borough Surveyor's Department.
Medical Officer of Health's Department.

R. It is practically impossible to concisely state the methods. Nearly every case is differently treated.

Q. (8) Is any establishment charge made upon invoices for goods supplied or work done in respect of :—

(*a*) Inter-departmental invoices.
(*b*) Other Local Authorities' Accounts.
(*c*) Private Individual accounts.

R. The same applies as to question 7.

One may be allowed to say perhaps what has been done in Chesterfield on this matter, and in doing so, you will see before the lecture is finished that I have laid myself open to an obvious criticism.

We have no Central Municipal Buildings in Chesterfield, and our position in this respect emphasises the difficulties of ever successfully dealing with the subject in standardised form.

Five separate buildings contain the following groups :—

(1) The Town Clerk and Borough Surveyor's Departments.
(2) The Borough Accountant's, Gas Engineer's, and Water Engineer's Departments.
(3) Medical Officer's Department and other smaller departments.
(4) Tramways and Electricity Departments.
(5) Education Offices.

In 1920 I submitted a report including certain statements upon the allocation of the Town Clerks' and my own Department's expenses.

These statements condensed, together with the Finance Committee's decisions, are now indicated.

STATEMENT OF ALLOCATION OF CENTRAL SALARIES.

	Borough Treasurer's, Borough Accountant's Department, Auditors' Fees, &c.				Town Clerk's Department
	Annual Income basis	Approximate work done basis	Suggested basis	Adopted basis	Suggested and adopted basis for Salaries and rent
	%	%	%	%	%
Borough Fund	13½	8½	10	10	20
Free Library	—	¾	¾	1	2½ (Free Library, Education and Cemeteries together)
Education ..	6½	5¼	5	5	
Cemeteries ..	—	¾	¾	1	
District Fund	28	20	25	25	30
Overseers ..	10	7	6	6	—
Total Rate Charge.	58	42¼	47½	48	52½
Allotments. ..	—	¼	—	—	—
Water ..	5	6	5	5	10
Markets ..	1	1	1	1	2½
Gas	18½	31½	25	25	15
Electricity	9½	7½	10	10	10
Tramways ..	*3½	3¾	5	5	5
Motor Buses..	*4½	4	5	5	5
Housing ..	—	3¾	1½	1	—
	100	100	100	100	100

* Half Annual Income.

The Rent, Rates, Heating, Lighting and Cleaning of the offices under Group 2 and the composite Printing, Stationery and Postages for the Town Clerk's and my Department were allocated as shown in Table in next column.

This arrangement which still continues does not represent as fair and equitable a basis of charge as could be obtained, and it particularly hits the smaller departments, and I am hoping at an early date to revise the whole position as indicated later on.

A supervision charge of 10 per cent. is made upon all accounts rendered, including inter-departmental accounts, and capital work is charged 5 per cent., which is considered to be only a wear and tear allowance for tools and plant.

At this stage it may be of interest to quote Section 401 of the Chesterfield Corporation Act, 1923.

" In all cases in which the Corporation keep separate accounts for separate purposes they may apportion between those accounts or carry to either of them any receipts, credits, payments, and liabilities which from time to time it appears to them ought to be so apportioned or carried."

	Buildings, Group 2. Rent, Rates, Heating, Lighting and Cleaning (on basis of space occupied)	Composite Printing, Stationery and Postages. Town Clerk's and Borough Accountant's Department
	Per cent.	Per cent.
Borough Fund	5	10
Free Library	2½	1
Education	2½	3
Cemeteries	2½	1
District Fund	15	27½
Poor Rate	5	12½
Total Rate Charge	32½	55
Water	25	7½
Markets	2½	2½
Gas	25	20
Electricity	5	7½
Trams	5	3¾
Buses	5	3¾
	100	100

SUGGESTIONS FOR THE FUTURE.

A considerable space has been devoted upon the past and present day practice in the hope that the student may find it helpful to have in a moderately concise form all there is to be found upon the subject.

If for a moment a digression may be permitted, let me remark that for seventy years or more Rating Reform has been a municipal " Will of the Wisp." We are inclined to throw stones at Legislators or Administrators in London for the continued delay, but Mr. Patterson's " dangerous critic " has the obvious opportunity of suggesting the removal of the "beam" of "Allocation of Central Charges" from our eye ere we point out the existence of the " mote " of " Rating Reform " in that of others.

For more than 20 years the former has been recognised as of fundamental importance, and doubtless much time and thought has been expended in attempts to find a solution on a standardised basis.

It is reasonable to assume that many solutions may have emanated from the minds of those engaged upon the task, and without full knowledge of these facts, one naturally hesitates to criticise the absence of a scheme.

To the query " Is it capable of solution " the reply must be in the affirmative.

The solution is one *entirely in our own hands individually, viz. Costing.*

Serious examination of the factors involved in the problem, force me to the inevitable conclusion that standardisation, either by lump sum or percentage methods, is futile.

Lump sum methods are probably preferable to percentage schemes.

Both must be subjected to continual revision, and if any degree of accuracy is to be approached, much thought and labour must be expended.

Any percentage scheme in a Borough possessing undertakings or funds, some of which are stationary, the remainder making rapid progress, will lead to an unfair burden being placed upon the former to the advantage of the latter.

Accuracy in this matter ought surely to be expected of the strictest of all professions in matters of figures and results.

What are the advantages to be gained ?

Costing will—

Give accurate results and reliable data, by which we shall be enabled—

(a) To eliminate waste and, *inter alia*, to justify the introduction or extension of office machinery.

(b) To improve the " money sense " in ourselves and all members of the staff.

(c) To put up an unanswerable case to any criticism from Trading Departments.

(d) To enforce our rights to allowance from Government Departments.

(e) To create absolute confidence in the minds of the members of the Authorities we have the honour to serve.

(f) To obtain valuable comparison of administrative actual costs of one Authority with another.

Two quotations at this point it is hoped will be considered apposite.

The first is the last of the four classical maxims laid down by Adam Smith many years ago.

" Every tax ought to be so contrived as both to take out and keep out of the pockets of the people as little as possible over and above what it brings into the Public Treasury of the State."

The second is by Sir Henry Bunbury in a paper read to the Institute of Public Administration on the 24th January 1924 on " Control of Expenditure within Government Departments." He then said :—

" To secure this economy in expenditure, it was necessary to develop more and not less of the ' money sense ' in the Administrative Officials whose operations directly or indirectly lead to the extraction of money from the pockets of the taxpayer, and he thought that the solution lay in the establishment of a system based on principles, the first of which was :—

" Officials who were responsible for administering services should know continuously, in terms of pounds, shillings, and pence, the cost to the taxpayer of what they were doing."

It surely will be agreed that the principle herein enunciated is equally applicable to Local Authorities.

One rather suspects that the reason I was asked to prepare this paper was because, in attempting a model answer last session to a question of the 1924 examination, as set out hereunder :—

" Outline a suitable system, including draft forms, for recording *the time worked* and method of payment of salaries and wages in connection with the following services :—

(a) *Administration and Clerical Staffs.*

(b) School Teachers and Caretakers.

(c) Manual Workers."

I mentioned Unit or Time Sheets for Administrative Departments and hinted at internal costing in such departments.

Incidentally, it may be mentioned as an indication of the general attitude in this matter, that in a model answer to this question set out in a well-known book for students, the underlined part of the question was ignored.

About the year 1911 I first introduced a simple unit sheet into my office, and continued its use up to the year 1920.

In that year it was proved once more that :—

" The thing that has been done, it is that which shall be done,
And that which is done is that which shall be done,
And there is no new thing under the Sun."

for I discovered in Mr. Bateson's Municipal Office Organisation and Management several better specimens of such Unit Sheets.

After my " model " answer had appeared, many requests were received for specimens of the Unit Sheet, and finally one came from as far as South Africa. Most inquirers expressed the view that it appeared to fill a long felt want.

After all, what adequate reply is there to the point of view once put to me by an executive officer respecting the introduction of *Workmen's* Time Sheets as a basis for Works Costing :—

" You are asking my men, who are illiterate, to do that which your own staff, educated men, are not called upon to do."

We all know that in the offices of Solicitors and Commercial Accountants in private practice, time records are kept by all members of the staff, and a recent article in *The Accountant* shows this has apparently been much more highly developed in America.

If this is done for determining private charge, why should it be deemed impossible and impracticable where public money is concerned.

The value of these Unit Sheets, which are the base of the suggested Costing Scheme in respect of salaries has been abundantly proved in my own experience and leads me to the conviction that the larger the department, the more essential is something of the kind, to enable the Chief Financial Officer, or his deputy, and in the larger offices, the Sectional Chief Assistants, to properly keep in touch with the details of the department and to see fair play as between the individual members of the staff.

How many finance departments can readily answer such inquiries as the following :—

(a) What does it cost to prepare a rate demand note ?

(b) What is the tota cost of correspondence or the additional cost of correspondence and inquiries, resultant upon the abolition of outside collectors ?

(c) What is the total cost of all calculations and casting in the department ?

How many Municipal Accountants can tell what it costs complete, to produce a Revenue Account, Balance Sheet, &c., of any single trading undertaking, published in the annual Abstract of Accounts ?

When colleagues state that they cannot persuade the Finance Committee to allow them to introduce office machinery, the question always crosses one's mind what definite and convincing proof has been submitted of actual past cost and future probable cost and ultimate saving.

The main criticism against costing one expects to meet is that it will not be worth the trouble and it will involve expense which the results will not justify.

Whatever work it involves, it seems to me that the results are bound to justify it, but let us look at the process suggested and the work it involves.

Will you please look at the specimen unit sheet :—

The front page is filled in by the clerk according to the work he is doing, either :—

(a) As he completes an operation ; or
(b) At lunch time ; and/or
(c) At the close of the day.

My experience is that the time incurred in doing this is not worth recording.

The next morning, the Senior of the Section initials the sheet of each clerk in his section and satisfies himself it is a true record.

At the end of the week he also states shortly the position of each man's work whether "Current work" or "In arrears" and passes them to the Deputy, who, in turn, makes such notes as he deems necessary, and then passes to the Chief.

It is suggested that it is not necessary that *all* Unit Sheets be examined weekly, by even the Deputy or Chief Financial Officer in large offices, but sections might be taken in turn.

Your attention is next directed to the analysis columns at the back of this Unit Sheet, which it is intended to bring into operation in my department in the coming financial year.

Each man knows his price per hour.

Take two difficult examples of allocation.

(1) Cash Book Clerk getting £150 per annum with a 39½-hour week, this works out at 1s. 6d. per hour. He keeps columnar Cash Books :—

(a) Receipts.
(b) Payments.

And he knows at the end of the day, better than any-one else, on what funds his day's cost of roughly 10s. 6d. should be charged.

(2) *Cashiers and Counter Clerks.*

One day may be mainly concerned with rate demands payments, another Gas Accounts and so on. Surely these men can the most accurately allocate their time to the funds concerned, with the additional check of the Chief Cashier.

They therefore insert the value of their work in the respective columns.

At the end of the week—

(a) The Senior Clerk adds to his own total analysis (A) the total of each of his clerks (B).
(b) And the grand total of each section (C) is transferred from his sheet to a summary book, giving a page for each of the sections.

Each section total is carried periodically, either quarterly, half-yearly, or annually to a final summary which gives the figures chargeable to the respective funds for salaries.

The additional labour involved in a system as here outlined cannot be said by any stretch of imagination to be prohibitive, and if one may venture to prophesy, the results obtained when compared with those secured by the present haphazard methods will a tound most of us.

Having dealt with the most difficult part of the problem, viz. Salaries, it only remains for me to say that generally, I agree with the recommendations of the late esteemed Bo:ough Treasurer of West Ham in respect of the other items involved, and after all, my suggestions on the former item are only a development of his idea of "Diaries."

The following are shortly my views on the items remain ng to be considered :—

(a) Rents, Rates, Repairs to Buildings, Heating, Lighting and Cleaning.

Space occupied appears to be the best basis put forward, but here again from the costing of salaries might well emerge some better suggestions.

(b) Printing, Stationery and Postages, &c. should be charged as far as possible direct, e.g. Minutes, Abstract of Accounts, in accordance with pages occupied, the remainder—composite items—might follow the salary basis.

(c) *Expenses of Committee.*

(d) *Audit.*

(e) *Law Expenses.*

I entirely agree with his suggestions in all these matters (see *ante*).

Capital Accounts.

The record of Government Departments in the matter of salaries of permanent officials and the wages of permanent workmen has been peculiarly baffling, and any student will be well repaid by studying the varying form of covering letters to sanctions over a period of years received from the various Sanctioning Authorities.

Suffice it to say that whether the sanction permits of central charges being allocated to Loan Accounts or not, from an accountancy point of view a proper debit should be made to Capital Account for any legitimate charge, and if disallowed, should be provided by way of Revenue Contributions to Capital.

Assessment of Trading Undertakings.

This question is rather more remote from the subject under discussion, but as the Departmental Committee on Local Authorities Accounts pointed out, it is necessary to see that fair and equitable treatment is meted out to these undertakings, and it may well be imagined that continued growth or decline in a trading concern ignored by the Assessment Authorities would lead to inaccurate accounts and unfair rating incidence.

Differential Rating.

Emphasis must be placed upon the bearing that strict accounting and exact costing has upon this matter.

Parliament in its wisdom has decided that for some services, relief shall be given to certain groups and sections of ratepayers, e.g. Railways.

It is therefore obvious that the object of the Statute Law may be defeated if expenses rightfully chargeable to one Fund are placed upon the other.

In conclusion, let me say that whilst writing this paper, I have felt that possibly my method of dealing with the subject may be considered scarcely suitable for a students' lecture. I am hopeful however that it may produce considerable discussion and eventually lead to some practical results. Finally, I do want to make an appeal to you as students—

(a) To encourage new methods and particularly the introduction of labour saving office machinery ;
(b) To endeavour to develop the "money sense" in your daily occupation,

for I am convinced that only by all of us, whether we be called to high or low stations in the public service, endeavouring to reduce waste, cut unnecessary costs, and pull our weight, can we ever hope to see our old country weather the stress and storm of these difficult days and enter into the harbour of comfort and prosperity.

SPECIMEN UNIT SHEET

FRONT PAGE.
L.1.

BOROUGH ACCOUNTANT'S DEPARTMENT.

Name..

Week ending..........................192....

WEEKLY RECORD OF WORK.
FOR INSTRUCTIONS SEE BACK.

Code No.	Operation	M.		T.		W.		Th.		F.		S.		Remarks
		U.	T.	U.	T.	U.	T.	U.	T.	U.	T.	U.	T.	
	Exam. and Checking of Invoices.													
	Summarising of Invoices.													
	Despatch of Account Schedules.													
	Accounts posted to Ledgers.													
	Wages posted to Ledgers.													
	Ledger Cast and Balancing Sheet prepared and proved with Bank Sheet.													
	C. B. cross reference to Ledger.													
	Income posted to Ledger.													
	Sinking Fund and Annuity Tables.													
	Journal Adjustments. Ledgers examined by D. B. A.													
	Rev. Accounts and B. S. prepared.													
	Capital Statistical Statement.													
	Printer's copy of Abstract prepared.													
	Claims, Government, &c.													
	Annual Rate Estimates.													
	Annual Abstract.													
	Loan Indebt. Statement.													
	Epitome and other Returns.													
	Correspondence.													
	P. Pt. Collection Audit.													
	Miscellaneous :— (Enter full description.)													

BACK PAGE.

INSTRUCTIONS.

Every Official must fill in his Unit Sheet DAILY and for each item *give number of Units and time occupied*, also period dealt with, and get sheet initialled by 9.30 a.m. next morning.

Senior Clerks must initial these sheets and report anything exceptional AT ONCE to the Deputy Borough Accountant. Senior Clerks must collect these sheets, report on space provided below on general position of Section, particularly arrears, and hand to D. B. A. on Mondays by 10 a.m.

If the work done is current no remarks need be made in the last column, but if the work is not current, the date to which the work has been completed should be given in remarks column.

The D. B. A. to make any observations in space provided below, and hand to the Borough Accountant by noon.

Day		Monday ..	Tuesday ..	Wednesday ..	Thursday ..	Friday ..	Saturday ..	A.	B.	Rate per Hour. C.
Housing	£ s d									
Educa-tion	£ s d									
Borough Fund	£ s d									
Free Libr'ies	£ s d									
Gas	£ s d									
Water	£ s d									
Electric-ity	£ s d									
Trams	£ s d									
'Buses	£ s d									
Ceme-teries	£ s d									
Over-seers	£ s d									
Total	£ s d									

SENIOR CLERK'S REPORT.

D. B. A.'s REMARKS.

B. A.'s REMARKS.

A COMPARISON OF COMMERCIAL ACCOUNTS WITH MUNICIPAL ACCOUNTS

By Norman E. Lamb, F.S.A.A., A.I.M.T.A.

In this paper Mr. Lamb makes an interesting critical comparison between company accounts and the accounts of municipal corporations, concentrating upon the disagreements. Many of the points dealt with apply, of course, to other classes of commercial concerns and local authorities.

PART I.—A BROAD SURVEY.

(a) INTRODUCTORY.

(1) To compare things it is necessary to set them together to ascertain how far they agree or disagree.

Reflecting on the title of this lecture, one first of all finds it necessary to determine definitely how the terms "Commercial Accounts" and "Municipal Accounts" are to be interpreted for the purpose of a limited dissertation. So far as the former is concerned it could embrace the accounts of individuals, partnerships, companies and the many other organisations (whatever be their designations) engaged in commercial pursuits; while the latter might—in its widest sense—be deemed to include (by common usage of the term) the accounts of County Councils, County Borough Councils, non-County Borough Councils, Urban District Councils, Rural District Councils, &c.

(2) If it were decided to adopt these comprehensive definitions, we should, indeed, be faced with an unenviable task, for the component parts of each group possess their own peculiar characteristics. With different types of commercial concerns and dissimilar classes of local authorities we are confronted, not only with variations in the accounts of the two main groups, but also with differences in the accounts of the several concerns and authorities within these groups.

(3) It is at once apparent, therefore, that what may be styled the internal variations—i.e. the differences as between the accounts of one commercial concern and another, and one local authority and another—must be ignored for present purposes. Sweeping aside internal variations then, it becomes necessary to select, for comparison, the most representative examples from each group.

(4) I think I shall be anticipating your wishes in choosing Company Accounts (i.e. the accounts of statutory companies and companies registered under the Companies Acts, 1908 to 1917) and the accounts of Municipal Corporations (i.e. the accounts of county and non-county boroughs). Hence, my subsequent remarks will be directed to these accounts in particular—unless otherwise mentioned—although much that we shall consider will apply to the accounts of other classes of commercial concerns and local authorities respectively.

(5) Thus, with the two fields of research more clearly defined, one attempts to visualise them side by side and still is conscious of the magnitude of each. To encompass the ground and bring it within effective focus a further process of elimination is necessary. The comparison reveals similarities and dissimilarities. One's next step is therefore obvious. Where commercial accounts agree with municipal accounts they must be excluded from the "margin of consciousness" (as psychologists say), leaving the vision concentrated upon the disagreements.

(b) SOME ELEMENTARY ENQUIRIES.

(6) With our plan of investigation decided, let us commence straight away with the most elementary enquiries.

(7) First of all, is there any difference in the bookkeeping theory ?

The A B C of the accountant student's studies is the theory of double-entry bookkeeping, and—although seemingly a very elementary point—experience proves that it is well for the student of municipal accounts to realise, at the outset, that the same theory which applies to commercial accounts applies—unadulterated—to municipal accounts.

(8) Hazarding a guess at the student's next interrogation, might it not be somewhat on these lines ?

> "The accounts of the principal commercial concerns are chiefly kept on the Income and Expenditure basis and seldom on the Receipts and Payments principle. Which method is adopted by municipalities ?"

In answer it can be said that nowadays income and expenditure is the method generally employed by local authorities and that the bulk of the leading municipalities keep their accounts on the most complete lines, with effective Stocks and Stores Accounts and Cost Accounts.

(9) Still endeavouring to follow the student's train of thought, one senses a further question such as this :—

> "The accounts of commercial concerns lead up to the preparation of a Trading Account, a Profit and Loss Account (or a Revenue Account and Net Revenue Account) and a Balance Sheet. Sometimes there are separate Capital Accounts, Reserve Funds, Renewals Funds, &c., in addition.
>
> "Are Municipal Accounts designed similarly ?"

They are not, and consequently a brief review of such accounts is desirable.

(c) A PRELIMINARY GLIMPSE OF MUNICIPAL ACCOUNTS.

(10) Confining our attention at this stage to the framework of municipal accounts, we find that a municipality's income and expenditure can be classified under two main heads, viz. :—

(1) Rate Funds.
   (a) The Borough Fund.
   (b) The General District Fund.
(2) Trading Undertakings.

A lecture delivered before the South Wales and West of England Students' Society of the Institute of Municipal Treasurers and Accountants

(i) Rate Funds.

(11) Broadly stated, it may be said that a municipal corporation acts in a double capacity :—

(1) As a civic authority under the Municipal Corporations Act, 1882.

(2) As a public health authority under the Public Health Acts; the Act of 1875 being the principal Act.

In the former capacity the law requires a municipal corporation to keep a Borough Fund and in the latter a General District Fund. Besides the expenses chargeable to the funds under the above principal Acts, there is charged the expenditure imposed upon the municipality by numerous other Acts (General and Local) passed from time to time. Similarly, income arising under the provisions of the Acts must be carried to one or the other of these two funds according to the directions of the Acts.

(12) Where the income of the Borough Fund is insufficient to meet the expenditure of the fund a "Borough Rate" (which usually forms part of the Poor Rate) has to be levied. Likewise a General District Rate must be levied to meet a deficiency on the General District Fund. Invariably it will be found that the rates are the chief sources of income on the funds.

(13) But what (the student will ask) is the reason for this division into two funds ?—a question which raises one of the most important and perplexing problems in local government, namely, the incidence of rating. The incidence of the two rates varies considerably, the rates differing in respect of :—

(*a*) The area of assessment.

(*b*) The basis of assessment and rating.

(*c*) The mode of collection.

(*d*) Compounding allowances to owners of property paying rates instead of occupiers.

(14) The importance of correctly allocating income and expenditure between the two funds (supplemented by rates differing so widely in their incidence) will at once be apparent. If justice is to be done between the conflicting interests of the varying sections of ratepayers contributing to the expenditure of the municipality, the statutory provisions (i.e. of the general Acts and of the local Acts peculiar to a particular town) which determine the allocations, must be faithfully observed. This is a matter of considerable moment, calling for wide knowledge and involving questions of law as well as accounts.

(15) It might be mentioned here (in parenthesis, so to speak) that within recent years about thirty local authorities—including Cardiff, Newport and Swansea—have, by local legislation, unified the two funds into one general fund and amalgamated the two rates into one general rate. Unfortunately, we cannot, without digressing (even if time permitted), attempt to explain the steps which must be taken to bring about consolidations of funds and rates. Suffice it to say, in passing, that consolidation is a valuable reform which effects large savings in labour and money. The average saving to the thirty towns mentioned is equivalent to the produce of a penny rate per annum.

(16) The correct apportionment of expenditure between capital and revenue is another very important matter, for, as we shall see later, there are many vital considerations affecting the capital transactions of local authorities. Due regard to these considerations is imperative if equitable treatment is to be preserved between the ratepayers of to-day and those of "to-morrow."

(17) We have already observed that the rates levied constitute the main income of the rate funds. These rates—raised in advance—are based upon estimates of prospective requirements. Time and space alike preclude any elaboration of the subject of "estimates," but it will be manifest to all that they require the most careful attention if undue fluctuations in the rate burden are to be avoided.

(ii) Trading Undertakings.

(18) Municipalities may possess numerous trading undertakings, e.g. under the Tramways Acts, Electric Lighting Acts, Gas Works Clauses Acts, Water Works Clauses Acts, Light Railways Act, &c.

(19) The accounts in respect of these undertakings are, for the sake of convenience, shown separately, but the general law recognises only the two main rate funds referred to above.

(20) Whatever the result of a municipal trading undertaking's operations—be it profit or loss—this profit or loss virtually forms part of, or falls on, one of the two rate funds. The final balance of the Trading Undertaking Revenue Account is either carried forward or transferred to the rate fund to which it is statutorily attached, i.e. to the Borough Fund or the General District Fund. Thus a profit transferred to the rate fund will relieve such fund—and consequently the appropriate rate—to the extent of the sum credited. On the other hand, if a loss is transferred, the rate fund will be correspondingly burdened.

(iii) General Conclusions.

(21) So far as Rate Funds are concerned, therefore, it will be seen that there is nothing analogous to them in commercial accounts. Such funds differ materially from commercial trading accounts. Whereas the main object of a commercial organisation is that of "profit," that of a municipality must be "service." No question of profit or loss can arise with rate funds, except as regards transfers from the trading undertakings, as previously mentioned.

(22) It is in the separate accounts kept by municipalities in respect of their trading undertakings that we find the greatest similarity to the accounts of commercial concerns. These accounts are practically alike as regards income and working expenses. There are, however, certain marked differences in other respects, the chief of which relate to :—

(*a*) Capital transactions.

(*b*) The treatment of depreciation.

(*c*) The annual loan charges.

The repayment of debt is a statutory obligation imposed upon local authorities but not upon public companies. Each trading undertaking Revenue Account has to bear the annual interest on the loan debt and the annual contribution towards debt redemption in respect of the undertaking. This important feature comes under fuller review in a later part of our investigations.

(23) With the foregoing broad view as our background, it is now my intention to invite you to look particularly at those phases of the accounts, or

matters appertaining thereto, wherein are exhibited the principal contrasts between commercial and municipal accounts.

PART II.—A FOCUSSED VIEW OF PRINCIPAL CONTRASTS.

(24) The first accounting transactions of a new scheme—commercial or municipal—deal with the raising of capital. Taking first things first then, let us look into:

(d) CAPITAL TRANSACTIONS.

(i) *Methods of Raising Capital.*

(a) *Companies.*

(25) The capital of companies may be divided into two classes, viz:—

(1) Share Capital—i.e. capital subscribed by the *members* of the company, e.g. Preference and Ordinary Shares, &c., and

(2) Loan Capital—being capital raised from persons who are not members but *creditors* of the company, e.g. Debentures, Loans and Overdrafts.

Statutory companies derive their borrowing powers from the Acts under which they are formed. The Act would state the amount of share capital authorised and, usually, would provide that the company may only exercise borrowing powers when the whole of the capital has been subscribed and at least half has been paid up, and then only to the extent of one-third of the authorised capital.

(26) Companies registered under the Companies Acts 1908-1917 may issue share capital not exceeding the amount authorised by the Memorandum of Association. The power to borrow otherwise is also derived from the Memorandum and Articles, but in the case of a *trading* company the power so to borrow may be implied. Any restrictions imposed by the Memorandum or Articles must be strictly adhered to.

(27) Companies may raise capital by the following methods:—

(1) Issue of shares of different classes, which may later, when fully paid, be converted into stock. (Statutory Companies may issue stock direct.)

(2) Issue of debentures (either Simple or Mortgage Debentures) or debenture stock.

(3) Mortgage Loans.

(4) Bank Overdraft.

(5) Reserve Funds—whether Revenue or Capital.

(b) *Local Authorities.*

(28) Before a local authority may raise any money for capital purposes, it must possess a "borrowing power." This borrowing power, or sanction to borrow, is obtainable in one of the following ways:—

(1) The sanction of a Government department, acting under the general law, e.g. Public Health Act, 1875.

(2) A Provisional Order of a Government department, which must later be embodied in a Confirmation Bill and presented to Parliament for approval.

(3) A Local Act of Parliament, authorising the borrowing of certain moneys.

(4) Under General Law in a few cases, e.g. loans on the credit of sewage lands under Public Health Act, 1875.

(29) Each type of borrowing power states the period within which the loan must be repaid.

The methods by which the loans are raised in pursuance of the duly authorised powers fall chiefly into the following categories:—

(1) Mortgage Loans.

(2) Stock Issues—with the consent of the Ministry of Health—under Public Health (Amendment) Act, 1890.

(3) Debentures, Debenture Stock, &c., under Local Loans Act, 1875.

(4) Bills of Exchange.

(5) Bank Overdraft.

(6) Utilisation of Sinking Funds.

(7) Housing Bonds.

(8) Loans from Public Works Loans Commissioners.

(ii) *Nature of Capital.*

(a) *Companies.*

(30) The share capital of a company is a *permanent* liability and in this respect is dissimilar to the capital raised by a local authority, who are under an obligation to repay the amounts borrowed within stipulated periods.

Whether dividends will be paid on the share capital of a company, depends on the availability of profits.

(b) *Local Authorities.*

(31) Municipal loans are repayable in accordance with the terms of the borrowing power, and are secured—in respect of both interest and principal—by a mortgage of the particular rates or revenues affected, or in some cases by a general charge over the whole of the rates and revenues.

The security thus afforded in respect of the loans of local authorities reflects itself in the much lower rate of interest at which such loans may be borrowed when compared with loans raised by commercial companies.

(iii) *Capital Expenditure.*

(a) *Companies.*

(32) It is entirely within the discretion of the directors of a company to charge what expenditure they think proper to capital account. Consequently, it frequently happens that what one company treats as capital expenditure, another company charges direct to revenue.

There is, of course, the restraining influence of the audit over the capital allocations, but such control is nothing like so rigid as that applying to local authorities.

There is some restriction imposed on those statutory companies which have to publish their accounts in a prescribed form. For instance, a gas company must publish its balance sheet on the Double Account System, and a detailed capital account is required.

(b) *Local Authorities.*

(33) The only expenditure which local authorities may defray out of capital is that authorised by the sanction to raise the loan. They have therefore little or no discretion vested in them to decide what may or may not be treated as capital expenditure. Control in this respect is exercised by:—

(1) The appropriate Government department which sanctions the loan.

(2) The Town Council.

(3) The Auditors.

(iv) Working Capital—Statutory Provisions.

(a) Companies.

(34) There is nothing to prevent a company from providing a working balance out of its capital funds, and this is the usual course adopted.

(b) Local Authorities.

(35) Until the passing of the Local Authorities (Financial Provisions) Act, 1921, there was no means under the General Law by which a local authority could borrow for the purpose of providing working capital, except in one isolated case, viz. the Education (Working Balances) Act, 1903. A few of the larger authorities had, however, obtained powers in this direction by Local Act.

Under the provisions of the Local Authorities (Financial Provisions) Act, 1921, local authorities may borrow temporarily for the purpose of meeting current expenses. The loan must be sanctioned by the Minister of Health and must be repaid out of the revenue of the year during which it is raised.

It is worthy of note that most local authorities in Scotland have power to borrow temporarily for the purpose of meeting *capital or revenue* expenditure, without any sanction being necessary.

(v) Working Capital—Methods of Providing.

(a) Companies.

(36) Companies may obtain their working capital from the following sources :—

(1) Share capital.
(2) Loans.
(3) Debentures.
(4) Bank Overdraft.
(5) Reserve Funds.

The practice of setting aside revenue for the purpose of providing working capital is not common in the case of companies, but is quite usual in the case of private traders and firms, as in these cases the profit and loss accounts of the proprietors are nothing more than sub-divisions of their capital accounts.

(b) Local Authorities.

(37) Local authorities may provide working capital in the following ways :—

(1) By a specific loan for the purpose—if sanctioned :—
 (*a*) By a Local Act ; or
 (*b*) Under the Local Authorities (Financial Provisions) Act, 1921.
(2) By a bank overdraft, the legality of which is doubtful.
(3) By reserving profits (i.e. from revenue without recourse to borrowing).

(vi) Capitalisation of Interest.

(a) Companies.

(38) Companies registered under the Companies (Consolidation) Act, 1908, may, under certain conditions and with the sanction of the Board of Trade, pay interest on share capital out of capital during the construction of works. The conditions are contained in Section 91 of the Act, which reads as follows :

"Where any shares of a company are issued for the purpose of raising money to defray the expenses of the construction of any works or buildings or the provision of any plant which cannot be made profitable for a lengthened period, the company may pay interest on so much of that share capital as is for the time being paid up for the period and subject to the conditions and restrictions in this section mentioned, and may charge the same to capital as part of the cost of construction of the work or building, or the provision of plant:

Provided that :—

(1) No such payment shall be made unless the same is authorised by the articles or by special resolution.
(2) No such payment, whether authorised by the articles or by special resolution, shall be made without the previous sanction of the Board of Trade.
(3) Before sanctioning any such payment the Board of Trade may, at the expense of the company, appoint a person to inquire and report to them as to the circumstances of the case, and may, before making the appointment, require the company to give security for the payment of the costs of the inquiry.
(4) The payment shall be made only for such period as may be determined by the Board of Trade; and such period shall in no case extend beyond the close of the half-year next after the half-year during which the works or buildings have been actually completed or the plant provided.
(5) The rate of interest shall in no case exceed four per cent. per annum or such lower rate as may for the time being be prescribed by Order in Council.
(6) The payment of the interest shall not operate as a reduction of the amount paid up on the shares in respect of which it is paid.
(7) The accounts of the company shall show the share capital on which, and the rate at which, interest has been paid out of capital during the period to which the accounts relate.
(8) Nothing in this section shall affect any company to which the Indian Railways Act, 1894, as amended by any subsequent enactment applies."

(b) Local Authorities.

(39) Local authorities may only charge interest to capital when they have the authority of a provision in a Local Act. Parliament is very reluctant to give this power and their attitude may be summed up in the following extract from the Report of the Select Committee on the Repayment of Loans of Local Authorities (1902) :—

"Some local authorities desire in the case of reproductive works not only to defer the payment of the first instalment in respect of capital, but also to pay interest during construction out of the money borrowed. This would relieve those whose representatives decide to borrow for such works from immediate liability to contribute anything in respect of the borrowing and should not in the opinion of the Committee be ever permitted.

"During the construction of works the district has in many cases the advantage of the expenditure within it of much of the money raised by the loan, and this may fairly be taken into consideration as some compensation for the fact that nothing is being earned by the works in the interval."

(40) In certain cases the abnormal cost of construction and the high rates of interest prevailing at the present time are factors which have made the capitalisation of interest essential during the constructional period when an undertaking is earning no revenue. A good local instance of these circumstances is afforded in the case of the Taf Fechan Water Supply Board, which has obtained power to charge Interest on Loans to capital during the period of construction.

(vii) Reduction of Capital.

(41) When a company has incurred heavy losses, it usually resolves to write down the value of the assets and make good the deficiency on the Profit and Loss Account by the expedient of reducing the nominal value of its shares. A company may also repay its shareholders any paid-up capital which is not required. In all cases the consent of the Court is necessary.

This is a feature peculiar to companies. Never to my knowledge has a local authority repudiated any loan or interest thereon.

(viii) Repayment of Loans.

(42) This phase of local authorities' accounts involves the vexed controversy of depreciation in its relation to loan redemption. I therefore propose to leave it for the moment so that we may consider it, in conjunction with the question of depreciation, which is dealt with later.

(*e*) BOOKKEEPING AND ACCOUNTS.

(i) Books prescribed by Statute.

(*a*) *Companies.*

(43) Companies incorporated under the Companies Acts are required to keep the following books :—

(1) A Minute Book for directors' and members' meetings (Section 71).

(2) A Register of Members, which must contain the particulars prescribed in the Act (Section 25).

(3) An Annual List and Summary. This book must contain (per Section 26), *inter alia*, the undermentioned particulars :—

(*a*) Particulars of changes in members during the year.

(*b*) Particulars of the shares held, transferred, and acquired by each member during the year.

(*c*) Names and addresses of directors.

(*d*) Particulars of mortgages and charges made by the company.

(*e*) The Balance Sheet of the company as audited by the auditors of the company. This statement need not include a statement of Profit and Loss. (*Note.*—Not required in the case of private companies.)

(4) A Register of Directors (Section 75).

(5) A Register of Mortgages, which contains particulars similar to the Registers of Mortgages of Local Authorities (Section 100).

The statutory books prescribed by the Companies Clauses Acts are :—

(*a*) Register of shareholders.

(*b*) Shareholder's Address Book.

(*c*) Register of Mortgages and Bonds.

(*d*) Register of Holders of Consolidated Stock.

(*e*) Minute Book.

(*f*) Register of Transfers.

(*g*) Register of Debenture Stock.

(*b*) *Local Authorities.*

(44) Local authorities under the Public Health Act, 1875, are required to keep :—

(*a*) A Register of Mortgages.

(*b*) A Register of Transfers of Mortgages.

There appear to be no similar provisions in the Municipal Corporations Act, 1882, but Section 233 of this Act refers to the inspection of Minute Books and Orders for the payment of money. The treasurer is also directed to make up his accounts half-yearly, but there is no indication of the form which these are to take.

(ii) Prescribed Methods of Accounting.

(*a*) *Companies.*

(45) The books of account which may be required and the special accounts to be prepared could not well be prescribed for commercial companies by a general Act of Parliament. Consequently there are no statutory enactments in regard thereto.

Provisions as to the accounts which a company must keep will be contained in its Articles of Association, but apart from such provisions, the directors, being both agents and trustees, are bound to keep accounts.

As regards statutory companies, while it is often provided that their accounts shall be made up in a prescribed form, there are no provisions as to the manner in which such accounts are to be kept. The bookkeeping is, however, influenced to a great extent by their published form.

(*b*) *Local Authorities.*

(46) The Ministry of Health have power under the District Auditors Act, 1879, as regards any local authority, whose accounts are subject to audit by a district auditor, to make regulations respecting :—

(1) The audit of the accounts ; and

(2) The form of keeping the accounts.

The Ministry are also *required* to prescribe forms of financial statements for each authority.

As regards provincial boroughs the general power of the Ministry of Health to prescribe forms of account applies only to their accounts under the Public Health Acts, Education Act, the Housing and Town Planning Act, 1919.

So far the only important regulations made which prescribe systems of accounting are :—

(1) General Order of Accounts of 1867, which prescribe the system of accounting to be used by Guardians.

(2) General Order of Accounts of 1880, which lays down rules as to the method of account-keeping to be adopted by the Local Boards of Health, which were the predecessors of the Urban District Councils.

(3) Housing Accounts Order, 1920, which makes provision for the bookkeeping system to be used in connection with the Assisted Housing Schemes.

(iii) Influences on Accounts.

(a) *Companies.*

(47) If the Articles of Association contain any regulations as to the books and accounts to be kept these must be observed. Table A, which must be adopted by companies not registering Articles of their own, contains the following :—

103. The directors shall cause true accounts to be kept :—
Of the sums of money received and expended by the company and the matter in respect of which such receipt and expenditure takes place ; and
Of the assets and liabilities of the company.

104. The books of account shall be kept at the registered office of the company, or at such other place or places as the directors think fit, and shall always be open to the inspection of the directors.

105. The directors shall from time to time deter mine whether and to what extent and at what times and places and under what conditions or regulations the accounts and books of the company or any of them shall be open to the inspection of members not being directors, and no member (not being a director) shall have any right of inspecting any account or book or document of the company except as conferred by statute or authorised by the directors or by the company in general meeting.

106. Once at least in every year the directors shall lay before the company in general meeting a profit and loss account for the period since the preceding account or (in the case of the first account) since the incorporation of the company, made up to a date not more than six months before such meeting.

107. A balance sheet shall be made out in every year and laid before the company in general meeting made up to a date not more than six months before such meeting. The balance sheet shall be accompanied by a report of the directors as to the state of the company's affairs, and the amount which they recommend to be paid by way of dividend, and the amount, if any, which they propose to carry to a reserve fund.

108. A copy of the balance sheet and report shall, seven days previously to the meeting, be sent to the persons entitled to receive notices of general meetings in the manner in which notices are to be given hereunder.

(48) The usual course followed by company directors is to obtain the advice of the auditor as to the books and the method of keeping them, the matter being one within the discretion of the directors, who are the real accounting parties.

Those companies for which statutory forms of accounts are prescribed (e.g. Statutory Companies and Life Assurance Companies) frame their accounting systems with a view to providing the information required in the prescribed forms.

(b) *Local Authorities.*

(49) The accounts of local authorities are influenced in the following manner :—

(1) *Government Returns.*

Local authorities are required to make numerous returns of their transactions to Government departments. Many of these returns form the basis upon which Government grants due to the authority are calculated. Hence, the accounts of a local authority are designed in such a way as will readily furnish the required information by the different Government returns. Examples of the returns made by local authorities are :—

(a) Epitome of Accounts.
(b) Education Account (annual statement).
(c) Police Grant Claim.
(d) Maternity and Child Welfare Claim.
(e) Agricultural Rates Act, 1923, Claim.
(f) Electricity Return to Electricity Commissioners.
(g) Housing (Assisted Scheme) Returns.
(h) Statements of Loan Debt, Sinking Funds, &c., under Local Acts.

(2) *Abstract of Accounts.*

The form of the annual Abstract of Accounts which a corporation is required to publish will, to a certain extent, reflect itself in the accounting system.

As we shall see later, local authorities having a free hand as to the structure of the " abstract," some prepare excellent publications which are models of conciseness and lucidity, while others issue formidable volumes often needlessly intricate and involved. If the local public call for a wealth of detail and it is sought to gratify the desire, the account-keeping must be adapted accordingly.

(iv) Accounting Periods.

(a) *Companies.*

(50) There is no prescribed accounting period for companies (the Companies (Consolidation) Act, 1908, containing no provision in this connection) so that, in the absence of contrary provisions in the company's Articles, the accounts may be made up as and when the directors think fit. A statement in the form of a balance sheet, duly audited, must, however, be included by public companies in the Annual List and Summary which must be prepared and filed once in each calendar year.

If the provisions of Table A are in force, the accounts must be laid before each annual meeting and must be made up to a date not more than six months previous to the date of the annual general meeting. The annual meeting must be held in each calendar year and must not be more than fifteen months after the previous annual meeting.

The accounts of statutory companies must, as a rule, be made up to the 31st day of December in each year, unless decided otherwise by the Board of Trade.

(b) *Local Authorities.*

(51) With a few exceptions (e.g. Metropolitan Guardians) the whole of the accounts of local authorities in England and Wales are made up yearly to 31st March in each year.

(To be continued.)

A COMPARISON OF COMMERCIAL ACCOUNTS WITH MUNICIPAL ACCOUNTS

By Norman E. Lamb F.S.A.A., A.I.M.T.A.

(Concluded from p. 326.)

The subject of local authority finance and accounts is an exceedingly wide one, requiring specialised study. The treatment of various items in municipal accounts is here contrasted with their treatment in commercial accounts.

(f) PUBLISHED ACCOUNTS.

(i) *Publication of Accounts.*

(a) *Companies.*

(52) Companies formed under the Companies Acts are not, apart from Table A or their own Articles as the case may be, under any obligation to publish accounts to their shareholders or to lay such accounts before the company in general meeting. It is, nevertheless, the invariable practice for the Articles of a company to require these things to be done.

There is, however, a statutory obligation to file a statement in the form of a balance sheet with the Annual List and Summary of Shareholders, Capital, &c., which must be in the following form :—

(1) Signed by the Company's Auditors.
(2) Contain a Summary of Share Capital.
(3) Contain a Summary of its assets and liabilities.
(4) Give such particulars as will disclose the nature of the assets and liabilities.
(5) Give such particulars as will show how the value of the fixed assets has been arrived at.
(6) Need *not* contain a statement of profit and loss.

This Annual Summary must be filed with the Registrar of Companies once in each calendar year, even if a general meeting is not held.

(53) The provisions contained in the Clauses Acts which apply to most public utility companies are probably not very well known and are worthy of note.

The Waterworks Clauses Act, 1847, provides that an annual Abstract of Accounts is to be prepared, and after audit is to be sent to the Clerk of the Peace for the county in which the waterworks are situated. The Clerk of the Peace is to keep this account open for public inspection at all reasonable hours on payment of one shilling for each inspection.

The Gas Works Clauses Act, 1847, contains a similar provision, but the terms of the Gas Works Clauses Act, 1871, are somewhat different. Under the 1871 Act, the undertakers must keep at their office copies of the annual statement made up in the prescribed form, and must sell the same to any applicant at a price not exceeding one shilling for each copy.

The provisions of the Electric Lighting Act, 1882, are similar to those contained in the last-mentioned Act.

A lecture delivered before the South Wales and West of England Students' Society of the Institute of Municipal Treasurers and Accountants.

(b) *Local Authorities.*

(54) The Municipal Corporations Act, 1882, requires all Town Councils to print and publish a full abstract of their accounts annually after audit.

Urban District Councils are required by the Public Health Act to publish an abstract of their audited accounts in a local newspaper. It is also the practice of many of the larger Urban District Councils to publish a *full* abstract of their accounts.

(ii) *Form of Published Accounts.*

(a) *Companies.*

(55) As previously stated, there is no statutory obligation on registered companies to print any accounts or balance sheets. If accounts are published it is entirely within the discretion of the directors to decide what form they shall take. Consequently it will be found that practice differs considerably as to the amount of information disclosed.

There being no statutory requirement as to the publication of Trading and Profit and Loss Account it is very unusual for any particulars at all to be found of the former account, and it is not uncommon to find no details of the latter account.

There is, however, some limit to the extent to which a published balance sheet can be condensed, because by Section 113 of the Companies (Consolidation) Act the auditor of the company is required to report "whether in his opinion the balance sheet referred to in the report is properly drawn up so as to exhibit a true and correct view of the state of the company's affairs, according to the best of his information and the explanations given to him and as shown by the books of the company." An auditor of any professional standing would not certify a balance sheet which by reason of its brevity was apt to be misleading.

(56) The balance sheet to be filed with the Annual List and Summary must give such information as will disclose the nature of the liabilities and assets, and it must be stated how the values of the assets have been arrived at. Hence, it is often more informative than the published balance sheet.

It is, of course, well known that the form of balance sheet published rarely coincides with that contained in the books of the company, since for business reasons a company cannot issue very detailed information without putting rival concerns in possession of valuable information.

(57) The balance sheets of ordinary commercial concerns are prepared on the Single Account system, but in the case of statutory companies the balance

sheets are compiled on Double Account lines. The Double Account system, modified to a certain extent, is the usual method adopted by local authorities, and herein lies the chief distinction between published municipal accounts and commercial accounts.

The Double Account system was first prescribed by the Regulation of Railways Act, 1868, and involves the division of the balance sheet into two sections, namely, the Capital Account and the Revenue Account (or as it is sometimes called, the General Balance Sheet). The primary purpose of the system is to show what capital has been raised and how it has been expended. It is thus particularly applicable to those concerns which sink large amounts of capital in works of a permanent nature, e.g. railways. The Double Account system involves the retention of the assets in the capital section of the balance sheet at their original cost, the repairs and renewals being met out of revenue. Hence, it is usual to set aside provision for depreciation and renewals so that charges therefor may be equalised as between one year and another.

The Double Account system is prescribed by statute for use in connection with the following public utility companies :—

(1) Gas Companies.
(2) Electric Lighting Companies.
(3) Railway Companies.

In practice it is used for the following undertakings also, viz. :—

(4) Water Companies.
(5) Tramway Companies.

(58) Forms of accounts are prescribed for statutory companies, which provide more information than it is usual to give in connection with ordinary commercial accounts. The following is a list of the accounts, &c., required by the Electric Lighting Act, 1882, and is indicative of the accounts required from other public utility companies :—

(1) Statement of Share Capital.
(2) Statement of Loan Capital.
(3) Detailed Capital Account.
(4) Revenue Account (detailed).
(5) Net Revenue Account (detailed).
(6) Reserve Fund Account.
(7) Depreciation Fund Account.
(8) General Balance Sheet.
(9) Statement of Electricity Generated, &c.

Statutory companies are invariably granted a monopoly for the purposes for which they are formed. It follows, therefore, that the need for withholding information from the public does not exist, but on the contrary the need for information may become a necessity.

Other concerns which are required to make up their accounts in a prescribed form are :—

(1) Building Societies.
(2) Friendly Societies.
(3) Industrial Societies.
(4) Savings Banks.
(5) Insurance Companies, &c.

(*b*) *Local Authorities.*

(59) Beyond the provision of the Municipal Corporations Act, 1882, that the Treasurer is to print an abstract of his annual accounts after audit, there is nothing in the Act which gives any guide as to the form which the printed accounts are to take.

As a general rule it is the practice for municipal balance sheets to be published on Double Account lines, and even where this does not obtain the distinction between capital and revenue is just as strictly observed.

Little or no uniformity is to be found in the published accounts of local authorities, either in their general arrangement, or in the quantity of detail given. An exception must, however, be made in the case of Trading Undertakings. Many of the published accounts of trading undertakings of local authorities are based upon the statutory returns and to this extent a certain measure of uniformity is achieved.

(60) Another factor which influences the form of the published accounts of a corporation are the Government Returns. The accounts of the services in respect of which these returns are made are usually framed with a view to obtaining the information required by the returns. An instance of this is seen in the Education Accounts. Since the Education Accounts (Annual Statements) Order, 1921, the published accounts of Education Income and Expenditure have tended to far greater uniformity than before.

The accounts of the Assisted Housing schemes are prescribed in the Housing Accounts Order, 1920, and the published accounts are invariably in accordance with this order.

(61) Another important factor to remember when comparing the form of the published accounts of municipalities and commercial concerns is that the need for secrecy does not apply to the affairs of a local authority. Consequently it will be found that municipal abstracts aim at giving very full and complete information to the ratepayers.

(*iii*) *Standardisation of Accounts.*

(62) Ignoring the question of expediency, it is probably true to say that the standardisation of the accounts of small competitive businesses is impossible owing to the very varied nature of the circumstances of each company.

With regard to the larger industrial concerns it might be possible through association to frame a uniform method of presenting their results. It is, however, extremely doubtful whether such accounts would ever be published in full.

The accounts of statutory companies have been standardised to a very great extent, but the conditions obtaining in this class are, as we have seen, quite different. The circumstances of each company are similar and this, coupled with the fact that there is an absence of competition, makes uniformity of published accounts possible.

(63) There would seem to be little reason why the accounts of local authorities should not be standardised to a far greater extent than exists at present. Already the Council of the Institute of Municipal Treasurers and Accountants have drafted suggested standardised forms of accounts for use by local authorities, and the adoption of these forms would to a great extent achieve the desired result.

(iv) Inspection of Accounts.

(a) Companies.

(64) The following are the provisions as to the inspection of books, &c., contained in the Companies Act, 1908 :—

(1) *Register of Members.*

The Register of Members is open to the inspection of the members gratis, and of other persons upon payment. Members and other persons are entitled to copies upon payment.

(2) *Register of Mortgages.*

Members and Creditors of a company are entitled to inspect the Register of Mortgages free of charge. Other persons may do so upon payment.

The Register of Mortgages kept by the Registrar of Joint Stock Companies is also open to inspection by any person upon payment.

(3) *Auditor's Report.*

The shareholders are entitled to inspect the auditor's report and are entitled to copies on payment. (This right does not apply to Preference Shareholders in Private Companies.)

(4) *Balance Sheet.*

Shareholders may require copies on payment. Whether any of the other books of account are open to inspection will depend upon the terms of the company's articles. Table A provides that the directors may determine to what extent these books shall be open to inspection.

The relative enactments applying to statutory companies differ from the foregoing, e.g. the Companies Clauses Act, 1845, provides that the books of the Company, together with the balance sheet, shall be open to inspection by shareholders during a specified period, or, if no period be prescribed, for fourteen days prior to each ordinary meeting and for one month thereafter at the principal office of the Company.

(b) Local Authorities.

(1) *Municipal Corporations.*

(65) Under Section 233 of the Municipal Corporations Act, 1882, a burgess may inspect the minutes (but not *draft* minutes) of the Council and orders for the payment of money, and may take extracts therefrom. Ratepayers may also inspect the Treasurer's Abstract of Accounts and may obtain copies upon payment of a reasonable price.

(2) *Urban District Councils, &c.*

(66) The Public Health Act, 1875, requires a copy of the accounts together with all other vouchers and documents referred to in such accounts to be deposited in the office of the authority for seven clear days prior to audit during which time they are open to public, inspection.

Notice of such deposit must be given in the local newspapers. The General Accounts Order, 1880, provides that the accounts are also to be open to inspection during audit. Provision is contained in the Act of 1875 for the public inspection of the Register of Mortgages without any charge being made.

(g) LOAN REPAYMENTS AND DEPRECIATION.

(i) Statutory Provisions.

(a) Companies.

(67) There are no statutory provisions *requiring* companies either to provide for the repayment of their capital or to make provision for depreciation. As to whether a company should provide for depreciation prior to payment of dividends depends on the nature of the assets and is subject to the decisions in a number of important legal cases.

(b) Local Authorities.

(68) All the capital of local authorities is raised subject to a statutory obligation to repay the loans within periods specified in the borrowing powers. Reference has already been made to this aspect of the capital of local authorities.

(ii) Is Loan Redemption Equivalent to Depreciation ?

(69) It was frequently contended in pre-war days by critics of municipal trading that local authorities ought to provide not only for the redemption of loans but also for the depreciation of assets as part of the working expenses of the undertakings. The basis of this contention was that sinking fund provision was a statutory provision to repay the loans of local authorities, and that there was no connection between this provision and the provision which should be made in respect of the depreciation of assets. The latter, it was said, was a charge against revenue, necessary to ascertain the true profit, while the sinking fund provision was an appropriation of profits, which was peculiar to municipal methods of finance.

(70) It may be safely assumed that, in the majority of cases, the periods prescribed for the repayment of the loans of local authorities do not exceed the estimated lives of the subjects of the loans. If, therefore, we compare the results obtained by setting aside a sinking fund to redeem a loan of £1,000 in ten years, and the effect of creating a depreciation fund in respect of an asset costing £1,000, the expected life of which is ten years, we find the position to be as follows :

(1) *Sinking Fund Provision.*

A fund of £1,000 is on hand to repay the loan outstanding in respect of the obsolete asset.

(2) *Depreciation Fund.*

A fund of £1,000 is available for the purpose of acquiring a new asset to replace the obsolete one.

In both cases wastage of capital to the extent of £1,000 has been charged to revenue. The only difference which exists between the two methods is the way in which the asset is financed. In the case of the local authority the asset is financed with borrowed money which must be repaid, and in the case of the company the asset has been financed out of permanent capital.

It is clear, therefore, that if the period for the redemption of the loan does not exceed the life of the subject of the loan, the sinking fund provision may justly be regarded as equivalent to depreciation.

(71) With regard to the periods allowed for the repayment of loans, the following extract from the report of the "Select Committee on the Repayment

of Loans by Local Authorities" shows the policy of the Government Departments very clearly :—

"Par 4 . . . it is obvious that the discretion left to the Government departments which fix the actual period for the repayment of each loan is a very wide one. Although some other departments have duties in respect of certain loans, by far the greater part of the work of controlling the borrowings of local authorities falls, in England and Wales, upon the Local Government Board.

The board has a staff of engineering and medical inspectors amongst whose duties is that of holding local enquiries, when directed to do so, into the circumstances under which it is sought to spread the expense of any work over a number of years by raising a loan for such work. Such an inquiry is in most cases obligatory under statute, if the new loan required will cause the indebtedness of the district to exceed one year's assessable value. At these enquiries the question of the probable durability and continuing utility of the work is gone into by the Inspector, and it is his duty and that of the chief engineering inspector to advise the board as to the period for which the loan should be sanctioned.

Par. 5.—The Local Government Board and the Board of Trade hold that the maximum periods mentioned in general Acts refer to the most durable items of the work for which borrowing powers are sought. It is, therefore, their practice to examine each item of the estimates for such work, and to assign to each group of items an appropriate term for the repayment of the loan required for it. In order to avoid a multiplication of separate loans, the course usually adopted is to grant an equated period for the whole loan, which is arrived at by considering the sums required for each group of items, and the term assigned to that group. The result of this severance and equation is to reduce the periods allowed below the maximum periods mentioned in the Acts, but equation is not practised where the sums included in each group are large, and the local authority express a preference for separate loans.

Par. 6.—The Local Government Board, being charged with the general supervision of local finance, takes into its consideration in fixing the period for redemption not only the probable useful life of each part of an undertaking for which a loan is desired, but also the probable future condition of localities with regard to debt, in order that the ratepayers of the future may not be unduly burdened, and so rendered less able to discharge efficiently the duties that are likely to come upon them.

Par. 7.—In addition to their borrowing powers under general statutes, most of the more important municipal authorities have acquired the right to borrow for various purposes under local Acts, and have so borrowed large sums to be repaid within periods fixed by or under those Acts. The committee have been unable to discover any general principles by which the periods allowed by local Acts are fixed.

Par. 11.—Standing Order 172 of the House of Commons provides that 'in the case of all Bills whereby any municipal corporation, district council, joint board or joint committee, or other local authority, in England or Wales, are authorised to borrow money for any matter within the jurisdiction of the Board of Trade or the Local Government Board, estimates showing the proposed application of the money for permanent works shall (except so far as the exercise of the borrowing power is made subject to the sanction of the respective boards) be recited in the Bill as introduced into Parliament, and proved before the Select Committee to which the Bill is referred.'

There is no doubt that one of the objects of this Standing Order is to provide the committee dealing with a Bill with materials upon which to found a judgment upon the question of the appropriate period to allow for the loans sought by the Bill. The committee are of opinion that this Standing Order is not satisfactorily complied with in many cases. The estimates as set out in many Bills are too general, and the proof of them is usually merely formal.

If a Bill is unopposed the preamble is taken as proved, and as the estimates and other particulars are recited in the preamble, no further compliance with the Standing Order is called for.

Par. 12.—In addition to the statutory limitations upon the periods for repayment already mentioned, there is a further provision, acting as a check in the case of some loans to which the committee desire to call attention.

If the borrowing authority obtains the loan from the Public Works Loan Board, the period for repayment is determined by the Commissioners who are empowered by statute to make regulations governing all the conditions of these loans.

Section 11 of the Public Works Loans Act, 1875, directs the Commissioners in making such regulations to have regard to the durability of the work and to the expediency of the cost being paid by the generation of persons who will immediately benefit.

The general policy of the Commissioners is 'to hold out inducements to accept short periods for repayment instead of throwing as much of the burden as possible upon posterity.' One of these inducements is the acceptance of a lower rate of interest for a short term than for a longer one."

(*Note.*—The Local Government Board has since been superseded by the Ministry of Health.)

(72) If time permitted, much could be added as to the various contentions respecting the depreciation provision for municipal undertakings. The period allowed for the repayment of the loans forms the crux of the question. If they do not esceed the lives of the assets, then it cannot be said that the present generation is escaping its just share of the debt burden.

If a loan period is in excess of the life of the asset, then sound finance demands that some additional provision to the loan redemption charge should be made.

(73) It is, perhaps, well to mention the three methods of treatment which stood out prominently during the controversy. They were as follows :—

(1) Regarding the Sinking Fund (or Debt Redemption) charge as sufficient to cover depreciation. This is the method which was then, and still is, most generally adopted.

(2) Charging adequate depreciation and sinking fund in addition (e.g. Glasgow).

(3) Charging revenue with proper depreciation and merging the sinking fund charge therein (e.g. Bolton).

(74) No doubt it will be within the recollection of many present that this subject was very fully explored by the first President of our I.M.T.A. Students' Society (also the ex-President of the Incorporated Accountants' District Society), Mr. Allcock—the esteemed City Treasurer of Cardiff—in connection with the Tramway and Electric Lighting Accounts of his authority. The result was, I believe, that Mr. Allcock established what might be called a compromise, i.e. the provision of a voluntary depreciation fund to the extent to which the sinking fund does not meet the full depreciation requirements.

(iii) Methods of Providing for Loan Redemption.

(75) The following are the methods used by local authorities for the repayment of loans :—

(1) The Instalment system, under which an equal annual or half-yearly instalment of principal is repaid to lender throughout the period of the loan, with interest on the balance outstanding from time to time.

(2) The annuity system, under which an equal yearly or half-yearly payment of interest and principal combined, which is sufficient to repay the loan with interest, in the prescribed period, is made to the lender.

(3) The Sinking Fund method, under which such an annual contribution is set aside each year as will be sufficient to repay the loan at the end of the prescribed period. Sinking funds may be either :—

(*a*) Accumulative ; or

(*b*) Non-accumulative.

(iv) Methods of Providing Depreciation.

(76) The following are the chief methods of providing for the depreciation of assets which are adopted by commercial concerns :—

(*a*) Fixed instalment of original cost of assets—which approximates to the instalment method of repaying aloan.

(*b*) Percentage of reducing balance.

(*c*) Annuity method—which is approximately the same as the annuity method of repaying a loan.

(*d*) Sinking Fund method—which corresponds with the repayment of a loan by sinking fund.

(*e*) Charging renewal of assets to revenue as and when they arise. This is obviously impossible except in very large concerns where the renewals tend to equalise themselves.

(*f*) Revaluation method—under which the assets are revalued annually and the depreciation thus ascertained charged to Revenue.

(v) Treatment in Accounts.

(a) Companies.

(77) The usual way of treating depreciation in the books of ordinary commercial companies is to write down the values of the assets. At the same time additional provision may be made towards the estimated cost of renewals so as to avoid any heavy charge falling upon the income of any one particular year.

(78) Statutory companies which adopt the Double Account system carry their provision for depreciation (if any) to a fund which may be called " Depreciation Fund " or " Renewals Fund." In this case the assets are retained in the balance sheet at cost, renewals of plant being charged to the depreciation or renewals fund.

(b) Local Authorities.

(79) The accounts of local authorities are usually kept on the Double Account system and the assets are therefore retained in the balance sheet at cost. The provision made for the redemption of loans is credited to the " surplus " account.

Some local authorities, however, make provision, over and above the statutory sinking fund provision, for equalising the cost of renewals and repairs. In doing this the authority must act within the powers given by its Local Act relating to the particular trading undertaking.

(*h*) SUSPENSION OF SINKING FUNDS.

(a) Companies.

(80) As previously pointed out, companies are under no obligation to set aside sinking funds, so that, strictly speaking, the suspension of the sinking fund provision has no application to them. A company need not make any provision for depreciation (similar to a local authority's sinking fund) during the period of the construction of works. In fact, the provision which a company makes for depreciation, being entirely within the discretion of the directors, it is not uncommon to find that the amount set aside varies directly with the amount of profits available.

(b) Local Authorities.

(81) Local authorities may, if authorised by Local Act, suspend the statutory sinking fund contributions in respect of new works during the period of construction.

The Local Authorities (Financial Provisions) Act, 1921, also contains a provision to this effect in respect of *revenue producing* undertakings. Local Authorities must, however, obtain the consent of the Ministry of Health.

The Electricity Supply Act, 1922, gives power to Local Authorities to suspend the annual provision for repayment of debt in respect of money borrowed after the passing of the Act, for the purposes of the Electricity Supply Acts, to be suspended while the expenditure out of such moneys remains unremunerative, for such period not exceeding five years as the Electricity Commissioners may determine.

(82) Ordinarily the first instalment of sinking fund should be contributed within one year of :—

(*a*) the date of borrowing ; or

(*b*) the date of the expenditure upon the works whichever is the sooner.

(*i*) APPLICATION OF SINKING FUNDS TO NEW CAPITAL PURPOSES.

(83) Local Authorities have power, under the Stock Regulations, 1901, to apply their Stock Redemption Funds to new capital purposes. Similar powers in regard to Mortgage Sinking Funds may be obtained by Local Act. The effect of this power is that local authorities, instead of investing their sinking funds or applying them in the extinction of debt, may utilise them for financing new capital schemes.

Commercial companies which set aside depreciation without investing the provision so made, do exactly the same thing, i.e. the amount set aside is retained in the business and is available as working capital or for financing new schemes.

(j) The Study of Municipal Accounts.

(84) The subject of Local Authority Finance and Accounts is an exceedingly wide one, involving the municipal student in years of training and specialised study. Not only is a sound grasp of accountancy essential, but also a good knowledge of the law of local government and of certain branches of commercial law as affecting financial matters. It is further necessary to be acquainted with the principles of finance and the working of the money market, including the raising of loans and the investment of funds. A knowledge of the law and practice of banking and of economics and statistics is also desirable.

(85) This being so, how is it possible for one outside, or just at the threshold of, municipal circles to understand municipal accounts ?

Restricting my answer to students possessing a knowledge of accountancy in its general application, I would advise them to obtain and closely study one or two municipal abstracts which, as we have seen, are issued annually by each Borough Treasurer and are obtainable by ratepayers at a reasonable price. Herein he will find ample material for study, and if he will keep in mind the principal contrasts—compared with commercial accounts—as we have reviewed them, it should not be difficult to follow, at least, the *structure* of municipal accounts.

(86) The " Treasurer's Abstract of Accounts " is not nearly so formidable as appearances would suggest. One admits that upon first acquaintance it is apt to appear a rather mysterious compilation, fully intelligible only to those who have been responsible for its preparation. But this impression is quickly dispelled once the features peculiar to municipal accounts are properly grasped. Hence the earnest student may be assured that—by study on the lines indicated—it is within his power to understand and interpret the published accounts of local authorities, although he does not possess the knowledge necessary either to operate the finances or to prepare the accounts.

(87) For the benefit of those who may be disposed to accept this advice let us take a glance at a typical " abstract " and, in a rapid survey, note the ground which is unfamiliar.

(88) From the contents page we observe that the volume runs into anything from two hundred to three hundred pages and comprises very broadly :—

(1) A Revenue Account, a Capital Account, and a Balance Sheet for
 (a) Each Rate Fund.
 (Probably some rate fund services will be shown separately.)
 (b) Each Trading Undertaking.
(2) An aggregate Balance Sheet.
(3) Accounts in connection with loans raised (e.g. Stock issues) showing, *inter alia*, how the loans have been appropriated by the various rate funds and trading undertakings.
(4) A large amount of statistical information.

(89) Dismissing items (3) and (4), and scanning the *Revenue Accounts*, we see that these are quite easily followed, for they present the closest resemblance to commercial accounts. Let us pass on then, simply observing that from the Revenue Accounts of the Rate Funds an excellent idea is obtained of the extent of the municipality's activities and the cost of the public services.

(90) Turning to the *Capital Accounts* we note they are on double account lines, with the capital moneys (i.e. the loans) raised on the credit side and the expenditure thereout for each purpose on the debit side. Looking at the balances, we try to trace them into the balance sheets but find that (unlike what we are accustomed to in the case of Statutory Companies, e.g. Railway Companies) the balances are not shown in the balance sheets, but the Capital Account, in a summarised and slightly modified form, is repeated instead.

(91) Pursuing our scrutiny of the *Balance Sheets*, it is seen that the bulk of the capital expenditure is shown at cost, as under the Double Account system.

Reserve Funds, Renewals Funds, &c., on the liabilities side are, it is noted, counterbalanced on the assets side by investments and balances uninvested, duly earmarked.

The commercial practice is different, for when Reserve Funds, &c., are not invested it is usual for the cash represented by the funds to be merged in the general Cash balance.

(92) Our attention is now particularly arrested by certain items quite different from those in commercial accounts. These are in respect of :—

(1) Loans outstanding.
(2) Capital Expenditure.
(3) The surplus of assets over liabilities, comprising : Loans redeemed and the funds accumulated for loan redemption (e.g. Sinking Funds), &c. &c.

(93) We have already observed that instead of the balance of the Capital Account being carried to the balance sheet as under the strict Double Account system, the Capital Account is itself repeated in modified form.

In comparing the Capital Account with the summarised version contained in the Balance Sheet, we note the following differences :—

(a) In the Balance Sheet, " Loans outstanding " takes the place of the item " Loans raised " which is found in the Capital Account.
(b) The surplus of assets over liabilities, which does not appear in the Capital Account.

It will immediately be apparent that the two items which appear in the Balance Sheet, viz. :—

(a) " Loans outstanding " and by " Loans Redeemed " will agree in amount with the item " Loans raised " which is shown in the Capital Account.

(94) But what exactly is the Surplus Account ? This is, perhaps, the most confusing item in the Municipal Balance Sheet, but when considered in relation to items (1) and (2) above, it may soon be understood. It arises in this way. When the Revenue Account is debited with the annual debt redemption charges (i.e. annual repayments or annual instalments of sinking fund) the accounts credited are those with some such designations as " Sinking

Funds for Redemption of Loans," "Loans Redeemed," "Loans paid off out of Revenue," "Loan debt extinguished," &c. These accounts are often brought together under one main heading styled "Surplus of Assets over Liabilities."

(95) But whether shown separately or under one main heading, they indicate the extent to which the corresponding assets (formerly paid for out of borrowed moneys) are now paid for by the repayment of loans out of revenue, or the extent to which sums have been provided by revenue in readiness for repayment.

(96) Sometimes assets are deleted from the balance sheet when loans raised for their acquisition have been paid off, e.g. assets of a non-realisable value, as Street Improvements. When this is done the Surplus Account is correspondingly reduced.

(97) There are several other kinds of "surpluses" to be seen in the "Surplus Account" (e.g. Capital expenditure defrayed from Revenue Account), but such may be quite readily followed.

(98) The number of separate balance sheets in the volume prompts the inquiry as to how one is to ascertain the complete financial position of the authority. Remembering the reference to an "*Aggregate Balance Sheet*" on the contents page, we turn this up and find that it gives the solution we require, for herein is incorporated—in summarised columnar form—all the separate balance sheets, so giving in one statement the key to the municipality's financial position.

Here we must close the book, leaving the student to resume his research when time does not call a halt.

(*k*) CONCLUSION.

(99) In bringing these observations to a close one is conscious of many other features peculiar to municipal finance which—reflected in the accounts—call for careful analysis when making a *critical* comparison of commercial with municipal accounts. To instance one or two at random, there are :—

(1) The artificial division of the separate rate funds for income-tax purposes.

(2) The differences n the treatment of income-tax on trading undertakings by reason of the "set-off" provisions.

(3) The possible inadequacy of the establishment charges borne by trading undertakings, if insufficient sums have been debited for the services rendered by other Departments of the Corporation (e.g. the Town Clerk's Department, the Treasurer's Department, the Collecting Department, &c.), since the cost of these departments is defrayed by the rate funds.

(100) Such matters, however, are outside the scope of a general survey such as we have made, and are, I observe, covered by other lectures in the joint scheme.

With so comprehensive a subject, it has not been easy to compress even the principal contrasts into reasonable compass.

If, therefore, you have been wearied by the numerous recitals I have felt it necessary to inflict upon you, dare I express the hope that you may receive some subsequent compensation if at a future time you should, perchance, find them serve a useful reference purpose.

ELECTRICITY ACCOUNTS AND COSTING

By H. Andrews, A.I.M.T.A.,

(Chief Audit Clerk, Newport, Mon.)

The subject of electricity supply has been much to the fore in recent years and it is a factor of increasing importance in the industrial and social life of the country. This lecture gives a brief survey of the legislative history of electricity supply in this country and deals with the accounting and costing systems most generally in use.

(A) Introduction

WHEN I was invited by your Executive Committee some time ago to read a paper before this Society on the subject of Electricity Supply, it was intended that I should deal particularly with the position under the Electricity (Supply) Act of 1926. It was subsequently suggested that I might widen the scope to cover the question of Electricity Accounts and Costing. At first it did not appear to me to be necessary to do so, having regard to the fact that a valuable lecture on this subject had already been given before the London Students Society by W. A. Henderson, Esq., F.S.A.A., the Accountant to the Willesden Urban District Council, in December 1921. However, on the grounds that your Society had not had an opportunity of discussing Mr. Henderson's lecture, and that new students were not in possession of copies, I concurred in the Committee's wishes. In attempting to deal with the subject generally, considerations of space have necessitated curtailment of that part dealing with the Act of 1926, and it has only been possible to treat the Costing section in a somewhat scanty manner.

(1) *Definitions.*—A number of technical terms are met with in electrical literature, and it is desirable that the assistant engaged on Electricity Accounts should understand the meaning of some of those most commonly used. With this end in view the following elementary definitions are given :—

(*a*) *The ampere* denotes the rate of flow of a current of electricity, or, as it is more popularly termed, the *strength* of the electric current.

(*b*) *The volt* denotes the pressure of the electric current.

(*c*) *The watt* represents electrical power and is the unit by which the rate of doing work electrically is measured. The power developed in an electrical circuit is determined by the product of the rate of flow of current and the difference of electrical pressure, and the relation between these units is such that amperes × volts = watts. One thousand watts = 1 kilowatt.

(*d*) *The Board of Trade Unit* is the commercial unit for work done or measurement of electrical energy supplied. It is equal to 1,000 watt-hours and is synonymous with the term *kilowatt-hour.*

A lecture delivered before the South Wales and West of England Students' Society of the Institute of Municipal Treasurers and Accountants.

(*e*) *The Load Factor* is the ratio of actual output in units generated to the possible output if the maximum load were constantly in use throughout the period of supply.

Thus—

$$\frac{\text{No. of units generated} \times 100}{\text{Maximum load in K.W.} \times \text{hrs. of supply}} = \text{X per cent.}$$

(*f*) *The Diversity Factor* is the ratio of actual load on feeders to the sum of the maximum demands of all consumers.

Thus—

$$\frac{\text{Maximum load on feeders in K.W.}}{\text{Sum of consumers M.D. in K.W.}} = \text{X per cent.}$$

(B) Electricity Supply prior to the Act of 1926

(2) The subject of electricity supply has been much to the fore in recent years and there can be no doubt that it is a factor of increasing importance in the industrial and social life of the country. It is recognised that an adequate supply of cheap electrical power is virtually as essential as labour and materials in so far as it affects economical production.

For the better appreciation of the vital post-war changes, culminating in the Electricity (Supply) Act of 1926, it is proposed to give a brief survey of the legislative history of electricity supply in this country from the year 1882, when the principal Act was passed.

(3) The principal Act of 1882 empowered the Board of Trade to grant concessions by means of Provisional Orders and Licenses to—

(*a*) any local authority as defined (i.e. in London, the City of London, the London County Council, and the Metropolitan Borough Councils; and in the Provinces the Councils of Boroughs and Urban and Rural District Councils ;

(*b*) any company ; or

(*c*) any person

for the supply of electricity *within any area*, although in practice applications for Provisional Orders were generally limited to the area of one local authority. The state of uncertainty as to whether optional powers of compulsory purchase would be exercised or not by the local authority acted as a deterrent to private enterprise. An impetus was given to electrical development by the Act of 1888 extending the periods within which the option might be exercised, but the business was divided between a large number of undertakers, each operating over small areas generally settled by geographical and political considerations.

(4) The Electric Lighting (Clauses) Act, 1899, contains a code of provisions to be incorporated in every Provisional Order (now Special Order) made after the passing of the Act, save so far as they are expressly varied or excepted by the Order. The sections which more particularly concern the financial side of electricity supply are dealt with later.

(5) As a result of the report of a Joint Select Committee of both Houses in 1898, facilities more consistent with the development of the application of electric power to industry were granted in several private Acts, under which "power companies" with rights of supply in bulk and for power purposes over wide areas were granted powers in perpetuity. Owing to restrictive clauses, however, the powers were not effectual in providing a comprehensive system of supply.

(6) The Electric Lighting Act, 1909, gave somewhat wider facilities to electrical undertakers, although it has been stated that an insufficiently large and comprehensive outlook characterised its provisions.

(7) During the period of the war, the difficulties of meeting the increased demand for electrical energy consequent upon the rapid expansion of munition factories emphasised the defects of the existing conditions of generation and distribution. When, in 1916, the Board of Trade urged the linking-up of supply systems, it was forcibly found that, owing to the absence of any attempt to standardise pressures and frequencies, the necessary co-operation between neighbouring undertakings was in many cases either technically difficult or financially impracticable.

Various committees appointed by the Government during the war reported on different aspects of the situation, arising out of the unsuitability of the legislation and conditions relating to the supply of electricity. The Electric Power Supply Committee's recommendations were, in the main, incorporated in a Bill, but the provisions as they emerged in the Electricity (Supply) Act of 1919 were somewhat emasculated. The Electricity (Supply) Act of 1922 to some extent remedied the deficiencies of the Act of 1919, but the absence of compulsory powers largely discounted their effectiveness. Taken together, these Acts provided, *inter alia* :—

(*a*) For the appointment of Electricity Commissioners for promoting, regulating and supervising the supply of electricity.

(*b*) For the transfer to the Ministry of Transport (with power to delegate to the Electricity Commissioners) of all the powers and duties of the Board of Trade in connection with the Electricity (Supply) Acts.

(*c*) For the determination of electricity districts by the Commissioners, the promotion of schemes for the improvement of the existing organisation for the supply of electricity, and the establishment of joint electricity authorities, or other bodies, to secure the provision of cheap and abundant supplies of electricity.

"Weir" Committee

(8) Successive Governments have since reviewed the matter of the further reorganisation of the supply of electricity in the light of the experience gained by the Electricity Commissioners and early in 1925, the Weir Committee was appointed.

The technical considerations governing the generation and main transmission of cheap electrical energy in an industrial area were briefly summed up by the Committee as follows :—

(*a*) Generation in large stations, favourably situated as regards fuel, water and load with units of plant of comparatively large capacity ;

(*b*) The minimum legitimate amount of stand-by plant ; and

(*c*) the highest obtainable load factor, to secure which stations should be inter-connected with one another.

(9) Sir John Snell, the chairman of the Electricity Commissioners was requested by the Committee to prepare and submit a definite and practical technical scheme calculated to secure efficient generation of H.T. energy in 1940, or, alternatively, at the date when the per capita demand had reached 500 units, ignoring all questions of administration, ownership and organisation of generation and supply.

The salient points of Sir John's scheme were as follows :—

(*a*) All energy to be generated in certain selected main and secondary power stations, of which 43 were existing and 15 new.

(*b*) Four hundred and thirty-two generating stations to eventually be closed down.

(*c*) A "gridiron" of high tension transmission mains to be erected inter-connecting all the selected stations and coupling up with existing regional transmission systems and other existing stations.

The essential financial and other data submitted with the scheme were given in comparison with the existing position in a table which is reproduced below.

	Present Position	Position in 1940 or when Consumption has reached 500 Units per Head
Units sold per head of Population	110	500
Maximum Load	1,844,000 K.W.	8,135,000 K.W.
K.W. Installed	3,096,000 K.W.	10,000,000 K.W.
Spare Plant	68 per cent.	25 per cent.
Units Sold	4,016,000,000	21,385,000,000
Load Factor	24.9 per cent.	30 per cent.
Total Capital— Generation	£73,680,000	£127,000,000
"Gridiron" Transmission	—	£29,000,000
Distribution	£88,070,000	£243,500,000
Total Revenue	£24,256,000	£88,100,000
Average price per Unit ..	2.047d.	1d. or under
No. of Main Stations ..	} 438 altogether	28
No. of Secondary Stations		30

The saving in the country's electricity bill by the adoption of the scheme, when the consumption had reached 500 units per head, was estimated as follows :

If the price remained at	2.047d.	..	£93,296,000 per annum
" fell to	1.75d.	..	£66,832,000 "
" "	1.5d.	..	£44,556,000 "

(C) Electricity (Supply) Act, 1926

(10) The Act gives effect very largely to the recommendations of Lord Weir's Committee, and brings

into operation a national policy with regard to the generation and high tension transmission of electricity without nationalisation of the industry. It may be said to be founded on three principles :—

(*a*) Minimum of State control ;
(*b*) Minimum of State interference ; and
(*c*) Maximum freedom to existing undertakers.

The Act provides for the setting up of a Central Electricity Board for Great Britain, who are charged with the duty of supplying electricity to authorised undertakers and others, subject to certain restrictions.

(11) *Schemes.*—The principal objective of the Act is the supersession of small scale generation at a multiplicity of power stations, as hitherto, and the eventual concentration of generation in a limited number of inter-connected stations to be operated by the owners on account of the Board and termed " selected " stations.

The Electricity Commissioners are charged with the duty of preparing schemes for transmission to the Board dealing, ***inter alia***, with the following matters :

(*a*) determining what generating stations (whether existing or new) are to be selected stations ;
(*b*) providing for the inter-connection, by means of main transmission lines (popularly referred to as the " grid "), of selected stations with one another and with the systems of authorised undertakers ;
(*c*) providing for such standardisation of frequency as may be essential to the carrying out of the proposals for such inter-connection ;
(*d*) enabling or requiring temporary arrangements pending and the full scheme coming into effect ;
(*e*) containing such supplemental, incidental and consequential provisions as may appear necessary or expedient. (Section 4 (1).)

The Board are required to publish every scheme received and, after considering the scheme and any representations from interested parties, they may " adopt " the scheme with or without modification and either generally or as respects any part of the specified area. As soon as the scheme has been adopted and published, it becomes the duty of the Board to carry out and give effect to the scheme. (Section 4 (2) (3).) Provision is made for any authorised undertakers who consider the obligations imposed by the scheme would be prejudicial to them to require the Board to refer the matter to arbitration.

With regard to the expenses of standardisation of frequency, the Electricity Commissioners are to repay to the Board the consequential loan charges annually, treating such sums as part of their expenses and apportioning the same among joint electricity authorities and authorised undertakers on the basis of revenue received from the sale of electricity other than that sold in bulk. (Section 9 (3).)

(12) *Obligations and Rights of Owners of Selected Stations.*—As from a date fixed by the Board, the owners of selected stations are under the obligation (*a*) to operate the station so as to generate such quantity of electricity, at such rates of output and at such times as the Board may direct, and to conduct such operations with due regard to economy and efficiency ; and (*b*) to sell to the Board all electricity generated at the station. (Section 7 (1).) Unless otherwise agreed, the price to be paid ***by the Board*** to the owners for electricity generated at a selected station is to be the cost of production ascertained on the basis of the following charges in respect of the year of account, ***so far as they are attributable to the station***:

(i) Expenditure upon fuel, oil, water, stores consumed, salaries, wages, &c., repairs and maintenance, and renewals not chargeable to Capital Account ;
(ii) Rents, rates and taxes (other than taxes on profits), and insurance ;
(iii) The proper proportion of management and general establishment charges ;
(iv) Any other expenses on Revenue Account ;
(v) Interest (exclusive of interest payable out of capital) on money properly expended for capital purposes (whether defrayed out of capital or revenue), and interest on working capital. The rate of interest is to be in the case of—
    (*a*) a joint electricity authority or a local authority—the average rate payable on money raised for the purpose ; and
    (*b*) a company—the average rate of dividends and interest paid during the preceding year, with a minimum of 5 and a maximum of 6½ per cent. per annum.
(vi) An allowance for depreciation of the following amounts :—
    (*a*) In the case of a joint electricity authority or local authority—an amount equal to the sinking fund charges plus a further allowance in respect of capital expenditure defrayed otherwise than by loan moneys.
    (*b*) In the case of a company—an amount determined in accordance with a scale fixed by special order, subject to a special proviso in the case of London companies. (Section 7 (3) and Second Schedule.)

Any question arising between the Board and the owner as to the cost of production will be decided by an auditor appointed by the Minister of Transport. (Section 7 (6).)

(13) The owners of a selected station are entitled to be supplied by the Board from that station with such quantity of electricity (not exceeding the amount generated at the station) as they require or their undertaking. (Sections 7 (2) and 10.) Unless otherwise agreed, the price to be charged by the Board is the cost of production determined as above, adjusted according to the load factor and power factor of the supply given to the owners, plus a proper proportion of the Board's expenses other than those incurred in the purchase and generation of electricity ; or according to the tariff fixed under the Act, whichever is the lower. (Section 7 (4), Section 11.)

Special provision is made for the adjustment of the charge in cases where the owners of a selected station prove to the Commissioners that the cost of taking a supply from the Board exceeds the cost which they would have incurred, had the Act not been passed, in themselves generating a like quantity of electricity. (Section 13.)

(14) *Obligation of Board to Supply Authorised Undertakers.*—As soon as the Board in respect of any area notify that they are in a position to supply electricity, they are obliged to supply, directly or

indirectly, to any authorised undertaker, on demand, such amount of electricity as they require for their undertakings. (Section 10 (1).) The price to be charged by the Board (subject to the special provisions relating to the owners of selected stations) is to be in accordance with a tariff fixed by the Board from time to time on a self-supporting basis over an approved period, with such margin as the Commissioners may allow. (Section 11 (1).) The tariff is to be framed so as to include as part of the charge a fixed kilowatt charges component and a running charges component, or otherwise if determined by an order of the Commissioners. (Section 11 (2).) If the Board think fit, the tariff may be different for different areas. (Section 11 (3).)

(15) *Undertakers owning Non-selected Stations.*—When any authorised undertakers owning a non-selected station demand a supply, the Board may, in certain circumstances, make it a condition that the undertakers shall take the whole quantity of electricity required for the undertaking from the Board. (Section 10 (3).) Provision is made for the closing down of non-selected generating stations in cases where the Board undertake to supply the quantity of electricity required for a period of, at least, seven years on terms less than the then prevailing cost of generating at the station excluding capital charges on the station. In case of dispute, the question as to whether the cost of production at the non-selected station substantially exceeded the cost of purchasing a like quantity of electricity from the Board, the undertakers may require the question to be submitted to arbitration. (Section 14 (2).)

(16) *Provisions for the Protection of the Consumer.*—The underlying object of the Act of 1926 is to secure a cheap and abundant supply of electricity. Elaborate provisions have been enacted with a view to producing the requisite supply of electricity at reduced costs. The whole scheme would be futile, however, unless adequate provisions were included to ensure that some portion at least of the benefits were passed on to the consumers.

Previously, Section 7 of the Schedule to the Electric Lighting (Clauses) Act, 1899, required local authority undertakers to carry the net surplus on revenue account and the annual proceeds of the reserve fund, when amounting to the prescribed limit, to the credit of the local rate, or at their option to the improvement of the district, or in reduction of loans raised for electricity purposes; *provided* that if the surplus in any year exceeded 5 per cent. upon the aggregate capital expenditure, such rateable reduction in the charge for energy should be made as would reduce the surplus to that maximum rate of profit.

(17) The fifth schedule to the Act of 1926 makes an important amendment to the provision above outlined, and applies like amendments to corresponding provisions contained in special Acts or Orders which do not incorporate the Electricity (Clauses) Act. The new provisions are as follows :—

"The undertakers shall apply the net surplus remaining in any year and the annual proceeds of the reserve fund, when amounting to the prescribed limit—

(*a*) in reduction of the charges for the supply of energy ; or

(*b*) in reduction of the capital moneys borrowed for electricity purposes ; or

(*c*) with the consent of the Electricity Commissioners, in payment of expenses chargeable to capital ; or

(*d*) in aid of the local rate :

Provided that—

(i) the amount which may be applied in aid of the local rate in any year shall not exceed one and a half per cent. of the outstanding debt of the undertaking ; and

(ii) after the 31st March 1930, no sum shall be paid in aid of the local rate unless the reserve fund amounts to more than one-twentieth of the aggregate capital expenditure on the undertaking."

Strenuous efforts were made in some quarters to resist any amendment of the provisions of the Clauses Act with respect to limitation of transfers in aid of rates, but having regard to the avowed object of the new legislation, it can hardly be denied that a reasonable settlement of a highly contentious principle connected with municipal trading has been achieved. It is, perhaps, difficult to appreciate why "outstanding debt" was preferred to "aggregate capital expenditure" as the basis of the percentage of rate aid. Authorities who defray expenditure of a capital nature out of revenue will be penalised by the basis adopted, as will be those who apply their sinking funds in reduction of debt.

(18) As distinct from the new restrictions applicable to the profits of power companies and company undertakers, the limitation of the amount of transfers in aid of rates is not conditional on receiving a supply of electricity from the Board.

The Electricity Commissioners have laid it down that the restrictions on rate aid cannot be suspended to enable a local authority to recoup advances made from rates in the past. Power companies are subject to a sliding scale of dividends and prices with power to recoup any deficiency in previous dividends as compared with the standard rates. By Section 31 of the Act of 1926, the Minister of Transport may revise the "maximum" or "standard" prices having regard to any change in the cost of electricity attributable to the Act and may repeal or limit the power to recoup deficiencies in previous dividends.

(19) *Schemes under the Act of* 1926.—To date, two schemes have been formulated under the Act, one for Central Scotland and the second for South-East England. The Scottish scheme has been formally "adopted" by the Central Electricity Board and comprises an area of some 4,980 square miles, covering large industrial, shipbuilding and coalfield areas. Ten existing generating stations are to be utilised under the scheme and two new capital stations are to be provided. The transmission system comprising two ring mains will be established at a cost of some two and a quarter million pounds.

The South-East England scheme, embracing London and the Home Counties, covers an area of about 8,828 square miles. Thirteen stations are scheduled as "selected" stations under the scheme and fifteen are to be utilised temporarily. It is proposed to instal additional plant in the selected stations, to erect three new capital stations and to construct a transmission system which is estimated to cost nine millions. The scheme has not yet been adopted by the Central Electricity Board, but it is hoped to commence work on the transmission system by the coming autumn.

It is understood that other schemes are in course of preparation by the Electricity Commissioners and financial officers will have an important duty to perform in examining the financial details of any proposal affecting their areas. A study of the lecture entitled "Local Generation *versus* Bulk Supply," given in December 1926 by Percy Craven, Esq., F.S.A.A., the Borough Treasurer of Hornsey, will prove very helpful in this connection.

(D) ACCOUNTS

(20) *Statutory Provisions and Prescribed Forms.*—There are no statutory provisions regulating the actual *accounts* to be kept by local authorities in respect of electricity undertakings, but standardised forms of *abstracts* of accounts and statistical returns have been prescribed by the Board of Trade and their successors, the Electricity Commissioners, under the authority of the following enactments, and the accounting system should obviously be designed with a view to the completion of the forms in question.

(*a*) *Electric Lighting Act*, 1882 (*Section* 9), as amended—

"The undertakers shall, on or before the 30*th day of June* in every year, fill up an annual statement of accounts of the undertaking made up to the 31*st day of March* then next preceding; and such statement shall be in such form and shall contain such particulars and shall be published in such manner as may from time to time be prescribed in that behalf of the Electricity Commissioners.

"The undertakers shall keep copies of such annual statement at their office, and sell the same to any applicant at a price not exceeding one shilling a copy.

"In case the undertakers make default in complying with the provisions of this section, they shall be liable to a penalty not exceeding forty shillings for each day during which such default continues."

(*b*) *Electricity* (*Supply*) *Act*, 1919 (*Section* 27)—

"It shall be the duty of joint electricity authorities and authorised undertakers to furnish to the Electricity Commissioners at such times and in such form and manner as the Commissioners may direct such accounts, statistics, and returns as they may require for the purposes of their powers and duties under this Act."

The form of abstract prescribed under (*a*) comprises the following sections :—

(i) Statement as to loans authorised for the purpose of the undertaking, indicating—
  (*a*) Amounts sanctioned ;
  (*b*) Amounts borrowed at various rates of interest ;
  (*c*) Amounts repaid ;
  (*d*) Amounts sanctioned but not borrowed.
(ii) Capital Account, showing "expenditure and receipts"—
  (*a*) Up to the 31st March ;
  (*b*) During the year ; and
  (*c*) Total.
(iii) Revenue Account.
(iv) Net Revenue Account.
(v) Sinking Fund Account.
(vi) Reserve Fund Account ; and
(vii) General Balance Sheet, incorporating the closing totals of the Capital Account (ii) before detailing the other liabilities and assets.

(21) Local authority undertakers appear to model their published abstracts substantially upon the lines of the prescribed form and/or that submitted by the Institute and incorporated in the Departmental Committee's Report published in 1907.

The statistical return to be rendered to the Commissioners under Section 27 of the Act of 1919 is divided into three sections, viz. (A) Administration, (B) Financial, and (C) Engineering.

The accounts are subject to audit, in the case of boroughs by the auditors for the borough and by district auditors in the case of other local authority undertakers.

(22) Section 48 of the Act of 1926 authorises any local authority undertaker to sell (but not to manufacture) electric fittings and appliances to their *consumers or intending consumers*; also to instal, repair, and maintain the fittings at such charges and upon such terms as may be agreed. The power is subject to the following restrictions :—

(*a*) The sale price to be not less than the recognised retail (or trade, as the case may be) prices.
(*b*) The prices to be so adjusted as to meet the whole of the expenditure in any year, including loan charges.
(*c*) The published accounts of the local authority to show separately their income and expenditure (including loan charges) in the operation of the section.

The view has been expressed by an acknowledged legal authority that the section enables local authority undertakers to establish showrooms. Showrooms are maintained primarily, of course, as a means of publicity, demonstration, and propaganda, all with the object of stimulating the demand for electrical energy.

It will be a matter of some difficulty to arrive at proper apportionments of showroom and management expenses attributable to the sale of fittings, and it may be necessary to guard against a tendency to have regard to what the account will bear rather than the value of services rendered.

The Electricity Commissioners propose to issue a standard form of Fittings Account, and a draft form is at present under consideration by the Incorporated Municipal Electrical Association and the Institute.

(23) *Accounting Systems.*—It is not proposed to outline a complete system of accounting, seeing that local circumstances must always be considered and the bookkeeping methods in each case will naturally reflect the views of the responsible accounting officer. Expenditure possesses no special features from an accounting point of view and does not call for detailed treatment. In the remarks which follow it has been the endeavour to touch on some of the more important subsidiary records relating to income.

(24) *Income.*—The principal sources of income to an electricity undertaking are set out below :—

(1) Sale of electrical energy—
  (i) Private consumers for lighting, power and heating, under ordinary tariff rates or subject to special agreements in the case of large power consumers ;

(ii) Public lighting; and
(iii) Traction (tramways).

(2) Meter rents;

(3) Hire of apparatus; and

(4) Sale of fittings (direct and on hire-purchase terms) and rechargeable work.

(25) *Sale of Energy.*—Before a supply is given it is customary for the department's regulations to require the prospective consumer to submit an application in a prescribed form, giving particulars of the lamps and other apparatus for which a supply is required, indicating the maximum demand.

The applicant states also whether he desires a prepayment or quarterly meter and whether or not he is the owner of the premises to which a supply is required. On receipt of the application, the department responsible decides whether some security in the form of a deposit or guarantee should be demanded.

On receipt of a " test notice " from the wiring contractor, works orders are issued to lay the necessary service, connect up to the mains, test the installation and fix the meter. The works orders may, with advantage, be consecutively numbered and in carbon duplicate, one copy being forwarded to the accountant's department after certification as to completion of the service and fixing of the meter. From the completed form, a meter readers' card is made out and an account opened in the consumers' rental, in the case of quarterly consumers: If a prepayment meter be fixed, a record will be made in the prepayment meter books.

It is usual to maintain a register of applications for the purpose of " following up " the works orders until the actual connections are made and for statistical purposes.

(26) *Prepayment Meters.*—The following is a brief outline of a system which has given satisfaction.

(i) *Prepayment Meter Book*—

A loose-leaf form, showing at the head the consumer's address and name and particulars as to the make and number of the meter with provision for changes. Columns are provided for—date, meter index, units consumed, coin register and advance, coins unused, receipt No., initials of collector, and remarks (meters faulty, &c.).

(ii) *Receipt* (*or Record*)—

This form is in carbon duplicate and is framed as a *record* instead of a receipt. The consumer's name, address, and No. are inserted on the left-hand side of the form, and columns provided for coins unused, units consumed, cash in box, rebate, and net amount received. The self-summing principle has been adopted with six receipts to a page.

(iii) *Prepayment Meter Summary*—

This is a bound book provided with headings similar to (ii) from which daily totals are transferred. The amounts collected should be compared with number of units priced at current rates and the amount " over " or " short " in the case of each collector shown. Further columns indicate the number of meters cleared by each man and the average for all.

(iv) *Register of Meters cleared*—

The object of this book is to safeguard against the failure of the collectors to clear meters regularly, as well as the accidental or deliberate loss of a meter card with the consequent risk of leakage of revenue. Consumers are entered in street order and columns provided for each month repeated for several years.

(27) *Quarterly Meters.*—The meter readers' records are generally of the loose-leaf or card type, enabling them to be maintained in street order. It is an advantage to provide them in distinctive colours for lighting, heating and power. Many authorities nowadays supply the consumer with a record card which is attached to the meter. This arrangement enables the meter readings to be omitted from the account for energy supplied, besides providing a secondary record in the event of the official meter reader's record being lost.

There would appear to be no particular advantage in the meter readers being on the staff of the Treasurer unless the same men read the gas and water meters as well.

Some authorities maintain an office record of meter readings, supplemented by the amount of the charge for energy, which is used as the basis of the invoice. The form may be justified in the light of local circumstances, but it is possible in some cases to insert the charge direct on to the invoice without using any intermediate record.

(28) *Consumers' Rental.*—Whilst some authorities keep individual ledger accounts with consumers on the card index or loose-leaf principle, the rental method appears to be the more generally adopted. It has the advantage of facilitating the ascertainment of the quarterly totals of units supplied and charges due for energy, and sectional agreement with the subsidiary journals or registers, e.g. hire, hire-purchase and sales. Balancing as a whole is speeded up and, if necessary, each page may be proved separately.

Insets enabling the consumer's name and address to stand for four quarters are generally favoured and typical headings are given below.

Consumer's No.
,, Name and address.

Units consumed (under lighting, heating and power).

Amount due—
Arrears brought forward.
Energy (under lighting, heating, power and balance of minimum charge).
Meter Rent.
Hire, hire-purchase and maintenance.
Sales and chargeable work.
Total.

Credits—
Reference or Receipt No
Cash.
Bad debts and allowances.

Arrears carried forward.

Where the number of different rates is not prohibitive, it is possible to obtain an arithmetical check on the total charge for energy, based on the number of units supplied at the various rates. A convenient method is to provide a few columns for the rates generally prevailing for lighting, heating and power, with a further column in each case for units sold at " other rates " to be specified. Page totals of the rental are transferred to a summary which contains sufficient columns to segregate the units sold for different purposes at every separate rate.

For income-tax purposes it is an advantage to bring all accounts for the various corporation undertakings and departments together, instead of allowing them to appear in the ordinary " street " order in the rental. The " duplicate posting " system is especially useful in connection with the posting of receipts.

(29) Public utility undertakings in the United States have for some years applied mechanical methods to their consumers' accounts, and a few local authorities and companies in this country have recently installed machines suitable for this class of work. The continuous growth in the number of electricity consumers and the increasing difficulty of coping with the work under existing conditions suggest that serious consideration must be given to mechanical methods which are claimed to do the work quicker, cheaper and more accurately.

Two machines which are being successfully used for the preparation of consumers' accounts are the Burroughs' Public Utility Machine and the Elliott-Fisher. Each machine simultaneously prepares the invoice and enters the debits in the consumers' rental, or, if preferred, in individual accounts, at the same time compiling an abstract of invoices rendered. In each case the style of invoice has to allow the items making up the total debit to be set out horizontally, and as the records on the other forms are produced by carbon paper, their rulings must correspond. The machines automatically add across (producing the total debit) and perpendicularly, carrying cumulative totals which can be recorded at the foot of the abstract. The Elliott-Fisher Machine has an alphabetical keyboard as well as the accounting features, but this is of no material advantage for the class of work under review.

(30) The claims made for most labour-saving machines varyin inverse ratio to the modesty of their salesmen, but it is safe to say that either of the machines mentioned will do the billing work much more quickly than it can be done by hand. At a reasonable estimate they would complete about 500 accounts per day, besides writing the individual ledger accounts and abstract. If speed is to be attained, all the data to be incorporated in the invoice must be available to the operator in a clear and convenient form. Thus the meter reading cards showing the number of units consumed will be supplemented with cash columns for the insertion of the amount of the charge for energy supplied. Particulars of standing charges, e.g. meter rent and hire of apparatus, may be set out at the head of the consumers' Ledger Account.

(31) Mr. Wetherall has just decided to instal an Elliott-Fisher machine at Swansea, primarily to deal with electricity consumers' accounts, and he has been good enough to furnish me with specimens of the forms he proposes to use, which are reproduced at the end of this paper.

It will be observed that Mr. Wetherall does not propose to use an electricity *rental*, which possesses serious disadvantages when considered in connection with machine methods. In its place he provides individual ledger accounts for consumers and an abstract of invoices rendered. This latter record is produced in duplicate (a copy being supplied to the electrical engineer) simultaneously with the invoice and ledger record.

The consumers' ledger accounts are on the card system and ruled to last three years, using both sides of the card. A novel feature of this form is the arrangement of the columns for recording the credits in the lower half of the debit columns, thereby keeping the form within a reasonable compass. The machine could, of course, post the credits to the ledger accounts, but Mr. Wetherall contemplates using it to better advantage in other directions.

(32) *Hire Purchase.*—Electricity undertakings are urged to adopt the hire-purchase system as a means of selling apparatus and installations, the initial cost of which might prove embarrassing to the purchasers.

Normally, the hire-purchase instalments consist of (*a*) interest, (*b*) proportion of principal, and (*c*) maintenance charge (if any), but in the case of electricity supply undertakings regard is sometimes had to the revenue-bearing nature of the apparatus when in use, with the result that (*a*) and (*c*) may not be charged in full. For convenience, a flat percentage addition on the cash sale price is sometimes adopted to arrive at the " hire-purchase " price, whether the quarterly repayments extend over one year or three years. This arrangement is not altogether equitable for the percentage addition should vary with the period for repayment.

Having regard to the relatively small individual amounts involved and the probability that orthodox principles may not be followed, there is some justification for adopting short-cut accounting methods. The plan adopted at Newport is to record the hire-purchase agreements in a register which is provided with thefollowing columns :—

No. and date of agreement.
Name and address of hire-purchaser.
Description of apparatus, &c., supplied.
Date supplied.
Cost.
Cash sale price.
Hire-purchase price.
Period for repayment.
Amount due each quarter for four years.

Each year's transactions are shown in separate groups and the amount due each quarter throughout the term is extended. The sale is regarded as extending over the period for repayment, each financial year receiving a flat proportion of the " profit " on the transaction.

(33) *Rentals of Apparatus on Hire.*—Before any apparatus is supplied to consumers on hire it is customary for an agreement providing for the terms, &c., to be entered into. It is an advantage for these agreements to be consecutively numbered by the printer, thereby ensuring that every agreement is accounted for. The relevant particulars extracted from the completed agreements are entered in a register and the actual date of issue of the apparatus with details thereof extracted from the delivery notes or requisitions. It is an advantage to reserve a special delivery book or requisition book for hired apparatus, ensuring that the whole of the transac-

tions are properly recorded and the hiring charge duly made.

(34) *Sales of Fittings.*—Sales of fittings will generally be effected at the showroom and may be divided into two classes, cash and credit transactions. A special receipt book should be reserved for cash sales, whilst where credit is allowed a sales "docket" or delivery note would be made out. If the sales dockets be produced in carbon triplicate, one copy could be issued at the time as a delivery note, the second could constitute the invoice to be rendered with the quarterly account, whilst the third would be the office copy.

(35) *Re-chargeable Work.*—It is most important that there should be adequate control over work done for consumers at their expense. No work of this nature should be carried out except on the authority of a works order issued by a responsible assistant at the head office, and care is necessary to ensure that all items are properly charged to consumers.

A system which has been designed on these lines provides for the rechargeable Works Order Book to contain three different forms as a set, viz.

(1) Official works order;
(2) Invoice; and
(3) Office copy of works order and invoice combined.

By means of carbon paper, when the works order is written, the name and address of the consumer and particulars of work to be done appear on (2) and (3). Form (1) is issued to the works department, and Form (2) placed aside until details of the charge have been ascertained. The back of Form (3) acts as a Cost Ledger and is ruled to accommodate details of labour, materials, direct expenses, and oncost chargeable to the job authorised by the works order opposite.

The arrangement ensures that an invoice is rendered for every chargeable order issued, obviates the necessity of a separate Cost Ledger, and automatically displays the cost records for every invoice which incidentally bears the same number as the job.

A register is provided to summarise the prime cost records (for reconciliation with the Control Account) and the amount of the invoices for agreement in total with the column in the consumers' rental. Further columns are intended to secure the prompt execution of orders.

(36) *Deposits.*—Section 71 of the Clauses Act provides that where any deposit is accepted by the undertakers as security for the payment of their charges they shall pay interest thereon at the rate of 4 per cent. per annum on every sum of ten shillings for every period of six months during which it remains in their hands.

A register should be maintained to record the receipt and appropriation or return of deposits, and the following form has been found convenient:—

Consecutive Number.
Consumer's Name and Address.
Deposit.
Date received.
Receipt Number.
Amount.
Date of return or appropriation.
Repeat columns for ten years.
Interest.
Amount returned or appropriated.

The practice with respect to the treatment of interest varies. Some authorities credit the consumers' rental with interest annually at the 31st March, others allow credit when the interest due aggregates to a given sum, say £1, whilst another practice is to pay the interest only when the deposit is returned. Whichever method is adopted, interest should be calculated annually and charged accordingly in the Net Revenue Account, income-tax being deducted when payment is being made to the consumer.

(37) *Basis of Tariffs for Electrical Energy.*—To the uninitiated the whole question of electricity tariffs appears unnecessarily complex, and their incidence not altogether equitable. Why, for example, should a lighting consumer be charged, say, at fivepence per unit while a power consumer pays on an average, say, less than one penny per unit? or, how can it be profitable to the undertaking to supply electrical energy to a large power consumer at a price which works out at less than the *average* cost of production plus loan charges? The explanation is that, in fixing tariffs, one must have regard to the probable actual cost of production of a *particular* consumer's or class of supply rather than to the average cost per unit sold.

Differential charges are necessitated primarily by the fact that electricity cannot be stored in large quantities and even in any quantity without loss. Consequently, the necessary plant in the generating station has to be kept at work in order to supply the largest quantity of current which the consumers *may* at any one time require. Meanwhile, certain expenses, e.g. loan charges, maintenance costs and management expenses, are proceeding at a uniform rate hour by hour throughout the year. It follows, then, in fixing a tariff, that the rate at which energy is taken by a consumer (or his "load factor") is of prime importance.

(38) To estimate the actual cost of a supply to a particular consumer, it is necessary to differentiate between "standing charges" and "running costs" on the undertaking and to take into account any charges specifically attachable to the particular consumer. No definite basis of apportionment can be laid down, local circumstances must always be taken into account. The following table is merely indicative.

(*a*) *Standing Charges*—
(i) Loan Charges in respect of
Service to consumers' premises.
Generating station.
Sub-stations.
Feeder cables.
Distributing mains.
(ii) Salaries and wages of generating sub-station staff.
(iii) Maintenance of mains and services.
(iv) General establishment charges.
(v) Management expenses.

(*b*) *Running Charges*—
(i) Fuel.
(ii) Oil, waste, water and general stores.
(iii) Repairs and maintenance.

Standing charges are not affected by the output of electrical energy, and the several items are allocated (broadly speaking) to a particular supply on the basis of the relation of the individual maximum demand to the total maximum demand on the station, or sub-station, &c., as the case may be. Running charges may, in many cases, be allocated at a flat rate over the number of units sold, although the fuel item needs careful consideration by the electrical engineer, especially in the case of large consumers.

(39) *Methods of Charge.*—Under Section 31 of the schedule to the Electric Lighting (Clauses) Act, 1899, undertakers may charge for energy supplied by them to any ordinary consumer (*otherwise than by agreement*)—

(1) By the actual amount of energy so supplied ; or
(2) By the electrical quantity contained in the supply ; or
(3) By such other method as may for the time being be approved by the Minister of Transport.

According to the Report of the Advisory Committee on Domestic Supplies of Electricity and Methods of Charge (appointed by the Electricity Commissioners), dated July 1926, no " other method " under subsection (3) has been approved by the Minister of Transport, and the only *statutory* methods of charge in operation at the present time other than the flat rate method are those scheduled to a few special Acts and Orders relating to particular areas of supply. Many undertakers, however, exercise their right to *offer* multipart tariffs consisting of a periodical fixed charge and a low charge per unit. As such tariffs are adopted by agreement with the consumer, the consumers have the option of being charged by the ordinary flat rate method, but as a matter of fact the multipart tariff is generally made sufficiently attractive to secure general acceptance.

(40) The following are a few of the methods of arriving at the periodical fixed charge selected from the tariffs adopted by a number of undertakers at the option of and by agreement with consumers.

(*a*) Rateable Value Method—
This is the method generally favoured by local authority undertakers, although it is open to the objections that the rateable value bears no relation to the rate of use of energy required and anomalies arise in districts where house values vary.

(*b*) " Weighted " Rateable Value Method—
In this method the rateable value is used as a rough basis and weighted by the electricity department to compensate for irregularities in the property which are not reflected in the electrical demand.

(*c*) Fixed charge based on number of lampholders or lighting points, or on aggregate watts capacity for lighting installed on the premises—
These are simple methods, but their success depends upon the honesty of the consumer and efficient and continuous inspection of premises by the department.

(*d*) Maximum Demand Method—
This is the most fundamentally correct method, but it leaves the consumer doubtful as to the amount he will have to pay, and may penalise him for some occasional abnormal demand which in fact does not embarrass the supply undertaking. Moreover it requires a maximum demand indicator as well as the ordinary integrating meter and this is not favoured for domestic supplies.

(41) Section 42 of the Electricity (Supply) Act 1926, enacts that undertakers may be authorised by special order or by approval under Section 31 of the schedule to the Electric Lighting (Clauses) Act, 1899, to charge any ordinary consumer by a two-part tariff consisting of a periodical fixed or service charge (which may include a charge for hire or hire-purchase of any meter, lines, fittings, &c., provided by the undertakers) together with a charge for energy supplied. The special order or approval, where expedient, may provide for an option to consumers to be charged by an authorised alternative method.

(42) *Special Agreements.*—In the case of large power consumers, the negotiation of terms calls for the fullest exercise of technical ability and business acumen on the part of the Committee's advisers. The particular circumstances applicable to the proposed supply must be considered and the terms ultimately settled and incorporated in an agreement, which may provide for a fixed sum per annum (or alternatively a fixed charge per K.W. of maximum demand) with a charge for the quantity of energy actually supplied, based upon working costs per unit, subject to adjustment according to fluctuations in the cost per ton of coal over or under a basic price.

(43) *Reserve Fund.*—Local authority undertakers are empowered, by Section 7 of the Electricity (Clauses) Act, 1899, to provide a reserve fund by setting aside such amounts as they think reasonable and investing the same and the resulting income thereof in trustee investments, other than their own securities. The maximum reserve fund permitted is an amount equivalent to one-tenth of the aggregate capital expenditure on the undertaking, and it is noteworthy that *after the 31st March* 1930 no contributions may be made in aid of rates unless the reserve fund stands at more than one-twentieth of the capital expenditure.

The fund may be applied " to answer any deficiency at any time happening in the income . . . . or to meet any extraordinary claim or demand . . . . arising against the undertaking." A few local authorities have obtained wider powers with respect to reserve funds by means of local legislation, in some cases extending the maximum of the reserve fund to one-fifth of the aggregate capital expenditure and the application of the fund to include expenditure of a capital nature. Power has also been obtained to invest the reserve funds in the local authorities' own securities.

The question of the investment of reserve funds has, of recent years, produced some weighty advocates in favour of departing from the long-established principle that such funds should be invested *outside* the business. Is there not, indeed, much to be said in favour of retaining reserve funds *inside* the business in the case of electricity undertakings, where a considerable amount of working capital is required ?

(44) *Working Capital.*—A number of local authority undertakers have obtained power under private Acts to borrow for the purpose of working capital; but in the opinion of Sir Harry Haward, one of the Electricity Commissioners, general legislation did not appear to be necessary in view of the provisions of Section 3 of the Local Authorities (Financial Provisions) Act, 1921.

In the case of well-established undertakings, where it is possible to carry forward an adequate balance on revenue account, no difficulty arises, as this balance is available for the purpose of working capital. Lest there be any doubt on the point, Sir Harry Haward's own words at the 1926 Conference of the Institute are quoted—

> " In this connection some misapprehension appears to exist as to the requirements of Section 7 of the Electric Lighting (Clauses) Act, 1899, which deals with the application of the 'net surplus' but is silent as to any carry forward. This section relates in terms to the application of moneys *received* (cash) and no auditor would require a local authority to apply the 'net surplus' in the manner specified therein unless there were cash available for the purpose; otherwise the result would be an overdraft on which there is no power to pay interest."

Presumably the foregoing remarks apply, notwithstanding the amendment of Section 7 of the Clauses Act by the fifth schedule of the Act of 1926.

(45) *Capital Expenditure.*—Power to borrow for the purpose of financing capital expenditure may be obtained by local Act or by the issue of a loan sanction by the Electricity Commissioners. Amounts borrowed for electricity purposes are not reckoned as part of the total debt of a local authority for the purpose of any limitation on borrowing powers. The maximum periods allowed by the Electricity Commissioners for different purposes are as follows :—

	Years
Land	60
Buildings	30
Main Transmission Lines (underground)	40
Mains and Services	25
Plant	20
Meters, Motors, &c.	10
Domestic Apparatus	7

Prior to the passing of the Act of 1926, it was the general practice of the Commissioners to grant the maximum loan periods in all cases, but recently the tendency to curtail the periods for repayment has been marked. One is aware of cases where 20 years has been granted in respect of buildings and 15 years for plant. In connection with one scheme where the local authority only obtained these *reduced* terms after making strong representations to the Commissioners, they were urged to make special provision out of reserve or otherwise with a view to completing the provision for repayment within 10 years.

The policy of the Commissioners is no doubt dictated by their conception of what is financially prudent having regard to the probable future developments of electrical supply, but the effect will undoubtedly tend to benefit the later consumers at the expense of those of the intervening period. Is there not something to be said in favour of the view that it is inequitable to curtail the loan periods ? Capital works will only be abandoned in the event of the developments being such as to enable the owners of the station to purchase in bulk the energy required for their undertaking at a price cheaper than the cost of production locally (excluding capital charges) with the result that they will be better able to bear the loan charges on the superseded plant.

(46) The argument applies perhaps with greater force to the question of dealing with superseded plant generally in the event of a station being closed down on receiving a supply from the Central Electricity Board. It is suggested that there should be no acceleration of the redemption of the outstanding loan debt on works superseded in such cases. Whether the particular loan expenditure has been wholly redeemed or not, the assets superseded should be written off from the appropriate head of capital expenditure. In the event of there being any unredeemed loan debt in respect of the items in question, a corresponding amount should be shown as a deferred charge on the assets side of the balance sheet under some such heading as " Other Displaced and Superseded Works." This item will diminish year by year until the provision for redemption is complete.

(47) Power is given to the Commissioners under Section 2 of the Electricity (Supply) Act, 1922, to authorise the suspension of the annual provision for the repayment of loans by a local authority undertaker while the capital expenditure remains unremunerative. The maximum period of suspension is five years, and as it is the Commissioners' practice not to extend the ultimate date for repayment, a bigger burden is thrown on the remaining period.

(48) It should be observed that Section 7 of the Electricity (Clauses) Act, 1899, as amended by the fifth schedule to the Act of 1926, authorises the application of the net surplus on revenue account and the *annual proceeds* of the reserve fund *when amounting to the prescribed limit* in payment—*inter alia*—of expenses chargeable to capital, subject to the consent of the Electricity Commissioners. In this connection the following circular letter to local authority undertakers from the Electricity Commissioners under date 19th December 1927 is important.

Electricity (Supply) Act, 1926

APPLICATION OF SURPLUS REVENUE

" SIR,—The Electricity Commissioners have had under consideration the provisions of Section 43 of and the fifth schedule to the abovementioned Act, in regard to the application of net surplus revenue in payment of expenses chargeable to capital, and desire to state their general views on the matter for the information and guidance of local authority undertakers who are subject to the provisions of Section 7 of the Schedule to the Electric Lighting (Clauses) Act, 1899, or provisions corresponding to those of that section which are amended by the said fifth schedule.

(1) The Commissioners are broadly in accord with the policy adopted by certain local authorities of meeting out of annual revenue the cost of regularly occurring expenditure on distribution works such as house services, meters, wiring of premises, and provision of apparatus on hire or hire-purchase, and other comparatively short-lived works.

(2) With the view of obviating as far as possible the necessity for individual applications for the consent of the Commissioners to the application of net surplus to such purposes, the Commissioners hereby give their formal consent for the purposes of paragraph (*c*) of the fifth schedule to the Act of 1926, to the application by local

authorities who are subject to the before-mentioned provisions of net surplus in payment of expenses of providing works as aforesaid in all cases *where the reserve fund of the Electricity Undertaking is not less than one-twentieth of the aggregate capital expenditure, subject, however, to the amount so applied being not more than 5 per cent. of the revenue of the year in which the surplus was obtained.*

(3) Where a local authority is desirous of applying net surplus to capital purposes not falling within the scope of the preceding consent, an application for the consent of the Commissioners should be accompanied by particulars showing:

(*a*) The amount of net surplus;

(*b*) The expenses chargeable to capital proposed to be met out of net surplus, and the purposes for which such expenditure is required; and

(*c*) The amount of reserve fund at the end of the financial year concerned.

(4) The Commissioners are prepared to consider giving a general consent in suitable cases permitting a specific maximum amount out of the annual net surplus to be applied in payment of expenses for the provision and equipment of small static sub-stations (including kiosks) and distributing mains.

(5) The Commissioners would require exceptional circumstances to be adduced in support of any application for their consent to the use of net surplus for defraying the cost of main transmission lines, high tension feeders and generating plant, except where the amount proposed to be so applied represented comparatively small items of expenditure in excess of loans previously sanctioned for the particular works."

I am, Sir,
Your obedient servant,
(*Sgd.*) R. T. G. French,
Secretary."

In cases where expenditure of a capital nature (including wages of permanent workmen) is defrayed out of revenue it is desirable to debit such items to the net revenue account (or better still to an appropriation account) instead of to the revenue account proper. All expenditure of a capital nature should be included as capital assets in the balance sheet whether defrayed out of loan moneys or revenue.

(49) With respect to the basis for the statement of capital assets in the balance sheet, the view of the Departmental Committee on Local Authority Accounts, 1907, that the original cost is the only satisfactory basis finds general acceptance. Care is necessary, however, to ensure the elimination of assets superseded or alienated. A useful practice is to maintain an inventory of capital plant, recording the initial cost and history of the respective items, and to require the engineer to certify as to their existence at the end of each year. Minutes of the committee, and proceeds of sales of superseded plant, often give a key to the alienation of assets.

(E) Costing

(50) I do not propose to embark on a discussion as to whether the cost accounts should be kept in the department of the electrical engineer or of the chief financial officer. The best results are probably obtained when both officers co-operate and complete harmony exists between the staffs of the two departments. In any case, the cost accounts should form an integral part of the financial accounts, or be capable of reconciliation therewith.

The system should be designed to serve the following purposes:—

(*a*) Detection and prevention of waste, leakages or inefficiency;

(*b*) Analysis of the elements of cost and the relativity of constituent items to each other;

(*c*) Presentation of results for statistical purposes, forecasts and interim statements of operation;

(*d*) Guide for future estimates, quotations and policy generally.

(51) *Method of Costing and Scope.*—In the case of an electricity undertaking there will normally be two methods of costing employed, viz.

(*a*) Operating costs—in connection with the generation and distribution of electrical energy; and

(*b*) Job costs—for
(i) Capital works, and
(ii) Rechargeable works.

(*a*) So far as operating cost is concerned, the routine and the detailed work involved need not be extensive. The cost allocations should be drawn up in collaboration with the electrical engineer and might conveniently follow the items of expenditure in the statutory form of account, amplified from time to time when it is desired to obtain information upon a particular item with a definite object. Some authorities favour very elaborate classification of generation and maintenance costs, but it is open to question whether the value of the results obtained is such as to justify the expense and trouble involved. Over-elaboration increases the possibility of error, and may produce a mass of detail of no particular significance when considered item by item.

It should be observed, however, that for the purposes of the Act of 1926 the cost of production, i.e. generation, is to include certain indirect expenses and the costs are to be divided into standing and running charges, in accordance with regulations to be prescribed by the Commissioners. When these regulations are issued it will probably be necessary to extend the cost system to meet the new situation.

(*b*) On capital account the cost accounts should indicate the expenditure under each item of the engineer's estimate upon which the application for loan sanction was based. Each mains extension job should be costed separately and it may be desirable to deal with services similarly. Rechargeable work carried out will also be dealt with on the job cost method, the prime cost being supplemented by a percentage for oncost calculated to be sufficient to cover the indirect expenses applicable to such work with such profit as may be decided upon.

(52) *Essential Features of System.*—The essential features of an efficient costing system include:—

(*a*) Effective control of stores and rigid adherence to routine which should only be amended with the sanction of the responsible accounting officer (*b*) Means of recording accurately and allocating promptly expenditure upon labour, material and other expenses.

(*c*) Prompt presentation of costing returns and other data.

(53) *Effective Control of Stores.*—It is not necessary to describe the use or rulings of the forms required for the stores system ; they would comprise :—

(i) Purchase requisition (and possibly a requisition book).

(ii) Official order.

(iii) Goods inwards book.

(iv) Requisitions and/or delivery receipts for materials issued and where required a goods outwards book.

(v) Returns inwards, returns outwards and/or transfer books.

(vi) Bin cards (for storekeeper's use).

(vii) Stock ledger accounts—loose leaf or card system including " control " account.

The difficulties connected with stocks and stores accounts are rarely appreciated by those who have not had practical experience of the work. Suitable accommodation is of prime importance and rigid adherence to stores routine no less essential.

A few suggestions respecting stores accounting may not be out of place.

(1) A standard list of stock articles giving the proper nomenclature, units for issue and bin numbers should be in the hands of the storekeepers stores ledger clerks and foremen principally concerned.

(2) The stock ledger should be on the card or loose-leaf system and the folios allotted to articles might with advantage correspond with the bin numbers in the stores. Some authorities contend that values are not necessary in the stores ledger; they afford some check on the accuracy of the postings, however, and often lead to detection of items posted to the wrong accounts.

(3) It is a common practice for goods delivered direct to the site of particular jobs to be charged direct instead of passing through the stores ledger. Could not special articles ordered for particular jobs but delivered to the stores be treated similarly and entered by the storekeeper into a " Direct Materials Book " recording their receipt and issue ?

(4) Stocktaking should not be regarded as a job to be undertaken only at the 31st March. Periodical tests at frequent intervals, with a view to checking every bin several times a year and the more valuable items also at the end of the financial year, are more effective and afford relief at a time of pressure. Where large stocks are carried by the different departments of a corporation, it may be desirable to employ a member of the audit staff almost continuously on this work.

(54) *Prompt and Accurate Allocation of Elements of Cost.*—To facilitate the allocation of the operating expenses, a " Standing Works Order number " is allotted to each item and a schedule compiled, copies of which are issued to all concerned, including head office staff, storekeepers, timekeepers, and foremen.

Special works orders are issued in those cases where the cost is to be separately ascertained, e.g. re-chargeable work and capital expenditure, and the individual " job number " should be quoted in addition to the standing order (or allocation) number on requisitions and time sheets.

Labour costs will be extracted from detailed daily time sheets and may with advantage be summarised in a columnar wages abstract, allocating the wages over the appropriate cost headings and agreeing in total with the amount of the wages paid for the week. Similarly, stores issued may be summarised in daily, weekly or monthly totals, and classified under cost headings in a columnar stores or materials abstract, the totals of which must correspond with the aggregate value of the stores issued for the period. The use of a suitable bookkeeping machine in conjunction with stores vouchers arranged so that perforated sections (or separate forms) accommodate one entry, facilitates the analysis of materials costs as well as the posting of the stores ledger. A haulage abstract may be kept if the volume of work renders this desirable.

Sundry direct expenses may be analysed in an expenditure journal through the medium of dissected orders on treasurer schedules.

(55) *Costing Returns.*—Belated returns are of very little, if any, use in costing, where " news " not " history " is required. The interim return of operating costs should not be too detailed ; the specimen given in the appendix is based largely on the expenditure section of the published accounts. There would not appear to be much advantage in preparing operating cost returns more frequently than monthly, many authorities favouring quarterly returns.

So far as the cost of labour, materials and certain direct expenses are concerned, accurate data is available, but with respect to rents, rates, insurances, loan charges, &c., resort will have to be made to estimates and apportionments in compiling the interim return of operating costs.

In connection with the operating returns, it will be necessary to ascertain the number of units generated and where possible the number of units sold. Where both figures are available the costs should be reduced to the basis of each. It is understood, however, to be practically impossible to correctly estimate the number of units sold, so that for interim periods between dates of successive meter readings the cost per unit *generated* may be the only one given.

The electrical engineer will ordinarily submit statistics as to output, fuel, consumers, and mains, and these are sometimes incorporated into a comprehensive return including the cost statement. Corresponding figures for the same period of the previous year are invariably given in costing returns for comparison.

(G) Conclusion

In concluding, one is conscious of the fact that some matters of importance have not been dealt with and that others have been treated but superficially. Much as one regrets this, considerations of space have left no alternative and it is hoped that the discussion will bring out points on which further information may be desired.

INVOICE

M

DR. TO THE SWANSEA CORPORATION

ELECTRICITY ACCOUNT

For Quarter ended

Units Consumed				Sale of Current				% Increase	Rents and Sundries	Arrears	Total Due	Discount offered Amount
Lighting Scale	Lighting Special	Power	Heating	Lighting	Power	Heating	Bal. of Min. Chg.					
												After this date no discount whatever can be allowed

LEDGER

A/c No.

Standing Charges :—

	Units Consumed				Sale of Current				% Increase	Rents and Sundries	Arrears	Amount Due	Discount Offered
	Lighting Scale	Lighting Special	Power	Heating	Lighting	Power	Heating	Bal. of Min. Chg.					
Quar. End.													
Mar. 1928							Date	Receipt No.	Allowances	Irrecoverable	Arrears Forward	Amount Paid	Discount Taken

ELECTRIC LIGHT CHARGES ABSTRACT

Units Consumed				Current Sold				% Increase	Rents & Sundries	Arrears	Amount Due	Discount Offered	Account No.
Lighting Scale	Lighting Special	Power	Heating	Lighting	Power	Heating	Bal. of Min.Chg.						

ELECTRICITY UNDERTAKING

OPERATING COST STATEMENT ended 19 .

LAST YEAR (units) *						THIS YEAR (units) *				
Wages	Mat-erials	Other Exp's	Total	Aver. per unit		Wages	Mat-erials	Other Exps.	Total	Aver. per unit
£ s d	£ s d	£ s d	£ s d	d		£ s d	£ s d	£ s d	£ s d	d
					(a) GENERATION EXPENSES					
					1. Fuel, including cost of handling and ash disposal					
					2. Oil, Waste and Engine Room Stores					
					3. Water					
					4. Salaries and Wages at Generating Stations					
					Repairs and Maintenance of—					
					5. Buildings, Yards, Roadways, &c.					
					6. Station Wiring Installations and Lighting					
					7. Steam Plant, Boilers, Turbines, &c.					
					8. Electrical Plant, Generators, Exciters, &c.					
					9. Auxiliary Plant					
					10. Switchgear, Instruments and Tools					
					11. Accumulators and Accessories					
					12. Energy purchased in Bulk					
					Sub-Total					
					(b) DISTRIBUTION EXPENSES*					
					1. Salaries and Wages of Distribution Staff					
					Repairs and Maintenance of—					
					2. Buildings, Yards, &c.					
					3. Wiring Installation and Lighting					
					4. Machinery					
					5. Switchgear and Instruments					
					6. Transformers					
					7. Overhead Lines					
					8. Mains					
					9. Services					
					10. Switches, Cut-outs and other Apparatus on Consumers' Premises					
					11. Meters, Indicators, &c.					
					Sub-Total					
					(c) RENTS AND RATES*					
					1. Rents					
					2. Rates					
					Sub-Total					
					(d) MANAGEMENT EXPENSES					
					1. Salaries					
					2. Printing and Stationery					
					3. General Establishment Charges					
					4. Insurances*					
					5. Publicity and Advertising					
					Sub-Total					
					Total Working Expenses					
					(e) OTHER CHARGES					
					1. Capital Charges *					
					2. Income Tax (Nett)					
					Total Costs					

*Memo.—1. Number of Units generated and/or sold.

2. Distribution Expenses might be sub-divided into Transmission, Conversion, and Distribution, if preferred.

3. Rents, Rates, Insurances and Capital Charges are sometimes allocated to appropriate heads—a., b., and d.

THE ACCOUNTS OF MUNICIPAL UNDERTAKINGS

By Arthur Collins, F.S.A.A., F.I.M.T.A.

A comparison of municipal trading undertakings and ordinary commercial undertakings is the main theme of this lecture and it is one with which many accountants are not very familiar. Mr. Collins has a world-wide reputation for knowledge and experience of municipal affairs and his advice is constantly sought by municipal authorities.

THE subject upon which I am going to address you to-night is not a very popular one: it is one which is in some respects technical. I shall, however, endeavour to interest those who have a close knowledge of municipal trading accounts, and those who rarely come in contact with them, by dwelling not too much upon the technical side, but upon comparative phases of the subject as between municipal trading undertakings and ordinary commercial undertakings.

Principles of Municipal Trading

Let me first remind you that there are certain underlying principles which to a certain extent dictate the policy of municipal authorities when running their trading undertakings. I will recall to you three or four of the leading features of those underlying principles. First of all there is the monopoly element. At one time the monopoly was absolute in gas, electricity, tramways and water: nobody could stand up to the municipal services with a competitive service of their own. Water is still immune from competition, and is quite a monopoly; gas and electricity may be in competition, whether they are both owned by the municipality, or whether at one time gas only was supplied by a corporation, and a private electricity company forthwith entered into competition with electricity. Tramways during the last few years have had to put up with severe competition. These elements, especially the private omnibus element, have been a cause of considerable concern to the municipal tramways undertakings. But broadly speaking, as a principle, what we have to observe in considering municipal trading concerns is the monopolistic basis upon which those concerns are founded.

Secondly, the object of municipal trading concerns is good service rather than good profits. A municipality has to ensure that all those citizens who desire the ordinary public services like water shall have them, although if they paid the true cost of that water it would be beyond their capacity to pay. The same is becoming increasingly true with gas and electricity in this sense, namely, that Parliament is becoming more and more inclined to insist upon cheap and efficient service rather than the profit-making element as an essential part of the conduct of the undertaking.

Thirdly, there is the security of all the properties in the city; the bricks and mortar in the dwelling or in the business premises of every citizen, which are pledged to back the investment of any lender to a municipal trading undertaking. The security in a company is, of course, the business itself, but the guarantee of a municipal trading concern is not only the undertaking itself, but the guarantee of the rates which stands behind it, those rates which are pledged on the security of the properties of the city from the rating point of view.

Fourthly, there is no permanent capital allowed as the capital in a trading undertaking belonging to a municipality. The capital invested in such an undertaking is subject to very rigid statutory provisions, which provide that that capital shall gradually be redeemed instead of standing permanently on the books as it would in the case of a private company supplying electricity, gas, water or tramways.

Effect of Principles upon Municipal Trading Accounts

The effect of these three or four main principles upon the accounts is quite marked. In the Revenue Account, wherein are contained the ordinary revenues and working expenses of any municipal concern, there is not much difference between the features of such accounts as operated by municipalities on the one hand, and those operated by private companies on the other. But when you pass from that, and come to the factor which in a commercial concern is called the gross profit, carried to the net Revenue Account, these distinctions at once begin to appear between the two classes of concern.

In the net Revenue Account of a corporation concern, there used at one time to be put in interest on capital, and provision for the redemption of debt, and the balance was considered the net profit of the undertaking, or the excess was considered the net loss. But of late years it has been the tendency of municipal accountants to regard the net Revenue Account as an account which should be brought more strictly into comparison with private concerns, by debiting in the net Revenue Account only interest on the debt, and carrying the balance down to Profit and Loss Appropriation Account, or net Revenue Appropriation Account. This balance on the net Revenue Account is regarded as being the equivalent of the distributable profit of a private commercial concern (regard being had in both accounts to the necessity for setting aside reserve funds, as I shall presently explain) and out of this net profit the redemption money towards amortisation of the debt is allocated.

Then in the Capital Account and Balance Sheet, you have in a municipal concern, not only a record of the capital invested in the undertaking, but also on the other side of the account a record of the statutory provision made for the redemption of that debt, there being no such provision in the case of a privately owned trading concern such as an electricity company. And in the Balance Sheet you will see the distinction between the capital snd revenue items more marked in the case of a corporation undertaking than in the case of a private concern. You will generally find an

A lecture delivered before the Birmingham Chartered Accountant Students' Society.

up-to-date form of Balance Sheet for a trading concern distinguishing between items on Capital Account and items of Revenue Account, so that you can see for instance whether the cash is overdrawn or in hand on capital as distinct from the cash overdrawn or in hand on revenue. You may also have your debtors and creditors separate, so that you may see which of your creditors and debtors are also on Capital Account as distinct from Revenue Account. In a corporation undertaking it is not legally necessary to make that distinction, but sound practice in municipal accounting ensures that that division is observed.

Capital of Trading Concerns

Now capital invested in municipal trading is raised in quite a different way, generally speaking, from that which is raised for gas or electricity, or water, or a tramway concern under company management. The distinctions with which you are all so familiar in commercial accounts, between mortgages, or mortgage debentures, preference stock or shares, ordinary shares, sub-ordinary or founders' shares—in short, all the various distinctions which you draw between one or other of the holdings of the lenders of capital to a commercial trading concern affecting their rights to dividends, or principal money on liquidations, are not distinctions which are observed, or are observable, in the case of municipal trading undertakings.

All capital in all municipal trading undertakings, generally speaking, is on the same footing. There is no preference in dividend ; no preference in security on winding-up. Remember that a municipal concern is conceived as a concern which runs on for ever : there is no conception of any corporation meeting a date upon which winding-up will be necessary, when the rights of various subscribers of capital may need to be observed in accordance with the memorandum and articles of association giving prior rights to certain securities, such as preference stock. All securities invested in a municipal trading concern stand on the same footing, not in four or five different classes.

First of all there is the capital invested in the form of what is called stock. For our purpose to-night this may be taken as being practically the same in a municipal concern as it is in an ordinary concern, with this feature present however, that a dividend on all the capital invested in a municipal concern is assured. If the revenues of the municipal trading concern do not pay dividends on the investments in the concern, then the rates have got to make up the difference. There is no such thing as "passing a dividend" in the case of a municipal undertaking.

A municipal undertaking may have invested in it stock alone, or it may also finance itself by the raising of loans on mortgage, or by the issue, as in modern practice of bonds (for which the Coventry Corporation got special powers last year, and Birmingham is applying this year), or by the issue of moneys secured by bills redeemable on short notice, in six or twelve months time, Birmingham being one of the few corporations which has special power to raise capital by that means. Or the capital may be temporary loans from the bank, or even in certain circumstances, temporary loans from private individuals.

But whatever that capital is, remember it is subject to two special considerations which do not apply to private trading concerns at all, namely, that the capital is always assured of a dividend, and secondly, that the capital is never to be permanent, but is to be subject to annual provision for redemption.

Then again, the capital is not subject to variable dividends. You are all so closely acquainted with commercial practice that as you know, whether it be an ironfounder, or a shopkeeper, or a limited company, the rate of dividend depends upon the amount of profit made in the particular year. All capital invested in a municipal concern is on a fixed dividend basis. If the City of Birmingham issue a stock paying interest at the rate of 4¾ per cent., the rate of interest is 4¾ per cent. for the whole life of the stock, and the stock is generally raised for periods of from 20 to 40 years. If the capital is raised by a loan taken on mortgage—a sort of standard document being handed to the lender which pledges to him a proportion (an arithmetical part) of the corporation's assets as security for his debt—the rate of interest on that mortgage is fixed at the time it is taken, and whether the mortgage is according to the agreement to run for three or twenty years, that is the rate of interest fixed and invariable throughout the period of the life of that mortgage.

If it is renewed at the expiration of the term for a new period, then another rate of interest is fixed according to the then conditions of the market, and that rate remains constant throughout the period of the renewed life of the mortgage. Bills, being temporary borrowings, fix a rate of interest for the life of the bill six or twelve months, and temporary loans may just carry the rate of interest charged for the time being by the bank, while steps are being taken to raise more permanent forms of capital, so that whether the concern does well or badly there is no doubt whatever about the dividend on the securities, stocks or other forms of securities being paid.

Rates Making Up Revenue to Assure Dividends or Yields on Capital

Let me illustrate that by a practical example with which all corporation men are familiar, but with which other Birmingham men may not be so familiar. In your own city you know probably that the water undertaking of the corporation is one which, on a commercial basis, does not pay. But although the water revenue does not cover, or may not in every year cover the actual costs of running the undertaking, the dividend on all water securities is paid to the full ; if the water revenues do not make it up, then the rates do. In my time here I remember the water undertaking was in a commercial sense losing at the rate of about £120,000 a year, a very heavy deficit on the undertaking, and representing a heavy proportion of the total revenue of the undertaking ; but, nevertheless, all capital lent to the corporation and invested in the water undertaking received its dividend, and if the water revenues did not pay it, then the general rates which came to the assistance of the department did. It is in a case like that that you see the significance of rates standing behind the revenues of a department. A company has no such collateral security, and therefore is always subject to the revenues of the year being sufficient to pay the interest or dividend on the capital for that year.

Redemption of Municipal Capital

Then I should like to bring to your notice the provision for the redemption of all capital invested in a municipal trading undertaking. First of all capital cannot be raised at all unless special sanction has been given outside the corporation to the raising of capital. It is not possible for a local authority to say: " We will build a new waterworks, or build a new electricity station, or reconstruct and rearrange our gas works," and forthwith proceed to do it out of capital. If they did, any public-spirited citizen—assuming there be such still left in these days (laughter)—might take an action against the corporation, at his own expense —(that is why I used the expression "public-spirited" just now)—and he could compel the corporation to refrain from proceeding with that action until the appropriate sanction had been given.

The appropriate sanction is either authority given by Act of Parliament or authority given by a State department under powers conferred upon that department by Parliament. I daresay you have seen at various times reports in the local papers of a local inquiry being held by an officer of the Ministry of Health into an application by the Corporation for permission to raise a loan of, say, £100,000 for a new reservoir for the water works. That is, briefly, what I am speaking of, i.e. an application by the corporation for the sanction of the appropriate State department to the raising of this capital to be invested in a municipal trading undertaking. It is rarely that the sanction is refused, although on some occasions it is.

Sometimes an extension of a trading department is so great that the corporation have not powers to carry it out even if they can get the sanction to the loan, unless they get special Parliamentary authority. For instance, when we went to Wales for our water works, the corporation could not pass a resolution buying up about 40,000 acres in Wales and construct works upon them, even if a Government department had sanctioned the money. The appropriation of property in certain conditions, e.g. property in the water itself, which a scheme like that involves, has to be sanctioned expressly by Parliament; therefore, in a scheme of magnitude of that kind, you have to go to Parliament direct, because although a State department may sanction the spending of money on the appropriation of land, you still want special powers to take that water away, and bring it through all the districts between Wales and here. There, of course, you are up against a good many interests, and it is necessary that the matter should be laid before Parliament before you can get sanction to do it, when protective clauses may have to be inserted to preserve the interests of landed proprietors and others who may be closely affected by the scheme.

So that, in the first place, any additional capital has to be sanctioned, and in the second place, sanction when given is coupled with a provision that the debt thereby sanctioned shall be redeemed over a given number of years. I would ask you to bear this point in mind, and it will help me to avoid repetition later on, namely, that when the sanction is given, it is given on the condition that the debt thereby authorised and created shall be redeemed over a specified number of years appropriate to the purpose for which the money is to be used. If the loan, for instance, is for a new electricity station, the sanction will provide that in so many years the cost of the building must be redeemed out of revenue and the debt paid off, that in so many less years the machinery must also have been repaid by provision from revenue, in so many years the cost of laying cables in the streets (for which you would get, say, forty years) must be paid off, and the amount raised for consumers' services would have to be redeemed, say, within ten years.

Of every loan sanctioned my old colleagues in the Treasurer's Department here have to keep a very careful record, and starting with the amount raised for every loan, they have to prepare a schedule insuring that that debt is to be paid off out of revenue by the date sanctioned when the loan was approved.

Methods of Paying Off Municipal Trading Loans

That debt may be paid off by various methods. If you have raised a loan of £10,000 for a new tram shed, the terms on which you raise that loan may provide for it to be repaid to the lender whose capital you used by equal annual instalments of that money. If you borrowed the money for 20 years you would pay off £500 a year, and annual interest on the balance. It may, however, be paid by an annuity, being an equal annual amount representing the principal and interest combined. That is known as the annuity system, and the annuity system provides again for a schedule of such repayments; if the loan is to be paid off within twenty years, an annual sum is computed which will pay off the principal and discharge the interest exactly over the period.

These methods are the two commonly followed by smaller authorities; the third method is rather a more complex one and is therefore adopted mostly only by the larger authorities. It is the provision of a sinking fund. Nobody has ever been able to understand why the phrase "sinking fund" is used: certainly, I have never been able to get any intelligent explanation, but the phrase is used to indicate that instead of paying off a debt either by fixed instalments or by an annuity you put aside into a fund or pool such an amount each year as when accumulated, with interest, will provide by a given date the amount required to pay off the loan by one cheque at the end of the sanctioned period.

If I were to proceed into technical details, which are of interest only to municipal accountants, I should endeavour to show you how modern practice has provided a pool for the redemption of its debts instead of treating each debt separately as I have done to-night. I do not want you to think I have overlooked that phase, but it would not greatly interest an audience of this kind, and if it did, would probably result in a series of technical questions at the finish, in which half a dozen municipal men and myself would enjoy ourselves immensely, while the rest of the audience would be wondering what we were talking about. (Laughter.)

Revenues of Trading Concerns

Let me now deal shortly with the control of the revenue of a municipal trading undertaking, and the incidence of the charges upon the consumers or users. Here again, all municipal trading undertakings have to observe the provisions of the authority given to them by Parliament to run that concern. The first point I want to remind you of is uniformity in charges to the same class of consumer. In the commercial world, you know as well as I do, that the head of a concern may either favour or disfavour some particular customer. I have had occasion sometimes to think that probably the only reason for favour or disfavour has been that the gentleman in power has not loved anybody with red hair. (Laughter.) But there is that power of distinction vested in the heads of commercial concerns which is not permitted in the case of a municipal concern. All charges must be uniform to the same classes of consumer. The only exception to that condition is some of those cases where a commodity, be it gas, water, electricity and so on, is supplied to consumers outside the area of the proprietors' undertaking.

It is common knowledge that Birmingham gas and water undertakings serve areas outside the City of Birmingham, whereas it is only the rates of the City of Birmingham which are responsible for the losses. In the case of Birmingham all its charges are uniform; no more is charged for water or gas to a consumer in Smethwick who may be supplied by Birmingham than is charged in Birmingham, but in some cases throughout the country the authority supplying is permitted to make rather a higher charge for commodities supplied outside its own area than the charge inside the city. But again, uniformity must be observed; there must be no difference in the charges made to the same class of consumers in the city, and no difference in the charges made to any consumers in the same circumstances outside the city.

But there are different classes of consumers to be considered. For instance, in gas or electricity you have a scale of charges covering domestic purposes, such as lighting, heating and cooking. For power, you may have large or small consumers of gas, electricity or water, and a scale of charges is prescribed for them; all consumers on that scale consuming the same quantity pay only the same charge.

You may have the pre-payment system, such as the penny-in-the-slot gas meter; in those cases you must charge all pre-payment customers alike, although you may charge them rather more per thousand cubic feet through a pre-payment meter, owing to the extra expense and trouble the system causes, than you charge for 1,000 feet to a consumer who pays his bills quarterly.

If we had time I think I could interest you in modern developments in arranging scientific scales of charges for these undertakings, especially electricity, but as there is practically no distinction between a municipal undertaking and a commercial trading undertaking running a public utility concern, in that particular respect, I will refrain from doing so, beyond making one or two general observations.

Development Policy

I have referred to the uniformity of charge; modern developments have caused quite a transformation to take place in the old methods of charging which were common in my young days. In the case of electricity, and in the case of gas, competition has brought this result, that instead of having a flat rate now for all charges to consumers for the same quantity, you endeavour to play psychologically upon the mind of the consumer. For that purpose you may adopt in lieu of a flat rate only a choice by a consumer between a flat rate and a two-part or three-part tariff. What is a two-part tariff? It is just an attempt to induce consumers to patronise your concern more extensively.

It is an important feature which arises according to the general policy of the concern, viz. that one council may believe it is better to sell a lot of the commodity cheaply than it is to sell a small quantity of it dearly. This policy has been particularly noticeable in the case of electricity companies perhaps more often than corporations, but I could name three or four electricity companies in the country whose policy clearly appears to be to sell a given quantity at a high price, instead of to sell the greatest possible quantity at the lowest price. Many of these trading concerns run by private companies, however, are being run on terms of tenure which give the local authority a right to buy the undertaking after a certain number of years. Under the old Electricity Acts of 1882 the standard provision was that 42 years after an undertaking was established the local authority could buy it out on terms. If you reckon 42 years from 1882 or just after that you will find we are now in the years in which the option to purchase arises, and many of these options are now coming into force.

One of the elements which a private electricity undertaking has to consider is this, that where they are going in for a policy of selling as much electricity (and selling it cheaply) as they can, it means that they have got to embark more capital in their undertaking to cater for the demand when they are not sure of the terms on which they might be bought out. They may say therefore—our policy is going to be to make as much profit as we can on a tariff or a scale which makes it unlikely that the demand will so much increase between now and the time we are due to be bought out that we have to put more capital into the concern. The tendency in this case is to restrict the possibilities of having to put more capital down for new buildings, machinery and plant just now.

In an ordinary concern where this circumstance does not operate, particularly in a municipal trading undertaking, the two-part tariff is arranged something like this: suppose you occupy a house with six rooms, you pay a fixed charge for each £1 of rental value or for each room, and then an extraordinarily low charge for each unit you burn. I referred to the psychological effect of these tariff arrangements. I will assume for the present, notwithstanding the youthful appearance of many of you, that you are fathers of families, and that you have your own domestic budget to consider. The electricity managers say to you: now you are going into a house which is well furnished with electricity; you will have to allow in your annual budget so much for heating, so much for lighting, so much for general domestic use, such for instance as machines for sweeping the floors, and even implements to dry your hair or clean your teeth. (Laughter.) All these electricity devices are provided to encourage the use of large quantities of electricity at cheap prices. It is for the greater part a day-load demand.

I put it to you as the up-to-date municipal trading concern puts it to its consumers: we charge you 10s. a room for your six-roomed house, that is £3, but we will supply you with every unit of electricity you want at, say, a farthing. After you have got your first two or three electricity bills and got over the shock—(laughter)—you begin to realise that the more units you burn the less per unit it costs you. You have a fixed and constant charge of £3; that does not vary whether you use 100 or 1,000 units, and therefore you begin to consider whether it is better to use electricity instead of coal, and electricity instead of gas. Generally speaking, it is found that where a choice of tariffs is given in that way at attractive prices, it comes down to this fact in its effect: that the price per unit is so low that when you consume a good many units, and divide it into a standing charge of £3, as in the illustration I have given to you, that it is better to use more electricity at low prices than to use coal or gas. I could, if you were domestically inclined—probably you are not—(laughter)—keep you some considerable time on the scientific (and even psychological) provisions of a tariff of that kind, which is a special feature of municipal trading at the present time, and is also a marked feature of company utility undertakings, subject always as I say to the fact that they have to consider always what the potentialities are in the way of purchase by the municipal concern.

Municipal Trading and its Effect on Local Rates

I proceed now to consider the relationship between the rates and municipal trading undertakings. The general policy approved by Parliament at the present time is for a trading undertaking to be made self-supporting by its own revenues, no more and no less. Parliament does not encourage municipal corporations whether they are going to run a new undertaking, or whether they are running an old one, to proceed upon the basis that their policy is to be to make as much profit as possibly can be made while still giving a decent service.

One of the reasons which no doubt influenced Parliament in taking that view is that at the present time it is desirable to take all possible steps in reducing the costs of production, so that industry shall not be charged for electricity, or gas or water a profit which is added on to the cost price, and goes to the relief of rates ; instead of that, the price charged to consumers, especially industrial consumers, shall be as nearly as possible to cost price.

It is, of course, true sometimes that it would suit a trader better to pay a higher price for gas, of which he may use very little, in order that other consumers may help to make a big profit on gas, which will go to reduce the amount he pays in local rates, but that is so uncertain a contingency, especially now that derating has arrived for industry, that Parliament has taken the line of assuring a more definite relief to industry, by saying that the prices of these commodities shall be as nearly as they can be calculated to cost prices. If a municipal trading undertaking makes more than a fair margin of profit after covering all charges, Parliament's provision is that the surplus profit shall be carried forward in the undertaking, and appear as a credit next year when charges can be reduced, instead of following the older policy of transferring that profit in relief of the rates.

But there are certain undertakings which cannot, in the face of circumstances, make a profit, and yet must have a loss. Our Birmingham water undertaking is—but I have not seen the accounts for the last year or two, so I will say was—in that category. The charges made for water were already considered to be so high that it was not in the interests of public health to try and increase them ; the tendency rather was to work towards reducing them ; and if the charge for water, which in my time was 3s. in the £ on the assessment, did not cover the cost, the balance had to be made up by subsidy from the rates. Parliament is cautious in seeing the price of water shall not be made prohibitive, and if a concern, such as we have in Birmingham, cannot pay its way on the water rates, there is nothing put into the wheels to hinder a corporation from making the undertaking pay its way with the assistance of a subsidy from the general rates.

In the case of the tramways, too, it is necessary to consider both charges and profits. The tramways are a curious branch of municipal trading. In the case of gas, water and electricity, if you like to do so, it is only a question of putting the price up to make it pay ; people have to have gas, electricity and water. If you don't like the prices charged you cannot go out into the street and buy gas, electricity or water from some other supplier, but in the case of tramways you cannot simply increase your charges and make them pay, nor can you do so on buses. Immediately the consumer (i.e. the user) says he would rather walk than pay your fares, you are done. The question there is, what charges the traffic will bear.

In the case of tramway undertakings, especially with the competition they have to face from the buses, it is becoming increasingly hard to make the tramways pay, when proper regard is had to the necessary reserves ; in fact, some tramways are only able to avoid showing a loss at the present time by having to cut very fine the provision they make for renewals and replacements.

Depreciation of Trading Assets

I have now to deal with the depreciation and obsolescence of municipal undertakings. It will save repetition if I bring back to your notice the statement I made earlier, that nowadays when a loan is sanctioned for new capital expenditure, it is sanctioned on condition that it is repaid within a given time. In my earlier days in municipal finance, I have the clearest recollection of thirty to sixty years being given in which to repay a loan which was going to be expended on concerns which experience has shown had not a life of more than twenty or twenty-five. Many electricity undertakings in this country between 1882 and 1900 were sanctioned on condition that the loans raised for the undertakings were redeemed within forty years ; sometimes thirty, sometimes twenty-five ; the period was contracting all the time. But before twenty-five years were up, much of the machinery was worn out, and a great deal was obsolete within twenty to thirty years ; and the sinking fund did not provide for what was in those cases true wastage of assets value.

It was not long, therefore, before municipal trading undertakings began to realise that a sinking fund for the redemption of the debt did not always entirely meet the case, and that it was necessary, although you were paying off your debt within certain prescribed times, to supplement that provision by way of sinking fund, by additional reserve and renewal funds. To-day when a State department sanctions a loan, they calculate the life of that loan as near as can be to the life of the asset. They do not give you 25 years for an electricity undertaking as a whole, some parts of which, the cables in the ground for instance, last 50 years, and other parts like plant, which might be useless or uneconomic in 15 to 20 years. They say—we will give you 50 years for buildings ; 40 years for cables ; 15 years for machinery ; 10 years for appliances and instruments ; 5 years for apparatus installed on consumers' premises, and so on. This calculation of life in years makes the sinking fund as nearly as may be the equivalent of a renewal fund, but you wipe off the debt by the provision of those moneys which, if they were put aside in a private commercial undertaking, would be equivalent to a true renewal and reserve fund, with the original capital outlay intact in the balance sheet.

In addition to writing-off by sinking fund, however, municipalities are increasingly making provision out of revenues for other purposes; for instance, renewals, contingencies, internal insurance funds, and provision for superannuation of officials.

I am glad to say also that a more cautious attitude is being adopted now than ten or twenty years ago, in utilising the gross profit of a municipal trading undertaking. The provision of a general reserve has been shown to be invaluable: a reserve set aside for no particular reason, but there to meet contingencies. One special use to which a general reserve fund has been put, and is increasingly being used, is to maintain steadiness in charges.

The costs of a municipal undertaking working on a self-supporting basis might be represented by X this year, but next year owing to some unexpected event, such as a coal strike, their costs would stand at X plus 50 per cent. Nobody could tell when a contingency of that kind was going to arise, but so bitter were the experiences of municipalities when they were caught by incidents like the war and the coal strike, when their charges to consumers went up and down like a rocket, making extremely variable markings on a chart, that they are now being sufficiently wise to keep a good general reserve fund in hand. To maintain steadiness in prices is a course increasingly becoming recognised as one of the primary causes for keeping a good general reserve fund, quite apart from a renewals fund and in addition to a sinking fund.

Constant Expenditure of a Capital Nature

I should also like to draw your attention to a growing practice amongst undertakings, especially municipal undertakings, which I have not observed being followed quite to the same extent in the various company undertakings with which I deal. I refer to the practice of charging direct to revenue constant expenditure which formerly used to be charged to capital. For instance, meters: every growing concern has to provide a certain number of meters for its consumers. The old practice used to be to charge all these meters to capital and write them off over 10 or 20 years. Nowadays the custom is much more common of charging them straight to revenue so as to be done with it. By this time some concerns within my knowledge have no figure in their capital account at all for meters, although one concern that I know of owns £100,000 worth of meters. They have been charging their meters to revenue for years, and by this time have completely written-off amounts charged to capital for meters in years gone by. The value of those assets should, of course, appear in the balance sheet, as they should not be lost sight of, and full inventories must be kept of all these things.

Audit of Municipal Trading Accounts

The last phase which I shall deal with, shortly, is the work of auditing the accounts of municipal trading undertakings. First the auditor should see that the internal audit of a department is an adequate and satisfactory one; that there is proper vouching of all items of income and expenditure, and adequate and efficient supervision of cash, of stores, and last, but by no means least, that all permanent articles that ought to be in the inventory are entered there. I have sometimes been surprised, where I have found the greatest care taken of cash, and adequate care taken of stores, that permanent articles like furniture, typewriters, tools, small electric machines and what not, have not been recorded at all, or where originally recorded, have not been revised after review regularly. If you have an inventory entered up once, it should be checked as frequently throughout the year as the stocks and stores books, or the cash account is checked.

Next it is the duty of the professional auditor to see that all the capital invested in the undertaking is authorised, to see the sanctions on which the money was approved, to check the capital received, and see that it is properly applied. It is the care of the auditor to see that nothing has been charged to capital which ought to have been charged to revenue. When you recollect that a good many boroughs have no more audit than the elective audit (on which I have talked before) there is practically no check whatever in many cases upon the accounts of trading undertakings.

Then the auditor has to see that provision for repayment is fully made in accordance with the sanction given when the loan was granted, and where the sinking fund system is used, to see that the sinking fund moneys are properly invested in accordance with the requirements of the statutes as appropriate to the various loans.

Fourthly, as a professional auditor of municipal accounts, I always take care to suggest that the reserve fund should be scientific; to require all the assets in a municipal undertaking to be set out according to the dates on which they were bought, or the years in which they were constructed. I would look closely into the provision made for the repayment of debt on those assets, and where in conference with the officers of the department it appears clear that the sinking fund is not sufficient for the purpose to recommend that it is supplemented by a renewal fund.

Discretion as to the use of the substantial profits made by some municipal undertakings, which are often transferred to the relief of the rates, does not vest in the auditor; the power lies in the hands of the council, but I am quite sure from my own experience that every council takes a great deal of notice of the professional auditor, and I think it is one of the duties of the auditor to put his views into writing for submission to the appropriate committee, if he is not satisfied that the profits of the undertaking are being dealt with sufficiently cautiously, by being dissipated and not sufficiently conserved, by their utilisation for the relief of rates.

Lastly, it is necessary that every auditor should make himself familiar with the general law governing these trading undertakings, and with the local law of the local authority concerned, which may have special acts of its own relating to trading undertakings, so that he is not left at the risk of overlooking some obligation put upon the local authority whose accounts he is auditing by law. It is a very complex and difficult matter, but it is one I ought to mention in any record that may be taken of these proceedings, and the advice I venture to give is this: It is impossible in my judgment for a professional auditor to give a certificate that everything has been done that ought to be done, and that all the corporation requirements and his requirements as auditor have been met, unless he has satisfied himself by a study of the general and local Acts that every duty cast upon the local authority governing its trading undertakings has been satisfactorily discharged.

This is a dull subject; most of these municipal accounting subjects are. I can only hope that somewhere amongst my discursive remarks you may have found something interesting to each class of student who is represented here to-night." (Applause.)

DISCUSSION

Mr. ASHBY asked if the lecturer did not think it an anomaly that the trading undertakings of a corporation which had the rates of the municipality at their back should themselves be rated on all their properties to that same municipality?

Mr. COLLINS: The question of rating both municipal and private trading undertakings is difficult and complex. There are different views on it: the first is that a municipal trading concern should not be rated at all; the second is that it should be rated heavily, and the third that it should be rated lightly. As regards not rating a municipal trading undertaking at all, a difficult situation would be created if that were to be established as a practice. Where you have a municipality running a gas works, and a company running an electricity undertaking, it would not be right for one to be rated and the other not; if there is to be rating, let both be rated. As to whether they should be rated at top figure, or lightly, is another matter. If you were to rate to your maximum legal capacity some of the water undertakings of the country, all you would be doing would be to make it impossible for the water undertaking to pay its way at a moderate charge for water; you would be adding to the expenses very considerably by taking out of one pocket and putting it in another.

Generally speaking the assessment of these undertakings is left with some discretionary power to the rating officers. You cannot be unfair, but you can exercise some discretion.

Mr. THATCHER said reference had been made to the tendency of Parliament to limit the prices charged for public utilities in order to help productive industry. One could think of the possibilities of a municipal trading undertaking so fixing its prices to productive industry at the expense not of the rates, but of the other consumers of the undertaking. One could think of the possibilities of the prices to industry being fixed at the actual cost price of manufacture with practically no addition for distribution and overhead charges.

Personally he was an advocate of the need for a general reserve fund to meet contingencies, the nature of which Mr. Collins had given; he also agreed that in the case of any asset the life of which did not coincide with the period of the redemption of the loan, additional provision should be made, but he was inclined to think there was a tendency to create additional reserves even to those mentioned, by creating a reserve specifically for the extension of undertakings. From the point of fairness in the incidence of charge to present-day users of that particular commodity, what was Mr. Collins' opinion?

Mr. COLLINS, in replying, reminded his hearers that when dealing with scales of charges he had said there were a good many aspects of that subject upon which he would like to dwell but as time would not permit he had selected one or two. "The particular point raised by Mr. Thatcher," continued Mr. Collins, "goes into the economics of the question."

It is necessary to take care in fixing a scale of charges to consider what is the cost price. The problem that every municipality is faced with is, what is, the cost of giving a day load of power, gas or electricity to a manufacturer when your plant is otherwise standing idle, compared with the cost of giving a supply of light between the hours in winter of 7 and 9 o'clock. I doubt if any two accountants in the room would agree upon that point. Some electricity engineers claim that it is better to supply a large power consumer during the light hours of the day at practically no more than the cost of coal, oil, waste and water, and something for wear and tear (all distribution being left out) on the ground that that distribution system is necessary anyway. It is unlikely that two of you would agree on the figure that should be charged in supplying big consumers during the day at a low price. It is in each case a question of degree as to what are standing charges and what are running expenses to be taken into account.

In regard to reserves for extensions, undertakings have to act with moderation. Parliament has approved reserve funds to provide for extensions of undertakings, but the building of a new works out of revenue might be doing a grave injustice to the present consumers for the benefit of future consumers. The best way is to so use your reserve fund powers as to take care not always to be running to Capital Account for every small thing required.

Mr. BONHAM asked what was the lecturer's opinion on the action of the Government in the De-rating Bill in not allowing any relief to local undertakings in regard to rates?

Mr. COLLINS said it would not be easy to find words to express his personal opinion—(laughter)—but looking at it from a national standpoint they would be able to see some of the difficulties which would arise if all undertakings of that kind were derated. He would mention one only. The statutory provisions given to some of those undertakings had been very carefully balanced between one district and another in the matter of charges, and between one class and another in the matter of prices, especially of water. If the average water undertaking were derated it would upset a good many calculations that had to be made under Parliamentary powers to determine what was the price of bulk supplies of water, how much of the derating was to be credited to bulk supply as distinct from distribution. When you started disturbing the incidence of rates like that considerable confusion would ensue. "It would be a grand thing for the likes of me," said the speaker, amid laughter, "I should have some lovely arbitrations." On the whole it was felt by the Government that as the corporation were concerned in two capacities, viz. as ratepayers and collectors, it was not worth while.

Mr. BARROWS referred to the transfer of profits from municipal undertakings to the relief of rates, a practice which he understood was not now favoured. Was it not correct that in Birmingham something like £33,000 was transferred last year to the relief of rates?

Mr. COLLINS said a good many corporations still retained their powers to use profits from trading undertakings; there was nothing to interfere with the discretionary power vested in such corporations. It was only as corporations came to Parliament for new powers that that condition as to charging cost price for water, and often for gas, was being applied. Some corporations used their profits in that way to a larger extent than Birmingham, and in certain seaside towns it was the practice during the holiday season to make substantial profits on trams and buses, deliberately, to help to pay for promenades, &c., for summer seasonal visitors.

Mr. DAVIS asked if capital items charged to revenue should always be included in the assets in the balance sheet.

Mr. COLLINS: The answer is, yes, certainly.

Mr. LANCASTER pointed out that in Birmingham there were perpetual annuities in the gas and water departments for which there did not appear to be any provision for redemption. Could Mr. Collins explain?

Mr. COLLINS explained that those old gas and water annuities were unredeemable as far as the holder was concerned. The corporation could not call upon him to hand over an annuity for cash, but the corporation provided sums which they set aside for the redemption of those annuities by purchase when they came into the market. In that way they were gradually being bought up, although any holder who wished to hold them for ever could do so.

Mr. LANCASTER then asked how the charge for such a fund was calculated?

Mr. COLLINS said if he remembered rightly, in Birmingham, they capitalised an annuity at 20 years' purchase for the purpose of calculating provision for repayment. If any man held a gas annuity of £10 the corporation would set aside a sum of £200 as the proper capital sum to be provided by revenue in anticipation of that annuity coming into the market and being available for purchase.

Mr. WILES said the Coventry Corporation in a Bill promoted by them last year sought powers to create a new fund on the lines of the Scottish Common Good, to transfer profits or surpluses on their trading undertakings, if any, for purposes which would be tantamount to the relief of rates. That power was refused, but the committee concerned reported favourably to the Government. Was that not a direct contradiction to the tendency of Parliament to-day to refuse the power to transfer those balances to the relief of rates?

Mr. COLLINS, in replying, said he would hesitate to pit his memory against Mr. Wiles, who might be much better informed, but so far as he could recollect, after evidence was given, the committee approved a number of clauses, but only passed the principle of the Coventry clause in so far as it enabled the corporation to accept bequests and donations and gifts from public-spirited people. The committee expressed dissent from the particular suggestion that that fund should be built up by profits from trading concerns. That was the part they did not agree with, if he remembered rightly.

Mr. FURNESS said when the lecturer had talked of a renewals fund, did he mean renewals of large sections of the undertaking, or for the renewal of small units?

Mr. COLLINS said there had to be caution exercised in building up renewal funds for those major portions of the concern which were not adequately dealt with by the sinking fund, as distinct from the cases where the life of an asset in subsequent experience was proved to be longer than the term granted for repayment of the loan in the first instance. The two were often balanced against each other. There was everything to be said for setting up a renewal fund for small assets which required regularly renewing in order to avoid constant recurrence to capital. In dealing with small assets that wore out, if they were charged to capital in the first place it was really worth while to see that when they came to be renewed the council did not have to run into the capital account again, but were able to defray the costs out of a reserve fund.

(The Institute is not as a body responsible for or necessarily in agreement with the views and opinions expressed by the Author of the Paper, or by the speakers.)

STANDARDISATION OF ABSTRACTS OF ACCOUNTS

1. The subject of this paper may be described as " time worn " inasmuch as uniformity and standardisation of Accounts has been referred to in the Annual Reports in almost every year since this Institute was formed. But " time worn " as it may be, the subject has not diminished in importance and though in the last 40 years progress has undoubtedly been made, one is bound to admit that much remains to be achieved. The Accounts of the various Local Authorities throughout the country continue to be issued in a diversity of form and all will agree that the Institute will take yet another step forward to enhance its prestige if it can secure effective standardisation of the form in which the Abstract of Accounts of Local Authorities are published.

2. As a general principle it will be admitted without question that standardisation of the Accounts of Local Authorities is of importance and value. In the words of the President of 1906 in his Presidential Address :—

> " The ability readily to compare financial operations and results through the establishment of a uniform system stimulates the spirit of enquiry and research into causes and at the same time consciously or unconsciously promotes a healthy rivalry in the attainment of maximum results with a minimum of effort and cost. As to the particular line which uniformity should take, it may be difficult to suggest a scheme in all its completeness, which could be made applicable to all local authorities alike, having regard to distinctive legislative enactments which govern different classes of local authorities —county councils, urban and rural district councils, parish councils, and municipal boroughs. But apart from any special provision in the arrangement and order of accounts which may be imposed by existing statutes of Local Govern-

P*

ment Board regulations, certain broad features on uniform lines might easily be introduced and made common to each."

3. It may be appropriate to remind members that the Council of the Institute has expressed the opinion that uniformity in matters of general principle should be established between all the accounts of one local authority and further between the accounts of different local authorities of the same class.

4. In dealing with the subject matter of the paper I propose in the first instance to refer to the various steps which have already been taken by the Institute and other bodies to secure uniformity in the stating and keeping of accounts.

5. The first reference I can find in the history of the Institute is in 1889 when a paper entitled "Uniformity in the Form of Abstracts of Accounts," was read at the 4th Annual Meeting at Derby by the late Mr. Geo. Swainson, then Borough Treasurer of Bolton. In his paper Mr. Swainson indicated that a strong feeling was then growing that an effort should be made by the Institute to frame some uniform system of Corporate Bookkeeping with special regard to clearness and simplicity. He quoted an opinion from Burdett's Official Intelligence for 1889 that the desirability of securing a uniform system of accounts for Corporations throughout the kingdom was of paramount importance and should be dealt with by public Statute. The Institute was urged by the Editor of that publication to approach the Central Authority in London to try and arrange the actual form in which the Accounts should appear. Apparently at that time Accountants throughout the country had been discussing the subject from an auditor's point of view, pointing out serious faults which existed in the form of some Corporation accounts making it impossible to prepare an accurate Balance Sheet of their Assets and Liabilities. Curiously enough an eminent accountant giving evidence recently before a Parliamentary Committee has expressed the view that the present day system of local authority accounting does not give a true picture of whether they are making profits or losses. One does not of course necessarily agree with this statement.

6. Resulting from Mr. Swainson's paper the matter was referred to the Executive Committee of the Institute for action to be taken.

7. The report of the Proceedings of the Annual General Meeting in 1890 contains the following statement by the President:—

"The year which has just closed has been an unusually active one for the Committee. As directed at the last Annual Meeting they have taken in hand the difficult question of "Uniformity in Corporation Accounts." After thoroughly discussing the matter they considered the best way to deal with it was to settle main principles, and then recommend (which is all they can do) that such principles be adopted in all Boroughs where they are not already in vogue. The following circular was sent out to each Accountant or Treasurer who was a member of the Institute, giving the results of the Committee's deliberations, and asking for his support in carrying them into practice.

CORPORATE TREASURERS' AND ACCOUNTANTS' INSTITUTE.

Town Hall,
Blackburn,
24th October, 1889.

DEAR SIR,

For some time the Committee of your Institute have had under their consideration the question of the lack of uniformity in Corporation Accounts, and particularly in the form of publishing the Abstracts of Accounts. From enquiries made, the Committee find that many of the most important Corporations already include in their Annual Statements the whole Income and Expenditure of each year, although in some cases such statements when shown in the published accounts are still headed "Receipts and Payments." On the other hand, some Corporations merely keep their accounts on a cash basis, ignoring important items relating to the outstanding Assets and Liabilities at the end of the financial year. The Committee are fully convinced that the proper plan of keeping the whole of the Accounts of every Corporation is that of including the Income and Expenditure of each year, the Income being shown on the right-hand page of the published Abstract and the Expenditure on the left-hand page. Each set of Accounts should include a Balance Sheet, embodying the whole of the Ledger Balances, the stock of Stores, the outstanding Liabilities and Assets which should include outstanding (and collectable) rates, and the balance shown on the Revenue Account. It is desirable that there should be shown for every Fund, a Revenue Account, a Capital Account, and a Balance Sheet. It is also desirable that a General or Aggregate Balance Sheet should be inserted in every Abstract. The Borrowing Powers, Capital Expenditure, and Sinking Funds, should also be clearly shown.

I am desired by the Committee of the Institute to ask each member to be good enough to loyally co-operate with them in their efforts to remove a palpable blot which has existed in many Corporation Accounts, for a long period. I have to ask that you will when you arrive at the end of your present financial year, as far as the circumstances of your case will allow, adopt the above suggestions if you have not already done so.

I am, Sir,

Yours faithfully,

J. H. BAILEY, *Hon. Sec.*

The Committee are satisfied that if these recommendations are carried out, it will be an easy matter for any gentleman interested in Corporation Accounts, to pick up at random the "Abstract" from any Borough and compare any item of Expenditure or Receipt contained therein with that of his own or any other Borough, and feel satisfied that the figures given are all upon one common basis. No doubt some Boroughs will not be able to see their way to adopt all the recommendations at once, but in a few years they will doubtless be brought to see the advantage of doing so."

8. An eminent statesman once remarked that reforms could be secured forty years after everybody had agreed upon them. The time, therefore, is now ripe for a further step forward by the Institute, because it will be generally admitted the desirable comparison referred to in the last paragraph of the extract is not yet possible. Incredible as it seems, there are still important Local Authorities whose accounts are published on the "Receipts and Payments" system.

9. In 1903 the Joint Select Committee on Municipal Trading reported as follows:—

> ". . . in view of the ever-increasing number and magnitude of municipal undertakings, it is most desirable that a high and uniform standard of account keeping should prevail throughout the country.
>
> The Committee are doubtful whether it would be possible to prescribe a standard form of keeping accounts for all municipal or other Local Authorities, having regard to the varying conditions existing in different districts. But they recommend that the Local Government Departments should invite the Institute of Chartered Accountants, the Incorporated Society of Accountants and Auditors, and the Institute of Municipal Treasurers and Accountants of England and Wales and the Society of Accountants, Glasgow, to confer and report upon the matter."

10. So far as I can ascertain, the recommendation referred to was not proceeded with, but in 1906 the President of the Local Government Board appointed a Departmental Committee to enquire and report on the system of account keeping of Local Authorities, and to recommend regulations which should be made, regard being had to the necessity for showing accurately the amounts raised by local taxation and the purposes for which they are applied.

11. The Institute was represented on this Departmental Committee (though only indirectly) by the late Mr. Richard Barrow,

City Controller of Liverpool (appointed as a representative of the Association of Municipal Corporations) and the late Mr. J. J. Burnley, Accountant of the Wallasey Urban District Council (representing the Urban District Councils Association).

12. The Committee, after hearing evidence (including representatives of the Institute) issued its Report in 1907, from which the following extracts are taken :—

> "It is evident that the accounts of Local Authorities are not kept on any uniform system, but on various systems.
>
> "The chief causes of this want of uniformity are (*a*) the vague terminology of Acts of Parliament, (*b*) the absence of sufficiently precise regulations and definitions, and (*c*) the increasing sense of the inadequacy of the purely cash system of account-keeping.
>
> "The returns and financial statements furnished to the Local Government Board are compiled from data derived from different systems of accounts, and the statistical information thus obtained is not uniform.
>
> "The Committee find that there is a substantial unanimity of opinion that uniformity is desirable, so far as it can be attained, both as regards the system on which the accounts of local authorities should be kept and *as regards the form of their publication*.
>
> "With regard to the system of the accounts, we are firmly convinced that general principles such as have been laid down in this Report should be clearly defined by regulation. In our opinion, it is both unnecessary and impracticable to attempt to insist upon a stereotyped uniformity, provided the careful observance of the general principles is secured.
>
> "Uniformity in the published abstracts of the accounts can be largely obtained. The differences are so many and so various in local conditions, in the requirements of local Acts, in methods of valuation, assessment and rating, and in many circumstances which cannot possibly be explained on the face of the

accounts, that direct comparisons may often be fallacious and misleading. But such uniformity as can be obtained is no doubt desirable in itself: the possibility of comparison, even if incomplete, tends to foster interest in the accounts, and to stimulate criticism and investigation which may lead to substantial improvements in administration.

"It is generally agreed that as wide publicity as is practicable should be given to the accounts of local authorities, and that they should be published in such form as to be intelligible to ratepayers possessed of average ability but without special knowledge of accountancy. A short newspaper summary may be suitable for most rural districts, but is obviously insufficient for the needs of a large county or a large borough, or an important urban district. On the other hand, some large authorities appear to have recognised that a full abstract of their accounts is not adapted to the requirements of the ordinary ratepayer, and have published a short summary in addition.

"The Committee consider that all local authorities of importance should be required to publish a short epitome of their accounts and a balance sheet, either in newspapers or in such form as is capable of wide distribution, and that in addition, all County and Borough Councils, and also authorities of other classes who possess any of the principal trading undertakings, should be required to prepare a fuller abstract of their accounts for distribution at a reasonable price to such ratepayers as may wish for it.

"We are, however, strongly of opinion that in any abstract of the accounts a great mass of detail is much to be deprecated. It renders the accounts confusing and unintelligible to the ordinary ratepayer; while those more skilled in matters of account should be enabled to ascertain any particulars they may require, without undue difficulty, by inspection of the accounts themselves.

STANDARDISATION OF ABSTRACTS OF ACCOUNTS—(*continued*).

"Complete uniformity in the presentment of accounts to ratepayers is not attainable; but it is important that the accounts should be published in a simple and easily intelligible form, and the more important authorities should also prepare fuller abstracts of their accounts for the use of ratepayers who require further information.

"The Committee are of opinion that regulations based generally upon the considerations presented in this Report should be drawn up and embodied in General Orders of the Local Government Board.

"The principles to be followed in the preparation of the chief accounts, balance sheets and published abstracts of each authority should be clearly set out; and generally the regulations should be designed to ensure as great a measure of uniformity in the presentation of accounts as may be obtained under varying local conditions.

"In the opinion of the Committee the regulations should deal with the form in which the abstracts of the accounts of the local authorities are to be published; for it is highly desirable that one pattern for each class of authority should be followed in the outline and arrangement of these abstracts, with a view to making them as useful and easy of comprehension to all persons interested therein as is possible.

"The essential elements of a proper abstract must comprise sufficiently detailed income and expenditure accounts for each separate fund (including the revenue and net revenue accounts of each trading undertaking, the capital and loan expenditure accounts, and accounts of the sinking funds and reserve funds); a short summary of all the income and expenditure; the separate and aggregate balance sheets; and a tabular statement in regard to the authorised loans and the provision made for their repayments.

"The regulations should not preclude any reasonable subdivision of the entries, provided the standard arrangement be preserved, nor the addition of statements giving information upon any special matters which local circumstances may render desirable.

"We believe that clear regulations on the lines here indicated will not only secure the preparation of the accounts on uniform principles and their publication in an easily intelligible form, but will also furnish both the staff and the authority and the auditors with adequate means for verifying their accuracy and completeness.

"We may perhaps be permitted to draw attention to certain points on which some alteration of the existing statutes may be involved in giving the fullest effect to our recommendations.

> (1) It is desirable that the system of account for all local authorities should be prescribed by one central authority. This power of regulation should be wide enough to ensure the preparation of accounts on sound and uniform principles, especially where statements of profit and loss are required; the satisfactory treatment of estimates for rates and their deposit for inspection by ratepayers; the due certification of the accounts by or on behalf of the local authority, and the proper distribution of the duties in regard to their preparation, their completion for audit within a reasonable period, and their publication in uniform and intelligible shape.
>
> (2) If it is held that in any case the statutory provisions do not admit of accounts being prescribed on a system of "income and expenditure," as distinguished from systems of "receipts and payments" or "receipts and expenditure," amendment would appear to be necessary; and similar amendment may be requisite in connection with the financial statements and local taxation returns."

13. Although much water has flowed under the bridges since the Report was issued many of the observations of the Departmental Committee are as true to-day as in 1907, and although great improvements have undoubtedly been made on the lines indicated by the

Departmental Committee yet much remains to be done to attain the standard of uniformity which the Committee stated could be largely obtained.

14. In discussing standardisation it must be remembered that Local Authorities are not free agents to devise and publish the whole of their accounts in the particular form which may appeal to them. The task of standardisation is complicated by the provisions of numerous Acts of Parliament and Ministerial Regulations issued under the authority of Acts of Parliament which must be complied with. For a proper consideration of the subject it is therefore necessary to draw attention to limitations imposed by the Statutes and Orders.

15. The following references to Statutory Enactments will, I think, be found complete.

ENGLAND AND WALES.

(1) *The Local Taxation Returns Acts*, 1860-1877, provide for a Return of sums levied or received by local authorities in respect of rates, etc., and of the expenditure thereof to be made annually to the Minister of Health in such form as the Minister may require.

(2) *The Public Health Act*, 1875, provides that where an urban authority are the council of a borough the accounts of its receipts and expenditure under this Act shall be published in like manner and at the same time as the municipal accounts. The same Act further provides that where an urban authority is *not* the council of a borough, the clerk of the authority shall publish an abstract of the accounts in some one or more of the local newspapers circulating in the district. These provisions are modified by the Fifth Schedule to the Local Authorities (Audit) Order, 1928, which provides that

(a) the council of a borough as respects such of their accounts as are subject to audit by a district auditor ;

(b) every district council not being the council of a borough

may on the completion of the audit, if they think fit, in lieu of publishing an abstract of their accounts in some one or more of the local newspapers, cause to be advertised in one or more of those newspapers notice that the audit had been completed and that the audited accounts, etc., will be open for inspection by any ratepayer within the period of fourteen days from some later date mentioned in the notice.

(3) *The District Auditors' Act*, 1879, confers on the Minister of Health powers from time to time to make, revoke, or vary such regulations as seem to him necessary or proper, respecting the audit and manner of keeping the accounts of any local authority subject by law to be audited by a district auditor. The Minister may prescribe the form of keeping such accounts.

(4) Under the *Municipal Corporations Act*, 1882, a full abstract of the borough treasurer's accounts for each year is to be printed after audit. Such abstract is to be open to the inspection of all ratepayers of the borough and copies thereof shall be delivered to a ratepayer on payment of a reasonable price for each copy.

(5) By the *Local Government Act*, 1888, the accounts of the receipts and expenditure of County Councils are to be made up to the end of each local financial year in a form prescribed by the Minister of Health. The provisions of the Municipal Corporations Act 1882 with respect to the accounts of the treasurer of a borough and to the inspection and abstract thereof apply to the accounts of a county council.

(6) *The Local Government Act*, 1894, provides that the enactments relating to the accounts of Urban Sanitary Authorties and to all matters incidental thereto and consequential thereon shall apply to the accounts of the receipts and payments of parish and district councils and parish meetings. Power was given by the Act to the Local Government Board to make rules modifying the enactments relating (*inter alia*) to the publication of Abstracts of Accounts, and this power was exercised in the General Order *re* Audit of Accounts, 1895,

which provides that every rural district council shall, on the completion of the audit, publish an abstract of their accounts in some one or more of the local newspapers circulated in the district, but parish councils are relieved of the obligation to publish an abstract of accounts.

(7) *The London Government Act*, 1899, provides that the accounts of every Metropolitan Borough Council shall be made up and audited in like manner and subject to the same provisions as the accounts of the County Council and the enactments relating to the audit of those accounts and to all matters incidental thereto and consequential thereon shall apply accordingly.

(8) *The Education Acts*, 1902 *and* 1921, enact that separate accounts are to be kept by the council of a borough of their receipts and expenditure under the Acts and that the statutes relating to the accounts of a county council including all matters incidental thereto and consequential thereon shall apply in lieu of the provisions of the Municipal Corporations Act, 1882, relating to accounts and audit.

(9) *Rating and Valuation Act*, 1925. A big step forward towards uniformity of accounts is due to the provisions of Section 10 of the Rating and Valuation Act, 1925, which provided for the unification of the then existing separate rate funds into one General Rate Fund.

(10) Section 17 of the *Local Government Act*, 1929, provides that separate accounts shall be kept by the Council of every County Borough of their receipts and expenditure in connection with Public Assistance and these accounts are to be made up and audited and be subject to the same provisions as in the case of a County Council and all enactments relating to the accounts of a County Council including all matters incidental thereto and consequential thereon shall apply.

Particular attention is drawn to the omnibus nature of Section 51 of the Local Government Act, 1929, which provides as follows :—

STANDARDISATION OF ABSTRACTS OF ACCOUNTS—(*continued*).

"The Council of any County or County Borough, or of any district, and the Common Council of the City of London and Council of any Metropolitan Borough and any joint Committee or Joint Board appointed jointly by any two or more Councils as aforesaid shall make to the Minister such reports and returns and give him such information with respect to their functions as he may require. This Section shall extend to the County of London."

(11) By the *Electricity (Supply) Act*, 1919, joint electricity authorities and authorised undertakers must furnish to the Electricity Commissioners such accounts, statistics and returns and in such form as the Commissioners may require.

(12) Under the *Gas Regulation Act*, 1920, all gas undertakers must furnish to the Board of Trade at such times and in such forms as the Board may direct an annual account and such statistics and returns as the Board may require. A copy of the annual account must be sent to the local authority of the area of supply and copies are to be placed on sale at a price not exceeding one shilling per copy.

(13) *The Waterworks Clauses Act*, 1847, requires an annual abstract of the receipts and expenditure of water undertakers to be prepared and certified, and a copy sent to the clerk of the peace for the county.

(14) *The Tramways Act*, 1870, enacts that a Local Authority shall keep separate accounts of all monies paid by them in applying for, obtaining, and carrying into effect a provisional order obtained under the Act and in the repayment of monies borrowed, and of all monies received by them by way of rent or tolls in respect of the Tramways authorised thereby.

SCOTLAND.

(1) The *Local Government (Scotland) Act*, 1889, provides that the Accounts of the receipts and expenditure of a County Council shall be made up and balanced to the 15th May in

every year in such form as the Secretary for Scotland shall prescribe. The Act authorises the Secretary for Scotland to prescribe the form of abstract of accounts and in pursuance of this power such a form has duly been prescribed.

(2) The accounts of Burghs in Scotland are regulated by the *Town Councils (Scotland) Act*, 1900, which laid down in some degree of detail the accounts to be kept and required that such accounts should exhibit a complete state of affairs. The Secretary for Scotland in 1902 prescribed a model form for Burgh accounts in accordance with the powers given to him in that behalf, but this has been revoked in favour of a new model form, incorporating the changes necessitated by the Local Government (Scotland) Act, 1929, and published in November, 1930.

(3) The Third Schedule to the *Local Government (Scotland), Act*, 1929, provides that an Abstract of the Accounts of every County Council and Town Council shall be made up, balanced and signed in such manner as the Secretary of State may prescribe.

16. The foregoing statutory provisions have been amplified and/or modified by a series of Statutory Rules and Orders which prescribe in some measure of detail the forms of accounts to which they relate. In a number of cases the prescribed form has become the basis for the publication of those accounts in the Abstract (*e.g.*, Housing (Assisted Scheme) Accounts) and to that extent has been the means of achieving a high degree of uniformity. Scotland appears to be in advance of England as model forms and abstracts have been prescribed by the Central Departments.

17. The following is a list of the Statutory Rules and Orders in force in England and Wales which I believe is comprehensive :—

Local Government Board.—General Order—Accounts (Urban District Councils, etc.), 22nd March, 1880.

Local Government Board.—General Order—Accounts (Urban District Councils, etc.), 8th March, 1881.

STANDARDISATION OF ABSTRACTS OF ACCOUNTS—(*continued*).

Local Government Board.—General Order—Accounts (Port Sanitary Authorities), 28th February, 1896.

Local Government Board.—General Order—Accounts (Metropolitan Boroughs), 26th March, 1901.

Electricity Commissioners—Form of Statement of Accounts for Electric Lighting Undertakings, 1919.

Ministry of Health.—Housing Accounts Order, 31st March, 1920.

Ministry of Health.—Financial Statements Order, 14th December, 1921.

Ministry of Health.—Rate Accounts (Boroughs and Urban District Councils) Order, 30th September, 1926.

Ministry of Health.—Local Authorities (Audit) Order, 19th March, 1928.

Ministry of Health.—Accounts (Boroughs and Metropolitan Boroughs) Regulations, 23rd January, 1930.

Ministry of Health.—Public Assistance Accounts (County Councils) Regulations, 23rd January, 1930.

18. It will thus be seen that various Government Departments have been given powers relating to the Accounts of Local Authorities. This in itself increases the difficulty of attaining complete standardisation. It seems a matter for regret that the function of co-ordinating the accounting practice of the various local authorities is not centralised in one Government Department instead of being divided between the Ministry of Health, the Electricity Commissioners, the Board of Trade, and so on. The Departmental Committee, whose Report I have referred to, contemplated that the accounts of local authorities should be prescribed by one central authority with wide powers to ensure the presentment of accounts on sound and uniform principles. It is also a point for criticism that the audit system of Local Authorities' Accounts is not unified. While the accounts of County Councils, Urban and Rural District Councils and Metropolitan Borough Councils are audited throughout

by the staff of the Minister of Health, those of Boroughs are partly audited by the District Auditors of the Ministry of Health and partly by independent Professional Auditors as well as the so-called "audit" of Elective Auditors. The system of audit in Scotland is again on different lines. A more general use should be made of the services of Chartered and Incorporated Accountants practising throughout the Country. In addition to bringing their experience in the audit of commercial businesses to bear it would undoubtedly assist in the earlier publication of Abstracts of Accounts or at any rate remove the unsatisfactory feature which exists to-day of accounts being published " subject to Audit."

19. Arising out of the deliberations of the Departmental Committee of 1907, certain standard forms of account were recommended for use, and in 1913 as a result of careful consideration, this Institute published suggested Standard Forms for the following Accounts, *viz.* :—

(*a*) Borough Fund (Revenue) Account.

(*b*) Borough Fund (Capital) Account.

(*c*) General District Fund (Revenue) Account.

(*d*) General District Fund (Capital) Account.

(*e*) Borough or General District Fund Balance Sheet.

(*f*) Exchequer Contribution Account.

(*g*) Burial Board Fund Accounts.

(*h*) Public Libraries (Revenue) Account.

(*i*) Baths (Revenue) Account.

(*j*) Markets (Revenue) Account.

(*k*) Small Holdings, etc. (Revenue and Capital) Accounts.

20. This at the time was considered a substantial contribution to the work commenced in 1905.

21. Since that date standard forms of account have been issued as follows :—

STANDARDISATION OF ABSTRACTS OF ACCOUNTS—(*continued*).

(1) The Epitome of Accounts (in place of the former " A " and " B," Return under the Local Taxation Returns Acts) introduced by the Minister of Health in 1921.

(2) Abstract of Stock and Redemption Fund Accounts—Minister of Health.

(3) Annual Return of Sinking Funds and Instalments—Minister of Health.

(4) Form of Accounts for Electrical Undertakings originally prescribed by the Board of Trade in 1882 and since revised by the Electricity Commissioners.

(5) Electricity Statistical Return prescribed by the Electricity Commissioners in 1919.

(6) Statistical Return for Electricity Supply in Rural Areas prescribed by the Electricity Commissioners.

(7) Home Office Annual Financial Statement *re* Cost of Police.

(8) Ministry of Transport Summary of Expenditure *re* Highways and Bridges.

(9) Return *re* Gas Undertakings prescribed by Board of Trade in 1920.

(10) Form of Annual Return, etc., for Tramways and Trackless Trolley Undertakings published under the auspices of the Ministry of Transport in 1923.

(11) Forms *re* Costs of Collection and Disposal of Refuse and Street Cleansing, published by the Ministry of Health in 1926.

(12) Forms of Accounts and Estimates for Libraries and Museums, drawn up by the I.M.T.A., in conjunction with the Libraries Association and the Museums Association in 1926.

(13) Forms of Accounts *re* Sale of Electricity Fittings, etc., published by the I.M.T.A., June, 1928.

(14) Consolidated Loans Fund—Model Scheme including *pro forma* Accounts published by the I.M.T.A., in May, 1929.

Q*

STANDARDISATION OF ABSTRACTS OF ACCOUNTS—(*continued*).

(15) Form of Accounts for Municipal Omnibus Undertakings--published by the I.M.T.A. in conjunction with the Municipal Tramways Association, October, 1929.

(16) Memorandum, etc., *re* Public Assistance Accounts, published by the I.M.T.A. in conjunction with the County Accountants Society, February, 1930.

(17) Form *re* Costs of Sewage Disposal Works—issued by the Ministry of Health after consultation with the I.M.T.A. and the Sewage Disposal Works Managers' Association, in January, 1931.

(18) Form of Accounts for Income and Expenditure in respect of Poor Relief, together with Costing Returns for Institutional Relief, Residential Treatment of Tuberculosis, Maternity Homes and General Hospitals, published by the Ministry of Health, May, 1931.

22. Before discussing the subject further it may be useful to attempt to set out the principal objects intended to be achieved by the Standardisation of published Accounts. These may be summarised as being :—

(1) To make the financial result of the services operated by local authorities available for the purposes of comparison :—

(*a*) As between one year and another.

(*b*) As between area and area throughout the Country, thereby tending to promote a wider and deeper interest in local affairs.

(2) To assist in an earlier publication of the Accounts.

(3) In some measure at least to reduce the number of Returns now required by Government Departments.

(4) To enable the appropriate Government Departments to produce with accuracy and dispatch grouped statistics relating to locally operated services.

(5) To afford Councillors and Officials a convenient and ready means of reference for information required from day to day in the course of their duties.

(6) To make more general the preparation and publication of detailed statements based on "unit costs" which constitute a valuable means of comparison, thereby encouraging both Councillors and Officials to take a keener interest in their work. (The Ministry of Health has stated that the costing of the Public Cleansing Service has helped to reduce expenditure and obtain a higher standard of service).

(7) To afford opportunities to civic workers and economists to arrive at reliable deductions, to prevent misleading figures being quoted, and to minimise as far as possible misrepresentation of facts.

(8) Since it is eminently desirable in the best interests of Local Government that there should be a free interchange of officers, to overcome the initial difficulties of officers new to their posts.

23. Against these undoubted advantages must be set the possible danger of stagnation which is present in most forms of standardisation. While the main principles may and should be closely defined there should not be a too rigid insistence upon detail. Sufficient scope should be left for each Financial Officer to express his own initiative and individuality within the limits of the main principles.

Suggested Form of Standardised Abstract.

24. It is with great trepidation that I embark upon suggestions for a model form of Standardised Abstract, but this paper will fail in its purpose unless some indication is given of a possible solution of the problem. If my suggestions do not find favour with the Conference the criticism which results will, I hope, be of such a constructive character that the object of the paper will be thereby indirectly achieved.

25. A Model Form of Standardised Abstract of Accounts on broad lines will consist of the following sections :—

(1). A concise and non-technical Summary or Epitome of the accounts of the Local Authority which can be issued separately in booklet form as well as forming a part of the Abstract.

(2). The Accounts of Trading Undertakings.

(3). The Accounts of those non-trading services for which separate accounts must be kept and which it is desirable to state separately from the Non-trading services comprised within the General Rate Fund.

(4). The Accounts of the General Rate Fund.

(5). Consolidated Loans Accounts.

(6). The Accounts of the Rating Authority.

(7). The Accounts of the Superannuation Fund.

(8). The Aggregate Balance Sheet.

(9). A Statement as to Borrowing Powers, Loans, and Sinking Funds.

(10). A Statistical Appendix.

(11). A detailed Index.

The foregoing is suggested as an arrangement which will embrace the functions of almost all authorities.

Section 1.—Summary or Epitome.

26. Under the provisions of the Local Taxation Returns Acts, 1860, and 1877, and other enactments certain Returns as to local expenditure must be submitted to the Ministry of Health. In 1920/21 and 1921/22 the Ministry, after consulting the Council of the Institute, issued a revised and less complicated form of Return than had hitherto been in use.

27. The Ministry indicated that in revising the Return which is now designated " Epitome of Accounts " not only had the requirements of the Government been considered, but also the desirability of interesting ratepayers in the finance of their local authorities had been kept in mind. The Ministry therefore suggested that it may become the practice for each Council to publish the Epitome, contained in a few pages, for the information of the ratepayers. Certain local authorities now make a practice of doing this.

28. Whilst in entire agreement with the object of the Ministry, I am of the opinion, however, that the Ministry's form is still too technical and cumbersome for the purpose of interesting ratepayers, and further it suffers from the serious disadvantage that comparable figures for previous years are not included.

29. I suggest that the ideal form of Epitome should consist of a series of concise tabulated statements drawn up in as simple a form as possible—each table dealing with one phase only of the financial operations of the Authority.

Table 1 may comprise general " key " statistics as to area, population, valuation, total indebtedness, amount of Rates, Product of 1d. Rate, etc., and should comprise comparable figures for each of five years.

Table 2 should detail for a period of five years the surplus or deficiency of each of the Funds which are kept, and also the balance standing to the credit of the Reserve or Renewals Accounts. The totals should be linked up and referenced to the Aggregate Balance Sheet.

Table 3 might show, with comparable figures for the previous year, a summary of the income and expenditure of the principal non-trading services, *e.g.*, Health, Highways, Police, Education, etc., provided by the Corporation, with equivalent in Rate poundage. Details of the amounts contributed in rate relief by trading undertakings, and any deficiencies on such undertakings charged to rates should be included. The Statement should be completed by inserting the amount added to or taken from balances, and be reconciled with the actual true product of the rate levied.

Table 4 would be confined to the affairs of the Trading Undertakings, and show the Gross Profit from each, and how such gross profit has been appropriated. The position of the Reserve Funds, the Capital Expenditure, and the Debt should also be summarised. This Table would also give comparative figures for two years. An additional Table might be utilised to tabulate the results of each of the Trading Departments for a period of five years, including unit costs. It is surely more illuminating and interesting to show, for example, that the expenditure on generating and distributing electricity has *decreased* from 1·26 pence to ·74 pence per unit in a period of five years, than simply to record that the expenditure has *increased* from £100,155 to £145,157.

Table 5 might be used to summarise the accounts and statistics in respect of all Housing operations.

Table 6 may give in condensed form the transactions relating to Education.

Table 7 should be utilised to summarise the cost of Public Assistance.

Table 8 could usefully record in a few lines the total capital expenditure of each Fund at the end of the previous year, and the amount expended in the year of review.

Table 9 would deal with the Net Debt of each fund at the end of the previous year, and show how this has increased or decreased at the end of the current year. A column could usefully be added to show the amount which has had to be provided from Revenue to meet the interest and repayment charges during the year.

Table 10 might group together for each of the principal services (including trading undertakings) the amounts paid during the year for Interest on Debt, and the amount charged to the Revenue Account for redemption.

Table 11 may be a summary showing the extent to which the funds of the Authority have been assisted from the National Exchequer.

Table 12 could be a statement giving details of all Loan Sanctions received during the financial year. This is useful, both for reference purposes and for indicating to members of the public the channels into which the new activities of the council have been directed.

Table 13. The Tables would be completed by a print of the Aggregate Balance Sheet.

30. Each of the Tables should be referenced to the Abstract proper, and in every respect " tie up " thereto, so that if, for any purpose further details are required, these can be readily inspected.

31. The aim of the Tables or Epitome should be clarity and simplicity, and the danger of over-elaboration should be avoided. It is not intended that the Epitome should in itself become a miniature Abstract of Accounts. When issued as a separate booklet, the Tables may be accompanied by a short preface by the Chief Financial Officer, in which special attention could be drawn to any current outstanding features in the Accounts.

32. As a preliminary to discussing the remaining sections forming the Abstract, I propose to make one or two general observations which apply more or less to all the Accounts.

33. An examination of a number of Abstracts of Accounts discloses a noticeable lack of uniformity in the stating of Balance Sheets, so far as Capital Outlay is concerned. Four methods appear to be in use :—

(*a*) Capital Outlay shown at cost price.

(*b*) Capital Outlay shown at cost price, less loans redeemed.

(*c*) A combination of (*a*) and (*b*)—method (*a*) being applied to realisable assets and method (*b*) to unrealisable assets.

(*d*) Assets shown at a valuation.

In some towns no deductions are made when assets are alienated or exhausted—in others the amount of the outlay is eliminated when such is the case. In the case of Housing " Deferred Charges " are, by Ministry of Health regulations, written down annually.

34. For the purpose of the official accounts, my personal view is that valuation should not be resorted to, though, if desired, a note could be inserted on the Balance Sheet to show the market value. Objection can also be urged to the writing down of " non-realisable " assets by the amount of loan repayments. The value to the community of a non-realisable asset, such as a sewer, may actually increase year by year, and certainly may have an effective value long after the loan period has expired. I consider that the most satisfactory basis for the stating of Capital Outlay in all cases should be " cost price," and that when an asset is exhausted or alienated, its original cost should be removed from the Balance Sheet. I am aware that marked differences of opinion exist on this aspect of municipal finance ; this, however, is no excuse for lack of uniformity, the majority opinion should rule.

35. Another feature of the Accounts upon which there is no standard practice is the treatment of general establishment and standing charges. These charges should be grouped under one heading in the General Rate Fund, and each of the trading undertakings with such principal services as Housing, Education, Public Assistance, etc. should bear a proper share. The amount transferred to each service should be clearly shown as a deduction from the expenditure with a reference to the folio of the Abstract where the amount transferred appears.

36. Care should be taken that each Trading Undertaking is properly assessed for rating purposes. It is always a point of criticism that Trading Accounts of local authorities are not comparable with public companies as the former are unfairly relieved of charges which a Company would have to bear. The fact that payments are " out of one pocket into another " should not affect a

proper allocation of expenditure. The same remarks apply to all accounts—any department purchasing a commodity from another should always pay a fair price.

37. Investments which are almost invariably stated at cost price should in addition show the nominal amount of the security and as a note the stock exchange market value at the year end.

38. In the case of all accounts the comparable figures for the previous year should be given.

39. It is perhaps hardly necessary to add that the basis of all accounts should be "income and expenditure" and not "receipts and payments."

40. The amount of detail recorded in published Abstracts varies enormously in different towns. The value of an Abstract does not increase in proportion to the number of pages it contains—rather the reverse—and therefore non-essential detail should be ruthlessly cut out. The aim should be to produce a volume of convenient size. Much could be done if careful attention was paid to size of type and quality of paper.

Section 2.—Accounts of Trading Undertakings.

41. Generally speaking there is already a substantial degree of uniformity in the presentation of these accounts. The accounts of each Undertaking should be presented in the following order :—

(1) Revenue Account.

(2) Net Revenue Account.

(3) Net Revenue Appropriation Account.

(4) Reserve or Renewals Fund Account.

(5) Sinking Fund Account.

(6) Capital Account.

(7) Balance Sheet.

In each case the comparable figures for the previous year should be given and in the case of the Revenue and Net Revenue Accounts against each item in the accounts should be shown the appropriate unit equivalent, *i.e.*, per unit sold for Electricity, per car or bus mile in the case of Transport, etc.

42. Private Trading Companies, as a rule, give a minimum of information in their accounts to the public, the excuse being that they do not wish to convey valuable information as to their costs to their competitors. This perfectly good excuse for Companies is an equally good reason why local authorities accounts should be published in such a way as will facilitate comparison.

Section 3.—Education, Housing and Public Assistance Accounts.

43. The expenditure on these services involves a considerable call on the public purse. Standard forms have already been published and no further comment is therefore necessary.

Section 4.—The Accounts of the General Rate Fund.

44. It is in this Section that the greatest lack of uniformity prevails so far as the order in which the expenditure and income is stated. I see no precise virtue in any particular order. It is of little moment whether Public Health precedes Highways or *vice versa*, but it will be convenient to adopt the order followed in the Ministry of Health epitome of accounts. For purely local reasons it may be thought more convenient to group the services under headings of the Committees responsible for their administration. The duties allocated to Committees in various towns, however, differ considerably, and as for comparative purposes the cost of the service is more important than the expenditure of any particular Committee, the purely local convenience should give way in the wider interest. For the sake of comparison town with town it is obviously desirable that the same order should be followed.

45. The General Rate Fund will comprise—

(*a*) a Revenue Account which concludes with the balances brought and carried forward.

(*b*) a Sinking Fund Account,

(*c*) a Capital Account,

(*d*) a Balance Sheet

and any necessary subsidiary accounts such as Transport Renewals Funds, Plant Accounts, etc., which should be kept as few as possible.

46. The credits to the Rate Fund comprising the Rate Precept and Profits contributed from Trading Undertakings in relief of rates, etc., on the one hand, and Precepts on the Rate Fund for Education, Housing, and any calls on the Rates to meet Trading Undertaking losses on the other, should be grouped at the end of the Revenue Account.

47. The Capital Account should contain sufficient detail to show how the cost of capital works has been made up.

Section 5.—The Consolidated Loans Account.

48. This is an important section of the Abstract of Accounts and practice has proved it to be convenient that the whole of the Loans and Debt transactions should be aggregated into one set of accounts, comprising :—

(*a*) an account of Revenue transactions ;

(*b*) a Capital Account ; and

(*c*). a Balance Sheet.

No doubt as time proceeds each local authority will obtain powers to consolidate the whole of the loan operations irrespective of the class of security involved. When this eventuates the model standard form which has been prepared by the Institute and approved by the Ministry of Health will doubtless be employed. Until that day it is still possible to deal with the Loans transactions in one set of accounts.

Section 6.—*Accounts of the Rating Authority.*

49. These accounts comprising—

(*a*) Rate Income Account,

(*b*) Rate Income Appropriation Account,

(*c*) Transferred Assets Account,

(*d*) General Expenses Account, and

(*e*) Balance Sheet,

have been prescribed within recent times by the Ministry of Health with resultant uniformity in all areas.

Section 7.—*Accounts of the Superannuation Fund.*

50. There is a noticeable lack of uniformity in the manner in which these accounts are presented. The majority of Abstracts, however, show simply

(*a*) Revenue Account, and

(*b*) Balance Sheet,

and this would seem to be all that is required.

Section 8.—*The Aggregate Balance Sheet.*

51. This is a most important section of the Abstract in that it brings together the financial position of the Local Authority in respect of all its functions.

52. It is usual to find the Aggregate Balance Sheet stated in columnar form, and this, in practice, is the most convenient for reference. A convenient form of Aggregate Balance Sheet will comprise one line for each Fund and a separate column for each of the following headings :—

STANDARDISATION OF ABSTRACTS OF ACCOUNTS—(*continued*).

Left-hand Side.—Liabilities and Credits.

Column 1. Fund.
,, 2. Folio in Abstract (on which the detailed figures appear).
,, 3. Loan Debt.
,, 4. Redemption of Debt—Debt Extinguished.
,, 5. Redemption of Debt—Sinking Fund unapplied.
,, 6. Amount of Capital Expenditure met direct from Revenue and from Reserve, etc., Funds.
,, 7. Sundry Creditors on Capital Account.
,, 8. Bank and Cash on Capital Account.
,, 9. Sundry Creditors on Revenue Account.
,, 10. Bank and Cash on Revenue Account.
,, 11. Revenue Balances at credit.
,, 12. Depreciation, Renewal, and Reserve Funds—Amount at credit.
,, 13. Suspense Accounts.
,, 14. Total.

Right-hand Side.—Assets and Outlay.

Column 1. Fund.
,, 2. Folio in Abstract (on which the detailed figures can be found).
,, 3. Capital Assets and Outlay.
,, 4. Investments on Capital Account.
,, 5. Sundry Debtors, etc., on Capital Account.
,, 6. Bank and Cash, etc., on Capital Account.
,, 7. Stocks and Stores.
,, 8. Sundry Debtors on Revenue Account.
,, 9. Revenue Balances.
,, 10. Investments on Revenue Account.
,, 11. Bank and Cash on Revenue Account.
,, 12. Suspense Accounts.
,, 13. Total.

Below the totals for each of the columns can be added the comparable figures for each of the previous five years in order to indicate any significant changes during the period. After all, the Aggregate Balance Sheet is intended to give a " birds-eye " view of the financial position of the Local Authority as a whole.

Section 9.—*Statement of Borrowing Powers, Loans and Sinking Funds.*

53. No Abstract would be considered complete without a detailed statement showing how the Local Authority stands with regard to its Borrowing Powers. Each separate Borrowing Power should be recorded with the following particulars :—

1. Sanctioning Authority, Date of Sanction and Amount.
2. Period allowed for repayment.
3. Amount of Sanction exercised.
4. Total Capital Expenditure on the sanctioned work.
5. If (4) exceeds (3), amount of expenditure in excess of sanction.
6. Amount of unexpended Loans.
7. Debt redeemed.
8. Outstanding Debt.
9. Unexpired period.

A summary should be added with columns 4, 7 and 8, reconciled with the figures in the Aggregate Balance Sheet.

Section 10.—*Statistical Appendix.*

54. Apart from the Accounts of the year it is usual to include in the Abstract a collection of statistics covering a period of years. These prove valuable to show the progress of the Authority both for historical purposes and also for use in Parliamentary proceedings, etc.

The following is a statement of some useful tables :—

1. A statement recording valuation of the town and rates levied over an extended period of years.
2. Statements showing the charges for gas, water, and electricity, etc., over a period of at least five years.

3. A Schedule of Investments.

4. A Statement showing the amount of Loans falling due for repayment in each of the following 10 years.

5. A Statement showing the amount of debt which will be extinguished in each of the following 10 years.

6. Statistical Information for each of the Trading Undertakings.

7. A Schedule of property owned by the Authority.

8. A Table classifying the Rateable Value showing the number of hereditaments and the amount of rateable value in each class.

Section 11.—*Index.*

55. For all books of reference a carefully compiled Index is necessary. Having regard to the different accounts in which the same item will appear, it will save space if the index is in columnar form—with columns for Revenue Account, Capital Account, Balance Sheet, and Miscellaneous.

56. Throughout my paper I have emphasized the importance of " unit costs." Recently a publication entitled, " Aggregate Tabulations of Departmental Costs " was issued by the Corporation of the City of Dundee. This is an outstanding example of the use to be made of " unit costs." It is prefaced by the following " Foreword " of the Chairman of the Finance Committee—a clear call for a standardisation of accounts :—

> " This epitome of expenditure has been prepared in order to give a clear view of the activities of the various Departments.
>
> " Complete Departmental Costs for years prior to 1928/29 are not available for comparative purposes, but in future issues of this booklet it is intended to contrast the results of one year with those of another. These comparisons should prove most helpful, especially as exposing excesses or economies.
>
> " If, as is hoped, this or a similar form of tabulation is issued by other municipalities, more extended comparisons will be facilitated."

R

57. This booklet gives full particulars of unit costs not only for Trading Undertakings, but also for the Non-trading Services. In some instances as many as four " units " are shown for the same service.

58. At the present time " unit costs " in the published Abstracts of the great majority of towns are conspicuous by their absence; whilst even in the cases of those who do publish them, most, if not all, confine their attention to the Trading Funds.

59. It will no doubt be said that the chief difficulties at the moment are to determine the appropriate unit to be used for each particular service, and to ensure that all towns compile their costs on a strictly comparable basis. But I suggest that these difficulties are not insuperable, and that collective action on the part of the Institute is desirable and might solve the problem to the advantage of all concerned.

60. In concluding, I desire to urge the desirability of an early publication of the Abstract of Accounts. " The Accountant," in a leading article on May 23rd last, referring to this matter, stated that the average time taken by one hundred Public Companies (records for which were extracted indiscriminately) to produce their accounts was three and-a-half months after the closing of the books. As compared with this it was pointed out that the accounts of the " Big Five " Banks were all published within twenty-three days of their year end, the Railway Groups within less than two months, and the three leading Gas Companies within one month. The accounting organisation of Local Authorities should not be less efficient than the Banks, Railways, or Gas Companies, and therefore scope exists for a greater celerity in the publication of the Abstracts. The value of up-to-date information will be generally appreciated. It is the exception to find the Abstract of Accounts of any Authority published before the end of June in each year, and the average date is probably two or three months later.

STANDARDISATION OF ABSTRACTS OF ACCOUNTS—DISCUSSION.

THE PRESIDENT: The Paper is now open for discussion.

MR. SYDNEY CRESSEY (Borough Treasurer, Ealing): I should like to pay a tribute to the writer of the paper as an old student who owes a great deal in his early days to Mr. Boucher's efforts.

I must say that I wish to disagree with him on two points. Turning first to paragraph 46, he says: "The credits to the Rate Fund, comprising the Rate precept and the profits contributed from Trading Undertakings in relief of rates, etc., on the one hand, and precepts on the Rate Fund for Education, Housing, and any calls on the Rates to meet Trading Undertaking losses on the other, should be grouped at the end of the Revenue Account." The word I disagree with, and I think you will agree with me, is the word "precepts". Personally I hold the opinion that Education precepts do not exist now; it is simply a question of transfer, and in the interest of uniformity of terms, I suggest "precept" should be dropped.

Secondly, in paragraph 49 indirect reference is made to the Rate Accounts Order of 1926, an Order coming from the Ministry obviously with the intention of bringing about the standardisation of Rating Accounts, and he concludes the paragraph with the words "resultant uniformity in all areas". Personally I beg to differ from that. That order provided only for the uniformity of accounting. The first year I waited to see what was going to happen because I noticed there was no definite provision for the form of presentation. I waited for Birmingham (that is an Authority one can always rely upon, and I believe in following a good City). I copied Birmingham because I think that is as near as what was intended. Recently I reviewed twenty or thirty Abstracts and I did not find two alike in the presentation of these accounts.

I consider that standardisation cannot be brought about by agreement, but by compulsion in the way of an Order, not issued by the Ministry of Health and receiving the agreement of the Institute, but *issued by the Institute* and receiving the agreement of the Ministry of Health. Personally I find, while the Ministry have the best intention, they do not realise the necessary details.

I am very pleased to note Mr. Boucher's remarks with regard to "Epitomes of Accounts", and I shall be pleased to see that method used by the smaller authorities. I should be glad if my

(Mr. Sydney Cressey).
brother officers in non-county boroughs will see that it is issued in their own areas. That form of publication can be standardised in half-a-dozen tables. Thank you, Mr. President.

Councillor S. H. Baker (Chairman of the Finance Committee, Hornsey): I was very pleased to read this paper, Mr. President, not only because it is useful to ratepayers, but because it has an interest for me as an accountant. I, having that privilege, therefore have perhaps a better knowledge of this subject than many Chairmen of Finance Committees who come to this gathering.

Now there were one or two things which struck me in connection with the paper, to which I would like to draw your attention.

In paragraph 23 the author (and I congratulate him on this paper, which I think is quite an excellent one) states that there are disadvantages in standardisation, and there should not be too rigid insistence upon detail, and with that I agree. I hope certain latitude will be given to each Council to deal with their accounts in some different form, although in principle they should do it on the same lines.

Then in paragraph 25 the reference to the issue of an Epitome is, I think, an excellent suggestion, and is followed at any rate in the Borough and the County of which I have the pleasure and privilege of being a member.

Then he refers in paragraph 27 to a remark made by the Ministry, in which he mentions the desirability of interesting the ratepayers in the finances of their local authorities. That is really the point I want specially to speak about. Now in the accounts of industrial concerns we often use terms which we as accountants understand, but which the ordinary man does not comprehend, and I expect municipal treasurers are the same in the accounts which they issue for ratepayers. The difficulty which I have found on many occasions, and which Borough Treasurers must have found, is to train one's staff to realise that it may not be accountants who read their reports. It would be a good thing if we could remember to try and place ourselves, when we are preparing accounts or any report in connection with them, in the place of the dullest gentleman who we know is going to read our remarks. If we follow this principle we shall find that we shall prepare our figures and make our accounts so that they are understandable to all and clearer than they sometimes are even to ordinary accountants. Borough and County accounts are very complicated ; terms are used which are not usually those of the ordinary business man, and if one is not aware or has had no previous experience of them it becomes increasingly difficult to read the accounts intelligently. For instance, I recollect that when I went to Hornsey and to the County, I found myself up against many terms which I did not understand at the time. It seems absurd to you, perhaps, for me to say that when I saw the term " Borough Fund " I had to ask what it meant and what was placed there. I think it would be useful if each account were prefaced by a little statement from the Treasurer stating exactly what is placed to the Fund which the account represents, so that anybody who has no knowledge of them can get some grasp of the figures set out in the accounts.

I had difficulty to understand the County accounts when I first became a member, and I took the opportunity of making use of the good services of my friend, Mr. Rattenbury, who kindly gave me an evening and explained each account to me. That was very kind of him, as it took up a good deal of his time, and I feel if a little preface, similar to the explanation he gave me, were placed before each account, it would be a great help to those who have not an accountant-mind like you and me.

There was one other matter, Mr. President, referred to, which I want to mention, and that is in paragraph 29, the writer says :

" Table 10 might group together for each of the principal services (including trading undertakings) the amounts paid during the year for Interest on Debt, and the amount charged to the Revenue Account for redemption."

I have tried on many occasions to get a division of interest and capital payments, and I have always been told that it is very difficult to carry out, but I do think it would be far better if interest were divided from the loan repayments, and it would help to make the account clearer.

As regards paragraph 34—" I consider that the most satisfactory basis for the stating of Capital Outlay in all cases should be the ' cost price ' and that when an asset is exhausted or alienated, its original cost should be removed from the Balance Sheet." This, I think, is the soundest method of dealing with it.

(Councillor S. H. Baker).

There is one other point, and that is in paragraph 52, where the writer refers to the order of the Aggregate Balance Sheet. There are several schools of thought as to the order in which the assets should be placed in the Balance Sheet, particularly with regard to trading concerns. I, personally, and it is only an expression of opinion, at the present time believe in putting the liquid assets first. I always like to know what we have got liquid before we get to the other part. (Laughter.)

MR. A. R. A. MILLER (Borough Treasurer, Darwen) : Mr. President and Gentlemen, I was gratified to find that " Standardisation of Abstracts of Accounts " had been chosen as the subject of a paper. I entirely agree with the speakers who have paid tribute to Mr. Boucher for submitting a further valuable contribution to this " well-worn " subject.

May I be allowed a personal reference ? In October last, I was privileged to read a paper to the East Lancashire Section of the North Western Students' Society upon this subject. The title may not have been the same as that chosen by Mr. Boucher, but the subject matter was on parallel lines. In the November issue of the FINANCIAL CIRCULAR, the Editor was good enough to publish a leader upon " The Treasurer's Abstract," with particular reference to certain suggestions I made. The subject also cropped up in the three issues of the CIRCULAR immediately following. It is therefore good to find it already under the broad searchlight of an Annual Conference.

There are five points in Mr. Boucher's paper to which I would direct the attention of the Conference :

(1) In paragraph 44, it is correctly stated that the duties allocated to committees in various towns differ considerably and that whereas for purely local reasons it may be thought convenient to group the services under headings of the committees responsible for administration yet, as for comparative purposes, the cost of the service is more important than the expenditure of any particular committee; the purely local convenience should give way in the wider interest. I suggest, Mr. President, that we might first talk of " Standardisation of Committees ". " Standardisation of Accounts " would be a comparatively simple sequence. The cost

of each particular committee is a local convenience which cannot be put in the background, any more than can the cost of individual services. Why not, therefore, group in such a manner as to facilitate both requirements ?

(2) The improvements made in the Epitome in recent years amply support the belief that " Standardisation of Accounts " is a practical proposition. The manner in which the Epitome is published, however, leads me to suggest that three or four *pro forma* sets of accounts will be necessary. The county council Epitome is not suitable for a county borough, nor that of the latter authority for an urban district. The same point must of necessity apply to any publications which have for their objective standardisation.

(3) Standardisation of accounts would tend to increase the number of accounts to be published separately from the Rate Fund. This would, in itself, be a retrograde step, as an increase in the size of the Abstract would necessarily follow. I am glad Mr. Boucher points out that the value of an Abstract tends to vary inversely with the number of pages it contains.

(4) I anticipated that Mr. Boucher would have said more regarding the Accounts (Boroughs and Metropolitan Boroughs) Regulations, 1930. These Regulations go a long way towards achieving financial standardisation. If all chief financial officers would apply these Regulations to accounts not subject to district audit, standardisation would be a comparatively simple matter. Perhaps the first step should be a Ministry of Health Order, making the Regulations compulsory to all accounts of local authorities.

(5) An examination of the Statutory Rules and Orders detailed in paragraph 21 suggests that little import is paid to the balance sheet. Mr. Boucher rightly points out that uniformity in the stating of balance sheets is a necessary preliminary to standardisation, and it is regretted that this point appears to have been overlooked in the various Statutory Rules and Orders, with the notable exception of the 1930 Regulations.

After reading Mr. Boucher's paper, I picked up his Abstract of Accounts and, as expected, found that his suggested form of standardised abstract was a faithful survey of the Wallasey Abstract. That is one way of commending your own wares. This

Standardisation of Abstracts of Accounts—
Discussion (*continued*).

(Mr. A. R. A. Miller).

Conference is not the place to suggest the directions in which an abstract might be improved, but I am presuming sufficiently to mention two or three matters.

(1) *Aggregate Balance Sheet.*

(*a*) This statement forms section 8 of Mr. Boucher's model; in the majority of abstracts it is at the commencement. Probably the reason for this is the thought that the reader will consume the detail more readily once he has digested the summary of the whole position, and knows the worst.

(*b*) I hope I have misconstrued Mr. Boucher's intention, but I notice his *pro forma* aggregate balance sheet does not provide for the separate balancing of capital and revenue.

(*c*) If time permitted, I might be tempted to say why I disagree with the suggestion that the aggregate balance sheet is a most important section of the abstract.

(2) *Statement of Borrowing Powers, Loans and Sinking Funds.*

I suggest, with all deference to Mr. Boucher, that the statement outlined in paragraph 53, might be amplified by the following information :

(*a*) Unexercised Borrowing Powers ;
(*b*) Revenue, etc., Contributions ; and
(*c*) Net Loan Debt after deducting Sinking funds in hand.

(3) *Treasurer's Report.*

Apparently this " old friend " disappears. I do not think that the proposal will be received too kindly, despite the fact that the majority of reports read will not be missed. The stereotyped form year by year has long since become of no interest but I suggest that a short report, calling attention to unusual features, such as :

(*a*) any improvement in the form or re-arrangement of the accounts as compared with previous years ; and
(*b*) any outstanding financial feature of the year ;

is a desirable part of the Abstract.

STANDARDISATION OF ABSTRACTS OF ACCOUNTS—
DISCUSSION (*continued*).

(4) *Comparative Figures of previous years.*

I am in accord with comparative figures being inserted, but Mr. Boucher would rather overdo this point. For instance, what real use will the comparable figures for each of the previous five years be in the aggregate balance sheet. I also doubt whether it is in the best interest of public administration to carry the reader about too much.

In conclusion, I hope every chief financial officer present will return to his town with the intention of remodelling his abstract upon lines suitable for standardisation. This would show an earnest desire which might, in due course, come to the knowledge of "the powers that be," and lead to some definite action being taken.

MR. R. D. LAMBERT (Borough Treasurer, West Hartlepool): I do not wish to detain the meeting for a great length of time but I should like Mr. Boucher when he replies to be good enough to deal with one point in which I am very interested and which I think is one where uniformity is very desirable.

I have in mind the disposal of the results of trading undertakings. For example, I hold the view, rightly or wrongly, that a deficit or a surplus on a trading undertaking at the close of the year should remain on the accounts of that undertaking as a deficit or a surplus and be dealt with in the following year. There is no uniformity in the accounts of local authorities in that respect. In some cases a deficit is taken straight away to the debit of the Reserve Fund or the Rating Fund.

I suggest that the disposal is a matter for the Committee or Council to deal with after the closing of the accounts as is the practice in public companies. A Treasurer cannot know what may be the wishes of the Committee with regard to a deficit. In many cases it is provided by legislation that a deficit shall be met out of the rate made next after its ascertainment or out of the next following rate. It is obvious under these conditions that the Committee finally concerned with the accounts should have the right of saying whether the whole deficit is to be provided out of the next rate or the following rate, or whether part of it is to be met out of one rate and the balance out of the next following rate. Similarly with regard to surpluses. They should be left to the Committee to deal with as they think proper.

STANDARDISATION OF ABSTRACTS OF ACCOUNTS—
DISCUSSION (*continued*).

MR. J. STEWART SEGGIE (Chief Accountant, Department of Health for Scotland): Mr. President and Gentlemen: It is rather unfortunate that on the last day of your conference I should be called upon to take my place on this rostrum. I am not accustomed to being placed on the rostrum, nor am I accustomed to the hospitality I have received during the last three days. If it had been the first day of the Conference, you might have got the best from Scotland. There is a slogan "Come to Scotland" sounding at the present moment, and whilst I was listening to your discussions, it has occurred to me. If you go to Scotland, as you are going to do next year, you may certainly get some education of an instructive character to assist you in this and similar matters. (Laughter and applause.)

I have been to your conferences for five or six years and this is the first occasion I have had the privilege of listening to my own voice in your Conference meetings, and I find that the differences between Scotland and England are such that you cannot make a complete comparison in any of these matters.

I am, for instance, still at a loss to know how many different local authorities there are in England for whom accounts are necessary. Perhaps the speaker will let us know how many different classes there are, such as County Councils, Rural District Councils and Urban District Councils. I have heard of District Councils and Borough Councils and so on, but what I want to know is how many there are? The first essential, Sir, is to set out how many different local authorities' accounts are necessary, and by that I mean the different classes. In Scotland, for example, we have only three classes, the County Councils, the Burghs and the District Councils and it was a simple matter indeed, with the assistance of the Scottish Branch of the Institute to sit down and decide on a standard form for, first of all, the Housing Accounts; and then when the Act of 1929 came along, again it was a simple matter to produce a model or standard form of accounts. After getting those drafts set out we got together one or two members of the executive Committee of the Scottish Branch of the Institute and showed them what we proposed to do.

Now this big question as to whether the accounts should be on a cash basis or on an income and expenditure basis—one could go on with that question to eternity, but your whole finance with the exception of the trading undertakings is on a receipts and payments basis, and consequently to my mind, and from the point of view of the majority of the local authorities, apart from Edinburgh, Glasgow, Greenock and a few others who can prepare their accounts how they like, according to Local Acts—the principal form of setting out the accounts should be on a cash basis, and the receipts and payments system is easily understood and can be easily grasped.

Now I think in regard to this question of the standardisation of accounts, that it is a constructive question—one which has had to be considered, according to the speaker, for forty years by your Council. You have many eminent men on your Council, with great educational experience and great accounting experience. It would be the simplest thing in the world to classify your local authorities, draw out a skeleton form,get into touch with the Ministry of Health, and let them say to the Ministry : " These are the forms which we should like ; these are what the local authorities would like. Let us confer together." You will find that the Ministry of Health, as well as the Department of Health for Scotland, are only too willing to confer and co-operate in any matters which are going to be beneficial to the community at large.

I dare not speak in any detail with regard to English accounts, because if I made it appear that I knew about them, and if I gave my own view as to what to do in England, I am afraid they might lose a good man from Scotland. (Laughter.) It may be I should be sent down to the Ministry of Health to co-operate with the Institute in this great work which has been under consideration for forty years. (Applause.)

Mr. Edwin C. Riding (Borough Treasurer, Torquay) : Mr. President, I want to say at the outset how much I appreciate the excellent work which has been done by Mr. Boucher in the preparation of this paper. There are, however, one or two points on which I am not entirely in agreement with him.

I should, first of all, like to ask him what virtue there is in the actual order in which he places the accounts or funds in paragraph 25 of the paper. If there is to be uniformity in the compilation of their Abstracts in all towns, it appears to me that the General Rate Fund Account must come first. It is the one account which

(Mr. Edwin C. Riding).

is common to all Local Authorities, other than Counties, and it appears essential to me that if there is to be uniformity it must commence here.

I am afraid I shall be considered to be a " cat among the pigeons " when I say that a voluminous index to the Abstract of Accounts is pure verbiage. My view is that with a Table of Contents, and with an Epitome referenced in the way which Mr. Boucher suggests in paragraph 30, an Index can be dispensed with. It is expensive, and accounts in many instances for a big proportion of the space of the Abstract. It is far better to make the Epitome a key to the Abstract itself.

In paragraphs 51 and 52 Mr. Boucher deals with the Aggregate Balance Sheet. On consideration, I am suggesting that it is better to take the Funds in columns across the page and the details down the page. If Mr. Boucher's method is adopted, the result is a huge inset in the Abstract, and the flyleaf is very easily torn off. The accounts must of necessity be less in number than the detailed headings.

So far as the publication of the Abstract is concerned, I want it to be remembered in comparing the time involved with that of a public company, that the Corporation's Abstract consists of a considerable number of separate Funds or Undertakings. The delay is in the aggregating of these accounts, but it must be remembered that in most towns these separate funds or undertakings are published separately within a very short time after the end of the financial year. The Electricity, Water, Tramways and other accounts are presented to the respective Committees within a month or six weeks, and it is the aggregation of these accounts into a considerable volume which entails an immense amount of time in printing the whole book.

I note with regret that the Treasurer's Report in the Abstract is gradually disappearing. These Reports, to my mind, are very valuable to the ratepayers in this sense. As the average Press man would have considerable difficulty in getting a general view of the finances merely from the accounts, if the Treasurer will take the time to explain in a popular way the details and the salient features of the accounts, the Press is usually only too willing to take that Report and print it *in extenso*.

I disagree entirely with Mr. Cressey with regard to the uniformity of Rating Accounts. As is fairly well known, I have taken particular interest in the method of treatment of these Accounts, and I must confess that I was surprised after the second year—it was not fair to judge the first year because certain methods of treatment of Rating Accounts were entirely new—to find how excellently the Rating Accounts were presented and the degree of uniformity which was achieved.

Mr. Sydney Larkin (City Treasurer, Coventry): Mr. President: There is one point in Mr. Boucher's very excellent paper which possibly has been dealt with by each of the preceding speakers. (Laughter.) But in case it has not, I should like to mention it. (Laughter.) You know how heresies creep into the Church, and how difficult it is to rout them out, and unless someone has drawn attention to this particular point I think I ought to from this high eminence. (Laughter.)

Mr. Boucher has set out in his paper the accounts in the abstract, and he puts amongst them immediately before the Aggregate Balance Sheet, the accounts of the Superannuation Fund, and that rather implies—I do not think many people here think it is so—that the Superannuation Fund belongs to the Corporation. It is quite clear to me that that Fund does not belong to the Corporation, and therefore I think it would be far better if Mr. Boucher would give consideration in his revised report to the question of placing the accounts of the Superannuation Fund after the Aggregate Balance Sheet.

Mr. F. W. Rattenbury (County Accountant, Middlesex C.C.): Mr. President: It was a happy thought on your part when you asked Mr. Stewart Seggie, from over the Border, to address the Conference this morning, because, although he was speaking in a more or less foreign tongue, we were able to hear every word he said. (Laughter.) We have a great admiration for Scotland, and it was hardly necessary for Mr. Seggie to tell us that what Scotland drinks to-day, England will drink to-morrow. (Laughter.)

Mr. Sydney Baker's remarks were very much to the point. I wonder how many Financial Officers are satisfied with their Abstract of Accounts? I venture to suggest that there is not one, because

(Mr. F. W. Rattenbury).

we do realise this, that the man in the street—it is very difficult to define this term, which we keep having thrown at us—cannot possibly understand the Abstract of Accounts as published to-day, and we have been thinking and thinking for many years past how we can, by some manner of means, remedy that defect. Mr. President, I suggest that this is a matter which might very appropriately be considered by the Research Committee for which Mr. Henry Brown, of Rochester, has shown such enthusiasm.

MR. G. E. MARTIN (Borough Treasurer, Poplar) : Mr. President : There are one or two things perhaps I might call attention to in the paper.

The first is : that if standardisation ever comes about, I should like the regulations to go a little further than the paper suggests. In paragraph 50, Mr. Boucher suggests with regard to the accounts of the Superannuation Fund that the only things necessary are a Revenue Account and a Balance Sheet. I should certainly like to see it laid down with regard to this Fund that there should also be compulsory statistics. If statistics are valuable for other accounts, they certainly are essential for this account when there is an actuary who has to forecast what will happen in the future.

We have been running a Superannuation Fund in Poplar since 1911, and have always included in our Abstract financial statistics, and also what I might call vital statistics, showing the number of contributors, age groups, deaths, average age of retirement, pensioners dying, and so on. I certainly think that in years to come these statistics will be of great value, and if every Superannuation Fund compiled statistics on these lines, then the Actuaries in forty or fifty years' time will be able to check what they forecast in previous days. So I should like the regulations to go a little further on that point.

Then in paragraph 34 I notice that Mr. Boucher considers that capital outlay should be in all cases stated at cost price, and he seems to include in that such things as Highways and Sewers.

Personally I disagree, with great respect, because to make a figure of that kind of any value, you would have to include in your accounts the value of your Sewers and Highways that have been put in from time immemorial, and I cannot see that that would be possible even if it were of any value. I think that the proper method to deal with Highways and Sewers and other assets that are considered unrealisable is the method adopted in London, *i.e.*, bring them in at cost price, subject to reduction by the amount of loan repayment, so that when the loan expires the whole of the unrealisable asset is extinguished and disappears from the balance sheet.

Councillor E. C. Fawley (Member of the Finance Committee, Middlesex C.C.): I am going to speak, Mr. President, from a somewhat different angle from those who have spoken already. The greater part of my time has been spent in trying to understand municipal government, and I have had from time to time a great deal of difficulty in trying to find out what Financial Officers and others intended to imply, so that the man in the street would know what he had got to find, and when we are told, as we appear to be by the Author of this paper, that the Abstract which at one time in my memory occupied 35 pages, to-day has gone up to the enormous number of 350, all double-sized pages, I wonder whether or not it is really understood, and whether it will justify any expenditure which may be called for with a view to supplying the machinery which the officers will require for the purposes of producing the abstract.

When you talk of the man in the street, you talk of the man who looks at his demand note and says "I have £15 or £20 to pay"; and I do not think he is concerned whether it appears in an abstract of 100 or 300 pages. What he wants to see is that the officers are keeping the expenditure down to the lowest possible limit and the more figures you give the more staff you require to produce them and the larger the abstract will be and the less it will be understood. The Officer will understand it, but he is the only one who will—(Laughter)—well, of course, there is a gentleman on my left who says "perhaps?" (Laughter). Well, I agree, there are a few others who would understand it, and I count myself amongst them. (Laughter.)

But when you come back to the Council, what does it consist of? I am not going to refer to any particular body, but you have a body of perhaps 100 men and women, and you know women do not take any interest in financial questions—well, that is my experience

(Councillor E. C. Fawley).

of public bodies. Then you have about ten or twelve members of the Council who will take the trouble to understand the finance, and all they care about is how soon they can get into the meeting and how soon they can get out of it. That is what you get with the bulk of the members of public authorities—and I speak from some experience, as I have attended many bodies, such as the old London School Board, the London County Council, the old Local Boards, the District Councils and the County Council of Middlesex from the first day I sat, so I think I can say with some knowledge what local government is.

My point is this, whatever this abstract shall be, it shall be produced in the smallest possible space and give to the ratepayer knowledge of what he has got to pay.

MR. A. B. GRIFFITHS (City Treasurer, Sheffield) : Mr. President, Ladies and Gentlemen : I have been interested in Mr. Boucher's paper, and I should like to offer him my hearty congratulations.

It may be of interest if I tell you of an experience I had a few weeks ago. A business man wrote to me a kind letter after I had sent him an Abstract of Accounts and an Epitome. He sent his hearty congratulations on the Epitome, but he said the Abstract of Accounts was rather bulky. I agree with Mr. Rattenbury when he says that none of us are satisfied with our Abstract of Accounts.

There is one point upon which I should have liked Mr. Boucher's views, and that is the question of buying assets out of Revenue. Some Authorities shew Revenue contributions to Capital for all assets acquired out of Revenue, but in some instances this policy is not adopted. Where Loan Sanctions are exceeded and the excess expenditure charged to Revenue, the necessary adjustments should be made in the Balance Sheet. This also applies to new school furniture, which has been bought out of Revenue. It is advisable at the end of each financial year to take these and similar items into account, in order that the Balance Sheet may shew the exact position, but I have some doubt as to whether all Local Authorities carry this particular point far enough.

THE PRESIDENT : As no one else seems to wish to take part in the discussion, I will call on Mr. Boucher to reply to the various points raised.

Standardisation of Abstracts of Accounts—
Discussion (*continued*).

Mr. James Boucher : Mr. President : The discussion has taken quite a varied form and we have had I think some interesting contributions. Mr. Cressey, the Borough Treasurer of Ealing, who has made several useful contributions to local authority financial matters through the pages of the *Financial Circular* set the ball rolling by correcting me on one or two points. I admit the correction on paragraph 46 is merited and that it is incorrect to describe calls on the Rate Fund for Education and Housing as " precepts." Mr. Riding answered his second point and I still maintain there is substantial uniformity in the main principles of the Rating Account. I do not ask for rigid uniformity as to details but I think we should have uniformity so far as the main principles are concerned.

Mr. Councillor Sydney Baker, Chairman of the Finance Committee of Hornsey, made some interesting remarks and I agree with him that so far as possible the Abstract and especially the Epitome should be drawn up in a non-technical form. We cannot obviously get away from accepted accountancy principles so far as the Abstract proper is concerned but we have an opportunity in the Epitome to arrange matters in a different form so as to appeal to the uneducated—perhaps that is hardly the correct word to use —ratepayer who is not familiar with accountancy terms. For instance, in the main accounts we use the expression "deferred charges " for Housing. This was thrust upon us, but surely the layman cannot be expected to understand what is implied by " deferred charges." It, of course, comprises the cost of raising loans. I think we should endeavour as far as possible to use expressions which indicate as closely as possible the nature of the expenditure. Mr. Sydney Baker made a very good suggestion that the accounts might be prefaced by a short statement indicating the purpose of the accounts. We have already an example of that in the accounts of our friend Mr. Sydney Larkin of Coventry who does put a short preface before each of his accounts indicating its purpose.

I did not hear Mr. Miller's observations very clearly. He is an earnest student, and I have no doubt what he said was worth listening to. He and other speakers apparently place a good deal of importance upon a report from the Treasurer. This is all very well, but my experience is that these reports are apt to develop into

S

(Mr. James Boucher).
prosy paragraphs which leave you worse off in the end that you were before. It is a good idea if you are particularly anxious to put the financial affairs of the authority in a readable and popular form—always of course drawing attention to increases in rates and reductions in salaries—to write an article for the local newspaper which can appear after the publication of the Abstract.

Mr. Lambert of West Hartlepool asked me to deal with the treatment of trading department results and as to whether deficits or surpluses should be dealt with in the next or the following year. My view is that these should be dealt with in the year of account and I submit that while he is perfectly right in his suggestion that the Committees and Council should decide what to do with them and that the proper way is to submit the accounts in draft to the Finance Committee before they are actually closed and take instructions as to the disposal of surpluses or the method to be adopted to deal with losses. As a matter of fact I submitted the Trading Accounts of my Corporation to the Finance Committee last month and the accounts of the Rate Fund will be submitted next week and the Committee has or will give its decision as to what shall be done with the surplus or deficit. I certainly do not think deficits on trading undertakings should be carried forward year after year—I think if a deficit arises it should be dealt with at once, even at the expense of charging it to the Rates.

We had some very interesting remarks from Mr. Seggie of the Department of Health for Scotland. We are glad to hear he has enjoyed himself at Brighton, apparently not like the Englishman who went to Aberdeen and who, when asked : " How did they treat you ? " replied : " They did not." (Loud laughter). We are always willing to learn from Scotland and there is no doubt they are in some respects in advance of us so far as their accounts are concerned, but I suggest, with all respect to Mr. Seggie, that we are not willing to learn anything from Scotland on the lines of substituting a cash basis for our accounts in place of income and expenditure.

As regards the remarks of Mr. Riding of Torquay : I think he answered himself on the first point. He asked me what virtue there was in the particular order in which I placed the accounts and then went on to give us a reason for the delay in the publication of the accounts, namely, the difficulty of collecting them together for printing. The only virtue, I think, of printing the trading undertaking accounts first is that the accounts of trading undertakings are invariably ready first, and consequently we have about two-thirds of the abstract which can be printed off almost before the Rate is balanced. At any rate, before I left home one-half of my Abstract was printed, which included the trading accounts. On the question of the index, I do not think he was serious. With regard to the aggregate balance sheet, there are differences of opinion as to the form in which this should be set out. The only reason why I set out the order which I have done in the paper is that at the foot of the aggregate balance sheet I insert comparable figures for a period of three or four years, which serves a usefu purpose. Mr. Riding also referred to the Treasurer's Reports and the remarks I have already made—that the purpose could be served by writing articles for the press—apply equally to Mr. Riding's observations.

Mr. Larkin drew attention to the Superannuation Fund and suggested I might alter the order in which the accounts appear. This may be done, but after all the Superannuation Fund may be a liability to the Corporation, as any deficiency has to be made good —that is if it is under the Act of 1922.

Mr. Martin of Poplar, also on the question of the Superannuation Fund, suggested that certain statistics might be printed in the abstract for use in subsequent years. I have dealt with that in Section 10, paragraph 54. I do not mention Superannuation itself, but if it is thought desirable, then that is the place in which the statistics should appear. He dealt, also, with the question as to whether it is correct to state capital outlay at cost or whether to bring it in at cost less loan repayment. I expected we should get disagreement here, and apparently we have got it, because Councillor Sydney Baker agrees with me. He is a chartered accountant and his opinion must be of value. Mr. Martin disagrees. I leave it to you, but personally I think the proper system is cost price with assets removed from the balance sheet when exhausted or alienated.

Councillor Fawley of Middlesex made some interesting remarks and apparently advocates the Abstract being cut down as much as possible. It is all very well to say that years and years ago the

S*

(Mr. James Boucher).

Abstracts consisted of 25 pages and now it has gone up to 300 pages, but what about the growth of the services, such as Housing, Public Assistance and matters like these, all of which require pages devoted to them. I have suggested the Abstract in two forms, the Epitome, and the Abstract proper. The Epitome, if it is properly "tied up" with the Abstract will serve the purpose Councillor Fawley wants. The main functions of the Corporation can be summarised in the contents of a few tables. I suggest that is the best way. In paragraph 40 of the paper I suggest we should ruthlessly cut out any non-essential detail.

Then we had an interesting contribution from Mr. Griffiths of Sheffield. I do not know whether Sheffield pay for assets out of revenue and do not put them in their balance sheet, but I should be surprised if they do. Any payment for assets out of revenue should be brought into the balance sheet. So far as school furniture is concerned, my impression is that you would have extraordinary difficulty with the Board of Education, if you wanted to charge up the furniture for a new school direct to revenue. I cannot imagine they would grant it, and in any case surely the usual thing is to get a Loan Sanction. If you get a Loan Sanction it almost necessarily goes to the Capital Account and any renewals would be a proper charge to revenue.

I think, Mr. President, those are the only observations that I need reply to. Mr. Rattenbury submitted that the matter might be referred to the Research Committee of the Institute, and I suggest that this should be done.

Mr. William C. Coxall (Borough Treasurer, Chesterfield) : Mr. President : I have been listening on the outskirts of the conference room this morning to the discussion, and very candidly I am surprised at the great interest that this subject has created in this Conference, particularly amongst the representatives of the authorities. I did not think that our Abstracts would rouse such keen interest, and I rise to move that the matter be referred to the Council for consideration and report.

There is always a danger in standardisation or uniformity that individuality might be lost, and I should be very sorry for that to happen. I do not think our Abstract ought to be cut down absolutely to the condition of a Government return, and I would suggest to the Council one or two points, after having studied during the past year fifty or sixty Abstracts before I wrote an article in the *Financial Circular* on Epitomes.

The first things that ought to go out of the Abstract are, I think, those wretched folders. I never trouble to open one; I would sooner look at an Abstract, even if it were an inferior one, without these folders. With regard to the aggregate balance sheet: I think that could be cut to half a page, or, at the very outside, a page. The other point I should like to suggest is that the trading costs per unit should be shown, and that the profit and loss items should be shown in different type, which could be sighted more easily.

I formally move that the matter be referred to the Council.

(*The Resolution, being duly seconded, was put to the meeting and carried unanimously.*)

The Secretary: I am sure you will all be pleased to know that we have here with us to-day Mr. Gunner, of Croydon. (Applause.)

Mr. William Gunner (Borough Treasurer, Croydon): I wish to thank you, Gentlemen, for the very kind way in which my name has been received. I cannot help taking my mind to the first meeting when our Institute was formed. It was held in Manchester, and I think I was the only municipal officer from south of the Trent at that meeting, and on seeing the great number with us to-day, compared with what there was at that first meeting, I can only say I heartily congratulate the Institute on its progress. (Applause.)

COST ACCOUNTS AS APPLIED TO MUNICIPALITIES

By John Allcock, O.B.E., F.S.A.A.
(City Treasurer and Controller of Cardiff)

In these days of growing municipal enterprise, when, moreover, fresh responsibilities are constantly being laid upon local authorities, while at the same time there is a continual call for economy, an efficient costing system is an essential part of the organisation of a municipality. Mr. Allcock explains in broad outline the principles on which a system of cost accounting should be based and operated as an aid to economical administration.

IN the interests of economy and efficiency, it is recognised that cost accounts, and their far-reaching application to industrial organisations, or municipal services, have, during recent years, figured very prominently and are now a very important branch of accountancy.

The fierce business competition of to-day, with trading problems becoming more complex and economic measures definitely laid by Ministries of the Government upon local authorities, have caused cost accounts to become imperative for the business-like control, and efficient management of any industry, or municipal service.

To those who have devoted attention to the science of costing, it will be apparent that cost accounting does not merely consist in the recording of figures, but in the scientific analysis of the various items of the actual costs during the stages of manufacturing processes, or working operations, thus supplying information which points the way to economical action.

Advantages of Cost Accounts

Experience has proved that the advantages derived from an effective and well organised system of cost accounting cannot be overstated in the administrative and financial control of public works departments, tramways, motor omnibuses, electricity, gas and waterworks undertakings, &c.

In these days of municipal enterprise and activity, the executive officers of a corporation (and this term implies city engineer and surveyor, electrical engineer, gas engineer, waterworks engineer, tramways and motor omnibus manager) realise the various works they control are so varied and extensive and involve the expenditure of such considerable sums of money that personal contact on the part of the executive officer with every detail and working operation is entirely out of the question.

With the aid of an efficient costing system the position of each of the respective operations can be readily ascertained by the production of data at frequent and regular periods to warn and guide those committees and chief officers who are responsible for expenditure incurred by their respective departments.

Some technical men do not always take kindly to figures, but graphs or charts prepared from cost sheets supplied by the financial officer readily appeal to them, and show at a glance and in a more effective degree the comparative position between actual and estimated expenditure at stages during the process of manufacturing and operating costs, and the general progress of works.

Essentials for Cost Accounts

It is necessary that the records for building up cost accounts should be statements of actual facts, otherwise the results will be entirely misleading.

It is also essential that the persons responsible for cost accounting should have a full knowledge of the practical side of the business in order to deal with technicalities arising from the requirements of executive officers.

The scheme of a cost accounting system should be skilfully and economically planned so as to promptly give the information it is expected to afford, namely, to reveal the cost of the various grades of labour employed, material, plant and machinery used, and the accurate allocation and distribution of oncost charges to locate waste, extravagance or leakage of material. At the same time careful consideration must be given so that the expense involved does not outweigh the advantages gained.

Costing systems are now materially aided by the use of various types of mechanical appliances, such as calculating, adding and listing and public utility machines.

These appliances not only reduce the expense of costing to a minimum but materially expedite the work.

Objections to cost accounting by some business concerns are not unknown even in these times of keen industrial competition, but sooner or later it will be realised that costing systems are indispensable if one wishes to proceed on right lines.

Local conditions and full co-operation of the departments concerned must be considered so as to secure the best results, and also as to which department of a municipality or under whose control the actual cost accounts should be prepared.

The following reasons are advanced for the cost accounts being compiled by the finance department:—

(1) The executive officers, being fully occupied with the technical sides of their departments, cannot reasonably be expected to specialise in the preparation of cost accounts.

(2) As cost accounts are incorporated with the general accounts of a local authority, it appears obviously to be within the province of the financial officer to determine the system of accounts to be adopted.

(3) The finance department not having any direct interest will not tend to be partial in the treatment of accounts relating to any particular department.

On the other hand it may be contended that the executive officers would not receive the information

A lecture delivered to the local societies of the Chartered Accountants Students, the Incorporated Accountants Students, and the Institute of Chartered Secretaries at the City Hall, Cardiff, on the 31st October 1932.

they desire as promptly as they might if the cost accounts were directly under their control. This suggestion, however, can only be made in connection with an inefficient finance department.

Classification of Cost Accounts

Cost accounts are classified to conform to the special nature of a business undertaking or service carried out, for example :—

Classification	*Application*
1. Unit Cost.	Cost per unit of electricity generated. Cost per ton of stone quarried.
2. Multiple Cost.	Cost of varieties of manufactured products.
3. Process Costs.	Cost of each process of work carried out by a succession of processes until completed.
4. Operating Costs.	Applicable to railways, tramways, omnibuses, electric light, waterworks and gas undertakings.
5. Terminal Costs.	Apply to the cost or contract for completion of works.

There are three groups of expenditure, of which it is necessary to understand their relative importance in order to acquire an effective grasp when compiling cost accounts, for example :—

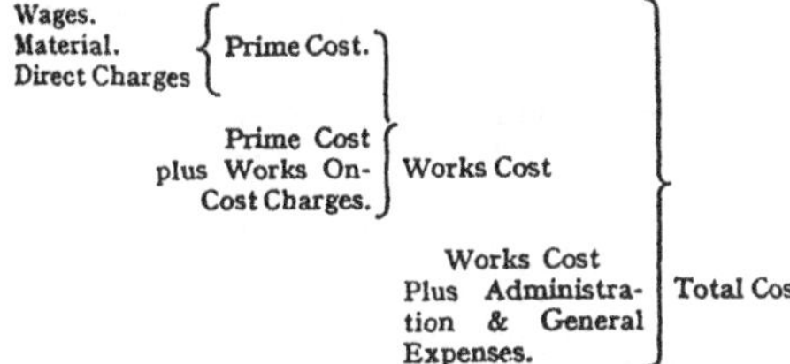

Municipal authorities have recognised, by the introduction of cost accounts, the advantages gained as a guide for future policy, particularly when comparisons are made with the unit costs of the services of other municipalities.

The following will illustrate the scope of unit costs as adopted by municipal authorities :—

Trading Undertakings.

Service	*Unit Adopted*
Tramways.	Average cost per car mile.
Motor Omnibus.	Average cost per 'bus mile.
Electricity Works.	Cost per unit generated.
Waterworks.	Cost per 1,000 galls. consumption.
Gas Works.	Cost per therm of gas produced.

Non-Trading Undertakings.

Refuse Collection.	Cost per 1,000 houses or premises. Cost per ton.
Street Cleansing.	Cost per 10,000 sq. yds. cleansed. Cost per 1,000 population.
Education.	Cost per pupil in average attendance.
Hospital.	Cost per patient week.
Police.	Cost per member of force.

Other Services.

Mechanical vehicles (various classes).	Cost per hour or day.	
Horse, cart, and driver.	,,	,,
Steam rollers.	,,	,,
Asphalt macadam plant.	,,	,,
Stone crushing plant.	,,	,,
Concrete mixers, &c.	,,	,,

Preparation of Cost Accounts

To deal with cost accounts and their application to each of the respective trading concerns of a corporation would be too large for the scope of this lecture, for each department's costing operations are so extensive as to necessitate a lecture unto itself although it may be said that the costing principles are much of the same character subject to such detailed variation as may be found necessary to meet the needs of the department concerned.

I propose therefore to confine myself to the cost accounts of a municipal authority's public works department which consist of the following elements :—

Wages.
Materials.
Cartage.
Mechanical Transport Services.
Plant.
Oncost Charges :
 Workshop Services.
 Establishment Charges.

After which an exposition will be given of the cost accounts kept in my department by reference to the actual books of account.

Wages.—A very important element in cost accounts relates to wages. There are various ways in which these can be recorded, one being by the use of automatic time-recording machines, but this method hardly lends itself to returns of time worked on jobs which are spread practically all over the city and other means have had to be adopted. One method is to provide each workman with a weekly time sheet. This is entered up by him showing the time occupied, the class of work, and where the work was executed, leading up to the total wages earned. In this case such wages sheets are certified by the foreman in charge, thus confirming the correctness of the time recorded by the workman. An improvement, however, has been made on this. In actual practice it is found highly desirable to institute a time sheet which is filled up in such a way as to act as a summary of the entries, which would be found in detail on the ordinary time sheet first mentioned. This would mean that if a man was engaged on two or more different classes of work in a week, the record would reach the office in such a way as to show instantly, without any further analysis, the time worked on each job, and in this case the time-keeper would enter the sheet in question from the foremen's records, this system greatly facilitates the compiling of the cost accounts when compared with the previous and somewhat out-of-date system of separate time sheets.

The importance of this will be realised when one takes into consideration that sometimes a gang will consist of from 200 to 300 men.

The time sheets are checked by the executive officer's department who prepare the pay sheets and forward them to the finance office where the money columns are checked and the actual payment of wages is carried out by an assistant of the financial officer.

With reference to the payment of wages a declaration is made at the foot of each pay sheet by the pay clerk to the effect that he has paid the workmen whose numbers and names appear on the pay sheet with the exception of any absentees whose pay numbers are stated in such declaration. This is witnessed by the foreman in charge of the men who is present at the time of payment.

In cases where workmen fail to put in an appearance for their wages, the pay clerk enters the particulars in an unclaimed wages book and hands such money to the chief cashier to the financial officer who is responsible for the custody of same until authoritatively claimed.

Pay sheets afford a fruitful and easy form of fraud. We have all heard of " dead men " and there is a risk of their introduction. It is therefore wise to adopt a policy which will reduce to a minimum the possibility of fraud by introducing as many different people as is reasonably possible so as to practically eliminate collusion.

In the case of the Cardiff Corporation it would be necessary in order for fraud to be perpetrated that there should be collusion between the time-keeper, the foreman, the wages clerk and the pay cashier. The pay clerks should not know the pay stations they have to attend until immediately before leaving the office and the duties of the pay clerks should be constantly changed. It is unwise to permit pay clerks to continually pay in the same pay stations week after week.

The detailed analyses of wages under the respective heads of service form the debit of the wages item in the cost accounts.

Stock and Stores.—These, wherever possible, should be placed in a central position in the works department so that the storekeeper may expeditiously issue such stores as may be requisitioned by the various trades carried on in the workshops and to minimise the loss which would otherwise ensue by what is known as " walking time " and in all probability in consequence thereof idleness of machinery and plant.

It is important that the goods and materials in charge of the storekeeper should be arranged in methodical order so as to expedite their issue. It should be the duty of the storekeeper to keep posted up to date either bin cards (and these are recommended for small goods) or a stock and stores register. He should also provide himself with particulars of the maximum and minimum quantities required of each class of materials so that he may immediately realise the goods which must be ordered from time to time. This will prevent delay of work which would arise if the necessary material was not expeditiously delivered and it will also obviate the accumulation of obsolete stock.

Material Inwards.—Annual contracts should be entered into for the supply of materials but it is found that however careful one may be in drawing up such contracts, occasions will arise from time to time calling for the purchase of materials not covered by such contracts. In these cases competitive quotations should be obtained and these should be examined by the finance department when the tradesmen's accounts are checked. Centralisation of contracting for the requirements common to all departments permits of contracts being placed on far more reasonable terms than would otherwise obtain.

An important element in financial control is to be found in the introduction of a requisition book. In this book the head of each department must enter his probable requirements, say for a month ahead, and obtain the approval of the committee to the ordering of the items entered in the requisition book. I have heard it said that it is impossible to keep a requisition book but I deny this absolutely. The fact that I have had over 30 years' experience of the use and easy working of requisition books is a sufficient reply to this objection. Still when materials are required between committee meetings then from a purely business point of view they must be obtained, otherwise delay will occur. The way in which this can be met is by requiring the head of the department to enter all orders placed by him of this character in red ink in the requisition book. The Committee will then automatically see how far he is complying with the regulations that as far as possible the authority of the Committee should be given to the head of the department *before* placing orders for materials. If there are many red ink items in the requisition book the Committee will naturally want to know the reason.

When an order has been placed by the executive officer the storekeeper should be notified so that he may make the necessary arrangements for the reception of the goods which in all cases must be accompanied by advice notes. The storekeeper will check the quantity and quality of the goods and on finding both correct he would enter the goods, day by day, on the goods inward sheet and forward this sheet daily to the executive officer's department with the advice notes attached.

All invoices should be forwarded by contractors and tradesmen direct to the executive department for the purpose of being checked and for posting to the goods inwards sheets. These inward sheets fulfil a two-fold purpose, namely (*a*) the checking of contractors' and tradesmen's accounts, and (*b*) they provide the medium of posting the quantities together with the money values to the debit side of the individual stock ledger accounts.

The invoices are then handed to the finance department and it is a matter of importance that no account relating to stock and stores should be passed by that department, unless it can be checked from the goods inward sheet.

When the finance department are satisfied as to the correctness of the accounts, they are presented to the Committee in the ordinary way so that payment may be authorised. These accounts are subsequently used for posting the money value of the materials to the debit side of stock and stores account in the impersonal ledger.

Materials Outwards.—It is obvious unless a strict check is kept upon the issue of materials that fraud may creep in here. It should therefore be a strict condition that goods or materials (even of the smallest quantity) should not leave the custody of the storekeeper except on the signed requisition of an authorised person. On such an order being sent to the storekeeper the materials will be issued together with details entered on a receipt delivery note made out in carbon duplicate, the receipt form on this note must be signed by the person receiving the goods on the job, which is then returned to the storekeeper, and dealt with as follows :—The first form is forwarded direct to the costing section for pricing from the stock ledger accounts, calculating values, allocating debits and preparation of the material abstract.

The second form is retained by the storekeeper for reference, from which he posts his stock register or bin cards.

The method of pricing materials should be the actual price of each purchase inclusive of transport or other oncost charges.

Analysis of Materials.—These have to be dealt with from two points of view :—

(*a*) As debits to the impersonal accounts, for instance, highways, public improvements, sewers, &c.

(*b*) As credits to the various stock and stores accounts.

It is therefore necessary to analyse these transactions so as to obtain in the most convenient form the debit and credit above mentioned.

Actual experience will dictate as to the extent of the analyses. It will be found in some instances that the headings will be relatively few, but in some cases, more especially where works departments and trading undertakings are in existence, the analyses will cover almost every head of service.

Cartage.—Most corporations have stables of their own, but it is not economical to keep such a number of horses as will be necessary to meet the maximum demand. Recourse has therefore to be had to hiring. In the latter case, the basis of allocation for charges to the particular jobs will be from daily returns made by the time-keeper, of the loads delivered, or hours worked, or per ton mile. This will be certified by the foreman in charge of the works and analysed in the finance department, thus creating a charge to each cost account for hired haulage service.

These returns of hired haulage service are used to check the haulage contractor's accounts.

Where the local authority possesses its own stables it is necessary to keep a stables account on practically the same lines as a trading undertaking. The items debited to a stables account are as follows :—

Drivers' wages.
Provender, corn-crushing and chaff cutting.
Shoeing horses.
Cleaning horses, stables, &c.
Rent of grazing land (if any).
Repairs to buildings.
Repairs to harness.
Repairs and renewals of wagons, vans, &c.
Gas, electricity, water and miscellaneous.
Stud renewals fund.
Rates, taxes and insurances.
Interest and sinking fund on stable buildings, or rental.

When the annual rate estimates are being prepared a careful estimate must be made of an all-in charge per day, based upon the estimated number of working days in respect of cartage service for the ensuing year, as this item will form a considerable element in the anticipated cost of carrying out works.

All such possibilities as variation in rates of wages, cost of fodder, &c., or maintenance of buildings, must be taken into consideration, and an all-in rate fixed which, when charged to the accounts using stable services, will approximately be equal to the total debits in the stables account; obviously this is somewhat difficult and it may be necessary to adjust the rate chargeable during the course of the year. Circumstances must guide as to the disposal of any balance on the account at the end of the financial year.

If the charges made during the year for stables services have been too small, there will be a deficiency on the account, and the correct method would be to apportion such loss *pro rata* over the accounts utilising such services.

If the charge for cartage services has been made at too high a rate during the year, it will lead to a surplus on the account, and it can be dealt with by crediting the principal accounts utilising such services; there is, however, another alternative.

The stud renewals account is built up by setting aside a certain percentage on the value of horses, and out of this fund new horses are purchased.

The adequacy or otherwise of this fund is contingent on prices paid for houses, and on the health of the horses.

I feel that a very useful purpose would be served by transferring the profit on stables account, if it should be a reasonable amount, to the stud renewals account.

Mechanical Transport, Steam Rolling, &c.—It is very important that detailed and informative accounts should be kept of the cost of running all machinery.

These accounts are dealt with exactly on the same principles as stables account, the debits to the respective accounts consisting of repairs and maintenance costs, oils, cleaning, insurances, road licences, depreciation on purchase price if provided out of revenue, sinking fund, if the machinery was purchased out of capital, and interest on the debt thus created.

The respective accounts of each different class of machinery are credited monthly by charging an "all-in" rate per hour, or per day, based on services rendered. These items form the debits to the accounts receiving such services.

In the case of works aided by Government grants, the Ministry of Transport stipulates in Circular No. 375 : Roads, the maximum rate allowed to cover maintenance, interest, and replacement in respect of transport and steam rolling plant of each class. To this daily rate has to be added an average daily rate of the cost of drivers' wages and the average daily cost of fuel.

It will be obvious to you all that these accounts are extremely valuable to the executive officer, as the information therein contained will enable him to ascertain the cost of each class of machinery employed by him, and as a consequence he will know whether such machinery is running economically or not. He will be able to make up his mind whether it would be wise to dispense with some which may be replaced by more economical machinery and thus lead to economical working.

Use of Plant.—The charges for use of plant are divided as follows :—

(*a*) Those relating to machinery of considerable value.

(*b*) Those relating to small plant and tools.

In the case of the former, such as asphalt and tar macadam plant, concrete mixers, mechanical tar sprayers, stone crushers, &c., each type of plant should have a separate account and be debited with all charges which come against it and credited with an estimated all-in charge for services to meet such debits.

Charges for the use of light plant and tools can conveniently be based upon a percentage charge on the total wages cost of the work and posted to the credit of tools and light plant account. Actual experience will indicate to what extent any modification of such charge is necessary.

There is, however, another opinion, viz. that the correct method is to base such charge upon wages and materials combined, but I desire to point out that wages and materials combined would at times form a faulty basis because in one case materials may be delivered to a job from a depot, such materials having incurred cost of handling, whereas on another job the materials may be carted direct from a railway siding and in respect of which there are practically no handling charges, and again, some materials might possibly represent a very high percentage of the combined cost of wages and materials, whereas in another case such percentage might be relatively small.

It may be stated that with regard to claims upon the Ministry of Transport, an allowance of 1½ per cent. is made in respect of light tools, based upon the total cost of the job, exclusive of work carried out by contract, so you can see how largely opinions vary on this particular matter.

Workshop Services.—Most corporations provide themselves with workshops attached to the main depot, comprising the following trades :—

Engineering.
Blacksmiths.
Carpenter.
Wheelwright.
Plumbers' and Painters' Shops.

Wages of men engaged in the workshops are charged direct to the jobs on which they are engaged.

A separate account must be kept for each workshop. The items debited to the respective accounts comprise repairs and maintenance of machinery and plant, electric light and power, or gas, fuel, loan charges (if any), ground rent, rates and taxes, insurances, and interest on capital (if any).

The credits on the workshops account are the amounts included in the charges made to the accounts in respect of which services have been rendered. These percentage rates are based on previous records of working capacity and a very careful estimate of all the items forming the debit of the workshop accounts.

A further method with which I have no doubt you are all acquainted is the hourly machine rate generally adopted in factory costing. This is based on operatives wages, depreciation, and interest on the initial cost and upkeep of each machine during the time it is in use, and all other items relating to the ascertaining of an hourly machine rate charge.

Establishment Charges.—This expenditure by its very nature cannot be charged direct to the works concerned. I do not think I need trouble you with the details of such an account.

This account is credited with the percentage amounts charged to the various heads of services. Care should be exercised in observing at frequent periods during the financial year, that the total debits to the establishment charges account are balanced by the credits. If there is a marked difference the matter should at once be investigated and adjustments made by fixing an equitable charge.

This difference may be accounted for by the total value of work in one year being normal, while in another year it may far exceed the normal, and in consequence operating directly upon the percentage which should be debited to the accounts in respect of establishment charges.

Stocktaking

By test checks of stocks during the year and comparing results with the stock ledger accounts, and inquiry in case of discrepancy, not only is a better control exercised but the economic value is great; for this system overcomes the necessity of actually taking stock of each article at the end of the year, and prevents delay in closing the books and the publication of the abstract of accounts; moreover storekeepers and all concerned are more careful and alert when they know that instead of an annual stocktaking a test check of their stores may be made at any time.

The question as to how stocks and stores are to be priced at stocktaking period gives room for a variety of opinions. The method suggested, and which is generally adopted, is to value the stores at the net cost including handling charges. Any deterioration which the goods on hand may undergo by being out of date, or through other causes, should be written off and the stock brought down to realisable value. When stocks become obsolete they should be reduced to scrap value.

May I say it is not intended that these remarks should be regarded as an exhaustive treatise on this important subject, but I hope this broad outline will serve to demonstrate the principles on which a cost accounting system should be based, and operated as an essential aid to the economical administration of a local authority.

Before closing I wish to place on record the fact that I have been materially assisted in the preparation of this paper by Mr. J. Spencer, the principal assistant in the costing section of my department.

After discussion the meeting proceeded to examine in detail the actual accounts kept in the costing section of the City Treasurer's department.

Memo. 150/Accts.

Memorandum to accompany the Accounts (Boroughs and Metropolitan Boroughs) Regulations, 1930.

The General Scheme of the Regulations.

1. The Regulations define the principles upon which the accounts are to be kept and the results which are to be attained: it is only in respect of the chief accounts of the Council that they define the form and method of the book-keeping.

They require that prompt record shall be kept of all facts and transactions which concern the accounts of the Council, and that, wherever it is desirable to relieve the chief accounts of detail by analysing, classifying and summarising matter so recorded, this shall be done in subsidiary books or statements of appropriate form. All matters concerning accounts are to be dealt with in a series of records, statements and accounts duly linked together and inter-referenced up to the point where the resultant figures are entered in the Council's ledger accounts.

They do not prescribe forms for these primary records, statements and accounts, but leave it to the Councils to adopt those which are most appropriate in dealing with the widely differing circumstances and conditions which obtain. With regard to Public Assistance however, it is considered desirable for the time being to follow generally the forms prescribed in the Poor Law Orders for the Accounts of Relieving Officers, Collectors and Institutions. Apart from this the provisions of existing Orders remain in force in regard to the forms to be used only in certain branches of the accounts where uniformity is of special importance; and these Orders and the systems they illustrate can be regarded as exemplifications of the methods by which many of the results required by these Regulations can best be attained.

The Chief Accounts of the Council.

2. The double-entry ledger accounts constitute the official record and classification of the Council's transactions in each year, and their balance sheets are intended to present a complete statement of the financial position at the close of each year, and of all matters then outstanding which concern the accounts of the succeeding year.

The personal control accounts, the final accounts and the balance sheets should be contained in consecutively folioed volumes. For the convenience of those who refer to the ledgers it is useful to arrange the impersonal accounts in the order of the entries in the Official Epitome of the Council's accounts and in their published Abstracts.

It is undesirable that these ledger accounts should include any lists of similar items which can be introduced in total without detracting from the value of the accounts as a record of the year's transactions; and, therefore, in addition to summarising in control accounts the transactions with tradesmen, stockholders, mortgagees, depositors and certain other creditors, with ratepayers and many other groups of debtors, and with collecting and disbursing officers and storekeepers, certain postings to and from the cash book can also be made in periodical totals, e.g., collecting officers' deposits, payments to tradesmen and salary cheques.

Special virtues of double-entry accounts aided and simplified by the control account system are the security which they provide against any subsequent alteration of closed accounts, and the fact that they ensure that all sums recorded as due to or from the Council and other matters outstanding at the close of the year will be followed up in succeeding periods.

3. *Cash Book.*—The cash book required by the Regulations is an account of the sums paid into the bank which acts as custodian of the Council's funds and of the cheques or other authorities for payment by the bank which have been issued. Cheques which have not been issued should not be included in this account as payments made, nor should cheques which have been dishonoured be allowed to remain in account as sums received.

The Regulations (except in Art. 17 which relates to accounts submitted in part to one auditor and in part to another) do not call for any separate banking accounts. Unnecessary division of the bank accounts is, for various reasons, undesirable; and apart from any statutory requirement, the only cases in which it may be useful are those where accurate apportionment of bank interest is a matter of importance, and the work involved in making this apportionment in the Council's offices would be greater than the trouble involved in keeping the bank accounts apart.

Separate cash book accounts for departments whose cash transactions are in the main distinct from those of other departments are often desirable, but it is to be noted that the only requirements of the Regulations in this regard are those contained in Art. 17 and in the schedule relating to general loans. There are, however, a number of requirements in regard to cash balances being shown separately upon the balance sheets, or upon subsidiary statements connected therewith, e.g., those of loan moneys, capital receipts, and sinking funds unapplied. These latter requirements do not involve the keeping of separate cash accounts. The balance of an aggregate cash account can be apportioned to any number of funds or accounts for balance sheet purposes provided a statement be entered in the cash book identifying its balance with the items carried therefrom to the balance sheets.

4. *Officers' Accounts.*—It is not necessary that a separate account should be opened in the ledger for each officer; it may be more convenient to aggregate in one account, the transactions of a group of officers, e.g., one wagepayers' account or one rate collectors' account; but in each such case a statement must be entered upon the face of the account showing to what extent each officer is responsible for the balance shown therein.

5. *Debtors' Accounts.*—The requirement to open debtors' accounts does not extend to cash income, i.e., to those branches of income where payment has always to be made at the time of charge. It applies to all credit income, i.e., that in regard to which payment is not necessarily made at the time of charge. It is of special importance in connection with each source of income in respect of which items may be written off or recoverable arrears have to be kept on record.

The system of account keeping illustrated in the Rate Accounts (Borough and Urban District Councils) Order, 1926, and the circular letter accompanying that Order should be followed as far as is practicable and appropriate in connection with each source of income where payment does not always accompany the charge. Where the basis and calculation of each charge cannot be set out in appropriate columns of the income account book a reference to the subsidiary statement in which the particulars are set out should be given in that book in respect of each charge.

A matter of great importance in connection with each source of income, whether it be cash or credit income, is that the amounts due to the Council should be promptly and completely entered. To secure this the system of primary records should be as complete and reliable as is practicable, and where possible such as to establish that the total charge is correct.

6. *Creditors' Accounts.*—It is recognised that the requirement to keep current account with tradesmen and to bring the items of expenditure into account when the claims fall due for payment instead of when the payments are made, will in many cases necessitate an alteration in the system of account keeping.

When the current accounts do not include the unpaid bills, the spending Committees need for the proper discharge of their work separate statements showing how much has been spent up to date under each head or sub-head for which separate account is required. Hence a direction that the accounts themselves shall provide this information does not of necessity involve any increase in the account keeping work.

The classification of the items involves the same work whether it be a classification from paid or unpaid bills, and passing the transactions through creditors' accounts makes but a small addition to the clerical work, especially if the postings are made in aggregated totals as the Regulations permit.

The keeping of prompt account with debtors and creditors is regarded as a matter of the first importance in all commercial and industrial systems, and in so far as the debtors' accounts are concerned this may be said to be recognised in practice for all accounts of local authorities.

It is left to each Council to decide whether or to what extent the accounts of these creditors are to be aggregated, and by what method the credit entries are to be analysed, classified and summarised for posting to the impersonal and to the storekeepers' accounts of the ledger system.

There are certain creditors' accounts which require separate and special treatment—*e.g.*, the account with the Inland Revenue and the account with the Insurance Commissioners in respect of the contributions due from the Council and its employees.

Apportionment of Recurring Charges.

7. In order to give a completely accurate statement of the financial position of a trading undertaking at the close of each year, and of its profit or loss, account must be taken of (a) the proportion of sums payable and receivable after the end of the year which relate to periods within the year, and (b) the proportions of sums paid or received within the year which relate to periods after its close.

The correct way of bringing these proportions into account is that of maintaining in the account a provision equal to the net amount necessary to cover them. This is because items which are not due for receipt or payment cannot lawfully be included in the debtors' or creditors' accounts at the end of the year, and do not come within the limits prescribed by Art. 6(1) of the Regulations for the income and expenditure entries.

In connection with trading revenues the Regulations in Art. 7(2) make provision for account being taken of these proportions where it is desired to do so for the Council's own purposes or for providing figures to be entered in statements of account required by Government Departments. It is not thought that there is much advantage in elaborating rate fund accounts in this way. And it is to be noted that the provision does not extend to housing accounts.

The need for this elaboration of account is in some cases removed or reduced by arranging that the periods of interest, sinking fund, insurance and other payments terminate on the last day of the financial year.

Records of Capital Assets.

8. The Regulations do not *require* records of the original cost of capital assets to be maintained in the accounts along with per contra entries showing to what extent such cost is still borne by loan, and to what extent it has been otherwise defrayed, and do not preclude any Council, if it so elects, from dealing with all its loan expenditure on the simpler plan known as the deferred charge principle.

These records of capital are clearly valuable where trading undertakings of any importance are concerned, and are indeed necessary in such cases in order properly to complete the returns prescribed by Government Departments. In other than trading accounts they are of historical interest, and may also have value in presenting the securities which the Council can offer to lenders.

Although the Regulations do not limit local discretion in regard to the extent to which properties or works shall be treated as capital assets, they do require that the properties and works which are so treated shall be specified in the balance sheets, and that there shall be shown there to what extent the records relate to realisable assets such as trading plant, real property, and the permanent equipment thereof, and to what extent, if any, they relate to works such as pavements, sewers, street improvements, or sea defences.

Records of this nature would obviously be valueless and deceptive if they included any alienated or exhausted items, or if, by the inclusion of loan expenditure upon replacement, they were made to include the same asset more than once. Hence considerable elaboration of record is involved wherever the capital treatment is adopted. In the case of a trading undertaking it involves the keeping of an inventory of capital plant which should be annually certified as to its unexhausted condition by the chief engineer and as to its cost by the chief financial officer. In the case of highway, sewer, sea defence and other works, it involves keeping on record each item of outlay included in a Capital Asset Account in order that such Asset may be removed when exhausted or replaced by other work.

If in any case an asset is thus written off when loan is still owing in connection with it, it is clearly desirable that the remaining loan debt should at once be discharged or counterbalanced by sinking fund provision. Where this is not done, the only way of presenting the matter in account is by setting up the remaining outlay as a "deferred charge" until the loan debt has been redeemed.

The figures entered in the operative columns of the capital accounts must in all cases represent original cost. If valuations are noted in the accounts or balance sheets (*e.g.*, where the original cost of real estate is unknown or where the property came by gift), the date of the valuation and its authority should be stated.

Capital Receipts.

9. All receipts which cannot properly be treated as revenue receipts should be dealt with in the Capital Receipts Accounts prescribed by the Regulations. Whether a receipt is a revenue or a capital receipt is a question of law, but it is seldom necessary to refer the matter beyond the Auditor for decision. It is obvious that none which come into the following groups can properly be treated as current income.

a. Sums received in recoupment of loan expenditure;
b. Sums received for the sale of real estate or any interest or easement therein;
c. Sums received in consideration of the assumption of continuing liabilities—*e.g.*, for road maintenance where other persons are liable *ratione tenuræ* or otherwise, for the upkeep of graves, etc.;
d. Sums to be held in trust for application of the income to special purposes;
e. Donations and contributions in aid of capital outlay.

It is perhaps unnecessary to point out that any interest or rent derived from loan outlays, from special capital funds, or from unspent or recouped loan money is to be treated as revenue income.

In the case where the receipts are such as will normally cover the whole of the loan expenditure—as in the case of loans under the Small Holdings and the Small Dwellings Acquisition Acts, loans to other local authorities, loans for private street works or private improvement works and loans for the purchase of goods for sale or hire-purchase, the Capital Receipts Account will or should effect a continuous balance between the assets and liabilities connected with the transactions—e.g., the balances of the following accounts in regard to private street expenses should constitute a self-balancing section:

Outstanding loans for private street work.	Repayments due from frontagers. Expenditure unapportioned (if any). Unspent loan money (if any). Recovered loan money in hand.

The statutory instalments of loan repayment or the sinking fund contributions can be paid out of this recovered loan money. In order to comply with statutory requirements or for other reasons it may be necessary to show this balance of recovered loan money in two amounts, viz., (i) sinking fund in hand, (ii) other recovered loan money in hand. If at any time the amount needed for loan repayment exceeds the recovered loan money an overdrawn cash balance should appear on the liability side, which would indicate that revenue has temporarily provided the necessary amount. But neither in this case nor in other cases should any effective charge for loan repayment appear in the revenue account: it is only with realised profit or loss on the transactions that this account is concerned.

10. The Regulations have not dealt with the application of unspent balances of loans or of capital moneys received from the sale of land or otherwise in partial recoupment of loan outlay. In some cases this matter is the subject of statutory or departmental direction. Where no such directions apply the appropriate treatment depends upon the circumstances, and the following principles should be adopted:—

(i) *Loans repayable by instalments.*

(a) Unspent balances of quite small amount may, with due authority, be carried to the account which bears the charge of loan repayment. Sums under £2 may be so treated in the case of Public Works Loan Board loans.

(b) If the lender is willing to take the amounts back and to allow the remaining instalments to be reduced proportionately, this should be done. It is a simple procedure when the instalments are fractional, but where they are governed by an annuity table a recast of the table is involved.

(c) In other cases the amounts should be carried to a special sinking fund account, and should be applied in annual amounts which will give to the revenue account which bears the charge of loan repayment the same proportion of relief in each year; e.g., if the amount of unspent or recovered loan money is £500 and the outstanding debt is £5,000, the amount to be transferred to the revenue account in each year should be one-tenth of the fractional or annuity instalment to be repaid in that year. The interest earned on the amount unapplied should be transferred as it arises to the same revenue account.

(ii) *Loans for which sinking funds are provided.*

The amounts should be added to the sinking fund as and when they arise, and—

(a) If no payment to the sinking fund has yet become due, then, subject to any statutory requirements, the calculation of the amounts to be carried to the fund in succeeding years should be based on the debt as reduced by the amount so added.

(b) If the additions are not of sufficient amount to warrant a revision of the annual contributions they may be allowed to operate automatically in relief of the final contribution.

(c) In other cases the sums to be added to the fund in each succeeding year should be reduced proportionately. For instance, if the amount carried in is £500 and the loan debt for which provision has not yet been made is £5,000, each succeeding year's contribution to the fund would be reduced by one-tenth of the total addition due to the fund in that year, including both revenue contribution and interest accretion.

General Loans.

11. Art. 9 and the Second Schedule contain directions for the account keeping where the Council make use of general loans as therein mentioned.

Some Councils have recourse only to those lenders who are prepared to accept repayment in instalments suited to the conditions and extending over the whole periods of their respective borrowing powers. In these cases the loans are all earmarked to particular borrowing powers, and Art. 9 and the Second Schedule of the Regulations have no application.

But, where loans are raised on conditions as to amount, period, recall and method of repayment designed to suit the convenience of the lenders rather than that of the borrowers, any unnecessary earmarking to borrowing powers leads to much complication in the accounts and to other disadvantages.

It is sometimes assumed that each loan so raised must be attached in the accounts at any given time to a particular borrowing power, but may if required be transferred to another borrowing power. There is, however, no necessity so to attach it in the first instance; and if it is in fact so attached it is not clear that there is in law any power to transfer it to another borrowing power. All that is needed is that the amount of the general loans outstanding should balance with the total of the debt outstanding on the borrowing powers to which it is applied.

The method is applicable not only to mortgages issued in the common form authorised by a number of local Acts and charged on all the rates funds and revenues of the Council, but also to mortgages issued under the Public Health Act, the Education Act, and other Acts which apply the Public Health Act provisions; but in the latter case it can only be applied to and within the group of mortgages issued under the particular statutory authority which is cited as the authority for the mortgages.

The regulations contained in the Second Schedule will give a simple and clear presentation of the facts, and at the same time will show how the conditions attaching to the borrowing powers are complied with, and how each sinking fund conforms to its appointed measure and is applied to the purposes for which it is compiled.

The system resembles that which applies to stock; but the borrowing powers to which the proceeds of stock issues are applicable are limited and defined. Statutory authority is needed before such proceeds can be treated indifferently with mortgage and other loans in the manner described, and a full scheme of loan consolidation cannot legally be adopted without this authority.

For the assistance of those who have to keep accounts which include general loans a skeleton exemplification is set out in the first Appendix to this Memorandum of

(a) The manner in which the Statement as to Borrowing Powers can be made to supply all desirable information in regard to compliance with conditions attaching thereto and of how this Statement can be made to serve for a number of years.

(b) The Interest Account in which the net total has to be apportioned to the borrowing accounts as none of the items therein pertain specifically to any borrowing powers.

Balance Sheets.

12. Suggestions in regard to the manner in which the requirements contained in the last two paragraphs of Article 10 of the Regulations can conveniently be met are set out in the second Appendix to this Memorandum.

General Provisions.

13. The Regulations do not contain any provisions which would limit the discretion of a Council in regard to the officers it employs or the duties it assigns to each. But, in view of the important bearing which wise allotment of duties has upon the efficiency, economy and security of the account keeping, it is thought desirable to refer

here to the principles which appear to be of chief value in this connection.

i. That the duty of providing information, calculating, checking and recording the sums due to or from the Council should be separated as completely as possible from the duty of collecting or disbursing those sums.

ii. That officers charged with the duty of examining and checking the accounts of cash transactions should not themselves be engaged in any of these transactions.

iii. That responsibility for the maintenance of current supervision of all accounts and records relating thereto should rest upon one chief financial officer, even when a separate departmental accountant is employed, as the efficiency of internal audit depends largely upon its independence. And that the officer charged with this duty of supervision should have access at any time and authority to apply any test or check to the accounts and records.

iv. That responsibility for the organisation of efficient accounting systems should also rest upon this officer. But that he should in all cases consult the chief officer of the department concerned as to the form and manner of keeping any records, statements or accounts which have to be kept in that department, due regard being paid on the one hand to the provision of prompt, reliable and complete information for the preparation and verification of accounts, and on the other hand, to the avoidance of unnecessary delay or increase of cost in the execution of work.

Ministry of Health,
Whitehall,
S.W. 1.
29th January, 1930.

APPENDIX I.

General Loans.

STATEMENT AS TO BORROWING POWERS.

Borrowing Account (*a*)........................

Borrowing Power.					Advances made.			Year 19 –19			Year 19 –19		Last two columns repeated for as many further years as may be desired.
Date.	Authority.	Purpose.	Amount.	Period.	Year of advance.	Amount.	Year of expiry.	Out-standing advance brought forward.	Reduction during year.	Out-standing advance carried forward.	Reduction during year.	Out-standing advance carried forward.	

(*a*) A separate section of the statement should be used for each borrowing account, the totals being brought together in a summary (*see* p. 11).

SUMMARY—YEARS 19   TO 19 .

Borrowing Account.	Advances: Totals for 19 –19 .			Totals for 19 –19 .		
	Additions during year.	Reductions during year.	Outstanding at end of year.	Additions during year.	Reductions during year.	Outstanding at end of year.
Add unapplied balance of General Loan Cash Account (if any).						
Total, agreeing with total of general loans outstanding.						

INTEREST ACCOUNT.

Mortgagees' Account.	Gross Interest due in year.	Investment Accounts.	Gross dividends due in year.
Cash Book.	Interest on General Loan Account overdraft.	Cash Book.	Interest on credit balances of General Loan Account.
		Borrowing Accounts.	Apportioned shares of net interest. (*a*)

(*a*) These apportionments will normally be made in the ratio of the total outstanding advances to each borrowing account.

There is no call to apportion separately in respect of each borrowing power.

The calculation can be eased by making the 31st March the normal date for advances and for instalment repayments, special advances repayments being made at evenly spaced dates, *e.g.*, quarterly. The apportionment basis can then be the outstanding debt of each account on the first day of the year, after adding (or deducting) the appropriate fractions of the special advances (or repayments). It can be further eased by confining the advances and their repayments to integral pounds.

APPENDIX II.

Aggregate Balance Sheet.

Liabilities.	Assets.
Loan and Capital Section.	
Loans Outstanding	Capital Properties and Works
Cash (Overspent balance on Loan Accounts)	Loans to other Authorities or persons
Total of Capital Liabilities	Sinking Fund and other investments
	Cash in hand on Capital Loan and Sinking Fund Accounts
Capital Provisions made	Total of Capital Assets
Capital Receipts unapplied	Deferred Charges
Total of Section.	*Total of Section.*
Revenue Section.	
Outstanding Liabilities to Tradesmen and Contractors	Uncollected Income
Depositors	Various Income Accounts
Precepting Authorities	Special Accounts
Other Creditors (Special accounts)	Stores
Advances to provide working balances	Rechargeable works in progress
	Special Fund Investments
Cash (overspent balances)	Cash (unspent balances)
Total of Revenue Liabilities	Total of Revenue Assets
Fund Balances (To be specified)	Fund Balances (To be specified)
Total of Section.	*Total of Section.*
Grand Total	Grand Total ....

General Notes.

In some cases creditor and debtor balances, stores and rechargeable work in progress may concern the Loan and Capital Section as well as the Revenue Section.

The items appearing in the Loan and Capital Section will reproduce the totals shown in the tabular statements required by Article 14 (3) of the Regulations, for which forms are suggested below (p. 17). On these forms all the balances connected with each borrowing power, each capital asset and each deferred charge will be shown. On the balance sheets themselves subdivision should not be extended further than is desirable for a clear presentation of the position in connection with each fund.

NOTES ON PARTICULAR ITEMS IN THE BALANCE SHEET.

Loans Outstanding.—It is desirable to show separately—

The nominal amount of each Stock or Debenture Issue.
The total of the mortgage loans.
The loans from Pension, Reserve or other fund of the Council.
The capital value of Annuities.
Any other loans, e.g., Bank Loans or Money Bills.

N.B.—(*a*) With regard to general loans as described in Article 9 and the second Schedule, usually one ledger control account will suffice for these. It can reproduce the totals shown in a Mortgagees' Account Book, which should have columns for the number of the loans (as in the Register of Mortgages), the name of the lender, the period and terms as to recall, and the following money columns:—

Loans outstanding when year begins	Loans repaid during year
	Interest Payments
Loans received during year	Income Tax retentions
Gross interest due in year	Loans outstanding when year ends

(*b*) In the case of Annuities it is desirable to add the percentage basis of the capitalisation. The value of terminable annuities should be reduced each year in accordance with an appropriate annuity table.

Capital Properties and Works.—It is only where it is desired to maintain a record of the original cost of capital assets that any items will appear under this heading. Art. 10 (5) of the Regulations must be observed when this record forms part of the accounts.

Capital Provisions Made.—The balances appearing under this heading show to what extent the cost of the properties treated as capital assets has been covered by

(*a*) Loan repayment or sinking fund provision.
(*b*) The appropriation of capital receipts.
(*c*) Direct charge on revenue.

Deferred Charges.—The balances under this heading show to what extent expenditures borne by loan have yet to be covered by revenue contributions.

Loan expenditures which do not create capital assets must be classed as deferred charges, e.g., expenses of, and discounts on, Stock issues, Loans for renewal of pavements or for the mere replacement of plant and loans to cover compensation or financial adjustment payments.

Where all loan expenditures are treated as deferred charges there will be no entries under the heading "capital properties and works" or "capital provisions made."

Loans to other Authorities or Persons.—Where loans have been raised for the purpose of making loans to others, any difference between the loan debts due from and to the Council should constitute a cash balance in the loan section of the balance sheet. In these cases the repayment transactions do not concern the revenue accounts.

Capital Receipts Unapplied.—Balances will appear under this heading where the Authority has received and has not yet applied to an authorised purpose any premiums on Stock issues, any donations towards prospective capital expenditure, any sums received on the sale or transfer of capital assets in excess of the loan owing thereon, or any other sums of a capital nature.

Investments (of all kinds).—These should be shown at cost price clear of any brokerage or stamp duty charges.

Cash Balances in Loan and Capital Sections.—These will comprise (a) unspent and overspent loan balances, (b) sinking fund balances uninvested, and (c) capital receipts unapplied.

Outstanding Liabilities—Tradesmen and Contractors.—This balance will come from the ledger control account, which summarises the transactions with all ordinary creditors.

Depositors.—E.g., Deposits as security for trade income, gas or electricity, etc., including accrued interest, if any. Deposits by tenderers and contractors. Payments in respect of income due in later years.

Precepting Authorities.—The balances appearing under this heading will be unpaid portions of the sums due under the precepts. Overpayments (if any) would appear per contra.

Surpluses or deficiencies in the levies made on behalf of the Precepting Authorities rank as fund balances (see below).

Other Creditors (Special Accounts).—E.g., Income Tax deductions retained pending settlement with the Inland Revenue, and sums due to other Local Authorities on agency or other special accounts.

Uncollected Income.

(*a*) *Various Income Accounts.*

These balances will come from the control accounts which reproduce the totals shown in the several income account books, e.g., those relating to Rates, Water, Gas and Electricity Charges, Private Work Charges, Rents, Sales, Costs and Fines, Hall Letting, etc.

(*b*) *Special Accounts.*

These items will cover such matters as set-off claims against the Inland Revenue, grants or subsidies due but not paid, special amounts due from other local authorities and other uncollected charges.

Main Fund Balances.—These will include the balances on the General Rate Fund Account, the Trading Revenues, the Education, Housing or other subsidised funds of which separate account has to be kept, and, where the Council elect to treat them as main funds, the Adoptive Act Funds.

Special Area Funds.—Where any expenditure has to be borne by part of the Council's area, or any income has to be credited to part, an account of this order is needed, and the produce of any additional item of the general rate levied in that part will be credited to such account.

Reserve and Other Subsidiary Funds.—These will include reserves for contingencies and provisions in respect of Accruing Charges in trading accounts; reserves for contingent liabilities or for bad debts; equalisation reserves in connection with repair and upkeep of Real Property or other recurring charges.

(In order to take account of accrued proportions it is only necessary to make one ledger posting in each year, viz., a transfer to or from this provision of the amount necessary to adjust it to the net total shown on a schedule of accrued proportions. Such a schedule can serve for a number of years, if it is provided with columns for recording annual variations.)

Trust Funds.—These will include Pension, Superannuation or Thrift Funds.

Surplus (or Deficient) Rate Levies on Precept or Other Accounts.—These balances, which will be shown on the Rate Income Appropriation Account or elsewhere, will be items which have to be taken into account for adjustment when the poundages of the several levies to be included in the next general rate are being settled.

APPENDIX II—(*continued*).

Tabular Statements of Balances.

DETAILED STATEMENT OF BALANCES—CAPITAL ACCOUNTS.

Description or number of Loan or Advance from Loan Fund.	Liabilities.			Capital Provision.			Totals.	Description of Property or Works.	Assets.		
	Out-standing Loan debt.	Over-spent Cash Balance (if any).	Other Liabilities (if any).	By Loan repay-ment or Sinking Fund.	By direct charge on revenue.	By use of capital receipts.			Original cost (less portions alienated or dis-carded).	Unspent Cash Balance (if any).	Unapplied Sinking Fund (if any).
	£ s. d.	£ s. d.	£ s. d.	£ s. d.	£ s. d.	£ s. d.	£ s. d.		£ s. d.	£ s. d.	£ s. d.

DETAILED STATEMENT OF BALANCES—DEFERRED CHARGE ACCOUNTS.

Description or number of Loan or Advance from Loan Fund.	Liabilities.			Totals.	Loan purpose.	Amount of Deferred Charge.	Assets.	
	Outstanding Loan.	Overspent Cash Balance (if any).	Other Liabilities (if any).				Unspent Cash Balance (if any).	Unapplied Sinking Fund (if any).
	£ s. d.	£ s. d.	£ s. d.	£ s. d.		£ s. d.	£ s. d.	£ s. d.

BOROUGH ACCOUNTS

See also titles :

ACCOUNTS OF LOCAL AUTHORITIES;
AUDIT;
AUDITORS;
BORROWING;
COSTING;
FINANCE;
FINANCE DEPARTMENT;
RATE ACCOUNTS, and financial titles *passim*, a complete list of which will be found at the head of title FINANCE.

General.—The statutory regulation and consequent organisation of the accounts of a municipal borough depend ultimately upon the power to levy a general rate, and in a broad sense the borough accounts may be said to be the accounts of the general rate fund.

Within the ambit of the general rate fund account, transactions may be classified according to the different services administered and certain accounts may be kept quite separate (see *post*, p. 155), in particular the accounts of trading undertakings. Even these latter accounts are associated with the rate fund for such purposes as the transfer of surplus profits or the provision of deficiencies.

Formerly a municipal borough levied two rates, the borough rate and the general district rate, and the accounts, however subdivided, had to be organised in such a way as to provide a rigid separation of the borough fund from the general district fund. These two funds were amalgamated by sect. 10 (1) of the R. & V.A., 1925 (*a*), as from the date when the first new valuation list under that Act came into force (*i.e.* either April 1, 1928, or April 1, 1929) into a general rate fund.

The borough council, acting as the rating authority, is also required to keep certain accounts (including a general rate fund account), but these are dealt with in the title RATE ACCOUNTS.

Sect. 185 of the L.G.A., 1933 (*aa*), provides that all receipts of a borough council, including rents and profits of all corporate land, shall be carried to the general rate fund and all liabilities be discharged thereout. Under sect. 187 (1), all payments to and out of the general rate fund shall be made to and by the treasurer. Payments out of this fund must be made in pursuance of an order of the council signed by three members and countersigned by the town clerk. [317]

(*a*) 14 Statutes 631.
(*aa*) See 26 Statutes 407.

The exceptions to this general rule are payments made:

(a) In pursuance of the specific requirement of any enactment.

(b) In pursuance of an order of a competent court or of a justice of the peace acting in discharge of his judicial functions.

(c) In respect of any remuneration of:
- (i.) the mayor;
- (ii.) the recorder in his capacity either of recorder or of judge of the borough civil court;
- (iii.) the stipendiary magistrate;
- (iv.) the clerk of the peace, when paid by salary;
- (v.) the clerk of the borough justices;
- (vi.) any other officer or person whose remuneration is payable by the council.

(d) In respect of the remuneration and allowances certified by the Treasury to be payable to them in relation to an election petition.

(e) In respect of the remuneration certified by the recorder to be due to an assistant recorder, assistant clerk of the peace, or additional crier (sect. 187 (2)) (*b*). **[318]**

As stated, the transactions to be entered in the account of the general rate fund may, and should, be classified according to the different services administered, and the following services are usually included under this heading:

Salaries and Establishment Expenses.
Municipal Elections.
Quarter Sessions, Assizes and Coroners' Inquisitions.
Police, Fire Brigade and Probation of Offenders.
Town Hall and Municipal Offices.
Parks and Recreation Grounds.
Markets.
Refuse Collection, etc., Sewerage and Sewage Treatment.
Highways and Streets and Public Lighting.
Maternity and Child Welfare, Sanatoria, Dispensaries, etc.

In other cases separate accounts are required to be kept by statute or order, *e.g.* Housing, Public Assistance, Education and Public Baths and Libraries, whilst in some cases it is the custom to keep separate accounts for services ordinarily included under the general rate fund, *e.g.* Police, Probation of Offenders, Sewage Farms and Markets. In all these cases, however, the separate accounts remain subsidiary to the general rate fund and any deficiencies will be chargeable thereto. This applies equally to the trading undertakings of an authority, *e.g.* Transport, Gas, Electricity and Water, the surplus or deficiency upon which accounts may be transferred in whole or in part to the general rate fund. Exceptions to the general rule are found in the Trust and Charity Funds often administered by municipalities. **[319]**

A differentiation must also be observed between county boroughs and non-county boroughs. The wider range of duties allocated by the legislature to the former results in a corresponding increase in the number of funds and accounts administered by them. For example county boroughs operate the following services, which in the case of a non-county borough would usually be administered by the county council: public assistance, lunacy and mental deficiency institutions, tuber-

(*b*) 26 Statutes 408.

culosis and venereal diseases treatment, motor taxation and main roads in their areas. [320]

Metropolitan borough accounts are similar in many respects to those of provincial boroughs, the differences being due to special enactments which are applicable to London in many cases. The L.C.C. is the authority in London for main drainage, education and fire brigade, whilst in connection with housing the clearance of large insanitary areas is also undertaken by the county council. Another important distinction is that borrowing by the metropolitan boroughs requires the sanction of the L.C.C., which latter advances the money also in the majority of cases. [321]

Power of Minister of Health to Prescribe Accounts.—Sect. 235 of the L.G.A., 1933 (*bb*), confers on the Minister of Health wide powers with regard to the form in which local authorities' accounts are to be made up. It is therein provided, *inter alia*, that the Minister may make regulations generally with respect to the preparation and audit of accounts which are subject to audit by a district auditor, including:

(1) The financial transactions which are to be recorded in the accounts.

(2) The mode of keeping the accounts of the authority and of their officers, and the form of those accounts.

(3) The mode in which, if it is so prescribed, the accounts are to be certified by the authority or any officer of the authority.

(4) The publication of information with respect to the audited accounts.

(5) The making of an abstract of the accounts as audited.

It will be observed that this power does not extend to accounts not subject to district audit, but some borough councils have by local act or provisional order or by resolution under the powers conferred by the Municipal Corpns. (Audit) Act, 1933, or sect. 239 of the L.G.A., 1933 (which replaced the Municipal Corpns. (Audit) Act) (*c*), adopted the district audit for all accounts, in which case sect. 235 will apply to all accounts. The accounts of metropolitan boroughs are subject to district audit.

Similar powers to the above were available formerly to the Minister under the District Auditors Act, 1879 (*cc*), the whole of which is repealed by the L.G.A., 1933. The following are the more important orders dealing with accounts made under sect. 5 of the 1879 Act, still remaining in force:

(1) *Housing Accounts Order (Local Authorities)*, 1920 (*d*).—This order sets out a list of prescribed ledger accounts to be opened and the method of treating the various transactions in the accounts. The forms of the various books to be used are also prescribed, and the memorandum accompanying the order contains explanatory matter regarding special points in connection with Housing (Assisted Scheme) Accounts.

(2) *Financial Statements Order*, 1921 (*e*).—A new form of financial statement was prescribed hereunder, to be used for the purpose of arriving at the amount of stamp duty payable at audit.

(3) *Accounts (Payment into Bank) Order*, 1922 (*f*).—Every officer paying money into the bank on behalf of the local authority

(*bb*) 26 Statutes 432.
(*c*) *Ibid.*, 290, 434.
(*cc*) 10 Statutes 571 *et seq.*
(*d*) S.R. & O., 1920, No. 487.
(*e*) S.R. & O., 1921, No. 1902.
(*f*) S.R. & O., 1922, No. 1404.

is required by this order to keep a duplicate of the paying-in slip. In addition some note must be made on the slip and counterfoil in respect of each cheque, in order to identify the latter with the debt in discharge of which it was received.

(4) *The Rate Accounts (R.D.C.) Order*, 1926, *and The Rate Accounts (Borough and U.D.C.) Order*, 1926 (*ff*). (See title RATE ACCOUNTS.)

(5) *The Local Authorities (Audit) Order*, 1928 (*g*). (See title AUDIT.)

(6) *The Accounts (Boroughs and Metropolitan Boroughs) Regulations*, 1930 (*g*), which are dealt with immediately below. [322]

The Accounts (Boroughs and Metropolitan Boroughs) Regulations, 1930 (*h*).—These regulations were made in January, 1930, and came into force on April 1, 1930. They apply to all accounts of Metropolitan boroughs and to those accounts of provincial boroughs which are subject to district audit. In the case of a county borough, the regulations are applicable also to the public assistance accounts dealing with the poor law functions transferred under the L.G.A., 1929 (*i*), so far as they continue to be administered under the provisions of the Poor Law Act, 1930 (*j*) (formerly the Poor Law Act, 1927). Where the power of giving assistance under alternative enactments is exercised by the council, the regulations will not apply unless all the borough accounts are subject to district audit. Although not directly applicable to boroughs whose accounts are not subject to the Government audit, the majority of such boroughs have adopted the principles laid down in the regulations in whole or in part.

The chief financial officer is made responsible for the punctual keeping of a balancing system of double entry ledger accounts, which must include personal accounts, impersonal accounts, final accounts and balance sheet.

Personal Accounts.—The prescribed personal accounts include a cash book for recording the council's bank transactions, *i.e.* sums received on behalf of the council by their bankers, and payments ordered to be made thereout. When the account is balanced, a reconciliation statement as between pass book and cash book is to be prepared.

An account must be kept in respect of each officer who collects, receives or disburses money or stores and materials on behalf of the council, and personal accounts must also be opened in respect of debtors during the year.

It is provided, however, that where primary records can conveniently be classified, totals only may be posted in the personal accounts, which thus become total or " control " accounts, and must agree in total with the details contained in the primary records. [323]

Impersonal Accounts.—Accounts of income and expenditure hereunder are to be set up for each heading of account as appearing in the annual epitome of accounts, or other return required to be furnished to the Minister, with such further classification as may be deemed desirable by the council. In all cases, however, the income and expenditure in connection with the following must be shown separately :

(*ff*) S.R. & O., 1926, Nos. 1123 and 1178.
(*g*) S.R. & O., 1928, No. 177.
(*h*) S.R. & O., 1930, No. 30.
(*i*) 10 Statutes 883 *et seq.*
(*j*) 12 Statutes 968 *et seq.*

(a) Each head of account.
(b) Each area of charge.
(c) Each institution.
(d) Each work chargeable to loan or capital account.
(e) Each work or service the cost of which is chargeable to other persons.

The accounts must include all items of income and expenditure which fall due within or at the close of the year. [324]

Final Accounts.—Final accounts are necessary in respect of revenue and capital, and in the former case must bring out a balance between the income and expenditure of:

(a) The general rate fund.
(b) Each undertaking or service where a separate account is by law required or is needed for the purpose of the council.
(c) Each part of the borough for which a separate account is needed.
(d) Each reserve, pension or other fund of which continuous account has to be kept.

Income and expenditure are to be shown gross, except where a "contra" entry is necessary to correct an overstatement. In the case of trading undertakings, the final account may be divided into a revenue and net revenue account.

The capital section must contain the following accounts:

(a) Capital Asset Accounts, containing a correct record of each work or property treated as a capital asset.
(b) A Capital Provisions Account, showing the provision made other than by loan towards the cost of capital assets, *e.g.* sinking funds, revenue contributions, and in some cases loans redeemed.
(c) A Deferred Charge Account in respect of loan expenditure other than that included in a capital asset account showing the extent to which it remains to be provided out of revenue.
(d) A Capital Receipts Account, showing receipts of a capital nature other than loan receipts.
(e) An account of each fund provided for the purpose of loan repayment.

Where capital assets are not realisable, the capital provision in respect thereof is to be shown separately, and where any capital asset passes out of the council's possession or ceases to be serviceable, an amount equal to the cost is to be written off the capital asset account, and the capital provisions account reduced by the appropriate amount included therein in respect of the asset. Any loan outstanding in connection with such an asset is to be treated as a deferred charge until redeemed. Records must be kept showing the operation of this provision in order to ensure its due observance. [325]

Balance Sheet.—Balance sheets must be prepared showing the assets and liabilities, and the financial position of each of the funds or revenues of the council at the close of the year. Where there is more than one balance sheet, an aggregate balance sheet must be entered in the ledger, and in all cases the capital and revenue sections must be balanced separately. Liabilities and fund surpluses on the one side, and assets and fund deficiencies or deferred charges on the other, must be clearly distinguished. [326]

Primary Records and Accounts.—The regulations prescribe in some detail the primary records necessary to provide the material for posting the ledger. Collecting and disbursing officers are each to keep detailed records of the moneys passing through their hands, and accounts must be kept for debtors in respect of credit income, together with a separate account of each source of income. All sums due to the council must be recorded in the credit income accounts, which must show a detailed record of how the items are dealt with, and interlock with the collecting officer's accounts and appropriate debtors' accounts. [327]

Expenditure and Cost Accounts.—The primary records must provide such information as is necessary properly to classify the council's expenditure in the ledger and to charge debtors with the correct cost of recoverable works. For this purpose time-sheets and wages-sheets or books must be used in respect of workmen's wages and a summary wages classification prepared to show the charge in respect of each work or service. This classification is to bring out a total agreeing with the gross wage charge during the period.

With regard to subsidiary services such as the daily services of horses, rollers, vehicles, etc., such records must be kept as will enable the cost to be properly charged or apportioned.

The regulations provide for detailed stores accounts showing quantities received into store, issued from store, returned to store, and remaining in store. The detailed stores accounts are to be controlled by a total account showing stores transactions as above in total, the two sets of accounts being maintained in agreement. A stocktaking return must be used showing side by side book quantities and actual quantities of stores, the two being brought into agreement by such adjustments as appear to accord with the facts after the cause of the difference has been properly investigated. [328]

Loan and Capital Accounts.—The following records must be kept under this heading:

(1) A tabular and summarised account of each group of stockholders, mortgagees, annuitants and other lenders to whom debts of the same order are owing.

(2) A statement as to borrowings, showing:

  (a) the date, authority, purpose, period and amount of each borrowing power;

  (b) the amount borrowed in each year in respect of each borrowing power;

  (c) the amount repaid during the year and the amount outstanding; and the sinking fund (if any) held at the end of the year.

(3) A statement showing in respect of each capital asset or deferred charge the exact correspondence of the balance connected therewith at the end of each year.

(4) A record of each sinking or redemption fund for the discharge of loan debt showing year by year in parallel columns:

  (a) the total amount of debt repaid out of the fund to the end of the year;

  (b) the amount remaining in the fund invested or uninvested,

together with any other information necessary for the compilation of any return required to be made to the Minister.

Where accounts of a borough council are subject in part only to audit by the district auditor, the part subject to such audit must be kept in a separate set or sets of books. Any accounts and records relating to transactions which concern that part in common with the part not subject to district audit, must also be submitted to the district auditor.

The first schedule to the regulations explains that the final ledger accounts should be presented for audit permanently bound in a volume, of which each folio or page should bear a consecutive number.

The second schedule deals with the accounting treatment of "general loans," *i.e.* loans raised by mortgage or bonds available in law for all or any statutory borrowing powers, or such borrowing powers under a particular enactment. A separate cash account must be kept recording receipt, application and repayment of such loans, and any borrowing power exercised is to be treated as an advance therefrom to the appropriate fund. A register of all such advances must be kept. Interest on general loans must be apportioned between the various borrowing accounts on the basis of advances outstanding at the beginning or end of the year, allowance being made for part periods. Sinking fund accumulations must be shown as balances unapplied on the various fund balance sheets, unless repaid to the general loans account, when they become available for loan redemption or new capital purposes, and are treated as having been repaid by the original borrowing fund. [329]

Date of Closing Accounts.—Under sects. 223 and 240 of the L.G.A., 1933 (*k*), all accounts of a borough council must now be made up yearly to March 31 in each year, or such other date as the Minister of Health directs, or the council, with the consent of the Minister, may determine. Sect. 26 of the Municipal Corpns. Act, 1882, which required accounts to be made up half-yearly is repealed by the L.G.A., 1933. [330]

Publication of Accounts. (1) *Abstract of Accounts.*—Sect. 240 (c) of the L.G.A., 1933 (*k*), provides that after the audit of the accounts for each financial year the treasurer of the borough shall print an abstract of such of the accounts for that year as are not subject to district audit. Sect. 235 empowers the Minister of Health to make regulations as to the making of an abstract of accounts as audited in cases where the district audit applies. Apart from publication, the accounts of the council and of their treasurer must be open to the inspection of any member of the council, who may make a copy of them or extract therefrom (sect. 283 (3)) (*l*).

Most borough councils have availed themselves to the fullest extent of their powers to publish an abstract of their accounts, and many of the abstracts now published present a comprehensive summary of the whole of the council's financial transactions for the period covered. It may be observed that such a publication provides a convenient means of conveying to the ratepayers information concerning the council's financial position and activities, since any local government elector of the borough is entitled to inspect the same without payment, and copies are required to be delivered to any such elector on payment of a reasonable sum for each copy (sect. 283 (4)) (*l*).

It is customary, therefore, to find very full and complete expositions of accounts and statistics in these publications, which normally contain the following sections :

(*k*) 26 Statutes 427, 435.
(*l*) *Ibid.*, 455.

(a) Introductory preface by the chief financial officer pointing out the main features of the accounts, and directing attention to any important developments.
(b) Revenue accounts, capital accounts and balance sheets for the various funds of the council, including the general rate fund. A net revenue account and net revenue appropriation account is usually included in the trading undertaking accounts.
(c) Accounts in respect of special funds, *e.g.* rating authority accounts, trusts and charities.
(d) Loan tables showing details of borrowing powers, sanctions exercised, repayments and loans outstanding.
(e) Other statistics, such as area, rateable value, population, charges for commodities, comparative statements, and an index.

Opportunity is often taken to extend the scope of the publication to provide useful statistics regarding the authority. Diagrams showing pictorially the growth of loan debt, the proportions of the authority's net expenditure borne by rates and taxes respectively, and the rateable capacity of the area, which are often included, are instances in point. No regulations have been made prescribing the form which an abstract is to take, and it will thus be found that no two books are quite similar in design or in the setting out of the information contained. This makes it difficult to compare the transactions of one authority with those of another. [331]

(2) *Epitome of Accounts.*—In view of the complexity and extent of the accounts of the more important boroughs, there has evolved a practice in recent years for such authorities to issue a small booklet, called an Epitome of Accounts, which shows the finances and statistics of the authority in condensed form. These publications should not be confused with the Epitome of Accounts rendered annually to the Minister of Health. These booklets contain only the "key" figures of the accounts, and are published with the object of providing the layman, who might otherwise be confused by the more complex Abstract of Accounts, with information concerning the authority in "tabloid" form. Such an epitome would usually consist of the following:

(1) Statistics showing area, population, rateable values, rates levied, loan debt, etc., with comparative figures for previous years.
(2) A summary of the total income and expenditure of the council, also with comparative figures.
(3) Tables showing the cost in terms of rate poundage, of the various rate services, showing the amount borne by rates and by taxes.
(4) A summary of the income and expenditure of the trading undertakings and the disposal of surpluses and deficiencies.
(5) Details of loan debt outstanding and redeemed, and capital expenditure divided between productive and non-productive purposes.
(6) An aggregate balance sheet.

In some cases a short report or preface is included directing attention to the more important particulars, and pointing out conclusions which may be drawn therefrom. It is often referenced to the relative parts of the Abstract of Accounts where more detailed information is available. Brevity is the essence of these publications, however, and they are usually limited to twenty or twenty-four pages. [332]

Financial Returns.—The duty of making a return of income and expenditure yearly to March 31 to the M. of H. is laid on every local authority by sect. 244 of the L.G.A., 1933 (*m*). Any person in default is liable on summary conviction to a fine not exceeding £20, and notwithstanding the recovery of any such fine, the making of the return may be enforced, at the instance of the Minister, by *mandamus*. Similar provisions contained in the Municipal Corpns. Act, 1882, and the Local Taxation Returns Acts, 1860 and 1877, were repealed by the above Act.

This return is known as the Epitome of Accounts, and must be compiled from the accounts for the year ended March 31 on forms supplied by the M. of H., detailed instructions as to the method of compilation also being supplied. A return need not, unless the Minister requires, be made of income and expenditure included in accounts subject to district audit, if a copy of the financial statement relating to those accounts is sent to the Minister, and the financial statement is to be deemed the return (sect. 244 (5)). The return contains the following :

(1) *Table A.—General Statistics*, showing population, rateable value, rates levied, produce of 1*d*. rate, etc.

(2) *Table B.*—Provides for the income and expenditure on the main services of the general rate fund, including elementary and higher education, police, housing, highways, etc. Expenditure is divided between loan charges, revenue contributions to capital expenditure, and general expenditure and income as between amounts received from the county council, Government grants and other income. The net expenditure on income is extended and the equivalent rate in the £ shown.

(3) *Table C.*—Shows income and expenditure on each trading fund, including details as to the disposal of any balance at the end of the year, *e.g.* carried forward, transfers to or from rates, etc.

(4) *Table D.*—Deals with special funds, including sinking and redemption funds, trust and charity funds and reserve funds.

(5) *Table E, Aggregate Rate Fund Account.*—Includes the net expenditure from Table B, transfers to and from rates shown in Table C and other income and expenditure of the council during the year, together with the equivalent rate poundages.

(6) *Table F.*—Provides for a summary to be given of the loan and capital transactions during the year.

(7) *Table G.*—Refers to the Government grants received during the year analysed under the services for which received.

The Epitome of Accounts shows in summarised form the whole of the council's financial activities during the year under review, and the M. of H. Annual Report contains the figures for the whole country as abstracted from these returns. Many authorities publish the epitome as part of their abstracts of accounts, and the headings utilised therein are occasionally used as the basis of the headings in the accounts and abstract, thus facilitating the preparation of the return, whilst its standardised form assists in the comparison of costs and statistics relating to services in different towns. **[333]**

Sect. 199 of the L.G.A., 1933 (*n*), provides for a return of sinking or redemption funds, or other provision for the repayment of moneys borrowed by the council of a county, borough, district or parish being made to the Minister of Health on request. This provision follows the course adopted in recent local Acts authorising the borrowing of money, of making the duty of transmitting a return depend on the

(*m*) 26 Statutes 437. (*n*) *Ibid.*, 415.

receipt of a request for it from the Minister. The older form of clause in a local Act required a return to be furnished annually. It should be observed that sect. 199 of the Act of 1933 extends to returns of all moneys borrowed by any of the councils above mentioned, whether under a public general Act, or a local Act, or any order, rule or regulation, and that the section takes effect in substitution for any similar requirement in any such Act or statutory order (*o*), with the result that the existing requirement is repealed. The return is required to contain such particulars and to be made up to such date as the Minister may require. It must be certified by the treasurer or other person whose duty it is to keep the accounts of the authority, and, if the Minister so requires, is to be verified by a statutory declaration. A Government department also invariably requires a return as the basis of a claim to grant in cases where a Government grant is given, this being usually a condition of grant. Examples in point include Education Substantive Grant, Unemployment Scheme Grants, Housing Grants, etc. **[334]**

London.—The position in London is dealt with in the body of this title, as Part X. of the L.G.A., 1933, relating to Accounts and Audit, applies to London (sect. 243) (*p*); as also does Part XI. relating to Local Financial Returns, the expression "local authority" including a metropolitan borough council and the Common Council of the City of London (sect. 248) (*q*). (See also *ante*, p. 156.) **[335]**

(*o*) Defined in L.G.A., 1933, s. 305.
(*p*) 26 Statutes 437.
(*q*) *Ibid.*, 439.

COSTING

See also titles:
FINANCE;
FINANCE COMMITTEE;
FINANCE DEPARTMENT;
FINANCIAL OFFICER.

GENERAL

One of the methods by which local authorities seek to exercise financial control is by the operation of modern costing systems. Such systems include the supervision of methods of wage payment, the control of stocks and stores, departmental costing, the allocation of general expenses of administration, and the submission of full and accurate claims for Government grants.

Costing can be, and is, beneficially employed in connection with all the trading undertakings of local authorities as well as in most of the rate fund services.

Well established principles, mainly relating to labour, materials and overhead expenses can usefully be employed in all departments. Clerical salaries and wages are now allocated on rational lines and not as formerly charged to one general account. Where the number of types of materials dealt with is considerable, the introduction of machinery for purposes of dissection is usually an economical proposition, particularly when the costing work is centralised. Generally accepted rules with regard to requisition, order, receipt, custody and issue of stores are followed and all purchases of materials (and services) authenticated by official records. Weekly cost sheets are prepared for all works, the true cost of which it is essential should be available, by extracting the necessary details from original entries prior to the normal analysis of the expenditure for the accounts.

Costing as operated to-day in the local government service is a development of the recommendations appearing in the Report of the Departmental Committee on the Accounts of Local Authorities, 1907, and the resulting cost accounts are merely an extension of the classification of an authority's financial transactions. [248]

MECHANISATION

A comparatively recent feature of costing schemes is the introduction of mechanical devices for classifying and tabulating records. By the utilisation of such equipment written information, having first been transposed into suitable form, is so handled mechanically as to give results identical with those previously given by hand methods and to produce them much more expeditiously.

The basis of costing by machinery is the " coding " of all original particulars whether they refer to dates, descriptions, locations, or other details into numbers, so that all necessary information is reduced to a numerical basis before proceeding. The final results are naturally produced also as numbers which may need to be decoded for the benefit of those for whom the results are prepared.

Mechanical installations of this nature can be used, *inter alia*, for the following purposes: Distributing wages and materials charges; computing hours, amounts and overhead charges on completed jobs; checking estimates; making wage rate adjustments in accordance with the basis of payment of labour; preparing monthly statements of comparative costs; comparing hours, amounts and overheads of work in progress; analysing details of expenses; stores accounting and control.

The advantages to be gained by mechanisation of these processes need not be enumerated here, but generally it may be said that it gives greater scope for increased efficiency in costing at less expense. [249]

CENTRALISATION OF CONTROL

The consideration of mechanical costing leads naturally to the much debated question of centralisation.

Centralised costing would appear to be desirable in all, although it is usually only practicable in the case of the larger, local authorities. Many, however, advocate decentralisation irrespective of the size of the authority. Having regard to the fact that cost accounts are merely an extension of the classification of transactions adopted for the purpose of the financial accounts it would seem that they could be more satisfactorily controlled by the chief financial officer. Such control, however, does not necessarily imply centralisation, and control by the finance department may be quite effective when the costing work is decentralised. Centralisation, however, in its broadest sense means not only control, but the organisation of the entire costing of all departments in one central costing branch either attached to, or working in the closest co-operation with, the finance department.

With this underlying idea in mind, the following advantages of centralisation are suggested:

Organisation in the office of, as well as control by, the chief financial officer satisfies the principle of internal check and gives greater confidence in the published results.

The finance department has records of all charges, including loan charges, legal expenses, expenditure on purchases of property, central establishment allocations, etc., not immediately or directly available to executive departments, and is more likely, therefore, to compile a complete statement of the entire cost, including a full proportion of overhead expenses.

Reconciliation with the financial records is automatically secured.

Economies in staffing and machine " units " are facilitated.

Economies in other matters such as central stores are also facilitated (*a*).

(*a*) See Co-operative Purchasing, *post*, p. 105.

On the other hand the supporters of decentralisation urge that:

Costing records should be prepared by the department by which the works are carried out for reasons of convenience of reference to technicians, etc.;

Records are more quickly available to the technical staff;

The finance department is not competent to comment upon or interpret fairly cost records involving technical considerations;

Complete centralisation is impracticable except in the case of large authorities which have numerous accounting and costing sections of staffs of all undertakings housed in one administrative block of buildings.

It may be that in certain cases a middle course of supervision by the financial officer is preferable to one of complete centralisation or one of complete decentralisation, and in any event it is essential, if satisfactory results are to be obtained, that there should be the fullest co-operation between the finance and executive departments.

In many of the larger authorities a qualified cost clerk is in charge of the costing of each of the trading departments and of the more important of the rating departments. The cost clerks, in some cases, act under the supervision of a cost accountant who is a member of the staff of the chief financial officer. [250]

CO-OPERATIVE PURCHASING

The introduction of co-operative purchasing facilitates economy, which is the aim of all costings.

It involves the purchase of all supplies for a local authority by one department. It does not necessarily involve the formation of an entirely new department, as one of the departments already in being can be utilised as the central purchaser for all other departments.

It is necessary for the transition from one method to the other to be gradual in order to avoid dislocation and friction. In the early stages of the scheme, it is usually desirable to concentrate on consumable stores.

The methods adopted usually take the following form: executive departments render to the purchasing department statements of stores required over suitable periods; schedules for tender are prepared from these statements and the necessary contracts placed by the purchasing department; executive departments are then informed as to contracts, each department thus being enabled to place its own orders against the respective contracts, or alternatively, each department notifies the purchasing department of its immediate requirements, the latter dealing directly with the contractors and arranging for direct deliveries where necessary.

The advantages claimed for co-operative purchasing include: commodities of a similar nature required by the various departments can be standardised in type, and the resulting increased quantities are purchased at more economical prices; there is a concentration of purchasing power and a consequent accession of influence as a buyer; supplies are more promptly delivered and safeguards against leakage and abuse more easily effected; a staff specialised in buying is gradually evolved. [251]

DEPARTMENTAL COSTING STANDARDS

Complete benefits from costing by local authorities are obtainable only by means of schemes embodying standards scientifically computed.

A necessary preliminary is a rational arrangement in the presentation of departmental estimates. This generally entails a reclassification of expenditure, the grouping being amended in subsequent years as found necessary. Code references are determined and on the basis of these all expenditure allocations are made. The first item in each code group designates the department; the second ((a), (b), (c), etc.), the branch or section of that department; the third, the type of expenditure; and the fourth indicates the order in which items of each type of expenditure appear. Examples of expenditure groupings of the third class are: (A) Personal remuneration and emoluments (salaries, wages, pensions, gratuities, allowances, uniform, clothing). (B) Expenses of operation (consumable materials, carriage, haulage, cartage, implements, water, gas, electric current). (C) Office expenses (telephone service, printing and stationery, advertising, postages and telegrams, travelling expenses, conferences). (D) Rents, rates, taxes, licences, customs, insurances. (E) Repairs and maintenance. (F) Loan charges. (G) Special. (H) Other incidental outlays.

The appended tabulation of a portion of a classification sheet as applied to a Public Baths department illustrates the system of code reference adopted:

	Baths Establishments.		
	Central.	Northern.	Southern.
Wages - - - - - - -	9 (a) A1	9 (b) A2	9 (c) A3
National insurance - - - - -	,, D1	,, D4	,, D7
Coals and cartage - - - - -	,, B1	,, B5	,, B9
Towelling and soap - - - - -	,, B2	,, B6	,, B10
Water - - - - - - -	,, B3	,, B7	,, B11
Electric current - - - - - -	,, B4	,, B8	,, B12
Telephone service - - - - -	,, C1	,, C3	,, C5
Printing, stationery and advertising -	,, C2	,, C4	,, C6
Rent, rates and taxes - - - -	,, D2	,, D5	,, D8
Insurance - - - - - - -	,, D3	,, D6	,, D9
Property repairs - - - - -	,, E1	,, E2	,, E3
Other outlays - - - - - -	,, H1	,, H2	,, H3

The symbols are suggestive and staffs quickly become familiar with them. Care is taken that no combination can have two different interpretations.

Each account, pay roll, and stores allocation, passed to the finance department for payment or entry, is boldly marked with the code or codes referring to the expenditure involved, no narrative being necessary except in the cases of groups G and H. Other outlays, in addition to being described by the appropriate code references, are allocated in detail.

The expenditure for the first complete year of operation under this system is often selected as a standard for future comparisons, but care is necessary to secure that the figures used represent a normal outlay.

When the figures are available, standards are compiled not only for departments but also for the various groups of expenditure, thus :

Services.	Group Standards.								Departmental Standards.
	A	B	C	D	E	F	G	H	
	£	£	£	£	£	£	£	£	£
(i) Rate fund									
.... 1									
.... 2									
.									
.									
*Bath establishments 9									
.									
.									
(ii) Trading									
....									
....									
....									
....									

* See illustrative form, *ante.*

The expenditure records in the finance department being constructed so as to accommodate allocations according to code, it is a simple matter to inform executive departments at the close of each month, or other agreed period, of the expenditure to date under each head. This is done on columnar statements of the following type :

Code.	Standard.	Estimate. Year ending ....193 .			Actual. ...... months ended.........193 .			Actual percentage of:	
								Standard.	Estimate.
	£	£	*s.*	*d.*	£	*s.*	*d.*	per cent.	per cent.
3 (a) A1 –									
„ A2 –									
et seq. –									
„ B1 –									
„ B2 –									
„ B3 –									
„ . –									
„ . –									
„ H1 –									

For the purposes of these statements, however, only items of " controllable expenditure " are stated, expenses such as those attaching to interest payments, sinking fund contributions, rates, taxes and insurance, being expressly excluded as not being under the control of the executive departments.

By these or similar methods and by repeated amendments of code according to requirements all departmental costs are satisfactorily standardised.

If the foregoing procedure is followed it is a simple matter at the end of each financial year to compile useful aggregate tabulations of costs relating to all departments of the local authority.

In compiling statistics, in setting departmental standards, and in making comparisons particular attention is paid to the following points:

Loan charges. If more than the statutory amount is set aside in a particular year (including the standard year) a special note to that effect is made.

Standards are amended periodically in order to give effect to any extensions of departmental activities.

Variations from standards are stated not only as percentages but also as sterling aggregates.

Monthly standards take cognisance of charges recurring at quarterly or half-yearly intervals.

The selection of a standard year does not imply perfect efficiency in that particular year; it merely constitutes a basis for comparison. [252]

DEPARTMENTAL COSTS AND UNITS

The preceding section deals principally with internal comparisons; that is to say, with departmental costs of one local authority for comparison month by month and year by year.

In this section, the unit costs indicated are considered more from the point of view of comparison with other authorities.

A scheme of unit costs traces inefficiency and extravagance. Just as cost accountancy is a refinement of financial accountancy, so a system of unit costs is a classification of aggregate costs. The aim to control expenditure by means of costing can be fostered by the publication of tabulations of standard unit costs throughout the country.

In the subjoined sections, appropriate units for certain services to which costing methods can be beneficially applied are indicated immediately following each sub-title. [253]

Rate Fund Services.—It is only by adequate systems of control reinforced by modern financial regulations, and wisely conceived committee policy, that local rates can be confined within reasonable limits. All rate fund expenditure is, or should be, carefully scrutinised, and appropriate costs prepared, by officials fully qualified to undertake such duties. Unit costs of selected rate fund services are now considered.

Cleansing (*b*).

Main Accounts:

Refuse collection	per ton	per 1,000 of population
Refuse disposal	,,	,, ,,
Street cleansing	per mile	,, ,,

Subsidiary Accounts:

Horses, carts and stables Lorries and sweepers Workshops General administration	Allocated according to "user."

If the department has several branch depots a further analysis is necessary, as is also required of the cost of mechanical trans-

(*b*) The larger local authorities base their cleansing costs on the M. of H.'s Memorandum (March 1925) on the subject, and allocations are in accordance with the recommendations contained therein.

port, if the separate running costs of each vehicle are desired. All loads are stated in tons on daily slips issued to carters and lorrymen. If it is impossible, owing to lack of weighbridges, to obtain exact weights, estimates are based on weights of reliable sample loads.

Hospitals (*c*).

Wards	per occupied bed; per patient-day
Ambulance	per mile run
Dining-rooms	per person fed
Dispensary	per prescription
Nurses' Homes	per nurse

Among the factors on which hospital costs depend are:

(1) The design of the building, and its geographical position.
(2) The nature of the diseases treated and the extent to which the building is occupied throughout the year.
(3) The relative proportion of the number of staff to the number of patients.

Lighting.

(1) Per lamp. (2) Per mile of street. (3) Per 1,000 of population.

Main Accounts:

Gas: street lamps; private lamps.
Gas (automatic): street lamps.
Electricity: street lamps.
Lighting of public lamps of neighbouring authorities.

Subsidiary Accounts:

These show costs of different sizes of gas street lamps and of electrical street lamps, facilitating comparisons between different districts.

The cost of "change-over" from gas to electric lighting (or the reverse) should be specially noted in any tabulation of costs.

Parks.

Per acre.
Per 1,000 of population.

Tennis courts }
Bowling greens } per player.

Parks may in some cases include promenades, etc.

Works.

(i.) *Roads and Streets* (*d*).

Per mile. Per 1,000 of population.
The net cost of highways is suitably sub-divided thus:

1. Maintenance, including minor improvements.
2. Major improvements.
3. New constructions.

Subsidiary costs per square yard relating to different types of construction are also prepared.

(*c*) The M. of H. issues annual returns relating to hospital costs.
(*d*) Returns relating to road construction and repair are called for annually by the M. of T.

(ii.) *Private Street Works* (*e*).

In order to arrive at a reasonably accurate figure of cost of private street works carried out by direct labour, for the purposes of their recovery, percentages of varying magnitudes are usually added to the different elements of cost. By this method, if the percentages are carefully calculated, overhead expenses are fully recovered. Recoveries on account of haulage and rolling are made on the basis of fixed hourly rates designed to cover wages of drivers, cost of fuel, garaging, depreciation, repairs, oils, etc.

(iii.) *Sewers.*

Per mile.

(iv.) *Sewage Disposal Works.*

Cost divisions (*f*):

Screening and tank treatment.
Filtration and humus tank treatment.
Activated sludge treatment.
Land treatment other than sludge treatment.
Pumping.

(v.) *Subsidiary Accounts:*

Mechanical transport.
Workshops.
Plant operating.
Stables.
Rollers.
Stores expenses.
Implements.
Supervision.

The charge headings are varied to suit the circumstances. [254]

Trading Undertakings.—Costing and financial control in the trading undertakings of local authorities are of the utmost importance, not only to manufacturers and traders, but to the general public as well.

Electricity.

Per 1,000 units generated (or sold).
Per unit in lb. weight of coal consumed.

Subsidiaries:

Working costs per unit sold.
Coal account.
Generating station account.

There are special considerations applying to the costing of an electricity undertaking which do not arise in the other supply services. Extensive plant is idle for long periods owing to the peak load existing only for a small proportion of the hours of darkness, and storage in large quantities is impossible. These and other exceptional characteristics account for the otherwise surprising practice of supplying electricity for power, etc. in certain instances, at prices lower than the average cost of generating it.

(*e*) P.H.A., 1875, s. 150 (13 Statutes 686), and Private Street Works Act, 1892 (9 Statutes 193).

(*f*) In accordance with form of annual return accompanying Circular No. 1165, issued by the M. of H. to sanitary authorities in 1931.

Gas.

Per therm (or per 1,000 cubic feet) of gas made (or sold).
Per ton of coal carbonised.

Subsidiaries :

Motor vehicles, wagons, gas fire repairs, gas cooker repairs, depot maintenance, retorts and settings, water gas, workshops.

One of the most pressing of problems in a gas undertaking is that of costing the wear and tear, for which purpose statements are prepared at frequent intervals for submission to the gas engineer for his guidance.

Transport.

Per 100 seat-mile.
Per car, 'bus, or vehicle mile.
Per passenger carried.

Subsidiaries :

Cost per mile for current (tramcars and trackless trolley vehicles) Permanent way (tramways) :

Per mile of single track laid.
,, ,, (excluding concrete under-bed).

Maintenance : per mile of single track.

Garage account.

In comparing the running costs of tramcars with other forms of road passenger transport such as 'buses, it is advisable to utilise the 100 seat-mile unit in preference to others which give misleading ratios owing to the widely varying seating capacities of the different types of vehicle. On this basis, costs relating to tramcars usually compare favourably with those for 'buses and trackless trolley vehicles. General experience indicates that trackless trolley vehicles (*g*) can be run at a slightly lower rate per vehicle mile than can petrol 'buses The fuel oil engine 'bus, too, produces a lower working cost per mile than does the petrol 'bus, but as the former has not yet completely passed the experimental stage any conclusion should be drawn with caution.

Water.

Constructional :

Puddling, per cubic yard.
Pipe laying, per lineal yard.

Operating :

Per million gallons supplied (in £s.).
Per thousand ,, (in pence).
Per thousand of population.

Meter services.

The main point for comment is that great care must be exercised in the allocation of the wages factor in costs relating to water undertakings as between capital and revenue works. [255]

(*g*) Illuminating figures relating to trackless trolley undertakings as well as to the better known tramways and light railways are contained in the Returns of the M. of T., published annually by H.M. Stationery Office.

Housing—*Constructional* (*h*).

Sites A, B, C, etc.

Blocks 1, 2, 3, 4, 5, 6, etc.

Site A, Block 1.

(a) Excavating.	(k) Electrical.	
(b) Concreting.	(l) Roads (ppn)	According to frontage.
(c) Draining.	(m) Sewers (ppn)	According to frontage.
(d) Bricklaying.	(n) Site (ppn)	According to area.
(e) Tiling.	(o) Subsidiary transfers	Transport, plant, tools, etc. according to "user."
(f) Joinering.		
(g) Plastering.		
(h) Painting.		
(i) Plumbing.	(p) Overhead expenses.	

Other sub-divisions :

Type of construction :

Brick. Concrete. Steel.

Contractors :

P, Q, R, etc.

Acts : 1919, 1923, 1924, 1930, etc.

It is only by the operation of a sound costing system that the relative costs of house building by direct labour on the one hand and by contract on the other can be clearly defined. Comparisons are often vitiated because of very unsatisfactory and unconvincing methods of allocating overhead expenses. Obviously a local authority rate, including too small a proportion of the full quota of establishment and other charges, would be expected to be lower than a contract rate arrived at after the full amount of overhead charges had been brought into the estimate.

Maintenance.—Annual cost per house analysed under the various schemes and activities.

Repair work :

External painting.
External repairs (classified).
Internal painting and decorating.
Internal repairs.
Maintenance of adjoining open spaces.
Rechargeable repairs (cost of repairing wilful damage by tenants is recoverable). **[256]**

RECONCILIATION OF COSTING WITH FINANCIAL RECORDS

In the interests of sound finance it is essential that a complete reconciliation of departmental cost accounts should be effected with the financial accounts.

This reconciliation is secured by aggregate adjustment accounts which, in the cost ledgers, are credited with periodical totals of all postings in respect of stores, wages, establishment charges, etc., to the debit of the detailed cost accounts. **[257]**

(*h*) The costing of housing construction activities became compulsory on local authorities with the advent of the Housing, Town Planning, etc., Act, 1919.

EXPENSES OF ADMINISTRATION

See titles BOROUGH ACCOUNTS; COUNTY ACCOUNTS; RURAL DISTRICT COUNCIL ACCOUNTS; URBAN DISTRICT COUNCIL ACCOUNTS.

CONCLUSION

Costing in the local government service has probably made more progress in the compilation of unit costs than in any other direction. The value of such published costs, however, is discounted heavily owing to variations in local conditions which are not reflected in the figures (*i*).

In some cases comparisons are disturbed by the inclusion in returns of revenue contributions to capital outlay. Gifts of lands and buildings affect the loan charges factor in other instances.

It is for this reason that a Central Costs Bureau has been suggested which could undertake the collection of more exhaustive data from all local authorities, and the further research necessary for the setting up of suitable standard costs. Such costs would permit of reliable conclusions being drawn as to the relative efficiencies of comparable services in different localities. Considerable time might elapse in completing the preliminary survey, but the ultimate economies would be considerable. The establishment expenses of such a bureau need not be excessive as much voluntary help would be forthcoming from the professional associations interested in such a development. A small permanent staff would suffice to carry out a programme of investigations.

An interesting commentary on costing methods in this country is provided in the recent report of the International City Managers Association (U.S.A.), entitled "Some Observations on Municipal Practices in European Cities." The report incorporates comments by investigators who made their visit with the object of examining, amongst other matters, costing methods. Whilst holding that there is room for improvement the reporters indicate clearly that in costing technique this country is well ahead of many continental countries.

In this connection the recent report of the Committee on Local Expenditure (Cmd. 4200) refers to the importance of costing and standard costs, more particularly in relation to public health services. The committee were impressed by the results achieved by the establishment of standardised costs in relation to the cleansing service, and urged consideration and inquiry with a view to the establishment of other standardised costs of health services, especially maintenance costs in public health institutions and the capital cost of such institutions. The committee stressed the advantages of central purchasing and standardisation of supplies, and, further, expressed the view that the function of the M. of H. in regard to costing should not be limited to the collection and publication of results (paras. 183 to 194 inclusive). [258]

(*i*) In the preface to Part I. of the costing returns for the year ending March 31, 1934 (dated January, 1935), it is said that the "principal value" of costing returns is lost unless they are available for purposes of comparison to all local authorities with similar relevant functions. Stress is also laid in the covering letter on the importance of promptitude in submitting costing returns.

ACCOUNTS OF LOCAL AUTHORITIES

General Statutory Requirements.—The accounts and accounting procedure of local authorities have, generally speaking, been but little the subject of regulation by statute or order, until comparatively recent years. The District Auditors Act, 1879, and sect. 58 of the L.G.A., 1894 (*a*), allowed the Local Government Board to prescribe forms of account, but this power had not been fully utilised.

(*a*) 10 Statutes 814 ; repealed by L.G.A., 1933.

As respects the accounts of U.D.Cs., the General Order of 1880 had indeed been made under sect. 5 of the District Auditors Act, 1879 (*b*), and the manner in which the financial transactions were to be recorded had been prescribed in some detail, together with the keeping of minute books dealing with financial transactions, general ledgers, rate collection accounts and other matters. Whilst, however, headings for the various ledger accounts to be opened were indicated, sufficient instructions as to the principles on which the entries were to be posted were not given, and in addition, the orders assumed that accountancy work would be distributed between the clerk and the surveyor, the existence of an accountant who would be responsible for keeping the accounts apparently not being contemplated. In recent years the R. & V.A., 1925 (*c*), and the Rate Accounts Orders, 1926, have resulted in many of the regulations in the earlier order becoming obsolete, but prior to this it had been found impossible fully to comply with its terms, and in the case of the large U.D.Cs., where a separate finance department existed, it was usual to find the Order of 1880 almost completely ignored.

In the case of metropolitan borough councils, sect. 14 of the London Government Act, 1899 (*d*) conferred the necessary power, and an order was issued in 1901 dealing with the forms to be used in the making and collection of rates. County councils, provincial borough councils, and rural district councils, however, were not, in 1907, subject to any orders dealing with their accounts generally, although power to make such orders was available to the Local Government Board.

The District Auditors Act, 1879, is repealed by the L.G.A., 1933, and sect. 235 of that Act allows the Minister of Health to make regulations, enforceable by penalties, with respect to the preparation and audit of accounts which are subject to audit by a district auditor, including, among the matters not relating to audit, (1) the financial transactions which are to be recorded in the accounts; (2) the mode of keeping the accounts of the authority and of their officers and the form of the accounts; and (3) the mode in which, if it is so prescribed, the accounts are to be certified by the authority or any officer of the authority.

The Joint Select Committee on Municipal Trading, 1903, was of the opinion that in view of the ever increasing number and magnitude of municipal undertakings, it was most desirable that a high and uniform standard of account keeping should prevail throughout the country. They were, however, doubtful whether it would be possible to prescribe a standard form of keeping accounts for all municipal or other local authorities, having regard to the varying conditions existing in different districts. On the other hand, the Departmental Committee on the Accounts of Local Authorities, 1907, not only recognised the need for uniformity, but expressed the opinion that uniformity of published accounts could to a great extent be obtained. The report states: " With regard to the system of accounts we are firmly convinced that general principles such as have been here laid down should be clearly defined by regulations. But the details of the book-keeping may need a certain amount of elasticity in order that they may be adapted to the diversities of local requirements, and in our opinion it is both unnecessary and impracticable to attempt to insist upon a stereotyped

(*b*) 10 Statutes 573; repealed by L.G.A., 1933.
(*c*) 14 Statutes 617 *et seq.*
(*d*) 11 Statutes 1233.

uniformity, provided the careful observance of the general principles is secured." The report did not result in Governmental action, but the recommendations were widely recognised as being sound and practicable and were followed in whole or in part by many local authorities. [53]

Various regulations have been made in post-war years, dealing with particular sections of local authorities' accounts, among the more important of which may be mentioned :

(1) *Housing Accounts Order*, 1920 (*e*).—This order was made under sect. 5 of the District Auditors' Act, 1879, and dealt with the accounts necessary for houses built under the provisions of the Housing, Town Planning, etc., Act, 1919, under which the Government undertook to bear the deficiency on the revenue account in excess of a penny rate. The order contains a list of prescribed ledger accounts and the manner of treating various transactions in the accounts, and various forms of books to be used are given. [54]

(2) *Rate Accounts Orders*, 1926 (*f*).—These orders were necessitated by the fundamental changes in rating procedure involved under the Rating and Valuation Act, 1925 (*g*), and laid down in some detail the books to be used and their rulings, the manner in which they were to be posted, and the specific duties of the chief financial officer and rating officers respectively. Additions to the prescribed forms are permitted but otherwise the consent of the M. of H. is required to any alterations in the forms or any other departure from the terms of the order. [55]

(3) *The Accounts (Boroughs and Metropolitan Boroughs) Regulations*, 1930 (*h*).—This order came into force on April 1, 1930, and was made in pursuance of sect. 5 of the District Auditors Act, 1879. It deals in detail with the principles on which the accounts of a local authority should be kept and balanced, and in many directions is in accordance with the recommendations of the Accounts Committee of 1907. The operation of the regulations is, however, restricted, in that they do not apply to those accounts of provincial boroughs which are not subject to district audit, and, of course, not at all to authorities other than metropolitan and provincial borough councils. The regulations are of great interest and importance, representing as they do, an official pronouncement regarding the application of the principles of accountancy to the transactions of local authorities, and it is probable that many authorities, to whom the regulations do not apply compulsorily, will follow the principles enunciated therein. A summary of the regulations is given under the title BOROUGH ACCOUNTS. The regulations are cited in this section as the Regulations of 1930. Regulations have also been made under sect. 5 of the District Auditors Act, 1879, governing the accounts of county councils and their committees and officers in relation to the administration of poor relief (*i*). These regulations closely

(*e*) S.R. & O., 1920, No. 487.
(*f*) S.R. & O., 1926, Nos. 1123, 1178.
(*g*) 14 Statutes 617 *et seq.*
(*h*) S.R. & O., 1930, No. 30.
(*i*) Public Assistance Accounts (County Councils) Regulations, 1930 (S.R. & O., 1930, No. 29).

resemble the regulations of 1930 relating to borough accounts, and it will be necessary to refer only to the latter regulations for illustrations in the course of this article. [56]

General Principles of Local Authorities' Accounts.—The specific function of local authorities in providing services for the community, in many cases in conjunction with, and subject to the control of, the central authority, has an important bearing on the system of accounts adopted, and this is further affected by the numerous differences in local conditions. There are, however, several important principles which should be, and usually are, applied in the accounts of all local authorities.

Evidence submitted to the Departmental Committee in 1907 revealed that the double-entry system was utilised by almost all local authorities, but it was noted that whilst most of the larger authorities adopted the income and expenditure system, very many of the smaller, and some of the larger authorities, continued to use the receipts and payments basis. The system of receipts and payments takes account only of cash received and paid during any particular accounting period, irrespective of the date of the actual transactions which have resulted in the receipt or payment of cash. The impersonal accounts raised to show groups of like receipts or payments will consist merely of totals of the relative cash book items, the latter being the main book of account under this system. The system has the merit of simplicity, enabling accounts to be closed quickly at the end of a period. On the other hand, simplicity is obtained at the expense of completeness, it being difficult, if not impossible, to prepare a revenue account, or a profit and loss account, and balance sheet from accounts kept on this basis. Moreover, the system lends itself to manipulation, since payments may be deliberately deferred so as to exclude them from the accounts of the year to which they properly belong by the simple expedient of holding back tradesmen's accounts for payment until the succeeding accounting period. In the latter case, the accounts of two years would necessarily be wrongly stated, and the result would be the incorrect rating of the ratepayers of each year.

The income and expenditure system, on the other hand, takes account of all items of expenditure incurred or of income accrued during a particular accounting period without regard to the date of the actual payment or receipt of cash by which the transactions are ultimately to be completed. It is thus necessary to include in the accounts accrued proportions of such items as rents, salaries and wages, and interest on loans, and records of other transactions such as the consumption of materials and stores, which are not cash transactions though necessarily expressed in terms of money. As a result the transactions of each period are presented completely and accurately, showing a correct statement of the financial position, and each year's ratepayers are charged with the exact cost of the operations of that year, since the rate estimates must also be framed on the income and expenditure basis. The two main objections to this system are the undesirability of including estimated items in the accounts in cases where the actual amounts cannot be ascertained, and the delay in closing accounts, as compared with those on the cash basis. With regard to the first point the 1907 committee considered it preferable to insert estimates rather than to omit substantial items, and thought that with proper care and efficient audit the discrepancies should not be considerable. The second point is to a certain extent influenced by the first, and depends largely on the administrative machine. It is found in practice that little difficulty is experienced on this head where an efficient system is in force.

The committee dealt fully with the merits of the two systems, and recommended the income and expenditure basis as being the most efficient system of account keeping suitable for general application to local authorities. In addition the 1907 committee recommended and the Regulations of 1930 lay down that detailed stores accounts should be maintained so as to control all stores from purchase to consumption, and that full and complete cost accounts should be kept. The double-entry and income and expenditure bases are necessary corollaries to the keeping of such accounts. In settling the terms of clause 215 of the Local Government Bill (now sect. 219 of the L.G.A., 1933), the Chelmsford Committee omitted the words "receipts and expenditure," which appeared in sect. 247 of the P.H.A., 1875 (*j*), and which justified the accounts being kept on the basis of cash received and paid. The financial transactions to be recorded in the accounts are to be dealt with in the regulations of the Minister of Health under sect. 235 (1) (a) of the L.G.A., 1933.

The above principles are in accordance with general commercial practice, but in other respects there are divergences as between municipal and commercial accounts. Generally speaking the aim of the local authority is to effect a balance between each year's expenditure and income, which are arrived at by means of estimates, and a sufficient rate or precept is levied to meet the deficit disclosed by such estimates. The commercial concern, being actuated by motives of profit, regulates its expenditure by reference to its probable income. One consequent difference is that with regard to expenditure the local authority is concerned mainly with the impersonal aspect of the transactions, and as a result, detailed creditors' accounts are rarely maintained. The personal aspect of such transactions, is, however, of importance to the commercial concern, and it is usual to find one detailed account for each person dealing with the firm whether as creditor or debtor. **[57]**

The manner in which a commercial company and a local authority respectively acquire their capital assets and liabilities also affects the accounting principles involved. The following distinctions illustrate this:

(1) The company finances its capital requirements by an issue of permanent capital, *e.g.* stock or shares which normally are irredeemable during the lifetime of the company. Except in the case of certain public utility companies, the double account system under which capital assets and liabilities are balanced separately is not adopted, and the balance sheet will not disclose what assets were acquired from the proceeds of the capital issue.

The local authority, on the other hand, finances its capital requirements from borrowed money which must be repaid over the period of years sanctioned by the central authority having regard to the estimated life of the assets acquired, and the double account system is therefore adopted.

It should be noted that there are two methods of stating capital expenditure under this system. The "capital asset"

(*j*) 13 Statutes 728. For the L.G.A., 1933, see 26 Statutes, title "Local Government."

method consists in stating capital expenditure at original cost in the capital account and the capital section of the balance sheet, and *per contra* the sources from which the expenditure was financed, *i.e.* loans outstanding and capital provisions, *e.g.* loans repaid, revenue contributions to capital, etc. The capital provision items are in the nature of a surplus, in many cases being shown under the generic heading of " surplus of capital assets," and are inserted in the capital account as balancing items. By this method the historical record of capital expenditure is preserved in the accounts even where assets are exhausted or alienated. Under the alternative method, *i.e.* the " deferred charge " method, all loan expenditure, so far as not yet covered by revenue contributions, is recorded as deferred charges, the only balancing item necessary *per contra* being that of outstanding loan debt. This entails the writing down of all capital provision items in respect of such expenditure on both sides of the capital account and balance sheet. Alienated assets immediately disappear from the accounts, and other deferred charges are gradually exhausted within the sanction period. The Regulations of 1930 provide for either or both systems being applied in appropriate circumstances as explained *post.* **[58]**

(2) Consequent on (1) it becomes necessary in the case of a local authority using the " capital assets " system to adjust the capital account as and when loans are repaid or expenditure of a capital nature met from revenue, by opening a surplus account for such items representing the portions of the assets acquired by the repayment of debt from revenue, and functioning as a balancing item in the capital account. Alternatively these items would be written off the capital expenditure account. This procedure differs from that of a company whose assets are acquired out of the share capital subscribed, but parallel conditions do exist where capital expenditure is financed out of the proceeds of a debenture issue which is redeemed by means of a sinking fund provided out of " profits." A " surplus " arises as a result of what is known as " permutation " of the sinking fund. Debt is repaid, not out of the sinking fund, but by means of the assets representing such fund. The purpose of the sinking fund being thus exhausted by the redemption of the debt the fund changes its character, becoming a surplus. **[59]**

(3) The Companies Act, 1929 (*k*), contains stringent provisions as to the valuation of assets for the purpose of the company's balance sheet. In the case of fixed assets, the basis of valuation must be stated on the face of the balance sheet, and as the auditor to the company must examine the values placed on assets included in the balance sheet, it is certain that these valuations and the question of depreciation must be the subject of periodical review by the directors.

On the other hand, the strict observance of the double account system in the case of the local authority entails capital assets being allowed to remain in the capital account at cost,

(*k*) 2 Statutes 775 *et seq.*

even though alienated or depreciated below that value. This is subject to modification where the deferred charge system as explained above is used. In this connection some important suggestions were made by the Departmental Committee of 1907, their recommendation being that assets having an abiding or realisable value, including the whole of the assets and capital outlay in respect of each trading undertaking should be maintained in the balance sheet at original cost, so long as they remained in the possession of the local authority. Para. 8 (5) of the Regulations of 1930 directs that where any property treated as a capital asset passes out of the possession of the council or ceases to be serviceable, an amount equal to the cost thereof is to be written off the capital asset account. [60]

(4) The normal commercial practice is to write off as soon as possible, intangible assets such as expenses of capital issues, preliminary expenses, etc. In many cases also, such assets as goodwill, patent rights, etc., are written down below cost, frequently to merely nominal values.

The majority of local authorities' capital accounts contain items of this nature, *e.g.* promotion and opposition of bills in Parliament, sewerage works, street improvements, roads, etc., which are, by their nature, non-productive. The Departmental Committee of 1907 recommended that such capital expenditure should be written down by the amount of provision made for debt repayment. Para. 8 (5) of the Regulations of 1930 directs that where any properties or works which are not realisable assets are treated as capital assets, the capital provision in respect thereof (*e.g.* loans redeemed) shall be separately stated in the accounts and upon the balance sheet. It would seem, therefore, that under the terms of this order intangible assets, as mentioned above, may still be allowed to remain in the accounts. [61]

The conclusions to be drawn from the various considerations enumerated above indicate that the double entry, income and expenditure basis of accounting and estimating is indispensable to the proper financial administration of local services, whether compulsory or otherwise. With regard to the capital section of the accounts, the double account system would appear to provide the correct treatment, but whether the " capital asset " or " deferred charge " system should be applied must depend upon the circumstances of each case. If the former be adopted, the historical aspect of the capital expenditure is preserved even where assets may have become non-existent by alienation or obsolescence. On the other hand, where the " deferred charge " method is applied, the more correct view of the financial position will be exhibited but with some loss in the matter of historical record. There is, however, no reason why any necessary historical record should not be maintained in statements supplementary to the actual accounts. [62]

Methods of Accountancy. *Ordering of Goods* (*l*).—As mentioned above, the Departmental Committee of 1907 stressed the importance of an adequate control over the purchase and subsequent consumption of materials, and a system of stores accounts and balancing is included

(*l*) All local authorities except non-county boroughs and parish meetings must make standing orders relating to contracts for the supply of goods or materials. L.G.A., 1933, s. 266 (2), see 26 Statutes, title " Local Government."

in the Regulations of 1930. The first essential in such a system must be control over the ordering of goods.

With many authorities all materials required are entered in a requisition book which is then submitted for the approval of the appropriate committee. In cases where, due to urgency or allowed by custom, goods have already been ordered or supplied, the items are distinguished by being entered in red ink. After authorisation by the committee, official orders are made out, preferably in carbon triplicate, one being sent to the tradesman, one remaining in the book, the third copy being transmitted to the chief financial officer for purposes of check. The old system which provided that an official invoice should accompany the order is open to serious objections since it is preferable from an audit standpoint to allow each firm to render claims on its own forms, and is little used at the present day.

In some cases the requisition book system is dispensed with, and chief officials of the various departments are allowed to purchase materials not exceeding (say) £10 in value, other requirements having to be sanctioned by the committee prior to purchase. Where it is known that large quantities of materials will be required during a period, as for example, road materials, school supplies and stationery, it is usual to obtain prices or tenders for submission to the committee. On acceptance, orders are sent to the selected firms as and when supplies are required, at the stated price, and in the case of materials common to more than one department, each department is allowed to order its own supplies.

Order books are in many cases purchased and controlled by the chief financial officer, being issued to the several departments as required. An additional measure of control may be obtained where only the chief official or his chief assistant is authorised to sign the orders given.

On receipt the goods are checked off in the executive department against the copy of the order, which is then suitably marked and the invoice sent to the financial officer's department. In the case of materials going to store, particulars will first be entered in the "goods received" records, which will subsequently be compared with the copy of the order. This ensures that the goods are in accordance with the order both as to quantity and quality, and at the same time practically eliminates the possibility of duplicate payments by reason of the fact that in the event of a subsequent invoice or delivery note being received, the attempt to check the goods with the order will disclose that this has already been performed. At the end of an accounting period, outstanding creditors may be ascertained from the unmarked orders.

Before an account is passed for payment it is usual for a routine process of check to be applied to it, and the application of this check may be evidenced by means of a rubber stamp, which would show the following details on the invoice :

(1) Goods received by.
(2) Checked in executive department.
(3) Certified by head of executive department.
(4) Checked in financial officer's department.
(5) Chief financial officer.
(6) Member of committee.

The space against each item would be initialled by the person responsible for the particular line of check, and the head of the executive department and chief financial officer also would certify before submitting the bills to committee, when the invoice would be finally certified as correct by a member of the committee. Responsibility for the correctness of the invoice is in this manner spread over various persons, and tends to prevent fraud except by collusion. It is essential to the proper working of the system that it should not be allowed to degenerate into merely a mechanical check, and it is therefore advisable for test checks to be applied periodically by the internal audit department. It should be remembered that materials are equivalent to cash and in the same way are liable to misappropriation. If the above mentioned stamp is suitably designed it may be utilised in marking the particular expenditure account and sub-account to which the expenditure is to be posted. [63]

Payment of Accounts.—The system of paying accounts has an important bearing on the accountancy method, and although variations are found in practice, all systems are usually in accordance with certain well-defined principles. Sect. 187 (2) of the L.G.A., 1933, enacts that all payments out of the general rate fund of a borough shall only be made in pursuance of an order of the council signed by three members thereof and countersigned by the town clerk, and the same order may include several payments. This is subject to the exceptions for the periodical and other payments there set out (see BOROUGH ACCOUNTS).

Similar provisions apply to county councils under sect. 184 (2) of the above Act, and in practice the majority of other local authorities apply this system to the payment of accounts. This order for payment is an authority to the treasurer to issue cheques for or otherwise pay the account scheduled to the order (*ll*).

All payments to and out of the county fund and general rate fund are to be made to and by the county treasurer and borough treasurer respectively under the terms of the L.G.A., 1933 (*m*), and it is usual, therefore, for the chief financial officer to be responsible for the submission of all accounts to committees for approval. Although district councils are not subject to a similar provision, it is usual for this method to be adopted by them. For administrative convenience it is advisable to arrange for invoices to be sent to the chief financial officer's department several days prior to the meeting of the committee, after having been suitably checked, initialled and marked as to allocation to expenditure accounts in the executive department. After the finance department check has been applied, the invoices are listed on a schedule, the form of which will depend to some extent on the local accounting system, but will normally include columns for account number or other reference, tradesmen, particulars and amount of bill. It is also usual for a certificate to be included to the effect that the total of the amounts set out therein is recommended to the council for payment, this being signed by the chairman of the committee.

When all committees have met during a particular month it becomes necessary to prepare cheques in payment of the accounts approved by them, and various methods are adopted for this purpose. In some cases the invoices of all committees are first brought together and sorted into alphabetical order, so as to allow of one payment only being made to each tradesman. In others the same end is achieved by examining the separate schedules of accounts and arriving at the total

(*ll*) Where the treasurer is a banker the "order on the treasurer" may take the form of a cheque, separate orders being issued in respect of the various accounts for payment, but such a course is inconvenient. See p. 34.

(*m*) Ss. 184 (1), 187 (1). See 26 Statutes, title "Local Government."

for each tradesman who has submitted accounts to more than one committee. Where there are separate bank accounts, this may involve cheques being analysed as between funds, this being effected by a printed or stamped ruling on the back of the cheques. In some cases one of the above systems is adopted for the general rate or other main fund, separate series of cheques being used for special accounts of the fund, *e.g.* education, housing, trading undertakings, etc.

The accounts are not fully authorised until approved by the council, and to effect this a list of all the cheques, giving cheque number, amount and payee, and agreeing with the total of all schedules of accounts submitted to the various committees, must be prepared, or alternatively the lists of accounts passed for payment, printed in many cases in the minutes of committees, can be bound together so as to serve the same purpose. These lists are known as orders on treasurer, and normally will contain a certificate authorising the treasurer to pay the items set out therein. Such an order, on approval by the council, will be signed by three members and the clerk, and a copy sent to the banker as his authority to honour the cheques.

Regarding the signing of cheques, some of the smaller authorities make each separate cheque an order of the council on the treasurer signed by three members and the clerk, in which case the list of cheques described above operates merely as a letter of advice. The number of cheques issued, however, is usually such as to make this course decidedly inconvenient, if not impossible, in the case of the larger authorities, and there does not appear to be any advantage in it. Where the chief financial officer is the treasurer, no authority to sign cheques is required, although a copy of the order on treasurer, or other list of cheques, is sent to the bank as an advice that cheques are to be drawn. Where the treasurer is a bank manager, the chief financial officer may conveniently be authorised to sign cheques in accordance with the order on treasurer, the cheques being in fact addressed to the treasurer.

It sometimes happens that accounts, due to urgency or to secure discount, etc., have to be paid before sanction of the council in the usual manner can be obtained, and regulations as to the method of payment are necessary. One method, widely used, is to insert the details on a special bank order, to which the signatures of three members of the council, the clerk and the treasurer are appended, and arrangements are made with the bank whereby cheques issued in pursuance of such an order are honoured immediately. Such accounts would be submitted subsequently to the appropriate committee for authorisation after payment. Some authorities maintain a special bank account, out of which payments such as the above may be made, kept normally on the imprest system, under which disbursements must be subsequently approved by the committee, and paid into the account to bring the imprest up to its original figure. It is usual, under this system, to authorise the chief financial officer to draw cheques on the special bank account. Perhaps the most convenient method, particularly from the audit standpoint, is for a sub-committee of the finance committee to meet (say) each week for the purpose of sanctioning payments of this nature, but the decisions of the committee should be approved by the council at a subsequent meeting. None of these methods can be regarded as strictly complying with the law regarding payments of accounts where the urgent account is one which requires an "order on treasurer." [64]

Petty Cash.—Accounts of a trifling nature will usually be paid out of petty cash, but it is advisable that the number of such accounts should be as few as possible. Where, for example, all departments are housed in the same building, it may be convenient to have only one such balance, under the control of the chief financial officer, whilst in others, circumstances may necessitate each department's operating its own petty cash. In all cases the balance allotted should be merely such as is reasonably necessary, having regard to the class of payments to be made, and the latter should be closely defined as to nature and amount.

The method of recording petty cash should be that known as the imprest system, which is now largely used in both commercial and municipal accounting systems. Under this system, the petty cashier is advanced a round sum, sufficient to last for (say) a month, and this is debited to his petty cash account. All disbursements out of petty cash are recorded on the credit side of the petty cash account, which usually contains analysis columns allowing the expenditure to be allocated to the appropriate heads of account, and should in all cases be supported by vouchers. Printed slips should be utilised to obtain receipts, where, as in many cases, no other would be available. An account of disbursements, with vouchers, is submitted to a committee each month, and a cheque drawn in payment, as in the case of an ordinary tradesman creditor, and the refund of this amount will again bring up the petty cash balance to the amount of the original imprest.

Continuous and efficient internal audit is necessary in the case of these accounts, and at any time, the petty cashier should be able to produce cash and vouchers to the amount of his original balance. Subject to the imposition of such an audit, the main ledger need only contain a debit of the imprest advanced, which may be carried forward each year so long as the balance is not altered. [65]

Expenditure Accounts.—As mentioned previously, the local authority is concerned primarily with its expenditure, and it is therefore of great importance that this branch of its accounting system should be carefully systematised. The directions of the Regulations of 1930 are of considerable interest in this connection. Dealing with the chief accounts of the council, the regulations state that an account must be opened of the expenditure under each head of account which appears in the epitome of accounts or other returns to be furnished to the Minister of Health, or is needed for the purposes of preliminary classification together with such further classification under sub-heads as may be deemed necessary by the council. The classification of the council's expenditure in these accounts must be such as will show separately the expenditure in respect of:

(a) each head of account;
(b) each area of charge;
(c) each institution;
(d) each work chargeable to capital or loan account; and
(e) each work or service the cost of which is chargeable to other persons.

In addition, such preliminary classification accounts shall be kept as are necessary for a proper allocation of labour charges, cost of supervision, use of plant, handling of material, services of workshops and any other matters in which more than one head or sub-head of expenditure is concerned.

The majority of the expenditure accounts will be comprised in the revenue ledger or section of the ledger, and it is helpful to have these running in some definite order, *e.g.* alphabetically, or in the order of the estimates, epitome or abstract of accounts. All accounts relating to expenditure subject to audit by the district auditor must be kept in a separate set or sets of books under the Regulations of 1930.

In one form or another the expenditure journal system of posting the expenditure accounts is the method usually adopted. The ruling of this book, which can conveniently be on the loose leaf principle, includes columns for date, tradesman, particulars, folio, total, code numbers, etc., and a number of analysis columns, sufficient to accommodate the analysis required. Each invoice passed for payment is entered herein, either from the cash book, if this is detailed, or from the schedule of accounts submitted to the committee, the total then being analysed under the various headings and sub-headings, according to the allocation on the invoice. Various devices are in existence in order to economise the work involved in the above, as for example, providing the schedule of accounts with analysis columns, or attaching thereto sheets containing analysis columns, in order to make it function as an expenditure journal. In other cases a carbon copy of the schedule of accounts is utilised as the credit side of the cash book, the system to be adopted depending on local circumstances.

Normally the expenditure journal will be cast and posted monthly or quarterly, and the expenditure accounts will consequently disclose totals only, any detail required being the subject of reference back to the expenditure journal. The system, however, possesses the merit of not overburdening the ledger with a mass of detail.

The Regulations of 1930 also provide for the keeping of the necessary primary records, statements and accounts in order to arrive at the proper classification of the council's expenditure. With regard to labour charges, the records must include time sheets or records, wages sheets or books, and a classification of the wages charge so summarised as to disclose the charge in respect of each work, etc., and to agree with the gross wages charge. Such primary records will usually form part of the costing system, and will enable the wages account in the ledger to be cleared by transfer to the various expenditure accounts. Similar remarks apply to the stores accounts necessary under the regulations, with the addition in this case of stocktaking returns, and a summary account of stores received, issued and remaining on hand. With regard to subsidiary services such as horses, vehicles, rollers, etc., records must be kept of the daily services rendered so as to provide a basis for charging or apportioning the cost among the various expenditure accounts. [66]

Income Accounts.—The classification of the income accounts is provided for in the Regulations of 1930 on similar lines to those relating to expenditure, *i.e.*, an account must be opened under each head of account appearing in the epitome of accounts, or other return, or which is needed for the purposes of preliminary classification, together with such further classification as may be deemed desirable. The classification is to be such as will show separately the income in respect of:

(a) each head of account;
(b) each area of charge;
(c) each institution;
(d) each work chargeable to capital or loan account; and
(e) each work or service the cost of which is chargeable to other persons.

Considerations which make it generally unnecessary to keep detailed personal accounts with creditors do not apply to debtors and the necessity for detailed personal accounts will be apparent. The regulations provide for debtors' accounts to be kept in respect of all credit income, each of which must contain a punctual and detailed record of:

(a) the amounts receivable by the council;
(b) the amounts received in respect thereof;
(c) the number and date of each receipt given in respect thereof;
(d) the items (if any) written off as irrecoverable;
(e) the authority, and, either by reference or by entry, the reason for each such writing off;
(f) the items carried forward as recoverable arrears.

The regulations provide for the detailed debtors' accounts to be controlled by total main ledger accounts, by means of summarising and balancing each account of credit income at the close of each year, and at such other times as may be required, the results thus shown being reproduced in the corresponding total debtors' account in the ledger. It is also provided that in each income account, the total of the amounts received shall agree with the total of the corresponding receipts appearing in the collecting officer's accounts, and that a separate account shall be kept in respect of cash income.

In the generality of cases, the above principles are observed by all local authorities, usually in one of two ways. In cases where the debtors' ledgers are written up direct from the original records, *e.g.* tabular records such as gas, electricity and water rentals, etc., and card ledgers, a summary of the postings for the period is made, and the totals utilised in raising the necessary control accounts in the ledger. In other cases an income journal is compiled from the primary records, and the postings in detail to the debtors' ledgers and in total to the main ledger effected therefrom.

The treatment of capital income in most cases is the same. Repayments of Housing and Small Dwellings Acquisition Act advances and hire-purchase receipts can usually be dealt with by a tabular record or card ledger. It is, however, important in these cases to observe that the repayment and interest portions of the income are taken to separate accounts. Sales of capital assets, lump sum grants towards capital expenditure and similar capital receipts of a more or less sporadic nature may each be the subject of a separate income account, referred to in the Regulations of 1930 as a "Capital Receipts Account," and this must be kept so as to show how such receipts have been appropriated, and the extent to which they remain unappropriated. **[67]**

Vouchers.—Vouchers may be said to include anything which will afford independent evidence of a *bona fide* payment, receipt or existence of an asset, and in auditing the accounts of a local authority, the auditor will normally require such vouchers to be produced to him. Vouchers may be classified broadly as between those relating to income, and those relating to expenditure, but whilst there is this distinction, it should be noted that in some cases the two are interdependent. For example, in checking the expenditure debited against the recoverable works account, the auditor will at the same time be verifying the total amount to be repaid by the persons on whose behalf the work was done.

The main consideration from the financial officer's point of view consists of filing those vouchers which form the basis of the accounting system in some suitable order, so as to be readily producible when required. There should be a prime record in existence for each transaction involving income or expenditure, and in cases where this would not be so, *e.g.* certain petty cash payments, the system should provide for some voucher being brought into existence. Examples of income vouchers are:

(1) Counterfoils of all invoices rendered to debtors except in the case of rates, electricity, etc.
(2) Recoverable works records, or job cost accounts on the basis of which invoices are rendered to debtors.
(3) Meter reading cards, meter fixed records, hire and hire-purchase agreements, etc.
(4) Counterfoil receipt books.
(5) Register of receipts.
(6) Copies of tenancy agreements, leases and other deeds of title.

Miscellaneous items of income which arise periodically, such as ground rents, rents of property, etc., should be noted in a register of receipts, or card record kept for this purpose. In the case of land purchased, the title deeds and conveyance will not only show the purchase-money paid, but will provide information as to any income to be received, *e.g.* from rents. Receipt books, which should be under the control of the internal audit department, should be suitably numbered, and in many cases can be conveniently purchased in blocks so as to last for one complete year. In auditing the accounts for any particular year, the auditor may then be given the whole of the receipt book counterfoils for that year to be filed away together after use.

It is, however, in connection with expenditure that the subject of vouchers must receive chief consideration, mainly as a result of the different accountancy method adopted. As, in the case of income detailed personal accounts are usually kept, the accounting system will in itself contain detailed original records, but this is not normally the case where expenditure is concerned, and apart from such occasional vouching instruments as minutes and correspondence, the chief classes of expenditure vouchers consist of:

(1) Creditors' invoices and statements;
(2) Cheques returned after payment by the bank;
(3) Workmen's time sheets; and
(4) Contracts for works and supply of materials.

It will be appreciated that if no detailed personal ledger accounts are kept with creditors, the invoices themselves fulfil this function, and consequently they must be carefully preserved, and filed in some convenient order. Where the system of paying accounts (see *ante*) results in the invoices for a particular month being grouped together in alphabetical order under the names of the tradesmen, they can be filed together in that order, provided each invoice or group of invoices, is given a number, which is also inserted in the expenditure journal and committee schedule, against the appropriate item or items. Where, on the other hand, invoices are kept separately as between committees, then it is probably better to file them separately in the same way, numbering each record as explained above, and in each case filing the invoices in strong binders, containing legible descriptions and numbers on the cover. The numbering is important to enable ready reference to be made to the invoices where necessary.

Paid cheques should be obtained periodically from the bank and filed either separately at the back of the invoice to which they relate or together in separate binders. Although the former method aids the auditor to some extent, since he is able simultaneously to examine the tradesman's invoice and paid cheque, it is often considered preferable to file cheques together, since they are all of the same size, and consequently easy to handle, whilst the former method creates difficulties where one cheque is divided over various funds and invoices are filed as between committees.

Workmen's time sheets are usually ruled to last for one week, and in addition to containing details of time worked, should show the total wage payable for the week, agreeing with the gross wage payable as per the wages sheet, allocated over the various expenditure headings to which the work relates. The time sheets will then provide the basis for posting the cost accounts, and will usually be retained and filed by the costing department. It is desirable in this case that the time sheets be numbered in order of the wages sheets or abstracts, and filed in the same order, keeping those relating to each week in separate bundles. They will then be readily available, and the method will facilitate any check which the auditor might require to apply. **[68]**

Cash Book.—The cash book is the personal ledger account of the council's bank transactions, and under the Regulations of 1930 must contain an account of the sums received on behalf of the council by their bankers, and of the payments ordered to be made from the bank balance by a cheque or other authority.

Cash books in use generally by local authorities may be classified between those showing:

(1) Debit and credit analysis;
(2) Credit but not debit analysis; and
(3) Totals only on both sides.

The form to be used depends somewhat on the accounting system in force. It was usual to find form (1) in operation where the basis of the accounts was receipts and payments, but this is rapidly falling out of use. Form (2) may be used in substitution for an expenditure journal although the two are often found together; whilst form (3) demands both detailed cash and expenditure records to enable posting totals to be arrived at. It has to be remembered that the cash book is merely a ledger account kept separately for the sake of convenience, and since it is desirable that detail should be relegated to the primary records and so far as possible kept out of the ledger, there would seem to be little justification for either of the first two methods.

In utilising the third method, the material necessary for posting the debit side of the cash book will be found in total in the cashier's collecting and deposit book which records sums received as per the counterfoil receipts, and payments over to bank. This procedure is simplified if the rule be made that all receipts should be paid in through the cash office, and never direct to bank. In some cases, however, receipts are credited direct to the bank, notably in the case of Government grants, and the cash book entry should then be made, in principle, from the grant notification rather than the bank pass book. The credit side may be posted in total from the bank order or each committee schedule according to the number of cash books and bank accounts.

Whatever the method of keeping the cash book, it is necessary periodically to reconcile the balance appearing thereon with that shown in the bank pass book, and this also is provided for in the Regulations of 1930. This is effected by deducting from the balance of the pass book cheques issued but unpresented and bank credits not yet passed through the cash book, the subsequent agreement being expressed in the form of a reconciliation statement which should be written into the cash book yearly or half-yearly. Reconciliation necessitates the marking off of all pass book items with the corresponding entries in the cash book, and where the latter consists only of totals, resort must be had to such primary records as bank orders, cheque counterfoils, etc.

Cash books may be designed to distinguish capital and revenue and transactions relating to different funds, or separate cash books may be kept in respect of any or each thereof.

The cashier should have no part in writing up any cash book apart from his own collecting and deposit book, and in many cases, where the size of the staff allows, the cash book is written up by a clerk not responsible for the posting of any ledger. **[69]**

Bank Accounts.—Bearing in mind that all payments must be made to and by the treasurer, who need not be a banker, the question whether bank accounts should be in the name of the authority or its treasurer is largely academic. The question of the number of bank accounts to be opened is one of practical convenience rather than principle. In the case of a borough, however, whose accounts are not wholly subject to district audit, a separate banking account or accounts would appear to be desirable in respect of the accounts so subject.

The advantage attaching to separate banking accounts is that the allocation of bank interest and charges is effected by the bank, and if arrangements are made whereby all balances are aggregated for the purpose of arriving at the amount of interest or charges, this course need not involve any loss of interest or additional bank charges.

Separate bank accounts, however, tend to create confusion, especially in the case of the larger authorities, by reason of the number necessary, and the numerous transfers which are required as between funds, this being accentuated at the close of the accounting period. The position of the various funds and accounts should be readily ascertainable from the ledger accounts and cash books, the necessary agreement as between pass book and cash book being obtained in total.

A certain degree of separation, however, is probably necessary in practice in order to facilitate sectional balancing, and it is the practice usually to open separate accounts in respect of funds subject to audit by the district auditor, and in respect of trading undertakings. The Departmental Committee of 1907 considered that it might be found convenient to open separate capital and revenue accounts for each distinct fund or undertaking, but it is found in many cases where a separate banking account for each fund is maintained, that capital and revenue can be merged without inconvenience.

A further type of bank account is occasionally utilized in the modern municipal accountancy system, usually known as a "Pool Account." On the expenditure side, payments which are to be apportioned between various funds are transferred therefrom to this account, from which cheques are met when presented; an example of this is the Dividends Account in connection with a loans pool. A similar account is often used in connection with income where a cash register or other cash machine is operated. In this case the total collections are paid into the pool, subsequently being transferred to the appropriate funds, the transfer being performed by some officer other than the cashier, usually the internal auditor. Such a bank account is merely a temporary resting place for cash due to various funds and should be cleared daily. **[70]**

The Journal.—The function of the journal is to record transactions as opposed to that of the ledger which is to classify transactions. In both commercial and municipal accounting systems it has, however, been found convenient to make a preliminary classification of transactions in the books of record. The journal has therefore been subdivided, and thus Bought and Sold day books are usually found in the commercial system, whilst Income and Expenditure journals fulfil a similar function in the municipal system. Such books are, of course, parts of the journal, segregated for the purpose of convenience, and the use of the journal proper, including its sections, is now confined to recording transfers between main ledger accounts which would not be shown in any other book of first entry.

It will be used during the accounting period to record transfers such as wages, stores, etc., from the total wages and stores accounts, in detail to the debit of the various expenditure accounts, on the basis of the costing records, or, for example, as debiting the collector with the total collections during a period, as shown in the collecting and deposit book, and crediting in detail to the income and/or total debtors' accounts. Errors can be corrected through the medium of the journal, but it will be utilised mostly at the end of the accounting period when numerous transfers will require to be made in order to close the books. Especially is this the case where books are kept on the receipts and payments basis during the year and converted at the end of the year to the basis of income and expenditure. In this case all amounts due but unpaid, both debtors and creditors, will require to be passed through the journal.

The ruling of the book consists of date, narrative, folio, and two cash columns, and a concise explanatory narrative should be appended to each entry, or series of entries, where dealing with the same matter, so as to display on the face of the entry that it is correct. Since each entry must in the majority of cases link up with some voucher or prime record, as for example with the wages summary, or collecting and deposit book, it is desirable also that the narrative should contain some reference thereto. Where transfers are necessary as between funds having separate bank accounts, it is preferable to have in lieu of the journal, a system of bank transfer slips on the carbon duplicate system, one copy being sent to the bank for the purpose of the cash transfer, and the carbon copy serving as the journal entry. [71]

The Ledger.—All the financial transactions of the local authority are classified in the ledger, whether it be comprised in one book only or divided into several volumes. Where the accounts of an authority are not wholly subject to audit by the district auditor, as in the case of the majority of borough councils, the part subject to such audit must be kept in a separate set or sets of books.

The First Schedule to the Regulations of 1930 contains instructions as to the keeping of the ledger, which may well be applied to all accounts, *viz.*:

(1) The title of each ledger account shall be such as to define its purpose, and where it is a personal account shall bear the name of the person or group of persons whose account with the council it represents.

(2) The ledger accounts shall be grouped with due regard to their nature, and to bringing together the totals required for entry in any epitome of accounts or return required to be furnished to the Minister of Health.

(3) Each item in a ledger account shall be adequately described and referenced to its corresponding debit or credit, and a statement of the reasons and authority for each item relating to adjustment, allocation, transfer of charge or other special matter shall be given, by entry or by reference.

(4) The final ledger accounts shall be presented for audit permanently bound in volumes of which each folio or page shall bear a consecutive number.

With regard to the last paragraph it is found in practice that the district auditors will accept a ledger bound on the loose leaf principle.

[72]

The regulations also lay down the ledger system to be adopted, including the following accounts :

Personal Accounts.

(1) Cash book—see *ante.*
(2) Officers.—An account for each officer who collects or receives money on behalf of the council, each officer who disburses money on behalf of the council, and each officer charged with the receipt or issue of stores or materials.
(3) Debtors.—An account for each person or group of persons from whom money is due and owing to the council during the year.
(4) Creditors.—An account for each person or group of persons to whom money is due and owing by the council during the year.

Impersonal Accounts.

(1) Income.—See *ante.*
(2) Expenditure.—See *ante.*

Final Accounts.

(1) Revenue.—An account bringing out a balance between the income and expenditure of :
    (a) the General Rate Fund, other than income and expenditure of which separate account has to be taken as hereinafter provided ;
    (b) each undertaking or service in respect of which separate account is by law required or is needed for the purposes of the council ;
    (c) each part of the borough for which a separate account of income and expenditure is needed ; and
    (d) each reserve, pension, or other fund of which continuous account has to be kept.
(2) Loan and Capital.—Five classes of accounts are prescribed hereunder, *viz.* capital asset account, capital provision account, deferred charge account, capital receipts account, and an account of each fund provided for the purpose of loan repayment, these being dealt with *post.*

Balance Sheets.

Balance sheets showing the assets and liabilities and the financial position of each of the funds or revenues of the council at the close of the year.

Referring to the personal accounts to be kept with officers, it will be noted that such an account is necessary with each officer collecting or receiving money on behalf of the authority. The collecting and deposit book kept by the cashier would comply with this direction, and similar books will also be necessary in other cases, *e.g.* town clerk in respect of legal fees, etc., depots in respect of sundry sales of materials, etc. Petty cash accounts on the imprest system will ordinarily prove sufficient in the case of officers who are responsible for the disbursement of cash. It will also be noted that an account must be kept with each officer charged with the receipt or issue of stores or materials, so that the stores account—an impersonal account—will be utilised also as a personal account, and in addition it would seem necessary to open separate accounts where there are several depots and storekeepers.

The directions as to final accounts are followed substantially in the majority of cases, the general rate fund in boroughs, etc., being replaced in the case of county councils by the general county fund. The requirement that separate final accounts should be kept where necessary for each part of the borough would apply where differential rating was in force. In some cases it is necessary to prepare separate revenue accounts for this purpose, whilst in others it is found possible to raise one revenue account for expenditure common to the whole area, together with separate accounts for additional items of expenditure chargeable only on one or more parts of the area. The latter principle is applied in counties to the funds for general and special county purposes, and in rural districts to general and special expenses. The final, or revenue, account in respect of each fund or undertaking as above, will be compiled by debiting and crediting thereto the balances disclosed by the expenditure and income accounts appropriate to the particular revenue account. Alternatively, the totals of the debit and credit sides of such accounts can be respectively debited and credited thereto. The balance then exhibited by the revenue account is usually taken to a net revenue account, which will also include the balance brought forward from the previous year, and the net balance of this account will be inserted in the balance sheet, and carried forward to the subsequent year. **[73]**

Income Tax Accounts.—In order to facilitate the local authority's income tax settlement it is advisable to centralise all tax transactions in one account each year. It will be appreciated that if payments of tax due under the various schedules, and tax deductions from interest paid, are posted to particular expenditure and income accounts, the labour of extracting the figures necessary for the computation is considerable, with the attendant risk of items being omitted. The account to be opened is known usually as the Income Tax Suspense Account, and such an account will be required in the general rate fund or other parent fund of the authority, and also in the case of each trading undertaking which is assessed to tax under Schedule D, *e.g.* gas, electricity, water, tramways, etc. The method then is to debit all tax paid or suffered by deduction, and to credit all tax deducted from interest on loans, rents, etc., to this account.

Reference should be made (*post*) for the detailed settlement of the local authority's tax liability, but with regard to the accounts, the income tax suspense account should be completed by transfers in accordance with the details of that settlement. Thus, in the generality of cases, transfers will be necessary in respect of the following :

(1) Income tax under Schedule A, on properties owned and occupied by the authority, not being available as set-off, must be transferred and debited to the appropriate revenue account.

(2) Schedule A tax on properties owned and let by the authority is available for set-off against tax deductions. Such tax should, in the first place, be transferred to the debit of the revenue account, as in (1) above, and where the authority's computation shows that such items have been set-off against other tax liability, *e.g.* tax deducted from loan interest or rents payable, an equivalent amount of the latter is available for transfer to the credit of the revenue account as " income tax recovered by set-off."

(3) In the case of a trading undertaking which discloses a liability for excess of the Schedule D assessment over deductions from interest, etc., such excess is normally available for set-off in whole or in part in the authority's general computation.

(4) In the case of Housing, 1923 and 1924 Acts Accounts, where there is an excess of tax deductions over the Schedule A liability, there will be no charge in the revenue account for income tax. Where the reverse position operates, there should normally be a debit in the revenue account for the excess Schedule A, but in many cases, where this can be utilised as set-off in the rate fund, the benefit of the latter is allowed to enure to the housing accounts, and there will again be no charge in the revenue account. Any such charge would, in the majority of cases, operate to increase by a like amount the rate contribution to the schemes. For this reason, the tax transactions of these housing funds are often included in the rate fund income tax suspense account as part and parcel thereof.

The precise treatment of these income tax adjustments in the accounts is a question upon which there is some difference of opinion.

In regard to the adjustment referred to in (3) above, the Institute of Municipal Treasurers and Accountants has expressed the view that the benefit should accrue to the rate fund, and this is in keeping with the fact that the liability of the local authority to income tax is a single liability, the net charge being most appropriately shown in the Rate Fund Revenue Account.

It would also seem to be inconsistent to charge Schedule A tax (see (1) above) on, say, a sewage pumping station as an establishment charge in the sewage revenue account, when Schedule A on another subject (see (2) above) is not so charged or is charged in part only.

It should also be borne in mind that recovery by way of set-off only arises as a result of the consideration of the liability of the local authority as a whole.

Many adjustments of a like nature to the above will generally be found necessary, according to the type of authority and local circumstances, and as it is normally impossible in practice to complete each year's tax computation in the year of assessment, there will usually be a balance on the income tax suspense to carry forward *via* the balance sheet. In lieu of taking all surplus set-off, as arrived at, to the credit of the revenue account, many authorities prefer to equalise such transfers at a similar yearly figure.

It may be mentioned that as respects interest accruing in sinking funds the set-off of tax allowed by sect. 79 of the P.H.A., 1925 (*n*), has been extended to county councils and parish councils, and to loans raised under Acts other than the P.H.A., 1875, by sub-sect. (3) of sect. 213 of the L.G.A., 1933. Sect. 79 is repealed by the Act of 1933

(*n*) 13 Statutes 1152.

and replaced by the sub-section in question, which closely resembles the repealed provision. By sub-sect. (6) of sect. 218, the new enactment applies to an accumulating sinking fund established by a local authority under any enactment for the repayment of moneys borrowed by way of mortgage, in like manner as it applies to such a sinking fund established under Part IX. of the Act. County councils, borough and district councils and parish councils are all local authorities within the sub-section; see the definition of " local authority " in sect. 305. [74]

The " Negative " System of Accounting.—In recent years what is known as the " principle of negation " has been applied with success to the posting of certain of the primary records of a local authority. The method is applicable in any case where there is a large number of similar payments or receipts to be accounted for, which occur at regular and frequent intervals, such as the payment of police pensions and collection of housing rents at weekly or monthly intervals. In cases such as these where each particular item of receipt or payment to be made at each interval is the same, it is more important to be able to see, and requires less labour to account for, only the comparatively small number of irregular payments or non-payments, than the comparatively large number of regular payments made. The system therefore proceeds along the lines of accounting in detail for all irregular items, and in total for all regular items, and in the case of the collection of housing rents, to which the system is particularly applicable, its application would be as follows:

The usual columnar tenants' rental will be utilised, with a cash column for each of the twenty-six weeks in the half-year, and instead of posting against each tenant under the appropriate weekly column, the amount paid by such tenant in that particular week, and leaving a blank where no payment was made, the procedure is reversed. Thus, where the regular weekly payment was made, as it would be in the majority of cases, no entry would be made in the rental. On the other hand, where a tenant failed to pay the full week's rent, a black ink item would be inserted for the amount left unpaid, and similarly, where a payment in advance of more than one week's rent was made, the amount of pure over-payment would be posted to the credit of the tenant in red ink. Where a house was empty during a period, the amount of rent lost, *i.e.* the void allowance, would be entered in green ink against the particular house. The next step is to prove these figures with the cash actually collected, and this is done, each week, by adding together:

(1) The weekly debit for all the houses;
(2) The arrears brought forward at the commencement of the week; and
(3) The overpayments carried forward at the end of the week.

From this total is deducted the total of:

(1) Overpayments brought forward at the beginning of the week;
(2) Arrears carried forward at the end of the week; and
(3) Voids during the week.

The resultant figure is the cash actually collected from housing tenants during the week, and should agree with the amount paid in by the collector. The debit for any particular week can easily be arrived at by multiplying the number of houses by the rent per week of each, whilst arrears and overpayments brought forward in any week are the same as the figures carried forward the previous week. It will be seen that there is a large saving of time over the method under which individual amounts of rent paid are posted to the credit of the particular tenant, and the whole column cast in order to arrive at the amount of cash collected. In addition, the tenants' rental will always show at a glance which tenants are in arrear, and the amount of such arrears, since a blank space will mean that payments are up to date, and the figures utilised will be taken from balanced accounts.

The system above described has been further developed by the use of duplicate posting strips, such strips being ruled so as to fit one weekly column in the tenants' rental, and providing a column on the left-hand side for arrears or overpayments brought forward, a middle column for actual cash paid, and a right-hand column for arrears or overpayments carried forward at the end of the week. Tenants' rent cards are also ruled in a similar manner, and a receipt for rent paid will be posted on to the rent card through the duplicate posting strip, together with the arrears or overpayment which will be extended in the right-hand column. As each rent strip " fits " a column of the rental, all that is necessary in posting is to line up the strip on the appropriate page, and copy in the arrears or overpayments at the end of the week in the correctly coloured ink, or the rent strip may be gummed in the rental, thus eliminating any posting whatsoever. A summary as above will then disclose the amount of cash collected, and if the right-hand column of the rent strip be perforated, it can be detached and used as the left-hand column of the succeeding week's duplicate posting strip.

The system is not solely applicable to the collection of housing rents, although its adoption by local authorities is mostly in this direction, but can be utilised in other directions where the incidents of the transactions are similar to those of housing rents. **[75]**

Loan and Capital Accounts.—The methods of dealing with capital expenditure and borrowings in the case of a local authority are influenced to a certain extent by the control of the Government, and the necessity for the repayment of all capital borrowings, which, as explained *ante*, necessitate separate and distinct treatment as compared with similar items in the accounts of a commercial concern.

The larger portion of the local authority's capital expenditure is financed out of borrowed money, and before loans can be raised, it is necessary, unless a local Act is obtained, to apply for and obtain the formal sanction of a government department, which is usually the M. of H. It is advisable, therefore, to keep a primary record of sanctions applied for and obtained, showing details as to date, amount, period, etc. The period of the loan is fixed by the sanctioning authority having regard to the probable life of the asset to be acquired.

The majority of the smaller authorities raise a specific loan to finance each sanction, in which case all loan and capital transactions can be accommodated in the capital ledger. Where, however, money is raised by means of a stock issue, or is borrowed continuously by means of short term mortgages, a separate set of accounts is necessary in respect of the borrowings, advances being made thereout to the various funds incurring capital expenditure, on the basis of the loan sanctions. The accounts necessary under the Stock Regulations include a dividends fund and a redemption fund, to which are credited contributions by borrowing funds on account of interest on and redemption of debt (see title STOCK, *post*). Similar accounts are necessary in the case of a consolidated loans fund, where stock, mortgages, bills, etc., are issued by the one fund, advances being made thereout in a similar manner to stock (see title CONSOLIDATED LOAN FUND, *post*). [76]

In the case of borrowings by means of short term mortgages or bonds, which are available in law for the purpose of:

(1) All or any statutory borrowing powers ; or
(2) All or any statutory borrowing powers under a particular enactment,

the Regulations of 1930 lay down the accounting procedure to be observed in relation to accounts to which the regulations apply. A separate cash account must be kept of all moneys raised in the above manner—referred to as " general loans "—and of the application and repayment of such moneys. Whenever any such moneys are applied in the exercise of a statutory borrowing power, the amount so applied—referred to as an " advance "—is to be transferred from this cash account to that of the borrowing fund, and debited in the loan accounts as a loan to the borrowing account concerned. Apart from the cash account, the loans accounts will normally consist of a credit balance on the mortgagees' and bondholders' accounts representing amounts owing by the fund, and a debit balance on the advances accounts for the amounts owing to the fund.

Interest payable on loans will be debited in the first place to an interest account, which must be apportioned each year between the borrowing accounts on the basis of the outstanding advances against each, either at the beginning or close of the year, after the necessary adjustments have been made for advances outstanding for part of the year only. [77]

The advances will be made to each borrowing fund on the basis of sanctions held by it, and repayments of advances will be transferred to the loans fund in accordance with the conditions as to period, etc., attaching to the statutory borrowing powers. If not so transferred the amounts provided for repayment must be carried to the sinking fund accounts in respect of the borrowing powers, and be shown on the balance sheet as sinking funds unapplied. It is usual in practice, however, to transfer yearly the amounts as shown by the sinking fund schedules, and for the borrowing funds to treat a like amount of debt as having been redeemed. Such repayments are then available in the loans fund for repayment of loans, or for further advances in the exercise of statutory borrowing powers.

A register of advances must be kept recording each advance, and the arrangements made for complying with the conditions of the statutory borrowing powers, and this can usefully incorporate the records of sanctions mentioned above. A ruling of such a record is given in Appendix I. to the Memorandum accompanying the Regulations of 1930, and the matter is also dealt with *post*.

The final accounts of the loans fund will include a revenue account showing on the credit side the balance brought forward of loan moneys unallocated at the commencement of the year, and loans raised and redemption moneys received during the year, and on the debit side advances made and loans repaid during the year, together with the balance unallocated at the end of the year. The loans fund balance sheet will then disclose on the credit side advances outstanding and cash in hand, and on the debit side mortgages and bonds outstanding, unallocated balance of the interest account (if any), creditors, and cash due to bank. [78]

Dealing with loan and capital accounts to be maintained by the various funds of the authority, the Regulations of 1930 provide for the raising of five classes of accounts, *viz.* :

(1) *Capital Asset Account.*—An account of the cost of each work or property treated as a capital asset.
(2) *Capital Provision Account.*—An account or accounts of the provision made otherwise than by loan in respect of the cost of capital assets.
(3) *Deferred Charge Account.*—An account of each authorised loan expenditure other than that which is included in a capital asset account.
(4) *Capital Receipts Account.*—An account of each receipt or group of similar receipts of a capital nature other than loan receipts.
(5) An account of each fund provided for the purpose of loan repayment.

The local authority is, under the Regulations, given the option of treating all or any of its loan expenditure as capital assets, or of dealing with all its loan expenditure on the deferred charge principle, referred to below. Where, however, any such expenditure is dealt with as a capital asset, it must be specified in the balance sheet, and the latter must show to what extent the records relate to realisable assets such as trading plant, real property and permanent equipment, and to what extent they relate to works such as pavements, sewers, etc. In order to maintain the capital asset treatment as above, a clear description of the properties and works treated as capital assets must be maintained in the capital account, and it is obvious that considerable elaboration of record is necessary in order to ensure that expenditure on replacement and original cost are not both included, or that exhausted and alienated assets are definitely excluded. A record is also necessary in the case of non-realisable assets in order that the item may be removed from the capital account when exhausted or replaced. [79]

The capital provision account contains the items necessary to balance the capital account under the double account system, *viz.* :

(1) Revenue contributions to capital outlay.
(2) Capital receipts appropriated in defraying loan expenditure.
(3) Loan repayments or sinking funds in hand.

Each deferred charge account is to be kept so as to show the extent to which the loan expenditure to which it relates remains to be provided out of revenue. Thus, where non-realisable assets are treated on this basis, the loan expenditure would first be debited to a deferred charge account, as distinct from a capital asset account, and the balance of this account would be written down yearly by the amount of loan repayment in connection therewith, the capital provision account being reduced by a like amount. The ultimate effect of this treatment is to write off the value of the deferred charge over the life of the loan, at the end of which the balance of both the capital provision and deferred charge accounts would disappear from the accounts. This procedure can be adopted, as mentioned above, for the whole of a council's loan expenditure, but as stated in the Memorandum accompanying the Regulations of 1930, the records necessary to the capital asset treatment are clearly valuable in connection with trading undertakings, and indeed necessary in these cases in order to complete the returns required by Government departments. In other than trading accounts they are of historical interest, and may also be of value in illustrating the safety of the security for loans which the council can offer to lenders.

The course recommended by the Departmental Committee in 1907 would seem to be the most efficacious under these circumstances, *i.e.*:

(1) Trading undertaking assets to be shown in the capital account at cost.
(2) Other assets having an abiding or realisable value to be treated on the capital asset system as above.
(3) Non-realisable assets to be dealt with on the deferred charge system as above.

Where any property treated as a capital asset passes out of the possession of the local authority, or ceases to be serviceable, an amount equal to the cost must be written off the capital asset account concerned. In addition, on the other side of the accounts, the appropriate capital provision account is to be written down by the capital provision included therein in respect of the particular capital asset. Where the loan in respect of the asset is not fully redeemed, a proportion of the capital asset account equal to the balance of loan outstanding must be allowed to remain in the capital account, and be treated as a deferred charge until written off out of the loan repayments. [80]

The capital receipts account is to be kept so as to show how the receipts to which it relates have been appropriated and to what extent they remain unappropriated. The Memorandum accompanying the Regulations of 1930 specifies the following types of income to be regarded as capital receipts:

(1) Sums received in recoupment of loan expenditure, *e.g.* repayment of advances under Small Dwellings Acquisition Acts.
(2) Sums received in consideration of the assumption of continuing liabilities, *e.g.* for road maintenance, upkeep of graves, etc.
(3) Sums received from the sale of real estate or any interest or easement therein.
(4) Sums to be held in trust for application of the income to special purposes, *e.g.* bequests for the redemption of debt.
(5) Donations and contributions in aid of capital outlay.

In cases where the receipts are such as will normally cover the whole of the loan expenditure, as in the case of Small Dwellings Acquisition Acts advances, the capital receipts account should effect a continuous balance between the assets and liabilities connected with the transactions. Thus the latter account will show provision for the redemption of debt on the one hand, and amounts due from frontagers, mortgagors, etc., on the other. The balance of this account from time to time will be such as will balance an account containing on the one hand loans outstanding to outside lenders, and on the other, amounts outstanding on advances together with cash in hand (if any). [81]

The Regulations of 1930 provide for certain primary records in respect of loan and capital accounts which may advantageously be followed in all cases. A tabular and summarised account is to be kept of each group of stockholders, mortgagees or other lenders to whom debts of the same order are owing, and this implies both a detailed record of each loan and a summary in one form or another of each group of loans. In many cases, the register of mortgages, stock, etc., is utilised as the detailed account, the total loans outstanding summarised therefrom agreeing with the balance shown on the ledger

L.G.L. I.—4

control account, whilst in others the interest register, with the inclusion of a column for loans outstanding at the end of each interest period, is made to serve the same purpose.

A statement is also to be maintained in columnar form as to moneys borrowed under statutory borrowing powers. The statement may be ruled so as to include details for a number of years and must show:

(1) The date, authority, purpose, period and amount of each borrowing power;
(2) The amount borrowed in each year in the exercise of the borrowing power;
(3) The amount repaid during the year, the amount outstanding and the sinking fund (if any) held at the end of the year.

A ruling of the above statement is given in Appendix I. to the Memorandum accompanying the Regulations of 1930, although there is no column included therein for sinking funds in hand as mentioned above.

A sinking fund record must be compiled for each sinking or redemption fund showing year by year in parallel columns, the total amount of debt repaid out of the fund up to the end of the year, and the amount remaining in the fund invested or uninvested, together with any other information necessary for the compilation of returns required by the Minister. It is advisable in practice to head each sinking fund record with all relevant facts and details connected therewith, such as purpose, amount, term of years, rate of accumulation, dates raised, and instalments where allocated in this manner, etc. It is desirable also to have columns showing separately for each year, the ordinary revenue contributions, and any special contributions such as unspent loan balances repaid and other capital receipts, whilst the record may usefully be referenced to the statement of borrowing powers.

A statement is to be prepared in respect of each capital asset and each deferred charge, showing the exact correspondence of the balances connected therewith at the close of each year. Thus the balance sheet value of each capital asset will be counterbalanced by loan debt outstanding, and repaid, revenue contributions and other capital receipts. The original value placed on each deferred charge will be similarly accounted for, but in addition, the amounts written off each side for balance sheet purposes will also be shown. The details in these records when summarised would then interlock with the total figures included in the capital section of the balance sheet. [82]

The Balance Sheet.—The Regulations of 1930 contain directions as to the compilation of the balance sheet and may be regarded as a clear exposition of the manner of displaying the various items.

As many separate balance sheets as are desirable or necessary should be prepared, and where more than one is thus necessary, an aggregate balance sheet summarising the balances appearing in the separate balance sheets, must be entered in the ledger. On each balance sheet other than the aggregate balance sheet, the loan and capital accounts must be grouped together and balanced separately from the revenue portion of the balance sheet. A clear distinction is to be maintained on one side of the balance sheet between liabilities and fund surpluses, and on the other between assets and fund deficiencies or deferred charges. A form of aggregate balance sheet is given in the Appendix to the Memorandum to the Regulations, the loan and capital section of which is balanced separately from the revenue, although as stated above, this is not compulsory in regard to the aggregate balance sheet. The Appendix to the Memorandum accompanying the Regulations also sets out explanatory notes on particular items in the balance sheet. With regard to the loans outstanding item, it is interesting to note that it is considered desirable to show loans from pension, reserve or other funds of the council, separately from stock, mortgages, annuities, etc. [83]

London.—Reference has already been made to sect. 14 of the London Government Act, 1899 (see p. 26, *ante*), and to the Accounts (Boroughs and Metropolitan Boroughs) Regulations, 1930 (see p. 27, *ante*). Parts X. and XI. of L.G.A., 1933, apply to London, and sect. 14 of the London Government Act, 1899, is repealed. Mention has also to be made of the Metropolitan Borough Councils (Form of Statement of Rate-borne Expenditure) Regulations, 1929 (*o*), the London County Council Precept Order, 1930 (*p*), and the Form of Demand Note (London) Rules, 1930 (*q*).

The finances of the L.C.C. are governed mainly by the L.G.A., 1888, and the Finance Committee are appointed in pursuance of sect. 80 (3) of that Act (*r*). The powers of the council with respect to the raising of money on capital account were consolidated in the L.C.C. (Finance Consolidation) Act, 1912. The accounts of the council, which are made up to the end of the local financial year (March 31), are kept throughout on the income and expenditure basis. Sect. 68 (7) of the Act of 1888 (*s*) requires the accounts to be kept in such a way as to prevent the whole county from being charged with the expenditure properly payable only by a portion of the county. The City of London is exempt from contributing towards part of the council's expenditure, and in respect of such expenditure a "Special County Account" is kept. Under sect. 41 (7) (*t*) the council and the city are empowered to come to an agreement for the cessation of this exemption, but no such agreement has been arrived at. For expenditure to which the whole of the administrative county contributes a "General County Account" is kept.

Since April 1, 1930, a fourth principal banking account of the County Fund has been kept, called the "Public Assistance Account," and all receipts in connection with public assistance (other than transferred schools) and hospitals, including transfers of rate money from the general account, are carried to this account. In pursuance of various statutory requirements, or for other special reasons, separate accounts are kept for various branches of the council's administration.

The transactions subject to the financial provisions of the Housing, Town Planning, etc., Act, 1919, are required by regulations issued by the Minister of Health to be separately recorded in the "Housing (Assisted Scheme) Account." Separate accounts are also kept of transactions subject to the Housing, etc., Act, 1923, the Housing (Financial Provisions) Act, 1924, and the Housing Act, 1930, respectively.

A separate account (the Mental Hospitals Account) is kept of the council's transactions as the Visiting Committee for London under the

(*o*) S.R. & O., 1929, No. 1044.
(*p*) S.R. & O., 1930, No. 119.
(*q*) S.R. & O., 1930, No. 540.
(*r*) 10 Statutes 751.
(*s*) *Ibid.*, 741.
(*t*) *Ibid.*, 721.

Lunacy Acts. The net expenditure in respect of the council's obligations, under the Act of 1888, to provide and administer mental hospitals, is ultimately charged to the Special County Account.

There is also a separate account, the " Consolidated Loans Fund " or debt account, a statutory account showing the whole of the transactions relating to interest on, and redemption of, debt (*u*). [84]

(*u*) The above particulars are taken from the Annual Report of the L.C.C., 1931, Vol. I., Part I.

For Product Safety Concerns and Information please contact our EU representative GPSR@taylorandfrancis.com Taylor & Francis Verlag GmbH, Kaufingerstraße 24, 80331 München, Germany